The American Intellectual Tradition

The American Intellectual Tradition

Volume I: 1630 to 1865

SEVENTH EDITION

Edited by

DAVID A. HOLLINGER

University of California, Berkeley

and

CHARLES CAPPER

Boston University

New York   Oxford

OXFORD UNIVERSITY PRESS

2016

Oxford University Press is a department of the University of Oxford.
It furthers the University's objective of excellence in research,
scholarship, and education by publishing worldwide.

Oxford   New York
Auckland   Cape Town   Dar es Salaam   Hong Kong   Karachi
Kuala Lumpur   Madrid   Melbourne   Mexico City   Nairobi
New Delhi   Shanghai   Taipei   Toronto

With offices in
Argentina   Austria   Brazil   Chile   Czech Republic   France   Greece
Guatemala   Hungary   Italy   Japan Poland   Portugal   Singapore
South Korea   Switzerland   Thailand   Turkey   Ukraine   Vietnam

For titles covered by Section 112 of the US Higher Education
Opportunity Act, please visit www.oup.com/us/he for the
latest information about pricing and alternate formats.

Published by Oxford University Press
198 Madison Avenue, New York, New York 10016
http://www.oup.com

Oxford is a registered trademark of Oxford University Press

The CIP Data is On-File at the Library of Congress.

ISBN: 978-0-19-026232-7

Printing number: 9 8 7 6 5 4 3 2 1

Printed in the United States of America
on acid-free paper

In Memory of Henry F. May

Contents

Part Three: Protestant Awakening and Democratic Order

Part Four: *Romantic Intellect and Cultural Reform*

Part Five: *The Quest for Union and Renewal*

Preface

If a tradition is a family of disagreements, the American intellectual tradition is a very extended family. Its members include arguments inspired by the interests and ideals of a variety of communities within the United States as well as arguments concerned with the national community itself. The family also embraces arguments responsive to Western, if not universal, issues in philosophy, science, religion, politics, literature, and the arts. Some of the most influential members of this family are intensely aware of their European ancestry, whereas others have married into European families, and still others remain always preoccupied with the family's Americanness. The family currently seems generally content with its extended state; its diverse and contested character is often a source of pride. But not everyone is agreed on just what makes it a family to begin with. And the family is divided, if not confused, over exactly which of its members ought to supervise the education of its young. What disagreements are primary? How should the tradition be structured to ensure its continuation and critical revision? What specific artifacts of discourse have played the greatest role historically in developing the American intellectual tradition?

Answers to these questions are necessarily implied by any sourcebook for the study of American intellectual history. In deciding what to include in this collection, we have been aware of the dynamism and diversity of our subject as well as highly conscious of the differing constructions of it offered by various scholars. We have sought the advice of numerous colleagues and accordingly have designed *The American Intellectual Tradition* to make available to students many of the documents now routinely assigned by teachers of this subject in colleges and universities throughout the United States. Hence these volumes are chiefly practical devices, not outlines of a systematic, comprehensive interpretation of American intellectual history. Yet certain priorities have shaped these volumes, and it is appropriate to make them explicit.

The American Intellectual Tradition is frankly intellectual in orientation. Most of the documents it contains are the result of someone's effort to make an analysis and to persuade others of the correctness of that analysis. Although these documents express "attitudes" and embody "ideas," we have been more sensitive to their status as arguments. Hence most of our selections are of the genres classically associated with purposive discourse: sermon, address, letter, treatise, and essay. We have tried to identify pieces of argumentation that became prominent points of reference for contemporaries or for Americans of later generations. In so doing, we have necessarily been drawn again and again to the work of men and women normally regarded as intellectual leaders: people who were relatively effective at making arguments.

Arguments can be addressed to an infinite number of issues, but the writings in this book respond to issues that have persistently generated extensive intellectual discussion. The bulk of our selections concern the theoretical basis for religious, scientific, artistic, political, social, and economic practice. Because the United States is above all a polity, the American family of disagreements includes a high proportion of arguments concerning the basis of politics. Because the public culture of America has often been caught up in the distinctive ethos of Protestant Christianity, many of our selections—especially in Volume I—are directed to religious issues. Because modern America has been a peculiarly science-preoccupied civilization, many of the selections in Volume II address the character of the scientific enterprise and debate the implications of scientific knowledge. We have also been mindful of categories of race, class, and gender, as well as themes in theology, cultural theory, and American foreign and transnational affairs that have risen to prominence in the humanities and social sciences over the last several decades, and consequently in recent editions we have devoted an increasing amount of space in the sourcebook to these subjects.

In order to give these issues historical shape, we have organized the documents around general themes or movements, which we address briefly in the introduction preceding each main section. Were this a textbook rather than a sourcebook, we would have attempted to indicate the entire structure of discourse surrounding the texts we discuss; here we can do no more than hint at this, leaving it to the instructor to fill in the missing arguments and counterarguments. In framing our selections, we have also tried to avoid what seems to us a failing in many previous anthologies: the packaging of each source as an example of a particular doctrine or movement. Throughout we have emphasized that most intellectual works are dynamic and multifaceted and therefore have meaning in more than one frame of reference. With this in mind, we have written headnotes that highlight the dense internal content of each document as well as the setting in which it was produced.

It is easy to list the names of historically significant American thinkers whose work does not appear in these volumes. Yet, we have resisted the impulse to reduce the length of our selections in order to make room for a greater number of authors. The multiplication of texts by cutting them into mere snippets might have enabled us to more effectively register the social and cultural diversity of American intellectual leadership. Every ideological persuasion and identity group might then find its representative listed in the table of contents. The plural and contested character of the American intellectual tradition might then be acknowledged even more compellingly than is acknowledged by the selections we have decided to include. But the reducing of texts to brief excerpts has a great cost. The rhetorical and discursive power that helped draw attention to a text in the first place can be easily lost. Tensions within a text can be silenced, rendering the authors more univocal than they were. Although we have sometimes printed only a brief selection from a longer work, most of the documents found in *The American Intellectual Tradition* are complete, or nearly complete, essays, addresses, or chapters of books. We hope that what this sourcebook offers in the depth of its selections will compensate for what it lacks in the range of its inclusions.

This seventh edition has been shaped in large part by the advice of colleagues who have used the previous editions in teaching. We have dropped a number of selections and added new ones in an effort to take account of recent scholarship that assigns new historical significance to certain authors and texts. Most of our changes are in the latter parts of Volume II because of greater fluctuations in the consensus of historians about who and what matters in the later twentieth century. We have also updated and in many cases expanded the commentary and citations in the Introductions and headnotes.

The chronologies at the end of each volume list almost as many European textual and sociopolitical events as American ones, reflecting our awareness that American intellectual history is bound up with the larger history of Europe, and indeed that of most of the world. The United States stands intellectually in much the same relation to Europe as Great Britain does: British intellectuals help constitute the discourse of Europe while simultaneously perpetuating and revising their own national tradition. The same can be said of intellectuals in Russia, Spain, Germany, Italy, or France, as well as of those in the United States. Moreover, national cultures are sites of differing international significance at different times. In the seventeenth century, for example, the discourse of an extended Europe went forward without much attention to what was being said in British North America, but in the twentieth century the United States became a major site for this discourse.

Students interested in how the field of American intellectual history has developed over time and is now being practiced will want to look at Joel Isaac, James T. Kloppenberg, and Jennifer Ratner-Rosenhagan, eds., *The Worlds of American Intellectual History* (New York, 2016). That volume includes essays on a variety of issues now being pursued by specialists and can be read in relation to an earlier state-of-the-field volume, John Higham and Paul K. Conkin, *New Directions in American Intellectual History* (Baltimore, 1979). Of the several journals that publish recent research in this field, the most important is *Modern Intellectual History* (Cambridge University Press). Other highly relevant journals are *The Journal of the History of Ideas* (University of Pennsylvania Press) and *Intellectual History Review* (Taylor and Francis).

We want to acknowledge the invaluable advice provided by a number of colleagues in the preparation of the seventh edition. Some of these have also consulted with us in one or more of the previous editions, but in this round we are especially indebted to the following: Benjamin Alpers of the University of Oklahoma; Betty Bergland of the University of Wisconsin-River Falls; Angus Burgin of The Johns Hopkins University; Leslie Butler of Dartmouth College; Jennifer Burns of Stanford University; Healan Gaston of Harvard University; Daniel Geary of Trinity College, Dublin; Nils Gilman of the University of California, Berkeley; Andrew Hartman of Illinois State University; Jennifer Hochschild of Harvard University; Daniel Immerwahr of Northwestern University; Joel Isaac of the University of Cambridge; Andrew Jewett of Harvard University; Richard King of the University of Nottingham, Amy Kittelstrom of Sonoma State University, James T. Kloppenberg of Harvard University; Michael O'Brien of the University of Cambridge; Mark Peterson of the University of California, Berkeley; Jennifer Ratner-Rosenhagen of the University of Wisconsin-Madison; Dorothy Ross of the Johns Hopkins University; David Sehat of Georgia State University; Nico Slate of Carnegie Mellon University; Werner Sollors of Harvard University; Richard Candida Smith of the University of California, Berkeley; Jonathan Spiro of Castleton College; Daniel Wickberg of the University of Texas, Dallas; Caroline Winterer of Stanford University, Molly Worthen of the University of North Carolina, and members of the Berkeley-Stanford Intellectual History Group.

The ways in which such colleagues as these have helped to shape the successive editions of this sourcebook are described in detail in David A. Hollinger, "What Is Our Canon? How American Intellectual Historians Debate the Core of Their Field," *Modern Intellectual History* 9 (2012), 185–200. Listed below are colleagues who have assisted us at one time or another in the preparation of editions one through six.

Their influence is still felt in this seventh edition, and we are glad for this opportunity to thank them again.

For advice regarding this sourcebook, we wish to thank the following individuals: Jennifer Burns of the University of Virginia; Patrick Allitt of Emory University; Joyce Appleby of the University of California, Los Angeles; Robert C. Bannister of Swarthmore College; Thomas Bender of New York University; Fred Beuttler of the University of Chicago; Casey Nelson Blake of Columbia University; Ruth H. Bloch of the University of California, Los Angeles; Eileen Boris of the University of California, Santa Barbara; Howard Brick of the University of Michigan; Jennifer Burns of the University of Virginia; Richard Bushman of Columbia University; E. Wayne Carp of Pacific Lutheran University; John Carson of the University of Michigan; Saul Cornell of Ohio State University; Charles Lloyd Cohen of the University of Wisconsin–Madison; George Cotkin of California State Polytechnic University at San Luis Obispo; David Brion Davis of Yale University; David Engerman of Brandeis University; Richard Wightman Fox of the University of Southern California; George M. Fredrickson of Stanford University; Lawrence J. Friedman of Indiana University; Daniel Geary of Trinity College Dublin; James B. Gilbert of the University of Maryland; Samuel Haber of the University of California, Berkeley; David D. Hall of the Harvard Divinity School; Thomas L. Haskell of Rice University; Hugh Hawkins of Amherst College; David Hoeveler of the University of Wisconsin—Milwaukee; E. Brooks Holifield of Emory University; James Hoopes of Babson College; Daniel Horowitz of Smith College; Daniel Walker Howe of Oxford University; David Johnson of Portland State University; John F. Kasson of the University of North Carolina at Chapel Hill; Linda K. Kerber of the University of Iowa; Richard King of the University of Nottingham; James T. Kloppenberg of Harvard University; Lloyd S. Kramer of the University of North Carolina at Chapel Hill; Bruce Kuklick of the University of Pennsylvania; Ralph Luker of Antioch College; Kevin Mattson of Ohio State University; Donald B. Meyer of Wesleyan University; Robert Moates Miller of the University of North Carolina at Chapel Hill; Jill Morawski of Wesleyan University; Michael O'Brien of Cambridge University; Lewis Perry of St. Louis University; Mark Pittenger of the University of Colorado; Christopher Phelps of the University of Nottingham; Jon H. Roberts of Boston University; Daniel T. Rodgers of Princeton University; Dorothy Ross of the Johns Hopkins University; Joan Shelly Rubin of the University of Rochester; Ethan Schrum of the University of Pennsylvania; Barbara Sicherman of Trinity University; Daniel Singal of Hobart and William Smith Colleges; Jeffrey Sklansky of the University of Illinois at Chicago; Richard Candida Smith of the University of California, Berkeley; Wilson Smith of the University of California, Davis; John W. Stewart of Princeton Theological Seminary; Justin Suran of the University of California, Berkeley; James Turner of the University of Notre Dame; Robert Westbrook of the University of Rochester; Daniel Wilson of Muhlenberg College; Rosemarie Zagarri of George Mason University; and members of the Triangle Intellectual History Seminar. Some of these colleagues would have preferred a somewhat different table of contents, but without their counsel *The American Intellectual Tradition* would be less representative of current teaching practice.

For assistance in preparing this seventh edition of *The American Intellectual Tradition* we wish to thank Rebekah Beaulieu and Gene Zubovich. We also wish to express our appreciation for the advice and assistance of Brian Wheel and the production team of Oxford University Press.

The editors have worked closely at every stage of the preparation of *The American Intellectual Tradition*, but responsibility for Volume I belongs to Charles Capper and for Volume II to David Hollinger.

Berkeley, Calif. D.A.H.
Boston, Mass. C.C.
June 2015

Note on the Texts in Volume 1

The date assigned to a text other than a letter is the year of its first regular publication or, in the case of an address or sermon, of its initial delivery. If the year of first publication varies significantly from the date of composition, the latter is given in parentheses preceding the text. Letters are identified by date of composition. Except for archaic letters, the original spelling, capitalization, and punctuation of all texts has been retained.

The American Intellectual Tradition

Part One

The Puritan Vision Altered

Introduction

To consider Puritan thinkers as part of an ongoing tradition of American intellectuals might seem perversely anachronistic. The very noun "intellectual" was never used by them, and key concepts commonly found in the writings represented in these volumes, such as "self-sufficient reason" or "the independent thinker," would have seemed to them absolutely abhorrent. Yet if the Puritans were not moderns, they were not archaic obscurantists either. The outpouring of scholarship on American Puritanism in the past seventy years has taught us to marvel at the highly articulated intellectuality of Puritan culture in both Old and New England. Nor should this be surprising. The Puritans were enthusiastic inheritors not only of Christian and biblical scholarship, but also of the new learning and culture of Renaissance humanism. From both sources they took materials that they strenuously manipulated in order to achieve the highest cultural goal of the religious intellectual—a justification of the ways of God to man and woman. Out of this striving necessarily came a complex synthesis of supernatural, rationalistic, and emotional elements that has remained—in large part *because* of its complexity—a powerful influence in American intellectual life down to the twenty-first century.

At the bottom of this Puritan synthesis was the idea of the covenant. This was a concept, developed first by late sixteenth and early seventeenth-century Continental and English Reformed theologians, that defined the relationship between God and humankind as being based on a covenant—a series of divinely ordained yet understandable rules and mutual responsibilities. So defined, the covenant or "federal" idea obviously had wide-ranging applicability, as is well shown in the first two selections. John Winthrop, in his lay sermon on Christian charity, used the concept both to expound a complete theory of political authority and social relations and to explain the world-historical significance of the entire New England venture. John Cotton's treatise on the theology of the covenant was no less comprehensive. Embracing the orthodox Puritan doctrine of God's promise of assured salvation for the elect, Cotton strove mightily at the same time to reconcile that grandly deterministic tenet with the necessity of humans' ethical duties and spiritual efforts.

New England Puritan covenantal thought, although vast in scope, was fraught with ambiguity and tensions. When conflict among its formulators consequently broke out in the first years of the Massachusetts Bay settlement, although the dissenters were few, the dissension brought into sharp focus some of the most basic elements of the Puritan intellectual vision. None of these was more basic than the ultimate evangelical questions raised in Cotton's treatise: What must I do to be saved? and (almost as momentous) How do I *know* that I am saved? The selection from the General Court's examination of Anne Hutchinson dramatically reveals the astonishingly broad range of answers that Puritan intellectuals sometimes gave to those questions. Religious dissension naturally raises the issue of toleration, a problem addressed by the Bay Colony's other great religious dissenter, Roger Williams. But for Williams the issue was not the familiar modern secular one of mutual tolerance achieved through rational discourse, but rather one that went, like Hutchinson's dissent, although from a different angle, to the heart of the New England covenantal way. In his treatise against religious persecution, Williams argued that "carnal" weapons used against religious dissenters, which the Massachusetts colony's intellectual leaders believed were essential to the implementation of God's word in this world, undermined the very foundation of biblically revealed Christianity.

By the end of the seventeenth century, New England Puritan culture was undergoing if not, as some historians once claimed, a complete "declension" from its initial founding, then certainly the erosion of much of its unifying social and political basis. The Puritan monopoly of political power in the Massachusetts Bay Colony had been broken with the new charter's substitution of property for church membership as the basis for suffrage, non-Puritan sects were growing in numbers, and competing Enlightenment currents were increasingly attracting the allegiance of Puritan and non-Puritan intellectuals. Meanwhile, ministers continued to preach jeremiads over what they saw as clear evidence of rising worldliness in their society. In this context a host of third- and fourth-generation New England Puritan leaders, like their Protestant counterparts in other parts of America and in Europe, lent support to organized efforts to revitalize their region's piety. The last selections by three leading ministerial intellectuals demonstrate the wide range of responses to these turbulent times. Cotton Mather, in his essay on the doing of good, sought feverishly to find in voluntaristic moral efforts avenues to Godly piety and community solidarity. By contrast, in reaction to the subsequent revivals of the Great Awakening, Charles Chauncy insisted on both Bible-based and rationalist reasons for staunchly opposing their putative "enthusiasm." Jonathan Edwards, on the other hand, in his sermon exhorting his listeners to an anguished awareness of their plight as determined sinners and especially in his treatise delineating the spiritual character of religious emotions, both creatively adapted and radically subverted emerging Enlightenment psychological and ethical paradigms in order to restore the majesty and integrity of a God-intoxicated Christian faith.

Recommendations for Further Reading
Perry Miller, *The New England Mind,* vol. 1: *The Seventeenth Century* (New York, 1939), and vol. 2: *From Colony to Province* (Cambridge, Mass., 1953); Edmund S. Morgan, *Visible Saints: The History of a Puritan Idea* (New York, 1963); Robert Middlekauff, *The Mathers: Three Generations of Puritan Intellectuals, 1596–1728* (New York, 1971); Sacvan Bercovitch, *The American Jeremiad* (Madison, Wis., 1978); Norman Fiering, *Moral Philosophy at Seventeenth-Century Harvard: A Discipline in Transition* (Chapel Hill, 1981); Charles E. Hambrick-Stowe, *The Practice of Piety: Puritan Devotional Disciplines in Seventeenth-Century New England* (Chapel Hill, 1982); Charles Lloyd Cohen, *God's Caress*: *The Psychology of Puritan Religious Experience* (New York, 1986); Harry S. Stout, *The New England Soul: Preaching and Religious Culture in Colonial New England* (New York, 1986); Andrew Delbanco, *The Puritan Ordeal* (Cambridge, Mass., 1989); David D. Hall, *Worlds of Wonder, Days of Judgment: Popular Religious Belief in Early New England* (New York, 1989); Jon Butler, *Awash in a Sea of Faith: Christianizing the American People* (Cambridge, Mass., 1990); Michael J. Crawford, *Seasons of Grace: Colonial New England's Revival Tradition in Its British Context* (New York, 1991); Stephen Foster, *The Long Argument: English Puritanism and the Shaping of New England Culture, 1570–1700* (Chapel Hill, 1991); Amanda Porterfield, *Female Piety in Puritan New England: The Emergence*

of *Religious Humanism* (New York, 1992); Francis J. Bremer, ed., *Puritanism: Transatlantic Perspectives on a Seventeenth-Century Anglo-American Faith* (Boston, 1993); Stephen Innes, *Creating the Commonwealth: The Economic Culture of Puritan New England* (New York, 1995); Michael P. Winship, *Seers of God: Puritan Providentialism in the Restoration and Early Enlightenment* (Baltimore, 1996); Mark A. Peterson, *The Price of Redemption: The Spiritual Economy of Puritan New England* (Stanford, 1997); Darren Staloff, *The Making of an American Thinking Class: Intellectuals and Intelligentsia in Puritan Massachusetts* (New York, 1998); Frank Lambert, *Inventing the "Great Awakening"* (Princeton, 1999); Joyce E. Chaplin, *Subject Matter: Technology, the Body, and Science on the Anglo-American Frontier, 1500–1676* (Cambridge, Mass., 2001); Lisa M. Gordis, *Opening Scripture: Bible Reading and Interpretive Authority in Puritan New England* (Chicago, 2003); E. Brooks Holifield, *Theology in America: Christian Thought from the Age of the Puritans to the Civil War* (New Haven, 2003); Nicholas Guyatt, *Providence and the Invention of the United States, 1607–1876* (New York, 2007). Thomas S. Kidd, *The Great Awakening: The Roots of Evangelical Christianity in Colonial America* (New Haven, 2007); Carla Gardina Pestana, *Protestant Empire: Religion and the Making of the British Atlantic World* (Philadelphia, 2009); Walter W. Woodward, *Prospero's America: John Winthrop, Jr., Alchemy, and the Creation of New England Culture, 1606–1676* (Chapel Hill, 2010); David D. Hall, *A Reforming People: Puritanism and the Transformation of Public Life in New England* (New York, 2011); David F. Holland, *Sacred Borders: Continuing Revelation and Canonical Restraint in Early America* (New York, 2011); Sarah Rivett, *The Science of the Soul in Colonial New England* (Chapel Hill, 2011); Michael P. Winship, *Godly Republicanism: Puritans, Pilgrims, and a City on a Hill* (Cambridge, Mass., 2012); Linford D. Fisher, *The Indian Great Awakening: Religion and the Shaping of Native Cultures in Early America* (New York, 2012).

JOHN WINTHROP

"A Modell of Christian Charity"
(1630)

As the first and very often annually reelected governor of the Massachusetts Bay Colony until his death, John Winthrop (1588–1649) was early New England's preeminent political leader. He was also its leading political theorist. His speeches on the limits of popular liberty and the importance of special prerogatives for elected magistrates constitute the most important body of governmental theory in the first years of settlement.

But his most philosophical discourse was the extraordinary lay sermon he probably delivered in England just before boarding the Puritan flagship *Arbella* bound for New England. In it he envisioned a polity that, however consensual in form and sometimes contractual in language, was organic and strongly theocratic. The ideal state, in Winthrop's schema, rested on a covenant with God, who both determined the fundamental moral laws regulating society and, through Christ's infusion of the power of love, created in the elect their desire to carry out His commandments. What gave Winthrop's abstract model its peculiar power, though, were two additional themes that he grafted onto it: his organically imaged and Bible-derived injunctions concerning the proper social and economic behavior befitting a community "knitt together" by Christ; and his strangely cosmic image of this tiny Puritan outpost bearing a terrible responsibility for fulfilling—or not fulfilling—God's plan for human redemption.

Edmund S. Morgan's *The Puritan Dilemma: The Story of John Winthrop* (Boston, 1958) is a classic portrait that still repays reading. For a recent biography that emphasizes Winthrop's embedded place in a transatlantic Tudor-Stuart political and religious world, see Francis J. Bremer, *John Winthrop: America's Forgotten Founding Father* (New York, 2003). Contrasting influential discussions of Winthrop and the founding Puritans' conception of their exemplary mission may be found in Perry Miller, "Errand into the Wilderness," in Miller's *Errand into the Wilderness* (Cambridge, Mass., 1956), 1–15; and Sacvan Bercovitch, *The American Jeremiad* (Madison, Wis., 1978), 3–61. For revisionary counterviews, see Theodore Dwight Bozeman, *To Live Ancient Lives: The Primitivist Dimension in Puritanism* (Chapel Hill, 1988), 81–119; and Bremer, *John Winthrop*, 173–84.

God Almightie in his most holy and wise providence hath soe disposed of the Condicion of mankinde, as in all times some must be rich some poore, some highe and eminent in power and dignitie; others meane and in subieccion.

The Reason Hereof.

1. REAS: *First,* to hold conformity with the rest of his workes, being delighted to shewe forthe the glory of his wisdome in the variety and differance of the Creatures and the glory of his power, in ordering all these differences for the preservacion and good of the whole, and the glory of his greatnes that as it is the glory of princes to have many officers, soe this great King will have many Stewards counting himselfe more honoured in dispenceing his guifts to man by man, then if hee did it by his owne immediate hand.

2. REAS: *Secondly,* That he might have the more occasion to manifest the worke of his Spirit: first, upon the wicked in moderateing and restraineing them: soe that the riche and mighty should not eate upp the poore, not the poore, and dispised rise upp against theire superiours, and shake off theire yoake; 2ly in the regenerate in exerciseing his graces in them, as in the greate ones, theire love mercy, gentlenes, temperance etc., in the poore and inferiour sorte, theire faithe patience, obedience etc:

3. REAS: Thirdly, That every man might have need of other, and from hence they might be all knitt more nearly together in the Bond of brotherly affeccion: from hence it appeares plainely that noe man is made more honourable then another or more wealthy etc., out of any perticuler and singuler respect to himselfe but for the glory of his Creator and the Common good of the Creature, Man; Therefore God still reserves the propperty of these guifts to himselfe as Ezek: 16, 17. he there calls wealthe his gold and his silver etc. Prov: 3.9. he claimes theire service as his due honour the Lord with thy riches etc. All men being thus (by divine providence) rancked into two sortes, riche and poore; under the first, are comprehended all such as are able to live comfortably by theire owne meanes duely improved; and all others are poore according to the former distribution. There are two rules whereby wee are to walke one towards another: JUSTICE and MERCY. These are allwayes distinguished in theire Act and in theire obiect, yet may they both concurre in the same Subject in eache respect; as sometimes there may be an occasion of shewing mercy to a rich man, in some sudden danger of distresse, and allsoe doeing of meere Justice to a poor man in regard of some perticuler contract etc. There is likewise a double Lawe by which wee are regulated in our conversacion one towardes another: in both the former respects, the lawe of nature and the lawe of grace, or the morrall lawe or the lawe of the gospell, to omitt the rule of Justice as not propperly belonging to this purpose otherwise then it may fall into consideracion in some perticuler Cases: By the first of these lawes man as he was enabled soe withall [is] commaunded to love his neighbour as himselfe upon this ground stands all the precepts of the morall law, which concernes our dealings with men. To apply this to the works of mercy this lawe requires two things first that every man afford his help to another in every want or distresse Secondly, That hee performe this out of the same affeccion, which makes him carefull of his owne good according to that of our Saviour Math: [7.12] Whatsoever ye would that men should doe to you. This was practised by Abraham and Lott in entertaineing the Angells and the old man of Gibea.

Source: Winthrop Papers, vol. 2 (Boston: Massachusetts Historical Society, 1931), 282–95. Notes altered. Reprinted by permission of the Massachusetts Historical Society, Copyright © 1931.

The Lawe of Grace or the Gospell hath some differance from the former as in these respectes first the lawe of nature was given to man in the estate of innocency; this of the gospell in the estate of regeneracy: 2ly, the former propounds one man to another, as the same fleshe and Image of god, this as a brother in Christ allsoe, and in the Communion of the same spirit and soe teacheth us to put a difference betweene Christians and others. Doe good to all especially to the household of faith; upon this ground the Israelites were to putt a difference betweene the brethren of such as were strangers though not of the Canaanites. 3ly. The Lawe of nature could give noe rules for dealeing with enemies for all are to be considered as friends in the estate of innocency, but the Gospell commaunds love to an enemy, proofe. If thine Enemie hunger feed him; Love your Enemies doe good to them that hate you Math: 5. 44.

This Lawe of the Gospell propoundes likewise a difference of seasons and occasions there is a time when a christian must sell all and give to the poore as they did in the Apostles times. There is a tyme allsoe when a christian (though they give not all yet) must give beyond theire abillity, as they of Macedonia. Cor: 2. 6. likewise community of perills calls for extraordinary liberallity and soe doth Community in some speciall service for the Churche. Lastly, when there is noe meanes whereby our Christian brother may be relieved in this distresse, wee must help him beyond our ability, rather than tempt God, in putting him upon help by miraculous or extraordinary meanes.

This duty of mercy is exercised in the kindes, Giveing, lending, and forgiveing.

QUEST. What rule shall a man observe in giveing in respect of the measure?

ANS. If the time and occasion be ordinary he is to give out of his aboundance—let him lay aside, as God hath blessed him. If the time and occasion be extraordinary he must be ruled by them; takeing this withall, that then a man cannot likely doe too much especially, if he may leave himselfe and his family under probable meanes of comfortable subsistance.

OBIECTION. A man must lay upp for posterity, the fathers lay upp for posterity and children and he is worse than an Infidell that provideth not for his owne.

ANS: For the first, it is plaine, that it being spoken by way of Comparison it must be meant of the ordinary and usuall course of fathers and cannot extend to times and occasions extraordinary; for the other place the Apostle speakes against such as walked inordinately, and it is without question, that he is worse then an Infidell whoe throughe his owne Sloathe and voluptuousnes shall neglect to provide for his family.

OBIECTION. The wise mans Eies are in his head (saith Salomon) and foreseeth the plague, therefore wee must forecast and lay upp against evill times when hee or his may stand in need of all he can gather.

ANS: This very Argument Salomon useth to perswade to liberallity. Eccle: [11.1.] cast thy bread upon the waters etc.: for thou knowest not what evill may come upon the land Luke 16. make you friends of the riches of Iniquity; you will aske how this shall be? very well, for first he that gives to the poore lends to the lord, and he will repay even in this life an hundred fold to him or his. The righteous is every mercifull and lendeth and his seed enjoyeth the blessing; and besides wee know what advantage it will be to us in the day of account, when many such Witnesses shall stand forthe for us to witnesse the improvement of our Tallent. And I would knowe of those whoe pleade soe much for layeing up for time to come, whether they hold that to be Gospell Math: 16. 19. Lay not upp for yourselves Treasures upon Earth etc. if they acknowledge it what extent will they allowe it; if onely to those primitive times lett them consider the reason whereupon our Saviour groundes it, the first is that they are subiect to the moathe, the rust the Theife. Secondly, They will steale away the hearte, where the treasure is there will the heart be alsoe. The reasons are of like force at all times therefore the exhortation must be generall and perpetuall which [applies] allwayes in respect of the love and affeccion to riches and in regard of the things themselves when any speciall service for the churche or perticuler distresse of our brother doe call for the use of them; otherwise it is not onely lawfull but necessary to lay upp as Joseph did to have ready uppon such occasions as the Lord (whose stewards wee are of them) shall call for them from us: Christ gives us an Instance of the first, when hee sent his disciples for the Asse, and bidds them answer the owner thus, the Lord hath need of him; soe when the Tabernacle was to be builte his [servant] sends to his people to call for their silver and gold etc.; and yeildes them noe other reason but that it was for his worke, when Elisha comes to the widowe of Sareptah and findes her prepareing to make ready her pittance for herselfe and family, he bids her first provide for him, he challengeth first gods parte which shee must first give before shee must serve her owne family, all these teache us that the lord lookes that when hee is pleased to call for his right in any thing wee have, our owne Interest wee have must stand aside, till his turne be served, for the other wee need looke noe further then to that of John 1. he whoe hath this worlds goodes and seeth his brother to neede, and shutts upp his Compassion from him, how dwelleth the love of god in him, which comes punctually to this Conclusion: if thy brother be in want and thou canst help him, thou needst not make doubt, what thou shouldst doe, if thou lovest god thou must help him.

QUEST: What rule must wee observe in lending?

ANS: Thou must observe whether thy brother hath present or probable, or possible meanes of repayeing thee, if ther be none of these, thou must give him according to his necessity, rather then lend as hee requires; if he hath present meanes of repayeing thee, thou art to looke at him, not as an Act of mercy, but by way of Commerce, wherein thou arte to walke by the rule of Justice, but, if his meanes of repayeing thee be onely probable or possible then is hee an obiect of thy mercy thou must lend him, though there be danger of looseing it Deut: 15. 7. If any of thy brethren be poore etc. thou shalt lend him sufficient that men might not shift off this duty by the apparent hazzard, he tells them that though the Yeare of Jubile were at hand (when he must remitt it, if hee were not able to repay it before) yet he must lend him and that chearefully: it may not greive thee to give him (saith hee) and because some might obiect, why soe I should soone impoverishe my selfe and my family, he adds with all thy Worke etc. for our Saviour Math: 5. 42. From him that would borrow of thee turne not away.

QUEST: What rule must wee observe in forgiveing?

ANS: Whether thou didst lend by way of Commerce or in mercy, if he have noething to pay thee [thou] must forgive him (except in cause where thou hast a surety or a lawfull pleadge) Deut. 15. 2. Every seaventh yeare the Creditor was to quitt that which hee lent to his brother if hee were poore as appeares ver: 8 [4]: save when there shall be noe poore with thee. In all these and like Cases Christ was a generall rule Math: 7. 22. Whatsoever ye would that men should doe to you doe yee the same to them allsoe.

QUEST: What rule must wee observe and walke by in cause of Community of perill?

ANS: The same as before, but with more enlargement towardes others and lesse respect towards our selves, and our owne right hence it was that in the primitive Churche they sold all had all things in Common, neither did any man say that that which he possessed was his owne likewise in theire returne out of the Captivity, because the worke was greate for the restoreing of the church and the danger of enemies was Common to all Nehemiah exhortes the Jewes to liberallity and readines in remitting theire debtes to theire brethren, and disposeth liberally of his owne to such as wanted and stands not upon his owne due, which hee might have demaunded of them, thus did some of our forefathers in times of persecucion here in England, and soe did many of the faithfull in other Churches whereof wee keepe an honourable remembrance of them, and it is to be observed that both in Scriptures and latter stories of the Churches that such as have beene most bountifull to the poore Saintes especially in these extraordinary times and occasions god hath left them highly Commended to posterity, as Zacheus, Cornelius, Dorcas, Bishop Hooper, the Cuttler of Brussells and divers others observe againe that the scripture gives noe causion to restraine any from being over liberall this way; but all men to the liberall and cherefull practise hereof by the sweetest promises as to instance one for many, Isaiah 58. 6: Is not this the fast that I have chosen to loose the bonds of wickednes, to take off the heavy burdens to lett the oppressed goe free and to breake every Yoake, to deale thy bread to the hungry and to bring the poore that wander into thy house, when thou seest the naked to cover them etc. then shall thy light breake forthe as the morneing, and thy healthe shall growe speedily, thy righteousnes shall goe before thee, and the glory of the lord shall embrace thee, then thou shalt call and the lord shall Answer thee etc. 2. 10: If thou power out thy soule to the hungry, then shall thy light spring out in darknes, and the lord shall guide thee continually, and satisfie thy Soule in draught, and make fatt thy bones, thou shalt be like a watered Garden, and they shall be of thee that shall build the old wast places etc. on the contrary most heavy cursses are layd upon such as are straightened towards the Lord and his people Judg: 5. [23] Cursse ye Meroshe because the[y] came not to help the Lord etc. Pro: [21.13] Hee whoe shutteth his eares from hearing the cry of the poore, he shall cry and shall not be heard: Math: 25. [41] Goe ye curssed into everlasting fire etc. [42.] I was hungry and ye fedd mee not. Cor: 2.9. 16.[6.] He that soweth spareingly shall reape spareingly.

Haveing allready sett forth the practise of mercy according to the rule of gods lawe, it will be usefull to lay open the groundes of it allsoe being the other parte of the Commaundement and that is the affeccion from which this exercise of mercy must arise, the Apostle tells us that this love is the fulfilling of the lawe, not that it is enough to love our brother and soe noe further but in regard of the excellency of his partes gieveing any motion to the other as the Soule to the body and the power it hath to sett all the faculties on worke in the outward exercise of this duty as when wee bid one make the clocke strike he doth not lay hand on the hammer which is the immediate instrument of the sound but setts on worke the first mover or maine wheele, knoeing that will certainely produce the sound which hee intends; soe the way to drawe men to the workes of mercy is not by force of Argument from the goodnes or necessity of the worke, for though this course may enforce a rationall minde to some present Act of mercy as is frequent in experience, yet it cannot worke such a habit in a Soule as shall make it prompt upon all occasions to produce the same effect but by frameing these affeccions of love in the hearte which will as natively bring forthe the other, as any cause doth produce the effect.

The deffinition which the Scripture gives us of love is this Love is the bond of perfection. First, it is a bond, or ligament. 2ly, it makes the worke perfect. There is noe body but consistes of partes and that which knitts these partes together gives the body its perfeccion, because it makes eache parte soe contiguous to other as thereby they doe mutually participate with eache other, both in strengthe and infirmity in pleasure and paine, to instance in the most perfect of all bodies, Christ and his church make one body: the severall partes of this body considered aparte before they were united were as disproportionate and as much disordering as soe many contrary quallities or elements but when christ comes and by his spirit and love knitts all these partes to himselfe and each to other, it is become the most perfect and best proportioned body in the world Eph: 4. 16. Christ by whome all the body being knitt together by every ioynt for the furniture thereof according to the effectuall power which is in the measure of every perfeccion of partes a glorious body without spott or wrinckle the ligaments hereof being Christ or his love for Christ is love 1 John: 4.8. Soe this definition is right. Love is the bond of perfection.

From hence wee may frame these Conclusions.

1 first all true Christians are of one body in Christ 1. Cor. 12. 12. 13. 17. [27.] Ye are the body of Christ and members of [your?] parte.

2ly. The ligaments of this body which knitt together are love.

3ly. Noe body can be perfect which wants its propper ligamentes.

4ly. All the partes of this body being thus united are made soe contiguous in a speciall relacion as they must needes partake of each others strength and infirmity, ioy, and sorrowe, weale and woe. 1 Cor: 12.26. If one member suffers all suffer with it, if one be in honour, all reioyce with it.

5ly. This sensiblenes and Sympathy of each others Condicions will necessarily infuse into each parte a native desire and endeavour, to strengthen defend preserve and comfort the other.

To insist a little on this Conclusion being the product of all the former the truthe herof will appeare both by precept and patterne 1. John. 3. 10. yee ought to lay downe your lives for the brethren Gal: 6. 2. beare ye one anothers burthens and soe fulfill the lawe of Christ.

For patterns wee have that first of our Saviour whoe out of his good will in obedience to his father, becomeing a parte of this body, and being knitt with it in the bond of love, found such a native sensiblenes of our infirmities and sorrowes as hee willingly yeilded himselfe to deathe to ease the infirmities of the rest of his body and soe heale theire sorrowes: from the like Sympathy of partes did the Apostles and many thousands of the Saintes lay downe theire lives for Christ againe, the like wee may see in the members of this body among themselves. 1. Rom. 9. Paule could have beene contented to have beene seperated from Christ that the Jewes might not be cutt off from the body: It is very observable which hee professeth of his affectionate part[ak]eing with every member: whoe is weake (saith hee) and I am not weake? whoe is offended and I burne not; and againe. 2. Cor: 7.13. therefore wee are comforted because yee were comforted, of Epaphroditus he speaketh Phil: 2. 30. that he regarded not his owne life to [do] him service soe Phebe and others are called the servantes of the Churche, now it is apparant that they served not for wages or by Constrainte but out of love, the like wee shall finde in the histories of the churche in all ages the sweete Sympathie of affeccions which was in the members of this body one towardes another, theire chearfullnes in serveing and suffering together how liberall they were without repineing harbourers without grudgeing and helpfull without reproacheing and all from hence they had fervent love amongst them which onely make[s] the practise of mercy constant and easie.

The next consideration is how this love comes to be wrought; Adam in his first estate was a perfect modell of mankinde in all theire generacions, and in him this love was perfected in regard of the habit, but Adam Rent in himselfe from his Creator, rent all his posterity allsoe one from another, whence it comes that every man is borne with this principle in him, to love and seeke himselfe only and thus a man continueth till Christ comes and takes possession of the soule, and infuseth another principle love to God and our brother. And this latter haveing continuall supply from Christ, as the head and roote by which hee is united get the predominency in the soule, soe by little and little expells the former 1 John 4. 7. love cometh of god and every one that loveth is borne of god, soe that this love is the fruite of the new birthe, and none can have it but the new Creature, now when this quallity is thus formed in the soules of men it workes like the Spirit upon the drie bones Ezek. 37. [7] bone came to bone, it gathers together the scattered bones or perfect old man Adam and knitts them into one body againe in Christ whereby a man is become againe a liveing soule.

The third Consideracion is concerning the exercise of this love, which is twofold, inward or outward, the outward hath beene handled in the former preface of this discourse, for unfolding the other wee must take in our way that maxime of philosophy, Simile simili gaudet or like will to like; for as it is things which are carved[1] with disafeccion to eache other, the ground of it is from a dissimilitude or [blank] ariseing from the contrary or different nature of the things themselves, soe the ground of love is an apprehension of some resemblance in the things loved to that which affectes it, this is the cause why the Lord loves the Creature, soe farre as it hath any of his Image in it, he loves his elect because they are like himselfe, he beholds them in his beloved sonne: soe a mother loves her childe, because shee throughly conceives a resemblance of herselfe in it. Thus it is betweene the members of Christ, each discernes by the worke of the spirit his owne Image and resemblance in another, and therefore cannot but love him as he loves himselfe: Now when the soule which is of a sociable nature findes any thing like to it selfe, it is like Adam when Eve was brought to him, shee must have it one with herselfe this is fleshe of my fleshe (saith shee) and bone of my bone shee conceives a greate delighte in it, therefore shee desires nearenes and familiarity with it: shee hath a greate propensity to doe it good and receives such content in it, as feareing the miscarriage of her beloved shee bestowes it in the inmost closett of her heart, shee will not endure that it shall want any good which shee can give it, if by occasion shee be withdrawne from the Company of it, shee is still lookeing towardes the place where shee left her beloved, if shee heare it groane shee is with it presently, if shee finde it sadd and disconsolate shee sighes and mournes with it, shee hath noe such ioy, as to see her beloved merry and thriveing, if shee see it wronged, shee cannot beare it without passion, shee setts noe boundes of her affections, nor hath any thought of reward, shee findes recompence enoughe in the exercise of her love towardes it, wee may see this Acted to life in Jonathan and David. Jonathan a valiant man endued with the spirit of Christ, soe soone as hee Discovers the same spirit in David had presently his hearte knitt to him by this linement of love, soe that it is said he loved him as his owne soule, he takes soe great pleasure in him that hee stripps himselfe to adorne his beloved, his fathers kingdome was not soe precious to him as his beloved David, David shall have it with all his hearte, himselfe desires noe more but that hee may be neare to him to reioyce in his good he chooseth to converse with him in the wildernesse even to the hazzard of his owne life, rather then with the greate Courtiers in his fathers Pallace; when hee sees danger towardes him, hee spares neither care paines, nor perill to divert it, when Iniury was offered his beloved David, hee could not beare it, though from his owne father, and when they must parte for a Season onely, they thought theire heartes would have broke for sorrowe, had not theire affections found vent by aboundance of Teares: other instances might be brought to shewe the nature of this affeccion as of Ruthe and Naomi and many others, but this truthe is cleared enough. If any shall object that it is not possible that love should be bred or upheld without hope of requitall, it is graunted but that is not our cause, for this

---

1. The text is here evidently corrupt.

love is allwayes under reward it never gives, but it allwayes receives with advantage: first, in regard that among the members of the same body, love and affection are reciprocall in a most equall and sweete kinde of Commerce.

2ly [3ly], in regard of the pleasure and content that the exercise of love carries with it as wee may see in the naturall body the mouth is at all the paines to receive, and mince the foode which serves for the nourishment of all the other partes of the body, yet it hath noe cause to complaine; for first, the other partes send backe by secret passages a due propor-cion of the same nourishment in a better forme for the strengthening and comforteing the mouthe. 2ly the labour of the mouthe is accompanied with such pleasure and content as farre exceedes the paines it takes: soe is it in all the labour of love, among christians, the partie loveing, reapes love againe as was shewed before, which the soule covetts more then all the wealthe in the world. 2ly [4ly]. noething yeildes more pleasure and content to the soule then when it findes that which it may love fervently, for to love and live beloved is the soules paradice, both heare and in heaven: In the State of Wedlock there be many comfortes to beare out the troubles of that Condicion; but let such as have tryed the most, say if there be any sweetnes in that Condicion comparable to the exercise of mutuall love.

From the former Consideracions ariseth these Conclusions.

1. First, This love among Christians is a reall thing not Imaginarie.

2ly. This love is as absolutely necessary to the being of the body of Christ, as the sin-ewes and other ligaments of a naturall body are to the being of that body.

3ly. This love is a divine spirituall nature free, active strong Couragious permanent under valueing all things beneathe its propper obiect, and of all the graces this makes us nearer to resemble the virtues of our heavenly father.

4ly, It restes in the love and wellfare of its beloved, for the full and certaine knowl-edge of these truthes concerning the nature use, [and] excellency of this grace, that which the holy ghost hath left recorded 1. Cor. 13. may give full satisfaccion which is needfull for every true member of this lovely body of the Lord Jesus, to worke upon theire heartes, by prayer meditacion continuall exercise at least of the speciall [power] of this grace till Christ be formed in them and they in him all in eache other knitt together by this bond of love.

It rests now to make some applicacion of this discourse by the present designe which gave the occasion of writeing of it. Herein are 4 things to be propounded: first the persons, 2ly, the worke, 3ly, the end, 4ly the meanes.

1. For the persons, wee are a Company professing our selves fellow members of Christ, In which respect onely though wee were absent from eache other many miles, and had our imploymentes as farre distant, yet wee ought to account our selves knitt together by this bond of love, and live in the excercise of it, if wee would have comforte of our being in Christ, this was notorious in the practise of the Christians in former times, as is testified of the Waldenses from the mouth of one of the adversaries Aeneas Sylvius, mutuo [solent amare] pene antequam norint, they use to love any of theire owne religion even before they were acquainted with them.

2ly. for the worke wee have in hand, it is by a mutuall consent through a speciall over-ruleing providence, and a more then an ordinary approbation of the Churches of Christ to seeke out a place of Cohabitation and Consorteshipp under a due forme of Government both civill and ecclesiasticall. In such cases as this the care of the publique must oversway all private respects, by which not onely conscience, but meare Civill pol-licy doth binde us; for it is a true rule that perticuler estates cannott subsist in the ruine of the publique.

3ly. The end is to improve our lives to doe more service to the Lord the comforte and encrease of the body of christe whereof wee are members that our selves and posterity may be the better preserved from the Common corrupcions of this evill world to serve the Lord and worke out our Salvacion under the power and purity of his holy Ordinances.

4ly for the meanes whereby this must bee effected, they are 2fold, a Conformity with the worke and end wee aime at, these wee see are extraordinary, therefore wee must not content our selves with usuall ordinary meanes whatsoever wee did or ought to have done when wee lived in England, the same must wee doe and more allsoe where wee goe: That which the most in theire Churches maineteine as a truthe in profession onely, wee must bring into familiar and constant practise, as in this duty of love wee must love brotherly without dissimulation, wee must love one another with a pure hearte fervently wee must beare one anothers burthens, wee must not looke onely on our owne things, but allsoe on the things of our brethren, neither must wee think that the lord will beare with such faileings at our hands as hee dothe from those among whome wee have lived, and that for 3 Reasons.

1. In regard of the more neare bond of mariage, betweene him and us, wherein he hath taken us to be his after a most strickt and peculiar manner which will make him the more Jealous of our love and obedience soe he tells the people of Israeli, you onely have I knowne of all the families of the Earthe therefore will I punishe you for your Transgressions.

2ly, because the lord will be sanctified in them that come neare him. Wee know that there were many that corrupted the service of the Lord some setting upp Alters before his owne, others offering both strange fire and strange Sacrifices allsoe; yet there came noe lire from heaven, or other sudden Judgement upon them as did upon Nadab and Abihu whoe yet wee may thinke did not sinne presumptuously.

3ly. When God gives a speciall Commission he lookes to have it stricktly observed in every Article, when hee gave Saule a Commission to destroy Amaleck hee indented with him upon certaine Articles and because hee failed in one of the least, and that upon a faire pretence, it lost him the kingdome, which should have beene his reward, if hee had observed his Commission: Thus stands the cause betweene God and us, wee are entered into Covenant with him for this worke, wee have taken out a Commission, the Lord hath given us leave to drawe our owne Articles wee have professed to enterprise these Accions upon these and these ends, wee have hereupon besought him of favour and blessing: Now if the Lord shall please to heare us, and bring us in peace to the place wee desire, then hath hee ratified this Covenant and sealed our Commission, [and] will expect a strickt performance of the Articles contained in it, but if wee shall neglect the observacion of these Articles which are the ends wee have propounded, and dissembling with our God, shall fall to embrace this present world and prosecute our carnall intencions, seekeing great things for our selves and our posterity, the Lord will surely breake out in wrathe against us be revenged of such a periured people and make us knowe the price of the breache of such a Covenant.

Now the onely way to avoyde this shipwracke and to provide for our posterity is to followe the Counsell of Micah, to doe Justly, to love mercy, to walk humbly with our God, for this end, wee must be knitt together in this worke as one man, wee must entertaine each other in brotherly Affeccion, wee must be willing to abridge our selves of our superfluities, for the supply of others necessities, wee must uphold a familiar Commerce together in all meekenes, gentlenes, patience and liberallity, wee must delight in eache other, make others Condicions our owne reioyce together, mourne together, labour, and suffer together, allwayes haveing before our eyes our Commission and Community in the worke, our Community as members of the same body, soe shall wee keepe the unitie of the spirit in the bond of peace, the Lord will be our God and delight to dwell among us, as his owne people and will commaund a blessing upon us in all our wayes, soe that wee shall see much more of his wisdome power goodnes and truthe then formerly wee have beene acquainted with, wee shall finde that the God of Israeli is among us, when tenn of us shall be able to resist a thousand of our enemies, when hee shall make us a prayse and glory, that men shall say of succeeding plantacions: the lord make it like that of New England: for wee must Consider that wee shall be as a Citty upon a Hill, the eies of all people are uppon us; soe that if wee shall deale falsely with our god in this worke wee have undertaken and soe cause him to withdrawe his present help from us, wee shall be made a story and a by-word through the world, wee shall open the mouthes of enemies to speake evill of the wayes of god and all professours for Gods sake; wee shall shame the faces of many of gods worthy servants, and cause theire prayers to be turned into Cursses upon us till wee be consumed out of the good land whether wee are goeing: And to shutt upp this discourse with that exhortacion of Moses that faithfull servant of the Lord in his last farewell to Israel: Deut. 30. Beloved there is now sett before us life, and good, deathe and evill in that wee are Commaunded this day to love the Lord our God, and to love one another to walke in his wayes and to keepe his Commaundements and his Ordinance, and his lawes, and the Articles of our Covenant with him that wee may live and be multiplyed, and that the Lord our God may blesse us in the land whether wee goe to possesse it: But if our heartes shall turne away soe that wee will not obey, but shall be seduced and worshipp [serve *cancelled*] other Gods our pleasures, and proffitts, and serve them; it is propounded unto us this day, wee shall surely perishe out of the good Land whether wee passe over this vast Sea to possesse it;

> Therefore lett us choose life,
> that wee, and our Seede,
> may live; by obeyeing his
> voyce, and cleaveing to him,
> for hee is our life, and
> our prosperity.

JOHN COTTON

Selection from *A Treatise of the Covenant of Grace* (1636)

Although the early New England Puritans could boast some of the greatest ministers in the Anglo-American world, John Cotton (1584–1652) was arguably their greatest. Erudite, eloquent, and immensely influential, he was a master of the precisely logical Puritan "plain style" with which he infused his forty volumes of sermons and treatises on virtually every controverted Puritan subject, from theology and social ethics to political theory and ecclesiastical government. But if there was one intellectually defining moment in Cotton's career, it was when he preached a series of sermons on the subject of grace and salvation three years after arriving in the Massachusetts Bay Colony in 1633.

In these sermons (later collected to form his *Treatise*), Cotton marked out a distinct path for Puritan theology. His starting point was its central doctrine—the covenant of grace—by which a divinely elected human remnant, no longer since Adam's fall able to achieve holiness through their works, were promised salvation conditioned by their faith. But to this metahistory Cotton added, more clearly than did most of his colleagues, the caveat that God fulfilled *both* of the new covenant's two sides: His promise of the salvation of the elect *and* their faith that "conditioned" it. Moreover, he scorned as strong evidence of a person's "justification" (God's imputation of Christ's virtue to an individual) various outward signs of "sanctification" (or the justified person's moral conduct) that many ministers encouraged their flocks to consider when deciding whether or not someone had been regenerated through grace. These views were not "antinomian" or (as the term literally meant) "against the law" in any heretical sense; Cotton always insisted that the Mosaic law was highly useful in God's plan as well as thoroughly binding on both the elect and nonelect. But for Cotton what was crucial for salvation were two spiritual processes: a person's preparations through the active yet selfless exercise of such holy "gifts" as contrition, humility, and love; and, above that, God's implantation of a spirit that transformed these otherwise spiritually impotent powers into divine facilitators of the yearning soul's exaltation into the eternal life of the saint. Just how the putative saints were succeeding with these inward procedures that year seems to have been to Cotton somewhat of an open question.

The best guide to Cotton's intellectual development remains Larzer Ziff, *The Career of John Cotton: Puritanism and the American Experience* (Princeton, 1962). For discussions of Cotton's position in the context of "preparationist" and "spiritist" traditions within mainstream orthodox Puritan theology, see William K. B. Stoever, *"A Faire and Easie Way to Heaven": Covenant Theology and Antinomianism in Early Massachusetts* (Middletown, Conn., 1978), chap. 3; and Janice Knight, *Orthodoxies in Massachusetts: Rereading American Puritanism* (Cambridge, Mass., 1994), chap. 5.

… Quest. 6. We come now unto a sixth question. If the Lord do give himself first in the Covenant of his Grace, this may then be a doubt, and a question in Christian soul; If God gives himself before any blessing, before any Promise in order of nature (though he giveth himself alwaies in a Promise)…, if we cannot claim any blessing from God at the first in any conditional promise, therefore not by any condition in our selves, but as we received all things from God, so we claim all things from God in Jesus Christ, and so do first seek for him, and for all things in him: If thus, *to what use then serveth the Law of God, which requireth such and such conditions in us? do we not abrogate the Law, and make it of none effect, and root it out from having any power over Christians?* And truly, some under pretence of the Covenant of Grace, have thought it altogether bootless to bind Christians unto the Law of God, and to look at it as any part of the direction of their course: because this is an imputation usually reflected upon the Convenant of Grace, let us consider therefore, and enquire *to what use serveth the Law of God, if God give himself first unto his people in the Covenant of his Grace?*

Answ. Though the Lord giveth himself freely to the soul, and his Son, and all the blessings of the Covenant of Grace, without respect unto any work of the *Law,* yet the *Law* is of special and notable use unto all the sons of men, both unto them which are not yet brought home unto God by converting Grace, and also to those that are Regenerate in Jesus Christ.…

First, unto *carnal* men, and they are of two sorts, some belong unto the *Election* of Grace, though they be not yet called; others are not written in the Lambs Book of Life, but will in the end finally perish: and yet the Law is of use unto both sorts of them.

1. For those that are the *Elect* of God, it is of use unto them, to aggravate their sin, and to multiply it unto them as it were; that is to say, to aggravate the apprehension of the hainousness of sin upon their Consciences, and to set home the burden of their sins unto their souls, thereby to drive them to feel their great need of the Lord Jesus Christ, whom otherwise they should for ever have despised. Thus the Apostle answereth in the place fore-named, *The Law was added because of transgressions:* that they might clearly appear, and be aggravated thereby; that a man might plainly discern how he hath made himself liable unto the wrath of God, by so manifold breaches of so many Commandments in one kind or other: the Law giveth clear knowledg of sin, and so much the more doth it set on the weight of it upon the Conscience, working fear in the heart, *Rom.* 8.15. and hence it is that the Apostle telleth us, *Gal.* 3.24. that *the Law was our School-master to Christ;* as a School-master driveth his Scholar through fear, unto this or that duty: so the Law of God driveth the soul though fear unto *Jesus Christ;* not that it doth reveal *Christ* a Saviour and Redeemer of Free Grace, but the soul being once brought down under the sense of sin by the terrors of the *Law,* will readily and diligently hearken unto the news of Christ a Saviour: for being once made sensible of his own inability to redeem himself, and unworthiness to be redeemed from the wrath of God, now is the Soul fitted to hear the voice of the Gospell, now is the news of *Jesus Christ* beautiful, and glad tidings: and of this use is the *Law* unto the *Elect* of God, before they come under the Covenant of the Grace of God.

2. But of what use is the Law unto other men? *Answ.* First, In regard of *disobedience* it is of use unto them, and 2. the *obedience* to it is of use,

1. In regard of *disobedience:* for if men had not known sin, it had been some pretence, though they had committed sin; but when men have the knowledge of the *Law,* and yet

Source: John Cotton, *A Treatise of the Covenant of Grace, As it is dispensed to the Elect Seed, effectually unto Salvation* (London: Peter Parker, 1671), 67–71, 72–76, 80–81, 87–101, 107–11.

commit sin willingly, now they have no Cloak for their sin.... Thus there is use of the Law unto disobedient persons, their disobedience will leave them without excuse when they sin against their Consciences, and against the means which the Lord hath administered unto them: for though the Lord never gave them such grace as did accompany Salvation, yet such *Illumination* he did give them, that they needed not to have broken his *Law* so many wayes, with such wicked hands as they have done: therefore when they have been enlarged to perform many duties, and might avoid much sin, and yet will sin against their Consciences, and tread underfoot those means of grace that were committed unto them; It is then most righteous with God that they should be condemned.

2. Of what use is the *obedience* of the Law unto such whom Gods soul taketh no pleasure in? Truely, it is of sad and dreadful use unto them; for it serveth to harden them in their sins, (though that be but an accidental use thereof) their sins are thereby made out of measure sinful, *Rom.* 7.13. They harden their hearts, 1. by their *obedience* to the Law. 2. By the *Comfort* which they take in that Obedience; both these do marvellously harden their hearts. For the first of these, The Apostle *Paul, Acts* 23.1. had kept so good a Conscience, that he knew not any sin against the *Law* that he lived in; but though he was unrebukable, he did count it all loss afterward, *Phil.* 3.7,8. those things that before he thought had been his gain, now he *counteth them but dung that he may win Christ:* when a man attaineth to outward conformity unto the *Law,* he is then ready to think it is indeed good for poor sinful men to look for Salvation by *Jesus Christ;* but for himself, he hopeth in his devotion, and that he is able to save himself: these are such as justifie themselves before men, to whom our Saviour speaketh, *Luke* 16.15. and of whom he saith, *That Publicans and Harlots shall go into the Kingdome of Heaven before them,* Matth. 21.31, 32. for many times you shall have the most deboist and profane wretches more humbled, and readier to hearken to the voice of Christ, and sooner convinced of the necessity of the Covenant of Grace, then those that are but morally righteous by the Law, *Rom.* 9.30, 31, 32.... Thus the *Law* becometh a snare unto them; and that which is of singular and wholsome use unto the Children of God, is made death unto them. And as their obedience to the *Law* is thus a snare unto them: so secondly, the *delight* and *comfort* which they take in their obedience is a greater snare then the other: the stony and thorny soil did hear the Word with joy, and so those Hypocrites, *Isa.* 59.2. *did delight to approach unto God:* but what followed upon the delight which they took in God, and in holy Duties? it made them ready to expostulate with God, why he did not answer them according to their works: the delight which they found, did so fill their hearts with assurance of the Grace of God, that they looked at their Duties as so many tokens of the love of God unto their souls; and then when men come to find more comfort in their obedience, then in the grace of God in *Jesus Christ,* it maketh them ready to expostulate with God, touching the worth of their own righteousness. *Isa.* 57.10. *Thou hast found the life of thine hand, therefore thou wast not grieved;* as long as a man findeth life and comfort in his own duties and performances, what need can he see to be grieved for the want of *Jesus Christ?* or at the best, if he do grieve, and find his heart comforted in grieving and delighting in the course of Humiliation, he then thinketh he hath no need of being farther solicitous about his spiritual estate. Thus we see plainly, that the *Law* of God is of marvellous use in the dayes of the Gospel, of great use unto those that belong unto God, to break their hearts for sin, and to drive them to *Jesus Christ;* and for others, the *disobedience* of the *Law,* leaves them without excuse, that so disobey it; again, the obedience of it, and comfort in that obedience, doth harden the hearts of others from *Jesus Christ.*

2. But what say you then unto men that are under a Covenant of Grace, and brought unto fellowship with Christ therein? of what use is the Law of God unto such? is it utterly antiquated, or is there any more to be done with it?

Answ. The Apostle answereth this Question, when he saith, *I am not without the Law to God, but under the law to Christ,* 1 Cor. 9.21. so (mind you) the *Law* is of use unto the Apostle *Paul,* but how? as the *Law* cometh under Christ, so *Paul* cometh under the *Law;* this is the sum of the Answer, but that would be further explained. What meaneth he when he saith, *I am under the Law to Christ?* In some sense a Christian is wholly freed from the *Law:* In some sense he is yet under the *Law.* So far as the *Law* is any way besides, or out of Christ, so far the Apostle is without the *Law:* So far as the *Law* is under Christ, so far he is under the *Law.* Keep close to these two Principles, and you shall safely avoid Rocks on every hand: thus by the use of the *Law* shall you not go aside to a Covenant of Works, nor by attendance unto Grace, shall you need to neglect the Law. How far is the *Law* under Christ? when it hath brought the soul nearer unto Christ, and in a remote manner prepared him, the *Law is* in *Christ,* and you subject to it in him. 1. As the *Law* is *given* by Christ. 2. As in Christ *help* is given to perform it. First, as the *Law is* given by Christ, as 1 *Thes.* 4.2, 3. *You know what Commandments we gave you by the Lord Jesus: for this is the will of God, even your Sanctification, &c.* and many other Commandments he gave them, all which are legal Commandments, and yet the Apostle gave them by the *Lord Jesus:* so Mat. 5.17. to the end of the Chapter: our Saviour Christ would not have us think that he came to destroy the Law or the Prophets, but to fulfill them. And to that end he doth there expound the spiritual and true meaning of the *Law,* that whereas the *Pharisees* held forth the outward letter of the *Law* to be observed only, as thinking that unless a man did commit the Act of Murder, he was not guilty of the breach of the sixth Commandment; and if he committed not the Act of Adultery, he transgressed not the seventh Commandment, and so of the rest: Our Saviour Christ expoundeth the Law more spiritually, shewing that anger against a mans brother is the breach of the sixth Commandment; and whosoever shall look on a Woman to lust after her, hath committed Adultery with her in his heart, and broken the seventh Commandment; thus Christ hath as it were revived *Moses:* but as the *Law* is given by Christ, it is not a Covenant of Works; but a Commandment of welldoing; and he having given it, we take our selves bound to be subject to it. The Apostle also presseth the Moral *Law* upon several relations of men, *Ephes.* 6.1, 2, 3, &c. It is an honour to *Jesus Christ,* that his servants should be holy, as he is holy; it is for the glory of God, and he requireth it: The Apostle *James* presseth it, chap. 2.8. to the end of the Chapter. *If you fulfill the Royal Law according to the Scripture, (Thou shalt love thy Neighbour as thy self) ye do well.* And again, *Whosoever shall keep the whole Law, and yet offend in one point, he is guilty of all.* Thus we see the Apostles of *Jesus Christ* put it upon Christians to keep the *Law* of God, and *Christ* himself beareth witness to the *Law:* for God will never justifie sin to be no sin, though he will justifie the person of a sinner.

Now as the Lord Jesus giveth the *Law,* and as it were reneweth it, so he doth also give his *Spirit* unto his servants, enabling them to keep it, *Jer.* 31.33. *Ezek.* 36.27. *I will put my spirit within you, and cause you to walk in my Statutes, and ye shall keep my Judgments, and do them.* And again, *I will put my Law in their hearts, and write it in their inward parts.* Now this *Law* would he not write in the hearts of his people, nor given unto them his holy *Spirit* enabling them to keep his *Law,* were it not his will in *Jesus Christ,* that the Law should be the rule of holiness and righteousness unto his people: hence it is, that the children of God, though they be not under the *Covenant* of the *Law,* yet take themselves to be bound to the obedience of it; for if Jesus Christ have given the *Law,* as well as *Moses,* and if he have ratified it by giving them his *Spirit,* to teach and strengthen them to keep it, though not perfectly, yet sincerely, then they take themselves bound to obey the *Law,* though they be under the *Covenant* of *Grace;* for do *we make void the Law through faith? God forbid: yea, we establish the Law.* For what need have Christians of free Justification by Christ, if they were not bound to obedience by the Commandment of the Law? Therefore the free Justification of men under a free Covenant of Grace, doth establish the obedience of the *Law,* otherwise what need they run to Christ to save them from the *curse* of the *Law?* Why do we still run to Christ for the continuance of our justification? But that we find our selves ungodly creatures against the righteous and holy *Law* of God: therefore if God have given men the *Law,* and his holy *Spirit* to strengthen them in the obedience of it, and his *grace* to save them from the *curse* of it; then Christians are to know that they are bound to keep the *Law;* they lie under the *authority* of it, and dare not pluck their necks from under that yoke....

But how is a Christian *not under the Law?*

So far forth as the *Law* is not under Christ; I mean, so far as it is without Christ freely justifying of us by his grace, so far a Christian is freed from under the *Law.* In one word, a Christian man under a Covenant of Grace, is not under a Covenant of Works. *Rom.* 6.14. *You are not under the Law, but under Grace:* he meaneth, not under the *Covenant* of the *Law,* nor under the *power* and *authority* of the *Law,* as of their husband, *Rom.* 7.1, 2, 3, 4. The husbandly *Jurisdiction* of the *Law* is taken away; *The Law is not made for a righteous man,* I Tim. 1.9. that is, not the *Covenant* of the *Law,* for else we are under the *Commandments* of the *Law* to *Christ,* but the Jewish Teachers taught more, to wit, the *Covenant* of the *Law* unto Salvation: not but that the *Law is good, if a man use it lawfully;* he meaneth the *Covenant* of the *Law:* but how shall a man use it lawfully? for it is not given unto a righteous man; but he reckoneth up the breakers of every Commandment, and unto them it is given; *to the lawless, and disobedient; to the ungodly, and sinners; to the unholy, and profane; to murtherers of fathers, and murtherers of mothers; to man-slayers, and whoremongers; and to them that defile themselves with man-kind; to men-stealers, to lyars, to perjured persons, and if there be any other things that are contrary to sound Doctrine;* the *Covenant* of the *Law* is given unto such (and unto none but such) to *convince* them of their sins against the *Law,* to *humble* them to the death, and to *drive* them out of themselves, and confidence in themselves. But how doth it appear that the *Covenant of* the *Law* is not given to the children of God? from hence it is manifest;

Because a Christian man neither looketh for Justification and *Salvation* from his *Obedience* to the *Law,* nor feareth *Condemnation* though he fail in his Obedience; and: this is a fruit of his exemption from under the *Covenant* of the *Law:* For if a man should look for Life by his Obedience to the *Law,* and fear condemnation by the breach of it, this would bring a man under the *Covenant of the Law:* for the sanctification of the *Covenant* of the *Law,* is life to them that obey; and to them that disobey, death, and the curse. But a Christian looketh not for Life by his Obedience; and that is plain, *Psal.* 143.2. *Enter not into Judgment with thy servant, for in thy sight shall no flesh living be justified.* So *Rom.* 3.20. *By the deeds of the Law there shall no flesh be justified, for by the Law is the knowledge of sin:* therefore no hope of Salvation from our Obedience to the *Law.* But methinks (you will say) a Christian may fear his *condemnation* because of his *Disobedience* to the *Law.* Truly this is a great snare, and this Doctrine will be scandalous to many a poor soul, but without cause: Indeed, if God give a man to be under the Covenant of Grace, and not to see it, then he may fear; but if a man know himself to be under the Covenant of Grace, then he doth not fear condemnation from his disobedience....

Use 1. If any therefore shall accuse the Doctrine of the Covenant of free Grace of *Anti-nomianism,* and say, it teacheth men freedome from the *Law of Moses;* any if they commit any sin, they plead they are not bound unto the *Law;* we see how false such an aspersion would be: for all the people of God know, that the Lord is an avenger of every such wickedness. There is none under a Covenant of Grace that dare allow himself in any sin; for if a man should negligently commit any sin, the Lord will school him throughly, and make him sadly to apprehend how he hath made bold with the treasures of the grace of God.... So that the children of the Covenant of grace will only tell you, that they are free from the Covenant of the *Law,* but not from the *Commandment* of it: for as it is given by *Jesus Christ,* and ratified in the Gospel; and as Christ hath given us his Spirit enabling us to keep it, we are under it so far, as to take our selves bound by the authority of it; and if we do transgress against it, we know it is sin in the sight of God, and therefore it is that the soul in such a case is sensible of the wrath and displeasure of God, whether it be his own sin, or the sin of his brethren: therefore he runneth unto God for mercy; which he would not do, if he did not know, that his desert according to the *Law* did utterly cut him off from mercy, else would he never pray for pardon of sin, nor rejoyce when the Lord helpeth him to do that which is right and just in his sight, not bless the Lord for strengthening him unto obedience, unless he thought it to be his duty: and therefore,

Use 2. It is of use also to teach the servants of God, how far they *are freed* from the *Law;* to wit, from the *Covenant* of it: so that they neither look for justification, nor salvation from it. And let it not be grievous to any soul, that a Christian should say, He doth not fear *condemnation* by his disobedience: he will be apt to fear in this kind, untill he be assured of the favor of God; but when he knoweth his portion in the Covenant, then indeed he doth not fear *condemnation* by his sin, nor doth he think that the Lord will cleave unto him because of his fruitfulness; he casteth not off his comfort, nor looketh at himself as divorced from Christ, because of his barrenness before the Lord; nor doth he look for his daily bread from all his obedience, but expecteth all goodness and blessing from the treasures of the free grace of God.

Use 3. This may also serve to teach men some kind of discernment of their own spirits, and state: if you look for Justification no longer then you are obedient, and fear eternal condemnation when you are disobedient; if you be afraid of divorce from Christ because of your sins, or if you look for any blessing, and challenge right to any promise, by vertue of any welldoing of your own; in such a case either thou art under a Covenant of works, or at the least thou art gone aside to a Covenant of works; and if ever the Lord open your eyes, and bestow his free grace upon you, you will know your redemption from such dependances as these be. I know a Christian man, that hath not been clearly taught the distinct differences of the two Covenants, may be misled into dangerous waies, that might tend unto the utter undoing of his soul, but it is a sin of ignorance, and the Lord will not leave his servants, but clear up his truth and grace unto them.

Use 4. May serve to teach the servants of God, that desire to walk in a way of constant comfort, how to build their faith and their hope: truly if they be grounded upon your own obedience, or righteousness, or sanctification; if they depend upon you, you will find your hearts ever unsetled: you may find comfort, as under the *Law* you shall; for if a man be married to the *Law,* the Law will cast in comfort upon him because of his obedience; but if you shall believe that Christ is yours, and comfort your selves because you have been by the power of the *Law* constrained to duties, and restrained from sin, and thereupon build your conjugal communion with Jesus Christ, you will find your souls full of sadness and fear ere long, specially if you have true grace in your hearts: and therefore it is the faithfulness and tenderness of the grace of God unto his people, that when Christians come into this Countrey, though they have been marvellous eminent in our native Countrey, they cannot pray fervently, nor hear the word with profit, nor receive the seals with comfort: they wonder what is become of their old prayers, and hearings, and Sacraments, and of their lively spirits in holy duties; truly the Lord hath disenabled them (as it were) from such things, because they did build their union and fellowship with Jesus Christ upon them, that so they might know the freedome of the grace of God, *that justifieth the Ungodly*; then will the poor soul be glad to seek after the Lord Jesus Christ and say (as the people of God sometimes did, *Hos.* 2.7.) *I will go, and return to my first husband; for then was it better with me then now*: now the soul will plainly see and discern, that he closed not with his true Husband, when as he built so much hope and comfort upon his duties; therefore he will find himself weak, and dead, (as it were) to all spiritual duties, and can find no life in them, no comfort from them; and it is the marvellous goodness, and free grace of God unto such a soul, whom the Lord will not suffer to bless himself in his works; for if a man should lay the foundation of his comfort in them, and be ready as it were to take it ill, if he should not find God accepting his works; *Wherefore have we fasted and thou regardest it not? Isa.* 58.3. If a man *rejoyce in the sparks which he hath kindled, this shall he receive at the hands of God, to lye down in sorrow, Isa.* 50.11. whereas the light of God shall graciously break forth unto the servants of God, though they wait upon him, though they be for present in darkness, and see no light. Trust not therefore in any legal comforts, but wait upon the free grace of God, both to *justifie, sanctifie, comfort,* and *glorifie* your soul; and this is the way of constant peace: and if the Lord do at any time check his servants, when they walk in by-wayes; it is, that he may build them upon a surer foundation. So that their salvation will not lye upon their obedience, nor damnation be procured by their disobedience: this is the way of constant peace and safety unto all the *Israel* of God.

Quest. 7. This Doctrine may serve in the next place, to answer a seventh Question, touching the necessity of *Sanctification*. For it may be demanded, If the Lord will give *himself* unto the soul in the Covenant of his Grace, not only his attributes, but his *person*, all that is God is given by vertue of this Covenant; If God will give *himself*, not only to choose us to life and glory, but his *Son* to redeem us, and his *holy Spirit* to sanctifie us, *Ezek.* 36.27. what need is there of Sanctification: for if the *Holy Ghost* will dwell in us, he can take our wits, and understanding, and understand all our Mediations for us, without any such actual concurrence of ours, as might be requisite for that end; if the Lord giveth himself to be my *righteousness,* and *holiness,* what need I then these gifts of holiness? So that this in sum is the Question, If the Lord will give unto us himself, what need we these gifts to work any thing, which God is much more able to perform then we can be? This springeth naturally from the Doctrine.

Ans. Though the Lord giveth us himself, and his holy Spirit to dwell in us, yet is it needful that we should be indued with all the gifts of the Spirit of Grace that do accompany salvation. You will say, What need is there then that the *Holy Ghost* should dwell in us? or will not these carry an end our souls unto immortality? Truly we have need that the Lord should give us his holy Spirit to dwell in us, notwithstanding all the gifts of his grace, though they indeed are necessary conditions to be found in the souls of all Gods servants, *Heb.* 12.14. *Follow peace and holiness, without which no man shall see the Lord.* As if he made it of absolute necessity to salvation, not only in another world, but for a comfortable condition in this world; *follow* Peace and Holiness, as if so be that they were ready to fly away from a man; and indeed the word doth imply no less: for διώκετε, doth signifie the pursuit of something that fleeth from a man, as peace will many times flee from one, and a man will have much ado to attain unto it, *Psal.* 120.6, 7. *My soul hath long dwelt with him that hateth peace: I am for peace, but when I speak, they are for war*: it is not easily attained unto, therefore should not be suffered to depart, but held fast when it is enjoyed. And so for *Holiness*: the Apostle would have us make an holy kind of pursuit after it, as if it were still withdrawing from us; which cometh through the corruptions of our heart; for we are soon weary of holy Duties, as Prayer, or Conference, or the like: if Holiness be in anything, it soon groweth wearisome to flesh and blood; but though our weak and feeble nature will be withdrawing us from holiness, yet the Lord would have us to *follow* it, and pursue it; and so shall a man be withdrawn from the world, and from the temptations and bad examples thereof. Do not say, What, shall we be wiser then our Fathers? and, Is not Moderation best in all things? but consider what the Apostle saith, *Follow* still after it, even unto perfection; and his words do intimate the reason of it, *without which no man shall see the Lord:* for what is *Holiness* in its own nature? it is that which giveth God his due, as *righteousness* giveth man his due. And this is a main ground why we are so slow in works of holiness: for were they of another nature, and did they serve our turns more, as we think, we should not then account them tedious; If I were to sit and tell money all day long, this is for my self (saith a man) and for my profit; and if it were for another, we should not think the time long, it may be, at that work neither: but (mind you) when it cometh to any thing which doth concern the Lord, then it's so far above a mans reach, whatsoever we have to do in the things of God, that we should soon be weary of reaching forth our hands all the day long unto the Lord, and to be constantly for God, from God, and with God, in all our Actions: our base spirits are soon ready to be withdrawing from the Lord; therefore the Apostle biddeth us *follow after Peace, and Holiness, without which no man shall see God:* so that great is the necessity of Holiness, and worthy to be followed after: for though a mans own heart, and the world, and men, and Satan withdraw us from it, yet *follow* after it, for *without it no man shall see God.* There is a kind of holiness which some men have attained unto, many a fair day ago, but 'tis a thousand to one, whether it be the holiness which doth accompany salvation, for that Holiness is not easily attained unto; but the other will easily cleave close unto a man.

1. *Quest.* Now if you shall ask me, wherefore the Lord will have us *pursue* after Holiness; and what needeth it, if the Spirit of Holiness dwell in me by an everlasting Covenant: if it did withdraw from us as it did from *Adam,* it was another matter; but though it may be quenched in us, yet *abideth* it for ever: what need then of gifts of Holiness?

Answ. That one word may be sufficient, which we find in 2 *Tim.* 2.21. *If any man purge himself from these evils, he shall be a vessel unto honour, satisfied and meet for the Masters use, and prepared unto every good work.* This sheweth us why gifts of Holiness are requisite to be in Gods people, namely that they might become meet instruments in the hands of God, and fitted unto every good word and work; therefore it is, that the Lord will have us to be filled with all the gifts of Righteousness, and fruits of his Spirit, that we might be more fit *Temples* for the Holy Ghost to dwell in: and this is the principal Reason of the Point.

2. *Qu.* If then there be such gifts of holiness, what need the *Holy Ghost dwell* in us? is it not enough that he should shed abroad these things into our hearts? cannot the Lord carry an end the work of our salvation of these gifts?

Answ. There is need that the *Holy Ghost* should dwell in us, notwithstanding. 1. To *keep* these gifts in us. 2. To *act* them in us. 3. To *witness* these unto our souls, for our comfort, and the good one of another. Some Scriptures for all these.

1. That there is need *of the Holy Ghost* to keep these things in us; 2 *Tim.* 1.14. *That good thus which was comitted unto thee, keep by the Holy Ghost which dwelleth in us.* There is a very worthy thing committed to us, how shall we keep it? not by our own wit and wisdom, careful watchfulness, and faithfulness, (though such things ought not to be wanting) but the charge is, *Keep those things by the Holy Ghost which dwelleth in us.* We stand in need of *gifts,* to be fit instruments in the hands of God; we stand in need of the *Spirit* of God, to maintain that which God giveth us: and though *Adams gifts* were in perfection, yet not having the *holy Ghost* to *keep* them for him, they all flie from him as soon as ever he had tasted of the forbiden fruit, and left him naked and desperate. Therefore in the Covenant of Grace the Lord giveth the *Holy Ghost* to *keep* strong possession in his servants, against the strong man armed. This is the first ground why the *Holy Ghost dwelleth* in us.

2. Its the *Holy Ghost,* that *acteth* the gifts given to us, and enableth them in us: for the *Holy Ghost* who keepeth possession, doth derive continued strength into our faith, which putteth life into all the gifts of God. And if you shall ask how *love,* and *patience,* and the rest of the gifts of God do work? The *Holy Ghost stirreth* up faith to look unto Christ, who returneth strength by his Spirit unto Faith: and so *faith worketh by love,* and by meekness, and by all the rest of the fruits of the Spirit. Thus the Spirit of God *acteth* according to what we read, *Rom.* 8.14. As *many as are led by the Spirit of God, are the sons of God:* come to any holy duty, and it is the *Holy Ghost,* that leadeth you along, and *Acteth* in you: so *Ezek.* 36.27. *I will put my Spirit within you, and cause you to walk in my statutes, and you shall keep my judgments, and do them.* And, *holy men of God speak as they were moved by the Holy Ghost.* It is the *Spirit* of God that *moveth* us to any good work, and that *acteth* the gifts of his grace in us.

3. The Spirit of God doth not only keep these gifts for us, and act them in us; but it is the same Spirit of God that *witnesseth* to these gifts, and sheweth what gifts he hath given us; for such is the blindness of the nature of all the Sons of men, and it is a wonder to see, that generally Christians when the Lord first worketh these gifts in them, not one of a thousand but they think they are in a sad and fearful condition, &c so they are very uncomfortable: but now lest that we should alwayes mistake that which the Lord hath given us, *we have received the Spirit of God, that we might know the things that are freely given unto us of God,* 1 Cor. 2.12. he indeed taketh his own time to discover it, to some sooner, to some later; but this is his intendment, that he might honour his grace unto us, by all the rich and gracious gifts which he hath given us.

He doth also reveal unto us the duties which he helpeth us to do, *Rom. 9.1. I say the truth in Christ, I lye not, my conscience also bearing me witness in the holy Ghost, That I have great heaviness, and continual sorrow in mine heart: For I could wish that my self were accursed from Christ, for my Brethren, my Kinsmen according to the flesh.* The *Holy Ghost* that wrought in him this brotherly-love, the same *Holy Ghost beareth* him *witness* that he doth not lie; and that he had continual sorrow in his heart, and that he could have wished to have been accursed from Christ, that they might be saved? it grieved him so much that the whole Nation should be destitute of the Lord Jesus Christ.

Thus we see how great need there is of the Holy Ghost to *dwell* in us, to *keep* all the gifts of his grace in us, to *act* them according to his will, and to *discover* to us what gracious gifts the Lord hath wrought in us, and what duties he hath helped us to do, that we may be able to give account of them by the *Holy Ghost* that *dwelleth in us,* and beareth witness with us. So there is necessity both of the *gifts* of grace, that we may be fit Temples for the *Holy Ghost* to dwell in, and fit instruments for him to work by: there is need also the *Holy Ghost* should dwell in us, for the causes we have spoken unto....

3 *Quest.* How may we then *imploy* and *improve* his *Sanctification* which the Lord hath given us, and which he keepeth and acteth in us by his Spirit, and whereunto he beareth witness? How, or to what end shall we imploy it, seeing the Lord undertaketh to do these things for us?

Answ. If so be it, that the Lord Jesus Christ by his Spirit giveth us these gifts: It is our part then first to see that we do not rest in any sanctification, which doth spring from Christ, conveyed unto us by his blessed Spirit. The Spirit knitteth us unto Christ, and Christ unto us; he worketh faith in us to receive whatsoever the Lord giveth unto us, and by the same faith worketh all our holiness for us, 1 *Cor.* 1.30. *Christ is made unto us of God, wisdom, and righteousness, and sanctification, and redemption:* therefore we are to see him principal author of all these things in us, and for us. This is the principal comfort of all, and the glory of all our safety, and so far as any of these lieth in our Sanctification, we ought to see that it be sanctification in Jesus Christ; and then it is sanctification in Jesus Christ, when the Lord giveth us to look unto the Lord Jesus in it, and to it in him; and as we look for our holiness to be *perfect* in Jesus Christ, so we look for continual *supply* of it from him: and this it is to make Christ our sanctification, when as whatsoever gift the Lord giveth us, we go not forth in the strength of it but in the strength of *Jesus Christ.* There may be a change in the soul, which may spring from a spirit of *Bondage,* and may captivate our consciences unto the *Law,* that may restrain us from sin and constrain us unto duties: but such holiness springeth not from *union* with *Jesus Christ;* for there may be a conscience of duty, without sence of our need of Jesus Christ: as it was with the Israelites at Mount *Sinai,* Deut 5.27. *Go thou neer* (say they to *Moses*) *and hear all that the Lord our God shall say, and speak thou unto us, all that the Lord our God shall speak unto thee, and we will hear it and do it: they have well said all that they have spoken, saith the Lord; O that there were an heart in them, that they would see me.* and so forth. This I say, therefore, is the first thing to be attended unto; as ever you would make a right use of your holiness, see that it be such as floweth from Jesus Christ, and that there be not only an heart awed with the *Law,* but waiting upon Jesus Christ to be all in all in us, and to us: so shall we neither neglect the gifts of God in us, nor Christ, and his Spirit, but shall give their due honour unto all of them together.

This may also teach all Christians not to *trust* upon the gifts of their *Holiness:* though they do spring from the *Holy Ghost* himself, though they be such as are unchangeable, though they spring from Jesus Christ, and knit your souls in Union with him; yet *trust* not in the gifts themselves: the Lord layeth it down as the Apostacy of *Israel,* Ezek. 16.14, 15. *Thy renown went forth among the Heathen, for thy beauty, for it was perfect through my comliness which I had put upon thee, saith the Lord God. But thou didst trust in thine own beauty, and playedst the Harlot, &c.* Trust not therefore in any of these; but let all our confidence be in Jesus Christ, not in any of the gifts of his Spirit, whatsoever. For a little further opening of it.

Trust not in any *gifts* that you have received for the *performance* of any duty, for it is not the strongest Christian that is able to put forth a good thought, 2 *Cor.* 3.5. *But our sufficiency is of God. He that abideth in me, and I in him, the same bringeth forth much fruit: for without me ye can do nothing. Joh.* 15.5. And the Apostle *Paul* cannot only not do any great matter by his own strength and grace, but nothing at all without Jesus Christ; and therefore he giveth us to understand, that *it is God that worketh in us both to will and to do,* Phil. 2.12. if therefore we have any new work to do, look to the Lord Jesus Christ afresh by Faith, that he may carry an end our works in us, and for us; otherwise it is not any strength or grace in us, that can produce any good work, word, or thought: And therefore (mind you) the Apostle maketh it a Principle of Christian Religion, that *The just man liveth by his Faith*; and he often mentioneth it, *Gal.* 2.20. *The life which I now live in the flesh, I live by the faith of the Son of God;* where he putteth it into his own experience: why? did he not live by Love, and Patience, and Zeal? *&c.* Yes truly, they were lively in him, if ever in any man, besides our blessed Saviour; and yet notwithstanding, he never attributed life to any of these gifts of his; but if he speak of his *Life,* he maketh this his Universal Life, *I live by the Faith of the Son of God,* and *I am able to do all things through Christ which strengthneth me,* Phil. 4.13. This is the true saviour of a Christian spirit, that when gifts are at the highest, the heart is then at the lowest: 1 *Cor.* 15.9,10. The Apostle *Paul* there acknowledgeth himself to be as one born out of due time; for (saith he) *I am less then the least of the Apostles not meet to be called an Apostle, because I persecuted the Church of God; I, but by the grace of God I am what I am, and his grace which was bestowed upon me was not in vain, but I laboured more abundantly then they all, yet not I, but the grace of God in me.* This is truly spiritual sanctification, that when the soul is full of the *Holy Ghost,* and *gifts* of the *Holy Ghost,* yet he is like a man in great penury, as having nothing of himself: This is a marvelous spiritual poverty, and you shall ever find (and I desire the Lord would open the hearts of his people to know what I speak) that if Christians have fallen, their greatest falls have been in their most exemplary gifts. If you shall mark the sins of all the servants of God, they have been chiefly found in the very exercise of their best gifts....

Furthermore, as we receive [comfort] from Christ, and trust not in it, but in Christ, and receive the witness of it in Christ, and in the holy Spirit of Christ; and as we receive joy and Comfort also, which the Lord doth minister unto us, in a sanctified course, by his holy *Spirit:* so we *grow up,* and *perfect* our Holiness, which we have received in his Name: there is *growth* in grace; this sanctification is not bed-rid; Christians are not as weak now, as they were seven years ago, nor do they stand at a stay, but go forward in Christianity: and hereupon the Apostle exhorteth the *Ephesians, Eph.* 4.6. to speak the truth in love, that *they may grow up unto him in all things, which is the head, even Christ,* implying, that men that enter into wayes of Holiness, ought to grow on unto perfection in the fear of God. *The Righteous shall hold on his way, and he that hath clean hands shall grow stronger and stronger,* Job 17.9. And many sweet means the Lord hath appointed for this end; the communion of Gods people tendeth hereunto, *Prov* 13.20. He *that walketh with the wise shall learn wisdom:* all the Ordinances of God are appointed for this end also, to beget and encrease faith and holiness; therefore a Christian in the use of all these Ordinances doth not stand at a stay, but is still thriving and growing; and that not in his own strength, but in the strength of Jesus Christ, seeking for his acceptance & help in every duty he goeth about: and this is that which the Apostle *Paul* doth exhort the *Colossians* unto *chap.* 2.6, 7. *As ye have received Christ Jesus the Lord, so walk ye in him, rooted and built up in him, and established in the faith.* This ought Christians mainly to attend unto; that as you see the branch, the more juice it sucketh from the root, the more fruitful it is: so also it becometh the people of God, to know, the more need we stand in to be fruitful, the more need we have to derive a continual fresh supply from the Lord Jesus Christ, that by his Spirit, renewing grace in us, we may be enlarged, and carried an end in the waies of God: whereas otherwise the hearts of Christians would soon fail to go on in those things, wherein they desire to be growing up unto perfection. What is the reason that so many servants of God, are not so lively in their profession, as they were wont to be many years ago? Truly, we attend upon Ordinances, but it is only upon the outward act of them, and not upon *Jesus Christ* in them. This is many times wanting in the hearts of Gods people; but truly if this be our constant frame, and we do not recover our selves, then is not our sanctification that which floweth from fellowship with Jesus Christ, and the Spirit of his grace; for you shall ever find this to be true, that there is no gift of Jesus Christ, nor sanctification accompanying salvation, but it doth knit us neerer and neerer unto Christ; for the more we are filled with true spiritual gifts, the more empty we are of our own strength, and of self-conceits, and so we ought to be; otherwise you shall constantly find this, that if the Lord do not preserve this empty frame in us, the more full we are of any gift, the more full shall we be of our own strength, and consequently we shall feel the less need of Jesus Christ; and if this be our constant frame, it will be a sad argument that our best sanctification will not endure, but fall away, unless we be knit unto Jesus Christ by the Spirit of his grace; for by all true sanctification, we are the more knit unto him: so that if any man would know whether the superscription of Christ and his image be stamped upon his sanctification, this you shall ever find to be the stamp of the grace of Jesus Christ; That the more you receive from him, the more need you stand in of him: insomuch, that notwithstanding all the gifts of the Spirit, there is not the ablest Minister of the New Testament, but (if your gifts flow from the Spirit of Christ, and knit you unto Christ) you will find as great need to cleave unto Jesus Christ, as ever you did the first day, when you came trembling into the Pulpit. If therefore we feel our selves full, so that the more we have received, the more sufficient we are; and go not about the duties we have in hand, in fear and trembling, but in self-confidence; if this be our usual, and constant practice, it is but counterfeit Christianity: I do not say, That the gifts are counterfeit, for they are from the Spirit of God, and men may by them be very serviceable to Church and Commonwealth: but this is certain, that the stronger and the more your gifts are if you sit loose from Christ, the emptier your hearts are of him. But you will say, May not a Christian be sometimes full of himself, and depend upon the strength of his own gifts? Yes, brethren, God forbid I should deny that, for the best Christians have gone astray in the exercise of their best gifts; and hereupon *Abraham* hath been wanting in *faith,* and *Moses* in *meekness,* and *Peter* in *courage,* and *Sarah* in her *modesty;* they have been so apt to trust upon those graces of God, wherein they have most abounded, that they have principally failed therein: but this you shall find, that if they have been overtaken once or twice, as the burnt child dreadeth the fire; so they grow to be more sensible of their need of Jesus Christ, more fearful of departing from him, more careful to cleave unto him, that they might grow up in his name to all well pleasing in his sight. If therefore there be a sanctification that standeth at a stay in any man, it is a great suspicion whether it flow from fellowship with Christ, or no: if gifts be truly spiritual, a man shall ordinarily grow up in them. *Habenti dabitur,* Imploy them, and multiply them; but if you have received gifts in your own strength, and you are now full of your own sanctification, truly this is but froathy work, and doth not convey true nor lively nourishment and comfort: but to him that in his most spiritual gifts is empty of himself, and only full of Jesus Christ to live or die, is his advantage. This is the use that I would commend unto you touching your Christian *Sanctification.* Thus we see sundry things have been clear'd from this Doctrine concerning the Covenant of Grace.

ANNE HUTCHINSON

"The Examination of Mrs. Anne Hutchinson at the Court at Newtown" (1637)

While in England Anne Hutchinson (1584–1652) had been an ardent admirer of John Cotton's preaching. After immigrating to the Massachusetts Bay Colony the year after Cotton's arrival, with her eleven children and politically influential merchant husband, she quickly established herself in Boston as a powerful religious teacher in her own right. Partly her authority derived from her charismatic leadership of large weekly assemblies of women and prominent men who met to discuss the previous Sunday's sermon. But mainly her influence—and certainly her notoriety—came from the radical doctrines she articulated at the meetings. First, she claimed that because almost all the ministers other than Cotton made the covenant of grace conditional, they preached a covenant of works, or the heresy that a person could *earn* salvation through human efforts. In addition she seems to have sometimes taught that a saint's inward assurance of saving holiness, rather than being (as most Puritan divines taught) at least somewhat testable by objective means, was totally unmediated by reason, nature, or (as she suggests in the selection that follows) biblical texts. For persisting in speaking these ideas, she was banished from the colony and, Cotton himself having abandoned her, soon thereafter excommunicated from his church. She went to Rhode Island and a few years later to New York, where she and most of her family were killed in an Indian raid.

For two fresh studies of the "antinomian" controversy, see Michael P. Winship, *Making Heretics: Militant Protestantism and Free Grace in Massachusetts, 1636–1641* (Princeton, 2002); and Theodore Dwight Bozeman, *The Precisianist Strain: Disciplinary Religion and Antinomian Backlash in Puritanism to 1638* (Chapel Hill, 2004). Adapted from his *Making Heretics* (2002), Winship's *The Times and Trials of Anne Hutchinson* (Lawrence, Kans., 2005) is a well-contextualized account of the theological debates engaged in by Hutchinson and her allies and accusers. For alternative interpretations of the religious issues at stake, see the works cited in the headnote for the selection from John Cotton's *Treatise of the Covenant of Grace*. Two older works are still useful for extending the story of Hutchinson's ideas and related strains of Puritan "enthusiasm" into later periods: Philip F. Gura, *A Glimpse of Sion's Glory: Puritan Radicalism in New England, 1620–1660* (Middletown, Conn., 1984), 237–75; and David S. Lovejoy, *Religious Enthusiasm in the New World: Heresy to Revolution* (Cambridge, Mass., 1985), 62–86. For a study of gender in the literary-historical image of Hutchinson, see Amy Schrager Lang, *Prophetic Woman: Anne Hutchinson and the Problem of Dissent in the Literature of New England* (Berkeley, 1987). David D. Hall has edited an indispensable collection of documents on the Hutchinson controversy, from which this selection from the transcript of the General Court's trial is taken.

The selection picks up the discussion at the point where it shifts from arguments about the legality of Hutchinson's meetings with women—which she parried with great effectiveness—to questions about her theological positions. Apart from Cotton and Hutchinson, the speakers are either members of the Court, including, most prominently, Governor Winthrop and Deputy Governor Thomas Dudley, or the accusing ministers.

Dep. gov. I would go a little higher with Mrs. Hutchinson. About three years ago we were all in peace. Mrs. Hutchinson from that time she came hath made a disturbance, and some that came over with her in the ship did inform me what she was as soon as she was landed. I being then in place dealt with the pastor and teacher of Boston and desired them to enquire of her, and then I was satisfied that she held nothing different from us, but within half a year after, she had vented divers of her strange opinions and had made parties in the country, and at length it comes that Mr. Cotton and Mr. Vane were of her judgment, but Mr. Cotton hath cleared himself that he was not of that mind, but now it appears by this woman's meeting that Mrs. Hutchinson hath so forestalled the minds of many by their resort to her meeting that now she hath a potent party in the country. Now if all these things have endangered us as from that foundation and if she in particular hath disparaged all our ministers in the land that they have preached a covenant of works, and only Mr. Cotton a covenant of grace, why this is not to be suffered, and therefore being driven to the foundation and it being found that Mrs. Hutchinson is she that hath depraved all the ministers and hath been the cause of what is fallen out, why we must take away the foundation and the building will fall.

Mrs. H. I pray Sir prove it that I said they preached nothing but a covenant of works.

Dep. Gov. Nothing but a covenant of works, why a Jesuit may preach truth sometimes.

Mrs. H. Did I ever say they preached a covenant of works then?

Dep. Gov. If they do not preach a covenant of grace clearly, then they preach a covenant of works.

Mrs. H. Not Sir, one may preach a covenant of grace more clearly than another, so I said.

D. Gov. We are not upon that now but upon position.

Mrs. H. Prove this then Sir that you say I said.

D. Gov. When they do preach a covenant of works do they preach truth?

Mrs. H. Yes Sir, but when they preach a covenant of works for salvation, that is not truth.

D. Gov. I do but ask you this, when the ministers do preach a covenant of works do they preach a way of salvation?

Mrs. H. I did not come hither to answer to questions of that sort.

D. Gov. Because you will deny the thing.

Mrs. H. Ey, but that is to be proved first.

D. Gov. I will make it plain that you did say that the ministers did preach a covenant of works.

Mrs. H. I deny that.

D. Gov. And that you said they were not able ministers of the new testament, but Mr. Cotton only.

Mrs. H. If ever I spake that I proved it by God's word.

Court. Very well, very well.

Source: *The Antinomian Controversy, 1636–1638: A Documentary History*, ed. David D. Hall (Middletown, Conn.: Wesleyan University Press, 1968), 317–19, 321, 323–26, 332, 333–38, 340–45, 347–48. Editor's notes altered. Reprinted by permission of David D. Hall and Wesleyan University Press, Copyright © 1968.

Mrs. H. If one shall come onto me in private, and desire me seriously to tell them what I thought of such an one. I must either speak false or true in my answer.

D. Gov. Likewise I will prove this that you said the gospel in the letter and words holds forth nothing but a covenant of works and that all that do not hold as you do are in a covenant of works.

Mrs. H. I deny this for if I should so say I should speak against my own judgment....

Mr. Weld. Being desired by the honoured court, that which our brother Peters had spoken was the truth and things were spoken as he hath related and the occasion of calling this sister and the passages that were there among us. And myself asking why she did cast such aspersions upon the ministers of the country though we were poor sinful men and for ourselves we cared not but for the precious doctrine we held forth we could not but grieve to hear that so blasphemed. She at that time was sparing in her speech. I need not repeat the things they have been truly related. She said the fear of man is a snare and therefore I will speak freely and she spake her judgment and mind freely as was before related, that Mr. Cotton did preach a covenant of grace and we a covenant of works. And this I remember she said we could not preach a covenant of grace because we were not sealed, and we were not able ministers of the new testament no more than were the disciples before the resurrection of Christ....

Mr. Shephard. I am loth to speak in this assembly concerning this gentlewoman in question, but I can do no less than speak what my conscience speaks unto me. For personal reproaches I take it a man's wisdom to conceal. Concerning the reproaches of the ministry of our's there hath been many in the country, and this hath been my thoughts of that. Let men speak what they will not only against persons but against ministry, let that pass, but let us strive to speak to the consciences of men, knowing that if we had the truth with us we shall not need to approve our words by our practice and our ministry to the hearts of the people, and they should speak for us and therefore I have satisfied myself and the brethren with that. Now for that which concerns this gentlewoman at this time I do not well remember every particular, only this I do remember that the end of our meeting was to satisfy ourselves in some points. Among the rest Mrs. Hutchinson was desired to speak her thoughts concerning the ministers of the Bay. Now I remember that she said that we were not able ministers of the new testament. I followed her with particulars, she instanced myself as being at the lecture and hearing me preach when as I gave some means whereby a Christian might come to the assurance of God's love. She instanced that I was not sealed. I said why did she say so. She said because you put love for an evidence. Now I am sure she was in an error in this speech for if assurance be an holy estate then I am sure there are not graces wanting to evidence it.

Mr. Eliot. I am loth to spend time therefore I shall consent to what hath been said. Our brethren did intreat us to write and a few things I did write the substance of which hath been here spoken and I have it in writing therefore I do avouch it.

Mr. Shephard. I desire to speak this word, it may be but a slip of her tongue, and I hope she will be sorry for it, and then we shall be glad of it.

Dep. Gov. I called these witnesses and you deny them. You see they have proved this and you deny this, but it is clear. You said they preached a covenant of works and that they were not able ministers of the new testament; now there are two other things that you did affirm which were that the scriptures in the letter of them held forth nothing but a covenant of works and likewise that those that were under a covenant of works cannot be saved.

Mrs. H. Prove that I said so. (*Gov.*) Did you say so?

Mrs. H. No Sir, it is your conclusion.

D. Gov. What do I do charging of you if you deny what is so fully proved.

Gov. Here are six undeniable ministers who say it is true and yet you deny that you did say that they did preach a covenant of works and that they were not able ministers of the gospel, and it appears plainly that you have spoken it, and whereas you say that it was drawn from you in a way of friendship, you did profess then that it was out of conscience that you spake and said The fear of man is a snare wherefore should I be afraid, I will speak plainly and freely.

Mrs. H. That I absolutely deny, for the first question was thus answered by me to them. They thought that I did conceive there was difference between them and Mr. Cotton. At the first I was somewhat reserved, then said Mr. Peters I pray answer the question directly as fully and as plainly as you desire we should tell you our minds. Mrs. Hutchinson we come for plain dealing and telling you our hearts. Then I said I would deal as plainly as I could, and whereas they say I said they were under a covenant of works and in the state of the apostles why these two speeches cross one another. I might say they might preach a covenant of works as did the apostles, but to preach a covenant of works and to be under a covenant of works is another business.

Dep. Gov. There have been six witnesses to prove this and yet you deny it.

Mrs. H. I deny that these were the first words that were spoken.

Gov. You make the case worse, for you clearly shew that the ground of your opening your mind was not to satisfy them but to satisfy your own conscience.

Mr. Peters. We do not desire to be so narrow to the court and the gentlewoman about times and seasons, whether first or after, but said it was.

Dep. Gov. For that other thing I mentioned for the letter of the scripture that it held forth nothing but a covenant of works, and for the latter that we are in a state of damnation, being under a covenant of works, or to that effect, these two things you also deny. Now the case stands thus. About three quarters of a year ago I heard of it, and speaking of it there came one to me who is not here, but will affirm it if need be, as he did to me that he did hear you say in so many words. He set it down under his hand and I can bring it forth when the court pleases. His name is subscribed to both these things, and upon my peril be it if I bring you not in the paper and bring the minister (meaning Mr. Ward) to be deposed.

Gov. What say you to this, though nothing be directly proved, yet you hear it may be.

Mrs. H. I acknowledge using the words of the apostle to the Corinthians unto him, that they that were ministers of the letter and not the spirit did preach a covenant of works. Upon his saying there was no such scripture, then I fetched the Bible and shewed him this place 2 Cor. iii. 6. He said that was the letter of the law. No said I it is the letter of the gospel.

Gov. You have spoken this more than once then.

Mrs. H. Then upon further discourse about proving a good estate and holding it out by the manifestation of the spirit he did acknowledge that to be the nearest way, but yet said he, will you not acknowledge that which we hold forth to be a way too wherein we may have hope; no truly if that be a way it is a way to hell.

Gov. Mrs. Hutchinson, the court you see hath laboured to bring you to acknowledge the error of your way that so you might be reduced, the time now grows late, we shall therefore give you a little more time to consider of it and therefore desire that you attend the court again in the morning.

The Next Morning.

......

Dep. Gov. Let her witnesses be called.

Gov. Who be they?

Mrs. H. Mr. Leveret and our teacher and Mr. Coggeshall....

Gov. Mr. Cotton, the court desires that you declare what you do remember of the conference which was at that time and is now in question.

Mr. Cotton. I did not think I should be called to bear witness in this cause and therefore did not labour to call to remembrance what was done; but the greatest passage that took impression upon me was to this purpose. The elders spake that they had heard that she had spoken some condemning words of their ministry, and among other things they did first pray her to answer wherein she thought their ministry did differ from mine, how the comparison sprang I am ignorant, but sorry I was that any comparison should be between me and my brethren and uncomfortable it was, she told them to this purpose that they did not hold forth a covenant of grace as I did, but wherein did we differ? why she said that they did not hold forth the seal of the spirit as he doth. Where is the difference there? say they, why saith she speaking to one or other of them, I know not to whom. You preach of the seal of the spirit upon a work and he upon free grace without a work or without respect to a work, he preaches the seal of the spirit upon free grace and you upon a work. I told her I was very sorry that she put comparisons between my ministry and their's, for she had said more than I could myself, and rather I had that she had put us in fellowship with them and not have made that discrepancy. She said, she found the difference. Upon that there grew some speeches upon the thing and I do remember I instanced to them the story of Thomas Bilney in the book of martyrs how freely the spirit witnessed unto him without any respect unto a work as himself professes. Now upon this other speeches did grow. If you put me in mind of any thing I shall speak it, but this was the sum of the difference, nor did it seem to be so ill taken as it is and our brethren did say also that they would not so easily believe reports as they had done and withal mentioned that they would speak no more of it, some of them did; and afterwards some of them did say they were less satisfied than before. And I must say that I did not find her saying they were under a covenant of works, nor that she said they did preach a covenant of works.

Gov. You say you do not remember, but can you say she did not speak so———*Here two lines again defaced.*

Mr. Cotton. I do remember that she looked at them as the apostles before the ascension.

Mr. Peters. I humbly desire to remember our reverend teacher. May it please you to remember how this came in. Whether do you not remember that she said we were not sealed with the spirit of grace, therefore could not preach a covenant of grace, and she said further you may do it in your judgment but not in experience, but she spake plump that we were not sealed.

Mr. Cotton. You do put me in remembrance that it was asked her why cannot we preach a covenant of grace? Why, saith she, because you can preach no more than you know, or to that purpose, she spake. Now that she said you could not preach a covenant of grace I do not remember such a thing. I remember well that she said you were not sealed with the seal of the spirit.

Mr. Peters. There was a double seal found out that day which never was.

Mr. Cotton. I know very well that she took the seal of the spirit in that sense for the full assurance of God's favour by the holy ghost, and now that place in the Ephesians doth hold out that seal.

Mr. Peters. So that was the ground of our discourse concerning the great seal and the little seal.

Mr. Cotton. To that purpose I remember somebody speaking of the difference of the witness of the spirit and the seal of the spirit, some to put a distinction called it the broad seal and the little seal. Our brother Wheelwright answered if you will have it so be it so.

Mrs. H. Mr. Ward said that.

Some three or four of the ministers. Mr. Wheelwright said it.

Mr. Cotton. No, it was not brother Wheelwright's speech but one of your own expressions, and as I remember it was Mr. Ward.

Mr. Peters …

Mr. Cotton. Under favour I do not remember that.

Mr. Peters. Therefore her answer clears it in your judgment but not in your experience.

Mrs. H. My name is precious and you do affirm a thing which I utterly deny.

D. Gov. You should have brought the book with you.

Mr. Nowell. The witnesses do not answer that which you require.

Gov. I do not see that we need their testimony any further. Mr. Cotton hath expressed what he remembered, and what took impression upon him, and so I think the other elders also did remember that which took impression upon them.

Mr. Weld. I then said to Mrs. Hutchinson when it was come to this issue, why did you let us go thus long and never tell us of it?

Gov. I should wonder why the elders should move the elders of our congregation to have dealt with her if they saw not some cause.

Mr. Cotton. Brother Weld and brother Shepard, I did[1] then clear myself unto you that I understood her speech in expressing herself to you that you did hold forth some matter in your preaching that was not pertinent to the seal of the spirit——*Two lines defaced.*

Dep. Gov. They affirm that Mrs. Hutchinson did say they were not able ministers of the new testament.

Mr. Cotton. I do not remember it.

Mrs. H. If you please to give me leave I shall give you the ground of what I know to be true. Being much troubled to see the falseness of the constitution of the church of England, I had like to have turned separatist; whereupon I kept a day of solemn humiliation and pondering of the thing; this scripture was brought unto me—he that denies Jesus Christ to be come in the flesh is antichrist—This I considered of and in considering found that the papists did not deny him to be come in the flesh, nor we did not deny him—who then was antichrist? Was the Turk antichrist only? The Lord knows that I could not open scripture; he must by his prophetical office open it unto me. So after that being unsatisfied in the thing, the Lord was pleased to bring this scripture out of the Hebrews. He that denies the testament denies the testator, and in this did open unto me and give me to see that those which did not teach the new covenant had the spirit of antichrist, and upon this he did discover the ministry unto me and ever since. I bless

---

1.   Later editions of Hutchinson's *History* include a "not": "I did not." [Thomas Hutchinson, *History of the Colony and Province of Massachusetts Bay* (Boston, 1767).]

the Lord, he hath let me see which was the clear ministry and which the wrong. Since that time I confess I have been more choice and he hath let me to distinguish between the voice of my beloved and the voice of Moses, the voice of John Baptist and the voice of antichrist, for all those voices are spoken of in scripture. Now if you do condemn me for speaking what in my conscience I know to be truth I must commit myself unto the Lord.

Mr. Nowell. How do you know that that was the spirit?

Mrs. H. How did Abraham know that it was God that bid him offer his son, being a breach of the sixth commandment?

Dep. Gov. By an immediate voice.

Mrs. H. So to me by an immediate revelation.

Dep. Gov. How! an immediate revelation.

Mrs. H. By the voice of his own spirit to my soul. I will give you another scripture, Jer. 46. 27, 28—out of which the Lord shewed me what he would do for me and the rest of his servants.—But after he was pleased to reveal himself to me I did presently like Abraham run to Hagar. And after that he did let me see the atheism of my own heart, for which I begged of the Lord that it might not remain in my heart, and being thus, he did shew me this (a twelvemonth after) which I told you of before. Ever since that time I have been confident of what he hath revealed unto me.

Obliterated} another place out of Daniel chap. 7. and he and for us all, wherein he shewed me the sitting of the judgment and the standing of all high and low before the Lord and how thrones and kingdoms were cast down before him. When our teacher came to New-England it was a great trouble unto me, my brother Wheelwright being put by also. I was then much troubled concerning the ministry under which I lived, and then that place in the 30th of Isaiah was brought to my mind. Though the Lord give thee bread of adversity and water of affliction yet shall not thy teachers be removed into corners any more, but thine eyes shall see thy teachers. The Lord giving me this promise and they being gone there was none then left that I was able to hear, and I could not be at rest but I must come hither. Yet that place of Isaiah did much follow me, though the Lord give thee the bread of adversity and water of affliction. This place lying I say upon me then this place in Daniel was brought unto me and did shew me that though I should meet with affliction yet I am the same God that delivered Daniel out of the lion's den, I will also deliver thee.——Therefore I desire you to look to it, for you see this scripture fulfilled this day and therefore I desire you that as you tender the Lord and the church and commonwealth to consider and look what you do. You have power over my body but the Lord Jesus hath power over my body and soul, and assure yourselves thus much, you do as much as in you lies to put the Lord Jesus Christ from you, and if you go on in this course you begin you will bring a curse upon you and your posterity, and the mouth of the Lord hath spoken it.

Dep. Gov. What is the scripture she brings?

Mr. Stoughton. Behold I turn away from you.

Mrs. H. But now having seen him which is invisible I fear not what man can do unto me.

Gov. Daniel was delivered by miracle do you think to be deliver'd so too?

Mrs. H. I do here speak it before the court. I look that the Lord should deliver me by his providence.

Mr. Harlakenden. I may read scripture and the most glorious hypocrite may read them and yet go down to hell.

Mrs. H. It may be so…

Mr. Endicot. I would have a word or two with leave of that which hath thus far been revealed to the court. I have heard of many revelations of Mr[2] Hutchinson's, but they were reports, but Mrs. Hutchinson I see doth maintain some by this discourse, and I think it is a special providence of God to hear what she hath said. Now there is a revelation you see which she doth expect as a miracle. She saith she now suffers and let us do what we will she shall be delivered by a miracle. I hope the court takes notice of the vanity of it and heat of her spirit. Now because her reverend teacher is here I should desire that he would please to speak freely whether he doth condescend to such speeches or revelations as have been here spoken of, and he will give a great deal of content.

Mr. Cotton. May it please you Sir. There are two sorts of revelations, there are [*defaced*] or against the word besides scripture both which [*defaced*] tastical and tending to danger more ways than one——there is another sort which the apostle prays the believing Ephesians may be made partakers of, and those are such as are breathed by the spirit of God and are never dispensed but in a word of God and according to a word of God, and though the word revelation be rare in common speech and we make it uncouth in our ordinary expressions, yet notwithstanding, being understood in the scripture sense I think they are not only lawful but such as Christians may receive and God bear witness to it in his word, and usually he doth express it in the ministry of the word and doth accompany it by his spirit, or else it is in the reading of the word in some chapter or verse and whenever it comes it comes flying upon the wings of the spirit.

Mr. Endicot. You give me satisfaction in the thing and therefore I desire you to give your judgment of Mrs. Hutchinson; what she hath said you hear and all the circumstances thereof.

Mr. Cotton. I would demand whether by a miracle she doth mean a work above nature or by some wonderful providence for that is called a miracle often in the psalms.

Mrs. H. I desire to speak to our teacher. You know Sir what he doth declare though he doth not know himself [*something wanting.*] now either of these ways or at this present time it shall be done, yet I would not have the court so to understand me that he will deliver me now even at this present time.

Dep. Gov. I desire Mr. Cotton to tell us whether you do approve of Mrs. Hutchinson's revelations as she hath laid them down.

Mr. Cotton. I know not whether I do understand her, but this I say, if she doth expect a deliverance in a way of providence—then I cannot deny it.

Dep. Gov. No Sir we did not speak of that.

Mr. Cotton. If it be by way of miracle then I would suspect it.

Dep. Gov. Do you believe that her revelations are true?

Mr. Cotton. That she may have some special providence of God to help her is a thing that I cannot bear witness against.

Dep. Gov. Good Sir I do ask whether this revelation be of God or no?

Mr. Cotton. I should desire to know whether the *sentence of* the court will bring her to any calamity, and then I would know of her whether she expects to be delivered from that calamity by a miracle or a providence of God.

Mrs. H. By a providence of God I say I expect to be delivered from some calamity that shall come to me.

2.   Apparently a misprint for "Mrs."

Gover. The case is altered and will not stand with us now, but I see a marvellous providence of God to bring things to this pass that they are. We have been hearkening about the trial of this thing and now the mercy of God by a providence hath answered our desires and made her to lay open her self and the ground of all these disturbances to be by revelations, for we receive no such   made out of the ministry of the word   and so one scripture after another, but all this while there is no use of the ministry of the word nor of any clear call of God by his word, but the ground work of her revelations is the immediate revelation of the spirit and not by the ministry of the word, and that is the means by which she hath very much abused the country that they shall look for revelations and are not bound to the ministry of the word, but God will teach them by immediate revelations and this hath been the ground of all these tumults and troubles, and I would that those were all cut off from us that trouble us, for this is the thing that hath been the root of all the mischief.

Court. We all consent with you.

Gov. Ey it is the most desperate enthusiasm in the world, for nothing but a word comes to her mind and then an application is made which is nothing to the purpose, and this is her revelations when it is impossible but that the word and spirit should speak the same thing.

Mr. Endicot. I speak in reference to Mr. Cotton. I am tender of you Sir and there lies much upon you in this particular, for the answer of Mr. Cotton doth not free him from that way which his last answer did bring upon him, therefore I beseech you that you'd be pleased to speak a word to that which Mrs. Hutchinson hath spoken of her revelations as you have heard the manner of it. Whether do you witness for her or against her.

Mr. Cotton. This is that I said Sir, and my answer is plain that if she doth look for deliverance from the hand of God by his providence, and the revelation be in a word or according to a word, that I cannot deny.

Mr. Endicot. You give me satisfaction.

Dep. Gov. No, no, he gives me none at all.

Mr. Cotton. But if it be in a way of miracle or a revelation without the word that I do not assent to, but look at it as a delusion, and I think so doth she too as I understand her.

Dep. Gov. Sir, you weary me and do not satisfy me.

Mr. Cotton. I pray Sir give me leave to express my self. In that sense that she speaks I dare not bear witness against it.

Mr. Nowell. I think it is a devilish delusion.

Gover. Of all the revelations that ever I read of I never read the like ground laid as is for this. The Enthusiasts and Anabaptists had never the like.

Mr. Cotton. You know Sir, that their revelations broach new matters of faith and doctrine.

Gover. So do these and what may they breed more if they be let alone. I do acknowledge that there are such revelations as do concur with the word but there hath not been any of this nature.

Dep. Gov. I never saw such revelations as these among the Anabaptists, therefore am sorry that Mr. Cotton should stand to justify her.

Mr. Peters. I can say the same and this runs to enthusiasm, and I think that is very disputable which our brother Cotton hath spoken [*wanting*] an immediate promise that he will deliver them [*wanting*] in a day of trouble.

Gover. It overthrows all.

Dep. Gov. These disturbances that have come among the Germans have been all grounded upon revelations, and so they that have vented them have stirred up their hearers to take up arms against their prince and to cut the throats one of another, and these have been the fruits of them, and whether the devil may inspire the same into their hearts here I know not, for I am fully persuaded that Mrs. Hutchinson is deluded by the devil, because the spirit of God speaks truth in all his servants.

Gov. I am persuaded that the revelation she brings forth is delusion.

All the court but some two or three ministers cry out, we all believe it—we all believe it.

Mr. Endicot. I suppose all the world may see where the foundation of all these troubles among us lies.

Mr. Eliot. I say there is an expectation of things promised, but to have a particular revelation of things that shall fall out, there is no such thing in the scripture.

Gov. We will not limit the word of God.

Mr. Collicut. It is great burden to us that we differ from Mr. Cotton and that he should justify these revelations. I would intreat him to answer concerning that about the destruction of England.

Gov. Mr. Cotton is not called to answer to any thing but we are to deal with the party here standing before us.

Mr. Bartholomew. My wife hath said that Mr. Wheelwright was not acquainted with this way until that she imparted it unto him.

Mr. Brown. Inasmuch as I am called to speak, I would therefore speak the mind of our brethren. Though we had sufficient ground for the censure before, yet now she having vented herself and I find such flat contradiction to the scripture in what she saith, as to that in the first to the Hebrews—God at sundry times spake to our fathers—For my part I understand that scripture and other scriptures of the Lord Jesus Christ, and the apostle writing to Timothy saith that the scripture is able to make one perfect—therefore I say the mind of the brethren—I think she deserves no less a censure than hath been already past but rather something more, for this is the foundation of all mischief and of all those bastardly things which have been overthrowing by that great meeting. They have all come out from this cursed fountain.

Gov. Seeing the court hath thus declared itself and hearing what hath been laid to the charge of Mrs. Hutchinson and especially what she by the providence of God hath declared freely without being asked, if therefore it be the mind of the court, looking at her as the principal cause of all our trouble, that they would now consider what is to be done to her.———

Mr. Coddington. I do think that you are going to censure therefore I desire to speak a word.

Gov. I pray you speak.

Mr. Coddington. There is one thing objected against the meetings. What if she designed to edify her own family in her own meetings may none else be present?

Gov. If you have nothing else to say but that, it is pity Mr. Coddington that you should interrupt us in proceeding to censure.

Mr. Coddington. I would say more Sir, another thing you lay to her Charge is her speech to the elders. Now I do not see any clear witness against her, and you know it is a rule of the court that no man may be a judge and an accuser too. I do not speak to disparage our elders and their callings, but I do not see any thing that they accuse her of witnessed against her, and therefore I do not see how she should be censured for that. And for the other thing which hath fallen from her occasionally by the spirit of God, you know the spirit of God witnesses with our spirits, and there is no truth in scripture but God bears witness to it by his spirit, therefore I would entreat you to consider whether those things you have alledged against her deserve such censure as you are about to pass, be it to banishment or imprisonment. And again here is nothing proved about the elders, only that she said they did not teach a covenant of grace so clearly as Mr. Cotton did, and that they were in the state of the apostles before the ascension. Why I hope this may not be offensive nor any wrong to them.

Gov. Pass by all that hath been said formerly and her own speeches have been ground enough for us to proceed upon.

Mr. Coddington. I beseech you do not speak so to force things along, for I do not for my own part see any equity in the court in all your proceedings. Here is no law of God that she hath broken nor any law of the country that she hath broke, and therefore deserves no censure, and if she say that the elders preach as the apostles did, why they preached a covenant of grace and what wrong is that to them, for it is without question that the apostles did preach a covenant of grace, though not with that power, till they received the manifestation of the spirit, therefore I pray consider what you do, for here is no law of God or man broken....

Gov. The court hath already declared themselves satisfied concerning the things you hear, and concerning the troublesomeness of her spirit and the danger of her course amongst us, which is not to be suffered. Therefore if it be the mind of the court that Mrs. Hutchinson for these things that appear before us is unfit for our society, and if it be the mind of the court that she shall be banished out of our liberties and imprisoned till she be sent away, let them hold up their hands.

All but three.

Those that are contrary minded hold up yours,

Mr. Coddington and Mr. Colborn, only.

Mr. Jennison. I cannot hold up my hand one way or the other, and I shall give my reason if the court require it.

Gov. Mrs. Hutchinson, the sentence of the court you hear is that you are banished from out of our jurisdiction as being a woman not fit for our society, and are to be imprisoned till the court shall send you away.

Mrs. H. I desire to know wherefore I am banished?

Gov. Say no more, the court knows wherefore and is satisfied.

ROGER WILLIAMS

The Bloudy Tenent of Persecution for Cause of Conscience
(1644)

Roger Williams (c. 1603–1683), the banished Massachusetts minister who founded the colony of Rhode Island, is rightly remembered for his bold stand in favor of religious freedom, which he most fully articulated in his book, *The Bloudy Tenent of Persecution*, published in London nine years after his banishment. Ostensibly the treatise is a dialogue between two interlocutors, "Truth" and "Peace," who relentlessly critique a private letter of Cotton's, later published, defending state punishment for acts and speech in opposition to divinely ordained fundamental doctrines or modes of worship. In actuality, Williams's tract pointed in two different intellectual directions. One was astonishingly "modern." On one hand, he advocated not just "toleration" of Protestant "dissenters" and Catholics, as the Church of England and colonial churches eventually would, but complete religious freedom, including for non-Christians and even atheists. Furthermore, by arguing that religious persecution threatened both the "Truth" of religion *and* the "Peace" of civil society, he advanced the broadest rationale in American political theory for the separation of church and state before Thomas Jefferson's articulation of the principle nearly a century and a half later. Williams's argument that establishing the truth of a belief depended on freely "testing" it would have also resonated with the rationalist Jefferson. On the other hand, the primary direction of Williams's argument against religious persecution was neither modern nor rationalist but biblical and supernatural: punishment for supposed heresy was abominable, not because it vitiated religious understanding but because it negated revealed Christianity, which eschewed external "carnal weapons" in the inward battle to break down spiritual barriers to conversion. Nor did Williams miss an opportunity to observe the double irony that since his banishers refused to break completely from the state Church of England, they committed in his view heresy, which, if he followed Cotton's doctrine, would have obliged him to support *their* persecution.

A useful biography that concentrates on Williams's public career is Edwin S. Gaustad, *Liberty of Conscience: Roger Williams in America* (Grand Rapids, Mich., 1991). Edmund S. Morgan's *Roger Williams: The Church and the State* (New York, 1967) is an excellent study of Williams's political ideas. For a more recent interpretation, see Timothy L. Hall, *Separating Church and State: Roger Williams and Religious Liberty* (Urbana, Ill., 1998). W. Clark Gilpin, *The Millenarian Piety of Roger Williams* (Chicago, 1979), is illuminating on Williams's eschatology. For an examination of Williams's biblical interpretive practices, see James P. Byrd, Jr., *The Challenges of Roger Williams: Religious Liberty, Violent Persecution, and the Bible* (Macon, Ga., 2002).

To Every Courteous Reader

While I plead the cause of truth and innocency against the bloody doctrine of persecution for cause of conscience, I judge it not unfit to give alarm to myself and men to prepare to be persecuted or hunted for cause of conscience.

Whether you stand charged with ten or but two talents, if you hunt any for cause of conscience, how can you say you follow the Lamb of God, who so abhorred that practice?

If Paul, if Jesus Christ, were present here at London, and the question were proposed, what religion would they approve of? The papists, prelatists, Presbyterians, Independents, etc., would each say, "Of mine, of mine"?

But put the second question: If one of the several sorts should by major vote attain the sword of steel, what weapons does Christ Jesus authorize them to fight with in his cause? Do not all men hate the persecutor, and every conscience, true or false, complain of cruelty, tyranny, etc.?

Two mountains of crying guilt lie heavy upon the backs of all men that name the name of Christ, in the eyes of Jews, Turks, and pagans.

First, the blasphemies of their idolatrous inventions, superstitions, and most unchristian conversations.

Secondly, the bloody, irreligious, and inhuman oppressions and destructions under the mask or veil of the name of Christ, etc.

Oh! how like is the jealous Jehovah, the consuming fire, to end these present slaughters of the holy witnesses in a greater slaughter! (Rev. 5)

Six years preaching of so much truth of Christ as that time afforded in King Edward's days kindles the flames of Queen Mary's bloody persecutions.

Who can now but expect that after so many scores of years preaching and professing of more truth, and among so many great contentions among the very best of Protestants, a fiery furnace should be heat, and who sees not now the fires kindling?

I confess I have little hopes, till those flames are over, that this discourse against the doctrine of persecution for cause of conscience should pass current, I say not among the wolves and lions, but even among the sheep of Christ themselves. Yet, *liberavi animam meam*, I have not hid within my breast my soul's belief. And, although sleeping on the bed either of the pleasures or profits of sin, think you your conscience bound to smite at him that dares to waken you? Yet in the midst of all these civil and spiritual wars, I hope we shall agree in these particulars.

First, however the proud (upon the advantage of a higher earth or ground) overlook the poor, and cry out schismatics, heretics, etc., shall blasphemers and seducers escape unpunished? Yet there is a sorer punishment in the gospel for despising of Christ than Moses, even when the despiser of Moses was put to death without mercy. (Hebrews 10: 28, 29.) *He that believes not shall be damned.* (Mark 16:16)

Secondly, whatever worship, ministry, ministration, the best and purest are practiced without faith and true persuasion that they are the true institutions of God, they are sin, sinful worships, ministries, etc. And however in civil things we may be servants unto men, yet in divine and spiritual things the poorest peasant must disdain the service of the highest prince. *Be ye not the servants of men.* (1 Cor. 7 [23]).

Source: The Bloudy Tenent of Persecution for Cause of Conscience, ed. Richard Groves (Macon, Ga.: Mercer University Press, 2001), 8–10, 19–20, *28*, 33–39, 73–74, 77–78, 87–89, 133–35. Editor's notes omitted. Reprinted by permission of Mercer University Press, Copyright © 2001.

Thirdly, without search and trial no man attains this faith and right persuasion. *Try all things.* (I Thessalonians 5 [21])

In vain have English parliaments permitted English Bibles in the poorest English houses, and the simplest man or woman to search the scriptures, if yet against their souls' persuasion from the scripture they should be forced, as if they lived in Spain or Rome itself without the sight of a Bible, to believe as the church believes.

Fourthly, having tried, we must hold fast (I Thessalonians 5 [21]), upon the loss of a crown. (Rev. 3 [2]). We must not let go for all the fleabitings of the present afflictions, etc. Having bought truth dear, we must not sell it cheap, not the least grain of it for the whole world; no, not for the saving of souls, though our own most precious; least of all for the bitter sweetening of a little vanishing pleasure—for a little puff of credit and reputation from the changeable breath of uncertain sons of men, for the broken bags of riches on eagles' wings, for a dream of these—any or all of these, which on our death-bed vanish and leave tormenting stings behind them. Oh! how much better is it from the love of truth, from the love of the Father of lights from whence it comes, from the love of the Son of God, who is the way and the truth, to say as he, *For this end was I born, and for this end came I into the world, that I might bear witness to the truth.* (John 18:37)....

The Answer of Mr. John Cotton, of Boston, in New England, to the Aforesaid Arguments Against Persecution for Cause of Conscience, Professedly Maintaining Persecution for Cause of Conscience

The question which you put is, whether persecution for cause of conscience be not against the doctrine of Jesus Christ, the King of Kings?

Now, by persecution for cause of conscience, I conceive you mean either for professing some point of doctrine which you believe in conscience to be the truth, or for practicing some work which in conscience you believe to be a religious duty.

Now in points of doctrine some are fundamental, without right belief whereof a man cannot be saved; others are circumstantial, or less principal, wherein men may differ in judgment without prejudice of salvation on either part.

In like sort, in points of practice, some concern the weightier duties of the law, as, what God we worship, and with what kind of worship, whether such as, if it be right, fellowship with God is held, if corrupt, fellowship with him is lost.

Again, in points of doctrine and worship less principal, either they are held forth in a meek and peaceable way, though the things be erroneous or unlawful, or they are held forth with such arrogance and impetuousness as tends and reaches (even of itself) to the disturbance of civil peace.

Finally, let me add this one distinction more: when we are persecuted for conscience' sake, it is either for conscience rightly informed, or for erroneous and blind *conscience.*

These things premised, I would lay down mine answer to the question in certain conclusions.

First, it is not lawful to persecute any for conscience' sake rightly informed; for in persecuting such, Christ himself is persecuted in them. (Acts 9:4)

Secondly, for an erroneous and blind conscience (even in fundamental and weighty points), it is not lawful to persecute any, till after admonition once or twice; and so the apostle directs (Titus 3:10), and gives the reason that in fundamental and principal points of doctrine or worship the word of God in such things is so clear that he cannot but be convinced in conscience of the dangerous error of his way after once or twice admonition, wisely and faithfully dispensed. And then, if anyone persist, it is not out of conscience, but against his conscience, as the apostle says (verse 11), he "is subverted, and sins, being condemned of himself," that is, of his own conscience. So that if such a man, after such admonition, shall still persist in the error of his way, and be therefore punished, he is not persecuted for cause of conscience, but for sinning against his own conscience.

Thirdly, in things of lesser moment, whether points of doctrine or worship, if a man hold them forth in a spirit of Christian meekness and love, though with zeal and constancy, he is not to be persecuted, but tolerated, till God may be pleased to manifest his truth to him. (Phil. 3:17; Rom. 14:1—4)

But if a man hold forth, or profess any error or false way, with a boisterous and arrogant spirit, to the disturbance of civil peace, he may justly be punished according to the quality and measure of the disturbance caused by him....

A Reply to the Aforesaid Answer of Mr. Cotton, in a Conference Between Truth and Peace

Chapter 1

Truth. In what dark corner of the world, sweet Peace, are we two met? How has this present evil world banished me from all the coasts and quarters of it? And how has the righteous God in judgment taken you from the earth? (Rev. 6:4)

Peace. It is lamentably true, blessed Truth, the foundations of the world have long been out of course; the gates of earth and hell have conspired together to intercept our joyful meeting and our holy kisses. With what a wearied, tired wing have I flown over nations, kingdoms, cities, towns, to find out precious Truth!

Truth. The like inquiries in my flights and travels have I made for Peace, and still am told she has left the earth, and fled to heaven.

Peace. Dear Truth, what is the earth but a dungeon of darkness, where Truth is not?

Truth. And what is the peace thereof but a fleeting dream, your ape and counterfeit?

Peace. Oh! Where is the promise of the God of heaven, that righteousness and peace shall kiss each other?

Truth. Patience, sweet Peace, these heavens and earth are growing old, and shall be changed like a garment. (Psalm 102 [26]) They shall melt away, and be burnt up with all the works that are therein; and the Most High Eternal Creator shall gloriously create new heavens and new earth, wherein dwells righteousness. (2 Pet. 3 [13]) Our kisses then shall have their endless date of pure and sweetest joys. Till then both you and I must hope, and wait, and bear the fury of the dragon's wrath, whose monstrous lies and furies shall with himself be cast into the lake of fire, the second death. (Rev. 20 [10, 14])....

Chapter III

Truth. In the answer, Mr. Cotton first lays down several distinctions and conclusions of his own, tending to prove persecution.

Secondly, answers to the scriptures and arguments proposed against persecution.

Peace. The first distinction is this: by persecution for cause of conscience, "I conceive you mean either for professing some point of doctrine which you believe in conscience to be the truth, or for practicing some work which you believe in conscience to be a religious duty."

Truth. I acknowledge that to molest any person, Jew or Gentile, for either professing doctrine, or practicing worship merely religious or spiritual, it is to persecute him; and such a person, whatever his doctrine or practice be, true or false, suffers persecution for conscience.

But withal I desire it may be well observed that this distinction is not full and complete.[1] For beside this, that a man may be persecuted because he holds or practices what he believes in conscience to be a truth, as Daniel did, for which he was cast into the lions' den (Daniel 6:16), and many thousands of Christians, because they dare not cease to preach and practice what they believed, was by God commanded, as the apostles answered (Acts 4,5), I say, besides this, a man may also be persecuted because he dares not be constrained to yield obedience to such doctrines and worships as are by men invented and appointed. So the three famous Jews, who were cast into the fiery furnace for refusing to fall down in a nonconformity to the whole conforming world, before the golden image (Daniel 3:21). So thousands of Christ's witnesses, and of late in those bloody Marian days, have rather chosen to yield their bodies to all sorts of torments than to subscribe to doctrines, or practice worships unto which the states and times (as Nebuchadnezzar to his golden image) have compelled and urged them.

A chaste wife will not only abhor to be restrained from her husband's bed as adulterous and polluted, but also abhor (if not much more) to be constrained to the bed of a stranger. And what is abominable in corporal is much more loathsome in spiritual whoredom and defilement.

The spouse of Christ Jesus, who could not find her soul's beloved in the ways of his worship and ministry (Canticles 1,3,5), abhorred to turn aside to other flocks, worships, etc., and to embrace the bosom of a false Christ. (Canticles 1:8)

Chapter IV

Peace. The second distinction is this: "In points of doctrine some are fundamental, without right belief whereof a man cannot be saved; others are circumstantial and less principal, wherein a man may differ in judgment without prejudice of salvation on either part."

Truth. To this distinction I dare not subscribe, for then I should everlastingly condemn thousands, and ten thousands, yea, the whole generation of the righteous, who since the falling away from the first primitive Christian state or worship, have and do err fundamentally concerning the true matter, constitution, gathering, and governing of the church. And yet, far be it from any pious breast to imagine that they are not saved and that their souls are not bound up in the bundle of eternal life.

We read of four sorts of spiritual, or Christian, foundations in the New Testament. First, the foundation of all foundations, the cornerstone itself, the Lord Jesus, on whom all depend—persons, doctrines, practices. (1 Cor. 3 [11])

2. Ministerial foundations. The church is built upon the foundation of the apostles and prophets. (Eph. 2: 20)

3. The foundation of future rejoicing in the fruits of obedience. (1 Tim. 6 [19])

4. The foundation of doctrines, without the knowledge of which there can be no true profession of Christ, according to the first institution—the foundation, or principles

---

1. "Conscience will not be restrained from its own worship, nor constrained to another." (Williams's footnote)

of repentance from dead works, faith towards God, the doctrine of baptism, laying on of hands, the resurrection, and eternal judgment. (Heb. 6 [1,2]) In some of these, to wit, those concerning baptisms and laying on of hands, God's people will be found to be ignorant for many hundred years; and I yet cannot see it proved that light is risen, I mean the light of the first institution, in practice.

God's people, in their persons, heart-waking (Canticles 5: 2), in the life of personal grace, will yet be found fast asleep in respect of public Christian worship.

God's people, in their persons, are his, most dear and precious. Yet in respect of the Christian worship they are mingled among the Babylonians, from whence they are called to come out, not locally, as some have said, for that belonged to a material and local Babel, and literal Babel and Jerusalem have now no difference, but spiritually and mystically to come out from her sins and abominations.

If Mr. Cotton maintain the true church of Christ to consist of the true matter of holy persons called out from the world (and the true form of union in a church government), and that also neither national, provincial, nor diocesan churches are of Christ's institution, how many thousands of God's people of all sorts, clergy and laity, as they call them, will they find, both in former and later times, captivated in such national, provincial, and diocesan churches? Yea, and so far from living in, yea, or knowing of any such churches, for matter and form, as they conceive now only to be true, that until of late years how few of God's people knew any other church than the parish church of dead stones or timber, it being a late marvelous light revealed by Christ Jesus, the Sun of Righteousness, that his people are a company or church of living stones? (I Peter 2:9)

And, however his own soul, and the souls of many others, precious to God, are persuaded to separate from national, provincial, and diocesan churches, and to assemble into particular churches, yet, since there are parish churches in England, but what are made up of the parish bounds within such and such a compass of houses, and that such churches have been and are in constant dependence on, and subordination to the national church, how can the New English particular churches join with the old English parish churches in so many ordinances of word, prayer, singing, contribution, etc., but they must needs confess, that as yet their souls are far from the knowledge of the foundation of a true Christian church, whose matter must not only be living stones, but also separated from the rubbish of anti-Christian confusions and desolations.[2]

Chapter V

Peace. With lamentation, I may add, how can their souls be clear in this foundation of the true Christian matter, who persecute and oppress their own acknowledged brethren, presenting light unto them about this point? But I shall now present you with Mr. Cotton's third distinction. "In points of practice," says he, "some concern the weightier duties of the law, as what God we worship, and with what kind of worship; whether such, as if it be right, fellowship with God is held; if false, fellowship with God is lost."

Truth. It is worth the inquiry what kind of worship he intends. For worship is of various signification. Whether in general acceptation he mean the rightness or corruptness of the church, or the ministry of the church, or the ministrations of the word, prayer, seals, etc.

---

2.   "Mr. Cotton and all the half-Separatists, halting between true and false churches, and consequently not yet clear in the fundamental matter of a Christian church." (Williams's footnote)

And because it pleases the Spirit of God to make the ministry one of the foundations of the Christian religion (Hebrews 6:1, 2), and also to make the ministry of the word and prayer in the church to be two special works, even of the apostles themselves (Acts 6: 2), I shall desire it may be well considered in the fear of God.

First, concerning the ministry of the word. The New English ministers, when they were new elected and ordained ministers in New England, must undeniably grant that at that time they were no ministers, notwithstanding their profession of standing so long in a true ministry in old England, whether received from the bishops, which some have maintained true, or from the people, which Mr. Cotton and others better liked, and which ministry was always accounted perpetual and indelible. I apply, and ask, will it not follow, that if their new ministry and ordination be true, the former was false? And if false, that in the exercise of it, notwithstanding abilities, graces, intentions, labors, and, by God's gracious, unpromised, and extraordinary blessings, some success, I say, will it not according to this distinction follow that, according to visible rule, fellowship with God was lost?

Secondly, concerning prayer. The New English ministers have disclaimed and written against that worshipping of God by the common or set forms of prayer, which yet themselves practiced in England, notwithstanding they knew that many servants of God, in great sufferings, witnessed against such a ministry of the word, and such a ministry of prayer.

Peace. I could name the persons, time, and place, when some of them were faithfully admonished for using of the Common Prayer, and the arguments presented to them, then seeming weak, but now acknowledged sound; yet, at that time, they satisfied their hearts with the practice of the author of the Council of Trent, who used to read only some of the choicest selected prayers in the mass-book, which I confess was also their own practice in their using of the Common Prayer. But now, according to this distinction, I ask whether or no fellowship with God in such prayers was lost?

Truth. I could particularize other exercises of worship, which cannot be denied, according to this distinction, to be of the weightier points of the law—to wit, what God we worship, and with what kind of worship?—wherein fellowship with God, in many of our unclean and abominable worships, has been lost. Only upon these premises I shall observe: first, that God's people, even the standard bearers and leaders of them, according to this distinction, have worshipped God in their sleepy ignorance, by such a kind of worship as wherein fellowship with God is lost; yea also, that it is possible for them to do, after much light is risen against such worship, and in particular, brought to the eyes of such holy and worthy persons.

Secondly, there may be inward and secret fellowship with God in false ministries of word and prayer (for that to the eternal praise of infinite mercy, beyond a word or promise of God, I acknowledge), when yet, as the distinction says, in such worship, not being right, fellowship with God is lost, and such a service or ministration must be lamented and forsaken.[3]

Thirdly, I observe that God's people may live and die in such kinds of worship, notwithstanding that light from God, publicly and privately, has been presented to them, able to convince; yet, not reaching to their conviction, and forsaking of such ways, contrary to a conclusion afterward expressed; to wit, "that fundamentals are so clear, that a man

---

3.   "It pleases God sometimes, beyond his promise, to convey blessings and comfort to his, in false worships." (Williams's footnote)

cannot be convinced in conscience, and therefore that such a person not being convinced, he is condemned of himself, and may be persecuted for sinning against his conscience."

Fourthly, I observe, that in such a maintaining a clearness of fundamentals or weightier points, and upon that ground a persecuting of men because they sin against their consciences, Mr. Cotton measures that to others which himself, when he lived in such practices, would not have had measured to himself. As first, that it might have been affirmed of him that in such practices he did sin against his conscience, having sufficient light shining about him.

Secondly, that he should or might lawfully have been cut off by death or banishment, as an heretic, sinning against his own conscience.

And in this respect the speech by King James was notable to a great nonconformitant converted to conformity, and counseling the king to persecute the nonconformists even unto death. "You beast," quotes the king, "if I had dealt so with you in your noncomformity, where had you been?"

Chapter VI

Peace. The next distinction concerns the manner of persons holding forth the aforesaid practices, not only the weightier duties of the law, but points of doctrine and worship less principal.

"Some," says he, "hold them forth in a meek and peaceable way; some with such arrogance and impetuousness, as of itself tends to the disturbance of civil peace."

Truth. In the examination of this distinction we shall discuss, first, what is civil peace (wherein we shall vindicate your name the better); secondly, what it is to hold forth a doctrine, or practice, in this impetuousness or arrogancy.

First, for civil peace, what is it but *pax civitatis,* the peace of the city, whether an English city, Scotch, or Irish city, or further abroad, French, Spanish, Turkish city, etc.

Thus it pleased the Father of lights to define it (Jeremiah 29:7), *Pray for the peace of the city,* which peace of the city, or citizens, so compacted in a civil way of union, may be entire, unbroken, safe, etc., notwithstanding so many thousands of God's people, the Jews, were there in bondage, and would neither be constrained to the worship of the city Babel, nor restrained from so much of the worship of the true God as they then could practice, as is plain in the practice of the three worthies, Shadrach, Meshach, and Abednego, as also of Daniel (Daniel 3, 6)—the peace of the city or kingdom being a far different peace from the peace of the religion, or spiritual worship, maintained and professed of the citizens. This peace of their worship, which worship also in some cities being various, being a false peace, God's people were and ought to be noncomformitants, not daring either to be restrained from the true, or constrained to false worship; and yet without breach of the civil or city peace, properly so called.

Peace. Hence it is that so many glorious and flourishing cities of the world maintain their civil peace; yea, the very Americans and wildest pagans keep the peace of their towns or cities, though neither in one nor the other can any man prove a true church of God in those places, and consequently no spiritual and heavenly peace, the peace spiritual, whether true or false, being of a higher and far different nature from the peace of the place or people, being merely and essentially civil and human.

Truth. Oh! how lost are the sons of men in this point! To illustrate this: the church, or company of worshippers, whether true or false, is like unto a body or college of physicians in a city, like unto a corporation, society, or company of East India or Turkey merchants, or any other society or company in London, which companies may hold their courts, keep their records, hold disputations, and in matters concerning their society may dissent, divide, break into schisms and factions, sue and implead each other at the law, yea, wholly break up and dissolve into pieces and nothing, and yet the peace of the city not be in the least measure impaired or disturbed, because the essence or being of the city, and so the well being and peace thereof, is essentially distinct from those particular societies; the city courts, city laws, city punishments distinct from theirs. The city was before them, and stands absolute and entire when such a corporation or society is taken down....

Chapter XXXIII

Peace. Yea, but it is said that the blind Pharisees, misguiding the subjects of a civil state, greatly sin against a civil state, and therefore justly suffer civil punishments; for shall the civil magistrate take care of outsides only, to wit, of the bodies of men, and not of souls, in laboring to procure their everlasting welfare?

Truth. I answer, it is a truth: the mischief of a blind Pharisee's blind guidance is greater than if he acted treasons, murders, etc.; and the loss of one soul by his seduction is a greater mischief than if he blew up parliaments, and cut the throats of kings or emperors, so precious is that invaluable jewel of a soul above all the present lives and bodies of all the men in the world! And therefore I affirm that justice, calling for eye for eye, tooth for tooth, life for life, calls also soul for soul; which the blind-guiding, seducing Pharisee, shall truly pay in that dreadful ditch, which the Lord Jesus speaks of. But this sentence against him, the Lord Jesus only pronounces in his church, his spiritual judicature, and executes this sentence in part at present, and hereafter to all eternity. Such a sentence no civil judge can pass, such a death no civil sword can inflict.

I answer, secondly, dead men cannot be infected. The civil state, the world, being in a natural state, dead in sin, whatever be the state-religion unto which persons are forced, it is impossible it should be infected. Indeed, the living, the believing, the church and spiritual state, that and that only is capable of infection; for whose help we shall presently see what preservatives and remedies the Lord Jesus has appointed.

Moreover, as we see in a common plague or infection the names are taken how many are to die, and not one more shall be struck than the destroying angel has the names of; so here, whatever be the soul-infection breathed out from the lying lips of a plaque-sick Pharisee, yet the names are taken, not one elect or chosen of God shall perish. God's sheep are safe in his eternal hand and counsel, and he that knows his material, knows also his mystical stars, their numbers, and calls them every one by name. None fall into the ditch on the blind Pharisee's back but such as were ordained to that condemnation, both guide and followers. (1 Peter 2:8; Jude 4) The vessels of wrath shall break and split, and only they, to the praise of God's eternal justice. (Rom. 9:22)....

.... I observe that he implies that beside the censure of the Lord Jesus, in the hands of his spiritual governors, for any spiritual evil in life or doctrine, the civil magistrate is also to inflict corporal punishment upon the contrary minded: whereas, first, if the civil magistrate be a Christian, a disciple or follower of the meek Lamb of God, he is bound to be far from destroying the bodies of men for refusing to receive the Lord Jesus Christ: for otherwise he should not know, according to this speech of the Lord Jesus, what spirit he was of, yea, and to be ignorant of the sweet end of the coming of the Son of Man, which was not to destroy the bodies of men, but to save both bodies and souls. (verses 55–56)

Secondly, if the civil magistrate being a Christian, gifted, prophesy in the church (1 Cor. 14:1)—although the Lord Jesus Christ, whom they in their own persons hold forth, shall be refused—yet they are here forbidden to call for fire from heaven, that is, to procure or inflict any corporal judgment upon such offenders, remembering the end of the Lord Jesus' coming not to destroy men's lives, but to save them.

Lastly, this also concerns the conscience of the civil magistrate. As he is bound to preserve the civil peace and quiet of the place and people under him, he is bound to suffer no man to break the civil peace, by laying hands of violence upon any, though as vile as the Samaritans, for not receiving of the Lord Jesus Christ.

It is indeed the ignorance and blind zeal of the second beast, the false prophet (Rev. 13:13), to persuade the civil powers of the earth to persecute the saints, that is, to bring fiery judgments upon men in a judicial way, and to pronounce that such judgments of imprisonment, banishment, death, proceed from God's righteous vengeance upon such heretics. So dealt divers bishops in France, and England, too, in Queen Mary's days, with the saints of God at their putting to death, declaiming against them in their sermons to the people, and proclaiming that these persecutions, even unto death, were God's just judgments from heaven upon these heretics....

Chapter XLIV

.... *Truth.* .... I hence observe that there being in this scripture held forth a twofold state, a civil state and a spiritual, civil officers and spiritual, civil weapons and spiritual weapons, civil vengeance and punishment and a spiritual vengeance and punishment: although the Spirit speaks not here expressly of civil magistrates and their civil weapons, yet, these states being of different natures and considerations, as far differing as spirit from flesh, I first observe, that civil weapons are most improper and unfitting in matters of the spiritual state and kingdom, though in the civil state most proper and suitable.

Chapter XLV

For, to keep to the similitude which the Spirit uses, for instance, to batter down a stronghold, high wall, fort tower, or castle, men bring not a first and second admonition, and, after obstinacy, excommunication, which are spiritual weapons, concerning them that be in the church: nor exhortations to repent and be baptized, to believe in the Lord Jesus, etc., which are proper weapons to them that be without, etc.; but to take a stronghold, men bring cannons, culverins, saker, bullets, powder, muskets, swords, pikes, etc., and these to this end are weapons effectual and proportionable.

On the other side, to batter down idolatry, false worship, heresy, schism, blindness, hardness, out of the soul and spirit, it is vain, improper, and unsuitable to bring those weapons which are used by persecutors, stocks, whips, prisons, swords, gibbets, stakes, etc., (where these seem to prevail with some cities or kingdoms, a stronger force sets up again what a weaker pulled down); but against these spiritual strongholds in the souls of men, spiritual artillery and weapons are proper, which are mighty through God to subdue and bring under the very thought to obedience, or else to bind fast the soul with chains of darkness, and lock it up in the prison of unbelief and hardness to eternity.

2. I observe that as civil weapons are improper in this business, and never able to effect aught in the soul: so although they were proper, yet they are unnecessary; for if, as the Spirit here says, and the answerer grants, spiritual weapons in the hand of church

officers are able and ready to take vengeance on all disobedience, that is, able and mighty, sufficient and ready for the Lord's work, either to save the soul, or to kill the soul of whomsoever be the party or parties opposite; in which respect I may again remember that speech of Job, *How have you helped him that has no power?* (Job 26:2)

Peace. Offer this, as Malachi once spoke, to the governors, the kings of the earth, when they besiege, beleaguer, and assault great cities, castles, forts, etc., should any subject pretending his service bring store of pins, sticks, straws, bulrushes, to beat and batter down stone walls, mighty bulwarks, what might his expectation and reward be, but a least the censure of a man distract, beside himself?

Truth. What shall we then conceive of his displeasure who is the Chief or Prince of the kings of the earth, and rides upon the word of truth and meekness, which is the white horse (Rev. 6, 19) with his holy witnesses, the white troopers upon white horses, when to his help and aid men bring and add such unnecessary, improper, and weak munition?

Will the Lord Jesus (did he ever in his own person, or did he appoint to) join to his breastplate of righteousness, the breastplate of iron and steel? To the helmet of righteousness and salvation in Christ, a helmet and crest of iron, brass, or steel? A target of wood to his shield of faith? His two-edged sword, coming forth of the mouth of Jesus, the material sword, the work of smiths and cutlers? Or a girdle of shoe-leather to the girdle of truth? Excellently fit and proper is that alarm and item (Psalm 2 [10]), *Be wise, therefore, Oh, you kings*—especially those ten horns (Rev. 17), who, under pretence of fighting for Christ Jesus, give their power to the beast against him—and *be warned, you judges of the earth:* kiss the Son, that is, with subjection and affection, acknowledge him only the King and Judge of souls, in that power bequeathed to his ministers and churches, lest his wrath be kindled, yea, but a little; then, blessed are they that trust in him....

Chapter LXXX

Peace. Yea, but, say they, the godly will not persist in heresy, or turbulent schism, when they are convinced in conscience, etc.

Truth. Sweet Peace, if the civil court and magistracy must judge, as before I have written, and those civil courts are as lawful, consisting of natural men as of godly persons, then what consequences necessarily will follow I have before mentioned And I add, according to this conclusion it must follow, that, if the most godly persons yield not to once or twice admonition, as is maintained by the answerer, they must necessarily be esteemed obstinate persons; for if they were godly, says he, they would yield.[4] Must it not then be said, as it was by one passing sentence of banishment upon some whose godliness was acknowledged, that he that commanded the judge not to respect the poor in the cause of judgment, commands him not to respect the holy or the godly person?

Hence, I could name the place and time when a godly man, a most desirable person for his trade, etc., yet something different in conscience, propounded his willingness and desire to come to dwell in a certain town in New England; it was answered by a chief of the place, This man differs from us, and we desire not to be troubled. So that in conclusion, for no other reason in the world, the poor man, though godly, useful, and peaceable, could

---

4. "The doctrine of persecution necessarily and most commonly falls heavily upon the most godly persons." (Williams's footnote)

not be admitted to a civil being and habitation on the common earth, in that wilderness, among them.

The latter part of the answer, concerning the heretic, or obstinate person, to be excommunicated, and the scandalous offender to be punished in the commonweal, which neither of both come near our question: I have spoken I fear too largely already.

Peace. Mr. Cotton concludes with a confident persuasion of having removed the grounds of that great error, viz., that persons are not to be persecuted for cause of conscience.

Truth. And I believe, dear Peace, it shall appear to them that with fear and trembling at the word of the Lord examine these passages, that the charge of error rebound back, even such an error as may well be called the bloody tenent—so directly contradicting the spirit, and mind, and practice of the Prince of Peace; so deeply guilty of the blood of souls, compelled and forced to hypocrisy in a spiritual and soul-rape; so deeply guilty of the blood of the souls under the altar, persecuted in all ages for the cause of conscience, and so destructive to the civil peace and welfare of all kingdoms, countries, and commonwealths.

Chapter LXXXI

Peace. To this conclusion, dear Truth, I heartily subscribe, and know the God, the Spirit, the Prince, the angels, and all the true awaked sons of peace, will call you blessed.

Truth. How sweet and precious are these contemplations, but oh! how sweet the actions and fruitions!

Peace. Thy lips drop as the honey-comb, honey and milk are under thy tongue; oh! that these drops, these streams, might flow without a stop or interruption!

Truth. The glorious white troopers (Rev. 19) shall in time be mounted, and he that is the most high Prince of princes, and Lord General of generals mounted upon the word of truth and meekness (Ps. 45) shall triumph gloriously, and renew our meetings. But hark, what noise is this?

Peace. These are the doleful drums, and shrill-sounding trumpets, the roaring, murdering cannons, the shouts of conquerors, the groans of wounded, dying, slaughtered righteous with the wicked. Dear Truth, how long? How long these dreadful sounds and direful sights? How long before my glad return and restitution?

Truth. Sweet Peace, who will believe my true report? Yet true it is, if I were once believed, blessed truth and peace should not so soon be parted.

Peace. Dear Truth, what welcome have you found of late beyond your former times, or present expectations?

Truth. Alas! my welcome changes as the times, and strongest swords and arms prevail: were I believed in this, that Christ is not delighted with the blood of men, but shed his own for his bloodiest enemies, that by the word of Christ no man for gainsaying Christ, or joining with the enemy Antichrist, should be molested with the civil sword; were this foundation laid as the Magna Charta of highest liberties, and good security given on all hands for the preservation of it, how soon should every brow and house be stuck with olive branches?

Peace. This heavenly invitation makes me bold once more to crave thy patient ear and holy tongue. Error's impatient and soon tired, but you are light, and like the Father of lights, unwearied in your shinings. Lo here! what once again I present to your impartial censure.

COTTON MATHER

Selection from *Bonifacius*
(1710)

If Roger Williams sought to narrow the worldly scope of religion in order to preserve its authenticity, Cotton Mather (1663–1728) strove heroically to expand it, it would seem, almost infinitely. Theories have abounded concerning the sources of this trait or (more controversially) compulsion, beginning, naturally, with his extraordinary lineage as the son and grandson of three of Puritan New England's greatest ministers. But whatever the causes, the result seems clear enough: Mather's voracious passion to experience the power of his Christian faith through a multiplicity of forms animated, for better or worse, virtually all his far-flung works, from his ill-fated search for evidences of witchcraft to his enthusiastic embrace of the new natural science.

One can also see this drive operating in his influential *Bonifacius*. Most of this tract was taken up with various benevolent and (to a modern eye) meddling practical proposals for "doing good." But in these opening and closing chapters, Mather was both bolder and more revealing. He carefully asserted the orthodox basis of his good works in the saving grace of God while showing how the doing of good might bring about social cohesion, worldwide political change, and a joyful fulfillment of a faith so anguished as to seem otherwise almost unbearable.

For an excellent discussion of Mather's religious thought, see Robert Middlekauff, *The Mathers: Three Generations of Puritan Intellectuals, 1596–1728* (New York, 1971), 191–367. The historical and theological significance of Mather's pietism is cogently discussed in Richard F. Lovelace, *The American Pietism of Cotton Mather: Origins of American Evangelicalism* (Grand Rapids, Mich., 1979). Mather is the subject of two biographies that shed much light on his intellectual life and character: David Levin, *Cotton Mather: The Young Life of the Lord's Remembrancer, 1663–1703* (Cambridge, Mass., 1978); and Kenneth Silverman, *The Life and Times of Cotton Mather* (New York, 1984).

[Chapter One:] Essays to Do Good

Such *glorious things are spoken* in the oracles of our good God, concerning them who *devise good,* that A BOOK OF GOOD DEVICES may very reasonably demand attention and acceptance from them that have any impressions of the most *reasonable religion* upon them. I am *devising such* a BOOK; but at the same time offering a sorrowful demonstration, that if men would set themselves to *devise good,* a world of *good* might be done, more than there is, in this *present evil world.* It is very sure, the world has *need enough.* There needs abundance to be done, that the great GOD and His CHRIST may be more known and served in the world; and that the *errors* which are *impediments* to the *acknowledgments* wherewith men ought to glorify their Creator and Redeemer, may be rectified. There needs abundance to be done, that the *evil manners* of the world, by which men are *drowned in perdition,* may be reformed; and mankind rescued from the epidemical corruption and slavery which has overwhelmed it. There needs abundance to be done, that the *miseries* of the world may have *remedies* and *abatements* provided for them; and that miserable people may be relieved and comforted. The world has according to the computation of some, above seven hundred millions of people now living in it. What an ample field among all these, to *do good* upon! In a word, *the kingdom of God* in the world calls for innumerable *services* from us. To do SUCH THINGS IS TO DO GOOD. Those men DEVISE GOOD, who shape any DEVICES to do things of such a tendency; whether the things be of a *spiritual* importance, or of a *temporal.* You see, Sirs, the general matter, appearing as yet but as a *chaos,* which is to be wrought upon. *Oh! that the good Spirit of God may now fall upon us, and carry on the glorious work which lies before us!*

§2. 'Tis to be supposed, my readers will readily grant, that it is an excellent, a virtuous, a laudable thing to be full of *devices,* to bring about such *noble purposes.* For any man to deride, or to despise my proposal, *that we resolve and study to do as much good in the world as we can,* would be so black a character, that I am not willing to make a supposal of it in any of those with [whom] I am concerned. Let no man pretend unto the name of a *Christian,* who does not approve the proposal of a *perpetual endeavor to do good in the world.* What pretension can such a man have to be *a follower of the Good One?* The primitive *Christians* gladly accepted and improved the name, when the pagans by a mistake styled them, *Chrestians;* because it signified, *useful ones.* The *Christians* who have no ambition to be so, shall be condemned by the pagans, among whom it was a term of the highest honor, to be termed, *a benefactor;* to have *done good,* was accounted *honorable.* The philosopher being asked why everyone desired so much to look upon a fair object, he answered, that *it was a question of a blind man.* If any man ask, as wanting the sense of it, "What is it worth the while to *do good* in the world?," I must say, "It sounds not like the question of a good man." The Αιθησιςπνευματικη, as *Origen* calls it, the *spiritual taste* of every good man will make him have an unspeakable *relish* for it. Yea, unworthy to be discoursed as a *man,* is he, who is not for *doing of good among men.* An *enemy* to the proposal, *that mankind may be the better for us,* deserves to be reckoned, little better than, *a common enemy of mankind.* How cogently do I bespeak, a good reception of what is now designed! I produce not only *religion,* but even *humanity* itself, as full of a *fiery indignation against the adversaries of the design.* Excuse me, Sirs; I declare, that if I could

Source: Cotton Mather. *Bonifacius: An Essay upon the Good,* ed. David Levin (Cambridge: The Belknap Press of Harvard University Press, 1966), 17–34, 138–44, 149–51, 152. Editor's notes altered. Reprinted by permission of Harvard University Press, Copyright © 1966 by the President and Fellows of Harvard College.

have my choice, I would never *eat* or *drink,* or *walk,* with such an one as long as I live; or, look on him as any other than one by whom *humanity* itself is debased and blemished. A very *wicked writer,* has yet found himself compelled by the force of *reason,* to publish this confession. "To love the public, to study an universal good, and to promote the interest of the whole world, as far as is in our power, is surely the highest of goodness, and makes that temper, which we call Divine." And, he goes on: "Is the doing of good for glory's sake so divine a thing? [Alas, too much *humane,* Sir!] Or, is it not a diviner to do good, even where it may be thought inglorious? Even unto the ungrateful, and unto those who are wholly insensible of the good they receive!" A man must be far gone in *wickedness,* who will open his mouth, against such *maxims* and *actions!* A better pen has remarked it; yea, the man must be much a stranger in history, who has not made the remark. *To speak truth, and to do good, were in the esteem even of the heathen world, most God-like qualities.* God forbid, that in the esteem of the *Christian world* for those qualities, there should be any abatement!

§3. I won't yet propose the *reward* of *well-doing,* and the glorious things which the *mercy* and *truth* of God will do, for them who *devise good,* because I would have to do with such, as will esteem it, a sufficient *Reward* unto itself. I will imagine that generous ingenuity, in my readers, which will dispose them to count themselves *well-rewarded* in the thing itself, if God will accept them to *do good* in the world. It is an invaluable *honor,* to *do good;* it is an incomparable *pleasure.* A man must look upon himself as *dignified* and *gratified* by GOD when an *opportunity* to *do good* is put into his hands. He must embrace it with *rapture,* as enabling him directly to answer the great END of his being. He must manage it with *rapturous delight,* as a most suitable business, as a most precious privilege. He must *sing in those ways of the Lord,* wherein he cannot but find himself, while he is *doing of good.* As the saint of old sweetly sang, "I was glad, when they said unto me, Let us go into the House of the Lord." Thus ought we to be *glad,* when any *opportunity* to *do good,* is offered unto us. We should need no *arguments,* to make us entertain the offer; but we should *naturally* fly into the matter, as most agreeable to the *divine nature* whereof we are *made partakers.* It should *oblige* us wonderfully! An ingot of gold presented unto us, not more obliging! Think, Sirs, *Now I enjoy what I am for! Now I attain what I wish for!* Some servants of God have been so strongly disposed this way, that they have cheerfully made a tender of any *recompense* that could be desired (yea, rather than fail, a *pecuniary* one) unto any friend that would *think* for them, and *supply* the *barrenness* of their thoughts, and *suggest* unto them any special and proper *methods,* wherein they may be *serviceable.* Certainly, to *do good,* is a thing that brings its own *recompense,* in the opinion of those, who reckon a kind *information* of a point wherein they may *do good,* worthy to be by them requited with a *recompense* to the *informer.* I will only say: "If any of you are strangers unto such a disposition as this, to look upon an *opportunity* to *do good,* as a thing that *enriches* you, and to look upon yourselves as *enriched,* and *favored* of God, when He does employ you to *do good:* I have done with you." I would pray them, to lay the *book* aside; it will disdain to carry on any further conversation with 'em! It handles a subject on which the wretches of the house of *Caleb,* will not be conversed withal. It is content with one of Dr. *Stoughton's* Introductions: "It is enough to me, that I speak to wise men, whose reason shall be my rhetoric, to Christians, whose conscience shall be my eloquence."

§4. Though the assertion fly never so much like a *chainshot* among us, and rake down all before it, I will again, and again assert it; *that we might every one of us do more good than we do.* And therefore, this is the FIRST PROPOSAL, to be made unto us: *to be exceedingly humbled, that we have done so little good in the world.* I am not *uncharitable,* in saying: I know not that *assembly* of Christians upon earth, which ought not to be a *Bochim,* in this consideration. Oh! tell me, what *Utopia* I shall find it in! Sirs, let us begin to bring forth some *good fruit,* by lamenting our own *great unfruitfulness.* Verily, *sins of omission* must be confessed and bewailed; else we add unto the number of them. The most *useful* men in the world, have gone out of it, crying to God, "Lord, let my sins of omission be forgiven to me!" Men that have made more than ordinary conscience about well-spending of their *time,* have had their deathbed made uneasy by this reflection: *The loss of time now sits heavy upon me.* Be sure, all *unregenerate* persons are, as our Bible has told us, *unprofitable* persons. 'Tis not for nothing, that the comparison of *thorns,* and *briars,* has been used, to *teach* us, what they are. An unrenewed sinner, alas, he never did *one good work* in all his *life!* In all his *life,* did I say? You must give me that word again! He is *dead* while he *lives;* he is *dead in sins;* he has never yet begun to *live unto God:* and, as is he, so are *all the works of his hands;* they are *dead works.* Ah! wretched *good-for-nothing.* Wonder, wonder at the patience of Heaven, which yet forbears *cutting down* such a *cumberer of the ground.* The best, and the first advice, to be given unto such persons, is, *immediately to do their best, that they may get out of their woeful unregeneracy.* Let them *immediately* acknowledge the *necessity* of their turning to God, but how *unable* they are to do it, and how *unworthy* that God should make them *able. Immediately* let them lift up their *cry* unto sovereign *grace,* to *quicken* them; and let them then *try,* whether they cannot with *quickened* Souls, *plead* the *sacrifice* and *righteousness* of a glorious Christ for their happy reconciliation to God; seriously resolve upon a life of *obedience* to God, and *serious religion;* and resign themselves up unto the *Holy Spirit,* that He may possess them, instruct them, strengthen them, and *for His name's sake lead them in the paths of holiness.* There will no *good* be done, till this be done. The very *first-born* of all *devices to do good,* is in being *born again,* and in *devising means, that a banished* soul may no longer be *expelled* from the presence of God. But you that have been brought home to God, have sad cause, not only to deplore the *dark days* of your unregeneracy, wherein you did none but the *unfruitful works of darkness;* but also, that you have done so *little,* since God has quickened you and enabled you, to *do,* the things that should be done. How little, how little have you lived up, to the strains of *gratitude,* which might have been justly expected, since God has brought you *into His marvellous light!* The best of us may mourn in our complaint: "Lord, how little good have I done, to what I might have done!" Let the sense of this cause us to *loathe* and *judge* ourselves before the Lord: let it fill us with shame, and abase us wonderfully! How can we do any other, than with *David,* even make a cauldron of our couch, and a bath of our tears, when we consider how little *good* we have done! *Oh! that our heads were waters,* because they have been so *dry* of all thoughts to *do good! Oh! that our eyes were a fountain of tears,* because they have been so little upon the *lookout* for objects and methods to *do good* upon! For the *pardon* of this *evil-doing,* let us fly to the Great *Sacrifice,* which is our only *expiation.* Plead the *blood* of that *Lamb of God,* whose universal *usefulness* is one of those admirable properties, for which He has been called, *a lamb.* The *pardon* of our *barrenness* at *good works* being thus obtained, by faith in that *blood which cleanses from all sin,* that is the way for us to be rescued from a condemnation to *perpetual barrenness.* The dreadful sentence of, *Let no fruit grow on thee forever!* will be reversed and prevented, by such a *pardon.* Sirs, a true, right, evangelical procedure to *do good,* must have this *repentance* laid in the foundation of it! We do not *handle the matter wisely,* if *a foundation* be not laid thus *low,* and in the deepest *self-abasement.*

§5. How full, how full of *devices* are we, for our own *secular advantage!* And how *expert* in *devising many little things,* to be done for ourselves! We apply our thoughts, with a mighty assiduity, unto the old question, *What shall I eat and drink, and where-withal shall I be clothed? It* is with a very strong application of our thoughts, that we study, what we shall do for ourselves, in our *marriages,* in our *voyages,* in our *bargains,* and in many, many other concerns, wherein we are solicitous to have our condition easy. We solicitously *contrive,* that we may accomplish *good bargains,* and that we may steer clear of ten thousand *inconveniences,* to which, without some *contrivance,* we may lie obnoxious. The *business* of our *personal callings* we carry on with numberless thoughts, how we may *do well,* in what is to be done. To accomplish our temporal *business,* in affairs that cannot be numbered, *we find out witty inventions.* But, O rational, immortal, Heaven-born SOUL, are thy wonderous faculties capable of no greater improvements, no better employments? Why should a *soul* of such high capacities, a *soul* that may arrive to be clothed in the bright *scarlet of angels,* yet *embrace a dunghill!* O let a *blush* coloring beyond *scarlet,* be thy clothing for thy being found so meanly occupied! Alas, *in the multitude of thy thoughts within thee,* hast thou no dispositions to raise thy soul, unto some thoughts, *what may be done for* GOD, *and* CHRIST, *and for my own* SOUL, *and for the most considerable interests?* How many hundreds of *thoughts* have we, how to obtain or secure some trifle for ourselves; to *one,* how we may serve the interests of the glorious LORD, and of His people in the world? How can we now pretend, that we *love Him,* or, that a carnal, and criminal *self-love,* has not the dominion over us? I again come in, upon a *soul of* an Heavenly extract, and *smite* it, as the angel did the sleeping prisoner: *Awake, shake off thy shackles, lie no longer fettered in a base confinement unto nothing but a meaner sort of business.* Assume and assert the liberty of now and then thinking on the *noblest question* in the world: *What good may I do in the world?* There was a time, when it was complained by no less a man, than *Gregory* the Great (the Bishop of *Rome): I am sunk into the world!* It may be the complaint of a *soul,* that minds all other things, and rarely calls to mind that *noblest question. Ah! star, fallen from Heaven,* and choked in dust, rise and soar up to something answerable to thy original. Begin a *course of thoughts,* which when begun, will be like a *resurrection from the dead.* They *which dwell in the dust, wake and sing,* and little anticipate the *life* which we are to live at the *resurrection of the dead,* when they livelily set themselves to think: *How may I be a blessing in the world?* And, *What may I do, that righteousness may more dwell in the world?*

§6. How much *hurt* may be done by *one wicked man?* Yea, sometimes *one wicked man,* of but small abilities, becoming an *indefatigable tool of the Devil,* may do an incredible deal of mischief in the world. We have seen some wretched instruments of *cursed memory,* ply the intention of *doing mischief,* at a strange rate; until they have undone a whole country; yea, unto the undoing of more than three kingdoms. 'Tis a melancholy consideration, which I am now upon: and I may say, an astonishing one! You will hardly find *one of a thousand,* who does near so much, to serve God and Christ, and his own soul, as you may see done by thousands to serve the Devil. *An horrible thing!*

"O my soul; thy *Maker,* and thy *Saviour,* so worthy of thy love, and thy all! A Lord, whose infinite goodness, will follow all that thou doest for Him, with remunerations, beyond all apprehension glorious! How little, how little, is it that thou doest for Him! At the same time, look into thy neighborhood; see there a monster of wickedness, who to his uttermost will serve a Devil, that will prove a *destroyer* unto him, and all whose *wages* will be *torments.* He *studies* how to serve the *Devil;* he is never weary of his *drudgery;* he racks his *invention* to go through with it. He *shames* me, he *shames* me wonderfully! O my God, *I am ashamed, and blush to lift up my face unto thee, my God.*"

There is a man, of whom we read: "He deviseth mischief upon his bed, he sets himself in a way that is not good." Now I beseech you, why should not we be as *active,* as *frequent, as forward,* in *devising of good;* and as full of *exquisite contrivance?* Why should not we be as *wise to do good,* as any people are *wise to do evil?* I am sure, we have a *better cause;* and there is more of *reason* for it. My friend, thou are one that makes but a *little figure* in the world, and a *brother of low degree,* behold, a vast encouragement! A *little* man may do a great deal of *hurt.* And then, why may not a *little* man, do a great deal *of good!* It is possible the *wisdom of a poor man,* may start a proposal, that may *save a city,* serve a nation! A *single hair* applied unto a *flyer,* that has other wheels depending on it, may pull up an *oak,* or pull down an *house.*

It is very observable, that when our Lord JESUS CHRIST would recommend the *zeal,* with which the *Kingdom of Heaven* is to be served, He did not mention an example of *honest wisdom;* no, but of an unrighteous and scandalous *dishonesty* (as of an *unjust steward*) for our emulation. The *wisdom* of our Lord in this matter, is much to be observed. His design is, not only to represent the *prudence,* but also the vast industry, ingenuity, resolution, and *heroic effort of soul,* necessary in them, that would seek and serve the Kingdom of Heaven. There is nowhere to be found among men, that *vivacity of spirit* in *lawful* actions, which there is to be found in *unlawful* ones. The ways of *honesty* are plain to men, and they require not so much *uneasiness* in the minds of men to manage them. Whereas your *thieves* and *cheats,* and men that follow courses of *dishonesty,* take ways that are full of difficulties: the *turns* and the *tricks* with which they must be carried through them, are innumerable. Hence among such fellows, you find the exercise of the most extraordinary *subtlety.* There is no such cunning, and nimble *application* to be anywhere else met withal. 'Tis very emphatical, to fetch from hence the colors of *heavenly wisdom!* That which I would now be at, is this: that we *do good* with as much *application,* as any men alive can use in *evil-doing.* When *wickedness proceeds from the wicked,* it is often done *with both hands,* and *greedily.* Why may not we proceed in our *usefulness,* even *with both hands,* and *greedily* watching for opportunities? We have no occasion for any *ill arts,* that we may carry on our designs to *do good.* God forbid, that we should ever imagine the uniting of such *inconsistencies.* But why cannot we carry on our *designs,* with as much, and as deep, and as copious *thought,* as the men of *ill arts?* And why may not we lay out our spirits, with as transporting a vigor, to do the things that will be *acceptable* to God, and *profitable* to men, as any wretches have, when they *weary themselves to commit iniquity?* To reprehend certain ecclesiastical drones, who had little inclination to *do good,* Father *Latimer* employed a coarse expression of this importance: "If you won't learn of good men, for shame learn of the Devil! He is never idle. He goes about, seeking what hurt he may do!" Truly, the indefatigable prosecution of their designs, which we may see in some, whom the Holy Word of God has called, *the children of the Devil,* may exceedingly put us to the blush. Our *obligations* to *do good* are infinite: they *do evil* against all *obligations.* The *compensations* made unto them who *do good,* are encouraging beyond all expression; they who *do evil,* get nothing to boast of, but *evil pursues the sinners.* If the *Devil* do *go about,* and people inspired by him also *go about, seeking what hurt they may do,* why do not we *go about,* and *seek,* and think, where and how to *do good?* Verily, 'twere a character for a *good angel,* to do so. O thou *child of God,* and *lover of all righteousness:* how canst thou find in thy heart at any time to *cease* from doing all the *good,* that can be done, in the *right ways of the Lord?* Methinks, that *Word of the Lord,* may be a *burden* unto us; if we have any true *honor* in us, it will be so! *The children of this world,* are in (and *for*) *their generation, wiser than the children of light.* Yea, they pursue the *works of darkness* more livelily, than any of us *walk in the light,* wherewith our Great Saviour has favored us.

§7. To the title of GOOD WORKS there do belong, those *essays to do good,* which are now urged for. To produce them, the *first* thing, and indeed the ONE thing, that is *needful,* is, a glorious work of GRACE on the soul, renewing and quickening of it, and *purifying* of the sinner, and rendering him *zealous of good works:* a *workmanship of God* upon us, *creating* us over again, by JESUS CHRIST, *for good works.* And then, there is needful, what will necessarily follow upon such a *work:* that is, a *disposition* to *do good works* upon true, genuine, generous, and evangelical *principles.* Those *principles* are to be *stated,* before we can go any further; when they are *active,* we shall go a great deal further.

It is in the first place, to be taken for granted: that the *end* for which we do *good works* must not be, to afford the matter of our *justification,* before the Law of the holy GOD. Indeed, no *good works* can be done by any man until he be *justified.* Until a man be united unto the glorious CHRIST, who is *our life,* he is a *dead man.* And, I pray, what *good works* to be expected from such a man? They will all be *dead works.* For, "Severed from me ye can do nothing," saith our Savior. The *justification of a* sinner, *by faith, before good works, and in order to them,* is one of those truths, which may say to the Popish innovations, "With us are the gray-headed, and very aged men, much elder than they Father." It was an old maxim of the faithful, *Bona opera sequuntur justificatum, non præcecedunt justificandum.*[1] It is the *righteousness of* the *good works* done by our Saviour and *Surety,* not our own, that *justifies* us before God, and answers the demands of His Law upon us. We do *by faith* lay hold on those *good works* for our *justifying righteousness* before we arrive to do our own. 'Tis not our *faith* itself, either as doing of *good works,* or as being itself one of them, which entitles us to *the justifying righteousness* of our Saviour. But it is *faith,* only *as* renouncing of our own righteousness, and relying on that of our Saviour, provided for the *chief of sinners,* by which we are *justified.* Sir, all your attempts at *good works* will come to nothing, till a *justifying faith* in your Saviour, shall carry you forth unto them. This was the divinity of the ancients; Jerome has well expressed it: *Sine Christo omnis virtus est in vitie.*[2] Nevertheless; first, you are to look upon it, as a glorious truth of the Gospel, that the *moral law* (which prescribes and requires *good works)* must by every Christian alive be made the *rule* of his life. *Do we make void the Law through faith? God forbid. Yea, we establish the Law.* The *rule,* by which we are to *glorify* God, is given us in the law of *good works,* which we *enjoy* (I will express it *so!)* in the *Ten Commandments.* It is impossible for us, to be released from all obligations to glorify God by a conformity to this *rule;* sooner shall we cease to be creatures. The *conformity* to that rule in the *righteousness,* which our Saviour by His obedience to it, has *brought in,* to *justify* us, has forever *magnified the Law, and made it honorable.* Though our Saviour has furnished us, with a perfect and spotless *righteousness,* when His obedience to the *Law,* is placed unto our account; yet it is a *sin* for us at all to fall short in our own obedience to the *Law:* we must always loathe and judge ourselves for the *sin.* We are not under the *Law* as a *covenant of works.* Our own exactness in doing of *good works,* is not now the *condition* of our *entering into life.* Woe unto us if it were! But still, the *Covenant of Grace* holds us to it, as our *duty;* and if we are in the *Covenant of Grace,* we shall make it our *study,* to *do* those *good works* which once were the terms of our *entering into life. Manet lex tota pietatis,*[3] that

---

1. Good works follow justification; they do not precede justification.
2. Without Christ, all virtue is vice.
3. The entire law of duty [or obedience to God] remains.

was the divinity in *Tertullian's* days! There must be such an esteem for the *law of good works* retained forever in all the *justified: a law* never to be abrogated; never to be abolished! And then, secondly, though we are *justified* by a *precious faith* in the *righteousness of God our Saviour,* yet good works are demanded of us, to *justify* our *faith; to demonstrate,* that it is indeed that *precious faith. A justifying faith* is a *jewel,* which may be *counterfeited.* But now the *marks of a faith,* which is no counterfeit, are to be found in the *good works* whereto a servant of God is inclined and assisted by his *faith.* It is by a *regenerating work* of the Holy Spirit, that *faith* is wrought in the souls of the chosen people. Now the same *work* of God, and of *grace,* which does in a *regeneration* dispose a man to make his flight by *faith,* unto the *righteousness* of his only Saviour, will also dispose him to the *good works* of a *Christian life.* And the same *faith* which goes to the Saviour for a part in His *righteousness,* will also go to Him, for an heart and strength to do the *good works,* which are *ordained, that we should walk in them.* If our *faith* be not such *a faith,* 'tis a *lifeless* one, and it will not bring to *life, A workless faith* is a *worthless faith.* My friend, suppose thyself standing before the *Judgment-seat of* the glorious LORD. A needful, a prudent, supposal; it ought to be a very *frequent* one. The *Judge* demands, "What hast thou to plead, for a portion in the blessedness of the righteous?" The plea must be:

"O my glorious Judge, Thou hast been my sacrifice. Oh! Judge of all the earth, give poor dust and ashes leave to say, 'My righteousness is on the bench. Surely in the Lord I have my righteousness. O my Saviour, I have received it, I have secured it, upon Thy gracious offer of it.'"

The *Judge* proceeds:

"But what hast thou to plead, that thy faith should not be rejected, as the faith and hope of the hyprocrite?"

Here the plea must be:

"Lord, my faith was Thy work. It was a faith which disposed me to all the good works of Thy holy religion. My faith sanctified me. It carried me to Thee, O my Saviour, for grace to do the works of righteousness. It embraced that for my Lord as well as for my Saviour. It caused me with sincerity to love and keep Thy commandments; with assiduity to serve the interests of Thy Kingdom in the world." Thus you have *Paul* and *James* reconciled. Thus you have *good works* provided for. The aphorism of the physician, is, *Per brachium fit judicium de corde.* The *doings* of men are truer and surer indications, than all their *sayings,* of what they are *within.* But there is yet a further consideration, upon which you must be *zealously affected* for them. You must consider *good works,* as the *way* to, yea, as a *part* of, the *great salvation,* which is purchased and intended for you, by your blessed Saviour. Without an *holy heart you* can't be fit for an *holy heaven; meet for the inheritance of the holy ones* in that *light,* which admits no *works of darkness,* where none but *good works* are done for eternal ages. But an *holy heart* will cause a man to do *good works* with all his heart. The motto on the gates of the Holy City is: NONE BUT THE LOVERS OF GOOD WORKS TO ENTER HERE. 'Tis implied, in what we read, *without holiness no man shall see the Lord.* Yea, to be *saved* without *good works,* were to be *saved* without *salvation.* Much of our *salvation* lies in doing of *good works.* When our *souls* are *enlarged* and *unfettered,* it is that we may *do* such things. *Heaven* is begun upon *earth* in the doing of them. Doubtless, no man shall come up to *Heaven,* who is not so persuaded. I will mention but one more of those *principles,* which *good works* grow upon. 'Tis that noble one, of GRATITUDE. The believer cannot but inquire, "What shall I render to my Saviour?" The result of the inquiry will be, *with good works to glorify Him.* We read, "Faith works by love." Our *faith* will first show us the matchless and marvelous *love* of God, in saving us. And the *faith* of this *love* will work upon our hearts, until it has raised in us, an unquenchable flame of *love* unto Him that hath so *loved* us, and *saved* us.

These, these are to be our dispositions:

"O my Saviour, hast Thou done so much for me? Now will I do all I can for Thy Kingdom, and people in the world? Oh! What service is there that I may now do for my Saviour, and for His people in the world!"

These are the principles to be proceeded on! And on them, I will observe to you a notable thing. 'Tis worthy of observation, that there are no men in the world, who so abound in *good works,* as the men who have most of all abandoned all pretense to *merit* by their *works.* There are *Protestants* who have outdone *Papists,* in our days, as well as in Dr. *Willet's.* No *merit-mongers* have gone beyond some holy Christians, who have done *good works,* upon the *assurance* of their being already justified and entitled unto life eternal.

I take notice, that our Apostle, casting a just contempt on the *endless genealogies,* and long, intricate, perplexed pedigrees, which the *Jews* of his time, stood so much upon; proposes instead thereof to be studied, *charity, out of a pure heart, and a good conscience, and faith unfeigned.* As if he had said, I will give you a *genealogy* worth ten thousand of theirs, first, from *faith unfeigned* proceeds a *good conscience:* from a *good conscience proceeds* a *pure heart:* from a *pure heart* proceeds a *charity* to all about us. 'Tis admirably stated!

§8. It is to be feared, that we too seldom *inquire* after our Opportunities to Do Good. Our *opportunities to do good* are our Talents. An awful account must be rendered unto the great GOD, concerning our use of the Talents, wherewith He has entrusted us, in these precious *opportunities.* We do not *use* our *opportunities,* many times because we do not *know* what they are; and many times, the reason why we do not *know,* is because we do not *think.* Our *opportunities to do good,* lie by unregarded, and unimproved, and so 'tis but a mean account that can be given of them. We *read* of a thing, which we *deride as* often as we behold: *there is, that maketh himself poor, and yet has great riches.* It is a thing too frequently exemplified, in our *opportunities to do good,* which are some of our most valuable *riches.* Many a man seems to reckon himself destitute of those *talents;* as if there were *nothing* for him to do: he pretends he is not in a condition to *do* any *good. Alas! poor man; what can he do?* My friend, *think* again; *think often.* Inquire what your *opportunities* are. You will doubtless find them, to be more than you were *aware* of. *Plain men dwelling in tents,* persons of a very *ordinary character,* may in a way of bright piety, prove persons of *extraordinary usefulness.* A poor *John Urich* may make a *Grotius* the better for him. I have read of a pious *Weaver,* of whom some eminent persons would say, "Christ walked as it were alive upon the Earth in that man." And a world of *good* was done by that man. A mean *mechanic,* who can tell what an *engine* of good he may be, if humbly and wisely applied unto it!

This then is the next Proposal. Without abridging yourselves of your *occasional thoughts* on the question, often every day, *What good may I do?,* state a *time* now and then for more *deliberate thoughts* upon it. Can't you find a *time* (suppose once a week, yea, and how agreeably, on the *Lord's* day) to take that question into your consideration: What Is There That I May Do, For the Service of the Glorious Lord, and for the Welfare of Those, for Whom I Ought to Be Concerned? Having implored the *direction* of God, who is the *Father of Lights,* and the Author and Giver of *good thoughts, consider* on the matter, in the various aspects of it. *Consider* till you have *resolved* on something. The *resolutions* which you *take up,* immediately *write down.* Examine what *precept* and what *promise,* you can find in the Word of God, that may countenance the intentions, in these your *memorials.* Look over the *memorials* at proper seasons afterwards, to see how far you have proceeded in the execution of them. The advantages of these *reserved* and *revised* MEMORIALS, no *rhetoric* will serve to commend them, no *arithmetic* to number them. There are some *animals,* of whom we say, "They do not know their own strength." *Christians,* why should you be *they?*

§9. Let us descend unto PARTICULARS. But in doing so, let it not be imagined, that I pretend unto an enumeration of all the GOOD DEVICES, that are to be thought upon. Indeed, not a *thousandth* part of them, need or can be now enumerated. The *essay,* which I am now upon, is, only to dig open the several *springs* of *usefulness;* which having once begun to run, will spread into *streams,* which no *human foresight* can comprehend. *Spring up, O well!* So will every true *Israelite* sing, upon every PROPOSAL here exhibited. And the *nobles of Israel can* do nothing more agreeable to their own character, than to fall to work upon it. Perhaps almost every *proposal* to be now mentioned, may be like a *stone* falling on a *pool; reader,* keep thy mind *calm,* and see, whether the effect prove not so! That one *circle* (and *service*) will produce another, until they extend, who can tell, how far? and they cannot be reckoned up. The men who give themselves up to GOOD DEVICES, and who lake a due notice of their *opportunities to do good,* usually find a strange growth of their *opportunities.* The gracious and faithful Providence of the glorious Lord, grants this recompense unto His diligent servants, that He will *multiply* their *opportunities* to be *serviceable.* And when ingenious men have a little used themselves unto *contrivances,* in this or that way of pursuing the best intentions, their ingenuity will sensibly improve, and there will be more of *exquisiteness,* more of *expansion,* in their diffusive applications. Among all the dispensations of *special Providence,* in the government of the world, there is none more *uninterrupted,* than the accomplishment of that word, UNTO HIM THAT HATH, SHALL BE GIVEN. I will say this: O *useful Man,* take that for thy *motto:* HABENTI DABITUR. And, in a lively use of thy *opportunities to do good,* see how notably, it will be accomplished! Sir, see what accomplishment of that word will at last surprise you: "Though thy beginning were small, yet thy latter end shall greatly increase."...

[Chapter Twelve:] Desiderata

§22. We will not propose, that our *essays to do good,* should ever come to an end. But we will now put an end unto this, of tendering PROPOSALS for it. It shall conclude with a *catalogus desideratorum,* or a mention of some obvious, and general *services* for the Kingdom of God among mankind, whereto 'twere to be desired, that religious and ingenious men might be awakened.

A CATALOGUE OF DESIRABLES, waiting for the *zeal of good men* to prosecute them. (*Difficilem rem optas; generis humani innocentiam!*)[4]

I. The propagation of the holy and glorious *religion of* CHRIST; a religion which *emancipates* mankind from the worst of slaveries and miseries, and wonderfully *ennobles* it; and which alone prepares men for the blessedness of another world: why is this no more endeavored by the professors of it? PROTESTANTS, why will you be out-done by *popish idolaters!* Oh! the vast pains which those *bigots,* have taken, to carry on the *Romish* merchandises and idolatries! No less than six hundred clergymen, in that one order of the *Jesuits,* did within a few years, at several times, embark themselves for *China,* to win over

---

4. You choose a difficult thing, the righteousness of mankind.

that mighty nation unto their bastard-Christianity. No less than five hundred of them lost their *lives,* in the difficulties of their enterprise; and yet the survivors go on with it; expressing a sort of trouble, that it fell not unto their share to make a sacrifice of their *lives,* in enterprising the propagation of religion. O *my God, I am ashamed, and blush to lift up my face unto thee my God!* It were but a *Christian,* but a *grateful,* but an *equal* thing; but who can foretell what *prosperity* might be the recompense! If our *companies* and *factories,* would set apart a more considerable part of their *gains* for this work, and set upon a more vigorous prosecution of it. *Gordon's* proposal, unto all men of estates, to set apart a small part of their estates for this purpose (at the end of his *Geography),* should be taken into further consideration. What has been done by the *Dutch* missionaries at *Ceylon,* and what is doing by the *Danish* missionaries at *Malabar,* one would think, might animate us, to imitate them!

If men of a spirit for *evangelizing,* and *illuminating* a woeful world, would learn the *languages* of some nations that are yet *ungospellized,* and wait on the Providence of Heaven, to lead them to, and own them in, some *apostolical undertakings,* who can tell what might be done? We know, what *Ruffinus* relates concerning the conversion of the *Iberians;* and what *Socrates,* concerning the things done by *Frumentius* and *Ædesius,* in the *inner India.*

But on this *desirable* there are two things *remarkable.*

First, it is the conjecture of some *seers,* that until the *Temple* be *cleansed,* there will be no general appearance of the *nations* to worship in it. And the truth is, there will be danger, until then, that many persons active in *Societies for the Propagation of Religion,* may be more intent upon propagating their own little *forms* and *fancies* and *interests,* than the more *weighty matters of the Gospel.* Yea, 'twill be well, if they be not unawares imposed upon, to hurt *Christianity where* 'tis well-established, while places wholly *ungospellized* in the neighborhood may lie neglected. Let us therefore do what we can towards the Church's *reformation,* in order to its *dilatation.*

Secondly, it is probable, that the *Holy Spirit* in operations, like those of the first ages, whereby Christianity was first *planted,* will be again conferred from our *ascended Lord,* for the *spreading* of it. The *Holy Spirit,* who has withdrawn from the *apostate church,* will come, and *abide with* us, and render this world like a *watered garden.* His irresistible influences will cause whole *nations* to be *born at once;* He will not only *convert* but *unite,* His people. By Him, God shall *dwell with men.* Would not the *Heavenly Father give His Holy Spirit,* if it were more *asked* of Him!

II. 'Tis lamentable to see the *ignorance* and *wickedness,* yet remaining, even in many parts of the *British* dominions: in *Wales;* in the *Highlands;* and in *Ireland.* Are the *Gouges* all dead? There are pretended *shepherds,* in the world, that will never be able to answer before the Son of God, for their laying so little to heart, the *deplorable* circumstances, of so many people, whom they might, if they were not scandalously negligent, bring to be more acquainted with the only Saviour. And there might be more done, that some of the *American* colonies, may no longer be such *Cimmerian* ones.

III. Why is no more done, for the poor *Greeks,* and *Armenians,* and *Muscovites,* and other Christians, who have little *preaching,* and no *printing* among them? If we sent *Bibles,* and *Psalters,* and other *books of piety* among them, in their own languages, they would be *noble* presents, and, God knows, how *useful* ones!

IV. Poor *sailors,* and poor *soldiers,* call for our pity. They meet with *great and sore troubles.* Their *manners* are too commonly such, as discover no very good effects of their *troubles*. What shall be done to make them a *better sort of men?* There must, besides more *books of piety* distributed among them, other methods be thought upon; *Cadit asinus et est qui sublevat. Perit anima, et non est qui manum apponat?*[5] Let *Austin* awaken us.

V. The *Tradesman's Library* needs to be more enriched. We have seen, *Husbandry Spiritualized;* and, *Shepherdy Spiritualized;* and, *Navigation Spiritualized;* we have seen, the *weaver* also accommodated, with agreeable meditations. To spread the *nets of salvation* for men, in the ways of their *personal callings,* and convey good thoughts unto them, in the *terms* and *steps,* of their daily business, is a real service to the interests of piety. A Book also, that shall be an *onomatologia monitoria,* and shall advise people how to make their *names* become unto them, the *monitors* of their duty; might be of much use to the *Christened* world. And, a Book, that shall be, *The Angel of Bethesda,* and shall instruct people how to improve in agreeable points of piety, from the several maladies, which their *bodies* may be diseased withal; and at the same time, inform them of the most experimented, natural, specific *remedies* for their diseases, might be very useful to mankind. These two subjects, if not undertaken by any other hand, may be so shortly by that which now writes; except the glorious Lord of my life, immediately put an end unto it; and *my days are past, my purposes are broken off, even the thoughts of my heart!*

VI. *Universities* that shall have more *collegiae pietatis* in them, like those of the excellent *Franckius* in the lower *Saxony;* oh! that there were more of them!—*seminaries* in which the scholars may have a most polite education; but not be sent forth with recommendations for the evangelical ministry, till it be upon a strict examination found, that their souls are fired with the *fear* of God, and the *love* of Christ, and a *zeal* to do good, and a *resolution* to bear poverty, and obloquy, and all sorts of temptations, in the service of our holy religion; they would be the *wonders* of the world, and what *wonders* might they do in the world!

Let the *charity-schools,* also, *increase and multiply; charity-schools* which may provide subjects for the great Saviour, blessings for the next generation; *charity-schools,* not perverted unto the ill purposes of introducing a *defective Christianity.*

VII. Those things, that so far as we *understand by the books* of the sacred Prophecies, are to be, *the works of our day;* 'Tis *wisdom* to observe and pursue. When the time was arrived, that the *Antichrist* must enter his last *half-time,* one poor monk proves a main instrument of ravishing *half* his empire from him. Thus to fall in with the designs of the *Divine Providence,* is the way to be wonderfully prospered and honored. One small man, thus *nicking the time* for it, may do wonders!

I take the *works of our day* to be:

1. The *reviving of primitive Christianity;* to study and restore everything, of the *primitive* character. The *apostasy* is going off. The time for *cleansing the Temple* comes on. More *Edwardses* would be vast blessings, where the *primitive doctrines of Christianity* are depraved.

2. The persuading of the *European* powers, to shake off the chains *of popery.* This argument—there is no *popish nation,* but what by embracing the *Protestant religion,* would *ipso facto,* not only assert themselves into a glorious *liberty,* but also *double their wealth* immediately—'tis marvellous; that it is no more yet hearkened unto! Sirs, prosecute

---

5.   An ass falls, and there is someone to help lift up. A soul dies, and there is no one to help it.

it, with more of *demonstration*. One shows, that the abolishing of popery in *England,* is worth at least eight millions of pounds yearly to the nation. Let the argument be tried with other nations, the argument, *ab utili.*

3. The *forming* and *quickening* of that People, that are to be, The Stone Cut Out of the Mountain. Here, as well as in some other things, *none of the wicked shall understand, but the wise shall understand.* God will do His own work, in His own time, and in His own way. And *Austin* tells me, *Utile est ut taceatur aliquod verbum, propter incapaces.*[6]

[Chapter Thirteen:] The Conclusion

The *zeal of the Lord of Hosts will perform these things:* a *zeal* inspired and produced by the *Lord of Hosts* in His faithful servants, will put them upon the performance of such things. Nothing has been yet proposed, that is impracticable; *Non fortia loquor, sed possibilia.*[7] But, *Eusebius* has taught me, *Vere magnum est magna facere, et teipsum putare nihil.*[8] Sirs, under and after a course of such *actions,* which have a true glory in them, and really are more glorious than all the *actions* and *achievements,* whereof those bloody plunderers, whom we call *conquerors,* have made a wretched ostentation: and perhaps made inscriptions like those of *Pompey* on his Temple of *Minerva*—still *humility,* must be the *crown* of all. All, nothing without *humility;* nothing without a sense that you are *nothing,* a consent to be made *nothing.* You must first, most humbly acknowledge unto the great God, *that after you have done all, you are unprofitable servants;* and make your humble confession, that not only you have *done but that which was your duty to do,* but also that you have exceedingly fallen short of doing your *duty.* If God abase you with very *dark dispensations* of His Providence, after all your indefatigable and your disinterested essays to *glorify* Him, humble yourselves before Him; yet abate nothing of your *essays;* hold on, saying, "My God will humble me, yet will I glorify Him. Lord, Thou art righteous; but still I will do all I can to serve thy glorious Kingdom." This indeed, is a more easy *humiliation;* but then there is one to be demanded, of much greater difficulty: that is, that you humbly submit unto all the *diminutions,* among *men,* that God shall order for you. Your admirable Saviour was one who *went about* ever *doing of good;* mankind was never visited by such a *benefactor.* And yet we read, "He was One spoken against." Never anyone so vilified! Had He been the worst *malefactor* in the world, He could not have been worse dealt withal. He expostulated, "For which of my good works is it that you treat me so?" Yet they went on; they hated Him, they reproached Him, they murdered Him. *Austin* said very truly, *Remedium elationis est contuitus Dominicae crucis.*[9] It will also be the remedy of discouragement; it will keep you from *sinking,* as well as being *lifted up.* You are conformed unto your Saviour, in your watchful endeavors to *do good,* and be *fruitful in every good work.* But your conformity unto Him, yet *lacks one thing;* that is, after all, to be *despised and rejected of men;* and patiently to bear the contempt, and malice, and abuses of an *untoward generation.* One of the fathers, who sometimes wanted a little of this grace, could say, *Nihil est quod nos ita et hominibus et Deo gratos facit, quam si vitae merito magni, et humilitate infimi simus.*[10] 'Tis an excellent thing to come to *nothing.*

6. It is prudent to refrain from speaking.
7. I speak not of difficult things but of possibilities.
8. It is certainly noble to do great things and to think nothing of yourself.
9. The remedy for pride is the contemplation of the Cross.
10. Nothing makes us more pleasing to God and men than being low in humility even if we achieve greatness in our lives.

If you hear the hopes of disaffected men, to see you *come to nothing, hear it* with as much of satisfaction as they can *hope* it. Embrace *exinanitions;* embrace *annihilations.* I find a zealous and famous *doer of good,* much affected with the picture of a devout man, to whom a voice comes down from Heaven, *Quid vis fieri pro te?* Whereto he replies, *Nihil, Dornine, nisi pati et contemni pro te.*[11] Sirs, let it be seen somewhere else than in *picture;* be you the *substance* of it. Thus, *let patience have its perfect work!...*

Ye *useful men,* your *acceptance* with your Saviour, and with God through your Saviour, and *recompense* in the world to come, is to carry you cheerfully through all your *essays* at *usefulness.* To be *reprobate for every good work,* is a character, from which 'twill be the *wisdom* of all men, to fly with all the dread imaginable. But then, to be *always abounding in the work for the Lord,* this is always the truest and the highest *wisdom.* 'Tis the *wisdom which is from above,* that is full of *mercy and good fruits.* The *sluggards* who do no good in the world, are *wise in their own conceit;* but the men who are diligent in *doing of good,* can give such a *reason* for what they do, as proves them to be *really wise.* Men *leave off to be wise,* when they *leave off to do good.* The *wisdom* of it appears in this: 'tis the best way of spending our *time;* 'tis *well-spent,* when spent in *doing of good.* It is also a sure way, a sweet way, effectually to bespeak the *blessings* of God on ourselves. Who so likely to *find blessings,* as the men that *are blessings?* It has been said, *Qui bene vivit, semper orat,*[12] so I will say, *Qui bene agit, bene orta.*[13] Every *action* we do for the *Kingdom* of God, is in the efficacy of it, a *prayer* for the *kindness* of God. While we are *at work* for God, certainly, He will be *at work* for us, and ours: He will do for us, more than ever we have *done* for Him; far *more than we can ask or think!* There is a *voice* in every *good thing* that is done; 'tis that, *Oh! do good unto them that are good!* Thus my BONIFACIUS anon comes to wear the name of BENEDICTUS also. Yea, and there may be this more particular effect of what we do. While we *employ* our *wits* for the interests of God, it is very probable, that we shall *sharpen* them for our own. We shall become the more *wise for ourselves,* because we have been *wise to do good.* And of the man who is a *tree that brings forth fruit,* we read, *whatsoever he doth shall prosper.* Nor can a man take a readier way to *live joyfully, all the days of the life of our vanity, which God has given us under the sun.* For, now our *life* will not be thrown away in *vanity;* we don't *live in vain.* My friend, *go thy way* and be joyful; *for God accepteth thy works.* Our *few* and *evil* days are made much less so, by our *doing* of good in every one of them, as it rolleth over us. Yea, the Holy *Spirit* of God who is the *quickener* of them who *do good without ceasing,* will be their *comforter.* Every day of our *activity* for the Kingdom of God, will be in some sort a day of *Pentecost* unto us, a day of the Holy Spirit's coming upon us. The *consolations of God,* will *not be small,* with the man, who is full of *contrivances for God,* and for His Kingdom. In short, we read, "The valleys are covered over with corn; they shout for joy, they also sing." We may be in *low* circumstances: but if we abound in the fruits of *well-doing,* and if we feed many with our services, we are *covered over with corn.* We shall *shout for joy, and also sing,* if we be so. The *conscience of* what we do, and of what we aim to do, will be a *continual feast* unto us. *Our rejoicing is this, the testimony of our conscience!* And, *Recte fecisse merces est.*[14] Yea, the *pleasure* in doing of *good offices,* 'tis inexpressible; 'tis unparalleled; 'tis *angelical;* more to be envied than any *sensual pleasure;*

---

11.   What do you want me to do for you?...Nothing, Lord, but that I may suffer and be despised for your sake.
12.   He who lives well is always praying.
13.   He who does good, prays well.
14.   Virtue is its own reward.

a most *refined* one. Pleasure was long since defined, *the result of some excellent action.* 'Tis, a sort of *holy Epicurism.* O most *pitiable* they that will continue strangers to it! But, *memineris,* was the constant word of encouragement unto a soldier. I say, *remember;* there's more to be *remembered.*

When the *serviceable* man comes to his *Nunc Dimittis,*[15] then, he who did *live desired,* shall *die lamented.* It shall be witnessed and remembered of him, *that he was one who did good in Israel.* An *epitaph* the glory whereof is beyond that of the most superb and stately *pyramid!* When [*i.e.,* then] the calumniators, who once *licked the file* of his reputation, shall have only the impotence of their defeated malice to reflect upon....

... I will conclude with a TESTIMONY that I shall abide by. 'Tis this: were a man able to write in *seven languages:* could he converse daily with the sweets of all the *liberal sciences,* that more polite men ordinarily pretend unto; did he entertain himself with all ancient and modern *histories;* and could he feast continually on the *curiosities* which all sorts of learning may bring unto him; none of all this would afford the ravishing satisfaction, much less would any grosser delights of the *senses* do it; which he might find, in relieving the distresses of a poor, mean, *miserable neighbor;* and which he might much more find, in doing any *extensive service* for the kingdom of our great SAVIOUR in the world; or anything to redress the miseries under which mankind is generally languishing.

---

15. Permission to depart—that is, his death—in contentment that he has done all he can do.

CHARLES CHAUNCY

Enthusiasm Described and Caution'd Against
(1742)

Charles Chauncy (1705–1787), the great-grandson and namesake of the second president of Harvard College and the minister at Boston's prestigious First Church, was one of the most theologically liberal preachers in eighteenth-century New England. In the 1750s, along with other ministers of the wealthy mercantile-dominated congregations in eastern Massachusetts, he would espouse Arminianism, which asserted humans' ability to contribute to their salvation through the cultivation of a moral and rational mind-set. More provocatively, that same decade, he composed a manuscript defending universalism, or the belief in the eventual salvation of all men and women, which he would not publish for thirty years, in part out of deference to even his liberal colleagues' fear that the idea was destructive of moral responsibility.

However, his greatest contemporary fame came as a leading "Old Light" opponent of the massive religious revivals that swept through the colonies in the late 1730s and early 1740s, a position in his mind motivated by an earnest desire to conserve the Puritan Way from the "New Lights'" dangerous encouragement of excessive displays of emotion. Yet in his anti-revivalist sermons and tracts, he laid out an attack that, like the revivals themselves, defied easy labeling. In his *Seasonable Thoughts on the State of Religion in New England* (1743), he catalogued endless horror stories of ignorant itinerant ministers and lay "exhorters" imploring their hearers to shun "unconverted" established ministers while their audiences wallowed in the loud moaning and wild laughing deemed by many New Lights to be convincing evidence of a genuine conversion experience. The previous year, in his sermon *Enthusiasm Described and Caution'd Against,* using the term then widely used to stigmatize irrational and fanatical religion, Chauncy homed in on the wider consequences of this religious hobgoblin: social disorganization, biblical heresy, and an upending of the rational cognitive hierarchy undergirding both Puritan and Enlightenment faculty psychology. As if that was not enough, harking back to the charges made against Anne Hutchinson a century earlier, he associated these revivalist delusions with those of the radical insurrectionary sects of the Reformation. With such evils looming, it is no wonder that, after charging the revivalist extremists with dogmatism and intolerance, Chauncy saw no irony in his suggestion in *Seasonable Thoughts* that it would probably have been good to have given magistrates the power "to restrain some Men's *Tongues* with *Bit and Bridle.*" The young minister James Davenport, whom Chauncy addressed contemptuously in the preface to his sermon as the quintessential demagogic and slandering New Light, would reply in kind by pitching Chauncy's book into a great bonfire built to consume a pile of worldly fancy clothing and hell-facilitating works Davenport determined were "unsafe to be in the Hands of the People."

Edward M. Griffin, *Old Brick: Charles Chauncy of Boston, 1705–1787* (Minneapolis, 1980); and Charles H. Lippy, *Seasonable Revolutionary: The Mind of Charles Chauncy* (Chicago, 1981), are brief but useful intellectual biographies. In *The Hidden Balance: Religion and the Social Theories of Charles Chauncy and Jonathan Mayhew* (Cambridge, 1987), John Corrigan probes the connections between the social thought and the theology of Chauncy and his younger liberal contemporary. Conrad Wright's *The Beginnings of Unitarianism in America* (Boston, 1955) remains a superb guide to the Arminian liberal Christian movement that Chauncy helped to launch. For an instructive discussion of Chauncy, Edwards, and others who participated in the eighteenth-century controversy over interpreting religious emotions, see Ann Taves, *Fits, Trances, and Visions: Experiencing Religion and Explaining Experience from Wesley to James* (Princeton, 1999), 15–117.

A Sermon Preach'd at the Old Brick Meeting-House in Boston, the Lord's Day after Commencement, 1742.

1. C. O. R. XIV. xxxvii: "If any Man among you think himself to be a PROPHET, or SPIRITUAL, let him acknowledge that the Things that I write unto you are the Commandments of the. LORD."

Many Things were amiss in the *Church of Corinth*, when *Paul* wrote this Epistle to them. There were envyings, strife and divisions among them, on account of their ministers. Some cried up one, others another: one said, I am of PAUL, another I am of APPOLLOS. They had form'd themselves into parties, and each party so admired the teacher they followed, as to reflect unjust contempt on the other.

Nor was this their only fault. A spirit of pride prevailed exceedingly among them. They were conceited of their guts, and too generally dispos'd to make an osentatious shew of them. From this vain-glorious temper proceeded the forwardness of those that had the *gift* of *tongues* to speak in languages which others did not understand, to the disturbance, rather than edification of the church: And from the same principle it arose that they spake not by turns, but several at once, in the same place of worship, to the introducing such confusion, that they were in danger of being tho't mad.

Nor were they without some pretence to justify these disorders. Their great plea was, that in these things they were guided by the Spirit, acted under his immediate influence and direction. This seems plainly insinuated in the words I have read to you. *If any man think himself to be a prophet, or spiritual, let him acknowledge that the things that I write unto you are the commandments of the Lord.* As if the apostle had said, you may imagine your selves to be *spiritual* men, to be under a divine afflatus in what you do; but 'tis all imagination, meer pretence, unless you pay a due regard to the *commandments* I have here *wrote to you*; receiving them not as the *word of man, but of* GOD. Make trial of your spiritual pretences by this rule: If you can submit to it, and will order your conduct by it, well; otherwise you only cheat yourselves, while you think yourselves to be *spiritual* men, or *prophets:* You are nothing better than *Enthusiasts*; your being acted by the SPIRIT, immediately guided and influenced by him, is meer pretence; you have no good reason to believe any such thing.

From the words thus explained, I shall take occasion to discourse to you upon the following Particulars.

I. I shall give you some account of *Enthusiasm,* in its *nature* and *influence.*
II. Point you to a rule by which you may judge of persons, whether they are under the influence of *Enthusiasm*
III. Say what may be proper to guard you against this unhappy turn of mind,

The whole will then be follow'd with some suitable Application.
1. I am in the first place, to give you some account of *Enthusiasm*. And as this is a thing much talk'd of at present, more perhaps than as any other time that has pass'd over us, it will not be tho't unseasonable, if I take some pains to let you into a true understanding of it.

Source: Charles Chauncy, *Enthusiasm described and caution'd against: A Sermon Preach'd at the Old Brick Meeting-House in Boston, at the Lord's Day after the Commencement* (Boston: J. Draper, 1742), 1–21, 26–27.

The word, from its Etymology, carries in it a good meaning, as signifying *inspiration from* GOD: in which sense the prophets under the old testament, and the apostles under the new, might properly be called *Enthusiasts*. For they were under a divine influence, spake as moved by the HOLY GHOST, and did such things as can be accounted for in no way, but by recurring to an immediate extraordinary power, present with them.

But the word is more commonly used in a bad sense, as intending an *imaginary*, not *a real* inspiration: according to which sense, the *Enthusiast* is one, who has a conceit of himself as a person favoured with the extraordinary presence of the *Deity*. He mistakes the workings of his own passions for divine communications, and fancies himself immediately inspired by the SPIRIT of GOD, when all the while, he is under no other influence than that of an over-heated imagination.

The cause of this *enthusiasm* is a bad temperament of the blood and spirits; 'tis properly a disease, a sort of madness: And there are few; perhaps none at all, but are subject to it; tho' none are so much in danger of it as those, in whom *melancholy* is the prevailing ingredient in their constitution. In these it often reigns; and sometimes to so great a degree, that they are really beside themselves, acting as truly by the blind impetus of a wild fancy, as tho' they had neither reason nor understanding.

And various are the ways in which their *enthusiasm* discovers itself.

Sometimes, it may be seen in their countenance. A certain wildness is discernable in their general look and air; especially when their imaginations are mov'd and fired.

Sometimes, it strangely loosens their tongues, and gives them such an energy, as well as fluency and volubility in speaking, as they themselves, by their utmost efforts, can't so much as imitate, when they are not under the enthusiastick influence.

Sometimes, it affects their bodies, throws them into convulsions and distortions, into quakings and tremblings. This was formerly common among the people called Quakers. I was myself, when a Lad, an eye-witness to such violent agitations and foamings, in a boisterous female speaker, as I could not behold but with surprize and wonder.

Sometimes, it will unaccountably mix itself with their conduct, and give it such a tincture of that which is freakish or furious, as none can have an idea of, but those who have seen the behaviour of a person in a phrenzy.

Sometimes, it appears in their imaginary peculiar intimacy with heaven. They are, in their own opinion, the special favourites of GOD, have more familiar converse with him than other good men, and receive immediate, extraordinary communications from him. The tho'ts, which suddenly *rise up* in their minds, they take for suggestions of the SPIRIT; their very fancies are divine illuminations; nor are they strongly inclin'd to any thing, but 'tis an impulse from GOD, a plain revelation of his will.

And what extravagances, in this temper of mind, are they not capable of, and under the specious pretext too of paying obedience to the authority of GOD? Many have fancied themselves acting by immediate warrant from heaven, while they have been committing the most undoubted wickedness. There is indeed scarce anything so wild, either in *speculation* or *practice*, but they have given into it: They have, in many instances, been blasphemers of GOD, and open disturbers of the peace of the world.

But in nothing does the *enthusiasm* of these persons discover itself more, than in the disregard they express to the Dictates of *reason*. They are above the force of argument, beyond conviction from a calm and sober address to their understandings. As for them, they are distinguish'd persons; GOD himself speaks inwardly and immediately to their souls. "They see the light infused into their understandings, and cannot be mistaken; 'tis clear and visible there, like the light of bright sunshine; shews itself and needs no other proof but its own evidence. They feel the hand of God moving them within, and the impulses of his Spirit; and cannot be mistaken in what they feel. Thus they support themselves, and are sure reason hath nothing to do with what they see and feel, What they have a sensible experience of, admits no doubt, needs no probation."[1] And in vain will you endeavour to convince such persons of any mistakes they are fallen into. They are certainly in the right; and know themselves to be so. They have the Spirit opening their understandings and revealing the truth to them. They believe only as he has taught them: and to suspect they are in the wrong is to do dishonour to the Spirit; 'tis to oppose his dictates, to set up their own wisdom in opposition to his, and shut their eyes against that light with which he has shined into their souls. They are not therefore capable of being argued with; you had as good reason with the wind.

And as the natural consequence of their being thus sure of every thing; they are not only infinitely stiff and tenacious, but impatient of contradiction, censorious and uncharitable: they encourage a good opinion of none but such as are in their way of thinking and speaking. Those, to be sure, who venture to debate with them about their errors and mistakes, their weaknesses and indiscretions, run the hazard of being stigmatiz'd by them as poor unconverted wretches, without the Spirit, under the government of carnal reason, enemies to God and religion, and in the broad way to hell.

They are likewise positive and dogmatical, vainly fond of their own imaginations, and invincibly set upon propagating them: And in the doing of this, their Powers being awakened, and par as it were, upon the stretch, from the strong impressions they are under, that they are authorized by the immediate command of God himself, they sometimes exert themselves with a sort of *extatic* violence: And 'tis this that gives them the advantage, among the less knowing and judicious, of those who are modest, suspicious of themselves, and not too assuming in matters of conscience and salvation. The extraordinary fervour of their minds, accompanied with uncomnon bodily motions, and an excessive confidence and assurance, gains them great reputation among the populace; who speak of them as *men of GOD* in distinction from all others, and too commonly hearken to, and revere their dictate, as tho' they really were, as they pretend, immediately communicated to them from the Divine Spirit.

This is the nature of *Enthusiasm*, and this its operation, in a less or greater degree, in all who are under the influence of it. 'Tis a kind of religious Phrenzy, and evidently discovers it self to be so, whenever it rises to any great height.

And much to be pitied are the persons who are seized with it. Our compassion commonly works towards those, who, while under distraction, fondly imagine themselves to be Kings and Emperors: And the like pity is really due to those, who, under the power of *enthusiasm* fancy themselves, to be *prophets*; *inspired of God* and *immediately called* and *commissioned by him to deliver his messages to the world*: And tho' they should run into disorders, and act in a manner that cannot but be condemned, they should notwithstanding be treated with tenderness and lenity; and the rather, because they don't commonly act so much under the influence of a *bad mind,* as a *deluded imagination.* And who more worthy of christian pity than those, who, under the notion of serving God and the interest of religion, are filled with zeal, and exert themselves to the atmost, while all the time they are hurting and wounding the very cause they take so much pains to advance. 'Tis really a pitiable case; And tho' the honesty of their intentions won't legitimate their bad actions, yet it very much alleviates their guilt: We should think as favourably of them as may be, and be dispos'd to judge with mercy, as we would hope to obtain mercy.

---

1.   John Locke, *An Essay Concerning Human Understanding,* Book IV, Chap. 19.

But I come

II. In the second place, to point you to a *rule* by which you may judge of persons, whether they are *enthusiasts*, meer pretenders to the immediate guidance and influence of the SPIRIT. And this is, in general, *a regard to the bible, an acknowledgment that the things therein contained are the commandments of* GOD. This is the rule in the text. And 'tis an infallible rule of tryal in this matter: We need not fear judging amiss, while we keep closely to it.

'Tis true, it wont certainly follow, that a man, pretending to be a *prophet, or Spiritual,* really is so, if he owns the *bible,* and receives the truths therein revealed as the mind of GOD: But the conclusion, on the other hand, is clear and certain; if he pretends to be conducted by the SPIRIT, and disregards the scripture, pays no due reverence *to the things there delivered as the commandments of God,* he is a meer pretender, be his pretences ever so bold and confident, or made with ever so much seeming seriousness, gravity, or solemnity.

And the reason of this is obvious; viz. that the things contained in the scripture were wrote by holy men as they were moved by the HOLY GHOST: they were received from GOD, and committed to writing under his immediate, extraordinary influence and guidance. And the divine, ever-blessed SPIRIT is consistent with himself. He cannot be suppos'd to be the author of any *private* revelations that are contradictory to the *public standing ones,* which he has preserved in the world to this day. This would be to set the SPIRIT of truth at variance with himself; than which a greater reproach can't be cast upon him. 'Tis therefore as true, that those are *enthusiastical,* who pretend to the SPIRIT, and at the same time express a disregard *to* the scripture, as that the SPIRIT is the great revealer of the things therein declared to us. And we may depend upon the certainty of this conclusion. We have warrant to do so from the *inspired Paul;* and we have the more reason to rely upon the rule he has given us, as he has made it evident to the world, that he was a *prophet,* and *spiritual,* by signs and wonders which he did before the people, by the power of the SPIRIT of God.

But the *rule* in the text is yet more particular. It refers especially to *the things wrote by the apostle* PAUL, and which he wrote to the *church of Corinth, to* rectify the *disorders* that had crept in among them. And whoever the person be, that pretends to be *spiritual,* to be under the extraordinary guidance of the SPIRIT, and yet acts in contradiction to what the apostle has here wrote, he vainly imagines himself to be under the special guidance of the SPIRIT; he is a downright *enthusiast.*

And here suffer me to make particular mention of some of the things, the apostle has wrote in *this Epistle,* which, whoever will not acknowledge, in *deed* as well as *word,* to be the *commandments of God,* they are not guided by the SPIRIT, but vainly pretend to be so.

The first thing, in this kind, I would mention, is that which relates to *Ministers;* condemning an undue preference of one to another, the holding one in such admiration as to reflect disgrace on another. This was one of the disorders the Apostle takes notice of, as prevailing in the *church of Corinth*; and he is particular in his care to give check to this unchristian spirit, which had crumbled them into parties, and introduced among them faction and contention.

Now, whoever, under the pretence of being guided by the spirit, set up one minister in opposition to another, glory in this minister to the throwing undue contempt on that, thereby obstructing his usefulness, and making way for strife and divisions, they are not really acted by the SPIRIT, whatever they may pretend. For they evidently contradict what the apostle has wrote upon this very head: And if *he* was inspired the spirit *they* are influenced by, cannot be⁻ the SPIRIT of GOD.

Not that one minister may not be preferr'd another; this is reasonable: But no minister ought to be regarded, as tho' he was the author of our faith: nor, let his gifts and graces be what they will, is he to be so esteemed, as that others must be neglected, or treated in an unbecoming manner. But I shall not enlarge here, having spoken fully to this point; in a Sermon you may, some of you, have in your hands.

Another thing the apostle is particular in writing upon, is the *commandment of charity*. And this he declares to be a matter of such essential importance in true christianity, that if a man is really destitute of it, he is nothing in the sight of GOD: Nay, tho' his presences, his attainments, his gifts, be ever so extraordinary or miraculous; still, if he is without charity he will certainly be rejected of GOD and the LORD JESUS CHRIST. This is beautifully represented in the three first verses of the 13th chapter of this Epistle, in some of the boldest figures. "Tho' I speak, says the apostle, with the tongues of men and of angels, and have not charity, I am become as sounding brass, or a tinkling cymbal. And tho' I have the gift of prophecy, and understand all mysteries and all knowledge; and tho' I have all faith, so that I could remove mountains, and have not charity, I am nothing. And tho' I bestow all my goods to feed the poor, and tho' I give my body to be burned, and have not charity, it profiteth me nothing." As if the apostle had said, tho' a man had the languages of all nations, and could speak with the eloquence of angels; tho', like an inspired prophet, he had understanding in the deep counsels of GOD, and knew even all things sacred and divine; tho' he had the faith of miracles, and could do impossibilities; tho' he had the zeal of a martyr, and should give his body to be burned; tho' he had a disposition to alms-giving, and should bestow upon the poor his whole substance; still, if he was without charity, "that charity which suffereth long, and is kind; that charity which envyeth not, vaunteth not it self, is not puffed up; that charity which behaveth not it self unseemly; seeketh not her own, is not easily provoked, thinketh no evil, rejoiceth not in iniquity, but rejoiceth in the truth; that charity, in fine, which beareth all things, believeth all things, hopeth all things, endureth all things": I say, if he was without this charity, this love of his neighbor, these things would be all nothing; he would notwithstanding be out of favour with GOD, without any interest in CHRIST, and in such circumstances, as that unless there was a change in them, he would certainly perish.

This, in sum, is what the apostle has, in a distinct and peremptory manner, delivered concerning charity.

And in vain may any pretend to be under extraordinary guidance of the SPIRIT, while in their practice they trample upon this law of christian love. Men may talk of their *impulses* and *impressions*, conceive of them as the call of GOD, and go about, as moved by them, from place to place, imagining they are sent of GOD, and immediately commissioned by him: But if they are censorious and uncharitable; if they harbour in their minds evil surmisings of their brethren; if they slander and reproach them; if they claim a right to look into their hearts, make it their business to judge of their state, and proclaim them hypocrites, carnal unregenerate sinners, when at same time they are visibly of a good conversation in Christ: I say, when this is the practice of any, they do not acknowledge what the inspired PAUL has here *wrote as the commandment of GOD*: They are not therefore acted by the same SPIRIT with which he spake; but are evidently under a spirit of delusion: And this so obviously the case, that there is no reasonable room to one doubt upon the matter.

Charity, my brethren, is the commandment of the gospel by way of eminence. 'Tis the grand mark by which Christians are to distinguish themselves from all others. *By this,* says our Saviour,[2] *shall all men know that ye are my disciples, if ye have love to one another*: Yea, this is the grand criterion by which we are to judge, whither God *dwelleth in us by his Spirit. If we love one another, God dwelleth in us*||. And in the following Verse, *Hereby*, i.e. by our loving one another, *we know that we dwell in him, and begin us, because he hath given us of his Spirit*. To pretent therefore that we are led by the Spirit, and are under his extraordinary influence, when, in contradiction to the plain law of Jesus Christ, revealed by the Spirit, we *judge our brother*, and *set at naught our brother*, and plead a right to do so, and are in a disposition TO THANK GOD, THAT WE ARE ENABLED TO DO SO; there is not a more sure mark, in all the revelations of God, of a BAD HEART, or a DISTEMPERED MIND. If any thing will evidence a man to be a *prophet* and *spiritual*, only in his own conceit, this must do it: And if this is not allow'd to be sufficient proof, there is no knowing, when a man is under the influence of *enthusiastick* heat and zeal.

Another thing the apostle bespeaks this church upon, is that *self-conceit* which appear'd among them the exercise of *spiritual gifts*: And 'tis more than probable, there were those among them, who being vainly puffed up in their minds, behaved as tho' they were *apostles*, or *prophets*, or *teachers*; leaving their own station, and doing the work that was proper to others. It was to rectify such disorders, that the apostle, in the 12th chapter, addresses to them in that language, v. 29. *Are all apostles? Are all prophets? Are all teachers?* The question carries with it it's own answer, and means the same thing, as when he affirms in the foregoing verse *God hath set some in the church first apostles, secondarily prophets, thirdly teachers*, and so on. 'Tis evident from what the apostle here writes, and indeed from the current strain of this whole chapter, that there is in the body of Christ, the Church, a distinction of members; some intended for one use, others for another; and that it would bring confusion into the *body mystical*, for one member, to be employed in that service which is adapted another, and is its proper business.

'Tis not therefore the pretence of being moved by the Spirit, that will justify *private christians* in quitting their own proper station, to act in that which belongs to another. Such a practice as this naturally sends to destroy that order, God has constituted in the church and may be followed with mischiefs greater than we may be aware of.

'Tis indeed a powerful argument with many, in favour of these persons, their pretending to impulses, and a call from God; together with their insatiable thirst to do together good to soul. And 'tis owing to such pretences as these, that encouragement has been given to the rise of such numbers of *lay-exhorters and teachers*, in one place and another, all over the land. But if 'tis one of the things wrote by the apostle as the *commandment of God*, that there should be officers in the church, an order of men to whom it should belong, as their *proper, stated work*, to exhort and teach, this cannot be the business of others: And if any who think themselves to be *spiritual*, are under *impressions* to take upon them *this ministry*, they may have reason to suspect, whether their *impulses* are any other than the workings of their own imaginations: And instead of being under any divine extraordinary influence, there are just grounds of fear, whether they are not acted from the vanity of their minds: Especially, if they are but beginners in religion; men of weak minds, babes in understanding; as is most commonly the case. The apostle speaks of *novices*, as in danger of being *lifted up with pride, and falling into the comdemnation of the devil*: And it is a seasonable caution to this kind of persons. They should study themselves more, and they will feel less reason to think their disposition to exhort and teach to be from the SPIRIT OF

---

2. John 13. 35. || I John 4. 12.

GOD. And indeed, if the SPIRIT has bid men to *abide in their own callings*, 'tis not conceivable he should influence them to (leave their callings): And if he has set a mark of disgrace upon *busy-bodies in other men's matters*, 'tis impossible he should put men upon *wandring about from house to house, speaking the things they ought not.*

And it deserves particular consideration, whether the suffering, much more the encouraging WOMEN yea, GIRLS to speak in the assemblies for religious worship, is not a plain breach of that *commandment of the* LORD[3], wherein it is said, *Let your Women keep silence in the churches; for it is not permitted to them to speak—It is shame for Women to speak in the church.* After such an express constitution, designedly made to restrain WOMEN from speaking in the church, with what face can such a practice be pleaded for? They may pretend, they are moved by the SPIRIT, and such a tho't of themselves may be encouraged by others; but if the apostle *spake by the* SPIRIT, when he delivered *this commandment*, they can't act by the Spirit when they break it. 'Tis a plain case, these FEMALE EXHORTERS are condemned by the apostle; and if 'tis the *commandment of the Lord*, that they should not speak, they are *spiritual* only in their own tho'ts, while they attempt to do so.

The last thing I shall mention as written by the apostle, is that which obliges to a *just decorum in Speaking* in the *house of* GOD. It was an extravagance these *Corinthians* had fallen into, their speaking many of them together, and upon different things, while in the same place of worship. *How is it, brethren*, says the apostle? *When ye come together, every one hath a psalm; hath a doctrine; hath a tongue; hath a revelation; hath an interpretation.* It was this that introduced the confusion and noise, upon which the apostle declares, if an unbeliever should come in among them, he would take them to be mad. And the *commandment* he gives them to put a stop to this disorder, is, that they should *Speak in course, one by one*, and so as that *things might be done to edifying* ||.

And whoever the persons are, who will not acknowledge what the apostle has here said is the *commandment of* GOD, and act accordingly, are influenced by another spirit than that which moved in him, be their impressions or pretences what they will. The disorder of EXHORTING, and PRAYING, and SINGING, and LAUGHING, *in the same house of worship, at one and the same time*, is as great as was that, the apostle blames in the *church of Corinth*: And whatever the persons, guilty of such gross irregularity may imagine, and however they may plead their being under the influence of the SPIRIT, and mov'd by him, 'tis evidently a breach upon common order and decency: yea, a direct violation of the *commandment of* GOD, written on purpose to prevent such disorders: And to pretend the direction of the SPIRIT in such a flagrant instance of extravagant conduct; is to reproach the blessed SPIRIT, who is not, as the apostle's phrase is, *the author of confusion, but of peace, as in all the churches of the saints.*

In these, and all other instances, let us compare men's pretences to the SPIRIT by the SCRIPTURE: And if their conduct is such as can't be reconcil'd with an *acknowledgment of the things therein revealed, as the commandments of* GOD, their pretences are vain, they are *prophets* and *spiritual*, only in their own proud imaginations. I proceed now to

III. The third thing, which is to caution you against giving way to *enthusiastic impressions*. And here much might be said,

I might warn you from the *dishonour* it reflects upon the SPIRIT OF GOD. And perhaps none have more reproach'd the blessed SPIRIT, than men pretending to be under his

---

3. Context, V. 35. 26. †: v. 23. || 26, 27.

extraordinary guidance and direction. The veryest fancies, the vainest imaginations, the strongest delusions, they have father'd on him. There is scarce any absurdity in *principle*, or irregularity in *practice*, but he has been made the patron of it.—And what a stone of stumbling has the wildness of *Enthusiasm* been to multitudes in the world? What prejudices have been hereby excited in their minds against the very being of the SPIRIT? What temptations have been thrown in their way to dispute his OFFICE as the SANCTIFYER and COMFORTER of GOD's people? And how have they been over-come to disown HIS WORK, when it has been really wro't in the hearts of men?

I might also warn you from the damage it has done in the world. No greater mischiefs have arisen from any quarter. It is indeed the genuine source of infinite evil. POPERY it self han't been the mother of more and greater blasphemies and abominations: It has made strong attempts to destroy all property, to make all things common, *wives* as well as *goods*.—It has promoted faction and contention; filled the church oftentimes with confusion, and the state sometimes with general disorder.—It has, by its pretended, spiritual interpretations, made void the most undoubted laws of GOD. It has laid aside the *gospel sacraments* as weak and carnal things; yea; this *superior light within* has, in the opinion of thousands, render'd the *bible a useless dead letter*.—It has made men fancy themselves to be *prophets and apostles*; yea, some have taken themselves to be Christ Jesus; yea, the blessed God himself. It has, in one word, been a pest to the church in all ages, as great an enemy to real and solid religion, as perhaps the grossest *infidelity*.[4]

I might go on and warn you from the danger of it to yourselves. If you should once come under the influence of it, none can tell whither it would carry you. There is nothing so wild and frantick, but you may be reconcil'd to it. And if this shou'd be your case, your recovery to a right mind would be one of the most difficult things in nature. There is no coming at a thorow-pac'd *enthusiast*. He is proof against every method of dealing with him. Would you apply to him from reason? That he esteems a carnal thing, and flees from it as from the most dangerous temptation. Would you rise higher, and speak to him from *Scripture*? It will be to as little purpose. For if he pays any regard to it, 'tis only as it falls in with his own pre-conceiv'd notions. He interprets the scripture by *impulses* and *impressions*, and sees no meaning in it, only as he explains it from his own fancy.—'Tis infinitely difficult [to] convince a man grown giddy and conceited under the false notion, that the good *Spirit* teaches him every thing. His apprehended inspiration sets him above all means of conviction. He rather despises than hearkens to the most reasonable advices that can be given him.

But as the most suitable guard against the first tendencies towards *enthusiasm*, let me recommend to you the following words of counsel.

1. Get a true understanding of the *proper work of the* SPIRIT; and don't place it in those things wherein the gospel does not make it to consist. The work of the SPIRIT is different now from what it was in the first days of christianity. Men were then favoured with the extraordinary presence of the SPIRIT. He came upon them in miraculous gifts and powers; as a spirit of prophecy, of knowledge, of revelation, of tongue, of miracles: But the SPIRIT is not now to be expected in these ways. His grand business lies in preparing men's minds for the grace of God, by true *humiliation*, from an apprehension of sin, and the necessity of a *Saviour*; then in working in them *faith* and *repentance*, and such a *change* as shall *turn them from the power of sin* and *satan unto God*; and in fine, by carrying on the good work

---

4.   Undoubted instances of these, and many other things of a like nature, are well known to such as are, in any measure, acquainted with the *history* of the *church*.

he has begun in them: assisting them in duty, strengthening them against temptation, and in a *word*, preserving them blameless thro' faith unto salvation: And all this he does by the *word* and *prayer*, as the great means in the accomplishment of these purposes of mercy.

Herein, in general, consists the work of the SPIRIT. It does not lie in giving men *private revelations*, but in opening their minds to understand the *publick ones* contained in the scripture. It does not lie in *sudden impulses* and *impressions*, in *immediate calls* and *extraordinary missions*. Men mistake the business of the SPIRIT, if they understand by it such things as these. And 'tis, probably, from such unhappy mistakes, that they are at first betrayed into *enthusiasm*. Having a wrong notion of the *work of* the SPIRIT, 'tis no wonder if they take the uncommon fallies of their own minds for his influences.

You cannot, my brethren, be too well acquainted with what the *bible* makes the *work* of the HOLY GHOST in the affair of salvation: And if you have upon your minds a clear and distinct understanding of this, it will be a powerful guard to you against all *enthusiastical impressions*.

2. Keep close to the *Scripture*, and admit of nothing for an impression of the SPIRIT, but what agrees with that unerring rule. Fix it in your minds as a truth you will invariably abide by, that the *bible* is the grand test, by which every thing in religion is to be tried; and that you can, at no time, nor in any instance, be under the guidance of the SPIRIT of GOD, much less his *extraordinary* guidance, if what you are led to, is inconsistent with the things there revealed, either in point of *faith* or *practice*. And let it be your care to compare the motions of your minds, and the workings of your imaginations and passions, with the *rule* of GOD's *word*. And see to it, that you be impartial in this matter: Don't make the rule bend to your preconceiv'd notions and inclinations; but repair to the *bible,* with a mind dispos'd as much as may be, to know the truth as it lies nakedly and plainly in the *scripture* itself. And whatever you are moved to, reject the motion, esteem it as nothing more than a vain fancy, if it puts you upon any method of *thinking* or *acting,* that can't be evidently reconcil'd with *the revelation* of GOD in *his word.*

This adherence to the bible, my brethren, is one of the best preservatives against *enthusiasm*. If you will but express a due reverence to this *book* of GOD, making it the great rule of judgment, even in respect of the SPIRIT's *influences* and *operations,* you will not be in much danger of being led into delusion. Let that be your inquiry under all suppos'd *impulses* from the SPIRIT, *What faith the scripture? To the law, and to the testimony*: If your impressions, and imagined spiritual motions agree not therewith, 'tis because there is no hand of the SPIRIT of GOD in them: They are only the workings of your own imaginations, or something worse; and must at once, without any more ado, be rejected as such.

3. Make use of the *Reason* and *Understanding* GOD has given you. This may be tho't an ill-advis'd direction, but 'tis as necessary as either of the former. Next to the *Scripture*, there is no greater enemy to *enthusiasm*, than *reason*. 'Tis indeed impossible a man shou'd be an *enthusiast*, who is in the just exercise of his understanding; and 'tis because men don't pay a due regard to the sober dictates of a well inform'd mind, that they are led aside by the delusions of a vain imagination. Be advised then to shew yourselves men, to make use of your reasonable powers; and not act as the *horse* or *mule,* as tho' you had no undersanding.

'Tis true, you must not go about to set up your own *reason* in *opposition* to *revelation*: Nor may you entertain a tho't of making *reason* your *rule* instead of *scripture*. The *bible*, as I said before, is the *great rule* of religion, the grand test in matters of salvation: But then, you must use your reason in order to understand the *bible*: Nor is there any other possible way, in which, as a reasonable creature, you shou'd come to an understanding of.

You are, it must be acknowledged, in a corrupt state. The fall has introduc'd great weakness into your reasonable nature. You can't be too sensible of this; nor of the danger you are in of making a wrong judgment, thro' prejudice, carelessness, and the undue influence of sin and lust. And to prevent this, you can't be too solicitous to get your *nature sanctified:* Nor can you depend too strongly upon the divine grace to assist you in your search after truth: And 'tis in the way of due dependance on GOD, and the influences of his SPIRIT, that I advise you to the use of your reason: And in this way, you must make use of it. How else will you know what is a revelation from GOD? What shou'd hinder your entertaining the same tho't of a *pretended* revelation, as of a *real* one, but your reason discovering the falshood of the one, and the truth of the other? And when in the enjoyment of an undoubted revelation from GOD, as in the case of the *scripture,* How will you understand its meaning, if you throw by your reason? How will you determine, that this, and not that, is its true sense, in this and the other place? Nay, if no reasoning is to be made use of, are not all the senses that can be put on scripture equally proper? Yea, may not the most contrary senses be receiv'd at the same time, since reason only can point out the inconsistency between them? And what will be sufficient to guard you against the most monstrous extravagancies, in *principle* as well a*s practice,* if you give up your understandings? What have you left, in this case, to be a check to the wantoness of your imaginations? What shou'd hinder your following every idle fancy, 'till you have lost yourselves in the wilds of falshood and inconsistency?

You may, it is true, misuse your reason: And this is a consideration that shou'd put you upon a due care, that you may use it well; but no argument why you shou'd not use it at all: And indeed, if you shou'd throw by your reason as a useless thing, you would at once put your selves in the way of all manner of delusion.

But, it may be, you will say, you have committed yourselves to the *guidance* of the SPIRIT; which is the best preservative. Herein you have done well; nothing can be objected against this method of conduct: Only take heed of mistakes, touching the SPIRIT's *guidance.* Let me enquire of you, how is it the SPIRIT preserves from delusion? Is it not by opening the understanding, and enabling the man, in the due use of his reason, to perceive the truth of the things of GOD and religion? Most certainly: And, if you think of being led by the SPIRIT without understanding, or in opposition to it, you deceive yourselves. The SPIRIT of GOD deals with men as *reasonable* creatures: And they ought to deal with themselves in like manner. And while they do thus, making a wife and good use of the understanding, GOD has given them, they will take a proper means to prevent their falling into delusions; nor will there be much danger of their being led aside by *enthusiastic* heat and imagination.

4. You must not lay too great stress upon the *workings* of your *passions* and *affections.* These will be excited, in a less or greater degree, in the business of religion: And 'tis proper they shou'd. The passions, when suitably mov'd, tend mightily to awaken the *reasonable powers*, and put them upon a lively and vigorous exercise. And this is their proper use: And when address'd to, and excited to this purpose, they may be of good service: whereas we shall mistake the right use of the passions, if we place our religion *only* or *chiefly,* in the heat and fervour of them. The *soul* is the *man*: And unless the *reasonable nature* is suitably wro't upon, the *understanding* enlightned, the *judgment* convinc'd, the *will* perswaded, and the *mind* intirely chang'd, it will avail but to little purpose; tho' the passions shou'd be set all in a blaze. This therefore you shou'd be most concern'd about.

And if while you are sollicitous that you may be in transports of affection, you neglect your more noble part, your reason and judgment, you will be in great danger of being carried away by your imaginations. This indeed leads directly to *Enthusiasm*: And you will in vain, endeavour to preserve yourselves from the influence of it, if you a'nt duly careful to keep your passions in their proper place, under the government of a well informed understanding. While the passions are uppermost, and bear the chief sway over a man, he is in an unsafe state: None knows what he may be bro't to. You can't therefore be too careful to keep your passions under the regimen of a *sober judgment.* 'Tis indeed a matter of necessity, as you would not be led aside by delusion and fancy.

5. In the last place here, you must not forget to go to GOD by *prayer.* This is a duty in all cases, but in none more than the present. If left to yourselves, your own wisdom and strength, you will be insufficient for your own security; perpetually in danger from your *imaginations,* as well as the other enemies of your *souls.* You can't see too sensible of this; nor can you, from a sense of it, apply with too much importunity to the FATHER *of mercies,* to take pity upon you, and send you such a supply of grace as is needful for you. You must not indeed think, that your duty lies in the business of prayer, and nothing else. You must use your own endeavour, neglect nothing that may prove a guard to you: But together with the use of other means you must make known your request to GOD by prayer and supplication. You must daily commit the keeping of your soul to him; and this you must particularly be careful to do in times of more special hazard; humbly hoping in GOD to be your help: And if he shall please to undertake for you, no delusion shall ever have power over you, to seduce you but, possessing a found mind, you shall go on in the uniform, steady service of your maker and generation, till of the mercy of GOD, thro' the merits of the REDEEMER, you are crowned with eternal life.

But I shall now draw towards a close, by making some suitable *application* of what has been said....

Let us esteem those as *friends* to religion, and not *enemies,* who warn us of the danger of *enthusiasm,* and would put us upon our guard, that we be not led aside by it. As the times are, they run the hazard of being call'd *enemies* to the *holy* SPIRIT, and may expect to be ill-spoken of by many, and loaded with names of reproach: But they are notwithstanding the best friends to religion; and it may be, it will more and more appear, that they have all along been so. They have been stigmatised as OPPOSERS of the WORK OF GOD; but 'tis a great mercy of GOD, there have been such OPPOSERS; This land had, in all probability, been over-run with confusion and distraction, if they had acted under the influence of the *same heat and zeal,* which some others have been famous for.

'Tis really best, people shou'd know there is such a thing as *enthusiasm* and that it has been, in all ages, one of the most dangerous enemies to the church of GOD, and has done a world of mischief: And 'tis a kindness to them to be warn'd against it, and directed to the proper methods to be preserved from it. 'Tis indeed, one of the best ways of doing service *to real* religion, to distinguish it from that which is *imaginary*: Nor shou'd ministers be discouraged from endeavouring this, tho' they shou'd be ill-tho't, or evil-spoken of. They shou'd beware of being too much under the influence of that *fear of man, which bringeth a snare;* which is evidently the case, where they are either silent, or dare not speak out faithfully and plainly, left they shou'd be called PHARISEES or HYPOCRITES, and charged with LEADING SOULS TO THE DEVIL. 'Tis a *small matter* to be thus *judged* and *reviled*; and we shou'd be above being affrighted from duty by this, which is nothing more than the *breath* of poor, ignorant, frail man.

There is, I doubt not, a great deal of *real, substantial* religion in the land. The SPIRIT of GOD has wro't effectually on the hearts of many, from one time to another: And I make no question he has done so of late, in more numerous instances, it may be, than usual. But this, notwithstanding, there is, without dispute, a *spirit of enthusiasm*, appearing in one place and another. There are those, who make great pretences to the SPIRIT, who are carried away with their imaginations: And some, it may be, take themselves to be *immediately and wonderfully conducted by him*; while they are led only by their own fancies.

Thus it has been in other parts of the world. *Enthusiasm*, in all the *wildness*, and *fury*, and *extravagance* of it, has been among them, and sometimes had a most dreadfully extensive spread. *Ten thousand* wild *enthusiasts* have appear'd in arms, at the same time: and this too, in defence of *gross opinions*, as well as *enormous actions*. The first discovery therefore of such a spirit, unless due care is taken to give check to its growth and progress, is much to be feared; for there is no knowing, how high it may rise, nor what it may end in.—

The good LORD give us all wisdom; and courage, and conduct, in such a Day as this! And may both *ministers* and *people* behave after such a manner, as that religion may not suffer; but in the end, gain advantage, and be still more universally established.

And, may that grace of GOD, which has appeared to all men, bringing salvation, teach us effectually, to deny ungodliness and worldly lusts, and to live soberly, and righteously, and godlily in the world: so may we look with comfort for the appearing of our SAVIOUR JESUS CHRIST: And when he shall appear in the glory of his FATHER, and with his holy angels, we also shall appear with him, and go away into everlasting life; Which GOD, of his infinite mercy grant may be the portion of us all; for the sake of CHRIST JESUS.

AMEN.

JONATHAN EDWARDS

"Sinners in the Hands of an Angry God" (1741)

Selection from *A Treatise Concerning Religious Affections* (1746)

In his early years Jonathan Edwards (1703–1758) achieved considerable fame as a successful preacher and a moderate champion of the religious revivals. Indeed, his most comprehensive appraisal of them, *Some Thoughts Concerning the Present Revival of Religion in New-England* (1742), was partly the provocation for Chauncy's *Seasonable Thoughts* the following year, in which Chauncy directly replied to his great opponent. After that "Great Awakening" receded, Edwards composed a series of major treatises that would eventually establish him as American Puritanism's greatest theologian and America's foremost systematic philosopher before the Civil War. At the center of these works was the traditional Augustinian-Calvinist triad of divine excellency, human depravity, and grace-producing salvation for the divinely chosen few. Yet, undergirding this triad was a complex web of philosophical arguments that were deeply responsive to the same Enlightenment thinkers, beginning with Descartes and ending with the post-Lockean "moral sense" philosophers, whose rationalist, sentimental, and free-will claims were proving to a growing number of thinkers the system's undoing.

In the first of the two selections presented here—his famous sermon delivered on July 8, 1741, at Enfield, Massachusetts, in the midst of the most intense phase of the Great Awakening—Edwards demonstrated the experiential side of his "modern" reformulation of Calvinist theology. Specifically, in this sermon, which he delivered to a congregation heretofore resistant to the Awakening's spiritual outpouring, he exploited the genre of the hell-fire sermon, which early Puritan ministers had largely avoided. His purpose, though, was not simply to flog or terrify his hearers into displaying good behavior or a converted heart. Rather, it was to awaken in them, through psychologically expressive and culturally resonant metaphors, a potentially saving sense of the logic and reality of God's infinite wrath in the face of men's and women's inevitable rebellion against Him. In the second selection, his treatise on the religious affections, Edwards laid bare the positive cognitive basis and spiritual consequences of his new psychology of religion. To a large extent, of course, this treatise was a continuation of his earlier defenses of displays of religious emotions from aspersions cast by intellectualist ministers who had tried to discredit the revivals by equating their emotionalism with irrationalism. Edwards argued, on the contrary, that affections were the "spring of men's actions" and therefore at the center of all true religion. Furthermore, he contended, not all religious affections were truly religious, and most of the treatise was taken up by a discussion of various "signs" by which one might discern the difference. But Edwards's most important strategy—and the element that raised his treatise, philosophically speaking, above almost anything he ever wrote—was his construction of a new model of the human mind, which allowed him, as is shown in these extracts from *Religious Affections,* to root truly spiritual affections in a new sense of the heart. This new sense was, in true modern experimental idiom, a datum of consciousness but, unlike the materialist senses of Locke, was also an indwelling principle that allowed the soul to see and desire holiness. This holiness was therefore both a new kind of moral and aesthetic knowledge of being and a new inclination of the heart toward that knowledge. It was, in sum, grace in a new garb.

George M. Marsden's *Jonathan Edwards: A Life* (New Haven, 2003) is an excellent and now standard biography. Conrad Cherry's *Theology of Jonathan Edwards* (1966; Bloomington, Indiana 1990) remains the best overall introduction to Edwards's theology. For two probing studies of the historical and philosophical grounds of Edwards's religious thought, see Norman Fiering, *Jonathan Edwards's Moral Thought and Its British Context* (Chapel Hill, 1981); and Sang Hyun Lee, *The Philosophical Theology of Jonathan Edwards* (Princeton, 1988). Bruce Kuklick, *Churchmen and Philosophers: From Jonathan Edwards to John Dewey* (New Haven, 1985), traces the role of Edwardsian thought in the development of a post-Calvinist tradition of philosophical theology. Robert E. Brown, *Jonathan Edwards and the Bible* (Bloomington, 2002), helpfully analyzes Edwards's biblical criticism. Sang Hyun Lee, ed., *The Princeton Companion to Jonathan Edwards* (Princeton, 2005); and Stephen J. Stein, ed., *The Cambridge Companion to Jonathan Edwards* (Cambridge, 2007), are instructive collections of essays on Edwards's thought and legacy.

"Sinners in the Hands of an Angry God" (1741)

—Their foot shall slide in due time.

DEUT. xxxii. 35.

In this verse is threatened the vengeance of God on the wicked unbelieving Israelites, who were God's visible people, and who lived under the means of grace; but who, notwithstanding all God's wonderful works towards them, remained (as ver. 28.) void of counsel, having no understanding in them. Under all the cultivations of heaven, they brought forth bitter and poisonous fruit; as in the two verses next preceding the text.—The expression I have chosen for my text, *Their foot shall slide in due time,* seems to imply the following things, relating to the punishment and destruction to which these wicked Israelites were exposed.

1. That they were always exposed to *destruction;* as one that stands or walks in slippery places is always exposed to fall. This is implied in the manner of their destruction coming upon them, being represented by their foot sliding. The same is expressed, Psalm lxxiii. 18. "Surely thou didst set them in slippery places; thou castedst them down into destruction."

2. It implies, that they were always exposed to sudden unexpected destruction. As he that walks in slippery places is every moment liable to fall, he cannot foresee one moment whether he shall stand or fall the next; and when he does fall, he falls at once without warning: Which is also expressed in Psalm lxxiii. 18, 19. "Surely thou didst set them in slippery places; thou castedst them down into destruction: How are they brought into desolation as in a moment!"

3. Another thing implied is, that they are liable to fall *of themselves,* without being thrown down by the hand of another; as he that stands or walks on slippery ground needs nothing but his own weight to throw him down.

4. That the reason why they are not fallen already, and do not fall now, is only that God's appointed time is not come. For it is said, that when that due time, or appointed time comes, *their foot shall slide.* Then they shall be left to fall, as they are inclined by their own weight. God will not hold them up in these slippery places any longer, but will let them go; and then, at that very instant, they shall fall into destruction; as he that stands on such slippery declining ground, on the edge of a pit, he cannot stand alone, when he is let go he immediately falls and is lost.

The observation, from the words that I would now insist upon is this.—"There is nothing that keeps wicked men at any one moment out of hell, but the mere pleasure of God:"—By the *mere* pleasure of God, I mean his *sovereign* pleasure, his arbitrary will, restrained by no obligation, hindered by no manner of difficulty, any more than if nothing else but God's mere will had in the least degree, or in any respect whatsoever, any hand in

Source: The Works of President Edwards, vol. 6, ed. Edward Williams and Edward Parsons (London: James Black & Son, 1817), 450–64. Editors' notes altered.

the preservation of wicked men one moment.—The truth of this observation may appear by the following considerations.

1. There is no want of *power* in God to cast wicked men into hell at any moment. Men's hands cannot be strong when God rises up: The strongest have no power to resist him, nor can any deliver out of his hands.—He is not only able to cast wicked men into hell, but he can most easily do it. Sometimes an earthly prince meets with a great deal of difficulty to subdue a rebel, who has found means to fortify himself, and has made himself strong by the numbers of his followers. But it is not so with God. There is no fortress that is any defence from the power of God. Though hand join in hand, and vast multitudes of God's enemies combine and associate themselves, they are easily broken in pieces. They are as great heaps of light chaff before the whirlwind; or large quantities of dry stubble before devouring flames. We find it easy to tread on and crush a worm that we see crawling on the earth; so it is easy for us to cut or singe a slender thread that anything hangs by: thus easy is it for God, when he pleases, to cast his enemies down to hell. What are we, that we should think to stand before him, at whose rebuke the earth trembles, and before whom the rocks are thrown down?

2. They *deserve* to be cast into hell; so that divine justice never stands in the way, it makes no objection against God's using his power at any moment to destroy them. Yea, on the contrary, justice calls aloud for an infinite punishment of their sins. Divine justice says of the tree that brings forth such grapes of Sodom, "Cut it down, why cumbereth it the ground?" Luke xiii. 7. The sword of divine justice is every moment brandished over their heads, and it is nothing but the hand of arbitrary mercy, and God's mere will, that holds it back.

3. They are already under a sentence of *condemnation* to hell. They do not only justly deserve to be cast down thither, but the sentence of the law of God, that eternal and immutable rule of righteousness that God has fixed between him and mankind, is gone out against them, and stands against them; so that they are bound over already to hell. John iii. 18. "He that believeth not is condemned already." So that every unconverted man properly belongs to hell; that is his place; from thence he is. John viii. 23. "Ye are from beneath:" And thither he is bound; it is the place that justice, and God's word, and the sentence of his unchangeable law, assign to him.

4. They are now the objects of that very same *anger* and wrath of God, that is expressed in the torments of hell. And the reason why they do not go down to hell at each moment, is not because God, in whose power they are, is not then very angry with them; as he is with many miserable creatures now tormented in hell, who there feel and bear the fierceness of his wrath. Yea, God is a great deal more angry with great numbers that are now on earth; yea, doubtless, with many that are now in this congregation, who it may be are at ease, than he is with many of those who are now in the flames of hell.

So that it is not because God is unmindful of their wickedness, and does not resent it, that he does not let loose his hand and cut them off. God is not altogether such an one as themselves, though they may imagine him to be so. The wrath of God burns against them, their damnation does not slumber; the pit is prepared, the fire is made ready, the furnace is now hot, ready to receive them; the flames do now rage and glow. The glittering sword is whet, and held over them, and the pit hath opened its mouth under them.

5. The *devil* stands ready to fall upon them, and seize them as his own, at what moment God shall permit him. They belong to him, he has their souls in his possession, and under his dominion. The scripture represents them as his goods, Luke xi. 12. The devils watch them; they are ever by them, at their right hand; they stand waiting for

them, like greedy hungry lions that see their prey, and expect to have it, but are for the present kept back. If God should withdraw his hand, by which they are restrained, they would in one moment fly upon their poor souls. The old serpent is gaping for them; hell opens its mouth wide to receive them; and if God should permit it, they would be hastily swallowed up and lost.

6. There are in the souls of wicked men those hellish *principles* reigning, that would presently kindle and flame out into hell fire, if it were not for God's restraints. There is laid in the very nature of carnal men, a foundation for the torments of hell. There are those corrupt principles, in reigning power in them, and in full possession of them, that are seeds of hell fire. These principles are active and powerful, exceeding violent in their nature, and if it were not for the restraining hand of God upon them, they would soon break out, they would flame out after the same manner as the same corruptions, the same enmity does in the hearts of damned souls, and would beget the same torments as they do in them. The souls of the wicked are in scripture compared to the troubled sea, Isaiah lvii. 20. For the present, God restrains their wickedness by his mighty power, as he does the raging waves of the troubled sea, saying, "Hitherto shalt thou come, but no further;" but if God should withdraw that restraining power, it would soon carry all before it. Sin is the ruin and misery of the soul; it is destructive in its nature; and if God should leave it without restraint, there would need nothing else to make the soul perfectly miserable. The corruption of the heart of man is immoderate and boundless in its fury; and while wicked men live here, it is like fire pent up by God's restraints, whereas if it were let loose, it would set on fire the course of nature; and as the heart is now a sink of sin, so, if sin was not restrained, it would immediately turn the soul into a fiery oven, or a furnace of fire and brimstone.

7. It is no security to wicked men for one moment, that there are no visible means of death at hand. It is no security to a natural man, that he is now in health, and that he does not see which way he should now immediately go out of the world by any accident, and that there is no visible danger in any respect in his circumstances. The manifold and continual experience of the world in all ages, shews this is no evidence, that a man is not on the very brink of eternity, and that the next step will not be into another world. The unseen, unthought-of ways and means of persons going suddenly out of the world are innumerable and inconceivable. Unconverted men walk over the pit of hell on a rotten covering, and there are innumerable places in this covering so weak that they will not bear their weight, and these places are not seen. The arrows of death fly unseen at noon-day; the sharpest sight cannot discern them. God has so many different unsearchable ways of taking wicked men out of the world and sending them to hell, that there is nothing to make it appear, that God had need to be at the expence of a miracle, or go out of the ordinary course of his providence, to destroy any wicked man, at any moment. All the means that there are of sinners going out of the world, are so in God's hands, and so universally and absolutely subject to his power and determination, that it does not depend at all the less on the mere will of God, whether sinners shall at any moment go to hell, than if means were never made use of, or at all concerned in the case.

8. Natural men's prudence and care to preserve their own lives, or the care of others to preserve them, do not secure them a moment. To this, divine providence and universal experience do also bear testimony. There is this clear evidence that men's own wisdom is no security to them from death; that if it were otherwise we should see some difference between the wise and politic men of the world, and others, with regard to their liableness

to early and unexpected death; but how is it in fact? Eccles. ii. 16. "How dieth the wise man? even as the fool."

9. All wicked men's pains and *contrivance* which they use to escape hell, while they continue to reject Christ, and so remain wicked men, do not secure them from hell one moment. Almost every natural man that hears of hell, flatters himself that he shall escape it; he depends upon himself for his own security; he flatters himself in what he has done, in what he is now doing, or what he intends to do. Every one lays out matters in his own mind how he shall avoid damnation, and flatters himself that he contrives well for himself, and that his schemes will not fail. They hear indeed that there are but few saved, and that the greater part of men that have died heretofore are gone to hell; but each one imagines that he lays out matters better for his own escape than others have done. He does not intend to come to that place of torment; he says within himself, that he intends to take effectual care, and to order matters so for himself as not to fail.

But the foolish children of men miserably delude themselves in their own schemes, and in confidence in their own strength and wisdom: they trust to nothing but a shadow. The greater part of those who heretofore have lived under the same means of grace, and are now dead, are undoubtedly gone to hell; and it was not because they were not as wise as those who are now alive: it was not because they did not lay out matters as well for themselves to secure their own escape. If we could speak with them, and inquire of them, one by one, whether they expected, when alive, and when they used to hear about hell, ever to be the subjects of that misery; we, doubtless, should hear one and another reply, "No, I never intended to come here: I had laid out matters otherwise in my mind; I thought I should contrive well for myself: I thought my scheme good. I intended to take effectual care; but it came upon me unexpected; I did not look for it at that time, and in that manner; it came as a thief: Death outwitted me: God's wrath was too quick for me. Oh, my cursed foolishness! I was flattering myself, and pleasing myself with vain dreams of what I would do hereafter; and when I was saying, Peace and safety, then sudden destruction came upon me."

10. God has laid himself under *no obligation*, by any promise to keep any natural man out of hell one moment. God certainly has made no promises either of eternal life, or of any deliverance or preservation from eternal death, but what are contained in the covenant of grace, the promises that are given in Christ, in whom all the promises are yea and amen. But surely they have no interest in the promises of the covenant of grace who are not the children of the covenant, who do not believe in any of the promises, and have no interest in the Mediator of the covenant.

So that, whatever some have imagined and pretended about promises made to natural men's earnest seeking and knocking, it is plain and manifest, that whatever pains a natural man takes in religion, whatever prayers he makes, till he believes in Christ, God is under no manner of obligation to keep him a moment from eternal destruction.

So that, thus it is that natural men are held in the hand of God, over the pit of hell; they have deserved the fiery pit, and are already sentenced to it; and God is dreadfully provoked, his anger is as great towards them as to those that are actually suffering the executions of the fierceness of his wrath in hell, and they have done nothing in the least to appease or abate that anger, neither is God in the least bound by any promise to hold them up one moment; the devil is waiting for them, hell is gaping for them, the flames gather and flash about them, and would fain lay hold on them, and swallow them up; the fire pent up in their own hearts is struggling to break out; and they have no interest in any Mediator, there are no means within reach that can be any security to them. In short, they have no refuge, nothing to take hold of; all that preserves them every moment is the mere arbitrary will, and uncovenanted, unobliged forbearance of an incensed God.

APPLICATION

The use of this awful subject may be for awakening unconverted persons in this congregation. This that you have heard is the case of every one of you that are out of Christ.—That world of misery, that lake of burning brimstone, is extended abroad under you. There is the dreadful pit of the glowing flames of the wrath of God; there is hell's wide gaping mouth open; and you have nothing to stand upon, nor any thing to take hold of; there is nothing between you and hell but the air; it is only the power and mere pleasure of God that holds you up.

You probably are not sensible of this; you find you are kept out of hell, but do not see the hand of God in it; but look at other things, as the good state of your bodily constitution, your care of your own life, and the means you use for your own preservation. But indeed these things are nothing; if God should withdraw his hand, they would avail no more to keep you from falling, than the thin air to hold up a person that is suspended in it.

Your wickedness makes you as it were heavy as lead, and to tend downwards with great weight and pressure towards hell; and if God should let you go, you would immediately sink and swiftly descend and plunge into the bottomless gulf, and your healthy constitution, and your own care and prudence, and best contrivance, and all your righteousness, would have no more influence to uphold you and keep you out of hell, than a spider's web would have to stop a falling rock. Were it not for the sovereign pleasure of God, the earth would not bear you one moment; for you are a burden to it; the creation groans with you; the creature is made subject to the bondage of your corruption, not willingly; the sun does not willingly shine upon you to give you light to serve sin and Satan; the earth does not willingly yield her increase to satisfy your lusts; nor is it willingly a stage for your wickedness to be acted upon; the air does not willingly serve you for breath to maintain the flame of life in your vitals, while you spend your life in the service of God's enemies. God's creatures are good, and were made for men to serve God with, and do not willingly subserve to any other purpose, and groan when they are abused to purposes so directly contrary to their nature and end. And the world would spew you out, were it not for the sovereign hand of him who hath subjected it in hope. There are the black clouds of God's wrath now hanging directly over your heads, full of the dreadful storm, and big with thunder; and were it not for the restraining hand of God, it would immediately burst forth upon you. The sovereign pleasure of God, for the present, stays his rough wind; otherwise it would come with fury, and your destruction would come like a whirlwind, and you would be like the chaff of the summer threshing floor.

The wrath of God is like great waters that are dammed for the present; they increase more and more, and rise higher and higher, till an outlet is given; and the longer the stream is stopped, the more rapid and mighty is its course, when once it is let loose. It is true, that judgment against your evil works has not been executed hitherto; the floods of God's vengeance have been withheld; but your guilt in the mean time is constantly increasing, and you are every day treasuring up more wrath; the waters are constantly rising, and waxing more and more mighty; and there is nothing but the mere pleasure of God, that holds the waters back, that are unwilling to be stopped, and press hard to go forward. If God should only withdraw his hand from the flood-gate, it would immediately fly open, and the fiery floods of the fierceness and wrath of God, would rush forth with inconceivable fury, and would come upon you with omnipotent power; and if your strength were ten thousand times greater than it is, yea, ten thousand times greater than the strength of the stoutest, sturdiest devil in hell, it would be nothing to withstand or endure it.

The bow of God's wrath is bent, and the arrow made ready on the string, and justice bends the arrow at your heart, and strains the bow, and it is nothing but the mere pleasure of God, and that of an angry God, without any promise or obligation at all, that keeps the arrow one moment from being made drunk with your blood. Thus all you that never passed under a great change of heart, by the mighty power of the Spirit of God upon your souls; all you that were never born again, and made new creatures, and raised from being dead in sin, to a state of new, and before altogether unexperienced light and life, are in the hands of an angry God. However you may have reformed your life in many things, and may have had religious affections, and may keep up a form of religion in your families and closets, and in the house of God, it is nothing but his mere pleasure that keeps you from being this moment swallowed up in everlasting destruction. However unconvinced you may now be of the truth of what you hear, by and by you will be fully convinced of it. Those that are gone from being in the like circumstances with you, see that it was so with them; for destruction came suddenly upon most of them; when they expected nothing of it, and while they were saying, Peace and safety: Now they see, that those things on which they depended for peace and safety, were nothing but thin air and empty shadows.

The God that holds you over the pit of hell, much as one holds a spider, or some loathsome insect over the fire, abhors you, and is dreadfully provoked: his wrath towards you burns like fire: he looks upon you as worthy of nothing else, but to be cast into the fire; he is of purer eyes than to bear to have you in his sight; you are ten thousand times more abominable in his eyes, than the most hateful venomous serpent is in ours. You have offended him infinitely more than ever a stubborn rebel did his prince; and yet it is nothing but his hand that holds you from falling into the fire every moment. It is to be ascribed to nothing else, that you did not go to hell the last night; that you was suffered to awake again in this world, after you closed your eyes to sleep. And there is no other reason to be given, why you have not dropped into hell since you arose in the morning, but that God's hand has held you up. There is no other reason to be given why you have not gone to hell, since you have sat here in the house of God, provoking his pure eyes by your sinful wicked manner of attending his solemn worship. Yea, there is nothing else that is to be given as a reason why you do not this very moment drop down into hell.

O sinner! Consider the fearful danger you are in: it is a great furnace of wrath, a wide and bottomless pit, full of the fire of wrath, that you are held over in the hand of that God, whose wrath is provoked and incensed as much against you, as against many of the damned in hell. You hang by a slender thread, with the flames of divine wrath flashing about it, and ready every moment to singe it, and burn it asunder; and you have no interest in any Mediator, and nothing to lay hold off to save yourself, nothing to keep off the flames of wrath, nothing of your own, nothing that you ever have done, nothing that you can do, to induce God to spare you one moment.—And consider here more particularly,

1. *Whose* wrath it is: it is the wrath of the infinite God. If it were only the wrath of man, though it were of the most potent prince, it would be comparatively little to be regarded. The wrath of kings is very much dreaded, especially of absolute monarchs, who have the possessions and lives of their subjects wholly in their power, to be disposed of at their mere will. Prov. xx. 2. "The fear of a king is as the roaring of a lion: Whoso provoketh him to anger, sinneth against his own soul." The subject that very much enrages an arbitrary prince, is liable to suffer the most extreme torments that human art can invent, or human

power can inflict. But the greatest earthly potentates in their greatest majesty and strength, and when clothed in their greatest terrors, are but feeble, despicable worms of the dust, in comparison of the great and almighty Creator and King of heaven and earth. It is but little that they can do, when most enraged, and when they have exerted the utmost of their fury, All the kings of the earth, before God, are as grasshoppers; they are nothing, and less than nothing: both their love and their hatred is to be despised. The wrath of the great King of kings, is as much more terrible than theirs, as his majesty is greater. Luke xii. 4, 5. "And I say unto you, my friends, Be not afraid of them that kill the body, and after that, have no more that they can do. But I will forewarn you whom you shall fear: fear him, which after he hath killed, hath power to cast into hell; yea, I say unto you, Fear him."

2. It is the *fierceness* of his wrath that you are exposed to. We often read of the fury of God; as in Isaiah lix. 18. "According to their deeds, accordingly he will repay fury to his adversaries." So Isaiah lxvi. 15. "For behold, the Lord will come with fire, and with his chariots like a whirlwind, to render his anger with fury, and his rebuke with flames of fire." And in many other places. So, Rev. xix. 15. we read of "the wine-press of the fierceness and wrath of Almighty God." The words are exceeding terrible. If it had only been said, "the wrath of God," the words would have implied that which is infinitely dreadful: but it is "the fierceness and wrath of God." The fury of God! the fierceness of Jehovah! Oh, how dreadful must that be! Who can utter or conceive what such expressions carry in them! But it is also "the fierceness and wrath of *Almighty* God." As though there would be a very great manifestation of his almighty power in what the fierceness of his wrath should inflict, as though omnipotence should be as it were enraged, and exerted, as men are wont to exert their strength in the fierceness of their wrath. Oh! then, what will be the consequence! What will become of the poor worm that shall suffer it! Whose hands can be strong? And whose heart can endure? To what a dreadful, inexpressible, inconceivable depth of misery must the poor creature be sunk who shall be the subject of this!

Consider this, you that are here present, that yet remain in an unregenerate state. That God will execute the fierceness of his anger, implies, that he will inflict wrath without any pity. When God beholds the ineffable extremity of your case, and sees your torment to be so vastly disproportioned to your strength, and sees how your poor soul is crushed, and sinks down, as it were, into an infinite gloom; he will have no compassion upon you, he will not forbear the executions of his wrath, or in the least lighten his hand; there shall be no moderation or mercy, nor will God then at all stay his rough wind; he will have no regard to your welfare, nor be at all careful lest you should suffer too much in any other sense, than only that you shall *not suffer beyond what strict justice requires.* Nothing shall be withheld, because it is so hard for you to bear. Ezek. viii. 18. "Therefore will I also deal in fury, mine eye shall not spare, neither will I have pity; and though they cry in mine ears with a loud voice, yet I will not hear them." Now God stands ready to pity you; this is a day of mercy; you may cry now with some encouragement of obtaining mercy. But when once the day of mercy is past, your most lamentable and dolorous cries and shrieks will be in vain; you will be wholly lost and thrown away of God, as to any regard to your welfare. God will have no other use to put you to, but to suffer misery; you shall be continued in being to no other end; for you will be a vessel of wrath fitted to destruction; and there will be no other use of this vessel, but to be filled full of wrath. God will be so far from pitying you when you cry to him, that it is said he will only "laugh and mock," Prov. i. 25, 26, &c.

How awful are those words, Isa. lxiii. 3. which are the words of the great God, "I will tread them in mine anger, and will trample them in my fury, and their blood shall be sprinkled upon my garments, and I will stain all my raiment." It is perhaps impossible to conceive of words that carry in them greater manifestations of these three things, *viz.* contempt, and hatred, and fierceness of indignation. If you cry to God to pity you, he will be so far from pitying you in your doleful case, or shewing you the least regard or favour, that instead of that, he will only tread you under foot. And though he will know that you cannot bear the weight of omnipotence treading upon you, yet he will not regard that, but he will crush you under his feet without mercy; he will crush out your blood, and make it fly, and it shall be sprinkled on his garments, so as to stain all his raiment. He will not only hate you, but he will have you in the utmost contempt; no place shall be thought fit for you, but under his feet to be trodden down as the mire of the streets.

3. The *misery* you are exposed to is that which God will inflict to that end, that he might shew what that wrath of Jehovah is. God hath had it on his heart to shew to angels and men, both how excellent his love is, and also how terrible his wrath is. Sometimes earthly kings have a mind to shew how terrible their wrath is, by the extreme punishments they would execute on those that would provoke them. Nebuchadnezzar, that mighty and haughty monarch of the Chaldean empire, was willing to shew his wrath when enraged with Shadrach, Meshech, and Abednego; and accordingly gave orders that the burning fiery furnace should be heated seven times hotter than it was before; doubtless, it was raised to the utmost degree of fierceness that human art could raise it. But the great God is also willing to shew his wrath, and magnify his awful majesty and mighty power in the extreme sufferings of his enemies. Rom. ix. 22. "What if God, willing to shew his wrath, and to make his power known, endured with much long-suffering the vessels of wrath fitted to destruction?" And seeing this is his design, and what he has determined, even to shew how terrible the unrestrained wrath, the fury and fierceness of Jehovah is, he will do it to effect. There will be something accomplished and brought to pass that will be dreadful with a witness. When the great and angry God hath risen up and executed his awful vengeance on the poor sinner, and the wretch is actually suffering the infinite weight and power of his indignation, then will God call upon the whole universe to behold that awful majesty and mighty power that is to be seen in it. Isa. xxxiii. 12–14. "And the people shall be as the burnings of lime, as thorns cut up shall they be burnt in the fire. Hear ye that are far off, what I have done; and ye that are near, acknowledge my might. The sinners in Zion are afraid; fearfulness hath surprised the hypocrites," &c.

Thus it will be with you that are in an unconverted state, if you continue in it; the infinite might, and majesty, and terribleness of the omnipotent God shall be magnified upon you, in the ineffable strength of your torments. You shall be tormented in the presence of the holy angels, and in the presence of the Lamb; and when you shall be in this state of suffering, the glorious inhabitants of heaven shall go forth and look on the awful spectacle, that they may see what the wrath and fierceness of the Almighty is; and when they have seen it, they will fall down and adore that great power and majesty. Isa. lxvi. 23, 24. "And it shall come to pass, that from one new moon to another, and from one sabbath to another, shall all flesh come to worship before me, saith the Lord. And they shall go forth and look upon the carcases of the men that have transgressed against me; for their worm shall not die, neither shall their fire be quenched, and they shall be an abhorring unto all flesh."

4. It is *everlasting* wrath. It would be dreadful to suffer this fierceness and wrath of Almighty God one moment; but you must suffer it to all eternity. There will be no end to this exquisite horrible misery. When you look forward, you shall see a long for-ever, a boundless duration before you, which will swallow up your thoughts, and amaze your soul; and you will absolutely despair of ever having any deliverance, any end, any mitigation, any

rest at all. You will know certainly that you must wear out long ages, millions of millions of ages, in wrestling and conflicting with this almighty merciless vengeance; and then when you have so done, when so many ages have actually been spent by you in this manner, you will know that all is but a point to what remains. So that your punishment will indeed be infinite. Oh, who can express what the state of a soul in such circumstances is! All that we can possibly say about it, gives but a very feeble, faint representation of it; it is inexpressible and inconceivable: For "who knows the power of God's anger?"

How dreadful is the state of those that are daily and hourly in danger of this great wrath and infinite misery! But this is the dismal case of every soul in this congregation that has not been born again, however moral and strict, sober and religious, they may otherwise be. Oh that you would consider it, whether you be young or old! There is reason to think, that there are many in this congregation now hearing this discourse, that will actually be the subjects of this very misery to all eternity. We know not who they are, or in what seats they sit, or what thoughts they now have. It may be they are now at ease, and hear all these things without much disturbance, and are now flattering themselves that they are not the persons, promising themselves that they shall escape. If we knew that there was one person, and but one, in the whole congregation, that was to be the subject of this misery, what an awful thing would it be to think of! If we knew who it was, what an awful sight would it be to see such a person! How might all the rest of the congregation lift up a lamentable and bitter cry over him! But, alas! instead of one, how many is it likely will remember this discourse in hell? And it would be a wonder, if some that are now present should not be in hell in a very short time, even before this year is out. And it would be no wonder if some persons, that now sit here, in some seats of this meeting-house, in health, quiet and secure, should be there before to-morrow morning. Those of you that finally continue in a natural condition, that shall keep out of hell longest, will be there in a little time! your damnation does not slumber; it will come swiftly, and, in all probability, very suddenly upon many of you. You have reason to wonder that you are not already in hell. It is doubtless the case of some whom you have seen and known, that never deserved hell more than you, and that heretofore appeared as likely to have been now alive as you. Their case is past all hope; they are crying in extreme misery and perfect despair; but here you are in the land of the living and in the house of God, and have an opportunity to obtain salvation. What would not those poor damned hopeless souls give for one day's opportunity such as you now enjoy!

And now you have an extraordinary opportunity, a day wherein Christ has thrown the door of mercy wide open, and stands in calling and crying with a loud voice to poor sinners; a day wherein many are flocking to him, and pressing into the kingdom of God. Many are daily coming from the east, west, north and south; many that were very lately in the same miserable condition that you are in, are now in a happy state, with their hearts filled with love to him who has loved them, and washed them from their sins in his own blood, and rejoicing in hope of the glory of God. How awful is it to be left behind at such a day! To see so many others feasting, while you are pining and perishing! To see so many rejoicing and singing for joy of heart, while you have cause to mourn for sorrow of heart, and howl for vexation of spirit! How can you rest one moment in such a condition? Are not your souls as precious as the souls of the people at Suffield,[1] where they are flocking from day to day to Christ?

---

1.   A town in the neighbourhood.

Are there not many here who have lived long in the world, and are not to this day born again? and so are aliens from the commonwealth of Israel, and have done nothing ever since they have lived, but treasure up wrath against the day of wrath? Oh, sirs, your case, in an especial manner, is extremely dangerous. Your guilt and hardness of heart is extremely great. Do you not see how generally persons of your years are passed over and left, in the present remarkable and wonderful dispensation of God's mercy? You had need to consider yourselves, and awake thoroughly out of sleep. You cannot bear the fierceness and wrath of the infinite God.—And you, young men, and young women, will you neglect this precious season which you now enjoy, when so many others of your age are renouncing all youthful vanities, and flocking to Christ? You especially have now an extraordinary opportunity; but if you neglect it, it will soon be with you as with those persons who spent all the precious days of youth in sin, and are now come to such a dreadful pass in blindness and hardness.—And you, children, who are unconverted, do not you know that you are going down to hell, to bear the dreadful wrath of that God, who is now angry with you every day and every night? Will you be content to be the children of the devil, when so many other children in the land are converted, and are become the holy and happy children of the King of kings?

And let everyone that is yet out of Christ, and hanging over the pit of hell, whether they be old men and women, or middle aged, or young people, or little children, now hearken to the loud calls of God's word and providence. This acceptable year of the Lord, a day of such great favour to some, will doubtless be a day of as remarkable vengeance to others. Men's hearts harden, and their guilt increases apace at such a day as this, if they neglect their souls; and never was there so great danger of such persons being given up to hardness of heart and blindness of mind. God seems now to be hastily gathering in his elect in all parts of the land; and probably the greater part of adult persons that ever shall be saved, will be brought in now in a little time, and that it will be as it was on the great outpouring of the Spirit upon the Jews in the apostles' days; the election will obtain, and the rest will be blinded. If this should be the case with you, you will eternally curse this day, and will curse the day that ever you was born, to see such a season of the pouring out of God's Spirit, and will wish that you had died and gone to hell before you had seen it. Now undoubtedly it is, as it was in the days of John the Baptist, the axe is in an extraordinary manner laid at the root of the trees, that every tree which brings not forth good fruit, may be hewn down and cast into the fire.

Therefore, let everyone that is out of Christ, now awake and fly from the wrath to come. The wrath of Almighty God is now undoubtedly hanging over a great part of this congregation: Let every one fly out of Sodom: "Haste and escape for your lives, look not behind you, escape to the mountain, lest you be consumed."

Selection from
A Treatise Concerning Religious Affections
(1746)

I PET. 1:8: *Whom having not seen, ye love: in whom, though now ye see him not, yet believing, ye rejoice with joy unspeakable, and full of glory.*

In these words, the Apostle represents the state of the minds of the Christians he wrote to, under the persecutions they were then the subjects of. These persecutions are what he has respect to, in the two preceding verses, when he speaks of the trial of their faith, and of their being in heaviness through manifold temptations....

...[T]he proposition or doctrine, that I would raise from these words is this,

DOCT. True religion, in great part, consists in holy affections.

We see that the Apostle, in observing and remarking the operations and exercises of religion, in the Christians he wrote to, wherein their religion appeared to be true and of the right kind, when it had its greatest trial of what sort it was, being tried by persecution as gold is tried in the fire, and when their religion not only proved true, but was most pure, and cleansed from its dross and mixtures of that which was not true, and when religion appeared in them most in its genuine excellency and native beauty, and was found to praise, and honor, and glory; he singles out the religious affections of love and joy, that were then in exercise in them: these are the exercises of religion he takes notice of, wherein their religion did thus appear true and pure, and in its proper glory....

...It may be inquired, what the affections of the mind are?

I answer, the affections are no other, than the more vigorous and sensible exercises of the inclination and will of the soul.

God has induced the soul with two faculties: one is that by which it is capable of perception and speculation, or by which it discerns and views and judges of things; which is called the understanding. The other faculty is that by which the soul does not merely perceive and view things, but is some way inclined with respect to the things it views or considers; either is inclined to 'em, or is disinclined, and averse from 'em; or is the faculty by which the soul does not behold things, as an indifferent unaffected spectator, but either as liking or disliking, pleased or displeased, approving or rejecting. This faculty is called by various names: it is sometimes called the *inclination:* and, as it has respect to the actions that are determined and governed by it, is called the *will:* and the *mind,* with regard to the exercises of this faculty, is often called the *heart.*

The exercises of this faculty are of two sorts; either those by which the soul is carried out towards the things that are in view, in approving of them, being pleased with them, and inclined to them; or those in which the soul opposes the things that are in view, in

Source: The Works of Jonathan Edwards, ed. Perry Miller, vol. 2, *Religious Affections,* ed. John E. Smith (New Haven: Yale University Press, 1959), 93, 95, 96–97, 191, 197–213, 240–43, 249–53. Reprinted by permission of Yale University Press, Copyright © 1959.

disapproving them, and in being displeased with them, averse from them, and rejecting them.

And as the exercises of the inclination and will of the soul are various in their kinds, so they are much more various in their degrees. There are some exercises of pleasedness or displeasedness, inclination or disinclination, wherein the soul is carried but a little beyond a state of perfect indifference. And there are other degrees above this, wherein the approbation or dislike, pleasedness or aversion, are stronger; wherein we may rise higher and higher, till the soul comes to act vigorously and sensibly, and the actings of the soul are with that strength that (through the laws of the union which the Creator has fixed between soul and body) the motion of the blood and animal spirits begins to be sensibly altered; whence oftentimes arises some bodily sensation, especially about the heart and vitals, that are the fountain of the fluids of the body: from whence it comes to pass, that the mind, with regard to the exercises of this faculty, perhaps in all nations and ages, is called the *heart*. And it is to be noted, that they are these more vigorous and sensible exercises of this faculty, that are called the *affections*....

Shewing What Are Distingushing Signs of Truly Gracious and Holy Affections

[First Sign]

......

I. Affections that are truly spiritual and gracious, do arise from those influences and operations on the heart, which are *spiritual, supernatural* and *divine*.

I will explain what I mean by these terms, whence will appear their use to distinguish between those affections which are spiritual, and those which are not so.

We find that true saints, or those persons who are sanctified by the Spirit of God, are in the New Testament called spiritual persons. And their being spiritual is spoken of as their peculiar character, and that wherein they are distinguished from those who are not sanctified. This is evident because those who are spiritual are set in opposition to natural men, and carnal men. Thus the spiritual man, and the natural man, are set in opposition one to another; "The natural man receiveth not the things of the Spirit of God, for they are foolishness unto him; neither can he know them; because they are spiritually discerned. But he that is spiritual judgeth all things" (I Cor. 2:14–15). The Scripture explains itself to mean an ungodly man, or one that has no grace, by a natural man: thus the apostle Jude, speaking of certain ungodly men, that had crept in unawares among the saints, ver. 4 of his Epistle, says, ver. 19: "These are sensual, having not the Spirit." This the Apostle gives as a reason why they behaved themselves in such a wicked manner as he had described. Here the word translated "sensual," in the original is Ψυκικοι; which is the very same, which in those verses in I Cor. ch. 2 is translated "natural." In the like manner, in the continuation of the same discourse, in the next verse but one, spiritual men are opposed to carnal men: which the connection plainly shows mean the same, as spiritual men and natural men, in the foregoing verses: "and I, brethren, could not speak unto you, as unto spiritual, but as unto carnal"; i.e. as in a great measure unsanctified. That by carnal the Apostle means corrupt and unsanctified, is abundantly evident, by Rom. 7:25 and 8:1, 4–9, 12, 13; Gal. 5:16 to the end; cf. Col. 2:18. Now therefore, if by natural and carnal, in these texts, he intended "unsanctified"; then doubtless by spiritual, which is opposed thereto, is meant "sanctified" and gracious.

And as the saints are called spiritual in Scripture, so we also find that there are certain properties, qualities, and principles, that have the same epithet given them. So we read of a spiritual mind, Rom. 8:6–7 and of spiritual wisdom, Col. 1:9 and of spiritual blessings, Eph. 1:3.

Now it may be observed that the epithet "spiritual," in these and other parallel texts of the New Testament, is not used to signify any relation of persons or things to the spirit or soul of man, as the spiritual part of man, in opposition to the body, which is the material part: qualities are not said to be spiritual, because they have their seat in the soul, and not in the body: for there are some properties that the Scripture calls carnal or fleshly, which have their seat as much in the soul, as those properties that are called spiritual. Thus it is with pride and self-righteousness, and a man's trusting to his own wisdom, which the Apostle calls fleshy (Col. 2:18). Nor are things called spiritual, because they are conversant about those things that are immaterial, and not corporeal. For so was the wisdom of the wise men, and princes of this world, conversant about spirits, and immaterial beings; which yet the Apostle speaks of as natural men, totally ignorant of those things that are spiritual (I Cor. ch. 2). But it is with relation to the Holy Ghost, or Spirit of God, that persons or things are termed spiritual, in the New Testament. "Spirit," as the word is used to signify the third person in the Trinity, is the substantive, of which is formed the adjective "spiritual," in the Holy Scriptures. Thus Christians are called spiritual persons, because they are born of the Spirit, and because of the indwelling and holy influences of the Spirit of God in them. And things are called spiritual as related to the Spirit of God; "Which things also we speak, not in the words which man's wisdom teacheth, but which the Holy Ghost teacheth, comparing spiritual things with spiritual. But the natural man receiveth not the things of the Spirit of God" (I Cor. 2:13–14). Here the Apostle himself expressly signifies, that by spiritual things, he means the things of the Spirit of God, and things which the Holy Ghost teacheth. The same is yet more abundantly apparent by viewing the whole context. Again, "To be carnally minded is death: but to be spiritually minded is life and peace" (Rom. 8:6). The Apostle explains what he means by being carnally and spiritually minded, in what follows in the 9th verse, and shows that by being spiritually minded, he means a having the indwelling and holy influences of the Spirit of God in the heart. "But ye are not in the flesh, but in the Spirit, if so be the Spirit of God dwell in you. Now if any man have not the Spirit of Christ, he is none of his." The same is evident by all the context. But time would fail to produce all the evidence there is of this, in the New Testament.

And it must be here observed, that although it is with relation to the Spirit of God and his influences, that persons and things are called spiritual; yet not all those persons who are subject to any kind of influence of the Spirit of God, are ordinarily called spiritual in the New Testament. They who have only the common influences of God's Spirit, are not so called, in the places cited above, but only those, who have the special, gracious and saving influences of God's Spirit: as is evident, because it has been already proved, that by spiritual men is meant godly men, in opposition to natural, carnal and unsanctified men. And it is most plain, that the Apostle by spiritually minded, Rom. 8:6, means graciously minded. And though the extraordinary gifts of the Spirit, which natural men might have, are sometimes called spiritual, because they are from the Spirit; yet natural men, whatever gifts of the Spirit they had, were not, in the usual language of the New Testament, called spiritual persons. For it was not by men's having the gifts of the Spirit, but by their having the virtues of the Spirit, that they were called spiritual; as is apparent, by Gal. 6:1: "Brethren, if any man be overtaken in a fault, ye which are spiritual restore such an one in the spirit of meekness." Meekness is one of those virtues which the Apostle had just spoken of, in the verses next preceding, showing what are the fruits of the Spirit. Those qualifications are said to be spiritual in the language of the New Testament, which are truly gracious and holy, and peculiar to the saints.

Thus when we read of spiritual wisdom and understanding (as in Col. 1:9: "We desire that ye may be filled with the knowledge of his will, in all wisdom and spiritual understanding"). Hereby is intended that wisdom which is gracious, and from the sanctifying influences of the Spirit of God. For doubtless, by spiritual wisdom, is meant that which is opposite to what the Scripture calls natural wisdom; as the spiritual man is opposed to the natural man. And therefore spiritual wisdom is doubtless the same with that wisdom which is from above, that the apostle James speaks of, "The wisdom that is from above, is first pure, then peaceable, gentle," etc. (Jas. 3:17), for this the Apostle opposes to natural wisdom, ver. 15: "This wisdom descendeth not from above, but is earthly, sensual," the last word in the original is the same that is translated "natural," in I Cor. 2:14.

So that although natural men may be the subjects of many influences of the Spirit of God, as is evident by many Scriptures, as Num. 24:2; I Sam. 10:10 and 11:6 and 16:14; I Cor. 13:1–3; Heb. 6:4–6 and many others; yet they are not in the sense of the Scripture, spiritual persons; either are any of those effects, common gifts, qualities or affections, that are from the influence of the Spirit of God upon them, called spiritual things. The great difference lies in these two things.

1. The Spirit of God is given to the true saints to dwell in them, as his proper lasting abode; and to influence their hearts, as a principle of new nature, or as a divine supernatural spring of life and action. The Scriptures represent the Holy Spirit, not only as moving, and occasionally influencing the saints, but as dwelling in them as his temple, his proper abode, and everlasting dwelling place (I Cor. 3:16; II Cor. 6:16; John 14:16–17). And he is represented as being there so united to the faculties of the soul, that he becomes there a principle or spring of new nature and life.

So the saints are said to live by Christ living in them (Gal. 2:20). Christ by his Spirit not only is in them, but lives in them; and so that they live by his life; so is his Spirit united to them, as a principle of life in them; they don't only drink living water, but this living water becomes a well or fountain of water, in the soul, springing up into spiritual and everlasting life (John 4:14), and thus becomes a principle of life in them; this living water, this Evangelist himself explains to intend the Spirit of God (ch. 7:38–39). The light of the Sun of Righteousness don't only shine upon them, but is so communicated to them that they shine also, and become little images of that Sun which shines upon them; the sap of the true vine is not only conveyed into them, as the sap of a tree may be conveyed into a vessel, but is conveyed as sap is from a tree into one of its living branches, where it becomes a principle of life. The Spirit of God being thus communicated and united to the saints, they are from thence properly denominated from it, and are called spiritual.

On the other hand, though the Spirit of God may many ways influence natural men; yet because it is not thus communicated to them, as an indwelling principle, they don't derive any denomination or character from it; for there being no union it is not their own. The light may shine upon a body that is very dark or black; and though that body be the subject of the light, yet, because the light becomes no principle of light in it, so as to cause the body to shine, hence that body don't properly receive its denomination from it, so as to be called a lightsome body. So the Spirit of God acting upon the soul only, without communicating itself to be an active principle in it, can't denominate it spiritual. A body that continues black, may be said not to have light, though the light shines upon it; so natural men are said not to have the Spirit, Jude 19: "sensual," or natural (as the word is elsewhere rendered) "having not the Spirit."

2. Another reason why the saints and their virtues are called spiritual (which is the principal thing), is that the Spirit of God, dwelling as a vital principle in their souls, there produces those effects wherein he exerts and communicates himself in his own proper nature. Holiness is the nature of the Spirit of God, therefore he is called in Scripture the Holy Ghost. Holiness, which is as it were the beauty and sweetness of the divine nature, is as much the proper nature of the Holy Spirit, as heat is the nature of fire, or sweetness was the nature of that holy anointing oil, which was the principal type of the Holy Ghost in the Mosaic dispensation; yea, I may rather say that holiness is as much the proper nature of the Holy Ghost, as sweetness was the nature of the sweet odor of that ointment. The Spirit of God so dwells in the hearts of the saints, that he there, as a seed or spring of life, exerts and communicates himself, in this his sweet and divine nature, making the soul a partaker of God's beauty and Christ's joy, so that the saint has truly fellowship with the Father, and with his Son Jesus Christ, in thus having the communion or participation of the Holy Ghost. The grace which is in the hearts of the saints, is of the same nature with the divine holiness, as much as 'tis possible for that holiness to be, which is infinitely less in degree; as the brightness that is in a diamond which the sun shines upon, is of the same nature with the brightness of the sun, but only that it is as nothing to it in degree. Therefore Christ says, John 3:6: "That which is born of the Spirit is spirit"; i.e. the grace that is begotten in the hearts of the saints, is something of the same nature with that Spirit, and so is properly called a spiritual nature; after the same manner as that which is born of the flesh is flesh, or that which is born of corrupt nature is corrupt nature.

But the Spirit of God never influences the minds of natural men after this manner. Though he may influence them many ways, yet he never, in any of his influences, communicates himself to them in his own proper nature. Indeed he never acts disagreeably to his nature, either on the minds of saints or sinners: but the Spirit of God may act upon men agreeably to his own nature, and not exert his proper nature in the acts and exercises of their minds: the Spirit of God may act so, that his actions may be agreeable to his nature, and yet may not at all communicate himself in his proper nature, in the effect of that action. Thus, for instance, the Spirit of God moved upon the face of the waters, and there was nothing disagreeable to his nature in that action; but yet he did not at all communicate himself in that action, there was nothing of the proper nature of the Holy Spirit in that motion of the waters. And so he may act upon the minds of men many ways, and not communicate himself any more than when he acts on inanimate things.

Thus not only the manner of the *relation* of the Spirit, who is the operator, to the subject of his operations, is different; as the Spirit operates in the saints, as dwelling in them, as an abiding principle of action, whereas he doth not so operate upon sinners; but the influence and *operation itself* is different, and the effect wrought exceeding different. So that not only the persons are called spiritual, as having the Spirit of God dwelling in them; but those qualifications, affections and experiences that are wrought in them by the Spirit, are also spiritual, and therein differ vastly in their nature and kind from all that a natural man is or can be the subject of, while he remains in a natural state; and also from all that men or devils can be the authors of: 'tis a spiritual work in this high sense; and therefore above all other works is peculiar to the Spirit of God. There is no work so high and excellent; for there is no work wherein God does so much communicate himself, and wherein the mere creature hath, in so high a sense, a participation of God; so that it is expressed in Scripture by the saints being made "partakers of the divine nature" (II Pet. 1:4), and having God dwelling in them, and they in God (I John 4:12, 15–16, and ch. 3:21), and having Christ in them (John 17:21; Rom. 8:10), being the temples of the living God (2 Cor. VI:16), living by Christ's life (Gal. 2:20), being made partakers of God's holiness (Heb. 12:10), having Christ's love dwelling in them (John 17:26), having his joy fulfilled in them (John 17:13), seeing light in God's light and being made to drink of the river of God's pleasures (Ps. 36:8–9), having fellowship with God, or communicating and partaking with him (as the word signifies) (I John 1:3). Not that the saints are made partakers of the essence of God, and so are "Godded" with God, and "Christed" with Christ, according to the abominable and blasphemous language and notions of some heretics; but, to use the Scripture phrase, they are made partakers of God's fullness (Eph. 3:17–19; John 1:16), that is, of God's spiritual beauty and happiness, according to the measure and capacity of a creature; for so it is evident the word "fullness" signifies in Scripture language. Grace in the hearts of the saints, being therefore the most glorious work of God, wherein he communicates of the goodness of his nature, it is doubtless his peculiar work, and in an eminent manner, above the power of all creatures. And the influences of the Spirit of God in this, being thus peculiar to God, and being those wherein God does, in so high a manner, communicate himself, and make the creature partaker of the divine nature (the Spirit of God communicating itself in its own proper nature). This is what I mean by those influences that are divine, when I say that truly gracious affections do arise from those influences that are spiritual and divine.

The true saints only have that which is spiritual; others have nothing which is divine, in the sense that has been spoken of. They not only have not these communications of the Spirit of God in so high a degree as the saints, but have nothing of that nature or kind. For the apostle James tells us, that natural men have not the Spirit; and Christ teaches the necessity of a new birth, or a being born of the Spirit, from this, that he that is born of the flesh, has only flesh, and no spirit (John 3:6). They have not the Spirit of God dwelling in them in any degree; for the Apostle teaches, that all who have the Spirit of God dwelling in them are some of his (Rom. 8:9–11). And an having the Spirit of God is spoken of as a certain sign that persons shall have the eternal inheritance; for 'tis spoken of as the earnest of it (2 Cor. 1:22 and 5:5; Eph. 1:14), and an having anything of the Spirit is mentioned as a sure sign of being in Christ, "Hereby know we that we dwell in him, because he hath given us of his Spirit" (I John 4:30). Ungodly men, not only han't so much of the divine nature as the saints, but they are not partakers of it; which implies that they have nothing of it; for a being partaker of the divine nature is spoken of as the peculiar privilege of the true saints (II Pet. 1:4). Ungodly men are not partakers of God's holiness (Heb. 12:10). A natural man has no experience of any of those things that are spiritual: the Apostle teaches us that he is so far from it, that he knows nothing about them, he is a perfect stranger to them, the talk about such things is all foolishness and nonsense to him, he knows not what it means, "The natural man receiveth not the things of the Spirit of God; for they are foolishness to him; neither can he know them; because they are spiritually discerned" (I Cor. 2:14). And to the like purpose Christ teaches us that the world is wholly unacquainted with the Spirit of God, "Even the Spirit of truth, whom the world cannot receive; because it seeth him not, neither knoweth him" (John 14:17). And 'tis further evident, that natural men have nothing in them of the same nature with the true grace of the saints because the Apostle teaches us that those of them who go furthest in religion, have no charity, or true Christian love (I Cor. ch. 13). So Christ elsewhere reproves the Pharisees, those high pretenders to religion, that they had not the love of God in them (John 5:42). Hence natural men have no communion or fellowship with Christ, or participation with him (as these words signify), for this is spoken of as the peculiar privilege of the saints (I John 1:3, together with verses 6, 7, and I Cor. 1:8–9). And the Scripture speaks of the actual being of a gracious principle in the soul, though in its first beginning, as a seed there planted, as inconsistent with a man's being a sinner (I John 3:9). And natural men are represented in Scripture as having no spiritual light, no spiritual life, and no spiritual being; and therefore conversion is often compared to opening the eyes of the blind, raising the dead, and a work of creation (wherein creatures are made entirely new), and becoming newborn children.

From these things it is evident, that those gracious influences which the saints are subjects of, and the effects of God's Spirit which they experience, are entirely above nature, altogether of a different kind from anything that men find within themselves by nature, or only in the exercise of natural principles; and are things which no improvement of those qualifications, or principles that are natural, no advancing or exalting them to higher degrees, and no kind of composition of them, will ever bring men to; because they not only differ from what is natural, and from everything that natural men experience, in degree and circumstances; but also in kind; and are of a nature vastly more excellent. And this is what I mean by supernatural, when I say, that gracious affections are from those influences that are supernatural.

From hence it follows, that in those gracious exercises and affections which are wrought in the minds of the saints, through the saving influences of the Spirit of God, there is a new inward perception or sensation of their minds, entirely different in its nature and kind, from anything that ever their minds were the subjects of before they were sanctified. For doubtless if God by his mighty power produces something that is new, not only in degree and circumstances, but in its whole nature, and that which could be produced by no exalting, varying or compounding of what was there before, or by adding anything of the like kind; I say, if God produces something thus new in a mind, that is a perceiving, thinking, conscious thing; then doubtless something entirely new is felt, or perceived, or thought; or, which is the same thing, there is some new sensation or perception of the mind, which is entirely of a new sort, and which could be produced by no exalting, varying or compounding of that kind of perceptions or sensations which the mind had before; or there is what some metaphysicians call a new simple idea. If grace be, in the sense above described, an entirely new kind of principle; then the exercises of it are also entirely a new kind of exercises. And if there be in the soul a new sort of exercises which it is conscious of, which the soul knew nothing of before, and which no improvement, composition or management of what it was before conscious or sensible of, could produce, or anything like it; then it follows that the mind has an entirely new kind of perception or sensation; and here is, as it were, a new spiritual sense that the mind has, or a principle of new kind of perception or spiritual sensation, which is in its whole nature different from any former kinds of sensation of the mind, as tasting is diverse from any of the other senses; and something is perceived by a true saint, in the exercise of this new sense of mind, in spiritual and divine things, as entirely diverse from anything that is perceived in them, by natural men, as the sweet taste of honey is diverse from the ideas men get of honey by only looking on it, and feeling of it. So that the spiritual perceptions which a sanctified and spiritual person has, are not only diverse from all that natural men have, after the manner that the ideas or perceptions of the same sense may differ one from another, but rather as the ideas and sensations of different senses do differ. Hence the work of the Spirit of God in regeneration is often in Scripture compared to the giving a new sense, giving eyes to see, and ears to hear, unstopping the ears of the deaf, and opening the eyes of them that were born blind, and turning from darkness unto light. And because this spiritual sense is immensely the most noble and excellent, and that without which all other principles of perception, and all our faculties are useless and vain; therefore the giving this new sense, with the blessed fruits and effects of it in the soul, is compared to a raising the dead, and to a new creation.

This new spiritual sense, and the new dispositions that attend it, are no new faculties, but are new principles of nature. I use the word "principles," for want of a word of a more determinate signification. By a principle of nature in this place, I mean that foundation which is laid in nature, either old or new, for any particular manner or kind of exercise of the faculties of the soul; or a natural habit or foundation for action, giving a person ability and disposition to exert the faculties in exercises of such a certain kind; so that to exert the faculties in that kind of exercises, may be said to be his nature. So this new spiritual sense is not a new faculty of understanding, but it is a new foundation laid in the nature of the soul, for a new kind of exercises of the same faculty of understanding. So that new holy disposition of heart that attends this new sense, is not a new faculty of will, but a foundation laid in the nature of the soul, for a new kind of exercises of the same faculty of will.

The Spirit of God, in all his operations upon the minds of natural men, only moves, impresses, assists, improves, or some way acts upon natural principles; but gives no new spiritual principle. Thus when the Spirit of God gives a natural man visions, as he did Balaam, he only impresses a natural principle, viz. the sense of seeing, immediately exciting ideas of that sense; but he gives no new sense; neither is there anything supernatural, spiritual or divine in it. So if the Spirit of God impresses on a man's imagination, either in a dream, or when he is awake, any outward ideas of any of the senses, either voices, or shapes and colors, 'tis only exciting ideas of the same kind that he has by natural principles and senses. So if God reveals to any natural man, any secret fact; as for instance, something that he shall hereafter see or hear; this is not infusing or exercising any new spiritual principle, or giving the ideas of any new spiritual sense; 'tis only impressing, in an extraordinary manner, the ideas that will hereafter be received by sight and hearing. So in the more ordinary influences of the Spirit of God on the hearts of sinners, he only assists natural principles to do the same work to a greater degree, which they do of themselves by nature. Thus the Spirit of God by his common influences may assist men's natural ingeniosity, as he assisted Bezaleel and Aholiab in the curious works of the tabernacle: so he may assist men's natural abilities in political affairs, and improve their courage, and other natural qualifications; as he is said to have put his Spirit on the seventy elders, and on Saul, so as to give him another heart: so God may greatly assist natural men's reason, in their reasoning about secular things, or about the doctrines of religion, and may greatly advance the clearness of their apprehensions and notions of things of religion in many respects, without giving any spiritual sense. So in those awakenings and convictions that natural men may have, God only assists conscience, which is a natural principle, to do that work in a further degree, which it naturally does. Conscience naturally gives men an apprehension of right and wrong, and suggests the relation there is between right and wrong, and a retribution: the Spirit of God assists men's consciences to do this in a greater degree, helps conscience against the stupefying influence of worldly objects and their lusts. And so there are many other ways might be mentioned wherein the Spirit acts upon, assists and moves natural principles; but after all, 'tis no more than nature moved, acted and improved; here is nothing supernatural and divine. But the Spirit of God in his spiritual influences on the hearts of his saints, operates by infusing or exercising new, divine and supernatural principles;

principles which are indeed a new and spiritual nature, and principles vastly more noble and excellent than all that is in natural men.

From what has been said it follows, that all spiritual and gracious affections are attended with, and do arise from some apprehension, idea or sensation of mind, which is in its whole nature different, yea exceeding different from all that is or can be in the mind of a natural man; and which the natural man discerns nothing of, and has no manner of idea of (agreeable to I Cor. 2:14), and conceives of no more than a man without the sense of tasting can conceive of the sweet taste of honey, or a man without the sense of hearing can conceive of the melody of a tune, or a man born blind can have a notion of the beauty of the rainbow.

But here two things must be observed in order to the right understanding of this.

1. On the one hand it must be observed, that not everything which in any respect appertains to spiritual affections, is new and entirely different from what natural men can conceive of, and do experience; some things are common to gracious affections with other affections; many circumstances, appendages and effects are common. Thus a saint's love to God has a great many things appertaining to it, which are common with a man's natural love to a near relation: love to God makes a man have desires of the honor of God, and a desire to please him; so does a natural man's love to his friend make him desire his honor, and desire to please him: love to God causes a man to delight in the thoughts of God, and to delight in the presence of God, and to desire conformity to God, and the enjoyment of God; and so it is with a man's love to his friend; and many other things might be mentioned which are common to both. But yet that idea which the saint has of the loveliness of God, and that sensation, and that kind of delight he has in that view, which is as it were the marrow and quintessence of his love, is peculiar, and entirely diverse from anything that a natural man has, or can have any notion of. And even in those things that seem to be common, there is something peculiar: both spiritual love and natural, cause desires after the object beloved; but they be not the same sort of desires; there is a sensation of soul in the spiritual desires of one that loves God, which is entirely different from all natural desires: both spiritual love and natural love are attended with delight in the object beloved; but the sensations of delight are not the same, but entirely and exceedingly diverse. Natural men may have conceptions of many things about spiritual affections; but there is something in them which is as it were the nucleus, or kernel of them, that they have no more conceptions of, than one born blind has of colors.

It may be clearly illustrated by this: we will suppose two men; one is born without the sense of tasting, the other has it; the latter loves honey and is greatly delighted in it because he knows the sweet taste of it; the other loves certain sounds and colors: the love of each has many things that appertain to it, which is common; it causes both to desire and delight in the object beloved, and causes grief when it is absent, etc.: but yet, that idea or sensation which he who knows the taste of honey, has of its excellency and sweetness, that is the foundation of his love, is entirely different from anything the other has or can have; and that delight which he has in honey, is wholly diverse from anything that the other can conceive of; though they both delight in their beloved objects. So both these persons may in some respects love the same object: the one may love a delicious kind of fruit, which is beautiful to the eye, and of a delicious taste; not only because he has seen its pleasant colors, but knows its sweet taste; the other, perfectly ignorant of this, loves it only for its beautiful colors: there are many things seem, in some respect, to be common to both; both love, both desire, and both delight; but the love, and desire, and delight of the one, is altogether diverse from that of the other. The difference between the love of a natural man and spiritual man is like to this; but only it must be observed, that in one respect it is vastly greater, viz. that the kinds of excellency which are perceived in spiritual objects, by these different kinds of persons, are in themselves vastly more diverse, than the different kinds of excellency perceived in delicious fruit, by a tasting and a tasteless man; and in another respect it may not be so great, viz. as the spiritual man may have a spiritual sense or taste, to perceive that divine and most peculiar excellency, but in small beginnings, and in a very imperfect degree.

2. On the other hand, it must be observed, that a natural man may have those religious apprehensions and affections, which may be in many respects very new and surprising to him, and what before he did not conceive of; and yet what he experiences be nothing like the exercises of a principle of new nature, or the sensations of a new spiritual sense: his affections may be very new, by extraordinarily moving natural principles, in a very new degree, and with a great many new circumstances, and a new cooperation of natural affections, and a new composition of ideas; this may be from some extraordinary powerful influence of Satan and some great delusion; but there is nothing but nature extraordinarily acted. As if a poor man, that had always dwelt in a cottage, and had never looked beyond the obscure village where he was born, should in a jest, be taken to a magnificent city and prince's court, and there arrayed in princely robes, and set in the throne, with the crown royal on his head, peers and nobles bowing before him, and should be made to believe that he was now a glorious monarch; the ideas he would have, and the affections he would experience, would in many respects be very new, and such as he had no imagination of before; but all is no more, than only extraordinarily raising and exciting natural principles, and newly exalting, varying and compounding such sort of ideas, as he has by nature; here is nothing like giving him a new sense.

Upon the whole, I think it is clearly manifest, that all truly gracious affections do arise from special and peculiar influences of the Spirit, working that sensible effect or sensation in the souls of the saints, which are entirely different from all that it is possible a natural man should experience, not only different in degree and circumstances, but different in its whole nature: so that a natural man not only cannot experience that which is individually the same, but can't experience anything but what is exceeding diverse, and immensely below it, in its kind; and that which the power of men or devils is not sufficient to produce the like of, or anything of the same nature.

I have insisted largely on this matter, because it is of great importance and use, evidently to discover and demonstrate the delusions of Satan, in many kinds of false religious affections, which multitudes are deluded by, and probably have been in all ages of the Christian church; and to settle and determine many articles of doctrine, concerning the operations of the Spirit of God, and the nature of true grace.

Now therefore, to apply these things to the purpose of this discourse.

From hence it appears that impressions which some have made on their imagination, or the imaginary ideas which they have of God, or Christ, or heaven, or anything appertaining to religion, have nothing in them that is spiritual, or of the nature of true grace. Though such things may attend what is spiritual, and be mixed with it, yet in themselves they have nothing that is spiritual, nor are they any part of gracious experience.

Here, for the sake of the common people, I will explain what is intended by impressions on the imagination, and imaginary ideas. The imagination is that power of the mind, whereby it can have a conception, or idea of things of an external or outward nature (that is, of such sort of things as are the objects of the outward senses), when those things are not present, and be not perceived by the senses. It is called imagination from the word "image"; because thereby a person can have an image of some external thing in his mind, when that thing is not present in reality, nor anything like it. All such kind of things as we perceive by our five external senses, seeing, hearing, smelling, tasting and feeling, are external things: and when a person has an idea, or image of any of these sorts of things in his mind, when they are not there, and when he don't really see, hear, smell, taste, nor feel them; that is to have an imagination of them, and these ideas are imaginary ideas: and when such kind of ideas are strongly impressed upon the mind, and the image of them in the mind is very lively, almost as if one saw them, or heard them, etc. that is called an impression on the imagination. Thus colors, and shapes, and a form of countenance, they are outward things; because they are that sort of things which are the objects of the outward sense of seeing: and therefore when any person has in his mind a lively idea of any shape, or color, or form of countenance; that is to have an imagination of those things. So if he has an idea of such sort of light or darkness, as he perceives by the sense of seeing; that is to have an idea of outward light, and so is an imagination. So if he has an idea of any marks made on paper, suppose letters and words written in a book; that is to have an external and imaginary idea of such kind of things as we sometimes perceive by our bodily eyes. And when we have the ideas of that kind of things which we perceive by any of the other senses, as of any sounds or voices, or words spoken; this is only to have ideas of outward things, viz. of such kind of things as are perceived by the external sense of hearing, and so that also is imagination: and when these ideas are livelily impressed, almost as if they were really heard with the ears, this is to have an impression on the imagination. And so I might go on, and instance in the ideas of things appertaining to the other three senses of smelling, tasting and feeling.

Many who have had such things have very ignorantly supposed them to be of the nature of spiritual discoveries. They have had lively ideas of some external shape, and beautiful form of countenance; and this they call spiritually seeing Christ. Some have had impressed upon them ideas of a great outward light; and this they call a spiritual discovery of God's or Christ's glory. Some have had ideas of Christ's hanging on the cross, and his blood running from his wounds; and this they call a spiritual sight of Christ crucified, and the way of salvation by his blood. Some have seen him with his arms open ready to embrace them; and this they call a discovery of the sufficiency of Christ's grace and love. Some have had lively ideas of heaven, and of Christ on his throne there, and shining ranks of saints and angels; and this they call seeing heaven opened to them. Some from time to time have had a lively idea of a person of a beautiful countenance smiling upon them; and this they call a spiritual discovery of the love of Christ to their souls, and tasting the love of Christ. And they look upon it as sufficient evidence that these things are spiritual discoveries, and that they see them spiritually, because they say they don't see these things with their bodily eyes, but in their hearts; for they can see them when their eyes are shut. And in like manner, the imaginations of some have been impressed with ideas of the sense of hearing; they have had ideas of words, as if they were spoke to them; sometimes they are the words of Scripture, and sometimes other words: they have had ideas of Christ's speaking comfortable words to them. These things they have called having the inward call of Christ, hearing the voice of Christ spiritually in their hearts, having the witness of the Spirit, and the inward testimony of the love of Christ, etc.

The common, and less considerate and understanding sort of people, are the more easily led into apprehensions that these things are spiritual things, because spiritual things being invisible, and not things that can be pointed forth with the finger, we are forced to use figurative expressions in speaking of them, and to borrow names from external and sensible objects to signify them by. Thus we call a clear apprehension of things spiritual by the name of light; and an having such an apprehension of such or such things, by the name of seeing such things; and the conviction of the judgment, and the persuasion of the will, by the word of Christ in the gospel, we signify by spiritually hearing the call of Christ: and the Scripture itself abounds with such like figurative expressions. Persons hearing these often used, and having pressed upon them the necessity of having their eyes opened, and having a discovery of spiritual things; and seeing Christ in his glory, and having the inward call, and the like, they ignorantly look and wait for some such external discoveries, and imaginary views as have been spoken of; and when they have them, are confident that now their eyes are opened, now Christ has discovered himself to them, and they are his children; and hence are exceedingly affected and elevated with their deliverance and happiness, and many kinds of affections are at once set in a violent motion in them.

But it is exceeding apparent that such ideas have nothing in them which is spiritual and divine, in the sense wherein it has been demonstrated that all gracious experiences are spiritual and divine. These external ideas are in no wise of such a sort, that they are entirely, and in their whole nature diverse from all that men have by nature, perfectly different from, and vastly above any sensation which 'tis possible a man should have by any natural sense or principle, so that in order to have them, a man must have a new spiritual and divine sense given him, in order to have any sensations of that sort: so far from this, that they are ideas of the same sort which we have by the external senses, that are some of the inferior powers of the humane nature; they are merely ideas of external objects, or ideas of that nature, of the same outward sensitive kind; the same sort of sensations of mind (differing not in degree, but only in circumstances) that we have by those natural principles which are common to us, with the beasts, viz. the five external senses. This is a low, miserable notion of spiritual sense, to suppose that 'tis only a conceiving or imagining that sort of ideas which we have by our animal senses, which senses the beasts have in as great perfection as we; it is, as it were, a turning Christ, or the divine nature in the soul, into a mere animal. There is nothing wanting in the soul, as it is by nature, to render it incapable of being the subject of all these external ideas, without any new principles. A natural man is capable of having an idea, and a lively idea of shapes and colors and sounds when they are absent, and as capable as a regenerate man is: so there is nothing supernatural in them. And 'tis known by abundant experience, that 'tis not the advancing or perfecting humane nature, which makes persons more capable of having such lively and strong imaginery ideas, but that on the contrary, the weakness of body and mind, and distempers of body, makes persons abundantly more susceptive of such impressions....

[*Second Sign*]

......

II. The first objective ground of gracious affections, is the transcendently excellent and amiable nature of divine things, as they are in themselves; and not any conceived relation they bear to self, or self-interest.

I say that the supremely excellent nature of divine things, is the first, or primary and original objective foundation of the spiritual affections of true saints; for I do not suppose that all relation which divine things bear to themselves, and their own particular interest, are wholly excluded from all influence in their gracious affections. For this may have, and indeed has, a secondary and consequential influence in those affections that are truly holy and spiritual; as I shall show how by and by.

It was before observed, that the affection of love is as it were the fountain of all affection; and particularly, that Christian love is the fountain of all gracious affections: now the divine excellency and glory of God, and Jesus Christ, the Word of God, the works of God, and the ways of God, etc. is the primary reason, why a true saint loves these things; and not any supposed interest that he has in them, or any conceived benefit that he has received from them, or shall receive from them, or any such imagined relation which they bear to his interest, that self-love can properly be said to be the first foundation of his love to these things.

Some say that all love arises from self-love; and that it is impossible in the nature of things, for any man to have any love to God, or any other being, but that love to himself must be the foundation of it. But I humbly suppose it is for want of consideration, that they say so. They argue, that whoever loves God, and so desires his glory, or the enjoyment of him, he desires these things as his own happiness; the glory of God, and the beholding and enjoying his perfections, are considered as things agreeable to him, tending to make him happy; he places his happiness in them, and desires them as things, which (if they were obtained) would be delightful to him, or would fill him with delight and joy, and so make him happy. And so, they say, it is from self-love, or a desire of his own happiness, that he desires God should be glorified, and desires to behold and enjoy his glorious perfections. But then they ought to consider a little further, and inquire how the man came to place his happiness in God's being glorified, and in contemplating and enjoying God's perfections. There is no doubt, but that after God's glory, and the beholding his perfections, are become so agreeable to him, that he places his highest happiness in these things, then he will desire them, as he desires his own happiness. But how came these things to be so agreeable to him, that he esteems it his highest happiness to glorify God, etc.? Is not this the fruit of love? A man must first love God, or have his heart united to him, before he will esteem God's good his own, and before he will desire the glorifying and enjoying of God, as his happiness. 'Tis not strong arguing, that because after a man has his heart united to God in love, as a fruit of this, he desires his glory and enjoyment as his own happiness, that therefore a desire of this happiness of his own, must needs be the cause and foundation of his love: unless it be strong arguing, that because a father begat a son, that therefore his son certainly begat him. If after a man loves God, and has his heart so united to him, as to look upon God as his chief good, and on God's good as his own, it will be a consequence and fruit of this, that even self-love, or love to his own happiness, will cause him to desire the glorifying and enjoying of God; it will not thence follow, that this very exercise of self-love, went before his love to God, and that his love to God was a consequence and fruit of that. Something else, entirely distinct from self-love might be the cause of this, viz. a change made in the views of his mind, and relish of his heart; whereby he apprehends a beauty, glory, and supreme good, in God's nature, as it is in itself. This may be the thing that first draws his heart to him, and causes his heart to be united to him, prior to all considerations of his own interest or happiness, although after this, and as a fruit of this, he necessarily seeks his interest and happiness in God.

There is such a thing, as a kind of love or affection, that a man may have towards persons or things, which does properly arise from self-love; a preconceived relation to himself, or some respect already manifested by another to him, or some benefit already received or depended on, is truly the first foundation of his love, and what his affection does wholly arise from; and is what precedes any relish of, or delight in the nature and qualities inherent in the being beloved, as beautiful and amiable. When the first thing that draws a man's benevolence to another, is the beholding those qualifications and properties in him, which appear to him lovely in themselves, and the subject of them, on this account, worthy of esteem and goodwill, love arises in a very different manner, than when it first arises from some gift bestowed by another, or depended on from him, as a judge loves and favors a man that has bribed him; or from the relation he supposes another has to him, as a man who loves another because he looks upon him as his child. When love to another arises thus, it does truly and properly arise from self-love.

That kind of affection to God or Jesus Christ, which does thus properly arise from self-love, cannot be a truly gracious and spiritual love; as appears from what has been said already: for self-love is a principle entirely natural, and as much in the hearts of devils as angels; and therefore surely nothing that is the mere result of it, can be supernatural and divine, in the manner before described. Christ plainly speaks of this kind of love, as what is nothing beyond the love of wicked men, Luke 6:32: "If ye love them that love you, what thank have ye? For sinners also love those that love them." And the devil himself knew that that kind of respect to God which was so mercenary, as to be only for benefits received or depended on (which is all one), is worthless in the sight of God; otherwise he never would have made use of such a slander before God, against Job, as in Job 1:9–10: "Doth Job serve God for nought? Hast thou not made an hedge about him, and about his house?" etc. Nor would God ever have implicitly allowed the objection to have been good, in case the accusation had been true, by allowing that that matter should be tried, and that Job should be so dealt with, that it might appear in the event, whether Job's respect to God was thus mercenary or no, and by putting the proof of the sincerity and goodness of his respect, upon that issue.

'Tis unreasonable to think otherwise, than that the first foundation of a true love to God, is that whereby he is in himself lovely, or worthy to be loved, or the supreme loveliness of his nature. This is certainly what makes him chiefly amiable. What chiefly makes a man, or any creature lovely, is his excellency, and so what chiefly renders God lovely, and must undoubtedly be the chief ground of true love, is his excellency. God's nature, or the divinity, is infinitely excellent; yea 'tis infinite beauty, brightness, and glory itself. But how can that be true love of this excellent and lovely nature, which is not built on the foundation of its true loveliness? How can that be true love of beauty and brightness, which is not for beauty and brightness' sake? How can that be a true prizing of that which is in itself infinitely worthy and precious, which is not for the sake of its worthiness and preciousness? This infinite excellency of the divine nature, as it is in itself, is the true ground of all that is good in God in any respect; but how can a man truly and rightly love God, without loving him for that excellency in him, which is the foundation of all that is in any manner of respect good or desirable in him? They whose affection to God is founded first on his profitableness to them, their affection begins at the wrong end; they regard God only for the utmost limit of the stream of divine good, where it touches them, and reaches their interest; and have no respect to that infinite glory of God's nature, which is the original good, and the true fountain of all good, the first fountain of all loveliness of every kind, and so the first foundation of all true love....

And as it is with the love of the saints, so it is with their joy, and spiritual delight and pleasure: the first foundation of it, is not any consideration or conception of their interest in divine things; but it primarily consists in the sweet entertainment their minds have in the view or contemplation of the divine and holy beauty of these things, as they are in themselves. And this is indeed the very main difference between the joy of the hypocrite, and the joy of the true saint. The former rejoices in himself, self is the first foundation of his joy: the latter rejoices in God. The hypocrite has his mind pleased and delighted, in the first place, with his own privilege, and the happiness which he supposes he has attained, or shall attain. True saints have their minds, in the first place, inexpressibly pleased and delighted with the sweet ideas of the glorious and amiable nature of the things of God. And this is the spring of all their delights, and the cream of all their pleasures; 'tis the joy of their joy. This sweet and ravishing entertainment, they have in the view of the beautiful and delightful nature of divine things, is the foundation of the joy that they have afterwards, in the consideration of their being theirs. But the dependence of the affections of hypocrites is in a contrary order: they first rejoice, and are elevated with it, that they are made so much of by God; and then on that ground, he seems in a sort, lovely to them.

The first foundation of the delight a true saint has in God, is his own perfection; and the first foundation of the delight he has in Christ, is his own beauty; he appears in himself the chief among ten thousand, and altogether lovely: the way of salvation by Christ, is a delightful way to him, for the sweet and admirable manifestations of the divine perfections in it; the holy doctrines of the gospel, by which God is exalted and man abased, holiness honored and promoted, and sin greatly disgraced and discouraged, and free and sovereign love manifested; are glorious doctrines in his eyes, and sweet to his taste, prior to any conception of his interest in these things. Indeed the saints rejoice in their interest in God, and that Christ is theirs; and so they have great reason; but this is not the first spring of their joy: they first rejoice in God as glorious and excellent in himself, and then secondarily rejoice in it, that so glorious a God is theirs: they first have their hearts filled with sweetness, from the view of Christ's excellency, and the excellency of his grace, and the beauty of the way of salvation by him; and then they have a secondary joy, in that so excellent a Saviour, and such excellent grace is theirs.

But that which is the true saint's superstructure, is the hypocrite's foundation. When they hear of the wonderful things of the gospel, of God's great love in sending his Son, of Christ's dying love to sinners, and the great things Christ has purchased, and promised to the saints, and hear these things livelily and eloquently set forth; they may hear with a great deal of pleasure, and be lifted up with what they hear: but if their joy be examined, it will be found to have no other foundation than this, that they look upon these things as theirs, all this exalts them, they love to hear of the great love of Christ so vastly distinguishing some from others; for self-love, and even pride itself, makes 'em affect great distinction from others: no wonder, in this confident opinion of their own good estate, that they feel well under such doctrine, and are pleased in the highest degree, in hearing how much God and Christ makes of 'em. So that their joy is really a joy in themselves, and not in God.

And because the joy of hypocrites is in themselves, hence it comes to pass, that in their rejoicings and elevations, they are wont to keep their eye upon themselves; having received what they call spiritual discoveries or experiences, their minds are taken up about them, admiring their own experiences: and what they are principally taken and elevated with, is not the glory of God, or beauty of Christ, but the beauty of their experiences. They keep thinking with themselves, what a good experience is this! What a great discovery is this! What wonderful things have I met with! And so they put their experiences in the place of Christ, and his beauty and fullness; and instead of rejoicing in Christ Jesus, they rejoice in their admirable experiences: instead of feeding and feasting their souls in the view of what is without them, viz. the innate, sweet, refreshing amiableness of the things exhibited in the gospel, their eyes are off from these things, or at least they view them only as it were sideways; but the object that fixes their contemplation, is their experience; and they are feeding their souls, and feasting a selfish principle with a view of their discoveries: they take more comfort in their discoveries than in Christ discovered, which is the true notion of living upon experiences and frames; and not using experiences as the signs, on which they rely for evidence of their good estate, which some call living on experiences: though it be very observable, that some of them who do so, are most notorious for living upon experiences, according to the true notion of it.

The affections of hypocrites are very often after this manner; they are first, much affected with some impression on their imagination, or some impulse, which they take to be an immediate suggestion, or testimony from God, of his love and their happiness, and high privilege in some respect, either with or without a text of Scripture; they are mightily taken with this, as a great discovery; and hence arise high affections. And when their affections are raised, then they view those high affections, and call them great and wonderful experiences; and they have a notion that God is greatly pleased with those affections; and this affects them more; and so they are affected with their affections. And thus their affections rise higher and higher, till they sometimes are perfectly swallowed up: and self-conceit, and a fierce zeal rises withal; and all is built like a castle in the air, on no other foundation but imagination, self-love and pride.

And as the thoughts of this sort of persons are, so is their talk; for out of the abundance of their heart, their mouth speaketh. As in their high affections, they keep their eye upon the beauty of their experiences and greatness of their attainments; so they are great talkers about themselves. The true saint, when under great spiritual affections, from the fullness of his heart, is ready to be speaking much of God, and his glorious perfections and works, and of the beauty and amiableness of Christ, and the glorious things of the gospel; but hypocrites, in their high affections, talk more of the discovery, than they do of the thing discovered; they are full of talk about the great things they have met with, the wonderful discoveries they have had, how sure they are of the love of God to them, how safe their condition is, and how they know they shall go to heaven, etc.

A true saint, when in the enjoyment of true discoveries of the sweet glory of God and Christ, has his mind too much captivated and engaged by what he views without himself, to stand at that time to view himself, and his own attainments: it would be a diversion and loss which he could not bear, to take his eye off from the ravishing object of his contemplation, to survey his own experience, and to spend time in thinking with himself, what an high attainment this is, and what a good story I now have to tell others. Nor does the pleasure and sweetness of his mind at that time, chiefly arise from the consideration of the safety of his state, or anything he has in view of his own qualifications, experiences, or circumstances; but from the divine and supreme beauty of what is the object of his direct view, without himself; which sweetly entertains, and strongly holds his mind.

As the love and joy of hypocrites, are all from the source of self-love; so it is with their other affections, their sorrow for sin, their humiliation and submission, their religious desires and zeal: everything is as it were paid for beforehand, in God's highly gratifying their self-love, and their lusts, by making so much of them, and exalting them so highly, as things are in their imagination. 'Tis easy for nature, as corrupt as it is, under a notion of being already some of the highest favorites of heaven, and having a God who does so protect 'em and favor 'em in their sins, to love this imaginary God that suits 'em so well, and to extol him, and submit to him, and to be fierce and zealous for him. The high affections of many are all built on the supposition of their being eminent saints. If that opinion which they have of themselves were taken away, if they thought they were some of the lower form of saints (though they should yet suppose themselves to be real saints), their high affections would fall to the ground. If they only saw a little of the sinfulness and vileness of their own hearts, and their deformity, in the midst of their best duties and their best affections, it would knock their affections on the head; because their affections are built upon self, therefore self-knowledge would destroy them. But as to truly gracious affections, they are built elsewhere: they have their foundation out of self, in God and Jesus Christ; and therefore a discovery of themselves, of their own deformity, and the meanness of their experiences, though it will purify their affections, yet it will not destroy them, but in some respects sweeten and heighten them.

Part Two

Republican Enlightenment

Introduction

That massive Western intellectual reorientation known as the Enlightenment that began to emerge in the middle of the seventeenth century rested principally on two revolutionary ideas: that it was possible to understand the universe through the use of human faculties and that such understanding could be put to use to make society more rational and humane. In America a moderate version of the first of these ideas gradually entered the intellectual mainstream with little overt opposition. By the second half of the eighteenth century, even many Calvinistic intellectuals found it fairly easy to square revelation with some form of experiential reason. Simultaneously, under the influence of rising hopes fueled by the American Revolution, an increasing number of secular-minded intellectuals readily embraced the second idea of enlightened social amelioration. Yet the fact remains that however politically liberal, by European standards the American Enlightenment was intellectually comparatively tame. Even its most worldly spokesmen, like Franklin and Jefferson, rarely felt the necessity of making a public issue of their dismissal of Christian revelation. Nor did any American Hume or Voltaire come forward to suggest the corrosive power of empirical reason on commonly held beliefs in objective truth or morality.

Such intellectual ubiquity and moderation have sometimes led European writers to assert that the American Enlightenment meant simple blandness. This is obviously false. On the contrary, a good argument can be made to suggest that what made Enlightenment intellectuals in America so intriguing, not to mention influential, was precisely their ingenuity in absorbing and refashioning powerful religious and political currents that later generations would consider quite alien to the Enlightenment faith in reason and experiment. In the area of morality, no enlightened American intellectual exhibited these dialectical traits in more multiform ways than Benjamin Franklin. It is therefore fitting that Part Two open with a selection from Franklin's legendary narrative of post-Puritan ethics. In this section of his *Autobiography,* he showed through the guise of one of the most luminous personas in American literature how it was possible to make out of one's life an experiment in the ways to psychic autonomy and upward mobility.

Implicit in Franklin's moral code was a liberal, entrepreneurial yet public service–minded social and political vision that would have a long life in American culture. More immediately, American political thought was shaped by a more stringent complex of ideas that eighteenth-century thinkers called republicanism. In its full-blown ideological form, it asserted that the health of a polity was, on one hand, dependent on "virtue"—or the self-sufficiency and public spiritedness of its citizens—and, on the other hand, threatened by "corruption" promoted by overweening executive "power" in league with its self-seeking, luxury-loving minions. This ideology was a luxuriant tree with many roots and branches. It was linked with the civic humanism of ancient Greek and Roman authors as revived by Renaissance, Puritan Commonwealth, and

English parliamentary reform writers. In the American colonies it intertwined itself with Puritan and evangelical notions of the covenanted and benevolent faithful marching against the Antichrist in step with God's millennial scheme. Moreover, in the circumstances of the British-American colonial conflict, it gave lurid meaning to British encroachments. But in the hands of Revolutionary Enlightenment intellectuals, republicanism received a secular and to some extent liberal reshaping. This intellectual reconfiguration is well displayed in the three great Revolutionary texts presented here. In his *Dissertation on the Canon and the Feudal Law,* John Adams argued that it was knowledge and understanding that animated the New England form of liberty and power, whereas ignorance and superstition fueled their feudal and, by implication, partly British form. Likewise, Thomas Paine and Thomas Jefferson based their republican prescriptions for (in Paine's case) a monarchless state and (in Jefferson's) revolution on rationally agreed on "common sense" and "self-evident truths."

Historically, of course, the most important unadulterated political fruit of enlightened republicanism was the Constitution, whose intellectual complexity came out dramatically in the contentious debate over its ratification. After four years of post-Revolutionary political conflicts and rising fears for the security of the republic, political intellectuals were forced to contend with the greatest difficulty of a modern republican polity—how to reconcile conflicts of interest so that public virtue would remain intact. In addressing this problem, different thinkers arrived at sometimes very different conclusions. In his speech to the Constitutional Convention, Alexander Hamilton urgently presented his reasons for believing that only a centralized authoritative republican system would be sufficiently united and energetic to protect the national government from self-seeking interests and promote the Republic's welfare. Anti-Federalist opponents of the Constitution, such as "Brutus," on the other hand, argued just as forcefully after the Convention that the adopted document's plan of distantly representative bodies and partially mixed governmental authorities, together with its lack of explicit guarantees of citizens' individual rights, all betrayed the Revolution's ideal of resistance to excessive—and therefore virtue-corrupting—concentrations of power. By contrast, in the *Federalist* numbers 10 and 51, James Madison, the Constitution's leading architect, constructed a dynamically symmetrical representation of the new federal state that would be so extended and divided as to nurture a social pluralism and a popularly elected governing class that would work together to control liberty's vices. No greater monument to the American enlightened mind was produced than this passionately dispassionate discourse over the best rational model for the preservation of a virtuous republic.

The arguments over the ratification of the Constitution were part of a wider intellectual problem much debated in recent years by historians: the contradictory post-Revolutionary legacy of American republicanism. Most resonant perhaps today, the Revolution's proclamation of the rationality, equality, and opportunity of individuals naturally raised in the minds of many post-Revolutionary thinkers, if only mostly theoretically and temporarily, the issues of slavery and the subordination of women. In her essay "On the Equality of the Sexes," Judith Sargent Murray presented an especially compelling republican Enlightenment case for women's intellectual and (to a certain extent social and political) equality with men. But probably the most revealing entry into the ambiguities of post-Revolutionary republicanism may be found in a sampling of the writings of America's two great republican intellectuals, John Adams and Thomas Jefferson. In his letters to Samuel Adams and Jefferson,

John Adams earnestly pleaded his reasons for thinking that liberty was both nurtured and threatened by the people and aristocracies, advancing as a solution a republicanized version of a mixed government resting on different social orders. Jefferson, on the other hand, in the selection from his *Notes on the State of Virginia* and in his letter to John Adams, presented a contrasting case for a more egalitarian polity, although one that also admitted, on both Enlightenment and republican grounds, its own kind of noblesse oblige. Because much of what was nobly liberal about Jefferson and, to a lesser extent, John Adams, derived from their ethical and religious outlooks, three letters on those subjects round out these conversations of the American Enlightenment's polar souls. Finally, as Jefferson's tortured attempt in *Notes* to square the Enlightenment ideals that nurtured his antislavery sentiments with a science-based claim for the intellectual inferiority of blacks was most famously challenged by the Princeton president Samuel Stanhope Smith in his *Essay on the Causes of the Variety of Complexion and Figure in the Human Species,* an excerpt from this monument to the outer edges of Enlightenment liberalism concludes Part Two.

Recommendations for Further Reading

Alan Heimert, *Religion and the American Mind: From the Great Awakening to the Revolution* (Cambridge, Mass., 1966); Bernard Bailyn, *The Ideological Origins of the American Revolution* (Cambridge, Mass., 1967); Gordon S. Wood, *The Creation of the American Republic, 1776–1787* (Chapel Hill, 1969); J.G.A. Pocock, *The Machiavellian Moment: Florentine Political Thought and the Atlantic Republican Tradition* (Princeton, 1975): Henry F. May, *The Enlightenment in America* (New York, 1976); Donald H. Meyer, *The Democratic Enlightenment* (New York, 1976); Philip Greven, *The Protestant Temperament: Patterns of Child Rearing, Religious Experience and the Self in Early America* (New York, 1977); Linda K. Kerber, *Women of the Republic: Intellect and Ideology in Revolutionary America* (Chapel Hill,1980); Drew R. McCoy, *The Elusive Republic*: *Political Economy in Jeffersonian America* (Chapel Hill, 1980); Jay Fliegelman, *Prodigals and Pilgrims*: *The American Revolution Against Patriarchal Authority, 1750–1800* (Cambridge, 1982); Jan Lewis, *The Pursuit of Happiness: Family and Values in Jefferson's Virginia* (Cambridge, 1983); Ruth H. Bloch, *Visionary Republic: Millennial Themes in American Thought, 1756–1800* (Cambridge, 1985); Forrest McDonald, *Novus Ordo Seclorum: The Intellectual Origins of the Constitution* (Lawrence, Kans., 1985); Edmund S. Morgan, *Inventing the People The Rise of Popular Sovereignty in England and America* (New York, 1988); Mark A. Noll, *Princeton and the Republic, 1768–1822: The Search for a Christian Enlightenment in the Era of Samuel Stanhope Smith* (Princeton, 1989); Henry F. May, *The Divided Heart: Essays on Protestantism and the Enlightenment in America* (New York, 1991); Joyce Appleby, *Liberalism and Republicanism in the Historical Imagination* (Cambridge, Mass., 1992); Carl J. Richard, *The Founders and the Classics: Greece, Rome, and the American Enlightenment* (Cambridge, Mass., 1994); Barry Alan Shain, *The Myth of American Individualism: The Protestant Origins of American Political Thought* (Princeton, 1994); Jerome Huyler, *Locke in America*: *The Moral Philosophy of the Founding Era* (Lawrence, Kans., 1995); Jack N. Rakove, *Original Meanings*: *Politics and Ideas in the Making of the Constitution* (New York, 1996); Robert A. Ferguson, *The American Enlightenment, 1750–1820* (Cambridge, Mass., 1997); Ned C. Landsman, *From Colonials to Provincials: American Thought and Culture, 1680–1760* (New York, 1997); David S. Shields, *Civil Tongues and Polite Letters in British America* (Chapel Hill, 1997); Rogers M. Smith, *Civic Ideals: Conflicting Visions of Citizenship in U.S. History* (New Haven, 1997); Christopher Grasso, *A Speaking Aristocracy: Transforming Public Discourse in Eighteenth-Century Connecticut* (Chapel Hill, 1999); Leigh Eric Schmidt, *Hearing Things: Religion, Illusions, and the American Enlightenment* (Cambridge, Mass., 2000); Jonathan D. Sassi, *A Republic of Righteousness: The Public Christianity of the Post-Revolutionary New England Clergy* (New York, 2001);

J. David Hoeveler, *Creating the American Mind: Intellect and Politics in the Colonial Colleges* (Lanham, Md., 2002); Caroline Winterer, *The Culture of Classicism: Ancient Greece and Rome in American Intellectual Life, 1780–1910* (Baltimore, 2002); Ruth H. Bloch, *Gender and Morality in Anglo-American Culture, 1650–1800* (Berkeley, 2003); Holly Brewer, *By Birth or Consent: Children, Law, and the Anglo-American Revolution in Authority* (Chapel Hill, 2005); Chris Beneke, *Beyond Toleration: The Religious Origins of American Pluralism* (New York, 2006); James Delbourgo, *A Most Amazing Scene of Wonders: Electricity and Enlightenment in Early America* (Cambridge, Mass., 2006); Catherine Kerrison, *Claiming the Pen: Women and Intellectual Life in the Early American South* (Ithaca, 2006); Caroline Winterer, *The Mirror of Antiquity: American Women and the Classical Tradition, 1750–1810* (Ithaca, 2007); Nicole Eustace, *Passion Is the Gale: Emotion Power and the Coming of the American Revolution* (Chapel Hill, 2008); Catherine O'Donnell Kaplan, *Men of Letters in the Early Republic: Cultivating Forums of Citizenship* (Chapel Hill, 2008); Sarah Knott, *Sensibility and the American Revolution* (Chapel Hill, 2009); Eric Slauter, *The State as a Work of Art: The Cultural Origins of the Constitution* (Chicago, 2009); Alison L. LaCroix, *The Ideological Origins of American Federalism* (Cambridge, Mass., 2010); Jonathan Israel, *A Revolution of the Mind: Radical Enlightenment and the Intellectual Origins of Modern Democracy* (Princeton, 2010); Raúl Coronado, *A World Not to Come: A History of Latino Writing and Print Culture* (Cambridge, Mass., 2013); Eric Nelson, *The Royalist Revolution: Monarchy and the American Founding* (Cambridge, Mass., 2014).

BENJAMIN FRANKLIN

Selection from *The Autobiography*
(1784–88)

Scientist, businessman, statesman, journalist, diplomat, man of letters, and international celebrity, Benjamin Franklin (1706–1790) was the American Enlightenment's Proteus. In none of these roles, however, did Franklin achieve as much popular influence as in his ethical writings, and of these none was more important than his *Autobiography*. Here one can see in its fully nuanced complexity—as one cannot in his set pieces or cleverly sententious maxims—his essential message: Virtue is or should be both a code and an expression of life. In the selections that follow, written, like most of his memoir, in the last years of his life, Franklin advanced a large assortment of virtues drawn from a host of ancient and modern Western traditions, although he placed particular emphasis on the "Puritan" values of frugality, temperance, and industry. The means and ends of these virtues, of course, were quite un-Puritan. Not scrupulous introspection, but the alteration of habit was the way to virtue. Likewise, not holiness but human happiness—defined primarily as a condition of independence, self-control, and the power to promote the public welfare, and to be *seen* as such—appeared as, if not the highest, at least a perfectly sufficient goal. And throughout Franklin maintained a tone of warm but ironic appreciation of the self of his narrative, suggesting to the reader that this Franklin was perhaps every man or woman as *"Free and Easy"* as himself.

J. A. Leo Lemay's projected seven-volume *The Life of Benjamin Franklin*, 3 vols. (Philadelphia, 2006–), is an exhaustive biography. Alan Houston, *Benjamin Franklin and the Politics of Improvement* (New Haven, 2008), places the concept of improvement at the center of Franklin's social and political thought. For an interesting discussion of Franklin's project to create an exemplary self, see Mitchell Robert Breitwieser, *Cotton Mather and Benjamin Franklin: The Price of Representative Personality* (Cambridge, 1984), 171–305. For appraisals of Franklin's religion, see Alfred Owen Aldridge, *Benjamin Franklin and Nature's God* (Durham, N.C., 1967); and Kerry S. Walters, *Benjamin Franklin and His Gods* (Urbana, 1999). Joyce E. Chaplin, *The First Scientific American: Benjamin Franklin and the Pursuit of Genius* (New York, 2006), is a solid study of the connections between Franklin's scientific work and his multiform public life in a transatlantic setting. Sophus A. Reinert, "*The Way to Wealth* around the World: Benjamin Franklin and the Globalization of American Capitalism," *American Historical Review*, 120 (Feb. 2015), 61–97, provides a fresh look at Franklin's most popular text, its massive dissemination, and the misreadings of his economic philosophy encouraged by its aphoristic conceits.

Continuation of the Account of my Life. Begun at Passy, 1784.

It is some time since I receiv'd the...Letters, but I have been too busy till now to think of complying with the Request they contain. It might too be much better done if I were at home among my Papers, which would aid my Memory, and help to ascertain Dates. But my Return being uncertain, and having just now a little Leisure, I will endeavour to recollect and write what I can; if I live to get home, it may there be corrected and improv'd.

Not having any Copy here of what is already written, I know not whether an Account is given of the means I used to establish the Philadelphia Public Library, which from a small Beginning is now become so considerable, though I remember to have come down to near the Time of that Transaction, 1730. I will therefore begin here, with an Account of it, which may be struck out if found to have been already given.

At the time I establish'd myself in Pennsylvania, there was not a good Bookseller's Shop in any of the Colonies to the Southward of Boston. In New York and Philadelphia the Printers were indeed Stationers, they sold only Paper, etc., Almanacs, Ballads, and a few common School Books. Those who lov'd Reading were oblig'd to send for their Books from England. The Members of the Junto had each a few. We had left the Ale-house where we first met, and hired a Room to hold our Club in. I propos'd that we should all of us bring our Books to that Room, where they would not only be ready to consult in our Conferences, but become a common Benefit, each of us being at Liberty to borrow such as he wish'd to read at home. This was accordingly done, and for some time contented us. Finding the Advantage of this little Collection, I propos'd to render the Benefit from Books more common by commencing a Public Subscription Library. I drew a Sketch of the Plan and Rules that would be necessary, and got a skillful Conveyancer Mr. Charles Brockden to put the whole in Form of Articles of Agreement to be subscribed, by which each Subscriber engag'd to pay a certain Sum down for the first Purchase of Books and an annual Contribution for increasing them. So few were the Readers at that time in Philadelphia, and the Majority of us so poor, that I was not able with great Industry to find more than Fifty Persons, mostly young Tradesmen, willing to pay down for this purpose Forty shillings each, and Ten Shillings per Annum. On this little Fund we began. The Books were imported. The Library was open one Day in the Week for lending them to the Subscribers, on their Promissory Notes to pay Double the Value if not duly returned. The Institution soon manifested its Utility, was imitated by other Towns and in other Provinces, the Libraries were augmented by Donations, Reading became fashionable, and our People having no public Amusements to divert their Attention from Study became better acquainted with Books, and in a few Years were observ'd by Strangers to be better instructed and more intelligent than People of the same Rank generally are in other Countries.

When we were about to sign the above-mentioned Articles, which were to be binding on us, our Heirs, etc. for fifty Years, Mr. Brockden, the Scrivener, said to us, "You are young Men, but it is scarce probable that any of you will live to see the Expiration of the Term fix'd in this Instrument." A Number of us, however, are yet living. But the Instrument was after a few Years rendered null by a Charter that incorporated and gave Perpetuity to the Company.

Source: *Benjamin Franklin's Autobiography: An Authoritative Text, Backgrounds, Criticism*, ed. J. A. Leo Lemay and P. M. Zall (New York: W. W. Norton & Co., 1986), 62–79. Editors' notes altered. Reprinted by permission of W. W. Norton & Company, Inc., Copyright © 1986.

The Objections, and Reluctances I met with in Soliciting the Subscriptions, made me soon feel the Impropriety of presenting oneself as the Proposer of any useful Project that might be suppos'd to raise one's Reputation in the smallest degree above that of one's Neighbors, when one has need of their Assistance to accomplish that Project. I therefore put myself as much as I could out of sight, and stated it as a Scheme of *a Number of Friends,* who had requested me to go about and propose it to such as they thought Lovers of Reading. In this way my Affair went on more smoothly, and I ever after practic'd it on such Occasions; and from my frequent Successes, can heartily recommend it. The present little Sacrifice of your Vanity will afterwards be amply repaid. If it remains a while uncertain to whom the Merit belongs, someone more vain than yourself will be encourag'd to claim it, and then even Envy will be dispos'd to do you Justice, by plucking those assum'd Feathers, and restoring them to their right Owner.

This Library afforded me the Means of Improvement by constant Study, for which I set apart an Hour or two each Day; and thus repair'd in some Degree the Loss of the Learned Education my Father once intended for me. Reading was the only Amusement I allow'd myself. I spent no time in Taverns, Games, or Frolics of any kind. And my Industry in my Business continu'd as indefatigable as it was necessary. I was in debt for my Printing-House, I had a young Family coming on to be educated, and I had to contend with for Business two Printers who were establish'd in the Place before me. My Circumstances however grew daily easier: my original Habits of Frugality continuing. And My Father having among his Instructions to me when a Boy, frequently repeated a Proverb of Solomon, *"Seest thou a Man diligent in his Calling, he shall stand before Kings, he shall not stand before mean Men."* I from thence consider'd Industry as a Means of obtaining Wealth and Distinction, which encourag'd me: tho' I did not think that I should very literally stand before Kings, which however has since happened; for I have stood before five, and even had the honor of sitting down with one, the King of Denmark, to Dinner.

We have an English Proverb that says,

> He that would thrive
> Must ask his Wife,

it was lucky for me that I had one as much dispos'd to Industry and Frugality as myself. She assisted me cheerfully in my Business, folding and stitching Pamphlets, tending Shop, purchasing old Linen Rags for the Paper-makers, etc., etc. We kept no idle Servants, our Table was plain and simple, our Furniture of the cheapest. For instance my Breakfast was a long time Bread and Milk, (no Tea,) and I ate it out of a twopenny earthen Porringer with a Pewter Spoon. But mark how Luxury will enter Families, and make a Progress, in Spite of Principle. Being Call'd one Morning to Breakfast, I found it in a China Bowl with a Spoon of Silver. They had been bought for me without my Knowledge by my Wife, and had cost her the enormous Sum of three and twenty Shillings, for which she had no other Excuse or Apology to make, but that she thought *her* Husband deserv'd a Silver Spoon and China Bowl as well as any of his Neighbors. This was the first Appearance of Plate and China in our House, which afterwards in a Course of Years as our Wealth increas'd, augmented gradually to several Hundred Pounds in Value.

I had been religiously educated as a Presbyterian; and tho' some of the Dogmas of that Persuasion, such as the Eternal Decrees of God, Election, Reprobation, etc. appear'd to me unintelligible, others doubtful, and I early absented myself from the Public Assemblies of the Sect, Sunday being my Studying-Day, I never was without some religious Principles; I never doubted, for instance, the Existence of the Deity, that he made the World, and govern'd it by his Providence; that the most acceptable Service of God was the doing Good to Man; that our Souls are immortal; and that all Crime will be punished and Virtue rewarded either here or hereafter; these I esteem'd the Essentials of every Religion, and being to be found in all the Religions we had in our Country I respected them all, tho' with different degrees of Respect as I found them more or less mix'd with other Articles which without any Tendency to inspire, promote or confirm Morality, serv'd principally to divide us and make us unfriendly to one another. This Respect to all, with an Opinion that the worst had some good Effects, induc'd me to avoid all Discourse that might tend to lessen the good Opinion another might have of his own Religion; and as our Province increas'd in People and new Places of worship were continually wanted, and generally erected by voluntary Contribution, my Mite for such purpose, whatever might be the Sect, was never refused.

Tho' I seldom attended any Public Worship, I had still an Opinion of its Propriety, and of its Utility when rightly conducted, and I regularly paid my annual Subscription for the Support of the only Presbyterian Minister or Meeting we had in Philadelphia. He us'd to visit me sometimes as a Friend, and admonish me to attend his Administrations, and I was now and then prevail'd on to do so, once for five Sundays successively. Had he been, *in my Opinion,* a good Preacher perhaps I might have continued, notwithstanding the occasion I had for the Sunday's Leisure in my Course of Study: But his Discourses were chiefly either polemic Arguments, or Explications of the peculiar Doctrines of our Sect, and were all to me very dry, uninteresting and unedifying, since not a single moral Principle was inculcated or enforc'd, their Aim seeming to be rather to make us Presbyterians than good Citizens. At length he took for his Text that Verse of the 4th Chapter of Philippians, *Finally, Brethren, Whatsoever Things are true, honest, just, pure, lovely, or of good report, if there be any virtue, or any praise, think on these Things*; and I imagin'd in a Sermon on such a Text, we could not miss of having some Morality: But he confin'd himself to five Points only as meant by the Aposde, viz. 1. Keeping holy the Sabbath Day. 2. Being diligent in Reading the Holy Scriptures. 3. Attending duly the Public Worship. 4. Partaking of the Sacrament. 5. Paying a due Respect to God's Ministers.—These might be all good Things, but as they were not the kind of good Things that I expected from that Text, I despaired of ever meeting with them from any other, was disgusted, and attended his Preaching no more. I had some Years before compos'd a little Liturgy or Form of Prayer for my own private Use, viz, in 1728, entitled, *Articles of Belief and Acts of Religion.* I return'd to the Use of this, and went no more to the public Assemblies. My Conduct might be blameable, but I leave it without attempting farther to excuse it, my present purpose being to relate Facts, and not to make Apologies for them.

It was about this time that I conceiv'd the bold and arduous Project of arriving at moral Perfection. I wish'd to live without committing any Fault at anytime; I would conquer all that either Natural Inclination, Custom, or Company might lead me into. As I knew, or thought I knew, what was right and wrong, I did not see why I might not *always* do the one and avoid the other. But I soon found I had undertaken a Task of more Difficulty than I had imagined: While my Care was employ'd in guarding against one Fault, I was often supris'd by another. Habit took the Advantage of Inattention. Inclination was sometimes too strong for Reason. I concluded at length, that the mere speculative Conviction that it was our Interest to be completely virtuous, was not sufficient to prevent our Slipping, and that the contrary Habits must be broken and good Ones acquired and established, before we can have any Dependence on a steady uniform Rectitude of Conduct. For this purpose I therefore contriv'd the following Method.

In the various Enumerations of the moral Virtues I had met with in my Reading, I found the Catalogue more or less numerous, as different Writers included more or fewer Ideas under the same Name. Temperance, for Example, was by some confin'd to Eating and Drinking, while by others it was extended to mean the moderating every other Pleasure, Appetite, Inclination or Passion, bodily or mental, even to our Avarice and Ambition. I propos'd to myself, for the sake of Clearness, to use rather more Names with fewer Ideas annex'd to each, than a few Names with more Ideas; and I included after Thirteen Names of Virtues all that at that time occurr'd to me as necessary or desirable, and annex'd to each a short Precept, which fully express'd the Extent I gave to its Meaning.

These Names of Virtues with their Precepts were

1. TEMPERANCE.

Eat not to Dulness. Drink not to Elevation.

2. SILENCE.

Speak not but what may benefit others or your self. Avoiding trifling Conversation.

3. ORDER.

Let all your Things have their Places. Let each Part of your Business have its Time.

4. RESOLUTION.

Resolve to perform what you ought. Perform without fail what you resolve.

5. FRUGALITY.

Make no Expense but to do good to others or yourself: i.e. Waste nothing.

6. INDUSTRY.

Lose no Time. Be always employ'd in something useful. Cut off all unnecessary Actions.

7. SINCERITY.

Use no hurtful Deceit. Think innocently and justly; and, if you speak, speak accordingly.

8. JUSTICE.

Wrong none, by doing Injuries or omitting the Benefits that are your Duty.

9. MODERATION.

Avoid Extremes. Forbear resenting Injuries so much as you think they deserve.

10. CLEANLINESS.

Tolerate no Uncleanness in Body, Clothes or Habitation.

11. TRANQUILITY.

Be not disturbed at Trifles, or at Accidents common or unavoidable.

12. CHASTITY.

Rarely use Venery but for Health or Offspring; Never to Dulness, Weakness, or the Injury of your own or another's Peace or Reputation.

13. HUMILITY.

Imitate Jesus and Socrates.

My intention being to acquire the *Habitude* of all these Virtues, I judg'd it would be well not to distract my Attention by attempting the whole at once, but to fix it on one of them at a time, and when I should be Master of that, then to proceed to another, and so on till I should have gone thro' the thirteen. And as the previous Acquisition of some might facilitate the Acquisition of certain others, I arrang'd them with that View as they stand above. *Temperance* first, as it tends to procure that Coolness and Clearness of Head, which is so necessary where constant Vigilance was to be kept up, and Guard maintained, against the unremitting Attraction of ancient Habits, and the Force of perpetual Temptations. This being acquir'd and establish'd, *Silence* would be more easy, and my Desire being to gain Knowledge at the same time that I improv'd in Virtue, and considering that in Conversation it was obtain'd rather by the Use of the Ears than of the Tongue, and therefore wishing to break a Habit I was getting into of Prattling, Punning and Joking, which only made me acceptable to trifling Company, I gave *Silence* the second Place. This, and the next, *Order,* I expected would allow me more Time for attending to my Project and my Studies; RESOLUTION once become habitual, would keep me firm in my Endeavours to obtain all the subsequent Virtues; *Frugality* and *Industry,* by freeing me from my remaining Debt, and producing Affluence and Independence would make more easy the Practice of *Sincerity* and *Justice,* etc. etc. Conceiving then that agreeable to the Advice of Pythagoras in his Golden Verses, daily Examination would be necessary, I contriv'd the following Method for conducting that Examination.

I made a little Book in which I alloted a Page for each of the Virtues, I rul'd each Page with red Ink so as to have seven Columns, one for each Day of the Week, marking each Column with a Letter for the Day. I cross'd these Columns with thirteen red Lines, marking the Beginning of each Line with the first Letter of one of the Virtues, on which Line and in its proper Column I might mark by a little black Spot every Fault I found upon Examination, to have been committed respecting that Virtue upon that Day.

I determined to give a Week's strict Attention to each of the Virtues successively. Thus in the first Week my great Guard was to avoid every the least Offence against Temperance, leaving the other Virtues to their ordinary Chance, only marking every Evening the Faults of the Day. Thus if in the first Week I could keep my first Line marked T clear of Spots, I suppos'd the Habit of that Virtue so much strengthen'd and its opposite weaken'd, that I might venture extending my Attention to include the next, and for the following Week keep both Lines clear of Sports. Proceeding thus to the last, I could go thro' a Course complete in Thirteen Weeks, and four Courses in a Year. And like him who having a Garden to weed, does not attempt to eradicate all the bad Herbs at once, which would exceed his Reach and his Strength, but works on one of the Beds at a time, and having accomplish'd the first proceeds to a second; so I should have, (I hoped) the encouraging Pleasure of seeing on my Pages the Progress I made in Virtue, by clearing successively my Lines of their Spots, till in the End by a Number of Courses, I should be happy in viewing a clean Book after a thirteen Weeks' daily Examination.

This my little Book had for its Motto these Lines from *Addison's Cato,*

> Here will I hold: If there is a Pow'r above us,
> (And that there is, all Nature cries aloud
> Thro' all her Works) he must delight in Virtue,
> And that which he delights in must be happy.

Another from *Cicero.*

O Vitæ Philosophia Dux! O Virtutum indagatrix, expultrixque vitiorum! Unus dies bene, et ex preceptis tuis actus, peccanti immortalitati est anteponendus.[1]

Another from the Proverbs of Solomon speaking of Wisdom or Virtue;

Length of Days is in her right hand, and in her Left Hand Riches and Honors; Her Ways are Ways of Pleasantness, and all her Paths are Peace.

III, 16, 17

	S	M	T	W	T	F	S
T							
S	●	●	●		●	●	
O	●	●	●		●	●	●
R			●			●	
F		●			●		
I			●				
S							
J							
M							
Cl.							
T							
Ch							
H							

TEMPERANCE.

Eat not to Dulness.
Drink not to Elevation.

1. "O, Philosophy, guide of life! O teacher of virtue and corrector of vice. One day of virtue is better than an eternity of vice."

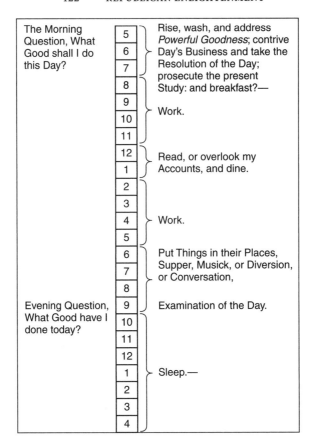

The Morning Question, What Good shall I do this Day?	5	Rise, wash, and address *Powerful Goodness*; contrive Day's Business and take the Resolution of the Day; prosecute the present Study: and breakfast?—
	6	
	7	
	8	
	9	Work.
	10	
	11	
	12	Read, or overlook my Accounts, and dine.
	1	
	2	Work.
	3	
	4	
	5	
	6	Put Things in their Places, Supper, Musick, or Diversion, or Conversation,
	7	
	8	
Evening Question, What Good have I done today?	9	Examination of the Day.
	10	Sleep.—
	11	
	12	
	1	
	2	
	3	
	4	

And conceiving God to be the Fountain of Wisdom, I thought it right and necessary to solicit his Assistance for obtaining it; to this End I form'd the following little Prayer, which was prefix'd to my Tables of Examination, for daily Use.

O Powerful Goodness! bountiful Father! merciful Guide! Increase in me that Wisdom which discovers my truest Interests; Strengthen my Resolutions to perform what that Wisdom dictates. Accept my kind Offices to thy other Children, as the only Return in my Power for thy continual Favors to me.

I us'd also sometimes a little Prayer which I took from *Thomson's* Poems, viz.

> Father of Light and Life, thou Good supreme,
> O teach me what is good, teach me thy self!
> Save me from Folly, Vanity and Vice,
> From every low Pursuit, and fill my Soul
> With Knowledge, conscious Peace, and Virtue pure,
> Sacred, substantial, neverfading Bliss!

The Precept of *Order* requiring that *every Part of my Business should have its allotted Time,* one Page in my little Book contain'd the following Scheme of Employment for the Twenty-four Hours of a natural Day.

I enter'd upon the Execution of this Plan for Self-examination, and continu'd it with occasional Intermissions for some time. I was surpris'd to find myself so much fuller of

Faults than I had imagined, but I had the Satisfaction of seeing them diminish. To avoid the Trouble of renewing now and then my little Book, which by scraping out the Marks on the Paper of old Faults to make room for new Ones in a new Course, became full of Holes: I transferr'd my Tables and Precepts to the Ivory Leaves of a Memorandum Book, on which the Lines were drawn with red Ink that made a durable Stain, and on those Lines I mark'd my Faults with a black Lead Pencil, which Marks I could easily wipe out with a wet Sponge. After a while I went thro' one Course only in a Year, and afterwards only one in several Years; till at length I omitted them entirely, being employ'd in Voyages and Business abroad with a Multiplicity of Affairs, that interfered. But I always carried my little Book with me.

My Scheme of ORDER, gave me the most Trouble, and I found, that tho' it might be practicable where a Man's Business was such as to leave him the Disposition of his Time, that of a Journeyman Printer for instance, it was not possible to be exactly observ'd by a Master, who must mix with the World, and often receive People of Business at their own Hours. *Order* too, with regard to Places for Things, Papers, etc. I found extremely difficult to acquire. I had not been early accustomed to it, and having an exceeding good Memory, I was not so sensible of the Inconvenience attending Want of Method. This Article therefore cost me so much painful Attention and my Faults in it vex'd me so much, and I made so little Progress in Amendment, and had such frequent Relapses, that I was almost ready to give up the Attempt, and content myself with a faulty Character in that respect. Like the Man who in buying an Axe of a Smith my Neighbor, desired to have the whole of its Surface as bright as the Edge; the Smith consented to grind it bright for him if he would turn the Wheel. He turn'd while the Smith press'd the broad Face of the Axe hard and heavily on the Stone, which made the Turning of it very fatiguing. The Man came every now and then from the Wheel to see how the Work went on; and at length would take his Axe as it was without farther Grinding. No, says the Smith, Turn on, turn on; we shall have it bright by and by; as yet 'tis only speckled. Yes, says the Man; but—*I think I like a speckled Axe best.*—And I believe this may have been the Case with many who having for want of some such Means as I employ'd found the Difficulty of obtaining good, and breaking bad Habits, in other Points of Vice and Virtue, have given up the Struggle, and concluded that *a speckled Axe was best.* For something that pretended to be Reason was every now and then suggesting to me, that such extreme Nicety as I exacted of myself might be a kind of Foppery in Morals, which if it were known would make me ridiculous; that a perfect Character might be attended with the Inconvenience of being envied and hated; and that a benevolent Man should allow a few Faults in himself, to keep his Friends in Countenance.

In Truth I found myself incorrigible with respect to *Order;* and now I am grown old, and my Memory bad, I feel very sensibly the want of it. But on the whole, tho' I never arrived at the Perfection I had been so ambitious of obtaining, but fell far short of it, yet I was by the Endeavour made a better and a happier Man than I otherwise should have been, if I had not attempted it; As those who aim at perfect Writing by imitating the engraved Copies, tho' they never reach the wish'd for Excellence of those Copies, their Hand is mended by the Endeavour, and is tolerable while it continues fair and legible.

And it may be well my Posterity should be informed, that to this little Artifice, with the Blessing of God, their Ancestor ow'd the constant Felicity of his Life down to his 79th Year in which this is written. What Reverses may attend the Remainder is in the Hand of Providence: But if they arrive, the Reflection on past Happiness enjoy'd ought to help his Bearing them with more Resignation. To *Temperance* he ascribes his long-continu'd Health, and what is still left to him of a good Constitution. To *Industry* and *Frugality* the early Easiness of his Circumstances, and Acquisition of his Fortune, with all that Knowledge which enabled him to be an useful Citizen, and obtain'd for him some Degree of Reputation among the Learned. To *Sincerity* and *Justice* the Confidence of his Country, and the honorable Employs it conferr'd upon him. And to the joint Influence of the whole Mass of the Virtues, even in their imperfect State he was able to acquire them, all that Evenness of Temper, and that Cheerfulness in Conversation which makes his Company still sought for, and aggreeable even to his younger Acquaintance. I hope therefore that some of my Descendants may follow the Example and reap the Benefit.

It will be remark'd that, tho' my Scheme was not wholly without Religion there was in it no Mark of any of the distinguishing Tenets of any particular Sect. I had purposely avoided them; for being fully persuaded of the Utility and Excellency of my Method, and that it might be serviceable to People in all Religions, and intending some time or other to publish it, I would not have anything in it that should prejudice anyone of any Sect against it. I purposed writing a little Comment on each Virtue, in which I would have shown the Advantages of possessing it,[2] and the Mischiefs attending its opposite Vice; and I should have called my Book the *Art of Virtue,* because it would have shown the *Means and Manner* of obtaining Virtue; which would have distinguish'd it from the mere Exhortation to be good, that does not instruct and indicate the Means; but is like the Apostle's Man of verbal Charity, who only, without showing to the Naked and the Hungry *how* or where they might get Clothes or Victuals, exhorted them to be fed and clothed. *James* II, 15, 16.

But it so happened that my Intention of writing and publishing this Comment was never fulfilled. I did indeed, from time to time put down short Hints of the Sentiments, Reasonings, etc. to be made use of in it; some of which I have still by me: But the necessary close Attention to private Business in the earlier part of Life, and public Business since, have occasioned my postponing it. For it being connected in my Mind with a *great and extensive Project* that required the whole Man to execute, and which an unforeseen Succession of Employs prevented my attending to, it has hitherto remain'd unfinish'd.

In this Piece it was my Design to explain and enforce this Doctrine, that vicious Actions are not hurtful because they are forbidden, but forbidden because they are hurtful, the Nature of Man alone consider'd: That it was therefore every one's Interest to be virtuous, who wish'd to be happy even in this World. And I should from this Circumstance (there being always in the World a Number of rich Merchants, Nobility, States and Princes, who have need of honest Instruments for the Management of their Affairs, and such being so rare) have endeavoured to convince young Persons, that no Qualities were so likely to make a poor Man's Fortune as those of Probity and Integrity.

My List of Virtues contain'd at first but twelve: But a Quaker Friend having kindly inform'd me that I was generally thought proud; that my Pride show'd itself frequently in Conversation; that I was not content with being in the right when discussing any Point, but was overbearing and rather insolent; of which he convinc'd me by mentioning several Instances; I determined endeavouring to cure myself if I could of this Vice or Folly among the rest, and I added *Humility* to my List, giving an extensive meaning to the Word. I cannot boast of much Success in acquiring the *Reality* of this Virtue; but I had a good deal with regard to the *Appearance* of it. I made it a Rule to forbear all direct Contradiction to the Sentiments of others, and all positive Assertion of my own. I even

2. "Nothing so likely to make a Man's Fortune as Virtue." [BF memo]

forbid myself, agreeable to the old Laws of our Junto, the Use of every Word or Expression in the Language that imported a fix'd Opinion; such as *certainly, undoubtedly,* etc. and I adopted instead of them, I *conceive,* I *apprehend,* or *I imagine* a thing to be so or so, or it so appears to me at present. When another asserted something that I thought an Error, I denied myself the Pleasure of contradicting him abruptly, and of showing immediately some Absurdity in his Proposition; and in answering I began by observing that in certain Cases or Circumstances his Opinion would be right, but that in the present case there *appear'd* or *seem'd* to me some Difference, etc. I soon found the Advantage of this Change in my Manners. The Conversations I engag'd in went on more pleasantly. The modest way in which I propos'd my Opinions, procur'd them a readier Reception and less Contradiction; I had less Mortification when I was found to be in the wrong, and I more easily prevail'd with others to give up their Mistakes and join with me when I hapen'd to be in the right. And this Mode, which I at first put on, with some violence to natural Inclination, became at length so easy and so habitual to me, that perhaps for these Fifty Years past no one has ever heard a dogmatical Expression escape me. And to this Habit (after my Character of Integrity) I think it principally owing, that I had early so much Weight with my Fellow Citizens, when I proposed new Institutions, or Alterations in the old; and so much Influence in public Councils when I became a Member. For I was but a bad Speaker, never eloquent, subject to much Hesitation in my choice of Words, hardly correct in Language, and yet I generally carried my Points.

In reality there is perhaps no one of our natural Passions so hard to subdue as *Pride.* Disguise it, struggle with it, beat it down, stifle it, mortify it as much as one pleases, it is still alive, and will every now and then peep out and show itself. You will see it perhaps often in this History. For even if I could conceive that I had completely overcome it, I should probably be proud of my Humility.

Thus far written at Passy, 1784.

I am now about to write at home, August 1788, but cannot have the help
expected from my Papers, many of them being lost in the War.
I have however found the following.

Having mentioned *a great and extensive Project* which I had conceiv'd, it seems proper that some Account should be here given of that Project and its Object. Its first Rise in my Mind appears in the following little Paper, accidentally preserv'd, viz.

Observations on my Reading History in Library, May 9, 1731.

"That the great Affairs of the World, the Wars, Revolutions, etc. are carried on and effected by Parties.

"That the View of these Parties is their present general Interest, or what they take to be such.

"That the different Views of these different Parties, occasion all Confusion.

"That while a Party is carrying on a general Design, each Man has his particular private Interest in View.

"That as soon as a Party has gain'd its general Point, each Member becomes intent upon his particular Interest, which thwarting others, breaks that Party into Divisions, and occasions more Confusion.

"That few in Public Affairs act from a mere View of the Good of their Country, whatever they may pretend; and tho' their Actings bring real Good to their Country, yet Men primarily consider'd that their own and their Country's Interest was united, and did not act from a Principle of Benevolence.

"That fewer still in public Affairs act with a View to the Good of Mankind.

"There seems to me at present to be great Occasion for raising an united Party for Virtue, by forming the Virtuous and good Men of all Nations into a regular Body, to be govern'd by suitable good and wise Rules, which good and wise Men may probably be more unanimous in their Obedience to, than common People are to common Laws.

"I at present think, that whoever attempts this aright, and is well qualified, cannot fail of pleasing God, and of meeting with Success.

B.F."

Revolving this Project in my Mind, as to be undertaken hereafter when my Circumstances should afford me the necessary Leisure, I put down from time to time on Pieces of Paper such Thoughts as occur'd to me respecting it. Most of these are lost; but I find one purporting to be the Substance of an intended Creed, containing as I thought the Essentials of every known Religion, and being free of everything that might shock the Professors of any Religion. It is express'd in these Words, viz.

"That there is one God who made all things.

"That he governs the World by his Providence.

"That he ought to be worshipped by Adoration, Prayer and Thanksgiving.

"But that the most acceptable Service of God is doing Good to Man.

"That the Soul is immortal.

"And that God will certainly reward Virtue and punish Vice either here or hereafter."

My Ideas at that time were, that the Sect should be begun and spread at first among young and single Men only; that each Person to be initiated should not only declare his Assent to such Creed, but should have exercis'd himself with the Thirteen Weeks' Examination and Practice of the Virtues as in the before-mention'd Model; that the Existence of such a Society should be kept a Secret till it was become considerable, to prevent Solicitations for the Admission of improper Persons; but that the Members should each of them search among his Acquaintance for ingenuous well-disposed Youths, to whom with prudent Caution the Scheme should be gradually communicated: That the Members should engage to afford their Advice, Assistance and Support to each other in promoting one another's Interest, Business and Advancement in Life: That for Distinction we should be call'd the Society of the *Free and Easy;* Free, as being by the general Practice and Habit of the Virtues, free from the Dominion of Vice, and particularly by the Practice of Industry and Frugality, free from Debt, which exposes a Man to Confinement and a Species of Slavery to his Creditors. This is as much as I can now recollect of the Project, except that I communicated it in part to two young Men, who adopted it with some Enthusiasm. But my then narrow Circumstances, and the Necessity I was under of sticking close to my Business, occasion'd my Postponing the farther Prosecution of it at that time, and my multifarious Occupations public and private induc'd me to continue postponing, so that it has been omitted till I have no longer Strength or Activity left sufficient for such an Enterprise: Tho I am still of Opinion that it was a practicable Scheme, and might have been very useful, by forming a great Number of good Citizens: and I was not discourag'd by the seeming Magnitude of the Undertaking, as I have always thought that one Man of tolerable Abilities may work great Changes, and accomplish great Affairs among Mankind, if he first forms a good Plan, and, cutting off all Amusements or other Employments that would divert his Attention, makes the Execution of that same Plan his sole Study and Business.

In 1732 I first published my Almanac, under the Name of *Richard Saunders,* it was continu'd by me about 25 Years, commonly call'd *Poor Richard's Almanac.* I endeavour'd to make it both entertaining and useful, and it accordingly came to be in such Demand that I reap'd considerable Profit from it, vending annually near ten Thousand. And observing that it was generally read, scarce any Neighborhood in the Province being without it, I consider'd it as a proper Vehicle for conveying Instruction among the common People, who bought scarce any other Books. I therefore filled all the little Spaces that occur'd between the Remarkable Days in the Calendar, with Proverbial Sentences, chiefly such as inculcated Industry and Frugality, as the Means of procuring Wealth and thereby securing Virtue, it being more difficult for a Man in Want to act always honestly, as (to use here one of those Proverbs) *it is hard for an empty Sack to stand upright.* These Proverbs, which contained the Wisdom of many Ages and Nations, I assembled and form'd into a connected Discourse prefix'd to the Almanac of 1757, as the Harangue of a wise old Man to the People attending an Auction. The bringing all these scatter'd Counsels thus into a Focus, enabled them to make greater Impression. The Piece being universally approved was copied in all the Newspapers of the Continent, reprinted in Britain on a Broadside to be stuck up in Houses, two Translations were made of it in French, and great Numbers bought by the Clergy and Gentry to distribute gratis among their poor Parishioners and Tenants. In Pennsylvania, as it discouraged useless Expense in foreign Superfluities, some thought it had its share of Influence in producing that growing Plenty of Money which was observable for several Years after its Publication....

JOHN ADAMS

A Dissertation on the Canon and the Feudal Law
(1765)

Vain, irritable, inordinately suspicious, yet disinterested, profound, scrupulously honest, and so passionate in his devotion to the right as to be lovable—so wrote Thomas Jefferson of the personality traits of his friend and comrade and soon to be political enemy John Adams (1735–1826).

These characteristics, which his biographers have come to denominate as quintessentially "Puritan" ones, also suffused a good deal of Adams's political writings, and nowhere more so than in his pre-Revolutionary *Dissertation on the Canon and the Feudal Law*. Adams had originally written its early sections in the form of letters to the Sodality, a private club of provincial lawyers to which he belonged. After news of Parliament's approval of the Stamp Act reached the colonies in the spring of 1765, he transformed his historical analysis into a full-blown public justification of American resistance to the legislation. This act, in Adams's view, was nothing less than an assault on the New England way. But to make his case, he had to republicanize his region's myth; liberty more than godliness, in Adams's reading, inspired Winthrop's "City upon a Hill." Even this version the enlightened Adams recast by making the passion for knowledge, which he ambiguously linked with "power," both the fundamental spring and the end of liberty. Finally, Adams portrayed such a starkly oppressive counter-system of priestcraft and feudal oppression that even small elements of such a system—like the Stamp Act—seemed tantamount to "a direct and formal design…to enslave all America."

For a good introduction to the development of Adams's political ideas, see John R. Howe, Jr., *The Changing Political Thought of John Adams* (Princeton, 1966). Paul Conkin delineates the Puritan cast of Adams's outlook in his *Puritans and Pragmatists: Eight Eminent American Thinkers* (New York, 1968), 109–48. Trevor Colbourn includes a useful chapter on the relation of Adams's views of history to his politics in *The Lamp of Experience: Whig History and the Intellectual Origins of the American Revolution* (Chapel Hill, 1965), 83–106. For additional studies of Adams's political thought, see the works cited in the headnote for John Adams's letters to Samuel Adams and Thomas Jefferson.

"Ignorance and inconsideration are the two great causes of the ruin of mankind." This is an observation of Dr. *Tillotson,* with relation to the interest of his fellow-men, in a future and immortal state: But it is of equal truth and importance, if applied to the happiness of men in society, on this side the grave. In the earliest ages of the world, *absolute monarchy* seems to have been the universal form of government. Kings, and a few of their great counsellors and captains, exercised a cruel tyranny over the people who held a rank in the scale of intelligence, in those days, but little higher than the camels and elephants, that carried them and their engines to war.

By what causes it was bro't to pass, that the people in the middle ages, became more *intelligent* in general, would not perhaps be possible in these days to discover: But the fact is certain; and wherever a general knowledge and sensibility have prevail'd among the *people,* arbitrary government, and every kind of oppression, have lessened and dis-appeared in proportion. Man has certainly an exalted soul! and the same principle in humane nature, that aspiring noble principle, founded in benevolence, and cherished by knowledge, I mean the love of power, which has been so often the cause of *slavery,* has, whenever freedom has existed, been the cause of *freedom.* If it is this principle, that has always prompted the princes and nobles of the earth, by every species of fraud and vio-lence, to shake off, all the *limitations* of their power; it is the same that has always stimu-lated the common people to aspire at independency, and to endeavor at confining the power of the great within the limits of *equity* and *reason.*

The poor people, it is true, have been much less successful than the great. They have seldom found either leisure or opportunity to form an union and exert their strength— ignorant as they were of arts and letters, they have seldom been able to frame and support a regular opposition. This, however, has been known, by the great, to be the temper of mankind, and they have accordingly laboured, in all ages, to wrest from the populace, as they are contemptuously called, the knowledge of their rights and wrongs, and the power to assert the former or redress the latter. I say RIGHTS, for such they have, undoubtedly, antecedent to all earthly government—*Rights* that cannot be repealed or restrained by human *laws*—*Rights* derived from the great legislator of the universe.

Since the promulgation of Christianity, the two greatest systems of tyranny, that have sprung from this original, are the *canon* and the *feudal* law. The desire of dominion, that great principle by which we have attempted to account for so much good, and so much evil, is, when *properly restrained,* a very useful and noble movement in the human mind: But when such restraints are taken off, it becomes an incroaching, grasping, restless and ungovernable power. Numberless have been the systems of iniquity, contrived by the great, for the gratification of this passion in themselves: but in none of them were they ever more successful, than in the invention and establishment of the *canon* and *the feudal law.*

By the *former* of these, the most refined, sublime, extensive, and astonishing consti-tution of policy, that ever was conceived by the mind of man, was framed by the *Romish* clergy for the aggrandisement of their own order. All the epithets I have here given to the Romish policy are just: and will be allowed to be so, when it is considered, that they even persuaded mankind to believe, faithfully and undoubtingly, that GOD almighty had intrusted *them* with the keys of heaven; whose gates *they* might open and close at

Source: The Adams Papers: Papers of John Adams, vol. 1, ed. Robert J. Taylor, Mary-Jo Kline, and Gregg L. Lint (Cambridge: The Belknap Press of Harvard University Press, 1977), 111–28. Editors' notes omitted. Reprinted by permission of Harvard University Press, Copyright © 1977 by the Massachusetts Historical Society.

pleasure—with a power of dispensation over all the rules and obligations of morality—with authority to licence all sorts of sins and crimes—with a power of deposing princes, and absolving subjects from allegiance—with a power of procuring or withholding the rain of heaven and the beams of the sun—with the management of earthquakes, pestilence and famine. Nay with the mysterious, awful, incomprehensible power of creating out of bread and wine, the flesh and blood of God himself. All these opinions, they were enabled to spread and rivet among the people, by reducing their minds to a state of sordid ignorance and staring timidity; and by infusing into them a *religious* horror of letters and knowledge. Thus was human nature chained fast for ages, in a cruel, shameful and deplorable servitude, to him and his subordinate tyrants, who, it was foretold, would exalt himself above all that was called God, and that was worshipped.

In the latter, we find another system similar in many respects, to the former: which altho' it was originally formed perhaps, for the necessary defence of a *barbarous* people, against the inroads and invasions of her neighbouring nations; yet, for the same purposes of tyranny, cruelty and lust, which had dictated the *canon* law, it was soon adopted by almost all the princes of Europe, and wrought into the constitutions of their *government*. It was originally, a code of laws, for a vast army, in a perpetual encampment. The general was invested with the sovereign propriety of all the lands within the territory. *Of him,* as his servants and vassals, the first rank of his great officers held the lands: and in the same manner, the other subordinate officers held of *them:* and all ranks and degrees held their lands, by a variety of *duties* and *services,* all tending to bind the chains the faster, on *every* order of mankind. In this manner, the common people were held together, in herds and clans, in a state of *servile* dependance on their lords; bound, even by the tenure of their lands to follow them, whenever they commanded, to their wars; and in a state of total ignorance of every thing divine and human, excepting the use of arms, and the culture of their lands.

But, another event still more calamitous to human liberty, was a wicked confederacy, between the *two systems* of tyranny above described. It seems to have been even *stipulated* between them, that the *temporal* grandees should contribute every thing in their power to maintain the ascendency of the *priesthood;* and that the spiritual grandees, in their turn, should employ that ascendency over the *consciences* of the *people,* in impressing on their minds, a *blind, implicit* obedience to civil magistracy.

Thus, as long as this confederacy lasted, and the people were held in ignorance; Liberty, and with her, Knowledge, and Virtue too, seem to have deserted the earth; and one age of darkness, succeeded another, till GOD, in his benign providence, raised up the champions, who began and conducted the *reformation.* From the time of the reformation, to the first settlement of *America,* knowledge gradually spread in Europe, but especially in *England;* and in proportion as *that* increased and spread among the people, *ecclesiastical* and *civil* tyranny, which I use as synonimous expressions, for the *canon* and *feudal* laws, seem to have lost their strength and weight. The people grew more and more sensible of the wrong that was done them, by these systems; more and more impatient under it; and determined at all hazards to rid themselves of it; till, at last, under the *execrable* race of the *Steuarts,* the struggle between the people and the confederacy aforesaid of temporal and spiritual tyranny, became formidable, violent and bloody.

It was this great struggle, that peopled America. It was not religion *alone,* as is commonly supposed; but it was a love of *universal Liberty,* and an hatred, a dread, an horror of the infernal confederacy, before described, that projected, conducted, and accomplished the settlement of America.

It was a resolution formed, by a sensible people, I mean the *Puritans,* almost in despair. They had become intelligent in general, and many of them learned. For this fact I have the testimony of archbishop *King* himself, who observed of that people, that they were more intelligent, and better read than even the members of the church whom he censures warmly for that reason. This people had been so vexed, and tortured by the powers of those days, for no other crime than their knowledge, and their freedom of enquiry and examination, and they had so much reason to despair of deliverance from those miseries, on that side the ocean; that they at last resolved to fly to the *wilderness* for refuge, from the temporal and spiritual principalities and powers, and plagues, and scourges, of their *native* country.

After their arrival here, they began their settlements, and formed their plan both of ecclesiastical and civil government, in *direct opposition* to the *canon* and the *feudal* systems. The leading men among them, both of the clergy and the laity, were men of sense and learning: To many of them, the historians, orators, poets and philosophers of *Greece* and *Rome* were quite familiar: and some of them have left libraries that are still in being, consisting chiefly of volumes, in which the wisdom of the most enlightened ages and nations is deposited, written however in languages, which their great grandsons, *tho' educated in European Universities,* can scarcely read.

Thus accomplished were many of the first Planters of these Colonies. It may be thought polite and fasionable, by many modern fine Gentlemen perhaps, to deride the Characters of these Persons, as enthusiastical, superstitious and republican: But such ridicule is founded in nothing but foppery and affectation, and is grosly injurious and false. Religious to some degree of enthusiasm it may be admitted they were; but this can be no peculiar derogation from their character, because it was at that time almost the universal character, not only of England, but of Christendom. Had this however, been otherwise, their enthusiasm, considering the principles in which it was founded, and the ends to which it was directed, far from being a reproach to them, was greatly to their honour: for I believe it will be found universally true, that no great enterprize, for the honour or happiness of mankind, was ever achieved, without a large mixture of that noble infirmity. Whatever imperfections may be justly ascribed to them, which however are as few, as any mortals have discovered their judgment in framing their policy, was founded in wise, humane and benevolent principles; It was founded in revelation, and in reason too; It was consistent with the principles, of the best, and greatest, and wisest legislators of antiquity. Tyranny in every form, shape, and appearance was their disdain, and abhorrence; no fear of punishment, not even of *Death* itself, in exquisite tortures, had been sufficient to conquer, that steady, manly, pertenacious spirit, with which they had opposed the tyrants of those days, in church and state. They were very far from being enemies to monarchy; and they knew as well as any men, the just regard and honour that is due to the character of a dispenser of the misteries of the gospel of Grace: But they saw clearly, that popular powers must be placed, as a guard, a countroul, a ballance, to the powers of the monarch, and the priest, in every government, or else it would soon become the man of sin, the whore of Babylon, the mystery of iniquity, a great and detestable system of fraud, violence, and usurpation. Their greatest concern seems to have been to establish a government of the church more consistent with the scriptures, and a government of the state more agreable to the dignity of humane nature, than any they had seen in Europe: and to transmit such a government down to their posterity, with the means of securing and preserving it, for ever. To render the popular power in their new government, as great and wise, as their principles and theory, i.e. as human nature and the christian religion require it should be, they endeavored to remove from it, as many of the feudal inequalities and dependencies, as could be spared, consistently with the preservation of a mild limited monarchy. And in this they discovered the depth of their wisdom, and the warmth of their friendship to human nature. But the first place is due to religion. They saw clearly, that of all the nonsense and delusion which had ever passed thro' the mind of man, none had ever been more extravagant than the notions of absolutions, indelible characters, uninterrupted successions, and the rest of those phantastical ideas, derived from the common law, which had thrown such a glare of mystery, sanctity, reverence and right reverence, eminence and holiness, around the idea of a priest, as no mortal could deserve, and as always must from the constitution of human nature, be dangerous in society. For this reason, they demolished the whole system of Diocesan episcopacy and deriding, as all reasonable and impartial men must do, the ridiculous fancies of sanctified effluvia from episcopal fingers, they established sacerdotal ordination, on the foundation of the bible and common sense. This conduct at once imposed an obligation on the whole body of the clergy, to industry, virtue, piety and learning, and rendered that whole body infinitely more independent on the civil powers, in all respects than they could be where they were formed into a scale of subordination, from a pope down to priests and fryars and confessors, necessarily and essentially a sordid, stupid, wretched herd; or than they could be in any other country, where an archbishop held the place of an universal bishop, and the vicars and curates that of the ignorant, dependent, miserable rabble aforesaid; and infinitely more sensible and learned than they could be in either. This subject has been seen in the same light, by many illustrious patriots, who have lived in America, since the days of our fore fathers, and who have adored their memory for the same reason. And methinks there has not appeared in New England a stronger veneration for their memory, a more penetrating insight into the grounds and principles and spirit of their policy, nor a more earnest desire of perpetuating the blessings of it to posterity, than that fine institution of the late chief justice Dudley, of a lecture against popery, and on the validity of presbyterian ordination. This was certainly intended by that wise and excellent man, as an eternal memento of the wisdom and goodness of the very principles that settled America. But I must again return to the feudal law.

The adventurers so often mentioned, had an utter contempt of all that dark ribaldry of hereditary indefeasible right—the Lord's anointed—and the divine miraculous original of government, with which the priesthood had inveloped the feudal monarch in clouds and mysteries, and from whence they had deduced the most mischievous of all doctrines, that of passive obedience and non resistance. They knew that government was a plain, simple, intelligible thing founded in nature and reason and quite comprehensible by common sense. They detested all the base services, and servile dependencies of the feudal system. They knew that no such unworthy dependences took place in the ancient seats of liberty, the republic of Greece and Rome: and they tho't all such slavish subordinations were equally inconsistent with the constitution of human nature and that religious liberty, with which Jesus had made them free. This was certainly the opinion they had formed, and they were far from being singular or extravagant in thinking so. Many celebrated modern writers, in Europe, have espoused the same sentiments. Lord Kaim's, a Scottish writer of great reputation, whose authority in this case ought to have the more weight, as his countrymen have not the most worthy ideas of liberty, speaking of the feudal law, says, "A constitution so contradictory to all the principles which govern mankind, can never be brought about, one should imagine, but by foreign conquest or native usurpations." Brit. Ant. P. 2. Rousseau speaking of the same system, calls it "That most iniquitous and absurd form of government by which human nature was so shamefully degraded." Social Compact, Page 164. It would be easy to multiply authorities, but it must be needless, because as the original of this form of government was among savages, as the spirit of it is military and despotic, every writer, who would allow the people to have any right to life or property, or freedom, more than the beasts of the field, and who was not hired or inlisted under arbitrary lawless power, has been always willing to admit the feudal system to be inconsistent with liberty and the rights of mankind.

To have holden their lands, allodially, or for every man to have been the sovereign lord and proprietor of the ground he occupied, would have constituted a government, too nearly like a commonwealth. They were contented therefore to hold their lands of their King, as their sovereign Lord, and to him they were willing to render homage: but to no mesne and subordinate Lords, nor were they willing to submit to any of the baser services. In all this, they were so strenuous, that they have even transmitted to their posterity, a very general contempt and detestation of holdings by quit rents: As they have also an hereditary ardor for liberty and thirst for knowledge.

They were convinced by their knowledge of human nature derived from history and their own experience, that nothing could preserve their posterity from the encroachments of the two systems of tyranny, in opposition to which, as has been observed already, they erected their government in church and state, but knowledge diffused generally thro' the whole body of the people. Their civil and religious principles, therefore, conspired to prompt them to use every measure, and take every precaution in their power, to propagate and perpetuate knowledge. For this purpose they laid, very early the foundations of colleges, and invested them with ample priviledges and emoluments; and it is remarkable, that they have left among their posterity, so universal an affection and veneration for those seminaries, and for liberal education, that the meanest of the people contribute chearfully to the support and maintenance of them every year, and that nothing is more generally popular than projections for the honour, reputation and advantage of those seats of learning. But the wisdom and benevolence of our fathers rested not here. They made an early provision by law, that every town consisting of so many families, should be always furnished with a grammar school. They made it a crime for such a town to be destitute of a grammar school master, for a few months, and subjected it to an heavy penalty. So that the education of all ranks of people was made the care and expence of the public in a manner, that I believe has been unknown to any other people ancient or modern.

The consequences of these establishments we see and feel every day. A native of America who cannot read and write is as rare an appearance, as a Jacobite or a Roman Catholic, i.e. as rare as a Comet or an Earthquake. It has been observed, that we are all of us, lawyers, divines, politicians and philosophers. And I have good authorities to say that all candid foreigners who have passed thro' this country, and conversed freely with all sorts of people here, will allow, that they have never seen so much knowledge and civility among the common people in any part of the world. It is true, there has been among us a party for some years, consisting chiefly not of the descendants of the first settlers of this country but of high churchmen and high statesmen, imported since, who affect to censure this provision for the education of our youth as a needless expence, and an imposition upon the rich in favour of the poor—and as an institution productive of idleness and vain speculation among the people, whose time and attention it is said ought to be devoted to labour, and not to public affairs or to examination into the conduct of their superiours. And certain officers of the crown, and certain other missionaries of ignorance, foppery, servility and slavery, have been most inclined to countenance and increase the same party. Be it remembered, however, that liberty must at all hazards be supported. We have a right to it, derived from our Maker. But if we had not, our fathers have earned, and bought it for us, at the expence of their ease, their estates, their pleasure, and their blood. And liberty cannot be preserved without a general knowledge among the people, who have a right from the frame of their nature, to knowledge, as their great Creator who does nothing in vain, has given them understandings, and a desire to know—but besides this they have a right, an indisputable, unalienable, indefeasible divine right to that most dreaded, and envied kind of knowledge, I mean of the characters and conduct of their rulers. Rulers are no more than attorneys, agents and trustees for the people; and if the cause, the interest and trust is insidiously betray'd, or wantonly trifled away, the people have a right to revoke the authority, that they themselves have deputed, and to constitute abler and better agents, attorneys and trustees. And the preservation of the means of knowledge, among the lowest ranks, is of more importance to the public, than all the property of all the rich men in the country. It is even of more consequence to the rich themselves, and to their posterity. The only question is whether it is a public emolument? and if it is, the rich ought undoubtedly to contribute in the same proportion, as to all other public burdens, i.e. in proportion to their wealth which is secured by public expences. But none of the means of information are more sacred, or have been cherished with more tenderness and care by the settlers of America, than the Press. Care has been taken, that the art of printing should be encouraged, and that it should be easy and cheap and safe for any person to communicate his thoughts to the public. And you, Messieurs Printers, whatever the tyrants of the earth may say of your paper, have done important service to your country, by your readiness and freedom in publishing the speculations of the curious. The stale, impudent insinuations of slander and sedition, with which the gormandizers of power have endeavor'd to discredit your paper, are so much the more to your honour; for the jaws of power are always opened to devour, and her arm is always stretched out if possible to destroy, the freedom of thinking, speaking and writing. And if the public interest, liberty and happiness have been in danger, from the ambition or avarice of any great man or number of great men, whatever may be their politeness, address, learning, ingenuity and in other respects integrity and humanity, you have done yourselves honour and your country service, by publishing and pointing out that avarice and ambition. These views are so much the more dangerous and pernicious, for the virtues with which they may be accompanied in the same character, and with so much the more watchful jealousy to be guarded against.

"Curse on such virtues, they've undone their country."

Be not intimidated therefore, by any terrors, from publishing with the utmost freedom, whatever can be warranted by the laws of your country; nor suffer yourselves to be wheedled out of your liberty, by any pretences of politeness, delicacy or decency. These as they are often used, are but three different names, for hypocrisy, chicanery and cowardice. Much less I presume will you be discouraged by any pretences, that malignants on this side the water will *represent* your paper as factious and seditious, or that the Great on the other side the water will take offence at them. This Dread of *representation,* has had for a long time in this province effects very similar to what the physicians call an hydropho, or dread of water. It has made us delirious. And we have rushed headlong into the water, till we are almost drowned, out of simple or phrensical fear of it. Believe me, the character of this country has suffered more in Britain, by the pusillanimity with which we have borne many insults and indignities from the creatures of power at home, and the creatures of those creatures here, than it ever did or ever will by the freedom and spirit that has been or will be discovered in writing, or action. Believe me my countrymen, they have imbibed an opinion on the other side the water, that we are an ignorant, a timid and a stupid people, nay their tools on this side have often the impudence to dispute your bravery. But I hope in God the time is near at hand, when they will be fully convinced of your understanding, integrity and courage. But can any thing be more ridiculous, were it not too provoking to be laughed at, than to pretend that offence should be taken at home for writings here? Pray let them look at home. Is not the human understanding exhausted there? Are not reason, imagination, wit, passion, senses and all, tortured to find out satyr and invective against the characters of the vile and futile fellows who sometimes get into place and power? The most exceptionable paper that ever I saw here, is perfect prudence and modesty, in comparison of multitudes of their applauded writings. Yet the high regard they have for the freedom of the Press, indulges all. I must and will repeat it, your Paper deserves the patronage of every friend to his country. And whether the defamers of it are arrayed in robes of scarlet or sable, whether they lurk and skulk in an insurance office, whether they assume the venerable character of a Priest, the sly one of a scrivener, or the dirty, infamous, abandoned one of an informer, they are all the creatures and tools of the lust of domination.

The true source of our sufferings, has been our timidity.

We have been afraid to think. We have felt a reluctance to examining into the grounds of our privileges, and the extent in which we have an indisputable right to demand them against all the power and authority, on earth. And many who have not scrupled to examine for themselves, have yet for certain prudent reasons been cautious, and diffident of declaring the result of their enquiries.

The cause of this timidity is perhaps hereditary and to be traced back in history, as far as the cruel treatment the first settlers of this country received, before their embarkation for America, from the government at Home. Every body knows how dangerous it was to speak or write in favour of any thing in those days, but the triumphant system of religion and politicks. And our fathers were particularly, the objects of the persecutions and proscriptions of the times. It is not unlikely therefore, that, although they were inflexibly steady in refusing their positive assent to any thing against their principles, they might have contracted habits of reserve, and a cautious diffidence of asserting their opinions publicly. These habits they probably brought with them to America, and have transmitted down to us. Or, we may possibly account for this appearance, by the great affection and veneration Americans have always entertained for the country from whence they sprang—or by the quiet temper for which they have been remarkable, no country having been less disposed to discontent than this—or by a sense they have, that it is their duty to acquiesce, under the administration of government, even when in many smaller matters gravaminous to them, and until the essentials of the great compact are destroy'd or invaded. These peculiar causes might operate upon them; but without these we all know, that human nature itself, from indolence, modesty, humanity or fear, has always too much reluctance to a manly assertion of its rights. Hence perhaps it has happened that nine tenths of the species, are groaning and gasping in misery and servitude.

But whatever the cause has been, the fact is certain, we have been excessively cautious of giving offence by complaining of grievances. And it is as certain that American governors, and their friends and all the crown officers have avail'd themselves of this disposition in the people. They have prevailed on us to consent to many things, which were grosly injurious to us, and to surrender many others with voluntary tameness, to which we had the clearest right. Have we not been treated formerly, with abominable insolence, by officers of the navy? I mean no insinuation against any gentleman now on this station, having heard no complaint of any one of them to his dishonor. Have not some generals, from England, treated us like servants, nay more like slaves than like Britons? Have we not been under the most ignominious contribution, the most abject submission, the most supercilious insults of some custom house officers? Have we not been trifled with, browbeaten, and trampled on, by former governors, in a manner which no king of England since James the second has dared to indulge towards his subjects? Have we not raised up one family, in them placed an unlimitted confidence, and been soothed and battered and intimidated by their influence, into a great part of this infamous tameness and submission? "These are serious and alarming questions, and deserve a dispassionate consideration."

This disposition has been the great wheel and the mainspring in the American machine of court politicks. We have been told that "the word 'Rights' is an offensive expression." That "the King his ministry and parliament will not endure to hear Americans talk of their Rights." That "Britain is the mother and we the children, that a filial duty and submission is due from us to her," and that "we ought to doubt our own judgment, and presume that she is right, even when she seems to us to shake the foundations of government." That "Britain is immensely rich and great and powerful, has fleets and armies at her command, which have been the dread and terror of the universe, and that she will force her own judgment into execution, right or wrong." But let me intreat you Sir to pause and consider. Do you consider your self as a missionary of loyalty or of rebellion? Are you not representing your King, his ministry and parliament as tyrants, imperious, unrelenting tyrants by such reasoning as this? Is not this representing your most gracious sovereign, as endeavouring to destroy the foundations of his own throne? Are you not putting language into the royal mouth, which if fairly pursued will shew him to have no right to the crown on his own sacred head? Are you not representing every member of parliament as renouncing the transactions at Runningmede, and as repealing in effect the bill of rights, when the Lords and Commons asserted and vindicated the rights of the people and their own rights, and insisted on the King's assent to that assertion and vindication? Do you not represent them as forgetting that the prince of Orange, was created King William by the People, on purpose that their rights might be eternal and inviolable? Is there not something extremely fallacious, in the common-place images of mother country and children colonies? Are we the children of Great-Britain, anymore than the cities of London, Exeter and Bath? Are we not brethren and fellow subjects, with those in Britain, only under a somewhat different method of legislation, and a totally different method of taxation? But admitting we are children; have not children a right to complain when their parents are attempting to break their limbs, to administer poison, or to sell them to enemies for slaves? Let me intreat you to consider, will the mother be pleased, when you represent her as deaf to the cries of her children? When you compare her to the infamous miscreant, who lately stood on the gallows for starving her child? When you resemble her to Lady Macbeth in Shakespear, (I cannot think of it without horror)

> Who "had given suck, and knew
> How tender 'twas to love the Babe that milk'd her."
> But yet, who could
> "Even while 'twas smiling in her Face,
> Have pluck'd her Nipple from the boneless Gums,
> And dash'd the Brains out."

Let us banish forever from our minds, my countrymen, all such unworthy ideas of the King, his ministry and parliament. Let us not suppose, that all are become luxurious effeminate and unreasonable, on the other side the water, as many designing persons would insinuate. Let us presume, what is in fact true, that the spirit of liberty, is as ardent as ever among the body of the nation, though a few individuals may be corrupted. Let us take it for granted, that the same great spirit, which once gave Cæsar so warm a reception; which denounced hostilities against John 'till Magna Charta was signed; which severed the head of Charles the first from his body, and drove James the second from his kingdom; the same great spirit (may heaven preserve it till the earth shall be no more) which first seated the great grand father of his present most gracious Majesty, on the throne of Britain, is still alive and active and warm in England; and that the same spirit in America, instead of provoking the inhabitants of that country, will endear us to them for ever and secure their good will.

This spirit however without knowledge, would be little better than a brutal rage. Let us tenderly and kindly cherish, therefore the means of knowledge. Let us dare to read, think, speak and write. Let every order and degree among the people rouse their attention and animate their resolution. Let them all become attentive to the grounds and principles of government, ecclesiastical and civil. Let us study the law of nature; search into the spirit of the British constitution; read the histories of ancient ages; contemplate the great examples of Greece and Rome; set before us, the conduct of our own British ancestors, who have defended for us, the inherent rights of mankind, against foreign and domestic tyrants and usurpers, against arbitrary kings and cruel priests, in short against the gates of earth and hell. Let us read and recollect and impress upon our souls, the views and ends, of our own more immediate forefathers, in exchanging their native country for a dreary, inhospitable wilderness. Let us examine into the nature of that power and the cruelty of that oppression which drove them from their homes. Recollect their amazing fortitude, their bitter sufferings! The hunger, the nakedness, the cold, which they patiently endured! The severe labours of clearing their grounds, building their houses, raising their provisions amidst dangers from wild beasts and savage men, before they had time or money or materials for commerce! Recollect the civil and religious principles and hopes and expectations, which constantly supported and carried them through all hardships, and patience and resignation! Let us recollect it was liberty! The hope of liberty for themselves and us and ours, which conquered all discouragements, dangers and trials! In such researches as these let us all in our several departments chearfully engage! But especially the proper patrons and supporters of law, learning and religion.

Let the pupil resound with the doctrines and sentiments of religious liberty. Let us hear the danger of thraldom to our consciences, from ignorance, extream poverty and dependance, in short from civil and political slavery. Let us see delineated before us, the true map of man. Let us hear the dignity of his nature, and the noble rank he holds among the works of God! that consenting to slavery is a sacriligious breach of trust, as offensive in the sight of God, as it is derogatory from our own honor or interest or happiness; and that God almightly has promulgated from heaven, liberty, peace, and good-will to man!

Let the Bar proclaim, "the laws, the rights, the generous plan of power," delivered down from remote antiquity; inform the world of the mighty struggles, and numberless sacrifices, made by our ancestors, in defence of freedom. Let it be known, that British liberties are not the grants of princes or parliaments, but original rights, conditions of original contracts, coequal with prerogative and coeval with government.—That many of our rights are inherent and essential, agreed on as maxims and establish'd as preliminaries, even before a parliament existed. Let them search for the foundations of British laws and government in the frame of human nature, in the constitution of the intellectual and moral world. There let us see, that truth, liberty, justice and benevolence, are its everlasting basis; and if these could be removed, the superstructure is overthrown of course.

Let the colleges join their harmony, in the same delightful concern. Let every declamation turn upon the beauty of liberty and virtue, and the deformity, turpitude and malignity of slavery and vice. Let the public disputations become researches into the grounds and nature and ends of government, and the means of preserving the good and demolishing the evil. Let the dialogues and all the exercises, become the instruments of impressing on the tender mind, and of spreading and distributing, far and wide, the ideas of right and the sensations of freedom.

In a word, let every sluice of knowledge be open'd and set a flowing. The encroachments upon liberty, in the reigns of the first James and the first Charles, by turning the general attention of learned men to government, are said to have produced the greatest number of consummate statesmen, which has ever been seen in any age, or nation. Your Clarendons, Southamptons, Seldens, Hampdens, Faulklands, Sidneys, Locks, Harringtons, are all said to have owed their eminence in political knowledge, to the tyrannies of those reigns. The prospect, now before us, in America, ought in the same manner to engage the attention of every man of learning to matters of power and of right, that we may be neither led nor driven blindfolded to irretrievable destruction. Nothing less than this seems to have been meditated for us, by somebody or other in Great-Britain. There seems to be a direct, and formal design on foot, to enslave all America. This however must be done by degrees. The first step that is intended seems to be an entire subversion of the whole system of our Fathers, by an introduction of the canon and feudal law, into America. The canon and feudal systems tho' greatly mutilated in England, are not yet destroy'd. Like the temples and palaces, in which the great contrivers of them, once worship'd and inhabited, they exist in ruins; and much of the domineering spirit of them still remains. The designs and labours of a certain society, to introduce the former of them into America, have been well exposed to the public by a writer of great abilities, and the further attempts to the same purpose that may be made by that society, or by the ministry or parliament, I leave to the conjectures of the thoughtful. But it seems very manifest from the S---p A-t itself, that a design is form'd to strip us in a great measure of the means of knowledge, by loading the Press, the Colleges, and even an Almanack and a News-Paper, with restraints and duties; and to introduce the inequalities and dependances of the feudal system, by taking from the poorer sort of people all their little subsistance, and conferring it on a set of stamp officers, distributors and their deputies. But I must proceed no further at present. The sequel, whenever I shall find health and leisure to pursue it, will be a "disquisition of the policy of the stamp act." In the mean time however let me add, These are not the vapours of a melancholly mind, nor the effusions of envy, disappointed ambition, nor of a spirit of opposition to government: but the emanations of an heart that burns, for its country's welfare. No one of any feeling, born and educated in this once happy country, can consider the numerous distresses, the gross indignities, the barbarous ignorance, the haughty usurpations, that we have reason to fear are meditating for ourselves, our children, our neighbours, in short for all our countrymen and all their posterity, without the utmost agonies of heart, and many tears.

THOMAS PAINE

Selection from *Common Sense* (1776)

An English Quaker staymaker's son, American Revolutionary pamphleteer, and elected deputy of the French Revolutionary National Convention, Thomas Paine (1737–1809) was the American Enlightenment's cosmopolitan radical. His radicalism, however, consisted less in the character of his life or his specific political positions—which in France were comparatively moderate—than in the fervent, self-assured way in his writings he assaulted inherited traditions that seemed to him to stand in the way of the free and rational ordering of human belief and conduct in accordance with Nature's laws. In his *Age of Reason* (1794–95) he furiously attacked Christianity on just these grounds, and it nearly destroyed his reputation in America.

By contrast Paine's earlier *Common Sense,* published on the eve of the American Revolution, made him overnight the most widely read and popularly acclaimed author in the colonies. Yet *Common Sense,* too, fundamentally assaulted an important American tradition: the English constitution and its mixed government of king, lords, and commons. Practically, of course, this position was revolutionary because it called for a break not just with Parliament, as did most resistance leaders, but with the king himself. More importantly, Paine's thoroughgoing assault on all forms of hereditary rule proclaimed the necessity for a wholly new form of republican government. Rather than promulgating the traditional radical Whig idea of preserving liberty and virtue in the state by dividing it into three separate and mutually checking branches resting on three distinct orders in society, Paine advocated the creation of a directly representative government produced by a social compact of equal individuals desirous of preserving their freedom and security and rationally pursuing their reciprocal commercial interests. It was this liberal ideal—together with Paine's secularized millennialist appeals to God as monarch and America as "an asylum for mankind"—that made *Common Sense* such a common *and* uncommon revolutionary treatise.

Jack Fruchtman, Jr., *Thomas Paine and the Religion of Nature* (Baltimore, 1993), is an illuminating study of Paine's religious worldview as it shaped his social and political thought. Contrasting discussions of Paine's ideology in the context of eighteenth-century ideas about society and politics may be found in Gregory Claeys, *Thomas Paine: Social and Political Thought* (Boston, 1989); and Jack Fruchtman, Jr., *The Political Philosophy of Thomas Paine* (Baltimore, 2009). For valuable studies of Paine's rhetorical conceits and literary methods, see Robert A. Ferguson, "The Commonalities of *Common Sense,*" in Ferguson's *Reading the Early Republic* (Cambridge, Mass., 2004), 84–119; and Edward Larkin, *Thomas Paine and the Literature of Revolution* (Cambridge, 2005). Sophia Rosenfeld, "Tom Paine's Common Sense and Ours," *William and Mary Quarterly,* 65 (October 2008) sheds light on the philosophical origins and character of Paine's pamphlet. Rosenfeld's *Common Sense: A Political History* (Cambridge, Mass., 2011) is a beautifully crafted history of appropriations of the phrase "common sense" for conservative, radical, and coercive political purposes.

Of the Origin and Design of Government in General, with Concise Remarks on the English Constitution

Some writers have so confounded society with government, as to leave little or no distinction between them; whereas they are not only different, but have different origins. Society is produced by our wants, and government by our wickedness; the former promotes our happiness *positively,* by uniting our affections; the latter *negatively,* by restraining our vices. The one encourages intercourse, the other creates distinctions. The first is a patron, the last a punisher.

Society in every state is a blessing, but government, even in its best state, is but a necessary evil; in its worst state, an intolerable one; for when we suffer, or are exposed to the same miseries *by a government,* which we might expect in a country *without government,* our calamity is heightened by reflecting that we furnish the means by which we suffer.

Government, like dress, is the badge of lost innocence; the palaces of kings are built on the ruins of the bowers of paradise. For, were the impulses of conscience clear, uniform, and irresistibly obeyed, man would need no other lawgiver; but that not being the case, he finds it necessary to surrender up a part of his property to furnish means for the protection of the rest; and this he is induced to do by the same prudence which in every other case, advises him out of two evils to choose the least.

Wherefore, security being the true design and end of government, it unanswerably follows, that whatever *form* thereof appears most likely to ensure it to us with the least expense and greatest benefit, is preferable to all others.

In order to give a clear and just idea of the design and end of government, let us suppose a small number of persons settled in some sequestered part of the earth, unconnected with the rest; they will then represent the first peopling of any country, or of the world. In this state of natural liberty, society will be their first thought. A thousand motives will excite them thereto; the strength of one man is so unequal to his wants, and his mind so unfitted for perpetual solitude, that he is soon obliged to seek assistance and relief of another, who in his turn requires the same.

Four or five united would be able to raise a tolerable dwelling in the midst of a wilderness; but *one* man might labor out the common period of life without accomplishing anything; when he had felled his timber he could not remove it, nor erect it after it was removed; hunger in the meantime would urge him from his work, and every different want call him a different way. Disease, nay even misfortune, would be death; for though neither might be mortal, yet either would disable him from living, and reduce him to a state in which he might rather be said to perish than to die.

Thus necessity, like a gravitating power, would soon form our newly-arrived emigrants into society, the reciprocal blessings of which would supersede and render the obligations of law and government unnecessary while they remained perfectly just to each other: but as nothing but heaven is impregnable to vice, it will unavoidably happen, that in proportion as they surmount the first difficulties of emigration, which bound them together in a common cause, they will begin to relax in their duty and attachment to each other; and this remissness will point out the necessity of establishing some form of government to supply the defect of moral virtue.

Source: Life and Writings of Thomas Paine, vol. 2, ed. Daniel Edwin Wheeler (New York: Vincent Parke & Co., 1908), 1–13, 19–21, 29, 51–54, 54–58, 89–92. Editor's notes omitted.

Some convenient tree will afford them a state-house, under the branches of which the whole colony may assemble to deliberate on public matters. It is more than probable that their first laws will have the title only of *Regulations,* and be enforced by no other penalty than public disesteem. In this first parliament every man, by natural right, will have a seat.

But as the colony increases, the public concerns will increase likewise, and the distance at which the members may be separated, will render it too inconvenient for all of them to meet on every occasion as at first, when their number was small, their habitations near, and the public concerns few and trifling. This will point out the convenience of their consenting to leave the legislative part to be managed by a select number chosen from the whole body, who are supposed to have the same concerns at stake which those have who appointed them, and who will act in the same manner as the whole body would were they present.

If the colony continue increasing, it will become necessary to augment the number of representatives, and that the interest of every part of the colony may be attended to, it will be found best to divide the whole into convenient parts, each part sending its proper number; and that the *elected* might never form to themselves an interest separate from the *electors,* prudence will point out the propriety of having elections often; because as the *elected* might by that means return and mix again with the general body of the *electors* in a few months, their fidelity to the public will be secured by the prudent reflection of not making a rod for themselves. And as this frequent interchange will establish a common interest with every part of the community, they will mutually and naturally support each other, and on this (not on the unmeaning name of king) depends the *strength of government and the happiness of the governed.*

Here, then, is the origin and rise of government; namely, a mode rendered necessary by the inability of moral virtue to govern the world; here, too, is the design and end of government, viz., freedom and security. And however our eyes may be dazzled with show, or our ears deceived by sound; however prejudice may warp our wills, or interest darken our understanding; the simple voice of nature and reason will say, it is right.

I draw my idea of the form of government from a principle in nature, which no art can overturn, viz., that the more simple anything is, the less liable it is to be disordered, and the easier repaired when disordered; and with this maxim in view, I offer a few remarks on the so much boasted Constitution of England. That it was noble for the dark and slavish times in which it was erected, is granted. When the world was overrun with tyranny, the least remove therefrom was a glorious rescue. But that it is imperfect, subject to convulsions, and incapable of producing what it seems to promise, is easily demonstrated.

Absolute governments (though the disgrace of human nature) have this advantage with them, that they are simple; if the people suffer, they know the head from which their suffering springs; they know likewise the remedy, and are not bewildered by a variety of causes and cures. But the Constitution of England is so exceedingly complex, that the nation may suffer for years together without being able to discover in which part the fault lies; some will say in one and some in another, and every political physician will advise a different medicine.

I know it is difficult to get over local or long-standing prejudices, yet if we will suffer ourselves to examine the component parts of the English Constitution, we shall find them to be the base remains of two ancient tyrannies, compounded with some new republican materials.

First—The remains of monarchical tyranny in the person of the King.

Secondly—The remains of aristocratical tyranny in the persons of the Peers.

Thirdly—The new republican materials in the persons of the Commons, on whose virtue depends the freedom of England.

The two first, by being hereditary, are independent of the people; wherefore in a *constitutional sense* they contribute nothing toward the freedom of the state.

To say that the Constitution of England is a *union* of three powers, reciprocally *checking* each other, is farcical; either the words have no meaning, or they are flat contradictions.

To say that the Commons is a check upon the King, presupposes two things:

First—That the King is not to be trusted without being looked after, or in other words, that a thirst for absolute power is the natural disease of monarchy.

Secondly—That the Commons, by being appointed for that purpose, are either wiser or more worthy of confidence than the Crown.

But as the same Constitution which gives the Commons a power to check the King by withholding the supplies, gives afterwards the King a power to check the Commons by empowering him to reject their other bills, it again supposes that the King is wiser than those whom it has already supposed to be wiser than him. A mere absurdity!

There is something exceedingly ridiculous in the composition of monarchy; it first excludes a man from the means of information, yet empowers him to act in cases where the highest judgment is required. The state of a king shuts him from the world, yet the business of a king requires him to know it thoroughly; wherefore the different parts, by unnaturally opposing and destroying each other, prove the whole character to be absurd and useless.

Some writers have explained the English Constitution thus: The King, say they, is one, the people another; the Peers are a house in behalf of the King, the Commons in behalf of the people.

But this hath all the distinctions of a house divided against itself; and though the expressions be pleasantly arranged, yet when examined, they appear idle and ambiguous; and it will always happen, that the nicest construction that words are capable of, when applied to the description of something which either cannot exist or is too incomprehensible to be within the compass of description, will be words of sound only, and though they may amuse the ear, they cannot inform the mind, for this explanation includes a previous question, viz.: *How came the King by a power which the people are afraid to trust, and always obliged to check?*

Such a power could not be the gift of a wise people, neither can any power, *which needs checking,* be from God; yet the provision, which the Constitution makes, supposes such a power to exist.

But the provision is unequal to the task; the means either cannot or will not accomplish the end, and the whole affair is a *felo de se;* for as the greater weight will always carry up the less, and as all the wheels of a machine are put in motion by one, it only remains to know which power in the Constitution has the most weight, for that will govern; and though the others, or a part of them, may clog, or, as the phrase is, check the rapidity of its motion, yet so long as they cannot stop it, their endeavors will be ineffectual; the first moving power will at last have its way, and what it wants in speed, is supplied by time.

That the Crown is this overbearing part in the English Constitution, needs not be mentioned, and that it derives its whole consequence merely from being the giver of places and pensions, is self-evident; wherefore, though we have been wise enough to shut and lock a door against absolute monarchy, we at the same time have been foolish enough to put the Crown in possession of the key.

The prejudice of Englishmen in favor of their own government by kings, lords and commons, arises as much or more from national pride than reason. Individuals are undoubtedly safer in England than in some other countries, but the *will* of a king is as much the *law* of the land in Britain as in France, with this difference, that instead of proceeding directly from his mouth, it is handed to the people under the more formidable shape of an act of Parliament. For the fate of Charles I hath only made kings more subtle— not more just.

Wherefore, laying aside all national pride and prejudice in favor of modes and forms, the plain truth is, that *it is wholly owing to the constitution of the people, and not to the constitution of the government,* that the Crown is not as oppressive in England as in Turkey.

An inquiry into the *constitutional errors* in English form of government is at this time highly necessary; for as we are never in a proper condition of doing justice to others, while we continue under the influence of some leading partiality, so neither are we capable of doing it to ourselves while we remain fettered by any obstinate prejudice. And as a man who is attached to a prostitute is unfitted to choose or judge of a wife, so any prepossession in favor of a rotten constitution of government will disable us from discerning a good one.

Of Monarchy and Hereditary Succession

Mankind being originally equals in the order of creation, the equality could only be destroyed by some subsequent circumstances; the distinctions of rich and poor may in a great measure be accounted for, and that without having recourse to the harsh, illsounding names of oppression and avarice. Oppression is often the *consequence,* but seldom or never the *means* of riches; and though avarice will preserve a man from being necessitously poor, it generally makes him too timorous to become wealthy.

But there is another and greater distinction, for which no truly natural or religious reason can be assigned, and that is, the distinction of men into KINGS and SUBJECTS. Male and female are the distinctions of nature, good and bad the distinctions of heaven; but how a race of men came into the world so exalted above the rest, and distinguished like some new species, is worth inquiring into, and whether they are the means of happiness or of misery to mankind.

In the early ages of the world, according to the Scripture chronology, there were no kings; the consequence of which was, there were no wars: it is the pride of kings which throws mankind into confusion. Holland without a king hath enjoyed more peace for this last century than any of the monarchical governments in Europe. Antiquity favors the same remark; for the quiet and rural lives of the first patriarchs hath a happy something in them, which vanishes away when we come to the history of Jewish royalty.

Government by kings was first introduced into the world by the heathens, from whom the children of Israel copied the custom. It was the most prosperous invention the devil ever set on foot for the promotion of idolatry. The heathens paid divine honors to their deceased kings, and the Christian world hath improved on the plan, by doing the same to their living ones. How impious is the title of *sacred majesty* applied to a worm who in the midst of his splendor is crumbling into dust!

As the exalting one man so greatly above the rest, cannot be justified on the equal rights of nature, so neither can it be defended on the authority of Scripture; for the will of the Almighty, as declared by Gideon and the prophet Samuel, expressly disapproves of the government by kings....

To the evil of monarchy we have added that of hereditary succession; and as the first is a degradation and lessening of ourselves, so the second, claimed as a matter of right, is an insult and imposition on posterity. For all men being originally equals, no *one* by *birth* could have a right to set up his family in perpetual preference to all others forever, and though himself might deserve *some* decent degree of honors of his contemporaries, yet his descendants might be far too unworthy to inherit them.

One of the strongest *natural* proofs of the folly of hereditary right of kings, is that nature disapproves it, otherwise she would not so frequently turn it into ridicule by giving mankind an *ass for a lion.*

Secondly, as no man at first could possess any other public honors than were bestowed upon him, so the givers of those honors could have no power to give away the right of posterity, and though they might say, "We choose you for *our* head," they could not, without manifest injustice to their children, say, "that your children and your children's children shall *reign* over ours for *ever.*" Because such an unwise, unjust, unnatural compact might, perhaps, in the next succession put them under the government of a rogue or a fool.

Most wise men in their private sentiments have ever treated hereditary right with contempt; yet it is one of those evils, which when once established is not easily removed; many submit from fear, others from superstition, and the more powerful part shares with the king the plunder of the rest.

This is supposing the present race of kings in the world to have had an honorable origin; whereas it is more than probable, that, could we take off the dark covering of antiquity and trace them to their first rise, we should find the first of them nothing better than the principal ruffian of some restless gang, whose savage manners or preeminence in subtility obtained him the title of chief among plunderers; and who by increasing in power, and extending his depredations, overawed the quiet and defenseless to purchase their safety by frequent contributions. Yet his electors could have no idea of giving hereditary right to his descendants, because such a perpetual exclusion of themselves was incompatible with the free and unrestrained principles they professed to live by....

Thoughts on the Present State of American Affairs

......

If there is any true cause of fear respecting independence, it is because no plan is yet laid down. Men do not see their way out; wherefore, as an opening into that business, I offer the following hints; at the same time modestly affirming, that I have no other opinion of them myself, than that they may be the means of giving rise to something better. Could the straggling thoughts of individuals be collected, they would frequently form materials for wise and able men to improve into useful matter.

Let the assemblies be annual, with a president only. The representation more equal. Their business wholly domestic, and subject to the authority of a continental congress.

Let each colony be divided into six, eight, or ten, convenient districts, each district to send a proper number of delegates to congress, so that each colony sends at least thirty.

The whole number in congress will be at least three hundred and ninety. Each congress to sit... and to choose a president by the following method: When the delegates are met, let a colony be taken from the whole thirteen colonies by lot, after which, let the whole congress choose (by ballot) a president from out of the delegates of that province.

In the next congress, let a colony be taken by lot from twelve only, omitting that colony from which the president was taken in the former congress and so proceeding on till the whole thirteen shall have had their proper rotation. And in order that nothing may pass into a law but what is satisfactorily just, not less than three-fifths of the congress to be called a majority. He that will promote discord, under a government so equally formed as this, would have joined Lucifer in his revolt.

But as there is a peculiar delicacy, from whom or in what manner this business must first arise, and as it seems most agreeable and consistent that it should come from some intermediate body between the governed and the governors, that is, between the congress and the people, let a *Continental Conference* be held, in the following manner, and for the following purpose:

A committee of twenty-six members of congress, viz., two for each colony. Two members from each house of assembly, or provincial convention; and five representatives of the people at large, to be chosen in the capital city or town of each province, for and in behalf of the whole province, by as many qualified voters as shall think proper to attend from all parts of the province for that purpose; or, if more convenient, the representatives may be chosen in two or three of the most populous parts thereof.

In this conference, thus assembled, will be united, the two grand principles of business, *knowledge* and *power*. The members of congress, assemblies, or conventions, by having had experience in national concerns, will be able and useful counsellors, and the whole, being empowered by the people, will have a truly legal authority.

The conferring members being met, let their business be to frame a *Continental Charter,* or Charter of the United Colonies; (answering to what is called the Magna Charta of England) fixing the number and manner of choosing members of congress, and members of assembly, with their date of sitting, and drawing the line of business and jurisdiction between them: always remembering, that our strength is continental, not provincial: securing freedom and property to all men, and above all things, the free exercise of religion, according to the dictates of conscience; with such other matter as is necessary for a charter to contain.

Immediately after which, the said conference to dissolve, and the bodies which shall be chosen conformable to the said charter, to be the legislators and governors of this continent for the time being; whose peace and happiness, may God preserve, Amen....

But where, say some, is the king of America? I'll tell you, friend, He reigns above, and doth not make havoc of mankind like the royal brute of Britain. Yet that we may not appear to be defective even in earthly honors, let a day be solemnly set apart for proclaiming the charter; let it be brought forth, placed on the divine law, the Word of God; let a crown be placed thereon, by which the world may know, that so far as we approve of monarchy, that in America *the law is king.*

For as in absolute governments the king is law, so in free countries the law ought to be king; and there ought to be no other. But lest any ill use should afterwards arise, let the crown at the conclusion of the ceremony be demolished and scattered among the people whose right it is.

A government of our own is our natural right: and when a man seriously reflects on the precariousness of human affairs, he will become convinced that it is infinitely wiser and safer to form a constitution of our own, in a cool deliberate manner, while we have it in our power, than to trust such an interesting event to time and chance. If we omit it now, some Masaniello may here after arise, who, laying hold of popular disquietudes, may collect together the desperate and the discontented, and by assuming to themselves the powers of government, may sweep away the liberties of the continent like a deluge.

Should the government of America return again into the hands of Britain, the tottering situation of things will be a temptation for some desperate adventurer to try his fortune; and in such a case, what relief can Britain give? Ere she could hear the news, the fatal business might be done; and ourselves suffering like the wretched Britains under the oppression of the Conqueror. Ye that oppose independence now, ye know not what ye do; ye are opening a door to eternal tyranny, by keeping vacant the seat of government.

There are thousands and tens of thousands who would think it glorious to expel from the continent that barbarous and hellish power which hath stirred up the Indians and negroes to destroy us; the cruelty hath a double guilt; it is dealing brutally by us and treacherously by them. To talk of friendship with those in whom our reason forbids us to have faith, and our affections, (wounded through a thousand pores,) instruct us to detest, is madness and folly. Every day wears out the little remains of kindred between us and them; and can there be any reason to hope that as the relationship expires the affection will increase, or that we shall agree better when we have ten times more and greater concerns to quarrel over than ever?

Ye that tell us of harmony and reconciliation, can ye restore to us the time that is passed? Can ye give to prostitution its former innocence? Neither can ye reconcile Britain and America. The last cord now is broken; the people of England are presenting addresses against us. There are injuries which nature cannot forgive; she would cease to be nature if she did. As well can the lover forgive the ravisher of his mistress, as the continent forgive the murders of Britain. The Almighty hath implanted in us these unextinguishable feelings for good and wise purposes. They are the guardians of His image in our hearts. They distinguish us from the herd of common animals. The social compact would dissolve and justice be extirpated from the earth, or have only a casual existence, were we callous to the touches of affection. The robber and the murderer would often escape unpunished, did not the injuries which our tempers sustain, provoke us into justice.

O ye that love mankind! Ye that dare oppose, not only the tyranny, but the tyrant, stand forth! Every spot of the old world is overrun with oppression. Freedom hath been hunted round the globe. Asia and Africa have long expelled her, Europe regards her like a stranger, and England hath given her warning to depart. O! receive the fugitive, and prepare in time an asylum for mankind …

Appendix

. . . . . .

I shall conclude these remarks with the following timely and well-intended hints. We ought to reflect, that there are three different ways by which an independency may hereafter be effected; and that one of those three will, one day or other, be the fate of America, viz., by the legal voice of the people in Congress; by a military power; or by a mob. It may not always happen that our soldiers are citizens, and the multitude a body of reasonable men; virtue, as I have already remarked, is not hereditary, neither is it perpetual. Should an independency be brought about by the first of those means, we have every opportunity and every encouragement before us, to form the noblest, purest constitution on the face of the earth. We have it in our power to begin the world over again. A situation, similar to the present, hath not happened since the days of Noah until now.

The birthday of a new world is at hand, and a race of men, perhaps as numerous as all Europe contains, are to receive their portion of freedom from the events of a few months. The reflection is awful—and in this point of view, how trifling, how ridiculous, do the little, paltry cavilings of a few weak or interested men appear, when weighed against the business of a world. Should we neglect the present favorable and inviting period, and independence be hereafter effected by any other means, we must charge the consequence to ourselves, or to those rather, whose narrow and prejudiced souls are habitually opposing the measure, without either inquiring or reflecting. There are reasons to be given in support of independence, which men should rather privately think of, than be publicly told of.

We ought not to be debating whether we shall be independent or not, but anxious to accomplish it on a firm, secure and honorable basis, and uneasy rather, that it is not yet begun upon. Every day convinces us of its necessity.

Even the Tories (if such beings yet remain among us) should, of all men, be the most solicitous to promote it; for as the appointment of committees at first, protected them from popular rage, so a wise and well established form of government will be the only certain means of continuing it securely to them. Wherefore, if they have not virtue enough to be *Whigs,* they ought to have prudence enough to wish for independence.

In short, independence is the only *bond* that can tie and keep us together. We shall then see our object, and our ears shall be legally shut against the schemes of an intriguing, as well as a cruel enemy. We shall then, too, be on a proper footing to treat with Britain; for there is reason to conclude, that the pride of that court will be less hurt by treating with the American states for terms of peace, than with those whom she denominates "rebellious subjects," for terms of accommodation. It is our delaying it that encourages her to hope for conquest, and our backwardness tends only to prolong the war. As we have, without any good effect there from withheld our trade to obtain a redress of our grievances, let us *now* try the alternative, by independently redressing them ourselves, and then offering to open the trade. The mercantile and reasonable part of England will be still with us; because peace *with* trade, is preferable to war *without* it. And if this offer be not accepted, other courts may be applied to.

On these grounds I rest the matter. And as no offer hath yet been made to refute the doctrine contained in the former editions of this pamphlet, it is a negative proof that either the doctrine cannot be refuted, or that the party in favor of it are too numerous to be opposed. *Wherefore,* instead of gazing at each other, with suspicious or doubtful curiosity, let each of us hold out to his neighbor the hearty hand of friendship, and unite in drawing a line, which, like an act of oblivion, shall bury in forgetfulness every former dissension. Let the names of Whig and Tory be extinct; and let none other be heard among us, than those of a *good citizen, an open and resolute friend,* and *a virtuous supporter of the* RIGHTS *of* MANKIND, *and of the* FREE AND INDEPENDENT STATES OF AMERICA.

THOMAS JEFFERSON

The Declaration of Independence
(1776)

The Declaration of Independence, as written by Thomas Jefferson (1743–1826) and amended and adopted by the Continental Congress, was *the* great political document of the American Enlightenment. This was not, of course, because of the originality of its particular ideas, which, as Jefferson later noted, were all stock notions of contemporary republican thought. What *was* original was the text as a whole: It was the first complete fusion in a public document of Enlightenment ideals and republican principles. After only the barest mention of "Nature's God," the Declaration boldly asserted as the foundation of its political principles "self-evident" truths that, because they were axiomatic, were to rational men "undeniable" (to use Jefferson's original adjective). Furthermore these rational truths were moral truths. They affirmed both the essential equality of men and certain individual human rights whose protection depended on forms of self-government that, as the "long train of abuses and usurpations" was meant to demonstrate, were sufficiently violated by the British king and his government as to evince "a design to reduce [the colonies] under absolute Despotism" and so justify a revolutionary separation. Finally, the Declaration announced the intention of the United States to establish for the first time in history a *nation* on the basis of these Enlightenment-republican principles. As such, the Declaration was both sweepingly universalistic and, as Jefferson later claimed, "an expression of the American mind." Garry Wills's *Inventing America: Jefferson's Declaration of Independence* (Garden City, N.Y., 1978), is a rich but controversial study of the Declaration in the context of Jefferson's moral and political theories. For a more technically philosophical interpretation, see Morton White, *The Philosophy of the American Revolution* (New York, 1978). Jay Fliegelman, *Declaring Independence: Jefferson, Natural Language, and the Culture of Performance* (Stanford, 1993), is an imaginative analysis of Jefferson's Declaration as a key artifact in a protodemocratic aesthetic revolution.

In *American Scripture: Making the Declaration of Independence* (New York, 1998), Pauline Maier appraises Revolutionary local and state proclamations, Declaration revisions, and subsequent interpretations of the evolving "text." For a challenging study of the Declaration as a global statement of sovereignty in the language of republicanism, see David Armitage, *The Declaration of Independence: A Global History* (Cambridge, Mass., 2007).

IN CONGRESS, JULY 4, 1776.
THE UNANIMOUS DECLARATION OF THE THIRTEEN UNITED STATES OF AMERICA,

When in the Course of human events, it becomes necessary for one people to dissolve the political bands which have connected them with another, and to assume among the powers of the earth, the separate and equal station to which the Laws of Nature and of Nature's God entitle them, a decent respect to the opinions of mankind requires that they should declare the causes which impel them to the separation. We hold these truths to be self-evident, that all men are created equal, that they are endowed by their Creator with certain unalienable Rights, that among these are Life, Liberty and the pursuit of Happiness. That to secure these rights, Governments are instituted among Men, deriving their just powers from the consent of the governed, That whenever any Form of Government becomes destructive of these ends, it is the Right of the People to alter or to abolish it, and to institute new Government, laying its foundation on such principles and organizing its powers in such form, as to them shall seem most likely to effect their Safety and Happiness. Prudence, indeed, will dictate that Governments long established should not be changed for light and transient causes; and accordingly all experience hath shewn, that mankind are more disposed to suffer, while evils are sufferable, than to right themselves by abolishing the forms to which they are accustomed. But when a long train of abuses and usurpations, pursuing invariably the same Object evinces a design to reduce them under absolute Despotism, it is their right, it is their duty, to throw off such Government, and to provide new Guards for their future security. Such has been the patient sufferance of these Colonies; and such is now the necessity which constrains them to alter their former Systems of Government. The history of the present King of Great Britain is a history of repeated injuries and usurpations, all having in direct object the establishment of an absolute Tyranny over these States. To prove this, let Facts be submitted to a candid world. He has refused his Assent to Laws, the most wholesome and necessary for the public good. He has forbidden his Governors to pass Laws of immediate and pressing importance, unless suspended in their operation till his Assent should be obtained; and when so suspended, he has utterly neglected to attend to them. He has refused to pass other Laws for the accommodation of large districts of people, unless those people would relinquish the right of Representation in the Legislature, a right inestimable to them and formidable to tyrants only. He has called together legislative bodies at places unusual, uncomfortable, and distant from the depository of their public Records, for the sole purpose of fatiguing them into compliance with his measures. He has dissolved Representative Houses repeatedly, for opposing with manly firmness his invasions on the rights of the people. He has refused for a long time, after such dissolutions, to cause others to be elected; whereby the Legislative powers, incapable of Annihilation, have returned to the People at large for their exercise; the State remaining in the mean time exposed to all the dangers of invasion from without, and convulsions within. He has endeavoured to prevent the population of these States; for that purpose obstructing the Laws for Naturalization of Foreigners; refusing to pass others to encourage their migrations hither, and raising the conditions of new Appropriations of Lands. He has obstructed the Administration of Justice, by refusing his Assent to Laws for establishing Judiciary powers. He has made Judges dependent on his Will alone, for the tenure of their offices, and the amount and payment of their salaries. He has erected a multitude of New Offices, and sent hither swarms of Officers to harass our people, and eat out their substance. He has kept among us, in times of peace, standing Armies without the Consent of our legislatures. He has affected to render the Military independent of and superior to the Civil power. He has combined with others to subject us to a jurisdiction foreign to our constitution, and unacknowledged by our laws; giving his Assent to their Acts of pretended Legislation: For Quartering large bodies of armed troops among us: For protecting them, by a mock Trial, from punishment for any Murders which they should commit on the Inhabitants of these States: For cutting off our Trade with all parts of the world: For imposing Taxes on us without our Consent: For depriving us in many cases of the benefits of Trial by Jury: For transporting us beyond Seas to be tried for pretended offences: For abolishing the free System of English Laws in a neighbouring Province, establishing therein an Arbitrary government, and enlarging its Boundries so as to render it at once an example and fit instrument for introducing the same absolute rule into these Colonies: For taking away our Charters, abolishing our most valuable Laws, and altering fundamentally the Forms of our Governments: For suspending our own Legislatures, and declaring themselves invested with power to legislate for us in all cases whatsoever. He has abdicated Government here, by declaring us out of his Protection and waging War against us. He has plundered our seas, ravaged our Coasts, burnt our towns, and destroyed the Lives of our people. He is at this time transporting large Armies of foreign Mercenaries to compleat the works of death, desolation and tyranny, already begun with circumstances of Cruelty & perfidy scarcely paralleled in the most barbarous ages, and totally unworthy the Head of a civilized nation. He has constrained our fellow Citizens taken Captive on the high Seas to bear Arms against their Country, to become the executioners of their friends and Brethren, or to fall themselves by their Hands. He has excited domestic insurrections amongst us, and has endeavoured to bring on the inhabitants of our frontiers, the merciless Indian Savages, whose known rule of warfare, is an undistinguished destruction of all ages, sexes and conditions. In every stage of these Oppressions We have Petitioned for Redress in the most humble terms: Our repeated Petitions have been answered only by repeated injury. A Prince, whose character is thus marked by every act which may define a Tyrant, is unfit to be the ruler of a free people. Nor have We been wanting in attentions to our Brittish brethren. We have warned them from time to time of attempts by their legislature to extend an unwarrantable jurisdiction over us. We have reminded them of the circumstances of our emigration and settlement here. We have appealed to their native justice and magnanimity, and we have conjured them by the ties of our common kindred to disavow these usurpations, which, would inevitably interrupt our connections and correspondence. They too have been deaf to the voice of justice and of consanguinity. We must, therefore, acquiesce in the necessity, which denounces our Separation, and hold them, as we hold the rest of mankind, Enemies in War, in Peace Friends.

We, therefore, the Representatives of the united States of America, in General Congress, Assembled, appealing to the Supreme Judge of the world for the rectitude of our intentions, do, in the Name, and by Authority of the good People of these Colonies, solemnly publish and declare, That these United Colonies are, and of Right ought to be

Free and Independent States; that they are Absolved from all Allegiance to the British Crown, and that all political connection between them and the State of Great Britain, is and ought to be totally dissolved; and that as Free and Independent States, they have full Power to levy War, conclude Peace, contract Alliances, establish Commerce, and to do all other Acts and Things which Independent States may of right do. And for the support of this Declaration, with a firm reliance on the protection of divine Providence, we mutually pledge to each other our Lives, our Fortunes and our sacred Honor.

ALEXANDER HAMILTON

"Constitutional Convention Speech on a Plan of Government" (1787)

As aide-de-camp to General Washington, brilliant secretary of treasury in the Washington administration, and ill-fated Federalist party leader, Alexander Hamilton (1755–1804) was American republicanism's sometimes consummate man of action. As treasury secretary, he was also the author of a series of influential financial reports that advocated the most far-reaching program of governmental support for capitalist economic development in the early Republic. But at the bottom of these public actions and policies, no less than with those of the more scholarly Adams and Jefferson, was a strongly held conception of the ideal republican state. The one text where Hamilton developed his conception most completely was his speech before the Constitutional Convention. This is ironic since in it he argued for a political system that was considerably more authoritative than the adopted one he would end up vigorously defending in the ensuing ratification debate. Nevertheless, in this pointed critique of the Convention's two plans for a new government, Hamilton canvassed several of his most fundamental ideas. One was his notion that a strong central state could be relied on to promote the public welfare better than state and local governments. A second was his claim that an industrious society inevitably nurtured clashing passions and interests that government needed to convert into springs of support for itself. And a third was his belief that both private and public virtue could be best promoted by making representation in the upper house and the executive branch as little subject to popular accountability as was still consistent with a nonhereditary republican society.

Forrest McDonald's *Alexander Hamilton: A Biography* (New York, 1979) is a useful guide to Hamilton's intellectual development. For a discerning study of Hamilton's political thought, see Gerald Stourzh, *Alexander Hamilton and the Idea of Republican Government* (Stanford, 1970). Cecelia M. Kenyon, "Alexander Hamilton: Rousseau of the Right," *Political Science Quarterly*, 73 (June 1958), 161–78, is an older yet still valuable counterview. For a probing discussion of the origins and legacy of Hamilton's and other Founders' ideas of the nation state, see Samuel H. Beer, *To Make a Nation: The Rediscovery of American Federalism* (Cambridge, Mass., 1993).

James Madison's Version

[Philadelphia, June 18, 1787]

MR. HAMILTON, had been hitherto silent on the business before the Convention, partly from respect to others whose superior abilities age & experience rendered him unwilling to bring forward ideas dissimilar to theirs, and partly from his delicate situation with respect to his own State, to whose sentiments as expressed by his Colleagues, he could by no means accede. The crisis however which now marked our affairs, was too serious to permit any scruples whatever to prevail over the duty imposed on every man to contribute his efforts for the public safety & happiness. He was obliged therefore to declare himself unfriendly to both plans. He was particularly opposed to that from N. Jersey, being fully convinced, that no amendment of the Confederation, leaving the States in possession of their Sovereignty could possibly answer the purpose. On the other hand he confessed he was much discouraged by the amazing extent of Country in expecting the desired blessings from any general sovereignty that could be substituted. As to the powers of the Convention, he thought the doubts started on that subject had arisen from distinctions & reasonings too subtle. A *federal* Govt. he conceived to mean an association of independent Communities into one. Different Confederacies have different powers, and exercise them in different ways. In some instances the powers are exercised over collective bodies; in others over individuals, as in the German Diet—& among ourselves in cases of piracy. Great latitude therefore must be given to the signification of the term. The plan last proposed[1] departs itself from the *federal* idea, as understood by some, since it is to operate eventually on individuals. He agreed moreover with the Honble gentleman from Va. (Mr. R.) that we owed it to our Country, to do on this emergency whatever we should deem essential to its happiness. The States sent us here to provide for the exigences of the Union. To rely on & propose any plan not adequate to these exigences, merely because it was not clearly within our powers, would be to sacrifice the means to the end. It may be said that the *States* can not *ratify* a plan not within the purview of the article of Confederation providing for alterations & amendments. But may not the States themselves in which no constitutional authority equal to this purpose exists in the Legislatures, have had in view a reference to the people at large. In the Senate of N. York, a proviso was moved, that no act of the Convention should be binding until it should be referred to the people & ratified; and the motion was lost by a single voice only, the reason assigned agst. it being, that it might possibly be found an inconvenient shackle.

The great question is what provision shall we make for the happiness of our Country? He would first make a comparative examination of the two plans—prove that there were essential defects in both—and point out such changes as might render a *national one,* efficacious. The great & essential principles necessary for the support of Government are 1. an active & constant interest in supporting it. This principle does not exist in the States in favor of the federal Govt. They have evidently in a high degree, the esprit de corps. They constantly pursue internal interests adverse to those of the whole. They have their

---

1. The New Jersey Plan.

Source: The Papers of Alexander Hamilton, vol. 4, ed. Harold C. Syrett and Jacob E. Cooke (New York: Columbia University Press, 1962), 187–95. Editors' notes altered. Reprinted by permission of Columbia University Press, Copyright© 1962.

particular debts—their particular plans of finance &c. All these when opposed to, invariably prevail over the requisitions & plans of Congress. 2. The love of power. Men love power. The same remarks are applicable to this principle. The States have constantly shewn a disposition rather to regain the powers delegated by them than to part with more, or to give effect to what they had parted with. The ambition of their demagogues is known to hate the controul of the Genl. Government. It may be remarked too that the Citizens have not that anxiety to prevent a dissolution of the Genl. Govt. as of the particular Govts. A dissolution of the latter would be fatal; of the former would still leave the purposes of Govt, attainable to a considerable degree. Consider what such a State as Virga. will be in a few years, a few compared with the life of nations. How strongly will it feel its importance & self-sufficiency? 3. An habitual attachment of the people. The whole force of this tie is on the side of the State Govt. Its sovereignty is immediately before the eyes of the people: its protection is immediately enjoyed by them. From its hand distributive justice, and all those acts which familiarize & endear Govt. to a people, are dispensed to them. 4. *Force* by which may be understood a *coertion of laws* or *coertion of arms*. Congs. have not the former except in few cases. In particular States, this coercion is nearly sufficient; tho' he held it in most cases, not entirely so. A certain portion of military force is absolutely necessary in large communities. Massts. is now feeling this necessity & making provision for it. But how can this force be exerted on the States collectively. It is impossible. It amounts to a war between the parties. Foreign powers also will not be idle spectators. They will interpose, the confusion will increase, and a dissolution of the Union will ensue. 5. *influence,* he did not mean corruption, but a dispensation of those regular honors & emoluments, which produce an attachment to the Govt. Almost all the weight of these is on the side of the States; and must continue so as long as the States continue to exist. All the passions then we see, of avarice, ambition, interest, which govern most individuals, and all public bodies, fall into the current of the States, and do not flow in the stream of the Genl. Govt. The former therefore will generally be an overmatch for the Genl. Govt. and render any confederacy, in its very nature precarious. Theory is in this case fully confirmed by experience. The Amphyctionic Council had it would seem ample powers for general purposes. It had in particular the power of fining and using force agst. delinquent members. What was the consequence. Their decrees were mere signals of war. The Phocian war is a striking example of it. Philip at length taking advantage of their disunion, and insinuating himself into their Councils, made himself master of their fortunes. The German Confederacy affords another lesson. The authority of Charlemagne seemed to be as great as could be necessary. The great feudal chiefs however, exercising their local sovereignties, soon felt the spirit & found the means of, encroachments, which reduced the imperial authority to a nominal sovereignty. The Diet has succeeded, which tho' aided by a Prince at its head, of great authority independently of his imperial attributes, is a striking illustration of the weakness of Confederated Governments. Other examples instruct us in the same truth. The Swiss cantons have scarce any Union at all, and have been more than once at war with one another. How then are all these evils to be avoided? only by such a compleat sovereignty in the general Governmt. as will turn all the strong principles & passions above mentioned on its side. Does the scheme of N. Jersey produce this effect? does it afford any substantial remedy whatever? On the contrary it labors under great defects, and the defect of some of its provisions will destroy the efficacy of others. It gives a direct revenue to Congs. but this will not be sufficient. The balance can only be supplied by requisitions: which experience proves can not be relied on. If States are to deliberate on the mode, they will also deliberate on the object of the supplies, and will grant or not grant as they approve or disapprove of it. The delinquency of one will invite and countenance it in others. Quotas too must in the nature of things be so unequal as to produce the same evil.

To what standard will you resort? Land is a fallacious one. Compare Holland with Russia: France or Engd. with other countries of Europe. Pena. with N. Carola. will the relative pecuniary abilities in those instances, correspond with the relative value of land. Take numbers of inhabitants for the rule and make like comparison of different countries, and you will find it to be equally unjust. The different degrees of industry and improvement in different Countries render the first object a precarious measure of wealth. Much depends too on *situation*. Cont. N. Jersey & N. Carolina, not being commercial States & contributing to the wealth of the commercial ones, can never bear quotas assessed by the ordinary rules of proportion. They will & must fail in their duty, their example will be followed, and the Union itself be dissolved. Whence then is the national revenue to be drawn? from Commerce? even from exports which notwithstanding the common opinion are fit objects of moderate taxation, from excise, &c &c. These tho' not equal, are less unequal than quotas. Another destructive ingredient in the plan, is that equality of suffrage which is so much desired by the small States. It is not in human nature that Va. & the large States should consent to it, or if they did that they shd. long abide by it. It shocks too much the ideas of Justice, and every human feeling. Bad principles in a Govt. tho slow are sure in their operation, and will gradually destroy it. A doubt has been raised whether Congs. at present have a right to keep Ships or troops in time of peace. He leans to the negative. Mr. Ps. plan provides no remedy. If the powers proposed were adequate, the organization of Congs. is such that they could never be properly & effectually exercised. The members of Congs. being chosen by the States & subject to recall, represent all the local prejudices. Should the powers be found effectual, they will from time to time be heaped on them, till a tyrannic sway shall be established. The general power whatever be its form if it preserves itself, must swallow up the State powers. Otherwise it will be swallowed up by them. It is agst. all the principles of a good Government to vest the requisite powers in such a body as Congs. Two Sovereignties can not co-exist within the same limits. Giving powers to Congs. must eventuate in a bad Govt, or in no Govt. The plan of N. Jersey therefore will not do. What then is to be done? Here he was embarrassed. The extent of the Country to be governed, discouraged him. The expence of a general Govt, was also formidable; unless there were such a diminution of expence on the side of the State Govts, as the case would admit. If they were extinguished, he was persuaded that great aeconomy might be obtained by substituting a general Govt. He did not mean however to shock the public opinion by proposing such a measure. On the other hand he saw no *other* necessity for declining it. They are not necessary for any of the great purposes of commerce, revenue, or agriculture. Subordinate authorities he was aware would be necessary. There must be district tribunals: corporations for local purposes. But cui bono, the vast & expensive apparatus now appertaining to the States. The only difficulty of a serious nature which occurred to him, was that of drawing representatives from the extremes to the center of the Community. What inducements can be offered that will suffice? The moderate wages for the 1st. branch would only be a bait to little demagogues. Three dollars or thereabouts he supposed would be the utmost. The Senate he feared from a similar cause, would be filled by certain undertakers who wish for particular offices under the Govt. This view of the subject almost led him to despair that a Republican Govt. could be established over so great an extent. He was sensible at the same time that it would be unwise to propose one of any other form. In his private opinion he had no scruple in declaring, supported as he was by the opinions of so many of the wise & good, that the British Govt was the best in the world: and that he doubted much whether any thing short of it would do in America. He hoped Gentlemen of different opinions would bear with him in this, and begged them to recollect the change of opinion on this subject which had taken place and was still going on. It was once thought that the power of Congs. was amply sufficient to secure the end of their institution. The error was now seen by every one. The members most tenacious of republicanism, he observed, were as loud as any in declaiming agst. the vices of democracy. This progress of the public mind led him to anticipate the time, when others as well as himself would join in the praise bestowed by Mr. Neckar on the British Constitution, namely, that it is the only Govt. in the world "which unites public strength with individual security." In every community where industry is encouraged, there will be a division of it into the few & the many. Hence separate interests will arise. There will be debtors & creditors &c. Give all power to the many, they will oppress the few. Give all power to the few, they will oppress the many. Both therefore ought to have power, that each may defend itself agst. the other. To the want of this check we owe our paper money, instalment laws &c. To the proper adjustment of it the British owe the excellence of their Constitution. Their house of Lords is a most noble institution. Having nothing to hope for by a change, and a sufficient interest by means of their property, in being faithful to the national interest, they form a permanent barrier agst. every pernicious innovation, whether attempted on the part of the Crown or of the Commons. No temporary Senate will have the firmness eno' to answer the purpose. The Senate (of Maryland) which seems to be so much appealed to, has not yet been sufficiently tried. Had the people been unanimous & eager, in the late appeal to them on the subject of a paper emission they would have yielded to the torrent. Their acquiescing in such an appeal is a proof of it. Gentlemen differ in their opinions concerning the necessary checks, from the different estimates they form of the human passions. They suppose seven years a sufficient period to give the senate an adequate firmness, from not duly considering the amazing violence & turbulence of the democratic spirit. When a great object of Govt. is pursued, which seizes the popular passions, they spread like wild fire, and become irresistable. He appealed to the gentlemen from the N. England States whether experience had not there verified the remark. As to the Executive, it seemed to be admitted that no good one could be established on Republican principles. Was not this giving up the merits of the question: for can there be a good Govt. without a good Executive. The English model was the only good one on this subject. The Hereditary interest of the King was so interwoven with that of the Nation, and his personal emoluments so great, that he was placed above the danger of being corrupted from abroad—and at the same time was both sufficiently independent and sufficiently controuled, to answer the purpose of the institution at home. One of the weak sides of Republics was their being liable to foreign influence & corruption. Men of little character, acquiring great power become easily the tools of intermedling Neibours. Sweeden was a striking instance. The French & English had each their parties during the late Revolution which was effected by the predominant influence of the former. What is the inference from all these observations? That we ought to go as far in order to attain stability and permanency, as republican principles will admit. Let one branch of the Legislature hold their places for life or at least during good behaviour. Let the Executive also be for life. He appealed to the feelings of the members present whether a term of seven years, would induce the sacrifices of private affairs which an acceptance of public trust would require, so as to ensure the services of the best Citizens. On this plan we should have in the Senate a permanent will, a weighty interest, which would answer essential purposes. But is this a Republican Govt., it will be asked? Yes if all the Magistrates are appointed, and vacancies are filled, by the people, or a process of election originating with the people. He was sensible that an Executive constituted as he proposed would have in fact but little of the power and independence that might be necessary. On the other plan of appointing him for 7 years, he thought the Executive ought to have but little power. He would be ambitious, with the means of making creatures; and as the object of his ambition wd. be to *prolong* his power, it is probable that in case of a war, he would avail himself of the emergence, to evade or refuse a degradation from his place. An Executive for life has not this motive for forgetting his fidelity, and will therefore be a safer depository of power. It will be objected probably, that such an Executive will be an *elective Monarch,* and will give birth to the tumults which characterize that form of Govt. He wd. reply that *Monarch* is an indefinite term. It marks not either the degree or duration of power. If this Executive Magistrate wd. be a monarch for life— the other propd. by the Report from the Comtte of the whole, wd. be a monarch for seven years. The circumstance of being elective was also applicable to both. It had been observed by judicious writers that elective monarchies wd. be the best if they could be guarded agst. the *tumults* excited by the ambition and intrigues of competitors. He was not sure that tumults were an inseparable evil. He rather thought this character of Elective Monarchies had been taken rather from particular cases than from general principles. The election of Roman Emperors was made by the *Army.* In *Poland* the election is made by great rival *princes* with independent power, and ample means, of raising commotions. In the German Empire, the appointment is made by the Electors & Princes, who have equal motives & means, for exciting cabals & parties. Might not such a mode of election be devised among ourselves as will defend the community agst. these effects in any dangerous degree? Having made these observations he would read to the Committee a sketch of a plan which he shd. prefer to either of those under consideration. He was aware that it went beyond the ideas of most members. But will such a plan be adopted out of doors? In return he would ask will the people adopt the other plan? At present they will adopt neither. But he sees the Union dissolving or already dissolved—he sees evils operating in the States which must soon cure the people of their fondness for democracies—he sees that a great progress has been already made & is still going on in the public mind. He thinks therefore that the people will in time be unshackled from their prejudices; and whenever that happens, they will themselves not be satisfied at stopping where the plan of Mr. R. wd. place them, but be ready to go as far at least as he proposes.

"BRUTUS"

Selection from "Essays of Brutus"
(1787–88)

Historians have generally given the Anti-Federalist opponents of the ratification of the Constitution the short shrift usually accorded losers in history. Yet their ideas contributed vitally to the shaping of the document, the nature of the defense made of it, and its later evolution. Furthermore, historians have at their disposal several Anti-Federalist texts that surpassed in their intellectual sophistication most pro-Constitution tracts. Among these are the essays of "Brutus," first printed, like the *Federalist Papers*, in New York newspapers and afterward widely reprinted in many states, where they were often referred to in subsequent articles and pamphlets.

In large part, what made Brutus's essays so influential was their coherent republican utilization of almost all the major Anti-Federalist objections to the Constitution. In these first and third letters, he dwelled on three fatal flaws: the allegedly federal but really "consolidated" character of the proposed national government, the Constitution's dangerously unrepublican reduction of representation in Congress, and, most theoretically important, its erection of a large unified republic inevitably oppressive and subversive of the public good. (In the second letter, here omitted, he also severely criticized the absence in the document of any bill of rights.) On two subtextual points Brutus was more ambiguous. One was the question of the sources of the Constitution's unrepublican effects—whether, that is, they would come about as unintended consequences or as a result of elites' conscious intentions to lead the people (as he said at one point) "wilfully" into an "absolute state of vassalage." The other matter was the pseudonym Brutus. Although historians have yet to agree upon whose identity the name masked, like similar ones used by many other debate participants, it clearly resonated with two salient phenomena of their discourse: their deep identification of their post-Revolutionary cause with the great heroes of classical and modern republican history and the impersonal and therefore disinterested personas so prized by eighteenth-century republican writers. In debating the Constitution, Brutus and his allies and opponents were trying to do more than just score points; they were striving to constitute the new nation's virtuous republican public sphere.

The best introduction to Anti-Federalist political thought is Herbert J. Storing's *What the Anti-Federalists Were For* (Chicago, 1981). Saul Cornell, *The Other Founders: Anti-Federalism and the Dissenting Tradition in America, 1788–1828* (Chapel Hill, 1999), presents the Anti-Federalists as founders of a seminal tradition of American localist political thinking. A valuable assortment of important contending interpretations of the ideological meaning of Federalist and Anti-Federalist debates may be found in "The Creation of the American Republic, 1776–1787: A Symposium of Views and Reviews," *William and Mary Quarterly*, 54 (July 1987), 549–640. For an influential study of the concept of the "public sphere" as it emerged in the West in the late eighteenth century, see Jürgen Habermas, *The Structural Transformation of the Public Sphere: An Inquiry into a Category of Bourgeois Society*, trans. Thomas Burger and Frederick Lawrence (Cambridge, Mass., 1989).

I

18 October 1787

To the Citizens of the State of New-York.

When the public is called to investigate and decide upon a question in which not only the present members of the community are deeply interested, but upon which the happiness and misery of generations yet unborn is in great measure suspended, the benevolent mind cannot help feeling itself peculiarly interested in the result.

In this situation, I trust the feeble efforts of an individual, to lead the minds of the people to a wise and prudent determination, cannot fail of being acceptable to the candid and dispassionate part of the community. Encouraged by this consideration, I have been induced to offer my thoughts upon the present important crisis of our public affairs.

Perhaps this country never saw so critical a period in their political concerns. We have felt the feebleness of the ties by which these United-States are held together, and the want of sufficient energy in our present confederation, to manage, in some instances, our general concerns. Various expedients have been proposed to remedy these evils, but none have succeeded. At length a Convention of the states has been assembled, they have formed a constitution which will now, probably, be submitted to the people to ratify or reject, who are the fountain of all power, to whom alone it of right belongs to make or unmake constitutions, or forms of government, at their pleasure. The most important question that was ever proposed to your decision, or to the decision of any people under heaven, is before you, and you are to decide upon it by men of your own election, chosen specially for this purpose. If the constitution, offered to your acceptance, be a wise one, calculated to preserve the invaluable blessings of liberty, to secure the inestimable rights of mankind, and promote human happiness, then, if you accept it, you will lay a lasting foundation of happiness for millions yet unborn; generations to come will rise up and call you blessed. You may rejoice in the prospects of this vast extended continent becoming filled with freemen, who will assert the dignity of human nature. You may solace yourselves with the idea, that society, in this favoured land, will fast advance to the highest point of perfection; the human mind will expand in knowledge and virtue, and the golden age be, in some measure, realised. But if, on the other hand, this form of government contains principles that will lead to the subversion of liberty—if it lends to establish a despotism, or, what is worse, a tyrannic aristocracy; then, if you adopt it, this only remaining assylum for liberty will be shut up, and posterity will execrate your memory.

Momentous then is the question you have to determine, and you are called upon by every motive which should influence a noble and virtuous mind, to examine it well, and to make up a wise judgment. It is insisted, indeed, that this constitution must be received, be it ever so imperfect. If it has its defects, it is said, they can be best amended when they are experienced. But remember, when the people once part with power, they can seldom or never resume it again but by force. Many instances can be produced in which the people have voluntarily increased the powers of their rulers; but few, if any, in which rulers have willingly abridged their authority. This is a sufficient reason to induce you to be careful, in the first instance, how you deposit the powers of government.

Source: The Complete Anti-Federalist, vol. 2, ed. Herbert J. Storing (Chicago: University of Chicago Press, 1981), 363–72, 377–82. Editor's notes omitted. Reprinted by permission of the University of Chicago Press, Copyright © 1981.

With these few introductory remarks, I shall proceed to a consideration of this constitution:

The first question that presents itself on the subject is, whether a confederated government be the best for the United States or not? Or in other words, whether the thirteen United States should be reduced to one great republic, governed by one legislature, and under the direction of one executive and judicial; or whether they should continue thirteen confederated republics, under the direction and controul of a supreme federal head for certain defined national purposes only?

This enquiry is important, because, although the government reported by the convention does not go to a perfect and entire consolidation, yet it approaches so near to it, that it must, if executed, certainly and infallibly terminate in it.

This government is to possess absolute and uncontroulable power, legislative, executive and judicial, with respect to every object to which it extends, for by the last clause of section 8th, article Ist, it is declared "that the Congress shall have power to make all laws which shall be necessary and proper for carrying into execution the foregoing powers, and all other powers vested by this constitution, in the government of the United States; or in any department or office thereof." And by the 6th article, it is declared "that this constitution, and the laws of the United States, which shall be made in pursuance thereof, and the treaties made, or which shall be made, under the authority of the United States, shall be the supreme law of the land; and the judges in every state shall be bound thereby, any thing in the constitution, or law of any state to the contrary notwithstanding." It appears from these articles that there is no need of any intervention of the state governments, between the Congress and the people, to execute any one power vested in the general government, and that the constitution and laws of every state are nullified and declared void, so far as they are or shall be inconsistent with this constitution, or the laws made in pursuance of it, or with treaties made under the authority of the United States.—The government then, so far as it extends, is a complete one, and not a confederation. It is as much one complete government as that of New-York or Massachusetts, has as absolute and perfect powers to make and execute all laws, to appoint officers, institute courts, declare offences, and annex penalties, with respect to every object to which it extends, as any other in the world. So far therefore as its powers reach, all ideas of confederation are given up and lost. It is true this government is limited to certain objects, or to speak more properly, some small degree of power is still left to the states, but a little attention to the powers vested in the general government, will convince every candid man, that if it is capable of being executed, all that is reserved for the individual states must very soon be annihilated, except so far as they are barely necessary to the organization of the general government. The powers of the general legislature extend to every case that is of the least importance—there is nothing valuable to human nature, nothing dear to freemen, but what is within its power. It has authority to make laws which will affect the lives, the liberty, and property of every man in the United States; nor can the constitution or laws of any state, in any way prevent or impede the full and complete execution of every power given. The legislative power is competent to lay taxes, duties, imposts, and excises;—there is no limitation to this power, unless it be said that the clause which directs the use to which those taxes, and duties shall be applied, may be said to be a limitation: but this is no restriction of the power at all, for by this clause they are to be applied to pay the debts and provide for the common defence and general welfare of the United States; but the legislature have authority to contract debts at their discretion; they are the sole judges of what is necessary to provide for the common defence, and they only are to determine what is for the general welfare; this power therefore is neither more nor less, than a power to lay and collect taxes, imposts, and excises, at their pleasure; not only [is] the power to lay taxes unlimited, as to the amount they may require, but it is perfect and absolute to raise them in any mode they please. No state legislature, or any power in the state governments, have any more to do in carrying this into effect, than the authority of one state has to do with that of another. In the business therefore of laying and collecting taxes, the idea of confederation is totally lost, and that of one entire republic is embraced. It is proper here to remark, that the authority to lay and collect taxes is the most important of any power that can be granted; it connects with it almost all other powers, or at least will in process of time draw all other after it; it is the great mean of protection, security, and defence, in a good government, and the great engine of oppression and tyranny in a bad one. This cannot fail of being the case, if we consider the contracted limits which are set by this constitution, to the late [state?] governments, on this article of raising money. No state can emit paper money—lay any duties, or imposts, on imports, or exports, but by consent of the Congress; and then the net produce shall be for the benefit of the United States: the only mean therefore left, for any state to support its government and discharge its debts, is by direct taxation; and the United States have also power to lay and collect taxes, in any way they please. Every one who has thought on the subject, must be convinced that but small sums of money can be collected in any country, by direct taxe[s], when the foederal government begins to exercise the right of taxation in all its parts, the legislatures of the several states will find it impossible to raise monies to support their governments. Without money they cannot be supported, and they must dwindle away, and, as before observed, their powers absorbed in that of the general government.

It might be here shewn, that the power in the federal legislative, to raise and support armies at pleasure, as well in peace as in war, and their controul over the militia, tend, not only to a consolidation of the government, but the destruction of liberty.—I shall not, however, dwell upon these, as a few observations upon the judicial power of this government, in addition to the preceding, will fully evince the truth of the position.

The judicial power of the United States is to be vested in a supreme court, and in such inferior courts as Congress may from time to time ordain and establish. The powers of these courts are very extensive; their jurisdiction comprehends all civil causes, except such as arise between citizens of the same state; and it extends to all cases in law and equity arising under the constitution. One inferior court must be established, I presume, in each state, at least, with the necessary executive officers appendant thereto. It is easy to see, that in the common course of things, these courts will eclipse the dignity, and take away from the respectability, of the state courts. These courts will be, in themselves, totally independent of the states, deriving their authority from the United States, and receiving from them fixed salaries; and in the course of human events it is to be expected, that they will swallow up all the powers of the courts in the respective states.

How far the clause in the 8th section of the 1st article may operate to do away all idea of confederated states, and to effect an entire consolidation of the whole into one general government, it is impossible to say. The powers given by this article are very general and comprehensive, and it may receive a construction to justify the passing almost any law. A power to make all laws, which shall be *necessary and proper,* for carrying into execution, all powers vested by the constitution in the government of the United States, or any department or officer thereof, is a power very comprehensive and definite [indefinite?], and may, for ought I know, be exercised in a such manner as entirely to abolish the state legislatures. Suppose the legislature of a state should pass a law to raise money to support their government and pay the state debt, may the Congress repeal this law, because it may prevent the collection of a tax which they may think proper and necessary to lay, to provide for the general welfare of the United States? For all laws made, in pursuance of this constitution, are the supreme lay of the land, and the judges in every state shall be bound thereby, any thing in the constitution or laws of the different states to the contrary not-withstanding.—By such a law, the government of a particular state might be overturned at one stroke, and thereby be deprived of every means of its support.

It is not meant, by stating this case, to insinuate that the constitution would warrant a law of this kind; or unnecessarily to alarm the fears of the people, by suggesting, that the federal legislature would be more likely to pass the limits assigned them by the constitution, than that of an individual state, further than they are less responsible to the people. But what is meant is, that the legislature of the United States are vested with the great and uncontroulable powers, of laying and collecting taxes, duties, imposts, and excises; of regulating trade, raising and supporting armies, organizing, arming, and disciplining the militia, instituting courts, and other general powers. And are by this clause invested with the power of making all laws, *proper and necessary,* for carrying all these into execution; and they may so exercise this power as entirely to annihilate all the state governments, and reduce this country to one single government. And if they may do it, it is pretty certain they will; for it will be found that the power retained by individual states, small as it is, will be a clog upon the wheels of the government of the United States; the latter therefore will be naturally inclined to remove it out of the way. Besides, it is a truth confirmed by the unerring experience of ages, that every man, and every body of men, invested with power, are ever disposed to increase it, and to acquire a superiority over every thing that stands in their way. This disposition, which is implanted in human nature, will operate in the federal legislature to lessen and ultimately to subvert the state authority, and having such advantages, will most certainly succeed, if the federal government succeeds at all. It must be very evident then, that what this constitution wants of being a complete consolidation of the several parts of the union into one complete government, possessed of perfect legislative, judicial, and executive powers, to all intents and purposes, it will necessarily acquire in its exercise and operation.

Let us now proceed to enquire, as I at first proposed, whether it be best the thirteen United States should be reduced to one great republic, or not? It is here taken for granted, that all agree in this, that whatever government we adopt, it ought to be a free one; that it should be so framed as to secure the liberty of the citizens of America, and such an one as to admit of a full, fair, and equal representation of the people. The question then will be, whether a government thus constituted, and founded on such principles, is practicable, and can be exercised over the whole United States, reduced into one state?

If respect is to be paid to the opinion of the greatest and wisest men who have ever thought or wrote on the science of government, we shall be constrained to conclude, that a free republic cannot succeed over a country of such immense extent, containing such a number of inhabitants, and these encreasing in such rapid progression as that of the whole United States. Among the many illustrious authorities which might be produced to this point, I shall content myself with quoting only two. The one is the baron de Montesquieu, spirit of laws, chap. xvi. vol. I [book VIII]. "It is natural to a republic to have only a small territory, otherwise it cannot long subsist. In a large republic there are men of large fortunes, and consequently of less moderation; there are trusts too great to be placed in any single sub-ject; he has interest of his own; he soon begins to think that he may be happy, great and glori-ous, by oppressing his fellow citizens; and that he may raise himself to grandeur on the ruins of his country. In a large republic, the public good is sacrificed to a thousand views; it is sub-ordinate to exceptions, and depends on accidents. In a small one, the interest of the public is easier perceived, better understood, and more within the reach of every citizen; abuses are of less extent, and of course are less protected." Of the same opinion is the marquis Beccarari.

History furnishes no example of a free republic, any thing like the extent of the United States. The Grecian republics were of small extent; so also was that of the Romans. Both of these, it is true, in process of time, extended their conquests over large territories of country; and the consequence was, that their governments were changed from that of free governments to those of the most tyrannical that ever existed in the world.

Not only the opinion of the greatest men, and the experience of mankind, are against the idea of an extensive republic, but a variety of reasons may be drawn from the reason and nature of things, against it. In every government, the will of the sovereign is the law. In despotic governments, the supreme authority being lodged in one, his will is law, and can be as easily expressed to a large extensive territory as to a small one. In a pure democracy the people are the sovereign, and their will is declared by themselves; for this purpose they must all come together to deliberate, and decide. This kind of government cannot be exercised, therefore, over a country of any considerable extent; it must be confined to a single city, or at least limited to such bounds as that the people can conveniently assemble, be able to debate, understand the subject submitted to them, and declare their opinion concerning it.

In a free republic, although all laws are derived from the consent of the people, yet the people do not declare their consent by themselves in person, but by representatives, chosen by them, who are supposed to know the minds of their constituents, and to be possessed of integrity to declare this mind.

In every free government, the people must give their assent to the laws by which they are governed. This is the true criterion between a free government and an arbitrary one. The former are ruled by the will of the whole, expressed in any manner they may agree upon; the latter by the will of one, or a few. If the people are to give their assent to the laws, by persons chosen and appointed by them, the manner of the choice and the number chosen, must be such, as to possess, be disposed, and consequently qualified to declare the sentiments of the people; for if they do not know, or are not disposed to speak the sentiments of the people, the people do not govern, but the sovereignty is in a few. Now, in a large extended country, it is impossible to have a representation, possessing the sentiments, and of integrity, to declare the minds of the people, without having it so numerous and unwieldly, as to be subject in great measure to the inconveniency of a democratic government.

The territory of the United States is of vast extent; it now contains near three millions of souls, and is capable of containing much more than ten times that number. Is it practicable for a country, so large and so numerous as they will soon become, to elect a representation, that will speak their sentiments, without their becoming so numerous as to be incapable of transacting public business? It certainly is not.

In a republic, the manners, sentiments, and interests of the people should be similar. If this be not the case, there will be a constant clashing of opinions; and the representatives of one part will be continually striving against those of the other. This will retard the operations of government, and prevent such conclusions as will promote the public good. If we apply this remark to the condition of the United States, we shall be convinced that it forbids that we should be one government. The United States includes a variety of climates. The productions of the different parts of the union are very variant, and their interests, of consequence, diverse. Their manners and habits differ as much as their climates and productions; and their sentiments are by no means coincident. The laws and customs of the several states are, in many respects, very diverse, and in some opposite; each would be in favor of its own interests and customs, and, of consequence, a legislature, formed of representatives from the respective parts, would not only be too numerous to act with any care or decision, but would be composed of such heterogenous and discordant principles, as would constantly be contending with each other.

The laws cannot be executed in a republic, of an extent equal to that of the United States, with promptitude.

The magistrates in every government must be supported in the execution of the laws, either by an armed force, maintained at the public expence for that purpose; or by the people turning out to aid the magistrate upon his command, in case of resistance.

In despotic governments, as well as in all the monarchies of Europe, standing armies are kept up to execute the commands of the prince or the magistrate, and are employed for this purpose when occasion requires: But they have always proved the destruction of liberty, and [are] abhorrent to the spirit of a free republic. In England, where they depend upon the parliament for their annual support, they have always been complained of as oppressive and unconstitutional, and are seldom employed in executing of the laws; never except on extraordinary occasions, and then under the direction of a civil magistrate.

A free republic will never keep a standing army to execute its laws. It must depend upon the support of its citizens. But when a government is to receive its support from the aid of the citizens, it must be so constructed as to have the confidence, respect, and affection of the people. Men who, upon the call of the magistrate, offer themselves to execute the laws, are influenced to do it either by affection to the government, or from fear; where a standing army is at hand to punish offenders, every man is actuated by the latter principle, and therefore, when the magistrate calls, will obey: but, where this is not the case, the government must rest for its support upon the confidence and respect which the people have for their government and laws. The body of the people being attached, the government will always be sufficient to support and execute its laws, and to operate upon the fears of any faction which may be opposed to it, not only to prevent an opposition to the execution of the laws themselves, but also to compel the most of them to aid the magistrate; but the people will not be likely to have such confidence in their rulers, in a republic so extensive as the United States, as necessary for these purposes. The confidence which the people have in their rulers, in a free republic, arises from their knowing them, from their being responsible to them for their conduct, and from the power they have of displacing them when they misbehave: but in a republic of the extent of this continent, the people in general would be acquainted with very few of their rulers: the people at large would know little of their proceedings, and it would be extremely difficult to change them. The people in Georgia and New-Hampshire would not know one another's mind, and therefore could not act in concert to enable them to effect a general change of representatives. The different parts of so extensive a country could not possibly be made acquainted with the conduct of their representatives, nor be informed of the reasons upon which measures were founded. The consequence will be, they will have no confidence in their legislature, suspect them of ambitious views, be jealous of every measure they adopt, and will not support the laws they pass. Hence the government will be nerveless and inefficient, and no way will be left to render it otherwise, but by establishing an armed force to execute the laws at the point of the bayonet—a government of all others the most to be dreaded.

In a republic of such vast extent as the United-States, the legislature cannot attend to the various concerns and wants of its different parts. It cannot be sufficiently numerous to be acquainted with the local condition and wants of the different districts, and if it could, it is impossible it should have sufficient time to attend to and provide for all the variety of cases of this nature, that would be continually arising.

In so extensive a republic, the great officers of government would soon become above the controul of the people, and abuse their power to the purpose of aggrandizing themselves, and oppressing them. The trust committed to the executive offices, in a country of the extent of the United-States, must be various and of magnitude. The command of all the troops and navy of the republic, the appointment of officers, the power of pardoning offences, the collecting of all the public revenues, and the power of expending them, with a number of other powers, must be lodged and exercised in every state, in the hands of a few. When these are attended with great honor and emolument, as they always will be in large states, so as greatly to interest men to pursue them, and to be proper objects for ambitious and designing men, such men will be ever restless in their pursuit after them. They will use the power, when they have acquired it, to the purposes of gratifying their own interest and ambition, and it is scarcely possible, in a very large republic, to call them to account for their misconduct, or to prevent their abuse of power.

These are some of the reasons by which it appears, that a free republic cannot long subsist over a country of the great extent of these states. If then this new constitution is calculated to consolidate the thirteen states into one, as it evidently is, it ought not to be adopted.

Though I am of opinion, that it is a sufficient objection to this government, to reject it, that it creates the whole union into one government, under the form of a republic, yet if this objection was obviated, there are exceptions to it, which are so material and fundamental, that they ought to determine every man, who is a friend to the liberty and happiness of mankind, not to adopt it. I beg the candid and dispassionate attention of my countrymen while I state these objections—they are such as have obtruded themselves upon my mind upon a careful attention to the matter, and such as I sincerely believe are well founded. There are many objections, of small moment, of which I shall take no notice—perfection is not to be expected in any thing that is the production of man—and if I did not in my conscience believe that this scheme was defective in the fundamental principles—in the foundation upon which a free and equal government must rest—I would hold my peace.

Brutus.

III

15 November 1787

To the Citizens of the State of New-York....

...Under these impressions, it has been my object to turn your attention to the principal defects in this system.

I have attempted to shew, that a consolidation of this extensive continent, under one government, for internal, as well as external purposes, which is evidently the tendency of this constitution, cannot succeed, without a sacrifice of your liberties; and therefore that the attempt is not only preposterous, but extremely dangerous; and I have shewn, independent of this, that the plan is radically defective in a fundamental principle, which ought to be found in every free government; to wit, a declaration of rights.

I shall now proceed to take a nearer view of this system, to examine its parts more minutely, and shew that the powers are not properly deposited, for the security of public liberty.

The first important object that presents itself in the organization of this government, is the legislature. This is to be composed of two branches; the first to be called the general assembly, and is to be chosen by the people of the respective states, in proportion to the number of their inhabitants, and is to consist of sixty five members, with powers in the legislature to encrease the number, not to exceed one for every thirty thousand inhabitants. The second branch is to be called the senate, and is to consist of twenty-six members, two of which are to be chosen by the legislatures of each of the states.

In the former of these there is an appearance of justice, in the appointment of its members—but if the clause, which provides for this branch, be stripped of its ambiguity, it will be found that there is really no equality of representation, even in this house.

The words are "representatives and direct taxes, shall be apportioned among the several states, which may be included in this union, according to their respective numbers, which shall be determined by adding to the whole number of free persons, including those bound to service for a term of years, and excluding Indians not taxed, three fifths of all other persons."—What a strange and unnecessary accumulation of words are here used to conceal from the public eye, what might have been expressed in the following concise manner. Representatives are to be proportioned among the states respectively, according to the number of freemen and slaves inhabiting them, counting five slaves for three free men.

"In a free state," says the celebrated Montesquieu, "every man, who is supposed to be a free agent, ought to be concerned in his own government, therefore the legislature should reside in the whole body of the people, or their representatives." But it has never been alledged that those who are not free agents, can, upon any rational principle, have any thing to do in government, either by themselves or others. If they have no share in government, why is the number of members in the assembly, to be increased on their account? Is it because in some of the states, a considerable part of the property of the inhabitants consists in a number of their fellow men, who are held in bondage, in defiance of every idea of benevolence, justice, and religion, and contrary to all the principles of liberty, which have been publickly avowed in the late glorious revolution? If this be a just ground for representation, the horses in some of the states, and the oxen in others, ought to be represented—for a great share of property in some of them, consists in these animals; and they have as much controul over their own actions, as these poor unhappy creatures, who are intended to be described in the above recited clause, by the words, "all other persons." By this mode of apportionment, the representatives of the different parts of the union, will be extremely unequal; in some of the southern states, the slaves are nearly equal in number to the free men; and for all these slaves, they will be entitled to a proportionate share in the legislature—this will give them an unreasonable weight in the government, which can derive no additional strength, protection, nor defence from the slaves, but the contrary. Why then should they be represented? What adds to the evil is, that these states are to be permitted to continue the inhuman traffic of importing slaves, until the year 1808—and for every cargo of these unhappy people, which unfeeling, unprincipled, barbarous, and avaricious wretches, may tear from their country, friends and tender connections, and bring into those states, they are to be rewarded by having an increase of members in the general assembly.

There appears at the first view a manifest inconsistency, in the apportionment of representatives in the senate, upon the plan of a consolidated government. On every principle of equity, and propriety, representation in a government should be in exact proportion to the numbers, or the aids afforded by the persons represented. How unreasonable, and unjust then is it, that Delaware should have a representation in the senate, equal to Massachusetts, or Virginia? The latter of which contains ten times her numbers, and is to contribute to the aid of the general government in that proportion? This article of the constitution will appear the more objectionable, if it is considered, that the powers vested in this branch of the legislature are very extensive, and greatly surpass those lodged in the assembly, not only for general purposes, but, in many instances, for the internal police of the states. The other branch of the legislature, in which, if in either, a f[a]int spark of democracy is to be found, should have been properly organized and established—but upon examination you will find, that this branch does not possess the qualities of a just representation, and that there is no kind of security, imperfect as it is, for its remaining in the hands of the people.

It has been observed, that the happiness of society is the end of government—that every free government is founded in compact; and that, because it is impracticable for the whole community to assemble, or when assembled, to deliberate with wisdom, and decide with dispatch, the mode of legislating by representation was devised.

The very term, representative, implies, that the person or body chosen for this purpose, should resemble those who appoint them—a representation of the people of America, if it be a true one, must be like the people. It ought to be so constituted, that a person, who is a stranger to the country, might be able to form a just idea of their character, by knowing that of their representatives. They are the sign—the people are the thing signified. It is absurd to speak of one thing being the representative of another, upon any other principle. The ground and reason of representation, in a free government, implies the same thing. Society instituted government to promote the happiness of the whole, and this is the great end always in view in the delegation of powers. It must then have been intended, that those who are placed instead of the people, should possess their sentiments and feelings, and be governed by their interests, or, in other words, should bear the strongest resemblance of those in whose room they are substituted. It is obvious, that for an assembly to be a true likeness of the people of any country, they must be considerably numerous.—One man, or a few men, cannot possibly represent the feelings, opinions, and characters of a great multitude. In this respect, the new constitution is radically defective.—The house of assembly, which is intended as a representation of the people of America, will not, nor cannot, in the nature of things, be a proper one—sixty-five men cannot be found in the United States, who hold the sentiments, possess the feelings, or are acquainted with the wants and interests of this vast country. This extensive continent is made up of a number of different classes of people; and to have a proper representation of them, each class ought to have an opportunity of choosing their best informed men for the purpose; but this cannot possibly be the case in so small a number. The state of New-York, on the present apportionment, will send six members to the assembly: I will venture to affirm, that number cannot be found in the state, who will bear a just resemblance to the several classes of people who compose it. In this assembly, the farmer, merchant, mecanick, and other various orders of people, ought to be represented according to their respective weight and numbers; and the representatives ought to be intimately acquainted with the wants, understand the interests of the several orders in the society, and feel a proper sense and becoming zeal to promote their prosperity. I cannot conceive that any six men in this state can be found properly qualified in these respects to discharge such important duties: but supposing it possible to find them, is there the least degree of probability that the choice of the people will fall upon such men? According to the common course of human affairs, the natural aristocracy of the country will be elected. Wealth always creates influence, and this is generally much increased by large family connections: this class in society will for ever have a great number of dependents; besides, they will always favour each other—it is their interest to combine—they will therefore constantly unite their efforts to procure men of their own rank to be elected—they will concenter all their force in every part of the state into one point, and by acting together, will most generally carry their election. It is probable, that but few of the merchants, and those the most opulent and ambitious, will have a representation from their body—few of them are characters sufficiently conspicuous to attract the notice of the electors of the state in so limited a representation. The great body of the yeomen of the country cannot expect any of their order in this assembly—the station will be too elevated for them to aspire to—the distance between the people and their representatives, will be so very great, that there is no probability that a farmer, however respectable, will be chosen—the mechanicks of every branch, must expect to be excluded from a seat in this Body—It will and must be esteemed a station too high and exalted to be filled by any but the first men in the state, in point of fortune; so that in reality there will be no part of the people represented, but the rich, even in that branch of the legislature, which is called the democratic.—The well born, and highest orders in life, as they term themselves, will be ignorant of the sentiments of the midling class of citizens, strangers to their ability, wants, and difficulties, and void of sympathy, and fellow feeling. This branch of the legislature will not only be an imperfect representation, but there will be no security in so small a body, against bribery, and corruption—It will consist at first, of sixty-five, and can never exceed one for every thirty thousand inhabitants; a majority of these, that is, thirty-three, are a quorum, and a majority of which, or seventeen, may pass any law—so that twenty-five men, will have the power to give away all the property of the citizens of these states—what security therefore can there be for the people, where their liberties and property are at the disposal of so few men? It will literally be a government in the hands of the few to oppress and plunder the many. You may conclude with a great degree of certainty, that it, like all others of a similar nature, will be managed by influence and corruption, and that the period is not far distant, when this will be the case, if it should be adopted; for even now there are some among us, whose characters stand high in the public estimation, and who have had a principal agency in framing this constitution, who do not scruple to say, that this is the only practicable mode of governing a people, who think with that degree of freedom which the Americans do—this government will have in their gift a vast number of offices of great honor and emolument. The members of the legislature are not excluded from appointments; and twenty-five of them, as the case may be, being secured, any measure may be carried.

The rulers of this country must be composed of very different materials from those of any other, of which history gives us any account, if the majority of the legislature are not, before many years, entirely at the devotion of the executive—and these states will soon be under the absolute domination of one, or a few, with the fallacious appearance of being governed by men of their own election.

The more I reflect on this subject, the more firmly am I persuaded, that the representation is merely nominal—a mere burlesque; and that no security is provided against corruption and undue influence. No free people on earth, who have elected persons to legislate for them, ever reposed that confidence in so small a number. The British house of commons consists of five hundred and fifty-eight members; the number of inhabitants in Great-Britain, is computed at eight millions—this gives one member for a little more than fourteen thousand, which exceeds double the proportion this country can ever have: and yet we require a larger representation in proportion to our numbers, than Great-Britain, because this country is much more extensive, and differs more in its productions, interests, manners, and habits. The democratic branch of the legislatures of the several states in the union consists, I believe at present, of near two thousand; and this number was not thought too large for the security of liberty by the framers of our state constitutions: some of the states may have erred in this respect, but the difference between two thousand, and sixty-five, is so very great, that it will bear no comparison.

Other objections offer themselves against this part of the constitution—I shall reserve them for a future paper, when I shall shew, defective as this representation is, no security is provided, that even this shadow of the right, will remain with the people.

Brutus.

JAMES MADISON

The Federalist, Number 10 and Number 51 (1787–88)

Republican party leader and fourth president of the United States, James Madison (1751–1836) is the only American statesman whose political theories have nearly eclipsed in historical importance his not inconsiderable career as a politician. This is mainly because of his contributions to the *Federalist,* the series of New York newspaper articles that he and Hamilton and John Jay contributed to win ratification of the Constitution. His *Federalist* writings remain to this day the most influential work in American political thought ever published, and for a very good reason: In them he achieved a modern breakthrough in American republican theory by placing its classical concerns for virtue on a new sociopolitical basis.

In the *Federalists* numbers 10 and 51, Madison presented the core of this theoretical foundation. In "Number 10" he argued that the proposed national government's extensive territory—which opponents of the Constitution feared would produce self-seeking factionalism or tyranny—would have precisely the opposite effect because it would multiply and thereby neutralize competing interests. He also argued that a large republic would produce popularly elected representatives who were more cosmopolitan in their vision and therefore likely wiser and more patriotic than those representing smaller states. Madison's revisionist argument in *Federalist* "Number 51," although less sociological, was no less elite-minded *and* protodemocratic. Here he detached the entire structure of mixed government from its historical roots in differing social orders and converted it into a system of popularly originated powers that, by checking each other, could thereby fulfill the traditional concern of republican ideology—the protection of liberty against the encroachments of power. With passions and interests so controlled and manipulated rather than suppressed or denied, self-government, Madison concluded, could be safely, if indirectly, guided by reason, either through the enlightened self-interest of the masses or through the wise and the virtuous who devised systems like those of the *Federalist*.

An outstanding interpretation of Madisonian and Federalist ideas of the Constitution may be found in Gordon S. Wood, *The Creation of the American Republic, 1776–1787* (Chapel Hill, 1969), 469–564. Morton White, *Philosophy, "The Federalist," and the Constitution* (New York, 1987); and Daniel W. Howe, "The Political Psychology of *The Federalist*," in Howe's *Making the American Self: Jonathan Edwards to Abraham Lincoln* (Cambridge, Mass., 1997), 48–103, illuminate the philosophical bases of Madison, Hamilton, and Jay's political theories. For an excellent study focusing on the evolution of Madison's republican thought in his post-Revolutionary years, see Lance Banning, *The Sacred Fire of Liberty: James Madison and the Founding of the Federal Republic* (Ithaca, 1995). Two of the freshest and most imaginative recent studies of Madison's political thought are by Colleen A. Sheehan: *James Madison and the Spirit of Republican Self-Government* (New York, 2009), which emphasizes Madison's deep engagement with European Enlightenment debates over the role of public opinion in a republican polity; and *The Mind of James Madison: The Legacy of Classical Republicanism* (New York, 2015), a compelling portrait of Madison as a scholar and political theorist.

Number 10

[22 November 1787]

Among the numerous advantages promised by a well constructed union, none deserves to be more accurately developed than its tendency to break and control the violence of faction. The friend of popular governments never finds himself so much alarmed for their character and fate, as when he contemplates their propensity to this dangerous vice. He will not fail therefore to set a due value on any plan which, without violating the principles to which he is attached, provides a proper cure for it. The instability, injustice and confusion introduced into the public councils, have in truth been the mortal diseases under which popular governments have everywhere perished; as they continue to be the favorite and fruitful topics from which the adversaries to liberty derive their most specious declamations. The valuable improvements made by the American constitutions on the popular models, both ancient and modern, cannot certainly be too much admired; but it would be an unwarrantable partiality, to contend that they have as effectually obviated the danger on this side as was wished and expected. Complaints are every where heard from our most considerate and virtuous citizens, equally the friends of public and private faith, and of public and personal liberty, that our governments are too unstable; that the public good is disregarded in the conflicts of rival parties; and that measures are too often decided, not according to the rules of justice, and the rights of the minor party; but by the superior force of an interested and over-bearing majority. However anxiously we may wish that these complaints had no foundation, the evidence of known facts will not permit us to deny that they are in some degree true. It will be found indeed, on a candid review of our situation, that some of the distresses under which we labour, have been erroneously charged on the operation of our governments; but it will be found at the same time, that other causes will not alone account for many of our heaviest misfortunes; and particularly, for that prevailing and increasing distrust of public engagements, and alarm for private rights, which are echoed from one end of the continent to the other. These must be chiefly, if not wholly, effects of the unsteadiness and injustice, with which a factious spirit has tainted our public administration.

By a faction I understand a number of citizens, whether amounting to a majority or minority of the whole, who are united and actuated by some common impulse of passion, or of interest, adverse to the rights of other citizens, or to the permanent and aggregate interests of the community.

There are two methods of curing the mischiefs of faction: The one, by removing its causes; the other, by controlling its effects.

There are again two methods of removing the causes of faction: The one by destroying the liberty which is essential to its existence; the other, by giving to every citizen the same opinions, the same passions, and the same interests.

It could never be more truly said than of the first remedy, that it is worse than the disease. Liberty is to faction, what air is to fire, an aliment without which it instantly expires. But it could not be a less folly to abolish liberty, which is essential to political life, because

Source: The Papers of James Madison, vol. 10, ed. Robert A. Rutland et al. (Chicago: University of Chicago Press, 1977), 263–70, 476–80. Editors' notes omitted. Reprinted by permission of the University of Chicago Press, Copyright © 1977.

it nourishes faction, than it would be to wish the annihilation of air, which is essential to animal life because it imparts to fire its destructive agency.

The second expedient is as impracticable, as the first would be unwise. As long as the reason of man continues fallible, and he is at liberty to exercise it, different opinions will be formed. As long as the connection subsists between his reason and his self-love, his opinions and his passions will have a reciprocal influence on each other; and the former will be objects to which the latter will attach themselves. The diversity in the faculties of men from which the rights of property originate, is not less an insuperable obstacle to an uniformity of interests. The protection of these faculties is the first object of government. From the protection of different and unequal faculties of acquiring property, the possession of different degrees and kinds of property immediately results: And from the influence of these on the sentiments and views of the respective proprietors, ensues a division of the society into different interests and parties.

The latent causes of faction are thus sown in the nature of man; and we see them every where brought into different degrees of activity, according to the different circumstances of civil society. A zeal for different opinions concerning religion, concerning government, and many other points, as well of speculation as of practice; an attachment to different leaders ambitiously contending for pre-eminence and power; or to persons of other descriptions whose fortunes have been interesting to the human passions, have in turn divided mankind into parties, inflamed them with mutual animosity, and rendered them much more disposed to vex and oppress each other, than to co-operate for their common good. So strong is this propensity of mankind to fall into mutual animosities, that where no substantial occasion presents itself, the most frivolous and fanciful distinctions have been sufficient to kindle their unfriendly passions, and excite their most violent conflicts. But the most common and durable source of factions, has been the various and unequal distribution of property. Those who hold, and those who are without property, have ever formed distinct interests in society. Those who are creditors, and those who are debtors, fall under a like discrimination. A landed interest, a manufacturing interest, a mercantile interest, a monied interest, with many lesser interests, grow up of necessity in civilized nations, and divide them into different classes, actuated by different sentiments and views. The regulation of these various and interfering interests forms the principal task of modern legislation, and involves the spirit of party and faction in the necessary and ordinary operations of government.

No man is allowed to be a judge in his own cause; because his interest would certainly bias his judgment, and, not improbably, corrupt his integrity. With equal, nay with greater reason, a body of men are unfit to be both judges and parties at the same time; yet what are many of the most important acts of legislation, but so many judicial determinations, not indeed concerning the rights of single persons, but concerning the rights of large bodies of citizens; and what are the different classes of legislators, but advocates and parties to the causes which they determine? Is a law proposed concerning private debts? It is a question to which the creditors are parties on one side, and the debtors on the other. Justice ought to hold the balance between them. Yet the parties are and must be themselves the judges; and the most numerous party, or, in other words, the most powerful faction must be expected to prevail. Shall domestic manufactures be encouraged, and in what degree, by restrictions on foreign manufactures? are questions which would be differently decided by the landed and the manufacturing classes; and probably by neither, with a sole regard to justice and the public good. The apportionment of taxes on the various descriptions of property is an act which seems to require the most exact impartiality, yet there is perhaps no legislative act in which greater opportunity and temptation are given to a predominant party, to trample on the rules of justice. Every shilling with which they over-burden the inferior number, is a shilling saved to their own pockets.

It is in vain to say, that enlightened statesmen will be able to adjust these clashing interests, and render them all subservient to the public good. Enlightened statesmen will not always be at the helm: Nor, in many cases, can such an adjustment be made at all, without taking into view indirect and remote considerations, which will rarely prevail over the immediate interest which one party may find in disregarding the rights of another, or the good of the whole.

The inference to which we are brought, is, that the *causes* of faction cannot be removed; and that relief is only to be sought in the means of controlling its *effects*.

If a faction consists of less than a majority, relief is supplied by the republican principle, which enables the majority to defeat its sinister views by regular vote: It may clog the administration, it may convulse the society; but it will be unable to execute and mask its violence under the forms of the constitution. When a majority is included in a faction, the form of popular government on the other hand enables it to sacrifice to its ruling passion or interest, both the public good and the rights of other citizens. To secure the public good, and private rights against the danger of such a faction, and at the same time to preserve the spirit and the form of popular government, is then the great object to which our enquiries are directed. Let me add that it is the great desideratum, by which alone this form of government can be rescued from the opprobrium under which it has so long labored, and be recommended to the esteem and adoption of mankind.

By what means is this object attainable? Evidently by one of two only. Either the existence of the same passion or interest in a majority at the same time, must be prevented; or the majority, having such co-existent passion or interest, must be rendered, by their number and local situation, unable to concert and carry into effect schemes of oppression. If the impulse and the opportunity be suffered to coincide, we well know that neither moral nor religious motives can be relied on as an adequate control. They are not found to be such on the injustice and violence of individuals, and lose their efficacy in proportion to the number combined together; that is, in proportion as their efficacy becomes needful.

From this view of the subject, it may be concluded that a pure democracy, by which I mean a society, consisting of a small number of citizens, who assemble and administer the government in person, can admit of no cure for the mischiefs of faction. A common passion or interest will, in almost every case, be felt by a majority of the whole; a communication and concert results from the form of government itself; and there is nothing to check the inducements to sacrifice the weaker party, or an obnoxious individual. Hence it is, that such democracies have ever been spectacles of turbulence and contention; have ever been found incompatible with personal security, or the rights of property; and have in general been as short in their lives, as they have been violent in their deaths. Theoretic politicians, who have patronized this species of government, have erroneously supposed, that by reducing mankind to a perfect equality in their political rights, they would, at the same time, be perfectly equalized, and assimilated in their possessions, their opinions, and their passions.

A republic, by which I mean a government in which the scheme of representation takes place, opens a different prospect, and promises the cure for which we are seeking. Let us examine the points in which it varies from pure democracy, and we shall comprehend both the nature of the cure, and the efficacy which it must derive from the union.

The two great points of difference between a democracy and a republic, are first, the delegation of the government, in the latter, to a small number of citizens elected by the rest; secondly, the greater number of citizens, and greater sphere of country, over which the latter may be extended.

The effect of the first difference is, on the one hand, to refine and enlarge the public views, by passing them through the medium of a chosen body of citizens, whose wisdom may best discern the true interest of their country, and whose patriotism and love of justice will be least likely to sacrifice it to temporary or partial considerations. Under such a regulation, it may well happen that the public voice pronounced by the representatives of the people, will be more consonant to the public good, than if pronounced by the people themselves convened for the purpose. On the other hand, the effect may be inverted. Men of factious tempers, of local prejudices, or of sinister designs, may by intrigue, by corruption, or by other means, first obtain the suffrages, and then betray the interests of the people. The question resulting is, whether small or extensive republics are most favourable to the election of proper guardians of the public weal; and it is clearly decided in favour of the latter by two obvious considerations.

In the first place it is to be remarked, that however small the republic may be, the representatives must be raised to a certain number, in order to guard against the cabals of a few; and that however large it may be, they must be limited to a certain number, in order to guard against the confusion of a multitude. Hence the number of representatives in the two cases not being in proportion to that of the constituents, and being proportionally greatest in the small republic, it follows, that if the proportion of fit characters be not less in the large than in the small republic, the former will present a greater option, and consequently a greater probability of a fit choice.

In the next place, as each representative will be chosen by a greater number of citizens in the large than in the small republic, it will be more difficult for unworthy candidates to practise with success the vicious arts, by which elections are too often carried; and the suffrages of the people being more free, will be more likely to centre on men who possess the most attractive merit, and the most diffusive and established characters.

It must be confessed, that in this, as in most other cases, there is a mean, on both sides of which inconveniencies will be found to lie. By enlarging too much the number of electors, you render the representative too little acquainted with all their local circumstances and lesser interests; as by reducing it too much, you render him unduly attached to these, and too little fit to comprehend and pursue great and national objects. The federal constitution forms a happy combination in this respect; the great and aggregate interests being referred to the national, the local and particular to the state legislatures.

The other point of difference is, the greater number of citizens and extent of territory which may be brought within the compass of republican, than of democratic government; and it is this circumstance principally which renders factious combinations less to be dreaded in the former, than in the latter. The smaller the society, the fewer probably will be the distinct parties and interests composing it; the fewer the distinct parties and interests, the more frequently will a majority be found of the same party; and the smaller the number of individuals composing a majority, and the smaller the compass within which they are placed, the more easily will they concert and execute their plans of oppression. Extend the sphere, and you take in a greater variety of parties and interests; you make it less probable that a majority of the whole will have a common motive to invade the rights of other citizens; or if such a common motive exists, it will be more difficult for all who feel it to discover their own strength, and to act in unison with each other. Besides other impediments, it may be remarked that, where there is a consciousness of unjust or dishonourable purposes, communication is always checked by distrust, in proportion to the number whose concurrence is necessary.

Hence it clearly appears, that the same advantage, which a republic has over a democracy, in controlling the effects of faction, is enjoyed by a large over a small republic—is enjoyed by the union over the states composing it. Does this advantage consist in the substitution of representatives, whose enlightened views and virtuous sentiments render them superior to local prejudices, and to schemes of injustice? It will not be denied, that the representation of the union will be most likely to possess these requisite endowments. Does it consist in the greater security afforded by a greater variety of parties, against the event of any one party being able to outnumber and oppress the rest? In an equal degree does the increased variety of parties, comprised within the union, increase this security. Does it, in fine, consist in the greater obstacles opposed to the concert and accomplishment of the secret wishes of an unjust and interested majority? Here, again, the extent of the union gives it the most palpable advantage.

The influence of factious leaders may kindle a flame within their particular states, but will be unable to spread a general conflagration through the other states: A religious sect may degenerate into a political faction in a part of the confederacy; but the variety of sects dispersed over the entire face of it, must secure the national councils against any danger from that source: A rage for paper money, for an abolition of debts, for an equal division of property, or for any other improper or wicked project, will be less apt to pervade the whole body of the union, than a particular member of it; in the same proportion as such a malady is more likely to taint a particular county or district, than an entire state.

In the extent and proper structure of the union, therefore, we behold a republican remedy for the diseases most incident to republican government. And according to the degree of pleasure and pride we feel in being republicans, ought to be our zeal in cherishing the spirit and supporting the character of federalists.

Publius.

Number 51

[6 February 1788]

To what expedient then shall we finally resort for maintaining in practice the necessary partition of power among the several departments, as laid down in the constitution? The only answer that can be given is, that as all these exterior provisions are found to be inadequate, the defect must be supplied, by so contriving the interior structure of the government, as that its several constituent parts may, by their mutual relations, be the means of keeping each other in their proper places. Without presuming to undertake a full development of this important idea, I will hazard a few general observations, which may perhaps place it in a clearer light, and enable us to form a more correct judgment of the principles and structure of the government planned by the convention.

In order to lay a due foundation for that separate and distinct exercise of the different powers of government, which to a certain extent, is admitted on all hands to be essential to the preservation of liberty, it is evident that each department should have a will of its own; and consequently should be so constituted that the members of each should have as little agency as possible in the appointment of the members of the others. Were this principle rigorously adhered to, it would require that all the appointments for the supreme executive, legislative and judiciary magistracies should be drawn from the same fountain of authority, the people, through channels having no communication whatever with one another. Perhaps such a plan of constructing the several departments would be less difficult in practice than it may in contemplation appear. Some difficulties, however, and some additional expence, would attend the execution of it. Some deviations therefore from the principle must be admitted. In the constitution of the judiciary department in particular, it might be inexpedient to insist rigorously on the principle; first, because peculiar qualifications being essential in the members, the primary consideration ought to be to select that mode of choice, which best secures these qualifications; secondly, because the permanent tenure by which the appointments are held in that department, must soon destroy all sense of dependence on the authority conferring them.

It is equally evident that the members of each department should be as little dependent as possible on those of the others, for the emoluments annexed to their offices. Were the executive magistrate, or the judges, not independent of the legislature in this particular, their independence in every other would be merely nominal.

But the great security against a gradual concentration of the several powers in the same department, consists in giving to those who administer each department, the necessary constitutional means, and personal motives, to resist encroachments of the others. The provision for defence must in this, as in all other cases, be made commensurate to the danger of attack. Ambition must be made to counteract ambition. The interest of the man must be connected with the constitutional rights of the place. It may be a reflection on human nature, that such devices should be necessary to control the abuses of government. But what is government itself but the greatest of all reflections on human nature? If men were angels, no government would be necessary. If angels were to govern men, neither external nor internal controls on government would be necessary. In framing a government which is to be administered by men over men, the great difficulty lies in this: You must first enable the government to control the governed; and in the next place, oblige it to control itself. A dependence on the people is no doubt the primary control on the government; but experience has taught mankind the necessity of auxiliary precautions.

This policy of supplying by opposite and rival interests, the defect of better motives, might be traced through the whole system of human affairs, private as well as public. We see it particularly displayed in all the subordinate distributions of power; where the constant aim is to divide and arrange the several offices in such a manner as that each may be a check on the other; that the private interest of every individual may be a sentinel over the public rights. These inventions of prudence cannot be less requisite in the distribution of the supreme powers of the state.

But it is not possible to give to each department an equal power of self-defence. In republican government the legislative authority necessarily predominates. The remedy for this inconveniency is to divide the legislature into different branches; and to render them by different modes of election, and different principles of action, as little connected with each other, as the nature of their common functions, and their common dependence on the society, will admit. It may even be necessary to guard against dangerous encroachments by still further precautions. As the weight of the legislative authority requires that it should be thus divided, the weakness of the executive may require, on the other hand, that it should be fortified. An absolute negative on the legislature appears, at first view, to be the natural defence with which the executive magistrate should be armed. But perhaps it would be neither altogether safe, nor alone sufficient. On ordinary occasions, it might not be exerted with the requisite firmness; and on extraordinary occasions, it might be perfidiously abused. May not this defect of an absolute negative be supplied by some quali-fied connection between this weaker department, and the weaker branch of the stronger department, by which the latter may be led to support the constitutional rights of the for-mer, without being too much detached from the rights of its own department?

If the principles on which these observations are founded be just, as I persuade myself they are, and they be applied as a criterion to the several state constitutions, and to the federal constitution, it will be found that if the latter does not perfectly correspond with them, the former are infinitely less able to bear such a test.

There are moreover two considerations particularly applicable to the federal system of America, which place that system in a very interesting point of view.

First. In a single republic, all the power surrendered by the people, is submitted to the administration of a single government; and the usurpations are guarded against by a divi-sion of the government into distinct and separate departments. In the compound republic of America, the power surrendered by the people, is first divided between two distinct governments, and then the portion allotted to each, subdivided among distinct and sepa-rate departments. Hence a double security arises to the rights of the people. The different governments will control each other; at the same time that each will be controlled by itself.

Second. It is of great importance in a republic, not only to guard the society against the oppression of its rulers, but to guard one part of the society against the injustice of the other part. Different interests necessarily exist in different classes of citizens. If a majority be united by a common interest, the rights of the minority will be insecure. There are but two methods of providing against this evil: The one by creating a will in the community independent of the majority, that is, of the society itself; the other by comprehending in the society so many separate descriptions of citizens, as will render an unjust combination of a majority of the whole very improbable, if not impracticable. The first method prevails in all governments possessing an hereditary or self-appointed authority. This at best is but a precarious security; because a power independent of the society may as well espouse the unjust views of the major, as the rightful interests of the minor party, and may possibly be turned against both parties. The second method will be exemplified in the federal republic of the United States. Whilst all authority in it will be derived from, and dependent on the society, the society itself will be broken into so many parts, interests and classes of citi-zens, that the rights of individuals or of the minority, will be in little danger from inter-ested combinations of the majority. In a free government, the security for civil rights must be the same as that for religious rights. It consists in the one case in the multiplicity of interests, and in the other, in the multiplicity of sects. The degree of security in both cases will depend on the number of interests and sects; and this may be presumed to depend on the extent of country and number of people comprehended under the same government. This view of the subject must particularly recommend a proper federal system to all the sincere and considerate friends of republican government: Since it shews that in exact proportion as the territory of the union may be formed into more circumscribed confed-eracies or states, oppressive combinations of a majority will be facilitated, the best security under the republican form, for the rights of every class of citizens, will be diminished; and consequently, the stability and independence of some member of the government, the only other security must be proportionally increased. Justice is the end of government. It is the end of civil society. It ever has been, and ever will be pursued, until it be obtained, or until liberty be lost in the pursuit. In a society under the forms of which the stronger faction can readily unite and oppress the weaker, anarchy may as truly be said to reign, as in a state of nature where the weaker individual is not secured against the violence of the stronger: And as in the latter state even the stronger individuals are prompted by the uncertainty of their condition, to submit to a government which may protect the weak as well as themselves: So in the former state, will the more powerful factions or parties be gradually induced by a like motive, to wish for a government which will protect all parties, the weaker as well as the more powerful. It can be little doubted, that if the state of Rhode-Island was separated from the confederacy, and left to itself, the insecurity of rights under the popular form of government within such narrow limits, would be displayed by such reiterated oppressions of factious majorities, that some power altogether independent of the people would soon be called for by the voice of the very factions whose misrule had proved the necessity of it. In the extended republic of the United States, and among the great variety of interests, parties and sects which it embraces, a coalition of a majority of the whole society could seldom take place upon any other principles than those of justice and the general good: Whilst there being thus less danger to a minor from the will of the major party, there must be less pretext also, to provide for the security of the former, by introducing into the government a will not dependent on the latter; or in other words, a will independent of the society itself. It is no less certain than it is important, notwithstanding the contrary opinions which have been entertained, that the larger the society, provided it lie within a practicable sphere, the more duly capable it will be of self government. And happily for the *republican cause*, the practicable sphere may be carried to a very great extent, by a judicious modification and mixture of *the federal principle*.

PUBLIUS.

JUDITH SARGENT MURRAY

"On the Equality of the Sexes"
(1790)

Along with her colleague the playwright and historian Mercy Otis Warren, Judith Sargent Murray (1751–1820) shared the spotlight as one of post-Revolutionary America's two chief women of letters. Even more so than Warren, Murray also shined as one of its cultural pioneers. Coming to embrace the country's most liberal religion, Universalism, she thereafter married the church's American founder, John Murray, with whom she established a loving and egalitarian partnership much in the tradition of the liberal Enlightenment age's ideal of companionate literary marriages. Also, in the 1790s she wrote the first American plays performed on Boston's long-banned stage, as well as a stream of essays published in the liberal *Massachusetts Magazine* (aptly subtitled *Monthly Museum of Knowledge and Rational Entertainment*), most of which were reprinted in her later expanded three-volume collection *The Gleaner* (1798). Dedicated to President Adams and written in the "polite" yet "casual" and lightly ironic style favored by the Neoclassical-minded age's Anglo-American critics, this collection was widely admired by the American luminaries of her day.

Murray's essays were also memorable because of the strong gender accents she often gave them, beginning with her multiple narrative masks. (On the title page of *The Gleaner*, she placed her female penname of "Constantia," while in the texts she maintained the fiction that they were written by the "Gleaner," Mr. Vigillius.) More to the ideological point, in a series of essays, she severely criticized the age-old exclusion of women from higher education and its allied public discourses. In her first essay on the subject, "On the Equality of the Sexes," which she initially wrote over a decade before Mary Wollstonecraft's famous comparable rationalist tract, *Vindication of the Rights of Woman* (1792), she showed how women's supposed foibles (including those of the "figure" of the biblical Eve), rather than proving their intellectual inferiority, demonstrated two opposite facts: women exercised in abundance all the Enlightenment philosophers' categories of mental faculties, and, insofar as women failed to do so, echoing another classic Enlightenment idea, it was clearly due to their inferior moral and educational opportunities. Most important, while (as with other republican educational reformers) she argued that expanding women's education would facilitate companionate marriages and rational families, she also argued for such reforms on liberal Enlightenment religious grounds as well: knowledge made women rational, sensible, and, most of all, appreciative of the "supreme Intelligence" and His rationally designed universe.

Sheila L. Skemp, *First Lady of Letters: Judith Sargent Murray and the Struggle for Female Independence* (Philadelphia, 2009), is now the standard biography. Much valuable information about Murray and her ideas may be found in two collections: Judith Sargent Murray, *The Gleaner*, ed. Nina Baym (Schenectady, N.Y., 1992); and Sharon M. Harris, ed., *Selected Writings of Judith Sargent Murray* (New York, 1995). For illuminating discussions of Murray and post-Revolutionary ideas about women's education and republican theory, respectively, see Linda K. Kerber, "Daughters of Columbia: Educating Women for the Republic, 1787–1805," and "'I Have Don…much to Carrey on the Warr': Women and the Shaping of Republican Ideology after the American Revolution," in Kerber's *Toward an Intellectual History of Women* (Chapel Hill, 1997), 23–40, 100–130.

Is it upon mature consideration we adopt the idea, that nature is thus partial in her distribution? Is it indeed a fact, that she hath yielded to one half of the human species to unquestionable a mental superiority? I know that to both sexes elevated understandings, and the reverse, are common. But, suffer me to ask, in what the minds of females are so notoriously deficient, or unequal. May not the intellectual powers be ranged under these four heads—imagination, reason, memory and judgment. The province of imagination hath long since been surrendered up to us, and we have been crowned undoubted sovereigns of the regions of fancy. Invention is perhaps the most arduous effort of the mind; this branch of imagination hath been particularly ceded to us, and we have been time out of mind invested with that creative faculty. Observe the variety of fashions (here I bar the contemptuous smile) which distinguish and adorn the female world; how continually are they changing, insomuch that they almost render the wise man's assertion problematical, and we are ready to say, *there is something new under the sun.* Now what a playfulness, what an exuberance of fancy, what strength of inventive imagination, doth this continual variation discover? Again, it hath been observed, that if the turpitude of the conduct of our sex, hath been ever so enormous, so extremely ready are we, that the very first thought presents us with an apology, so plausible, as to produce our actions even in an amiable light. Another instance of our creative powers, is our talent for slander; how ingenious are we at inventive scandal? what a formidable story can we in a moment fabricate merely from the force of a prolifick imagination? how many reputations, in the fertile brain of a female, have been utterly despoiled? how industrious are we at improving a hint? suspicion how easily do we convert into conviction, and conviction, embellished by the power of eloquence, stalks abroad to the surprise and confusion of unsuspecting innocence. Perhaps it will be asked if I furnish these facts as instances of excellency in our sex. Certainly not; but as proofs of a creative faculty, of a lively imagination. Assuredly great activity of mind is thereby discovered, and was this activity properly directed, what beneficial effects would follow. Is the needle and kitchen sufficient to employ the operations of a soul thus organized? I should conceive not. Nay, it is a truth that those very departments leave the intelligent principle vacant, and at liberty for speculation. Are we deficient in reason? we can only reason from what we know, and if an opportunity of acquiring knowledge hath been denied us, the inferiority of our sex, cannot fairly be deduced from thence. Memory, I believe, will be allowed us in common, since every one's experience must testify, that a loquacious old woman is as frequently met with, as a communicative old man; their subjects are alike drawn from the fund of other times, and the transactions of their youth, or of maturer life, entertain, or perhaps fatigue you, in the evening of their lives. "But our judgment is not so strong—we do not distinguish so well."—Yet it may be questioned, from what doth this superiority, in this determining faculty of the soul, proceed. May we not trace its source in the difference of education, and continued advantages? Will it be said that the judgment of a male of two years old, is more sage than that of a female's of the same age? I believe the reverse is generally observed to be true. But from that period what partiality! How is the one exalted, and the other depressed, by the contrary modes of education which are adopted! the one is taught to aspire, and the other is early confined and limited. As their years increase, the sister must be wholly domesticated, while the brother is led by the hand through all the flowery paths of science. Grant that their minds are by nature equal, yet who shall wonder at the *apparent* superiority, if indeed custom becomes *second nature;* nay if it taketh

Source: *Massachusetts Magazine,* 2 (March 1790), 132–35, and 2 (April 1790), 223–26.

place of nature, and that it doth the experience of each day will evince. At length arrived at womanhood, the uncultivated fair one feels a void, which the employments allotted her are by no means capable of filling. What can she do? to books she may not apply; or if she doth, *to those only of the novel kind,* lest she merit the appellation of a *learned lady;* and what ideas have been affixed to this term, the observation of many can testify. Fashion, scandal and sometimes what is still more reprehensible, are then called in to her relief; and who can say to what lengths the liberties she takes may proceed. Meantime she herself is most unhappy; she feels the want of a cultivated mind. Is she single, she in vain seeks to fill up time from sexual employments or amusements. Is she united to a person whose soul nature made equal to her own, education hath set him so far above her, that in those entertainments which are productive of such rational felicity, she is not qualified to accompany him. She experiences a mortifying consciousness of inferiority, which embitters every enjoyment. Doth the person to whom her adverse fate hath consigned her, possess a mind incapable of improvement, she is equally wretched, in being so closely connected with an individual whom she cannot but despise. Now, was she permitted the same instructors as her brother, (with an eye however to their particular departments) for the employment of a rational mind an ample field would be opened. In astronomy she might catch a glimpse of the immensity of the Deity, and thence she would form amazing conceptions of the august and supreme Intelligence. In geography she would admire Jehovah in the midst of his benevolence; thus adapting this globe to the various wants and amusements of its inhabitants. In natural philosophy she would adore the infinite majesty of heaven, clothed in condescension; and as she traversed the reptile world, she would hail the goodness of a creating God. A mind, thus filled, would have little room for the trifles with which our sex are, with too much justice, accused of amusing themselves, and they would thus be rendered fit companions for those, who should one day wear them as their crown. Fashions, in their variety, would then give place to conjectures, which might perhaps conduce to the improvement of the literary world; and there would be no leisure for slander or detraction. Reputation would not then be blessed, but serious speculations would occupy the lively imaginations of the sex. Unnecessary visits would be precluded, and that custom would only be indulged by way of relaxation, or to answer the demands of consanguinity and friendship. Females would become discreet, their judgments would be invigorated, and their partners for life being circumspectly chosen, an unhappy Hymen would then be as rare, as is now the reverse.

Will it be urged that those acquirements would supersede our domestic duties. I answer that every requisite in female economy is easily attained; and, with truth I can add, that when once attained, they require no further *mental attention.* Nay, while we are pursuing the needle, or the superintendency of the family, I repeat, that our minds are at full liberty for reflection; that imagination may exert itself in full vigor; and that if a just foundation is early laid, our ideas will then be worthy of rational beings. If we were industrious we might easily find time to arrange them upon paper, or should avocations press too hard for such an indulgence, the hours allotted for conversation would at least become more refined and rational. Should it still be vociferated, "Your domestic employments are sufficient"—I would calmly ask, is it reasonable, that a candidate for immortality, for the joys of heaven, an intelligent being, who is to spend an eternity in contemplating the works of Deity, should at present be so degraded, as to be allowed no other ideas, than those which are suggested by the mechanism of a pudding, or the sewing the seams of a garment? Pity that all such censurers of female improvement do not go one step further, and deny their future existence; to be consistent they surely ought.

Yes, ye lordly, ye haughty sex, our souls are by nature *equal* to yours; the same breath of God animates, enlivens, and invigorates us; and that we are not fallen lower than yourselves, let those witness who have greatly towered above the various discouragements by which they have been so heavily oppressed; and though I am unacquainted with the list of celebrated characters on either side, yet from the observations I have made in the contracted circle in which I have moved, I dare confidently believe, that from the commencement of time to the present day, there hath been as many females, as males, who, by the *mere force of natural powers,* have merited the crown of applause; who, thus unassisted, have seized the wreath of fame. I know there are who assert, that as the animal powers of the one sex are superior, of course their mental faculties also must be stronger; thus attributing strength of mind to the transient organization of this earth born tenement. But if this reasoning is just, man must be content to yield the palm to many of the brute creation, since by not a few of his brethren of the field, he is far surpassed in bodily strength. Moreover, was this argument admitted, it would prove too much, for occular demonstration evinceth, that there are many robust masculine ladies, and effeminate gentlemen. Yet I fancy that—Mr. Pope, though clogged with an enervated body, and distinguished by a diminutive stature, could nevertheless lay claim to greatness of soul; and perhaps there are many other instances which might be adduced to combat so unphilosophical an opinion. Do we not often see, that when the clay built tabernacle is well high dissolved, when it is just ready to mingle with the parent soil, the immortal inhabitant aspires to, and even attaineth heights the most sublime, and which were before wholly unexplored. Besides, were we to grant that animal strength proved any thing, taking into consideration the accustomed impartiality of nature, we should be induced to imagine, that she had invested the female mind with superior strength as an equivalent for the bodily powers of man. But waving this however palpable advantage, for *equality only,* we wish to contend.

I am aware that there are many passages in the sacred oracles which seem to give the advantage to the other sex; but I consider all these as wholly metaphorical. Thus David was a man after God's own heart, yet see him enervated by his licentious passions! behold him following Uriah to the death, and shew me wherein could consist the immaculate Being's complacency. Listen to the curses which Job bestoweth upon the day of his nativity, and tell me where is his perfection, where his patience—*literally* it existed not. David and Job were types of him who was to come; and the superiority of man, as exhibited in scripture, being also emblematical, all arguments deduced from thence, of course fall to the ground. The exquisite delicacy of the female mind proclaimeth the exactness of its texture, while its nice sense of honour announceth its innate, its native grandeur. And indeed, in one respect, the preeminence seems to be tacitly allowed us, for after an education which limits and confines, and employments and recreations which naturally tend to enervate the body, and debilitate the mind; after we have from early youth been adorned with ribbons, and other gewgaws, dressed out like the ancient victims previous to a sacrifice, being taught by the care of our parents in collecting the most showy materials that the ornamenting our exterior ought to be the principal object of our attention; after, I say, fifteen years thus spent, we are introduced into the world, amid the limited adulation of every beholder. Praise is sweet to the soul; we are immediately intoxicated by large draughts of flattery, which being plentifully administered, is to the pride of our hearts the most acceptable incense. It is expected that with the other sex we should commence immediate war, and that we should triumph over the machinations of the most artful. We must be constantly upon our guard; prudence and discretion must be our characteristics; and we must rise superior to, and obtain a complete victory over those who have been long adding to the native strength of their minds, by an unremitted study of men and books, and who have, moreover, conceived from the loose characters which they have seen portrayed in the extensive variety of their reading, a most contemptible opinion of the sex. Thus unequal, we are, notwithstanding, forced to the combat, and the infamy which is consequent upon the smallest deviation in our conduct, proclaims the high idea which was formed of our native strength; and thus, indirectly at least, is the preference acknowledged to be our due. And if we are allowed an equality of requirement, let serious studies equally employ our minds, and we will bid our souls arise to equal strength. We will meet upon even ground, the despot man; we will rush with alacrity to the combat, and, crowned by success, we shall then answer the exalted expectations, which are formed. Though sensibility, soft compassion, and gentle commiseration, are inmates in the female bosom, yet against every deep laid art, altogether fearless of the event, we will set them in array; for assuredly the wreath of victory will encircle the spotless brow. If we meet an equal, a sensible friend, we will reward him with the hand of amity, and through life we will be assiduous to promote his happiness; but from every deep laid scheme for our ruin, retiring into ourselves, amid the flowery paths of science, we will indulge in all the refined and sentimental pleasures of contemplation. And should it still be urged, that the studies thus insisted upon would interfere with our more peculiar department, I must further reply, that *early hours,* and close application, will do wonders; and to her who is from the first dawn of reason taught to fill up time rationally, both the requisites will be easy. I grant that niggard fortune is too generally unfriendly to the mind, and that much of that valuable treasure, time, is necessarily expended upon the wants of the body; but it should be remembered, that in embarrassed circumstances our companions have as little leisure for literary improvement, as is afforded to us; for most certainly their provident care is at least as requisite as our exertions. Nay, we have even more leisure for sedentary pleasures, as our avocations are more retired, much less laborious, and, as hath been observed, by no means require that avidity of attention which is proper to the employments of the other sex. In high life, or, in other words, where the parties are in possession of affluence, the objection respecting time is wholly obviated, and of course falls to the ground; and it may also be repeated, that many of those hours which are at present swallowed up in fashion and scandal, might be redeemed, were we habituated to useful reflections. But in one respect, O ye arbiters of our fate! we confess that the superiority is indubitably yours; you are by nature formed for our protectors; we pretend not to vie with you in bodily strength; upon this point we will never contend for victory. Shield us then, we beseech you, from external evils, and in return we will transact *your* domestick affairs. Yes, *your,* for are you not equally interested in those matters with ourselves? Is not the elegancy of neatness as agreeable to your sight as to ours; is not the well favoured viand equally delightful to your taste; and doth not your sense of hearing suffer as much, from the discordant founds prevalent in an ill regulated family, produced by the voices of children and many *et ceteras?*

CONSTANTIA.

By way of supplement to the foregoing pages, I subjoin the following extract from a letter, wrote to a friend in the December of 1780.

AND now assist me, O thou genius of my sex, while I undertake the arduous talk of endeavouring to combat that vulgar, that almost universal errour, which hath, it seems enlisted even Mr. P—under its banners. The superiority of your sex hath, I grant, been time out of mind seemed a truth incontrovertible; in consequence of which persuasion, every plan of education hath been calculated to establish this favourite tenet. Not long since, weak and presuming as I was, I amused myself with selecting some arguments from nature; reason, and experience, against this so generally received idea. I confess that to sacred testimonies I had not recourse. I held them to be merely metaphorical, and thus regarding them, I could not persuade myself that there was any propriety in bringing them to decide in this *very important debate*. However, as you, sir, confine yourself entirely to the sacred oracles, I mean to bend the whole of my artillery against those supposed proofs, which you have from thence provided, and from which you have formed an intrench-ment *apparently* so invulnerable. And first, to begin with our great progenitors; but here, suffer me to premise, that it is for mental strength I mean to contend, for with respect to animal powers, I yield them undisputed to that sex, which enjoys them in common with the lion, the tyger, and many other beasts of prey; therefore your observations respecting the *ribs, under the arm, at a distance from the head,* &c. &c. in no sort militate against my view. Well, but the woman was first in the transgression. Strange how blind *self love* renders you men; were you not wholly absorbed in a partial admiration of your own abili-ties, you would long since have acknowledged the force of what I am now going to urge. It is true some ignoramuses have absurdly enough informed us, that the beauteous fair of paradise, was seduced from her obedience, by a malignant demon, *in the guise of a baleful serpent;* but we, who are better informed, know that the fallen spirit presented himself to her view, *a shining angel still;* for thus, saith the critics in the Hebrew tongue, ought the word to be rendered. Let us examine her motive—Hark! the seraph declares that she shall attain a perfection of knowledge; for is there aught which is not comprehended under one or other of the terms *good* and *evil* It doth not appear that she was governed by any one sensual appetite; but merely by a desire of adorning her mind; a laudable ambition fired her soul, and a thirst for knowledge impelled the predilection so fatal in its consequences. Adam could not plead the same deception; assuredly he was not deceived; nor ought we to admire his superior strength, or wonder at his sagacity, when we so often confess that example is much more influential than precept. His gentle partner stood before him, a melancholy instance of the direful effects of disobedience; he saw her not possessed of that wisdom which she had fondly hoped to obtain, but he beheld the once blooming female, disrobed of that innocence, which had heretofore rendered her so lovely. To him then deception became impossible, as he had proof positive of the fallacy of the argument, which the deceiver had suggested. What then could be his inducement to burst the barri-ers, and to fly directly in the face of that command, which *immediately* from the mouth of deity *he* had received, since, I say, he could not plead that fascinating stimulus, the accu-mulation of knowledge, as indisputable conviction was so visibly portrayed before him. What mighty cause impelled him to sacrifice myriads of beings yet unborn, and by one impious act, which *he saw* would be productive of such fatal effects, entail undistinguished ruin upon a race of beings, which he was yet to produce. Blush ye vaunters of fortitude; ye boasters of resolution; ye haughty lords of the creation; blush when ye remember, that he was influenced by no other motive than a bare pusillanimous attachment to a woman! by sentiments so exquisitely soft, that all his sons have, from that period, when they have designed to degrade them, described as highly feminine. Thus it should seem, that all the arts of the grand deceiver (since means adequate to the purpose are, I conceive, invariably pursued) were requisite to mislead our general mother, while the father of mankind for-feited his own, and relinquished the happiness of posterity, merely in compliance with the blandishments of a female. The subsequent subjection the apostle Paul explains as a figure;

after enlarging upon the subject, he adds, *"This is a great mystery; but I speak concerning Christ and the church."* Now we know with what consummate wisdom the unerring father of eternity hath formed his plans; all the types which he hath displayed, he hath permitted *materially* to fail, in the very virtue for which *they* were famed. The reason for this is obvious, we might otherwise mistake his economy, and render that honour to the creature, which is due only to the creator. I know that Adam was a figure of him who was to come. The grace contained in this figure, is the reason of my rejoicing, and while I am very far from prostrating before the shadow, I yield joyfully in all things the preeminence to the second federal head. Confiding faith is prefigured by Abraham, yet he exhibits a contrast to affiance, when he says of his fair companion, she is my sister. Gentleness was the characteristick of Moses, yet he hesitated not to reply to Jehovah himself, with unsaintlike tongue he murmured at the waters of strife, and with rash hands he break the tables, which were inscribed by the finger of divinity. David, dignified with the title of the man after God's own heart, and yet how stained was his life. Solomon was celebrated for wisdom, but folly is wrote in legible characters upon his almost every action. Lastly, let us turn our eyes to man in the aggregate. He is manifested as the figure of strength, but that we may not regard him as any thing more than a figure, his soul is formed in no sort superior, but every way equal to the mind of her, who is the emblem of weakness, and whom he hails the gentle companion of his better days.

JOHN ADAMS

Letters to Samuel Adams, October 18, 1790; and to Thomas Jefferson, November 15, 1813; April 19, 1817

In the interval between his career as (in Jefferson's words) "the great Colossus" of the battle for independence in the Continental Congress and his presidency of the United States, John Adams published the two most systematic expositions of political theory produced in America before the nineteenth century. In his long, digressive but brilliantly pointed *Defence of the Constitutions of the United States* and *Discourses on Davila,* Adams spun out his arguments against the idea—first promulgated by Paine but later promoted in a more statist form by French revolutionaries—that republics ought to be dominated by unitary legislative bodies consisting of representatives elected by an undifferentiated electorate of equal citizens. Adams earnestly argued that such a system, if adopted in America, would inevitably lead to a self-seeking, class-conflicted, liberty-devouring state and society. As an alternative he put forward a republicanized version of the mixed government of the English constitution—a state consisting of a mutually checking executive and upper and lower house.

Besides being the new nation's most ambitious and knowledgeable political theorist, Adams was also, along with his friend Jefferson, one of the finest letter writers of the greatest letter-writing age in history, and so two letters are included here in which he presented succinct versions of these political ideas. In his letter to his cousin, the former revolutionary militant Samuel Adams, John Adams gave his reasons for thinking that neither reason nor virtue but only a rational "political architecture" of a balanced government could keep liberty from subverting virtue. In the second letter, taken from his touching and fascinating late correspondence with his once comrade-turned-enemy but now intimate philosophical friend Jefferson, Adams analyzed with great subtlety and passion the many sources and varied guises of the one element he regarded as the most important in his system, the "aristocracy." In the 1817 letter to Jefferson, Adams poignantly sketched what probably lay behind much of his political outlook—his curiously skeptical yet warmly humanized post-Puritan faith in this "best of all possible Worlds."

For a sympathetic study of Adams's later thought and intellectual personality, see Joseph J. Ellis, *Passionate Sage: The Character and Legacy of John Adams* (New York, 1993). For a penetrating discussion of Adams's republicanism, see Gordon S. Wood, *The Creation of the American Republic 1776–1787* (Chapel Hill, 1969), 567–92. C. Bradley Thompson, *John Adams and the Spirit of Liberty* (Lawrence, Kans., 1998), provides an admiring delineation of the theoretical context and rationale of Adams's political science. For an excellent comparative rendering of the mind-sets of Adams and Jefferson, see Henry F. May, *The Enlightenment in America* (New York, 1976), 278–302.

To Samuel Adams

New York, 18 October, 1790.

Dear Sir,—I am thankful to our common friend, as well as to you, for your favor of the fourth, which I received last night. My fears are in unison with yours, that hay, wood, and stubble, will be the materials of the new political buildings in Europe, till men shall be more enlightened and friendly to each other.

You agree, that there are undoubtedly principles of political architecture. But, instead of particularizing any of them, you seem to place all your hopes in the universal, or at least more general, prevalence of knowledge and benevolence. I think with you, that knowledge and benevolence ought to be promoted as much as possible; but, despairing of ever seeing them sufficiently general for the security of society, I am for seeking institutions which may supply in some degree the defect. If there were no ignorance, error, or vice, there would be neither principles nor systems of civil or political government.

I am not often satisfied with the opinions of Hume; but in this he seems well founded, that all projects of government, founded in the supposition or expectation of extraordinary degrees of virtue, are evidently chimerical. Nor do I believe it possible, humanly speaking, that men should ever be greatly improved in knowledge or benevolence, without assistance from the principles and system of government.

I am very willing to agree with you in fancying, that in the greatest improvements of society, government will be in the republican form. It is a fixed principle with me, that all good government is and must be republican. But, at the same time, your candor will agree with me, that there is not in lexicography a more fraudulent word. Whenever I use the word *republic* with approbation, I mean a government in which the people have collectively, or by representation, an essential share in the sovereignty. The republican forms of Poland and Venice are much worse, and those of Holland and Bern very little better, than the monarchical form in France before the late revolution. By the republican form, I know you do not mean the plan of Milton, Nedham, or Turgot. For, after a fair trial of its miseries, the simple monarchical form will ever be, as it has ever been, preferred to it by mankind. Are we not, my friend, in danger of rendering the word *republican* unpopular in this country by an indiscreet, indeterminate, and equivocal use of it? The people of England have been obliged to wean themselves from the use of it, by making it unpopular and unfashionable, because they found it was artfully used by some, and simply understood by others, to mean the government of their interregnum parliament. They found they could not wean themselves from that destructive form of government so entirely, as that a mischievous party would not still remain in favor of it, by any other means than by making the words *republic* and *republican* unpopular. They have succeeded to such a degree, that, with a vast majority of that nation, a republican is as unamiable as a witch, a blasphemer, a rebel, or a tyrant. If, in this country, the word *republic* should be generally understood, as it is by some, to mean a form of government inconsistent with a mixture of three powers, forming a mutual balance, we may depend upon it that such mischievous effects will be produced by the use of it as will compel the people of America to renounce,

Source: The Works of John Adams, ed. Charles Francis Adams (Boston: Charles C. Little and James Brown, 1851), vol. 6, 414–20; *The Adams-Jefferson Letters: The Complete Correspondence Between Thomas Jefferson and Abigail and John Adams*, 2 vols., ed. Lester J. Cappon (Chapel Hill: University of North Carolina Press, 1959), vol 2, 397–402, 508–10. Editor's notes in Cappon altered. Reprinted by permission of the University of North Carolina Press, Copyright © 1959.

detest, and execrate it as the English do. With these explanations, restrictions, and limitations, I agree with you in your love of republican governments, but in no other sense.

With you, I have also the honor most perfectly to harmonize in your sentiments of the humanity and wisdom of promoting education in knowledge, virtue, and benevolence. But I think that these will confirm mankind in the opinion of the necessity of preserving and strengthening the dikes against the ocean, its tides and storms. Human appetites, passions, prejudices, and self-love will never be conquered by benevolence and knowledge alone, introduced by human means. The millennium itself neither supposes nor implies it. All civil government is then to cease, and the Messiah is to reign. That happy and holy state is therefore wholly out of this question. You and I agree in the utility of universal education; but will nations agree in it as fully and extensively as we do, and be at the expense of it? We know, with as much certainty as attends any human knowledge, that they will not. We cannot, therefore, advise the people to depend for their safety, liberty, and security, upon hopes and blessings which we know will not fall to their lot. If we do our duty then to the people, we shall not deceive them, but advise them to depend upon what is in their power and will relieve them.

Philosophers, ancient and modern, do not appear to me to have studied nature, the whole of nature, and nothing but nature. Lycurgus's principle was war and family pride; Solon's was what the people would bear, &c. The best writings of antiquity upon government, those, I mean, of Aristotle, Zeno, and Cicero, are lost. We have human nature, society, and universal history to observe and study, and from these we may draw all the real principles which ought to be regarded. Disciples will follow their masters, and interested partisans their chieftains; let us like it or not, we cannot help it. But if the true principles can be discovered, and fairly, fully, and impartially laid before the people, the more light increases, the more the reason of them will be seen, and the more disciples they will have. Prejudice, passion, and private interest, which will always mingle in human inquiries, one would think might be enlisted on the side of truth, at least in the greatest number; for certainly the majority are interested in the truth, if they could see to the end of all its consequences. "Kings have been deposed by aspiring nobles." True, and never by any other. "These" (the nobles, I suppose,) "have waged everlasting war against the common rights of men." True, when they have been possessed of the *summa imperii* in one body, without a check. So have the plebeians; so have the people; so have kings; so has human nature, in every shape and combination, and so it ever will. But, on the other hand, the nobles have been essential parties in the preservation of liberty, whenever and wherever it has existed. In Europe, they alone have preserved it against kings and people, wherever it has been preserved; or, at least, with very little assistance from the people. One hideous despotism, as horrid as that of Turkey, would have been the lot of every nation of Europe, if the nobles had not made stands. By nobles, I mean not peculiarly an hereditary nobility, or any particular modification, but the natural and actual aristocracy among mankind. The existence of this you will not deny. You and I have seen four noble families rise up in Boston,—the Crafts, Gores, Dawes, and Austins. These are as really a nobility in our town, as the Howards, Somersets, Berties, &c., in England. Blind, undistinguishing reproaches against the aristocratical part of mankind, a division which nature has made, and we cannot abolish, are neither pious nor benevolent. They are as pernicious as they are false. They serve only to foment prejudice, jealousy, envy, animosity, and malevolence. They serve no ends but those of sophistry, fraud, and the spirit of party. It would not be true, but it would not be more egregiously false, to say that the people have waged everlasting war against the rights of men.

"The love of liberty," you say, "is interwoven in the soul of man." So it is, according to La Fontaine, in that of a wolf; and I doubt whether it be much more rational, generous, or social, in one than in the other, until in man it is enlightened by experience, reflection, education, and civil and political institutions, which are at first produced, and constantly supported and improved by a few; that is, by the nobility. The wolf, in the fable, who preferred running in the forest, lean and hungry, to the sleek, plump, and round sides of the dog, because he found the latter was sometimes restrained, had more love of liberty than most men. The numbers of men in all ages have preferred ease, slumber, and good cheer to liberty, when they have been in competition. We must not then depend alone upon the love of liberty in the soul of man for its preservation. Some political institutions must be prepared, to assist this love against its enemies. Without these, the struggle will ever end only in a change of impostors. When the people, who have no property, feel the power in their own hands to determine all questions by a majority, they ever attack those who have property, till the injured men of property lose all patience, and recur to finesse, trick, and stratagem, to outwit those who have too much strength, because they have too many hands to be resisted any other way. Let us be impartial, then, and speak the whole truth. Till we do, we shall never discover all the true principles that are necessary. The multitude, therefore, as well as the nobles, must have a check. This is one principle.

"Were the people of England free, after they had obliged King John to concede to them their ancient rights?" The people never did this. There was no people who pretended to any thing. It was the nobles alone. The people pretended to nothing but to be villains, vassals, and retainers to the king or the nobles. The nobles, I agree, were not free, because all was determined by a majority of their votes, or by arms, not by law. Their feuds deposed their "Henrys, Edwards, and Richards," to gratify lordly ambition, patrician rivalry, and "family pride." But, if they had not been deposed, those kings would have become despots, because the people would not and could not join the nobles in any regular and constitutional opposition to them. They would have become despots, I repeat it, and that by means of the villains, vassals, and retainers aforesaid. It is not family pride, my friend, but family popularity, that does the great mischief, as well as the great good. Pride, in the heart of man, is an evil fruit and concomitant of every advantage; of riches, of knowledge, of genius, of talents, of beauty, of strength, of virtue, and even of piety. It is sometimes ridiculous, and often pernicious. But it is even sometimes, and in some degree, useful. But the pride of families would be always and only ridiculous, if it had not family popularity to work with. The attachment and devotion of the people to some families inspires them with pride. As long as gratitude or interest, ambition or avarice, love, hope, or fear, shall be human motives of action, so long will numbers attach themselves to particular families. When the people will, in spite of all that can be said or done, cry a man or a family up to the skies, exaggerate all his talents and virtues, not hear a word of his weakness or faults, follow implicitly his advice, detest every man he hates, adore every man he loves, and knock down all who will not swim down the stream with them, where is your remedy? When a man or family are thus popular, how can you prevent them from being proud? You and I know of instances in which popularity has been a wind, a tide, a whirlwind. The history of all ages and nations is full of such examples.

Popularity, that has great fortune to dazzle; splendid largesses, to excite warm gratitude; sublime, beautiful, and uncommon genius or talents, to produce deep admiration; or any thing to support high hopes and strong fears, will be proud; and its power will be employed to mortify enemies, gratify friends, procure votes, emoluments, and power. Such family popularity ever did, and ever will govern in every nation, in every climate, hot and cold, wet and dry, among civilized and savage people, Christians and Mahometans, Jews and Heathens. Declamation against family pride is a petty, juvenile exercise, but unworthy of statesmen. They know the evil and danger is too serious to be sported with. The only way, God knows, is to put these families into a hole by themselves, and set two watches upon them; a superior to them all on one side, and the people on the other.

There are a few popular men in the Massachusetts, my friend, who have, I fear, less honor, sincerity, and virtue, than they ought to have. These, if they are not guarded against, may do another mischief. They may excite a party spirit and a mobbish spirit, instead of the spirit of liberty, and produce another Wat Tyler's rebellion. They can do no more. But I really think their party language ought not to be countenanced, nor their shibboleths pronounced. The miserable stuff that they utter about the *well-born* is as despicable as themselves. The εὐγενεῖς of the Greeks, the *bien nées* of the French, the *welgebohren* of the Germans and Dutch, the *beloved families* of the Creeks, are but a few samples of national expressions of the same thing, for which every nation on earth has a similar expression. One would think that our scribblers were all the sons of redemptioners or transported convicts. They think with Tarquin, "*In novo populo, ubi omnis repentina atque ex virtute nobilitas fit, futurum locum forti ac strenuo viro.*"[1]

Let us be impartial. There is not more of family pride on one side, than of vulgar malignity and popular envy on the other. Popularity in one family raises envy in others. But the popularity of the least deserving will triumph over envy and malignity; while that which is acquired by real merit, will very often be overborne and oppressed by it.

Let us do justice to the people and to the nobles; for nobles there are, as I have before proved, in Boston as well as in Madrid. But to do justice to both, you must establish an arbitrator between them. This is another principle.

It is time that you and I should have some sweet communion together. I do not believe, that we, who have preserved for more than thirty years an uninterrupted friendship, and have so long thought and acted harmoniously together in the worst of times, are now so far asunder in sentiment as some people pretend; in full confidence of which, I have used this freedom, being ever your warm friend.

JOHN ADAMS.

To Thomas Jefferson

Quincy November 15. [18]13

DEAR SIR

I cannot appease my melancholly commiseration for our Armies in this furious snow storm in any way so well as by studying your Letter of Oct. 28.

We are now explicitly agreed, in one important point, vizt. That "there is a natural Aristocracy among men; the grounds of which are Virtue and Talents."

You very justly indulge a little merriment upon this solemn subject of Aristocracy. I often laugh at it too, for there is nothing in this laughable world more ridiculous than the management of it by almost all the nations of the Earth. But while We smile, Mankind have reason to say to Us, as the froggs said to the Boys, What is Sport to you is Wounds and death to Us. When I consider the weakness, the folly, the Pride, the Vanity, the Selfishness, the Artifice, the low craft and meaning cunning, the want of Principle, the Avarice the unbounded Ambition, the unfeeling Cruelty of a majority of those (in all Nations) who are

---

1. "Amongst a new people, where all rank was of sudden growth and founded on worth, there would be room for a brave and strenuous man." Livy, 1.34.6.

allowed an aristocratical influence; and on the other hand, the Stupidity with which the more numerous multitude, not only become their Dupes, but even love to be Taken in by their Tricks: I feel a stronger disposition to weep at their destiny, than to laugh at their Folly.

But tho' We have agreed in one point, in Words, it is not yet certain that We are perfectly agreed in Sense. Fashion has introduced an indeterminate Use of the Word "Talents." Education, Wealth, Strength, Beauty, Stature, Birth, Marriage, graceful Attitudes and Motions, Gait, Air, Complexion, Physiognomy, are Talents, as well as Genius and Science and learning. Any one of these Talents, that in fact commands or influences true Votes in Society, gives to the Man who possesses it, the Character of an Aristocrat, in my Sense of the Word.

Pick up, the first 100 men you meet, and make a Republick. Every Man will have an equal Vote. But when deliberations and discussions are opened it will be found that 25, by their Talents, Virtues being equal, will be able to carry 50 Votes. Every one of these 25, is an Aristocrat, in my Sense of the Word; whether he obtains his one Vote in Addition to his own, by his Birth Fortune, Figure, Eloquence, Science, learning, Craft Cunning, or even his Character for good fellowship and a bon vivant.

What gave Sir William Wallace his amazing Aristocratical Superiority? His Strength. What gave Mrs. Clark, her Aristocratical Influence to create Generals Admirals and Bishops? her Beauty. What gave Pompadour and Du Barry the Power of making Cardinals and Popes? their Beauty. You have seen the Palaces of Pompadour and Du Barry: and I have lived for years in the Hotel de Velentinois, with Franklin who had as many Virtues as any of them. In the investigation of the meaning of the Word "Talents" I could write 630 Pages, as pertinent as John Taylors of Hazelwood. But I will select a single Example: for female Aristocrats are nearly as formidable in Society as male.

A daughter of a green Grocer, walks the Streets in London dayly with a baskett of Cabbage, Sprouts, Dandlions and Spinage on her head. She is observed by the Painters to have a beautiful Face, an elegant figure, a graceful Step and a debonair. They hire her to Sitt. She complies, and is painted by forty Artists in a Circle around her. The scientific Sir William Hamilton outbids the Painters, sends her to Schools for a genteel Education and Marries her. This Lady not only causes the Tryumphs of the Nile of Copinhagen and Trafalgar, but seperates Naples from France and finally banishes the King and Queen from Sicilly. Such is the Aristocracy of the natural Talent of Beauty. Millions of Examples might be quoted from History sacred and profane, from Eve, Hannah, Deborah Susanna Abigail, Judith, Ruth, down to Hellen Madame de Maintenon and Mrs. Fitcherbert. For mercy's sake do not compell me to look to our chaste States and Territories, to find Women, one of whom lett go, would, in the Words of Holopherne's Guards "deceive the whole Earth."

The proverbs of Theognis, like those of Solomon, are Observations on human nature, ordinary life, and civil Society, with moral reflections on the facts. I quoted him as a Witness of the Fact, that there was as much difference in the races of Men as in the breeds of Sheep; and as a sharp reprover and censurer of the sordid mercenary practice of disgracing Birth by preferring gold to it. Surely no authority can be more expressly in point to prove the existence of Inequalities, not of rights, but of moral intellectual and physical inequalities in Families, descents and Generations. If a descent from, pious, virtuous, wealthy litterary or scientific Ancestors is a letter of recommendation, or introduction in a Mans his favour, and enables him to influence only one vote in Addition to his own, he is an Aristocrat, for a democrat can have but one Vote. Aaron Burr had 100,000 Votes from the single Circumstance of his descent from President Burr and President Edwards.

Your commentary on the Proverbs of Theognis reminded me of two solemn Characters, the one resembling John Bunyan, the other Scarron. The one John Torrey: the other Ben. Franklin. Torrey a Poet, an Enthusiast, a superstitious Bigot, once very gravely asked my

Brother Cranch, "whether it would not be better for Mankind, if Children were always begotten from religious motives only?" Would not religion, in this sad case, have as little efficacy in encouraging procreation, as it has now in discouraging it? I should apprehend a decrease of population even in our Country where it increases so rapidly. In 1775 Franklin made a morning Visit, at Mrs. Yards to Sam. Adams and John. He was unusally loquacious. "Man, a rational Creature"! said Franklin. "Come, Let Us suppose a rational Man. Strip him of all his Appetites, especially of his hunger and thirst. He is in his Chamber, engaged in making Experiments, or in pursuing some Problem. He is highly entertained. At this moment a Servant Knocks, "Sir dinner is on Table." "Dinner! Pox! Pough! But what have you for dinner?" Ham and Chickens. "Ham"! "And must I break the chain of my thoughts, to go down and knaw a morsel of a damn'd Hogs Arse"? "Put aside your Ham." "I will dine tomorrow."

Take away Appetite and the present generation would not live a month and no future generation would ever exist. Thus the exalted dignity of human Nature would be annihilated and lost. And in my opinion, the whole loss would be of no more importance, than putting out a Candle, quenching a Torch, or crushing a Firefly, *if in this world only We have hope.*

Your distinction between natural and artificial Aristocracy does not appear to me well founded. Birth and Wealth are conferred on some Men, as imperiously by Nature, as Genius, Strength or Beauty. The Heir is honours and Riches, and power has often no more merit in procuring these Advantages, than he has in obtaining an handsome face or an elegant figure. When Aristocracies, are established by human Laws and honour Wealth and Power are made hereditary by municipal Laws and political Institutions, then I acknowledge artificial Aristocracy to commence: but this never commences, till Corruption in Elections becomes dominant and uncontroulable. But this artificial Aristocracy can never last. The everlasting Envys, Jealousies, Rivalries, and quarrells among them, their cruel rapacities upon the poor ignorant People their followers, compell these to sett up Caesar, a Demogogue to be a Monarch and Master, pour mettre chacun a sa place ["to put each one in his place"]. Here you have the origin of all artificial Aristocracy, which is the origin of all Monarchy. And both artificial Aristocracy, and Monarchy, and civil, military, political and hierarchical Despotism, have all grown out of the natural Aristocracy of "Virtues and Talents." We, to be sure, are far remote from this. Many hundred years must roll away before We shall be corrupted. Our pure, virtuous, public spirited federative Rupublick will last for ever, govern the Globe and introduce the perfection of Man, his perfectibility being already proved by Price Priestly, Condorcet Rousseau Diderot and Godwin.

"Mischief has been done by the Senate of U.S." I have known and felt more of this mischief, than Washington, Jefferson and Madison altoge[the]r. But this has been all caused by the constitutional Power of the Senate in Executive Business, which ought to be immediately, totally and eternally abolished.

Your distinction between the aristoi and pseudo aristoi, will not help the matter. I would trust one as soon as the other with unlimited Power. The Law wisely refuses an Oath as a witness in his own cause to the Saint as well as to the Sinner.

No Romance would be more amusing, than the History of your Virginian and our new England Aristocratical Families. Yet even in Rhode Island, where there has been no Clergy, no Church, and I had almost said, no State, and some People say no religion, there has been a constant respect for certain old Families. 57 or 58 years ago, in company with Col. Counsellor, Judge, John Chandler, whom I have quoted before, a Newspaper was brought in. The old Sage asked me to look for the News from Rhode Island and see how the Elections had gone there. I read the List of Wantons, Watsons, Greens, Whipples, Malbones etc. "I expected as much" said the aged Gentleman, "for I have always been of

Opinion, that in the most popular Governments, the Elections will generally go in favour of the most ancient families." To this day when any of these Tribes and We may Add Ellerys, Channings Champlins etc are pleased to fall in with the popular current, they are sure to carry all before them.

You suppose a difference Opinion between You and me, on the Subject of Aristocracy. I can find none. I dislike and detest hereditary honours, Offices Emoluments established by Law. So do you. I am for ex[c]luding legal hereditary distinctions from the U.S. as long as possible. So are you. I only say that Mankind have not yet discovered any remedy against irresistable Corruption in Elections to Offices of great Power and Profit, but making them hereditary.

But will you say our Elections are pure? Be it so; upon the whole. But do you recollect in history, a more Corrupt Election than that of Aaron Burr to be President, or that of De Witt Clinton last year. By corruption, here I mean a sacrifice of every national Interest and honour, to private and party Objects.

I see the same Spirit in Virginia, that you and I see in Rhode Island and the rest of New England. In New York it is a struggle of Family Feuds. A fewdal Aristocracy. Pensylvania is a contest between German, Irish and old English Families. When Germans and Irish Unite, they give 30,000 majorities. There is virtually a White Rose and A Red Rose a Caesar and a Pompey in every State in this Union and Contests and dissentions will be as lasting. The Rivalry of Bourbons and Noailleses produced The French Revolution, and a similar Competition for Consideration and Influence, exists and prevails in every Village in the World.

Where will terminate the Rabies Agri ["madness for land"]? The Continent will be scattered over with Manors, much larger than Livingstons, Van Ranselaers or Phillips's. Even our Deacon Strong will have a Principality among you Southern Folk. What Inequality of Talents will be produced by these Land Jobbers?

Where tends the Mania for Banks? At my Table in Philadelphia, I once proposed to you to unite in endeavours to obtain an Amendment of the Constitution, prohibiting to the separate States the Power of creating Banks; but giving Congress Authority to establish one Bank, with a branch in each State; the whole limited to Ten Millions of dollars. Whether this Project was wise or unwise, I know not, for I had deliberated little on it then and have never thought it worth thinking much of since. But you spurned the proposition from you with disdain.

This System of Banks begotten, hatched and brooded by Duer, Robert and Governeur Morris, Hamilton and Washington, I have always considered as a System of national Injustice. A Sacrifice of public and private Interest to a few Aristocratical Friends and Favourites. My scheme could have had no such Effect.

Verres plundered Temples and robbed a few rich Men; but he never made such ravages among private property in general, nor swindled so much out of the pocketts of the poor and the middle Class of People as these Banks have done. No people but this would have borne the Imposition so long. The People of Ireland would not bear Woods half pence. What Inequalities of Talent, have been introduced into this Country by these Aristocratical Banks!

Our Winthrops, Winslows, Bradfords, Saltonstalls, Quincys, Chandlers, Leonards Hutchinsons Olivers, Sewalls etc are precisely in the Situation of your Randolphs, Carters, and Burwells, and Harrisons. Some of them unpopular for the part they took in the late revolution, but all respected for their names and connections and whenever they fall in with the popular Sentiments, are preferred, cetoris paribus to all others. When I was young, the Summura Bonum in Massachusetts, was to be worth ten thousand pounds Sterling, ride in a Chariot, be Colonel of a Regiment of Miltia and hold a seat in his Majesty's Council. No Mans Imagination aspired to any thing higher beneath the Skies. But these Plumbs, Chariots, Colonelships and counsellorships are recorded and will never be forgotten. No great Accumulations of Land were made by our early Settlers. Mr. Bausoin a French Refugee, made the first great Purchases and your General Dearborne, born under a fortunate Starr is now enjoying a large Portion of the Aristocratical sweets of them.

As I have no Amanuenses but females, and there is so much about generation in this letter that I dare not ask any one of them to copy it, and I cannot copy it myself I must beg of you to return it to me, your old Friend

JOHN ADAMS

To Thomas Jefferson

Quincy April 19 1817

DEAR SIR

My loving and beloved Friend, Pickering, has been pleased to inform the World that I have "few Friends." I wanted to whip the rogue, and I had it in my Power, if it had been in my Will to do it, till the blood come. But all my real Friends as I thought them, with Dexter and Grey at their Head insisted "that I should not say a Word." "That nothing that such a Person could write would do me the least Injury. That it would betray the Constitution and the Government, if a President out or in should enter into a Newspaper controversy, with one of his Ministers whom he had removed from his Office, in Justification of himself for that removal or any thing else." And they talked a great deal about " *The Dignity*" of the Office of President, which I do not find that any other Persons, public or private regard very much.

Nevertheless, I fear that Mr. Pickerings Information is too true. It is impossible that any Man should run such a Gauntlet as I have been driven through, and have many Friends at last. This "all who know me know" though I cannot say "who love me tell."

I have, however, either Friends who wish to amuse and solace my old age; or Ennemies who mean to heap coals of fire on my head and kill me with kindness: for they overwhelm me with Books from all quarters, enough to offuscate all Eyes, and smother and stifle all human Understanding. Chateaubriand, Grim, Tucker, Dupuis, La Harpe, Sismondi, Eustace[.] A new Translation of Herodotus by Belloe with more Notes than Text. What should I do, with all this lumber? I make my "Woman kind" as the Antiquary expresses it, read to me, all the English: but as they will not read the French, I am obliged to excruciate my Eyes to read it myself. And all to what purpose? I verily believe I was as wise and good, seventy Years ago, as I am now.

At that Period Lemuel Bryant was my Parish Priest; and Joseph Cleverly my Latin School Master. Lemuel was a jolly jocular and liberal Schollar and Divine. Joseph a Scollar and Gentleman; but a biggoted episcopalian of the School of Bishop Saunders and Dr. Hicks, a down right conscientious passive Obedience Man in Church and State. The Parson and the Pedagogue lived much together, but were eternally disputing about Government and Religion. One day, when the Schoolmaster had been more than commonly fanatical, and declared "if he were a Monark, *He would have but one Religion in his Dominions*" The Parson coolly replied "Cleverly! You would be the best Man in the World, if You had no Religion."

Twenty times, in the course of my late Reading, have I been upon the point of breaking out, "This would be the best of all possible Worlds, if there were no Religion in it."!!!

But in this exclamati[on] I should have been as fanatical as Bryant or Cleverly. Without Religion this World would be something not fit to be mentioned in polite Company, I mean Hell. So far from believing in the total and universal depravity of human Nature; I believe there is no Individual totally depraved. The most abandoned Scoundrel that ever existed, never Yet Wholly extinguished his Conscience, and while Conscience remains there is some Religion. Popes, Jesuits and Sorbonists and Inquisitors have some Conscience and some Religion. So had Marius and Sylla, Caesar Cataline and Anthony, and Augustus had not much more, let Virgil and Horace say what they will.

What shall We think of Virgil and Horace, Sallust Quintillian, Pliny and even Tacitus? and even Cicero, Brutus and Seneca? Pompey I leave out of the question, as a mere politician and Soldier. Every One of these great Creatures has left indelible marks of Conscience and consequently of Religion, tho' every one of them has left abundant proofs of profligate violations of their Consciences by their little and great Passions and paltry Interests.

The vast prospect of Mankind, which these Books have passed in Review before me, from the most ancient records, histories, traditions and Fables that remain to Us, to the present day, has sickened my very Soul; and almost reconciled me to Swifts Travels among The Yahoo's. Yet I never can be a Misanthrope. Homo Sum ["I am a man"]. I must hate myself before I can hate my Fellow Men: and that I cannot and will not do. No! I will not hate any of them, base, brutal and devilish as some of them have been to me.

From the bottom of my Soul, I pitty my Fellow Men. Fears and Terrors appear to have produced an univer[s]al Credulity. Fears of Calamities in Life and punishments after death, seem to have possessed the Souls of all Men. But fear of Pain and death, here, do not seem to have been so unconquerable as fear of what is to come hereafter. Priests, Hierophants, Popes, Despots Emperors, Kings, Princes Nobles, have been as credulous as Shoeblacks, Boots, and Kitchen Scullions. The former seem to have believed in their divine Rights as sincerely as the latter. Auto de fee's in Spain and Portugal have been celebrated with as good Faith as Excommunications have been practiced in Connecticutt or as Baptisms have been refused in Phyladelphia.

How it is possible than [i.e., that] Mankind should submit to be governed as they have been is to me an inscrutable Mystery. How they could bear to be taxed to build the Temple of Diana at Ephesus, the Pyramyds of Egypt, Saint Peters at Rome, Notre Dame at Paris, St. Pauls in London, with a million Etceteras; when my Navy Yards, and my quasi Army made such a popular Clamour, I know not. Yet all my Peccadillos, never excited such a rage as the late Compensation Law!!![2]

I congratulate you, on the late Election in Connecticutt.[3] It is a kind of Epocha. Several causes have conspired. One which you would not suspect. Some one, no doubt instigated by the Devil, has taken it into his head to print a new Edition of "The independent Whig" even in Connecticut, and has scattered the Volumes through the State. These Volumes it is said, have produced a Burst of Indignation against Priestcraft Bigotry and Intollerance, and in conjunction with other causes have produced the late Election. When writing to you I never know when to Subscribe

JOHN ADAMS

2.   In 1816 and 1817 Congress passed several invalid-pension bills for veterans of the War of 1812. Adams apparently refers to the bill enacted on March 3, 1817.

3.   The campaign issue in the spring election of 1817 was "whether freemen shall be tolerated in the free exercise of their religious and political rights." Oliver Wolcott, father of the Constitution of 1818 (Connecticut's first), was elected governor.

THOMAS JEFFERSON

Selection from *Notes on the State of Virginia* (1787)

Letters to John Adams, October 28, 1813; to Benjamin Rush, with a Syllabus, April 21, 1803; and to Thomas Law, June 13, 1814

No American figure—not even Franklin—was more devoted to or pursued more successfully the Enlightenment ideal of a many-sided intellectual life in the service of the public good than Thomas Jefferson. Nor does one work reflect more completely his varied activities as scientist, architect, philosopher, and statesman than *Notes on the State of Virginia*, the book he produced out of his answers to a questionnaire circulated in 1780 by the secretary of the French legation at Philadelphia.

The selection from the four queries presented herein illustrates what might be called Jefferson's political sociology, or his pioneering effort at integrating his enlightened views of society and culture with his democratic politics and ethics. In his discussion of blacks and slavery, his two sets of interests seem painfully and tragically, if not completely, at odds. By contrast, in his discussions of public education and religious freedom, he argued compellingly that a hierarchical but enlightened educational system and a free, experimental approach to religious belief undergirded republican self-government and social progress. But the tour de force of Jefferson's republican sociology was his famous answer to the query about manufactures. Here he maintained that the spring of social and political virtue was economic independence, which, in turn, was nurtured by a commercial yet nonetheless self-sufficient kind of farming made possible by America's "immensity of land." As Jefferson's most succinctly political statement on the role of talent and virtue in a democratic polity was *his* side of the exchange with Adams over the nature of an aristocracy, this letter is printed following the *Notes*.

Finally, Jefferson's mature politics was most deeply rooted in his moral philosophy, which he developed in his usual serenely methodical, epistolary fashion. In his "Syllabus" on the doctrines of Jesus that he enclosed in his letter to Benjamin Rush, Jefferson argued for a severely ethicized and socialized Christianity that was as far from Paine's militantly rationalistic, anti-Christian deism as it was from Adams's skeptical pietism. But in his letter to Thomas Law, Jefferson presented his most developed case for the social efficacy of a moral philosophy. Jefferson's benevolent "moral sense" was as involuntary and democratic as any sense, yet tested, he conceded, by varying standards of "utility" and "general feeling."

Adrienne Koch, *The Philosophy of Thomas Jefferson* (New York, 1943), is a still useful introduction to Jefferson's thought. For more critical studies of Jefferson's naturalistic philosophy, see Daniel J. Boorstin, *The Lost World of Thomas Jefferson* (Boston, 1948); and Charles

A. Miller, *Jefferson and Nature: An Interpretation* (Baltimore, 1988). For important contrasting interpretations of Jefferson's views on blacks and slavery, see Winthrop D. Jordan, *White over Black: American Attitudes Toward the Negro, 1550–1812* (Chapel Hill, 1968), 429–81; and David Brion Davis, *The Problem of Slavery in the Age of Revolution, 1770–1823* (Ithaca, 1975), 164–212. Elizabeth Flower and Murray G. Murphey, in their *History of Philosophy in America,* vol. 1 (New York, 1977), 277–353, include a valuable analysis of Jefferson's ethics and metaphysics in the context of trends in eighteenth-century American philosophy. For a good discussion of Jefferson's religion, see Eugene R. Sheridan, "Introduction," in *Jefferson's Extracts from the Gospels: "The Philosophy of Jesus" and "The Life and Morals of Jesus,"* ed. Dickinson W. Adams, *The Papers of Thomas Jefferson, Second Series,* ed. Charles T. Cullen (Princeton, 1983), 3–42. In *The Limits of Optimism: Thomas Jefferson's Dualistic Enlightenment* (Charlottesville, 2011), Maurizio Valsania seeks to recover the coherency and realism of Jefferson's thought by placing it within contested traditionsof the Enlightenment.

circumstances, will divide us into parties, and produce convulsions which will probably never end but in the extermination of the one or the other race.—To these objections, which are political, may be added others, which are physical and moral. The first difference which strikes us is that of colour. Whether the black of the negro resides in the reticular membrane between the skin and scarf-skin, or in the scarf-skin itself; whether it proceeds from the colour of the blood, the colour of the bile, or from that of some other secretion, the difference is fixed in nature, and is as real as if its seat and cause were better known to us. And is this difference of no importance? Is it not the foundation of a greater or less share of beauty in the two races? Are not the fine mixtures of red and white, the expressions of every passion by greater or less suffusions of colour in the one, preferable to that eternal monotony, which reigns in the countenances, that immoveable veil of black which covers all the emotions of the other race? Add to these, flowing hair, a more elegant symmetry of form, their own judgment in favour of the whites, declared by their preference of them, as uniformly as is the preference of the Oran-ootan for the black women over those of his own species. The circumstance of superior beauty, is thought worthy attention in the propagation of our horses, dogs, and other domestic animals; why not in that of man? Besides those of colour, figure, and hair, there are other physical distinctions proving a difference of race. They have less hair on the face and body. They secrete less by the kidnies, and more by the glands of the skin, which gives them a very strong and disagreeable odour. This greater degree of transpiration renders them more tolerant of heat, and less so of cold, than the whites. Perhaps too a difference of structure in the pulmonary apparatus, which a late ingenious experimentalist has discovered to be the principal regulator of animal heat, may have disabled them from extricating, in the act of inspiration, so much of that fluid from the outer air, or obliged them in expiration, to part with more of it. They seem to require less sleep. A black, after hard labour through the day, will be induced by the slightest amusements to sit up till midnight, or later, though knowing he must be out with the first dawn of the morning. They are at least as brave, and more adventuresome. But this may perhaps proceed from a want of forethought, which prevents their seeing a danger till it be present. When present, they do not go through it with more coolness or steadiness than the whites. They are more ardent after their female: but love seems with them to be more an eager desire, than a tender delicate mixture of sentiment and sensation. Their griefs are transient. Those numberless afflictions, which render it doubtful whether heaven has given life to us in mercy or in wrath, are less felt, and sooner forgotten with them. In general, their existence appears to participate more of sensation than reflection. To this must be ascribed their disposition to sleep when abstracted from their diversions, and unemployed in labour. An animal whose body is at rest, and who does not reflect, must be disposed to sleep of course. Comparing them by their faculties of memory, reason, and imagination, it appears to me, that in memory they are equal to the whites; in reason much inferior, as I think one could scarcely be found capable of tracing and comprehending the investigations of Euclid; and that in imagination they are dull, tasteless, and anomalous. It would be unfair to follow them to Africa for this investigation. We will consider them here, on the same stage with the whites, and where the facts are not apocryphal on which a judgment is to be formed. It will be right to make great allowances for the difference of condition, of education, of conversation, of the sphere in which they move. Many millions of them have been brought to, and born in America. Most of them indeed have been confined to tillage, to their own homes, and their own society: yet many have been so situated, that they might have availed themselves of the conversation of their masters; many have been brought up to the handicraft arts, and from that circumstance have always been associated with the whites. Some have been liberally educated, and all have lived in countries where the arts and sciences are cultivated to a considerable degree, and have had before their eyes samples of the best works from abroad. The Indians, with no advantages of this kind, will often carve figures on their pipes not destitute of design and merit. They will crayon out an animal, a plant, or a country, so as to prove the existence of a germ in their minds which only wants cultivation. They astonish you with strokes of the most sublime oratory; such as prove their reason and sentiment strong, their imagination glowing and elevated. But never yet could I find that a black had uttered a thought above the level of plain narration; never see even an elementary trait of painting or sculpture. In music they are more generally gifted than the whites with accurate ears for tune and time, and they have been found capable of imagining a small catch. Whether they will be equal to the composition of a more extensive run of melody, or of complicated harmony, is yet to be proved. Misery is often the parent of the most affecting touches in poetry.—Among the blacks is misery enough, God knows, but no poetry. Love is the peculiar oestrum of the poet. Their love is ardent, but it kindles the senses only, not the imagination. Religion indeed has produced a Phyllis Whately; but it could not produce a poet. The compositions published under her name are below the dignity of criticism. The heroes of the Dunciad are to her, as Hercules to the author of that poem. Ignatius Sancho has approached nearer to merit in composition; yet his letters do more honour to the heart than the head. They breathe the purest effusions of friendship and general philanthropy, and shew how great a degree of the latter may be compounded with strong religious zeal. He is often happy in the turn of his compliments, and his stile is easy and familiar, except when he affects a Shandean fabrication of words. But his imagination is wild and extravagant, escapes incessantly from every restraint of reason and taste, and, in the course of its vagaries, leaves a tract of thought as incoherent and eccentric, as is the course of a meteor through the sky. His subjects should often have led him to a process of sober reasoning: yet we find him always substituting sentiment for demonstration. Upon the whole, though we admit him to the first place among those of his own colour who have presented themselves to the public judgment, yet when we compare him with the writers of the race among whom he lived, and particularly with the epistolary class, in which he has taken his own stand, we are compelled to enroll him at the bottom of the column. This criticism supposes the letters published under his name to be genuine, and to have received amendment from no other hand; points which would not be of easy investigation. The improvement of the blacks in body and mind, in the first instance of their mixture with the whites, has been observed by every one, and proves that their inferiority is not the effect merely of their condition of life. We know that among the Romans, about the Augustan age especially, the condition of their slaves was much more deplorable than that of the blacks on the continent of America. The two sexes were confined in separate apartments, because to raise a child cost the master more than to buy one. Cato, for a very restricted indulgence to his slaves in this particular, took from them a certain price. But in this country the slaves multiply as fast as the free inhabitants. Their situation and manners place the commerce between the two sexes almost without restraint.—The same Cato, on a principle of economy, always sold his sick and superannuated slaves. He gives it as a standing precept to a master visiting his farm, to sell his old oxen, old waggons, old tools, old and diseased servants, and every thing else become useless. "Vendat boves vetulos, plaustrum vetus, ferramenta, vetera, servum senem, servum morbosum, & si quid aliud supersit vendat." The American slaves cannot enumerate this among the injuries and insults they receive. It was the common practice to expose in the island of Æsculapius, in the Tyber, diseased slaves, whose cure was like to become tedious. The Emperor Claudius, by an edict, gave freedom to such of them as should recover, and first declared, that if any person chose to kill rather than to expose them, it should be deemed homicide. The exposing them is a crime of which no instance has existed with us; and were it to be followed by death, it would be punished capitally. We are told of a certain Vedius

Pollio, who, in the presence of Augustus, would have given a slave as food to his fish, for having broken a glass. With the Romans, the regular method of taking the evidence of their slaves was under torture. Here it has been thought better never to resort to their evidence. When a master was murdered, all his slaves, in the same house, or within hearing, were condemned to death. Here punishment falls on the guilty only, and as precise proof is required against him as against a freeman. Yet notwithstanding these and other discouraging circumstances among the Romans, their slaves were often their rarest artists. They excelled too in science, insomuch as to be usually employed as tutors to their master's children. Epictetus, [Diogenes, Phaedon], Terence, and Phædrus, were slaves. But they were of the race of whites. It is not their condition then, but nature, which has produced the distinction.—Whether further observation will or will not verify the conjecture, that nature has been less bountiful to them in the endowments of the head, I believe that in those of the heart she will be found to have done them justice. That disposition to theft with which they have been branded, must be ascribed to their situation, and not to any depravity of the moral sense. The man, in whose favour no laws of property exist, probably feels himself less bound to respect those made in favour of others. When arguing for ourselves, we lay it down as a fundamental, that laws, to be just, must give a reciprocation of right: that, without this, they are mere arbitrary rules of conduct, founded in force, and not in conscience: and it is a problem which I give to the master to solve, whether the religious precepts against the violation of property were not framed for him as well as his slave? And whether the slave may not as justifiably take a little from one, who has taken all from him, as he may slay one who would slay him? That a change in the relations in which a man is placed should change his ideas of moral right and wrong, is neither new, nor peculiar to the colour of the blacks. Homer tells us it was so 2600 years ago.

ἥμισυ γάρ τ᾽ ἀρετῆς ἀποαίνυται εὐρύοπα Ζεύς
ἀνέρος, εὖτ᾽ ἄν μιν κατὰ δούλιον ἦμαρ ἕλῃσιν. *Od.* 17.323

Jove fix'd it certain, that whatever day
Makes man a slave, takes half his worth away.

But the slaves of which Homer speaks were whites. Notwithstanding these considerations which must weaken their respect for the laws of property, we find among them numerous instances of the most rigid integrity, and as many as among their better instructed masters, of benevolence, gratitude, and unshaken fidelity.—The opinion, that they are inferior in the faculties of reason and imagination, must be hazarded with great diffidence. To justify a general conclusion, requires many observations, even where the subject may be submitted to the Anatomical knife, to Optical glasses, to analysis by fire, or by solvents. How much more then where it is a faculty, not a substance, we are examining; where it eludes the research of all the senses; where the conditions of its existence are various and variously combined; where the effects of those which are present or absent bid defiance to calculation; let me add too, as a circumstance of great tenderness, where our conclusion would degrade a whole race of men from the rank in the scale of beings which their Creator may perhaps have given them. To our reproach it must be said, that though for a century and a half we have had under our eyes the races of black and of red men, they have never yet been viewed by us as subjects of natural history. I advance it therefore as a suspicion only, that the blacks, whether originally a distinct race, or made distinct by time and circumstances, are inferior to the whites in the endowments both of body and mind. It is not against experience to suppose, that different species of the same genus, or varieties of the same species, may possess different qualifications. Will not a lover of natural history then, one who views the gradations in all the races of animals with the eye of philosophy, excuse an effort to keep those in the department of man as distinct as nature has formed them? This unfortunate difference of colour, and perhaps of faculty, is a powerful obstacle to the emancipation of these people. Many of their advocates, while they wish to vindicate the liberty of human nature, are anxious also to preserve its dignity and beauty. Some of these, embarrassed by the question "What further is to be done with them?" join themselves in opposition with those who are actuated by sordid avarice only. Among the Romans emancipation required but one effort. The slave, when made free, might mix with, without staining the blood of his master. But with us a second is necessary, unknown to history. When freed, he is to be removed beyond the reach of mixture....

Another object of the revisal is, to diffuse knowledge more generally through the mass of the people. This bill proposes to lay off every county into small districts of five or six miles square, called hundreds, and in each of them to establish a school for teaching reading, writing, and arithmetic. The tutor to be supported by the hundred, and every person in it entitled to send their children three years gratis, and as much longer as they please, paying for it. These schools to be under a visitor, who is annually to chuse the boy, of best genius in the school, of those whose parents are too poor to give them further education, and to send him forward to one of the grammar schools, of which twenty are proposed to be erected in different parts of the country, for teaching Greek, Latin, geography, and the higher branches of numerical arithmetic. Of the boys thus sent in any one year, trial is to be made at the grammar schools one or two years, and the best genius of the whole selected, and continued six years, and the residue dismissed. By this means twenty of the best geniuses will be raked from the rubbish annually, and be instructed, at the public expense, so far as the grammar schools go. At the end of six years instruction, one half are to be discontinued (from among whom the grammar schools will probably be supplied with future masters); and the other half, who are to be chosen for the superiority of their parts and disposition, are to be sent and continued three years in the study of such sciences as they shall chuse, at William and Mary college, the plan of which is proposed to be enlarged, as will be hereafter explained, and extended to all the useful sciences. The ultimate result of the whole scheme of education would be the teaching all children of the state reading, writing, and common arithmetic: turning out ten annually of superior genius, well taught in Greek, Latin, geography, and the higher branches of arithmetic: turning out ten others annually, of still superior parts, who, to those branches of learning, shall have added such of the sciences as their genius shall have led them to: the furnishing to the wealthier part of the people convenient schools, at which their children may be educated, at their own expense.—The general objects of this law are to provide an education adapted to the years, to the capacity, and the condition of every one, and directed to their freedom and happiness. Specific details were not proper for the law. These must be the business of the visitors entrusted with its execution. The first stage of this education being the schools of the hundreds, wherein the great mass of the people will receive their instruction, the principal foundations of future order will be laid here. Instead therefore of putting the Bible and Testament into the hands of the children, at an age when their judgments are not sufficiently matured for religious enquiries, their memories may here be stored with the most useful facts from Grecian, Roman, European and American history. The first elements of morality too maybe instilled into their minds; such as, when further developed as their judgments advance in strength, may teach them how to work out their own greatest happiness, by shewing them that it does not depend on the condition of life in which chance has placed them, but is always the result of a good conscience, good health, occupation, and freedom in all just pursuits.—Those whom either the wealth of their parents or the adoption of the state shall destine to higher degrees of learning, will go on to the grammar schools, which constitute the next stage, there to be instructed in the languages. The learning Greek and Latin, I am told, is going into disuse in Europe. I know not what their manners and occupations may call for: but it would be very ill-judged in us to follow their example in this instance. There is a certain period of life, say from eight to fifteen or sixteen years of age, when the mind, like the body, is not yet firm enough for laborious and close operations. If applied to such, it falls an early victim to premature exertion; exhibiting indeed at first, in these young and tender subjects, the flattering appearance of their being men while they are yet children, but ending in reducing them to be children when they should be men. The memory is then most susceptible and tenacious of impressions; and the learning of languages being chiefly a work of memory, it seems precisely fitted to the powers of this period, which is long enough too for acquiring the most useful languages ancient and modern. I do not pretend that language is science. It is only an instrument for the attainment of science. But that time is not lost which is employed in providing tools for future operation: more especially as in this case the books put into the hands of the youth for this purpose may be such as will at the same time impress their minds with useful facts and good principles. If this period be suffered to pass in idleness, the mind becomes lethargic and impotent, as would the body it inhabits if unexercised during the same time. The sympathy between body and mind during their rise, progress and decline, is too strict and obvious to endanger our being misled while we reason from the one to the other.—As soon as they are of sufficient age, it is supposed they will be sent on from the grammar schools to the university, which constitutes our third and last stage, there to study those sciences which may be adapted to their views.—By that part of our plan which prescribes the selection of the youths of genius from among the classes of the poor, we hope to avail the state of those talents which nature has sown as liberally among the poor as the rich, but which perish without use, if not sought for and cultivated.—But of all the views of this law none is more important, none more legitimate, than that of rendering the people the safe, as they are the ultimate, guardians of their own liberty. For this purpose the reading in the first stage, where *they* will receive their whole education, is proposed, as has been said, to be chiefly historical. History by apprising them of the past will enable them to judge of the future; it will avail them of the experience of other times and other nations; it will qualify them as judges of the actions and designs of men; it will enable them to know ambition under every disguise it may assume; and knowing it, to defeat its views. In every government on earth is some trace of human weakness, some germ of corruption and degeneracy, which cunning will discover, and wickedness insensibly open, cultivate, and improve. Every government degenerates when trusted to the rulers of the people alone. The people themselves therefore are its only safe depositories. And to render even them safe their minds must be improved to a certain degree. This indeed is not all that is necessary, though it be essentially necessary. An amendment of our constitution must here come in aid of the public education. The influence over government must be shared among all the people. If every individual which composes their mass participates of the ultimate authority, the government will be safe; because the corrupting the whole mass will exceed any private resources of wealth: and public ones cannot be provided but by levies on the people. In this case every man would have to pay his own price. The government of Great-Britain has been corrupted, because but one man in ten has a right to vote for members of parliament. The sellers of the government therefore get nine-tenths of their price clear. It has been thought that corruption is restrained by confining the right of suffrage to a few of the wealthier of the people: but it would be more effectually restrained by an extension of that right to such numbers as would bid defiance to the means of corruption.

Lastly, it is proposed, by a bill in this revisal, to begin a public library and gallery, by laying out a certain sum annually in books, paintings, and statues.

. . . . . .

Query XVII.

R E L I G I O N

The different religions received into that state?

… The error seems not sufficiently eradicated, that the operations of the mind, as well as the acts of the body, are subject to the coercion of the laws. But our rulers can have authority over such natural rights only as we have submitted to them. The rights of conscience we never submitted, we could not submit. We are answerable for them to our God. The legitimate powers of government extend to such acts only as are injurious to others. But it does me no injury for my neighbour to say there arc twenty gods, or no god. It neither picks my pocket nor breaks my leg. If it be said, his testimony in a court of justice cannot be relied on, reject it then, and be the stigma on him. Constraint may make him worse by making him a hypocrite, but it will never make him a truer man. It may fix him obstinately in his errors, but will not cure them. Reason and free enquiry are the only effectual agents against error. Give a loose to them, they will support the true religion, by bringing every false one to their tribunal, to the test of their investigation. They are the natural enemies of error, and of error only. Had not the Roman government permitted free enquiry, Christianity could never have been introduced. Had not free enquiry been indulged, at the æra of the reformation, the corruptions of Christianity could not have been purged away. If it be restrained now, the present corruptions will be protected, and new ones encouraged. Was the government to prescribe to us our medicine and diet, our bodies would be in such keeping as our souls are now. Thus in France the emetic was once forbidden as a medicine, and the potatoe as an article of food. Government is just as infallible too when it fixes systems in physics. Galileo was sent to the inquisition for affirming that the earth was a sphere: the government had declared it to be as flat as a trencher, and Galileo was obliged to adjure his error. This error however at length prevailed, the earth became a globe, and Descartes declared it was whirled round its axis by a vortex. The government in which he lived was wise enough to see that this was no question of civil jurisdiction, or we should all have been involved by authority in vortices. In fact, the vortices have been exploded, and the Newtonian principle of gravitation is now more firmly established, on the basis of reason, than it would be were the government to step in, and to make it an article of necessary faith. Reason and experiment have been indulged, and error has fled before them. It is error alone which needs the support of government. Truth can stand by itself. Subject opinion to coercion: whom will you make your inquisitors? Fallible men; men governed by bad passions, by private as well as public reasons. And why subject it to coercion? To produce uniformity. But is uniformity of opinion desireable? No more than of face and stature. Introduce the bed of Procrustes then, and as there is danger that the large men may beat the small, make us all of a size, by lopping the former and stretching the latter. Difference of opinion is advantageous in religion. The several sects perform the office of a Censor morum over each other. Is uniformity attainable? Millions of innocent men, women, and children, since the introduction of Christianity, have been burnt, tortured, fined, imprisoned; yet we have not advanced one inch towards uniformity. What has been the effect of coercion? To make one half the world fools, and the other half hypocrites. To support roguery and error all over the earth. Let us reflect that it is inhabited by a thousand millions of people. That these profess probably a thousand different systems of religion. That ours is but one of that thousand. That if there be but one right, and ours that one, we should wish to see the 999 wandering sects gathered into the fold of truth. But against such a majority we cannot effect this by force. Reason and persuasion are the only practicable instruments. To make way for these, free enquiry must be indulged; and how can we wish others to indulge it while we refuse it ourselves. But every state, says an inquisitor, has established some religion. No two, say I, have established the same. Is this a proof of the infallibility of establishments? Our sister states of Pennsylvania and New York, however, have long subsisted without any establishment at all. The experiment was new and doubtful when they made it. It has answered beyond conception. They flourish infinitely. Religion is well supported; of various kinds, indeed, but all good enough; all sufficient to preserve peace and order: or if a sect arises, whose tenets would subvert morals, good sense has fair play, and reasons and laughs it out of doors, without suffering the state to be troubled with it. They do not hang more malefactors than we do. They are not more disturbed with religious dissensions. On the contrary, their harmony is unparalleled, and can be ascribed to nothing but their unbounded tolerance, because there is no other circumstance in which they differ from every nation on earth. They have made the happy discovery, that the way to silence religious disputes, is to take no notice of them. Let us too give this experiment fair play, and get rid, while we may, of those tyrannical laws. It is true, we are as yet secured against them by the spirit of the times. I doubt whether the people of this country would suffer an execution for heresy, or a three years imprisonment for not comprehending the mysteries of the Trinity. But is the spirit of the people an infallible, a permanent reliance? Is it government? Is this the kind of protection we receive in return for the rights we give up? Besides, the spirit of the times may alter, will alter. Our rulers will become corrupt, our people careless. A single zealot may commence persecutor, and better men be his victims. It can never be too often repeated, that the time for fixing every essential right on a legal basis is while our rulers are honest, and ourselves united. From the conclusion of this war we shall be going down hill. It will not then be necessary to resort every moment to the people for support. They will be forgotten, therefore, and their rights disregarded. They will forget themselves, but in the sole faculty of making money, and will never think of uniting to effect a due respect for their rights. The shackles, therefore, which shall not be knocked off at the conclusion of this war, will remain on us long, will be made heavier and heavier, till our rights shall revive or expire in a convulsion.

Query XVIII.

MANNERS

The particular customs and manners that may happen to be received in that state?

It is difficult to determine on the standard by which the manners of a nation may be tried, whether *catholic,* or *particular.* It is more difficult for a native to bring to that standard the manners of his own nation, familiarized to him by habit. There must doubtless be an unhappy influence on the manners of our people produced by the existence of slavery among us. The whole commerce between master and slave is a perpetual exercise of the most boisterous passions, the most unremitting despotism on the one part, and degrading submissions on the other. Our children see this, and learn to imitate it; for man is an imitative animal. This quality is the germ of all education in him. From his cradle to his grave he is learning to do what he sees others do. If a parent could find no motive either in his philanthropy or his self-love, for restraining the intemperance of passion towards his slave, it should always be a sufficient one that his child is present. But generally it is not sufficient. The parent storms, the child looks on, catches the lineaments of wrath, puts on the same airs in the circle of smaller slaves, gives a loose to his worst of passions, and thus nursed, educated, and daily exercised in tyranny, cannot but be stamped by it with odious peculiarities. The man must be a prodigy who can retain his manners and morals undepraved by such circumstances. And with what execration should the statesman be loaded, who permitting one half the citizens thus to trample on the rights of the other, transforms those into despots, and these into enemies, destroys the morals of the one part, and the amor patriæ of the other. For if a slave can have a country in this world, it must be any other in preference to that in which he is born to live and labour for another: in which he must lock up the faculties of his nature, contribute as far as depends on his individual endeavours to the evanishment of the human race, or entail his own miserable condition on the endless generations proceeding from him. With the morals of the people, their industry also is destroyed. For in a warm climate, no man will labour for himself who can make another labour for him. This is so true, that of the proprietors of slaves a very small proportion indeed are ever seen to labour. And can the liberties of a nation be thought secure when we have removed their only firm basis, a conviction in the minds of the people that these liberties are of the gift of God? That they are not to be violated but with his wrath? Indeed I tremble for my country when I reflect that God is just: that his justice cannot sleep for ever: that considering numbers, nature and natural means only, a revolution of the wheel of fortune, an exchange of situation, is among possible events: that it may become probable by supernatural interference! The Almighty has no attribute which can take side with us in such a contest.—But is impossible to be temperate and to pursue this subject through the various considerations of policy, of morals, of history natural and civil. We must be contented to hope they will force their way into every one's mind. I think a change already perceptible, since the origin of the present revolution. The spirit of the master is abating, that of the slave rising from the dust, his condition mollifying, the way I hope preparing, under the auspices of heaven, for a total emancipation, and that this is disposed, in the order of events, to be with the consent of the masters, rather than by their extirpation.

Query XIX.

Manufactures

The present state of manufactures, commerce, interior and exterior trade?

We never had an interior trade of any importance. Our exterior commerce has suffered very much from the beginning of the present contest. During this time we have manufactured within our families the most necessary articles of cloathing. Those of cotton will bear some comparison with the same kinds of manufacture in Europe; but those of wool, flax and hemp are very coarse, unsightly, and unpleasant: and such is our attachment to agriculture, and such our preference for foreign manufactures, that be it wise or unwise, our people will certainly return as soon as they can, to the raising raw materials, and exchanging them for finer manufactures than they are able to execute themselves.

The political œconomists of Europe have established it as a principle that every state should endeavour to manufacture for itself: and this principle, like many others, we transfer to America, without calculating the difference of circumstance which should often produce a difference of result. In Europe the lands are either cultivated, or locked up against the cultivator. Manufacture must therefore be resorted to of necessity not of choice, to support the surplus of their people. But we have an immensity of land courting the industry of the husbandman. Is it best then that all our citizens should be employed in its improvement, or that one half should be called off from that to exercise manufactures and handicraft arts for the other? Those who labour in the earth are the chosen people of God, if ever he had a chosen people, whose breasts he has made his peculiar deposit for substantial and genuine virtue. It is the focus in which he keeps alive that sacred fire, which otherwise might escape from the face of the earth. Corruption of morals in the mass of cultivators is a phænomenon of which no age nor nation has furnished an example. It is the mark set on those, who not looking up to heaven, to their own soil and industry, as does the husbandman, for their subsistance, depend for it on the casualties and caprice of customers. Dependence begets subservience and venality, suffocates the germ of virtue, and prepares fit tools for the designs of ambition. This, the natural progress and consequence of the arts, has sometimes perhaps been retarded by accidental circumstances: but, generally speaking, the proportion which the aggregate of the other classes of citizens bears in any state to that of its husbandmen, is the proportion of its unsound to its healthy parts, and is a good-enough barometer whereby to measure its degree of corruption. While we have land to labour then, let us never wish to see our citizens occupied at a work-bench, or twirling a distaff. Carpenters, masons, smiths, are wanting in husbandry: but, for the general operations of manufacture, let our work-shops remain in Europe. It is better to carry provisions and materials to workmen there, than bring them to the provisions and materials, and with them their manners and principles. The loss by the transportation of commodities across the Atlantic will be made up in happiness and permanence of government. The mobs of great cities add just so much to the support of pure government, as sores do to the strength of the human body. It is the manners and spirit of a people which preserve a republic in vigour. A degeneracy in these is a canker which soon eats to the heart of its laws and constitution.

Letters to John Adams, October 28, 1813;
to Benjamin Rush, with a Syllabus, April 21, 1803;
and to Thomas Law, June 13, 1814

To John Adams

Monticello Oct. 28. [18]13.

DEAR SIR

According to the reservation between us, of taking up one of the subjects of our correspondence at a time, I turn to your letters of Aug. 16. and Sep. 2.

The passage you quote from Theognis, I think has an Ethical, rather than a political object. The whole piece is a moral *exhortation,* παράινεσιζ, and this passage particularly seems to be a reproof to man, who, while with his domestic animals he is curious to improve the race by employing always the finest male, pays no attention to the improvement of his own race, but intermarries with the vicious, the ugly, or the old, for considerations of wealth or ambition. It is in conformity with the principle adopted afterwards by the Pythagoreans, and expressed by Ocellus in another form. Περι δε τῆς ᾿εκ τῶν αλληλων ανθρωπων γενεσεως, etc.— ουχ῾ηδονης῾ενεκα῾ημιξις. Which, as literally as intelligibility will admit, may be thus translated. "Concerning the interprocreation of men, how, and of whom it shall be, in a perfect manner, and according to the laws of modesty and sanctity, conjointly, this is what I think right. First to lay it down that we do not commix for the sake of pleasure, but of the procreation of children. For the powers, the organs and desires for coition have not been given by god to man for the sake of pleasure, but for the procreation of the race. For as it were incongruous for a mortal born to partake of divine life, the immortality of the race being taken away, god fulfilled the purpose by making the generations uninterrupted and continuous. This therefore we are especially to lay down as a principle, that coition is not for the sake of pleasure." But Nature, not trusting to this moral and abstract motive, seems to have provided more securely for the perpetuation of the species by making it the effect of the oestrum implanted in the constitution of both sexes. And not only has the commerce of love been indulged on this unhallowed impulse, but made subservient also to wealth and ambition by marriages without regard to the beauty, the healthiness, the understanding, or virtue of the subject from which we are to breed. The selecting the best male for a Haram of well chosen females also, which Theognis seems to recommend from the example of our sheep and asses, would doubtless improve the human, as it does the brute animal, and produce a race of veritable αριστοι ["aristocrats"]. For experience proves that the moral and physical qualities of man, whether good or evil, are transmissible in a certain degree from father to son. But I suspect that the equal rights of men will rise up against this privileged Solomon, and oblige us

Source: *The Adams-Jefferson Letters: The Complete Correspondence Between Thomas Jefferson and Abigail and John Adams,* 2 vols., ed. Lester J. Cappon (Chapel Hill: University of North Carolina Press, 1959), vol. 2, 387–92; *The Papers of Thomas Jefferson, Second Series,* ed. Charles T. Cullen, *Jefferson's Extracts from the Gospels: "The Philosophy of Jesus" and "The Life and Morals of Jesus,"* ed. Dickinson W. Adams (Princeton: Princeton University Press, 1983), 331–34, 355–58. Editor's notes in Cappon altered; editor's notes in Adams omitted. Reprinted by permission of the University of North Carolina Press, Copyright © 1955; Princeton University Press, Copyright © 1983.

to continue acquiescence under the Ἀμαυρωσις γενεος᾽αστων ["the degeneration of the race of men"] which Theognis complains of, and to content ourselves with the accidental aristoi produced by the fortuitous concourse of breeders. For I agree with you that there is a natural aristocracy among men. The grounds of this are virtue and talents. Formerly bodily powers gave place among the aristoi. But since the invention of gunpowder has armed the weak as well as the strong with missile death, bodily strength, like beauty, good humor, politeness and other accomplishments, has become but an auxiliary ground of distinction. There is also an artificial aristocracy founded on wealth and birth, without either virtue or talents; for with these it would belong to the first class. The natural aristocracy I consider as the most precious gift of nature for the instruction, the trusts, and government of society. And indeed it would have been inconsistent in creation to have formed man for the social state, and not to have provided virtue and wisdom enough to manage the concerns of the society. May we not even say that that form of government is the best which provides the most effectually for a pure selection of these natural aristoi into the offices of government? The artificial aristocracy is a mischievous ingredient in government, and provision should be made to prevent it's ascendancy. On the question, What is the best provision, you and I differ; but we differ as rational friends, using the free exercise of our own reason, and mutually indulging it's errors. *You* think it best to put the Pseudo-aristoi into a separate chamber of legislation where they may be hindered from doing mischief by their coordinate branches, and where also they may be a protection to wealth against the Agrarian and plundering enterprises of the Majority of the people. I think that to give them power in order to prevent them from doing mischief, is arming them for it, and increasing instead of remedying the evil. For if the coordinate branches can arrest their action, so may they that of the coordinates. Mischief may be done negatively as well as positively. Of this a cabal in the Senate of the U.S. has furnished many proofs. Nor do I believe them necessary to protect the wealthy; because enough of these will find their way into every branch of the legislation to protect themselves. From 15. to 20. legislatures of our own, in action for 30. years past, have proved that no fears of an equalisation of property are to be apprehended from them.

I think the best remedy is exactly that provided by all our constitutions, to leave to the citizens the free election and separation of the aristoi from the pseudo-aristoi, of the wheat from the chaff. In general they will elect the real good and wise. In some instances, wealth may corrupt, and birth blind them; but not in sufficient degree to endanger the society.

It is probable that our difference of opinion may in some measure be produced by a difference of character in those among whom we live. From what I have seen of Massachusets and Connecticut myself, and still more from what I have heard, and the character given of the former by yourself, [vol. I. p. 3.] who know them so much better, there seems to be in those two states a traditionary reverence for certain families, which has rendered the offices of the government nearly hereditary in those families. I presume that from an early period of your history, members of these families happening to posses virtue and talents, have honestly exercised them for the good of the people, and by their services have endeared their names to them.

In coupling Connecticut with you, I mean it politically only, not morally. For having made the Bible the Common law of their land they seem to have modelled their morality on the story of Jacob and Laban. But altho' this hereditary succession to office with you may in some degree be founded in real family merit, yet in a much higher degree it has proceeded from your strict alliance of church and state. These families are canonised in the eyes of the people on the common principle "you tickle me, and I will tickle you." In

Virginia we have nothing of this. Our clergy, before the revolution, having been secured against rivalship by fixed salaries, did not give themselves the trouble of acquiring influence over the people. Of wealth, there were great accumulations in particular families, handed down from generation to generation under the English law of entails. But the only object of ambition for the wealthy was a set in the king's council. All their court then was paid to the crown and it's creatures; and they Philipised in all collisions between the king and people. Hence they were unpopular; and that unpopularity continues attached to their names. A Randolph, a Carter, or a Burwell must have great personal superiority over a common competitor to be elected by the people, even at this day.

At the first session of our legislature after the Declaration of Independence, we passed a law abolishing entails. And this was followed by one abolishing the privilege of Primogeniture, and dividing the lands of intestates equally among all their children, or other representatives. These laws, drawn by myself, laid the axe to the root of Pseudo-aristocracy. And had another which I prepared been adopted by the legislature, our work would have been compleat. It was a Bill for the more general diffusion of learning. This proposed to divide every county into wards of 5. or 6. miles square, like your townships; to establish in each ward a free school for reading, writing and common arithmetic; to provide for the annual selection of the best subjects from these schools who might receive at the public expense a higher degree of education at a district school; and from these district schools to select a certain number of the most promising subjects to be compleated at an University, where all the useful sciences should be taught. Worth and genius would thus have been sought out from every condition of life, and compleatly prepared by education for defeating the competition of wealth and birth for public trusts.

My proposition had for a further object to impart to these wards those portions of self-government for which they are best qualified, by confiding to them the care of their poor, their roads, police, elections, the nomination of jurors, administration of justice in small cases, elementary exercises of militia, in short, to have made them little republics, with a Warden at the head of each, for all those concerns which, being under their eye, they would better manage than the larger republics of the county or state. A general call of ward-meetings by their Wardens on the same day thro' the state would at any time produce the genuine sense of the people on any required point, and would enable the state to act in mass, as your people have so often done, and with so much effect, by their town meetings. The law for religious freedom, which made a part of this system, having put down the aristocracy of the clergy, and restored to the citizen the freedom of the mind, and those of entails and descents nurturing an equality of condition among them, this on Education would have raised the mass of the people to the high ground of moral respectability necessary to their own safety, and to orderly government; and would have completed the great object of qualifying them to select the veritable aristoi, for the trusts of government, to the exclusion of the Pseudalists: and the same Theognis who has furnished the epigraphs of your two letters assures us that ʿουδεμιαυ πω, Κυρν"αγαθοι πολιν ὤλεσαν'ανδρες ["Curnis, good men have never harmed any city"]'. Altho' this law has not yet been acted on but in a small and inefficient degree, it is still considered as before the legislature, with other bills of the revised code, not yet taken up, and I have great hope that some patriotic spirit will, at a favorable moment, call it up, and make it the key-stone of the arch of our government.

With respect to Aristocracy, we should further consider that, before the establishment of the American states, nothing was known to History but the Man of the old world, crouded within limits either small or overcharged, and steeped in the vices which that situation generates. A government adapted to such men would be one thing; but a very different one than for the Man of these states. Here every one may have land to labor for himself if he chuses; or, preferring the exercise of any other industry, may exact for it such compensation as not only to afford a comfortable subsistence, but wherewith to provide for a cessation from labor in old age. Every one, by his property, or by his satisfactory situation, is interested in the support of law and order. And such men may safely and advantageously reserve to themselves a wholsome controul over their public affairs, and a degree of freedom, which in the hands of the Canaille of the cities of Europe, would be instantly perverted to the demolition and destruction of every thing public and private. The history of the last 25. years of France, and of the last 40. years in America, nay of its last 200. years, proves the truth of both parts of this observation.

But even in Europe a change has sensibly taken place in the mind of Man. Science had liberated the ideas of those who read and reflect, and the American example has kindled feelings of right in the people. An insurrection has consequently begun, of science, talents and courage against rank and birth, which have fallen into contempt. It has failed in its first effort, because the mobs of the cities, the instrument used for its accomplishment, debased by ignorance, poverty and vice, could not be restrained to rational action. But the world will recover from the panic of this first catastrophe. Science is progressive, and talents and enter-prize on the alert. Resort may be had to the people of the country, a more governable power from their principles and subordination; and rank, and birth, and tinsel-aristocracy will finally shrink into insignificance, even there. This however we have no right to meddle with. It suffices for us, if the moral and physical condition of our own citizens qualifies them to select the able and good for the direction of their government, with a recurrence of elections at such short periods as will enable them to displace an unfaithful servant before the mischief he meditates may be irremediable.

I have thus stated my opinion on a point on which we differ, not with a view to controversy, for we are both too old to change opinions which are the result of a long life of inquiry and reflection; but on the suggestion of a former letter of yours, that we ought not to die before we have explained ourselves to each other. We acted in perfect harmony thro' a long and perilous contest for our liberty and independence. A constitution has been acquired which, tho neither of us think perfect, yet both consider as competent to render our fellow-citizens the happiest and the securest on whom the sun has ever shone. If we do not think exactly alike as to its imperfections, it matters little to our country which, after devoting to it long lives of disinterested labor, we have delivered over to our successors in life, who will be able to take care of it, and of themselves.

Of the pamphlet on aristocracy which has been sent to you, or who may be its author, I have heard nothing but thro' your letter. If the person you suspect[1] it may be known from the quaint, mystical and hyperbolical ideas, involved in affected, newfangled and pedantic terms, which stamp his writings. Whatever it be, I hope your quiet is not to be affected at this day by the rudeness of intemperance of scribblers; but that you may continue in tranquility to live and to rejoice in the prosperity of our country until it shall be your own wish to take your seat among the Aristoi who have gone before you. Ever and affectionately yours.

TH: JEFFERSON...

---

1. John Taylor of Caroline.

To Benjamin Rush, with a Syllabus

Washington April 21, 1803.

DEAR SIR

In some of the delightful conversations with you, in the evenings of 1798.99., which served as an Anodyne to the afflictions of the crisis through which our country was then labouring, the Christian religion was sometimes our topic: and I then promised you that, one day or other, I would give you my views of it. They are the result of a life of enquiry and reflection, and very different from that Anti-Christian system, imputed to me by those who know nothing of my opinions. To the corruptions of Christianity, I am indeed opposed; but not to the genuine precepts of Jesus himself. I am a Christian, in the only sense in which he wished any one to be; sincerely attached to his doctrines, in preference to all others; ascribing to himself every human excellence, and believing he never claimed any other. At the short intervals, since these conversations, when I could justifiably abstract my mind from public affairs, this subject has been under my contemplation. But the more I considered it, the more it expanded beyond the measure of either my time or information. In the moment of my late departure from Monticello, I received from Doctr Priestly his little treatise of "Socrates and Jesus compared." This being a section of the general view I had taken of the field, it became a subject of reflection, while on the road, and unoccupied otherwise. The result was, to arrange in my mind a Syllabus, or Outline, of such an Estimate of the comparative merits of Christianity, as I wished to see executed, by some one of more leisure and information for the task than myself. This I now send you, as the only discharge of my promise I can probably ever execute. And, in confiding it to you, I know it will not be exposed to the malignant perversions of those who make every word from me a text for new misrepresentations and calumnies. I am moreover averse to the communication of my religious tenets to the public; because it would countenance the presumption of those who have endeavored to draw them before that tribunal, and to seduce public opinion to erect itself into that Inquisition over the rights of conscience, which the laws have so justly proscribed. It behoves every man, who values liberty of conscience for himself, to resist invasions of it in the case of others; or their case may, by change of circumstances, become his own. It behoves him too, in his own case, to give no example of concession, betraying the common right of independent opinion, by answering questions of faith, which the laws have left between god and himself. Accept my affectionate salutations.

TH:JEFFERSON

ENCLOSURE

Syllabus of an Estimate of the merit of the doctrines of Jesus, compared with those of others.

In a comparative view of the Ethics of the enlightened nations of antiquity, of the Jews, and of Jesus, no notice should be taken of the corruptions of reason, among the ancients, to wit, the idolatry and superstition of their vulgar, Nor of the corruptions of Christianity by the over learned among its professors.

Let a just view be taken of the moral principles inculcated by the most esteemed of the sects of antt. philosophy, or of their individuals; particularly Pythagoras, Socrates, Epicurus, Cicero, Epictetus, Seneca, Antoninus.

I. Philosophers. 1. Their precepts related chiefly to ourselves, and the government of those passions which, unrestrained, would disturb our tranquility of mind.[2] In this branch of Philosophy they were really great.

2. In developing our duties to others, they were short and defective. They embraced indeed the circles of kindred and friends: and inculcated patriotism, or the love of our country in the aggregate, as a primary obligation: towards our neighbors and countrymen, they taught justice, but scarcely viewed them as within the circle of benevolence. Still less have they inculcated peace, charity, and love to our fellow men, or embraced with benevolence, the whole family of mankind.

II. Jews. 1. Their system was Deism, that is, the belief of one only god. But their ideas of him, and of his attributes, were degrading and injurious.

2. Their Ethics were not only imperfect, but often irreconcileable with the sound dictates of reason and morality, as they respect intercourse with those around us: and repulsive, and anti-social, as respecting other nations. They needed reformation therefore in an eminent degree.

III. Jesus. In this state of things among the Jews, Jesus appeared. His parentage was obscure, his condition poor, his education null, his natural endowments great, his life correct and innocent; he was meek, benevolent, patient, firm, disinterested, and of the sublimest eloquence.

The disadvantages under which his doctrines appear are remarkable.

1. Like Socrates and Epictetus he wrote nothing himself.

2. But he had not, like them, a Xenophon or an Arrian to write for him. On the contrary, all the learned of his country, entrenched in its power and riches, were opposed to him lest his labours should undermine their advantages:

and the committing to writing his life and doctrines, fell on the most unlettered, and ignorant of men:

who wrote too from memory, and not till long after the transactions had passed.

3. According to the ordinary fate of those who attempt to enlighten and reform mankind,

---

2.   To explain, I will exhibit the heads of Seneca's and Cicero's philosophical works, the most extensive of any we have recieved from the ancients. Of 10. heads in Seneca, 7. relate to ourselves, to wit, de irâ, Consolatio, de tranquilitate, de constantiâ sapientis, de otio sapientis, de vitâ beata, de brevitate vitae. 2. relate to others, de clementia, de beneficiis, and 1. relates to the government of the world, de providentiâ. Of II. tracts of Cicero, 5 respect ourselves, viz. de finibus, Tusculana, Academica, Paradoxa, de Senectute. 1. de officiis, partly to ourselves, partly to others. 1. de amicitiâ, relates to others: and 4. are on different subjects, to wit, de naturâ deorum, de divinatione, de fato, Somnium Scipionis. [T.J. note]

he fell an early victim to the jealousy and combination of the altar and
the throne;

at about 33. years of age, his reason having not yet attained the maximum of its energy,

nor the course of his preaching, which was but of about 3. years,
presented occasions for developing a compleat system of morals.

4. Hence the doctrines which he really delivered were defective as a whole.
And fragments only of what he did deliver have come to us, mutilated,
mistated, and often unintelligible.

5. They have been still more disfigured by the corruptions of schismatis-
ing followers,

who have found an interest in sophisticating and perverting the simple
doctrines he taught,

by engrafting on them the mysticisms of a Graecian Sophist, frittering
them into subtleties, and obscuring them with jargon,

until they have caused good men to reject the whole in disgust, and to
view Jesus himself as an impostor.

Notwithstanding these disadvantages, a system of morals is presented
to us, which,

if filled up in the true style and spirit of the rich fragments he left us,

would be the most perfect and sublime that has ever been taught by
man.

The question of his being a member of the god-head, or in direct communication with it,

claimed for him by some of his followers, and denied by others,

is foreign to the present view, which is merely an estimate of the intrinsic merit of his doctrines.

1. He corrected the Deism of the Jews, confirming them in their belief of
one only god,

and giving them juster notions of his attributes and government.

2. His moral doctrines relating to kindred and friends were more pure
and perfect, than those of the most correct of the philosophers,
and greatly more so than those of the Jews.

And they went far beyond both in inculcating universal philanthropy,
not only to kindred and friends, to neighbors and countrymen, but to all mankind, gathering all into one family, under
the bonds of love, charity, peace, common wants, and common
aids. A development of this head will evince the peculiar superiority of the system of Jesus over all others.

3. The precepts of Philosophy, and of the Hebrew code, laid hold of actions
only.

He pushed his scrutinies into the heart of man; erected his tribunal in
the region of his thoughts, and purified the waters at the fountain head.

4. He taught, emphatically, the doctrine of a future state: which was either
doubted or disbelieved by the Jews:

and wielded it with efficacy, as an important incentive, supplementary
to the other motives to moral conduct.

To Thomas Law

Poplar Forest near Lynchburg. June 13. [18] 14.

DEAR SIR

The copy of your Second thoughts on Instinctive impulses with the letter accompanying it, was received just as I was setting out on a journey to this place, two or three days distant from Monticello. I brought it with me, and read it with great satisfaction; and with the more, as it contained exactly my own creed on the foundation of morality in man. It is really curious that, on a question so fundamental, such a variety of opinions should have prevailed among men; and those too of the most exemplary virtue and first order of understanding. It shews how necessary was the care of the Creator in making the moral principle so much a part of our constitution as that no errors of reasoning or of speculation might lead us astray from its observance in practice. Of all the theories on this question, the most whimsical seems to have been that of Woollaston, who considers *truth* as the foundation of morality. The thief who steals your guinea does wrong only inasmuch as he acts a lie, in using your guinea as if it were his own. Truth is certainly a branch of morality, and a very important one to society. But, presented as its foundation, it is as if a tree, taken up by the roots, had its stem reversed in the air, and one of its branches planted in the ground.—Some have made the *love of god* the foundation of morality. This too is but a branch of our moral duties, which are generally divided into duties to god, and duties to man. If we did a good act merely from the love of god, and a belief that it is pleasing to him, whence arises the morality of the Atheist? It is idle to say as some do, that no such being exists. We have the same evidence of the fact as of most of those we act on, to wit, their own affirmations, and their reasonings in support of them. I have observed indeed generally that, while in protestant countries the defections from the Platonic Christianity of the priests is to Deism, in Catholic countries they are to Atheism. Diderot, Dalembert, D'Holbach, Condorcet, are known to have been among the most virtuous of men. Their virtue then must have had some other foundation than the love of god.

The το καλον of others is founded in a different faculty, that of taste, which is not even a branch of morality. We have indeed an innate sense of what we call beautiful: but that is exercised chiefly on subjects addressed to the fancy, whether thro' the eye, in visible forms, as landscape, animal figure, dress, drapery, architecture, the composition of colours &c. or to the imagination directly, as imagery, style, or measure in prose or poetry, or whatever else constitutes the domain of criticism or taste, a faculty entirely distinct from the moral one. Self-interest, or rather Self love, or *Egoism,* has been more plausibly substituted as the basis of morality. But I consider our relations with others as constituting the boundaries of morality. With ourselves we stand on the ground of identity, not of relation; which last, requiring two subjects, excludes self-love confined to a single one. To ourselves, in strict language, we can owe no duties, obligation requiring also two parties. Self-love therefore is no part of morality. Indeed it is exactly its counterpart. It is the sole antagonist of virtue, leading us constantly by our propensities to self-gratification in violation of our moral duties to others. Accordingly it is against this enemy that are erected the batteries of moralists and religionists, as the only obstacle to the practice of morality. Take from man his selfish propensities, and he can have nothing to seduce him from the practice of virtue. Or subdue those propensities by education, instruction, or restraint, and virtue remains without a competitor. Egoism, in a broader sense, has been thus presented as the source of moral action. It has been said that we feed the hungry, clothe the naked, bind up the wounds of the man beaten by thieves, pour oil and wine into them, set him on our own beast, and bring him to the inn, because we receive ourselves pleasure from these acts. So Helvetius, one of the best men on earth, and the most ingenious advocate of this principle, after defining "interest" to mean, not merely that which is pecuniary, but whatever may procure us pleasure or withdraw us from pain, [de l'Esprit.2.1.] says [ib. 2.2.] "the humane man is he to whom the sight of misfortune is insupportable and who, to rescue himself from this spectacle, is forced to succour the unfortunate object." This indeed is true. But it is one step short of the ultimate question. These good acts give us pleasure: but how happens it that they give us pleasure? Because nature hath implanted in our breasts a love of others, a sense of duty to them, a moral instinct in short, which prompts us irresistibly to feel and to succour their distresses; and protests against the language of Helvetius [ib. 2.5.] "what other motive than self interest could determine a man to generous actions? It is as impossible for him to love what is good for the sake of good, as to love evil for the sake of evil" The creator would indeed have been a bungling artist, had he intended man for a social animal, without planting in him social dispositions. It is true they are not planted in every man; because there is no rule without exceptions; but it is false reasoning which converts exceptions into the general rule. Some men are born without the organs of sight, or of hearing, or without hands. Yet it would be wrong to say that man is born without these faculties; and sight, hearing and hands may with truth enter into the general definition of Man. The want or imperfection of the moral sense in some men, like the want or imperfection of the senses of sight and hearing in others, is no proof that it is a general characteristic of the species. When it is wanting we endeavor to supply the defect by education, by appeals to reason and calculation, by presenting to the being so unhappily conformed other motives to do good, and to eschew evil; such as the love, or the hatred or rejection of those among whom he lives and whose society is necessary to his happiness, and even existence; demonstrations by sound calculation that honesty promotes interest in the long run; the rewards and penalties established by the laws; and ultimately the prospects of a future state of retribution for the evil as well as the good done while here. These are the correctives which are supplied by education, and which exercise the functions of the moralist, the preacher and legislator: and they lead into a course of correct action all those whose depravity is not too profound to be eradicated. Some have argued against the existence of a moral sense, by saying that if nature had given us such a sense, impelling us to virtuous actions, and warning us against those which are vicious, then nature must also have designated, by some particular ear-marks, the two sets of actions which are, in themselves, the one virtuous, and the other vicious: whereas we find in fact, that the same actions are deemed virtuous in one country, and vicious in another. The answer is that nature has constituted *utility* to man the standard and test of virtue. Men living in different countries, under different circumstances, different habits, and regimens, may have different utilities. The same act therefore may be useful, and consequently virtuous, in one country, which is injurious and vicious in another differently circumstanced. I sincerely then believe with you in the general existence of a moral instinct. I think it the brightest gem with which the human character is studded; and the want of it as more degrading than the most hideous of the bodily deformities. I am happy in reviewing the roll of associates in this principle which you present in your 2d. letter, some of which I had not before met with. To these might be added Ld. Kaims, one of the ablest of our advocates, who goes so far as to say, in his Principles of Natural religion, that a man owes no duty to which he is not urged by some impulsive feeling. This is correct if referred to the standard of general feeling in the given case, and not to the feeling of a single individual. Perhaps I may misquote him, it being fifty years since I read his book.

The leisure and solitude of my situation here has led me to the indiscretion of taxing you with a long letter on a subject whereon nothing new can be offered you. I will indulge myself no further than to repeat the assurances of my continued esteem & respect.

Th: Jefferson

SAMUEL STANHOPE SMITH

Selection from *An Essay on the Causes of the Variety of Complexion and Figure in the Human Species* (1810)

In the same year of 1787 that the quasi-deist Jefferson hesitantly jumped into a burgeoning debate among Enlightenment thinkers in Britain and the Continent over the nature of "race" and the place of "races" by suggesting in his *Notes on Virginia* that blacks were mentally inferior to whites, Samuel Stanhope Smith (1751–1819), the moderate Calvinist, pro-Federalist president of the College of New Jersey (later Princeton University), published the first work by an American on the science of race. In the Second Edition excerpted here he explicitly challenged the former president's claims. But what made Smith's book the most famous American ethnographic study for most of the nineteenth century was the Princeton president's engagement with all the larger questions of science, religion, and the human species entangled in this transatlantic controversy. Smith's work had a political resonance as well: during that year the Constitutional Convention met in Philadelphia, where the delegates grappled, often quite openly, with the problem of the legal status of enslaved African Americans, thereby luridly posing the further unanswered question of what *was* this new race of "Americans."

Smith's starting point was the biblical narrative of creation. Unqualifiedly accepting the Bible's monogenist narrative of a unified human lineage descended from Adam and Eve, he rejected out of hand the competing polygenist theory that posited that humanity was divided into several separately created distinct species. That heterodox hypothesis gained the adherence of many Enlightenment philosophers and scientists, including the influential Scottish jurist and author Lord Kames, whose discourse "On the Original Diversity of Mankind" (1776) Smith vigorously rebutted in a lengthy appendix. At the same time, while for Smith the stakes in the battle were thus religious, his chosen weapons were wholly secular. Embracing the same inductive Baconian science that polygenists like Kames adhered to, Smith also believed, as did most contemporary Protestant theologians, that as God's universe was one, there was nothing in his biblical revelations that contradicted scientifically demonstrated truth-claims. Consequently, Smith largely ignored questions of biblical interpretation and confidently made his monogenist case on purely naturalistic grounds. The various "races" that populated the globe were neither separately created nor permanently fixed but were instead variations of one species with different physical characteristics produced by the interaction among changing biological, climatic, and social circumstances. For African Americans, Smith said, the most crippling of these was their enslavement. Indeed, in his appended "Remarks" on a critique published three years earlier of the first edition of his *Essay,* by the British anatomist

Charles White, Smith pointedly tasked Jefferson, whose racist views in *Notes on Virginia* White had positively cited, for ignoring or downplaying this brutal fact. An inferior race did not give rise to slavery, Smith argued, but rather slavery helped create an inferior race.

Yet, as this last adjective might suggest, Smith's racial science colored his antislavery views every bit as much as Jefferson's stained his. While environmental circumstances would eventually produce a relatively stable race, Smith argued, altering them in the meantime could change its physical and mental makeup but only very slowly. Naturally, here agreeing with Jefferson, emancipation would and should also come only very gradually. However, like all pre-Darwinian scientists, Smith was fuzzy about the mechanisms by which these changes in color and character were transmitted to blacks' offspring. Nor was he entirely clear what would remain of their blackness. In his book he suggested ultimately none: blacks as blacks would ultimately disappear as they morphed into the superior character and appearance of whites. But that process had a radical implication. In a later published lecture to his students delivered shortly before he resigned the College presidency, he suggested that emancipated black slaves could be "whitened" very quickly, not by removing them to a colony in Africa, as Jefferson and other Founders had advocated, but by encouraging them instead to migrate to the West where they would be joined by whites with whom they would intermarry. Not even the most radical abolitionists would dare espouse such a taboo program of sexual "amalgamation," which would remain outlawed in many states through most of American history.

Mark A. Noll's excellent *Princeton and the Republic, 1768–1822: The Search for a Christian Enlightenment in the Era of Samuel Stanhope Smith* (Princeton, 1989) places Smith at the center of Princeton's efforts to shape American religious culture around the university's distinctive synthesis of moderate Calvinism, Scottish Common Sense philosophy, and republican ideology. The best discussion of Smith's *Essay* can be found in Winthrop Jordan's introduction to Harvard University Press's 1965 publication of the 1810 edition. For the Anglo-American racial discourses out of which Smith's theories emerged, see Jordan's classic *White over Black: American Attitudes Toward the Negro, 1550–1812* (Chapel Hill, 1968). Bruce Dain's *A Hideous Monster of the Mind: American Race Theory in the Early Republic* (Cambridge, Mass., 2002) helpfully situates Smith's racial ideas among those of lesser known antebellum black and white writers on race. For a wide-ranging study of the enormous influence biblical criticism had on four centuries of transatlantic debates about race, see Colin Kidd, *The Forging of Races: Race and Scripture in the Protestant Atlantic World, 1600–2000* (Cambridge, Eng., 2006).

THE unity of the human race, notwithstanding the diversity of colour, and form under which it appears in different portions of the globe, is a doctrine, independently of the authority of divine revelation, much more consistent with the principles of sound philosophy, than any of those numerous hypotheses which have referred its varieties to a radical and original diversity of species, adapted by the Creator, or by the necessary laws of the material world, to the respective climates which they were destined to inhabit. As there are several species of animals which seem to be confined by the physical laws of their constitution to a limited range of climate, and which either cannot exist, or do not attain the perfection of their nature, in regions either much farther to the North or to the South than those in which the Creator has planted them, superficial observers have been ready to conclude, from analogy, that different species of the human kind must have been originally circumscribed, by the forming hand of nature, within certain climatical limits, in which she has placed them, whence have sprung those varieties in external aspect, and in mental endowments, which distinguish the respective tribes of men from one another. But in contradiction to this principle, experience demonstrates that man is not exclusively confined in his range to any definite lines upon the earth. Although the fineness of texture, and delicacy of organization of the human constitution, renders it extremely susceptible of the impressions of climate, as well as of all other causes which act upon the animal frame, its peculiar flexibility, at the same time, enables it to adapt itself with wonderful facility, and without materially injuring the organs of life, to every degree of temperature from the extreme heats of the torrid, to the perpetual rigors of the frozen zone. We see commerce and war, ambition and avarice, transfer the same people to every clime upon the globe; and the American and European sailor reside equally at the pole, and under the equator. While the spirit of fanaticism carries the sun-burnt Saracen to the North, the love of war, and of plunder transplants the Tartar from the snows of Scythia to the burning plains of India. Why then should we, without necessity, assume the hypothesis that originally there existed different species of the human kind? And not only without necessity, but contrary to the principles of true philosophy, since all its varieties may be accounted for, which I hope to demonstrate in the course of this essay, by the known operation of natural causes.

Different species must be subject to different laws both in the physical and moral constitution of their nature. The whole philosophy of man, therefore, is confounded by that hypothesis which divides the *kind* into various *species,* radically different from one another. The laws of morals designed to regulate the mutual intercourse of mankind, we derive from examining our own nature, or collecting the common sentiments of men in society, united together by a common system of feelings and ideas. But how shall we apply rules, derived from these sources, to different nations, and to different individuals whose moral principles, resulting, in like manner, from the constitution of their natures, respectively, may be as various as their several aspects. Can they, indeed, be universally applied to fix an invariable moral code even for the same nation in different ages, after conquest, or commerce may have produced among them the most complicated mixture of species? *Varieties* may be created in the same species either in the animal or vegetable kingdom, by varying their culture, and, sometimes, by transferring them to a different soil, or climate; but to all these varieties, where there is no radical diversity of *kind,* the same general laws

Source: Samuel Stanhope Smith, *An Essay on the Causes of the Variety of Complexion and Figure in the Human Species,* Winthrop D. Jordan (Cambridge, Mass.: The Belknap Press of Harvard University Press, 1965), 7–9, 22–25, 41–45, 92–93, 99–101, 103–6, 118, 126, 148–50, 152–53, 160–67. Notes altered.

will still apply. To man, in like manner, may be applied the same general principles of moral and physical action, if it be ascertained that all their differences indicate only one original species. But, destroy this unity, and no certain and universal principles of human nature remain. We have no general and infallible standard by which to judge of the moral ideas and habits of different nations, or even of different men. Besides, if human nature actually embraces different species of men, by what criterion shall we distinguish them? What is their number? Where do they now exist pure and unmixed? . . .

If we compare together only those varieties of human nature by which the several sections of mankind differ most widely from one another, the difference is so great that, on the first view, it might very naturally lead to the conclusion that they must belong to distinct species. But, when we come to examine more particularly the intermediate grades which connect the extremes, and observe by what minute differences they approach, or recede from, one another; and when we observe further, that each of these minute gradations can be traced to obvious and natural causes, forming so many links, as it were, in the great chain connecting the extremes, we are ready to call in question our first impressions, and perceive the necessity of subjecting them to a new and more rigorous examination.

I have already remarked, that it is contrary to the laws of true philosophy to resort to the hypothesis of different original species of men in order to explain varieties which can otherwise be accounted for from the known operation of natural causes. Philosophy delights in tracing the most diversified results through various combinations, to the simplest elements. And, if we can find, in the laws of nature, powers sufficient to impress on the ground of the same original constitution of man all the varieties of complexion and form which have distinguished the race in different climes, and states of society, it is an homage which we owe to philosophy, as well as to religion, to refer all the different nations of the earth to the same original stock. It is a debt which we owe to humanity to recognize our brethren in every class of men into which society is divided, and under every shade of complexion which diversifies their various tribes from the equator to the poles.

I shall endeavour, in the following essay, to fulfil these obligations to science, and to charity. But, in the course of this disquisition, if some of the facts from which important conclusions are drawn, seem, at first view, to those who have not been accustomed to observe nature in her nicest operations, to be too minute to bear the consequences which are charged upon them, I trust that a closer attention to the very fine and almost insensible effects of many physical causes, which, in the end produce the greatest results, will convince the judicious inquirer that greater stress may not have been laid upon them than they are able to bear; so far at least as to prevent a hasty rejection of the principles, and to procure for them a fair, candid, and patient investigation.*

Of the chief causes of the varieties of the human species I shall treat under the heads *Of Climate—Of the State of Society—*and, *Of the Manner of Living.*

---

* It will be of importance to bear in mind throughout this essay, that the causes affecting the physical or moral constitution of man, and ultimately producing great distinctions between nations, seldom attain their full operation till after a long series of time. By almost imperceptible touches they produce their effects, till entering deeply, at length, into the habits and whole structure of our nature, they are transmitted from parents to their offspring. Even several generations may pass away before the ultimate results of the influences either of the climate, of the state of society, or of the manner of living, are perceived.

OF CLIMATE.

in tracing the various climates of the globe, advancing from the arctic circle to the equator, we find them marked with considerable regularity by the colour of the inhabitants. In the European continent, we meet, in the highest temperate latitudes, with a ruddy, and sanguine complexion, which is commonly conjoined with different shades of redness in the hair. We soon descend to a clearer mixture of red in white. And afterwards succeed the brown, the swarthy, and, passing over into Africa, the tawny, increasing by darker and darker shades as we approach the hottest temperature of the torrid zone. In the Asiatic continent we pass at once from the fair to the olive, and thence by various gradations in the darkness of the hue to the black colour which prevails in the southern provinces of the peninsulas of Arabia and India. The same distance from the sun, however, does not, in every region, indicate the same temperature of climate. Besides the latitude, many secondary causes must be taken into consideration to determine the character of the climate. Elevated and mountainous countries, in proportion to their altitude above the level of the sea, ascend towards that region of the atmosphere in which we find the dominion of perpetual cold. High mountains likewise arresting the clouds in their course, compel them to pour their frequent rains, as well as spread their cool shades over the vallies which lie between them. . . .

In these extensive countries in which the surface of the earth is more uniform than in Europe, and not so much broken and intersected by mountains, seas, and bays running far up into the land, the gradation of colour holds a more regular progression according to the latitude from the equator. But the influence of climate on the complexion is better illustrated by its effects on the Arabians and the Chinese, than on most other nations, who have been the subjects of frequent conquests, and great intermixtures with foreign tribes. These people have remained, from a very remote antiquity, almost wholly unmingled with foreign nations. The former, especially, can be traced by a clear, and undisputed genealogy to their origin in one family; and they have never been blended, either by conquest, or by commerce, with any other race. And yet we find every gradation of discolouration among them from the swarthy hue of the northern provinces to the deep black suffused with a yellowish tinge, which prevails in the southern angle of the Arabian peninsula.

But no example can carry with it greater authority on this subject than that of the Jews. Descended from one stock, prohibited by their most sacred institutions from intermarrying with strangers, and yet widely dispersed into every region on the globe, this one people is marked with the peculiar characteristics of every climate. In Britain and Germany they are fair, brown in France and in Turkey, swarthy in Portugal and Spain, olive in Syria and Chaldea, tawny or copper-coloured in Arabia and Egypt.

Another example of the power of climate to change the complexion, and even to introduce great alterations into the whole constitution, is presented to the view of the philosophic observer in the native population of the United States. Sprung, not long since, from the British, the Irish, and the German nations, who are the fairest people in Europe, they have extended themselves over the American continent from the thirty-first to the forty-fifth degree of northern latitude. And notwithstanding the recent period at which the first European establishments were made in America; and the continual influx of emigrants from the old continent, and their frequent intermarriages with the native Anglo-Americans; and, what is of not less consequence in this question, notwithstanding ideas of personal beauty derived from their ancestors which they sedulously cherish, and which the arts of civilized life have enabled them to preserve, as far as is possible, against the influence of the climate; yet have they undergone a visible and important change. A certain paleness of countenance, and softness of feature in the native American strikes a British traveller as soon as he arrives upon our shores. Many exceptions there are; but, in general, the American complexion does not exhibit so clear a red and white as the British, or the German. And there is a tinge of sallowness spread over it which indicates the tendency of the climate to generate bile. These effects are more obvious in the southern than in the northern states. They appear more strongly marked in the low lands near the ocean, than as you approach the mountainous regions to the North and West. And they are much more deeply impressed in the poorer classes of the people than in families of easy fortune who enjoy a more various and nutricious diet, and possess the means at once of improving their appearance, and guarding against the unfavourable influences of the climate. The people of New-Jersey, in the low and level country between the sea, and the extensive bay of the river Delaware, are generally darker in their complexion, than in those counties where the country rises into hills; and considerably darker than the inhabitants of Pennsylvania, which is every where diversified with hills, and frequently rises into lofty mountains. The depression of the land exposes it to greater heat; and the level surface of the country, not yet subjected to a high degree of culture, leaves it, in many places, covered with stagnant waters that impregnate the atmosphere with unwholesome exhalations, which greatly augment the secretion of bile. The increased heat of the sun in the low lands of Maryland and Virginia, near the coasts of the ocean, and of the wide bays which every where indent them, gives a visible heightening to the darkness of the complexion, especially in the poorest classes of the people who are most exposed to the force of the climate. Descending still farther to the South, along the sea coast of the Carolinas and Georgia, we often meet among the overseers of their slaves, and their laborious poor, with persons whose complexion is but a few shades lighter than that of the aboriginal Iroquois, or Cherokees. Compare these men with their British ancestors, and the change which has already passed upon them, will afford the strongest ground to conclude that, if they were thrown, like our native indians, into a state of absolute savagism, they would, in no great length of time, be perfectly marked with the same complexion, Not only is their complexion thus changed, but a visible and striking alteration seems to have been produced on their whole constitution. So thin and meagre frequently are they in their persons, that their limbs seem to have a disproportioned length to the body; and the figure of the skeleton appears often, very distinctly, through the skin. If these men, unmixed with others whose state in society enables them to enjoy in greater abundance the conveniences and comforts of living, and consequently the means of preserving themselves from the deteriorating impressions of the climate, had been found in a distant region where no memory of their origin remained, they would have furnished to the advocates of different species belonging to the human kind, an example as strong, and as much to the purpose of their argument, as most of those on which they now rely with the greatest confidence. . . .

Having, thus far, endeavoured to point out the power of CLIMATE in the production of many of the varieties which distinguish different portions of the human species, I proceed to illustrate the influence of the

STATE OF SOCIETY, AND THE
HABITS OF LIVING,

in creating other varieties, or in aggravating or correcting those which are occasioned by climate. . . .

For this purpose, I shall endeavour, in the first place, to evince by several facts and illustrations, that the state of society in which men live has a powerful influence in varying the character of the countenance, and even in changing the habit, and appearance of the whole person.

And, in the next place, to shew that some of the most distinguishing features of the savage, and particularly of the American savage, with whom we are best acquainted, naturally result from the rude condition in which he exists.

The influence of the state of society, and of the modes of life which prevail among different nations, or tribes of men, to produce some variety or change in the complexion, and even in the form and proportions of the person, may receive illustration from the variety of aspect exhibited by the higher and lower classes into which the people of almost all nations are divided; and who may be regarded, in some degree, as men in different states of society.

The poor and laboring part of the community in every country, are usually more dark in their complexion, more hard in their features, and more coarse and ill formed in their limbs, than persons of better rank, who enjoy greater ease, and more liberal means of subsistence. They want the delicate tints of colour, the pleasing regularity of features, and the elegant and fine proportions of the person so frequently seen in the higher classes. Many particular exceptions undoubtedly there are. Luxury may disfigure the one; a fortunate coincidence of circumstances may give a happy assemblage of features to the other.* But these exceptions will not invalidate the general observation. The distinctions which subsist between the several classes of society become more considerable by time, after families have held, for ages, nearly the same stations. But they are more conspicuous in those countries in which the laws or customs of the nation have made the most complete and permanent discrimination of ranks. In Scotland, for example, how wide is the difference between the chiefs of the Highland clans, and the tenants and laborers of the land! A similar distinction takes place between the nobility and peasantry of France, of Spain, of Italy, of Germany, and especially of Poland, because there the vassalage of the peasantry is more oppressive than in any other country in Europe. The noble, or military class in India has been pronounced by some travellers to be composed of a different race of men from the populace who are their traders, and artizans; because, the former, elevated by their rank above them, and devoted only to martial studies and achievements, are distinguished by that manly beauty so frequently found united with the profession of arms; the latter, poor and laborious, exposed to innumerable hardships and privations, and left, by their laws and their religion, without the hope of improving their condition, or the spirit to attempt it, have become timid and servile in the expression of their countenance, diminutive, and often deformed in their persons, and marked by a deeper shade than their superiors in their complexion. . . .

---

* It should be kept in mind through the whole of the following illustrations, that, when mention is made of the superior beauty of persons in the higher classes of society, the remark is general. It is not intended to deny that there exist many exceptions both of deformity among the great, and of beauty among the poor. And the general remark is intended to be applied only to those who enjoy their fortune with temperance; because luxury and intemperance tend equally with extreme poverty and hardships to disfigure the person.

In America we have not the distinction of patrician and plebeian ranks. And the frequency of migration, in a new and extensive country, has not suffered any peculiar habits of life or local manners, deeply to impress a distinctive character on the people of any state. Great equality of condition in the citizens of the United States, similarity of occupations, and nearly the same degree of cultivation, and social improvement pervading the whole, have produced such uniformity of character, that, as yet, they are not strongly marked by such differences in the expression of the countenance, the composition of their features, or generally in their personal properties, as, in other countries, mark the grades between the superior and inferior orders of the people. And yet there are beginning to be formed certain habits of countenance, the result chiefly of manners, which already serve, to a certain degree, to distinguish the natives of some of the states from those of others. Hereafter, doubtless, they will advance into more considerable, and characteristic distinctions.

If the white population of America affords us less conspicuous instances than many other nations, of that variety of countenance, and of personal beauty or defect arising from diversity of rank and refinement in society, the blacks in the southern states afford one that is highly worthy the attention of philosophers.

The field slaves are, in comparison with the domestics, badly fed, clothed, and lodged. They live together in small collections of huts on the plantations on which they labor, remote from the society and example of their superiors. Confined, in this manner, to associate only with themselves, they retain many customs of their African ancestors. And pressed with labor, and dejected by servitude, and the humiliating circumstances in which they find themselves, they have little ambition to improve their personal appearance; and their oppressed condition contributes to continue, in a considerable degree, the deformities of their original climate. The domestic servants, on the other hand, who remain near the persons, and are employed within the families of their masters, are treated with great lenity, their service is light, they are fed and clothed like their superiors; insensibly, they receive the same ideas of elegance and beauty, and discover a great facility in adopting their manners. This class of slaves, therefore, has advanced far before the others in acquiring the regular and agreeable features, and the expressive countenance, which can be formed only in the midst of civilized society. The former are, generally, ill shaped. They preserve, in a great degree, the African lips, nose, and hair. Their genius is dull, and the expression of their countenance sleepy and stupid. The latter frequently exhibit very straight and well proportioned limbs. Their hair is often extended to three and four inches, and, sometimes, to a greater length. The size and form of the mouth is, in many instances, not unhandsome, and sometimes even beautiful; the composition of their features is regular,* their capacity good, and their look animated *. . . .

---

* The features of the negroes in America, especially of those who reside immediately in the families of their masters, have undergone a great change, while the complexion is not yet sensibly altered. The form and expression of the countenance, and composition of the features being principally affected by the state of society, are constantly receiving some modification from that cause, to improve the negro visage. But the rays of the sun which require, in our climate, the greatest care to prevent them from darkening the fairest skin, may be sufficient, in the exposed condition of the slave, to prevent a skin already black from becoming fair. The countenance of the domestic slaves of the third and fourth race, and, in many instances, even of the second, affords a striking example of the influence of the state of society upon the features. And there is reason to believe that, if these people were perfectly free, and were admitted to all the civil privileges of their masters, they would, in a short period, have few of the distinctive traces of their African ancestors remaining, except their complexion. In the state of New-Jersey, where the hardships of slavery are scarcely felt, we see great numbers of negroes who have the nose as much raised from the face, the forehead as well arched, and the teeth as perpendicularly set in their sockets, as the whites. Some negroes I see daily in Princeton and its vicinity who have the nose turned with a handsome aquiline curve.

Mental capacity, which is as various as the human physiognomy, is equally susceptible of improvement, or deterioration, from the state of society, and the manners and pursuits, which may form the character of any people. The body and mind have such reciprocal influence upon each other, that we often see certain peculiar powers or tendencies of the rational faculty intimately connected with certain corporeal forms. And whenever the moral, not less than the physical causes, under the influence of which any people exist, have produced any visible effect on the form and expression of the countenance, they will also be found proportionally to affect the operations of the mind. . . .

It is frequently asked on this subject, why, unless there be an original difference in the species of men, are not the natives of all climates *born*, at least, with the same figure and complexion? To such enquiries it is sufficient to answer, that it is for the same reason, whatever that may be, that other resemblances of parents are communicated to children. Experience demonstrates that figure, stature, complexion, features, diseases, and even powers of the mind may become hereditary. To those who find no difficulty in acknowledging that these properties may be communicated to offspring according to the established laws of nature, the transmission of the climatical or national differences among men, of which we have treated, can contain nothing which ought to appear supernatural, or incredible.—If it be enquired, why, then, a sun burnt face, or a wounded limb, is not, by the same laws, if they exist, transmitted to posterity? we may justly reply, that these are only partial accidents which produce no change on the interior structure and temperament of the constitution. It is the *constitution* which is conveyed by birth. And when any change becomes incorporated, into the system, so as, in any considerable degree, to affect its organization, or the state of its secretions, it then becomes communicable to offspring along with all other constitutional properties. . . .

Having now concluded the investigation which I proposed into the causes of the principal varieties in complexion and figure which distinguish the different nations of men from one another, it gives me pleasure to observe on this, as on many other subjects which have been attempted to be formed into objections against the sacred history, that the most extensive and accurate researches into the actual state, and the powers of nature, have ever served, more and more to confirm the facts vouched to us by the authority of holy writ. A just philosophy will always be found coincident with the true theology. But I must repeat here an observation which I made in the beginning of this essay, and which I trust I am now entitled to make with more confidence, that the denial of the unity of the human species tends to impair, if not entirely to destroy, the foundations of duty and morals, and, in a word, of the whole science of human nature. No general principles of conduct, or religion, or even of civil policy, could be derived from natures originally and essentially different from one another, and, afterwards, in the perpetual changes of the world, infinitely mixed and compounded. The principles and rules which a philosopher might derive from the study of his own nature, could not be applied with certainty to regulate the conduct of other men, and other nations, who might be of totally different species; or sprung from a very dissimilar composition of species. The terms which one man would frame to express the ideas and emotions of his own mind must convey to another a meaning as different as the organization of their respective natures. But when the whole human race is known to compose only one species, this confusion and uncertainty is removed, and the science of human nature, in all its relations, becomes susceptible of system. The principles of morals rest on sure and immutable foundations.

Its unity I have endeavoured to confirm by explaining the causes of its variety. Of these, the first I have shewn to be *climate,* by which is meant, not so much the latitude of a country from the equator, as the degree of heat or cold, which often depends on a great variety of other circumstances. The next is *the state of society,* which may augment or correct the influence of climate, and is itself a separate and independent cause of many conspicuous distinctions among mankind. These causes may be infinitely varied in degree; and their effects may likewise be diversified by various combinations. And, in the continual migrations of mankind, these effects may be still further modified, by changes which have antecedently taken place in a prior climate, and a prior state of society. Even where all external circumstances seem to be the same, there may be causes of difference depending on many natural influences with which philosophy is not yet acquainted; as there are varieties among the children of the same family. Frequently we see, in the same country individuals resembling every nation on the globe. Such varieties prove, at least, that the human constitution is susceptible of all the modifications which exist among mankind, without having recourse, in order to account for them, to the unnecessary, and therefore unphilosophical hypothesis of there having existed from the beginning, different original species of men. It is not more astonishing in itself, or out of the order of nature, that nations sprung from the same stock, than that individuals should differ. In the one case we are assured of the fact from observation; in the other, we have reason to conclude, independently on the sacred authority of revelation, that from one pair have descended all the families of the earth.

MR. CHARLES WHITE

ON

CERTAIN STRICTURES MADE ON THE FIRST EDITION

OF THIS ESSAY,

BY MR. CHARLES WHITE (1799)

Mr. Charles White having, in a series of discourses delivered to the literary and philosophical society of Manchester in England, made several strictures on the first edition of this essay, and appealed to certain anatomical facts which he supposes to stand in opposition to its principles, I have conceived it to be a duty which I owe to myself, and a respect due to the ingenuity of Mr. White, to point out some mistakes in his facts, and some errors in the conclusions which he has drawn from them. The facts subjected to his own inspection were derived principally from an examination of a single African skeleton, though afterwards confirmed by other skeletons, and by some living subjects. . . .

Having made these preliminary observations I proceed to enter into a more particular consideration of those distinguishing properties which, according to our author, discriminate the negro of Africa from the fair native of Europe. . . .

The peculiar structure of the skull of an African, as delineated by Mr. White, is not a more certain criterion of diversity of species than those properties which have been already mentioned. Climate, modes of living, national customs and ideas, and the degree of civilization to which a people have arrived, all have an influence on the figure of this bony substratum of the head, as well as on the features of the countenance. Lavater says, he finds not a greater difference between the skulls of a German and an East-Indian, than between that of a German and a Hollander. And he observes further, that the skull of a Calmuc, or Nomade Tartar approaches very nearly that of an African. Lavater, indeed, without having accurately considered the changes which time, which civilization, or removal into different climates may produce in the same race, has confidently asked; "What care of education can arch the skull of a negro, like that of a star conversant astronomer?" It is not supposed that education alone can effect it on a negro who has already received the basis of his constitution, in Africa. But, that time, a more favorable climate, better diet, and habits of society, may in a series of descents accomplish such a change, in the West-India islands, and the American states, can be confirmed by many examples. We often see among the children of Africa both in insular and continental America, heads as finely arched, and persons as handsomely formed, as are ever seen among the descendents of Europeans. And it was remarked of the army of Toussaint in St. Domingo that many of his officers were not exceeded in elegance of form, and nobleness of aspect, by any in the army of Rochambeau, or Le Clerc.*

Nearly connected with the preceeding is the next characteristic distinction of the negro species which our author assigns, founded in the supposed deficiency of mental talent. For this fact, real, or pretended, he quotes the authority of Mr. Jefferson, in his notes on Virginia. "Comparing them (the negroes)," says he, "by their faculties of memory, reason, and imagination, it appears to me that in memory they are equal to the whites, in reason much inferior, and that, in imagination, they are dull, tasteless, and anomalous. It would be unfair," he adds, "to follow them to Africa for this investigation. We will consider them here on the same stage with the whites. But it will be right to make great allowances for the difference of condition, of education, of conversation, of the sphere in which they move. Yet, many of them have been so situated that they might have availed themselves of the conversation of their masters: many have been brought up to the handicraft arts, and, from that circumstance, have been always associated with the whites. Some have been liberally educated; and all have lived in countries where the arts and sciences have been cultivated to a considerable degree, and have had before their eyes samples of the best works from abroad. Never could I find that a black had uttered a thought above the level of plain narration. Misery," he continues, "is often the parent of the most affecting touches in poetry—Among the blacks *is* misery enough, God knows, but no poetry." He adds, "love is the peculiar œstrum of the poet. Their love is ardent, but it kindles the senses only, not the imagination. Religion, indeed, has produced a Phillis Whately; but it could not produce a poet. Ignatius Sancho has approached nearer to merit in composition; yet his letters do more honor to the heart, than to the head. He is often happy in the turn of his compliments, and his stile is easy and familiar. But his imagination is wild and extravagant; escapes incessantly from every restraint of reason and taste, and, in the course of its vagaries leaves a tract of thought as incoherent and eccentric as is the course of a meteor through the sky."—After this, Mr. Jefferson contrasts the enslaved Africans in the United States, with the Roman slaves, in order to shew the vast inferiority of the former in all the exercises of the mental powers.

These remarks upon the genius of the African negro appear to me to have so little foundation in true philosophy that few observations will be necessary to refute them.

If the principle maintained by Lavater, and by St. Gall, that the form of the skull is indicative of the peculiar talents, and even of the inclinations and dispositions of men, be founded in nature, will it not result, as a necessary consequence, that if the climate, the mode of living, or the state of society, or even accidental causes in early life, contribute

---

* The critical reviewers are pleased to insinuate that the fine persons of many of the West-India blacks arise from a mixture of white blood. There are undoubtedly, in the islands, mulattos and other mixtures of blood in different degrees. But the observation in the text is applicable to men and women who have a clear, undoubted African descent.

to vary the shape of that bony case which encompasses the brain, thereby pressing upon it in some points, and giving it scope in others; in some of its cells contracting this soft substance, and giving it a freer expansion in others, these causes must, in the same degree, assist, impede, or vary the operations of the mind, and affect the character of the national genius, or of the genius of a whole race of men placed in a particular climate, or existing in a particular state of society.

That the causes which have been just suggested, may have some effect in hebetating the mental faculties of the wretched savages of Africa, I am not prepared either to deny or affirm. I am inclined, however, to ascribe the apparent dullness of the negro principally to the wretched state of his existence first in his original country, where he is at once a poor and abject savage, and subjected to an atrocious despotism; and afterwards in those regions to which he is transported to finish his days in slavery, and toil. Genius, in order to its cultivation, and the advantageous display of its powers, requires freedom: it requires reward, the reward at least of praise, to call it forth; competition to awaken its ardor; and examples both to direct its operations, and to prompt its emulation. The abject servitude of the negro in America, condemned to the drudgery of perpetual labor, cut off from every mean of improvement,* conscious of his degraded state in the midst of freemen who regard him with contempt, and in every word and look make him feel his inferiority; and hopeless of ever enjoying any great amelioration of his condition, must condemn him, while these circumstances remain, to perpetual sterility of genius. It is unfair to compare the feeble efforts of the mind which we sometimes behold under slavish depression, with the noble ardor which is often kindled even in the wild freedom of the American forest.

The aboriginal natives of America often exhibit, as Mr. Jefferson justly remarks, some of the finest flights of imagination, and some of the boldest strokes of oratory. But we perceive these vigorous efforts of the soul only while they enjoy their rude independence, and are employed in their favorite exercises of hunting, or of war, which give ardor to their sentiments, and energy to their character. Whereas, if you cut them off from employments which, along with conscious freedom and independence, often awaken the untutored savage to the boldest enterprizes; if, in this condition, you place them in the midst of a civilized people with whom they cannot amalgamate, and who only humble them by the continual view of their own inferiority, you, at once, annihilate among them all the noble qualities which you had admired in their savage state; and the negro becomes a respectable man compared with the indian. . .

Judging by the criterion which Mr. White[,] after Mr. Jefferson, has endeavoured to establish, might not the Abbe Raynal, and other European writers who denounce the

---

*   How few are the negroes in America who enjoy access to the first elements of knowledge by being enabled either to read, or write. Mr. Jefferson says that many of them have been placed in situations in which they might have enjoyed the society of their masters. What society, alas, can subsist between a master, and a slave; not a polite and learned slave of Greece, such as was often seen at Rome, but a wretched and ignorant African slave? Besides, if they could enjoy an intercourse much more free and intimate than is possible from the nature of their respective situations, I ask, what would there be in that society, when we consider the general characters, occupations, and conversations, of those masters, favorable to improvement in science, or the arts; or calculated to draw forth, and cultivate any of the high powers of imagination[,] taste, or genius? The poems of Phillis Whately, a poor African slave, taught to read by the indulgent piety of her master, are spoken of with infinite contempt. But I will demand of Mr. Jefferson, or any other man who is acquainted with American planters, how many of those masters could have written poems equal to those of Phillis Whately? And with still greater reason might I ask the same question with regard to the letters of Ignatius Sancho.

American climate as unfavorable to the growth of animal bodies, and the energies of the human intellect, justify their conclusion, by the example of the Anglo-Americans? Among these descendents of the ingenious Europeans, since their settlement in America, have appeared fewer exquisite productions in the arts, fewer works of taste, erudition, or genius, than have adorned the kingdoms of Europe, in the same period. But is this to be imputed to the climate? and not rather to the peculiar labors, and occupations required in a new world, to draw it forth from its forests, and its marshes, which have diverted the efforts of the people to other objects of more immediate necessity? But besides this primary cause of deficiency in monuments of art, and works of taste, we may reckon the sparseness of our population which prevents that constant collision, and comparison of sentiment, which contributes to strike out the fire of genius, and to correct its eccentricities and errors; the want of men of leisure, and of wealth either to cultivate the arts, or to encourage and reward them. But because we have produced no such poets as Pope, or Milton; no such groupes of wits as adorned London or Paris in the age of Anne, and of Louis the fourteenth, has a philosopher of Europe, in the pride of her present improvements in every department of literature, a right to say, because one century has not yet produced the fruits of ten, that the American like what was fabled of the Beotian air, has hebetated the genius of this last and largest quarter of the globe? Whence arose the difference between the Athenian, and the Beotian, or Spartan wit, but from their different states of society? And the Anglo, or Gallo-American only affords another example of this powerful influence in diversifying, in maturing, or retarding the operations of the human mind. The period has not yet arrived for displaying the full powers of the American genius. But whoever will regard with a truly philosophic eye the works which it has accomplished, the almost new creation which it has produced, within the last century, over the face of an immense continent, will be disposed rather to respect its energy and enterprize than to disparage it by an unfair comparison with the results of the wealth and population of Europe, and the accumulated improvements of so many ages. Many particular instances America can already exhibit of scientific investigation, of political eloquence, of military skill and heroism, of invention, especially in the mechanic arts, and of execution in the fine arts, which have not been exceeded in any country. And circumstances are now daily occurring to call forth more and more the energies of the American character, and to display the vividness and force of the American genius, which will, in a short time place us above the fear of the contempt, or even the rivalship of any nation. And the reproaches of deficiency of talent cast upon America by philosophers who have had little opportunity, and perhaps less disposition to form an accurate judgment upon this subject, will be doubly retorted upon Europe; for she will then be in the period of her decline, while her young competitor will be advancing to the maturity of her powers, and her glory.

In returning from this slight digression, may I not be permitted to ask, if this criterion, which is applied so unfavorably to the Africans, be just, are the modern Greeks of the same race with those republican heroes who expelled the Persians from their country; with those illustrious scholars among whom Socrates and Plato only shone in the first rank? Would it now be possible to restore among these degraded subjects of Turkish despotism, the genius of Demosthenes, of Xenophon, or of Phidias? Or are the Copts, a people more dull and stupid than the negroes of Angola, the descendants of those Egyptians who were once the masters of the Greeks themselves? Innumerable causes may, for a long time, prevent the faculties of the human mind from arriving at full maturity in particular nations, or may totally restrain among them the growth, and development of the powers of

Part Three

Protestant Awakening and Democratic Order

Introduction

Four years before he died, Jefferson confidently predicted to a Unitarian correspondent that a thoroughly rationalized Unitarian Christianity would become within a generation the religion of America. He could hardly have been more wrong. In fact, at the very moment Jefferson wrote, there were occurring throughout the country stirrings of religious excitement that would soon swell into the greatest nationwide revival of emotion-laden Christian evangelicalism in American history. Indeed, by the time of the Civil War, evangelical Protestantism had virtually become the religion, if not of America, at least of most Americans. No greater proof would seem to be needed to show how little the American Enlightenment had accomplished in weakening the hold on American culture of generations of Puritan- and revival-nurtured piety.

Yet this era of the Second Great Awakening was not bereft of its own rationalistic elements. This was most obvious in the small but intellectually influential circles in Massachusetts and (to a much lesser extent) elsewhere that identified themselves as Liberal Christians or, as they soon called themselves, Unitarians. In his sermon "Unitarian Christianity" William Ellery Channing fervently argued that his denomination's supernatural rationalism, not the gloomy, servile theology of Calvinism, deserved the imprimatur as modern Christianity's robustly moral and deeply spiritual creed. Furthermore, even those more strictly evangelical antebellum revivalists, who claimed to stand in the tradition of the Calvinistic revivals of the First Great Awakening, often themselves appealed to didactically rational "common sense" and human ability. Indeed, Nathaniel William Taylor argued in his *Concio ad Clerum* that, though depraved by nature, individual men and women *must* be morally able to choose to obey God in order to ensure His cosmic plan of "moral government." In his *Lectures on Revivals of Religion,* Charles Grandison Finney went further in both his rationalism and his perfectionism. He asserted both that humans must exercise their moral freedom to obey in order to help achieve their salvation *and* that, after conversion, their capacity to strive for perfect holiness would likewise help to usher in God's kingdom on earth. No antebellum intellectual figure, however, went further than John Humphrey Noyes did in raising radical perfectionism to its apotheosis. In his essays from *The Berean,* Noyes argued that the essence of Bible religion consisted not in biblical testimony but rather the manifest indwelling of God, and that experience facilitated not merely an approach to perfection and progress toward the millennium but deliverance from all sins now in this world.

These activist impulses of antebellum America's evangelical age specifically encouraged a related but more broadly secular democratic notion—that Christianity was the egalitarian engine of social reform and progress. Mostly the reform movements that most liberal and evangelical Protestants supported were ones, such as temperance, that authoritatively inculcated an individualistic ethic of liberation from sin and therefore personal self-governance. Yet some writers derived from this conservative democratic strain, radical critiques of dominant values and structures of power as well as quasi-secular visions of a perfect society. In the excerpts from his *Thoughts on African Colonization* and from his newspaper the *Liberator,* William Lloyd Garrison delivered a withering assault on American slavery and white racism, while expressing a millennialist faith in the purely spiritual means and ends of their overcoming. In a more sober spirit Sarah Grimké, in her *Letters on the Equality of the Sexes, and the Condition of Woman,* took roughly the same evangelical perfectionist tack in addressing what in her view (and also Garrison's) was the plainly allied question of *women's* status. In particular, she offered both an individualistic *and* biblical critique of the ideology of female subordination as well as a powerful argument in favor of women's moral-minded political activism.

For an understanding of the political substance of antebellum democratic thought, though, one needs to turn to the period's political intellectuals, particularly those who identified with Andrew Jackson's Democratic party. Jacksonian democracy is often regarded as more or less continuous with Jeffersonian republicanism, which in several respects it was. Both ideologies associated economic independence with moral virtue, favored limited government, and were deeply hostile to government-engendered special privileges. But several pro-Jacksonian pundits broadened considerably the democratic implications of these republican Enlightenment stances in two important ways. First, they claimed that not only were ordinary people morally and politically trustworthy but they were so intellectually as well. George Bancroft was especially resourceful linking these moves. In his oration "The Office of the People," Bancroft defended, in both sweeping and circumspect ways, the philosophical validity and cultural utility of identifying majoritarian rule with nothing less than divine authority. Second, many Jacksonian intellectuals applied the republican Enlightenment philosophy of "equal rights," not only to the political process, but, even more broadly, to social and economic structures. Orestes Brownson provided unquestionably the most radical version of this application in his essay "The Laboring Classes," in which he concluded that equal rights required the virtual abolition of modern capitalism and the erection of a divinely sanctioned democratic state.

Like the Democratic party, the Whig party also had its intellectual defenders. And like their Jacksonian opponents, most of these Whig intellectuals too embraced the era's talisman of equality, although usually in a very different form. In their hands it appeared not as equality of rights or condition but of opportunity—to rise socially and economically or to benefit from increasing prosperity—that they believed was facilitated precisely by the tariffs, banks, internal improvements, and other programs of national institution building that the Jacksonians adamantly opposed. Consistent with their optimistic conservative nationalism, these Whigs also celebrated the given fact and public virtues of American democracy and therefore denounced as unnecessary and dangerous the class envy and hostility that they believed the Jacksonian assaults on privilege encouraged. There were other Whigs, however, who joined these notions with more nervously liberal views of America's prospects. More in line with the evangelicals or the morally concerned Protestant liberals from whom they drew many of their followers, they worried about the moral selfishness and social atomization that an expanding capitalist democracy seemed to them to be engendering. Intellectuals sometimes with only tenuous ties to the Whig party were particularly attracted to this kind of thinking, and the solutions they put forward were often Whiggish but with a distinct social and moral twist: They advocated promoting egalitarian opportunity and social cohesion by shoring up, through various political and voluntaristic means, America's ostensibly nonpolitical institutions, especially the family, the school, and the church. Catharine Beecher was a particularly fascinating representative of this current. Her *Treatise on Domestic Economy* linked Whiggish concern for upward mobility with the imperative of moral influence and social cohesion in the person of the American middle-class woman. Henry C. Carey accomplished something of the same synthesis in an even more sweeping form in the area of political economy. In his *Harmony of Interests,* Carey argued that the Whigs' program of government tariffs, if properly implemented, promoted nothing less than a "true Christianity" of equality, peace, and social benevolence unprecedented in the history of the world. Few evangelicals could have conjured up a more glorious picture of the coming age.

Recommendations for Further Reading
Whitney R. Cross, *The Burned-Over District: The Social and Intellectual History of Enthusiastic Religion in Western New York, 1800–1850* (Ithaca, 1950); Henry Nash Smith, *Virgin Land: The American West as Symbol and Myth* (Cambridge, Mass., 1950); Perry Miller, *The Life of the Mind in America: From the Revolution to the Civil War* (New York, 1965); Jerry Wayne Brown, *The Rise of Biblical Criticism in America, 1800–1870* (Middletown, Conn., 1969); Daniel Walker Howe, *The Unitarian Conscience: Harvard Moral Philosophy, 1805–1861* (Cambridge, Mass., 1970); D.H. Meyer, *The Instructed Conscience: The Shaping of the American National Ethic* (Philadelphia, 1972); Theodore Dwight Bozeman, *Protestants in an Age of Science: The Baconian Ideal and Antebellum American Religious Thought* (Chapel Hill, 1977); E. Brooks Holifield, *The Gentlemen Theologians: American Theology in Southern Culture, 1795–1860* (Durham, N.C., 1978); Herbert Hovenkamp, *Science and Religion in America, 1800–1860* (Philadelphia, 1978); Daniel Walker Howe, *The Political Culture of the American Whigs* (Chicago, 1979); John Ashworth, *'Agrarians' and 'Aristocrats': Party Political Ideology in the United States, 1837–1846* (London, 1983); Mary Kelley, *Private Woman, Public Stage: Literary Domesticity in Nineteenth-Century America* (New York, 1984); Bruce Kuklick, *Churchmen and Philosophers: From Jonathan Edwards to John Dewey* (New Haven, 1985); Nathan O. Hatch, *The Democratization of American Christianity* (New Haven, 1989); Kenneth Cmiel, *Democratic Eloquence: The Fight over Popular Speech in Nineteenth-Century America* (New York, 1990); Jonathan A. Glickstein, *Concepts of Free Labor in Antebellum America* (New Haven, 1991); Samuel Haber *The Quest for Authority and Honor in the American Professions, 1750–1900* (Chicago, 1991); Jean V. Matthews, *Toward a New Society: American Thought and Culture, 1800–1830* (Boston, 1991); Robert H. Abzug, *Cosmos Crumbling: American Reform and the Religious Imagination* (New York, 1994); John L. Brooke, *The Refiner's Fire: The Making of Mormon Cosmology, 1644–1844* (Cambridge, 1994); Mark Y. Hanley, *Beyond a Christian Commonwealth: The Protestant Quarrel with the American Republic, 1830–1860* (Chapel Hill, 1994); Paul K. Conkin, *The Uneasy Center: Reformed Christianity in Antebellum America* (Chapel Hill, 1995); Anne C. Rose, *Voices of the Marketplace: American Thought and Culture, 1830–1860* (New York, 1995); Paul K. Conkin, *American Originals: Homemade Varieties of Christianity* (Chapel Hill, 1997); Daniel Walker Howe, *Making the American Self: Jonathan Edwards to Abraham Lincoln* (Cambridge, Mass., 1997); Peter S. Field, *The Crisis of the Standing Order: Clerical Intellectuals and Cultural Authority in Massachusetts, 1780–1833* (Amherst, 1998); James L. Huston, *Securing the Fruits of Labor: The American Concept of Wealth Distribution, 1765–1900* (Baton Rouge, 1998); Nancy Isenberg, *Sex and Citizenship in Antebellum America* (Chapel Hill, 1998); Gilman M. Ostrander, *Republic of Letters: The American Intellectual Community, 1776–1865* (Madison, 1999); Marshall Foletta, *Coming to Terms with Democracy: Federalist Intellectuals and the Shaping of an American Culture* (Charlottesville, 2001); Mark A. Noll, *America's God: From Jonathan Edwards to Abraham Lincoln* (New York, 2002); Jeffrey

Sklansky, *The Soul's Economy: Market Society and Selfhood in American Thought, 1820–1920* (Chapel Hill, 2002); Steven Conn, *History's Shadow: Native Americans and Historical Consciousness in the Nineteenth Century* (Chicago, 2004); Maureen Konkle, *Writing Indian Nations: Native Intellectuals and the Politics of Historiography, 1827–1863* (Chapel Hill, 2004); Mary Kelley, *Learning to Stand and Speak: Women, Education, and Public Life in America's Republic* (Chapel Hill, 2006); Adam Tuchinsky, *Horace Greeley's New-York Tribune: Civil War–Era Socialism and the Crisis of Free Labor* (Ithaca, 2009). Elizabeth A. Clark, *Founding the Fathers: Early Church History and Protestant Professors in Nineteenth-Century America* (Philadelphia, 2011); Sandra M. Gustafson, *Imagining Deliberative Democracy in the Early American Republic* (Chicago, 2011); Kunal M. Parker, *Common Law, History, and Democracy in America, 1790–1900: Legal Thought before Modernism* (Cambridge, Eng., 2011); David Sehat, *The Myth of American Religious Freedom* (New York, 2011); Jon Gjerde, *Catholicism and the Shaping of Nineteenth-Century America,* edited by S. Deborah Kang (New York, 2012); Molly Oshatz, *Slavery and Sin: The Fight Against Slavery and the Rise of Liberal Protestantism* (New York, 2012); Eran Shalev, *American Zion: The Old Testament as a Political Text from the Revolution to the Civil War* (New Haven, 2013).

WILLIAM ELLERY CHANNING

"Unitarian Christianity"
(1819)

At his death, William Ellery Channing (1780–1842) was the most intellectually renowned minister in America. He was also the only American religious writer to be widely read in Europe, a distinction he would retain through the rest of the century. He derived much of his fame from his role as the most respected defender of Unitarianism when it first established itself in the 1810s and 1820s as a separate denomination, securing its dominance in eastern Massachusetts, the country's literary-intellectual center. But most of all his central message—human's "likeness to God"—reiterated in countless eloquent sermons, which he delivered for nearly forty years from his Federal Street Church, made him seem to his mostly urbane listeners and readers both spiritually inspiring and reassuringly true.

In his most famous sermon, later entitled "Unitarian Christianity," Channing set about to define, after a decade of his colleagues' pamphlet wars with their new church's Calvinist opponents, Unitarianism's rational yet supernatural contours. In fact, his discourse, which sold more copies than any American pamphlet yet published, was much more than a momentary intervention in a denominational skirmish. Dispensing with the traditional nervous arrogance of his eighteenth-century post-Calvinist predecessors' denunciations of religious "enthusiasm," he cogently and fervently presented the positive case for a unitary "Parental" God and a divinely mediating Jesus. Indeed, going on the offensive, he struck directly against the "immoral" Calvinists, insisting that the centrality of reason and ethics in Unitarianism, rather than subverting Christianity, sustained both its mind and its heart. His church's rational Christianity accomplished the first by asserting that the validity of the revelations of the Gospels, if they were to speak at all to humans, had to rest on a critical investigation of their supporting empirical and linguistic evidence. It accomplished the second by showing that man and woman, by cultivating their divine reason and moral sense, engendered as well their souls' never-ending growth toward divinity. The intended result was a Christian piety that would be rational, moral, and, while eschewing "strong excitements" and "disordered nerves," still strongly affective.

John White Chadwick's *William Ellery Channing: Minister of Religion* (Boston, 1903), remains the most intellectually useful Channing biography. A valuable interpretation of Channing's political outlook may be found in Andrew Delbanco, *William Ellery Channing: An Essay on the Liberal Spirit in America* (Cambridge, Mass., 1981). Daniel Walker Howe's study, *The Unitarian Conscience: Harvard Moral Philosophy, 1805–1861* (Cambridge, Mass., 1970), is indispensable for an understanding of the mind-set of Channing's generation of Unitarian intellectuals. For a cogent analysis of Channing's theological stance, see Conrad Wright, "The Rediscovery of Channing," in Wright's *The Liberal Christians* (Boston, 1970), 22–40, 126–28. For an excellent discussion of Channing's key theological concept of "self-culture," see David M. Robinson, "The Legacy of Channing: Culture as a Religious Category in New England Thought," *Harvard Theological Review,* 74 (April 1981), 221–39.

Discourse at the Ordination of the
Rev. Jared Sparks. Baltimore, 1819.

1 Thes. v. 21: "Prove all things; hold fast that which is good."

...There are two natural divisions under which my thoughts will be arranged. I shall endeavour to unfold, 1st, The principles which we adopt in interpreting the Scriptures. And 2dly, Some of the doctrines, which the Scriptures, so interpreted, seem to us clearly to express.

i. We regard the Scriptures as the records of God's successive revelations to mankind, and particularly of the last and most perfect revelation of his will by Jesus Christ. Whatever doctrines seem to us to be clearly taught in the Scriptures, we receive without reserve or exception. We do not, however, attach equal importance to all the books in this collection. Our religion, we believe, lies chiefly in the New Testament. The dispensation of Moses, compared with that of Jesus, we consider as adapted to the childhood of the human race, a preparation for a nobler system, and chiefly useful now as serving to confirm and illustrate the Christian Scriptures. Jesus Christ is the only master of Christians, and whatever he taught, either during his personal ministry, or by his inspired Apostles, we regard as of divine authority, and profess to make the rule of our lives.

This authority, which we give to the Scriptures, is a reason, we conceive, for studying them with peculiar care, and for inquiring anxiously into the principles of interpretation, by which their true meaning may be ascertained. The principles adopted by the class of Christians in whose name I speak, need to be explained, because they are often misunderstood. We are particularly accused of making an unwarrantable use of reason in the interpretation of Scripture. We are said to exalt reason above revelation, to prefer our own wisdom to God's. Loose and undefined charges of this kind are circulated so freely, that we think it due to ourselves, and to the cause of truth, to express our views with some particularity.

Our leading principle in interpreting Scripture is this, that the Bible is a book written for men, in the language of men, and that its meaning is to be sought in the same manner as that of other books. We believe that God, when he speaks to the human race, conforms, if we may so say, to the established rules of speaking and writing. How else would the Scriptures avail us more, than if communicated in an unknown tongue?

Now all books, and all conversation, require in the reader or hearer the constant exercise of reason; or their true import is only to be obtained by continual comparison and inference. Human language, you well know, admits various interpretations; and every word and every sentence must be modified and explained according to the subject which is discussed, according to the purposes, feelings, circumstances, and principles of the writer, and according to the genius and idioms of the language which he uses. These are acknowledged principles in the interpretation of human writings; and a man, whose words we should explain without reference to these principles, would reproach us justly with a criminal want of candor, and an intention of obscuring or distorting his meaning.

Were the Bible written in a language and style of its own, did it consist of words, which admit but a single sense, and of sentences wholly detached from each other, there would be no place for the principles now laid down. We could not reason about it, as about other writings. But such a book would be of little worth; and perhaps, of all books,

Source: The Works of William Ellery Channing, vol. 3 (Boston, 1843), 59, 60–71, 74–76, 82–88, 93–100.

the Scriptures correspond least to this description. The Word of God bears the stamp of the same hand, which we see in his works. It has infinite connexions and dependences. Every proposition is linked with others, and is to be compared with others; that its full and precise import may be understood. Nothing stands alone. The New Testament is built on the Old. The Christian dispensation is a continuation of the Jewish, the completion of a vast scheme of providence, requiring great extent of view in the reader. Still more, the Bible treats of subjects on which we receive ideas from other sources besides itself; such subjects as the nature, passions, relations, and duties of man; and it expects us to restrain and modify its language by the known truths, which observation and experience furnish on these topics.

We profess not to know a book, which demands a more frequent exercise of reason than the Bible. In addition to the remarks now made on its infinite connexions, we may observe, that its style nowhere affects the precision of science, or the accuracy of definition. Its language is singularly glowing, bold, and figurative, demanding more frequent departures from the literal sense, than that of our own age and country, and consequently demanding more continual exercise of judgment.—We find, too, that the different portions of this book, instead of being confined to general truths, refer perpetually to the times when they were written, to states of society, to modes of thinking, to controversies in the church, to feelings and usages which have passed away, and without the knowledge of which we are constantly in danger of extending to all times, and places, what was of temporary and local application.—We find, too, that some of these books are strongly marked by the genius and character of their respective writers, that the Holy Spirit did not so guide the Apostles as to suspend the peculiarities of their minds, and that a knowledge of their feelings, and of the influences under which they were placed, is one of the preparations for understanding their writings. With these views of the Bible, we feel it our bounden duty to exercise our reason upon it perpetually, to compare, to infer, to look beyond the letter to the spirit, to seek in the nature of the subject, and the aim of the writer, his true meaning; and, in general, to make use of what is known, for explaining what is difficult, and for discovering new truths.

Need I descend to particulars, to prove that the Scriptures demand the exercise of reason? Take, for example, the style in which they generally speak of God, and observe how habitually they apply to him human passions and organs. Recollect the declarations of Christ, that he came not to send peace, but a sword; that unless we eat his flesh, and drink his blood, we have no life in us; that we must hate father and mother, and pluck out the right eye; and a vast number of passages equally bold and unlimited. Recollect the unqualified manner in which it is said of Christians, that they possess all things, know all things, and can do all things. Recollect the verbal contradiction between Paul and James, and the apparent clashing of some parts of Paul's writings with the general doctrines and end of Christianity. I might extend the enumeration indefinitely; and who does not see, that we must limit all these passages by the known attributes of God, of Jesus Christ, and of human nature, and by the circumstances under which they were written, so as to give the language a quite different import from what it would require, had it been applied to different beings, or used in different connexions.

Enough has been said to show, in what sense we make use of reason in interpreting Scripture. From a variety of possible interpretations, we select that which accords with the nature of the subject and the state of the writer, with the connexion of the passage, with the general strain of Scripture, with the known character and will of God, and with the obvious and acknowledged laws of nature. In other words, we believe that God never contradicts, in one part of Scripture, what he teaches in another; and never contradicts, in revelation, what he teaches in his works and providence. And we therefore distrust every interpretation, which, after deliberate attention, seems repugnant to any established truth. We reason about the Bible precisely as civilians do about the constitution under which we live; who, you know, are accustomed to limit one provision of that venerable instrument by others, and to fix the precise import of its parts, by inquiring into its general spirit, into the intentions of its authors, and into the prevalent feelings, impressions, and circumstances of the time when it was framed. Without these principles of interpretation, we frankly acknowledge, that we cannot defend the divine authority of the Scriptures. Deny us this latitude, and we must abandon this book to its enemies.

We do not announce these principles as original, or peculiar to ourselves. All Christians occasionally adopt them, not excepting those who most vehemently decry them, when they happen to menace some favorite article of their creed. All Christians are compelled to use them in their controversies with infidels. All sects employ them in their warfare with one another. All willingly avail themselves of reason, when it can be pressed into the service of their own party, and only complain of it, when its weapons wound themselves. None reason more frequently than those from whom we differ. It is astonishing what a fabric they rear from a few slight hints about the fall of our first parents; and how ingeniously they extract, from detached passages, mysterious doctrines about the divine nature. We do not blame them for reasoning so abundantly, but for violating the fundamental rules of reasoning, for sacrificing the plain to the obscure, and the general strain of Scripture to a scanty number of insulated texts.

We object strongly to the contemptuous manner in which human reason is often spoken of by our adversaries, because it leads, we believe, to universal skepticism. If reason be so dreadfully darkened by the fall, that its most decisive judgments on religion are unworthy of trust, then Christianity, and even natural theology, must be abandoned; for the existence and veracity of God, and the divine original of Christianity, are conclusions of reason, and must stand or fall with it. If revelation be at war with this faculty, it subverts itself, for the great question of its truth is left by God to be decided at the bar of reason. It is worthy of remark, how nearly the bigot and the skeptic approach. Both would annihilate our confidence in our faculties, and both throw doubt and confusion over every truth. We honor revelation too highly to make it the antagonist of reason, or to believe that it calls us to renounce our highest powers.

We indeed grant, that the use of reason in religion is accompanied with danger. But we ask any honest man to look back on the history of the church, and say, whether the renunciation of it be not still more dangerous. Besides, it is a plain fact, that men reason as erroneously on all subjects, as on religion. Who does not know the wild and groundless theories, which have been framed in physical and political science? But who ever supposed, that we must cease to exercise reason on nature and society, because men have erred for ages in explaining them? We grant, that the passions continually, and sometimes fatally, disturb the rational faculty in its inquiries into revelation. The ambitious contrive to find doctrines in the Bible, which favor their love of dominion. The timid and dejected discover there a gloomy system, and the mystical and fanatical, a visionary theology. The vicious can find examples or assertions on which to build the hope of a late repentance, or of acceptance on easy terms. The falsely refined contrive to light on doctrines which have not been soiled by vulgar handling. But the passions do not distract the reason in religious, any more than in other inquiries, which excite strong and general interest; and this faculty, of consequence, is not to be renounced in religion, unless we are prepared to discard it universally. The true inference from the almost endless errors, which have darkened theology, is, not that we are to neglect and disparage our powers, but to exert them more patiently, circumspectly, uprightly. The worst errors, after all, having sprung up in that church, which proscribes reason, and demands from its members implicit faith. The most pernicious doctrines have been the growth of the darkest times, when the general credulity encouraged bad men and enthusiasts to broach their dreams and inventions, and to stifle the faint remonstrances of reason, by the menaces of everlasting perdition. Say what we may, God has given us a rational nature, and will call us to account for it. We may let it sleep, but we do so at our peril. Revelation is addressed to us as rational beings. We may wish, in our sloth, that God had given us a system, demanding no labor of comparing, limiting, and inferring. But such a system would be at variance with the whole character of our present existence; and it is the part of wisdom to take revelation as it is given to us, and to interpret it by the help of the faculties, which it everywhere supposes, and on which it is founded.

To the views now given, an objection is commonly urged from the character of God. We are told, that God being infinitely wiser than men, his discoveries will surpass human reason. In a revelation from such a teacher, we ought to expect propositions, which we cannot reconcile with one another, and which may seem to contradict established truths; and it becomes us not to question or explain them away, but to believe, and adore, and to submit our weak and carnal reason to the Divine Word. To this objection, we have two short answers. We say, first, that it is impossible that a teacher of infinite wisdom should expose those, whom he would teach, to infinite error. But if once we admit, that propositions, which in their literal sense appear plainly repugnant to one another, or to any known truth, are still to be literally understood and received, what possible limit can we set to the belief of contradictions? What shelter have we from the wildest fanaticism, which can always quote passages, that, in their literal and obvious sense, give support to its extravagances? How can the Protestant escape from transubstantiation, a doctrine most clearly taught us, if the submission of reason, now contended for, be a duty? How can we even hold fast the truth of revelation, for if one apparent contradiction may be true, so may another, and the proposition, that Christianity is false, though involving inconsistency, may still be a verity?

We answer again, that, if God be infinitely wise, he cannot sport with the understandings of his creatures. A wise teacher discovers his wisdom in adapting himself to the capacities of his pupils, not in perplexing them with what is unintelligible, not in distressing them with apparent contradictions, not in filling them with a skeptical distrust of their own powers. An infinitely wise teacher, who knows the precise extent of our minds, and the best method of enlightening them, will surpass all other instructors in bringing down truth to our apprehension, and in showing its loveliness and harmony. We ought, indeed, to expect occasional obscurity in such a book as the Bible, which was written for past and future ages, as well as for the present. But God's wisdom is a pledge, that whatever is necessary for *us,* and necessary for salvation, is revealed too plainly to be mistaken, and too consistently to be questioned, by a sound and upright mind. It is not the mark of wisdom, to use an unintelligible phraseology, to communicate what is above our capacities, to confuse and unsettle the intellect by appearances of contradiction. We honor our Heavenly Teacher too much to ascribe to him such a revelation. A revelation is a gift of light. It cannot thicken our darkness, and multiply our perplexities.

II. Having thus stated the principles according to which we interpret Scripture, I now proceed to the second great head of this discourse, which is, to state some of the views which we derive from that sacred book, particularly those which distinguish us from other Christians.

1. In the first place, we believe in the doctrine of God's UNITY, or that there is one God, and one only. To this truth we give infinite importance, and we feel ourselves bound to take heed, lest any man spoil us of it by vain philosophy. The proposition, that there is one God, seems to us exceedingly plain. We understand by it, that there is one being, one mind, one person, one intelligent agent, and one only, to whom underived and infinite perfection and dominion belong. We conceive, that these words could have conveyed no other meaning to the simple and uncultivated people, who were set apart to be the depositaries of this great truth, and who were utterly incapable of understanding those hair-breadth distinctions between being and person, which the sagacity of later ages has discovered. We find no intimation, that this language was to be taken in an unusual sense, or that God's unity was a quite different thing from the oneness of other intelligent beings.

We object to the doctrine of the Trinity, that, whilst acknowledging in words, it subverts in effect, the unity of God. According to this doctrine, there are three infinite and equal persons, possessing supreme divinity, called the Father, Son, and Holy Ghost. Each of these persons, as described by theologians, has his own particular consciousness, will, and perceptions. They love each other, converse with each other, and delight in each other's society. They perform different parts in man's redemption, each having his appropriate office, and neither doing the work of the other. The Son is mediator and not the Father. The Father sends the Son, and is not himself sent; nor is he conscious, like the Son, of taking flesh. Here, then, we have three intelligent agents, possessed of different consciousnesses, different wills, and different perceptions, performing different acts, and sustaining different relations; and if these things do not imply and constitute three minds or beings, we are utterly at a loss to know how three minds or beings are to be formed. It is difference of properties, and acts, and consciousness, which leads us to the belief of different intelligent beings, and, if this mark fails us, our whole knowledge falls; we have no proof, that all the agents and persons in the universe are not one and the same mind. When we attempt to conceive of three Gods, we can do nothing more than represent to ourselves three agents, distinguished from each other by similar marks and peculiarities to those which separate the persons of the Trinity; and when common Christians hear these persons spoken of as conversing with each other, loving each other, and performing different acts, how can they help regarding them as different beings, different minds? . . .

We also think, that the doctrine of the Trinity injures devotion, not only by joining to the Father other objects of worship, but by taking from the Father the supreme affection, which is his due, and transferring it to the Son. This is a most important view. That Jesus Christ, if exalted into the infinite Divinity, should be more interesting than the Father, is precisely what might be expected from history, and from the principles of human nature. Men want an object of worship like themselves, and the great secret of idolatry lies in this propensity. A God, clothed in our form, and feeling our wants and sorrows, speaks to our weak nature more strongly, than a Father in heaven, a pure spirit, invisible and unapproachable, save by the reflecting and purified mind.—We think, too, that the peculiar offices ascribed to Jesus by the popular theology, make him the most attractive person in the Godhead. The Father is the depositary of the justice, the vindicator of the rights, the avenger of the laws of the Divinity. On the other hand, the Son, the brightness of the divine mercy, stands between the incensed Deity and guilty humanity, exposes his meek head to the storms, and his compassionate breast to the sword of the divine justice, bears our whole load of punishment, and purchases with his blood every blessing which descends from heaven. Need we state the effect of these representations, especially on common minds, for whom Christianity was chiefly designed, and whom it seeks to bring to the Father as the loveliest being? We do believe, that the worship of a bleeding, suffering God, tends strongly to absorb the mind, and to draw it from other objects, just as the human tenderness of the Virgin Mary has given her so conspicuous a place in the devotions of the Church of Rome. We believe, too, that this worship, though attractive, is not most fitted to spiritualize the mind, that it awakens human transport, rather than that deep veneration of the moral perfections of God, which is the essence of piety.

2. Having thus given our views of the unity of God, I proceed in the second place to observe, that we believe in the unity of Jesus Christ. We believe that Jesus is one mind, one soul, one being, as truly one as we are, and equally distinct from the one God. We complain of the doctrine of the Trinity, that, not satisfied with making God three beings, it makes Jesus Christ two beings, and thus introduces infinite confusion into our conceptions of his character. This corruption of Christianity, alike repugnant to common sense and to the general strain of Scripture, is a remarkable proof of the power of a false philosophy in disfiguring the simple truth of Jesus.

According to this doctrine, Jesus Christ, instead of being one mind, one conscious intelligent principle, whom we can understand, consists of two souls, two minds; the one divine, the other human; the one weak, the other almighty; the one ignorant, the other omniscient. Now we maintain, that this is to make Christ two beings. To denominate him one person, one being, and yet to suppose him made up of two minds, infinitely different from each other, is to abuse and confound language, and to throw darkness over all our conceptions of intelligent natures. According to the *common* doctrine, each of these two minds in Christ has its own consciousness, its own will, its own perceptions. They have, in fact, no common properties. The divine mind feels none of the wants and sorrows of the human, and the human is infinitely removed from the perfection and happiness of the divine. Can you conceive of two beings in the universe more distinct? We have always thought that one person was constituted and distinguished by one consciousness. The doctrine, that one and the same person should have two consciousnesses, two wills, two souls, infinitely different from each other, this we think an enormous tax on human credulity....

3. Having thus given our belief on two great points, namely, that there is one God, and that Jesus Christ is a being distinct from, and inferior to, God, I now proceed to another point, on which we lay still greater stress. We believe in the *moral perfection of God* [.] We consider no part of theology so important as that which treats of God's moral character; and we value our views of Christianity chiefly as they assert his amiable and venerable attributes.

It may be said, that, in regard to this subject, all Christians agree, that all ascribe to the Supreme Being infinite justice, goodness, and holiness. We reply, that it is very possible to speak of God magnificently, and to think of him meanly; to apply to his person high-sounding epithets, and to his government, principles which make him odious. The Heathens called Jupiter the greatest and the best; but his history was black with cruelty and lust. We cannot judge of men's real ideas of God by their general language, for in all ages they have hoped to soothe the Deity by adulation. We must inquire into their particular views of his purposes, of the principles of his administration, and of his disposition towards his creatures.

We conceive that Christians have generally leaned towards a very injurious view of the Supreme Being. They have too often felt, as if he were raised, by his greatness and sovereignty, above the principles of morality, above those eternal laws of equity and rectitude, to which all other beings are subjected. We believe, that in no being is the sense of right so strong, so omnipotent, as in God. We believe that his almighty power is entirely submitted to his perceptions of rectitude; and this is the ground of our piety. It is not because he is our Creator merely, but because he created us for good and holy purposes; it is not because his will is irresistible, but because his will is the perfection of virtue, that we pay him allegiance. We cannot bow before a being, however great and powerful, who governs tyrannically. We respect nothing but excellence, whether on earth or in heaven. We venerate not the loftiness of God's throne, but the equity and goodness in which it is established.

We believe that God is infinitely good, kind, benevolent, in the proper sense of these words; good in disposition, as well as in act; good, not to a few, but to all; good to every individual, as well as to the general system.

We believe, too, that God is just; but we never forget, that his justice is the justice of a good being, dwelling in the same mind, and acting in harmony, with perfect benevolence. By this attribute, we understand God's infinite regard to virtue or moral worth, expressed in a moral government; that is, in giving excellent and equitable laws, and in conferring such rewards, and inflicting such punishments, as are best fitted to secure their observance. God's justice has for its end the highest virtue of the creation, and it punishes for this end alone, and thus it coincides with benevolence; for virtue and happiness, though not the same, are inseparably conjoined.

God's justice thus viewed, appears to us to be in perfect harmony with his mercy. According to the prevalent systems of theology, these attributes are so discordant and jarring, that to reconcile them is the hardest task, and the most wonderful achievement, of infinite wisdom. To us they seem to be intimate friends, always at peace, breathing the same spirit, and seeking the same end. By God's mercy, we understand not a blind instinctive compassion, which forgives without reflection, and without regard to the interests of virtue. This, we acknowledge, would be incompatible with justice, and also with enlightened benevolence. God's mercy, as we understand it, desires strongly the happiness of the guilty, but only through their penitence. It has a regard to character as truly as his justice. It defers punishment, and suffers long, that the sinner may return to his duty, but leaves the impenitent and unyielding, to the fearful retribution threatened in God's Word.

To give our views of God in one word, we believe in his Parental character. We ascribe to him, not only the name, but the dispositions and principles of a father. We believe that he has a father's concern for his creatures, a father's desire for their improvement, a father's equity in proportioning his commands to their powers, a father's joy in their progress, a father's readiness to receive the penitent, and a father's justice for the incorrigible. We look upon this world as a place of education, in which he is training men by prosperity and adversity, by aids and obstructions, by conflicts of reason and passion, by motives to duty and temptations to sin, by a various discipline suited to free and moral beings, for union with himself, and for a sublime and ever-growing virtue in heaven.

Now, we object to the systems of religion, which prevail among us, that they are adverse, in a greater or less degree, to these purifying, comforting, and honorable views of God; that they take from us our Father in heaven, and substitute for him a being, whom we cannot love if we would, and whom we ought not to love if we could. We object, particularly on this ground, to that system, which arrogates to itself the name of Orthodoxy, and which is now industriously propagated through our country. This system indeed takes various shapes, but in all it casts dishonor on the Creator. According to its old and genuine form, it teaches, that God brings us into life wholly depraved, so that under the innocent features of our childhood is hidden a nature averse to all good and propense to all evil, a nature which exposes us to God's displeasure and wrath, even before we have acquired power to understand our duties, or to reflect upon our actions. According to a more modern exposition, it teaches, that we came from the hands of our Maker with such a constitution, and are placed under such influences and circumstances, as to render certain and infallible the total depravity of every human being, from the first moment of his moral agency; and it also teaches, that the offence of the child, who brings into life this ceaseless tendency to unmingled crime, exposes him to the sentence of everlasting damnation. Now, according to the plainest principles of morality, we maintain, that a natural constitution of the mind, unfailingly disposing it to evil and to evil alone, would absolve it from guilt; that to give existence under this condition would argue unspeakable cruelty, and that to punish the sin of this unhappily constituted child with endless ruin, would be a wrong unparalleled by the most merciless despotism.

This system also teaches, that God selects from this corrupt mass a number to be saved, and plucks them, by a special influence, from the common ruin; that the rest of mankind, though left without that special grace which their conversion requires, are commanded to repent, under penalty of aggravated woe; and that forgiveness is promised them, on terms which their very constitution infallibly disposes them to reject, and in rejecting which they awfully enhance the punishments of hell. These proffers of forgiveness and exhortations of amendment, to beings born under a blighting curse, fill our minds with a horror which we want words to express.

That this religious system does not produce all the effects on character, which might be anticipated, we most joyfully admit. It is often, very often, counteracted by nature, conscience, common sense, by the general strain of Scripture, by the mild example and precepts of Christ, and by the many positive declarations of God's universal kindness and perfect equity. But still we think that we see its unhappy influence. It tends to discourage the timid, to give excuses to the bad, to feed the vanity of the fanatical, and to offer shelter to the bad feelings of the malignant. By shocking, as it does, the fundamental principles of morality, and by exhibiting a severe and partial Deity, it tends strongly to pervert the moral faculty, to form a gloomy, forbidding, and servile religion, and to lead men to substitute censoriousness, bitterness, and persecution, for a tender and impartial charity. We think, too, that this system, which begins with degrading human nature, may be expected to end in pride; for pride grows out of a consciousness of high distinctions, however obtained, and no distinction is so great as that which is made between the elected and abandoned of God.

The false and dishonorable views of God, which have now been stated, we feel ourselves bound to resist unceasingly. Other errors we can pass over with comparative indifference. But we ask our opponents to leave to us a GOD, worthy of our love and trust, in whom our moral sentiments may delight, in whom our weaknesses and sorrows may find refuge. We cling to the Divine perfections. We meet them everywhere in creation, we read them in the Scriptures, we see a lovely image of them in Jesus Christ; and gratitude, love, and veneration call on us to assert them. Reproached, as we often are, by men, it is our consolation and happiness, that one of our chief offences is the zeal with which we vindicate the dishonored goodness and rectitude of God.

4. Having thus spoken of the unity of God; of the unity of Jesus, and his inferiority to God; and of the perfections of the Divine character; I now proceed to give our views

of the mediation of Christ, and of the purposes of his mission. With regard to the great object which Jesus came to accomplish, there seems to be no possibility of mistake. We believe, that he was sent by the Father to effect a moral, or spiritual deliverance of mankind; that is, to rescue men from sin and its consequences, and to bring them to a state of everlasting purity and happiness. We believe, too, that he accomplishes this sublime purpose by a variety of methods; by his instructions respecting God's unity, parental character, and moral government, which are admirably fitted to reclaim the world from idolatry and impiety, to the knowledge, love, and obedience of the Creator; by his promises of pardon to the penitent, and of divine assistance to those who labor for progress in moral excellence; by the light which he has thrown on the path of duty; by his own spotless example, in which the loveliness and sublimity of virtue shine forth to warm and quicken, as well as guide us to perfection; by his threatenings against incorrigible guilt; by his glorious discoveries of immortality; by his sufferings and death; by that signal event, the resurrection, which powerfully bore witness to his divine mission, and brought down to men's senses a future life; by his continual intercession, which obtains for us spiritual aid and blessings; and by the power with which he is invested of raising the dead, judging the world, and conferring the everlasting rewards promised to the faithful....

5. Having thus stated our views of the highest object of Christ's mission, that it is the recovery of men to virtue, or holiness, I shall now, in the last place, give our views of the nature of Christian virtue, or true holiness. We believe that all virtue has its foundation in the moral nature of man, that is, in conscience, or his sense of duty, and in the power of forming his temper and life according to conscience. We believe that these moral faculties are the grounds of responsibility, and the highest distinctions of human nature, and that no act is praiseworthy, any farther than it springs from their exertion. We believe, that no dispositions infused into us without our own moral activity, are of the nature of virtue, and therefore, we reject the doctrine of irresistible divine influence on the human mind, moulding it into goodness, as marble is hewn into a statue. Such goodness, if this word may be used, would not be the object of moral approbation, any more than the instinctive affections of inferior animals, or the constitutional amiableness of human beings.

By these remarks, we do not mean to deny the importance of God's aid or Spirit; but by his Spirit, we mean a moral, illuminating, and persuasive influence, not physical, not compulsory, not involving a necessity of virtue. We object, strongly, to the idea of many Christians respecting man's impotence and God's irresistible agency on the heart, believing that they subvert our responsibility and the laws of our moral nature, that they make men machines, that they cast on God the blame of all evil deeds, that they discourage good minds, and inflate the fanatical with wild conceits of immediate and sensible inspiration.

Among the virtues, we give the first place to the love of God. We believe, that this principle is the true end and happiness of our being, that we were made for union with our Creator, that his infinite perfection is the only sufficient object and true resting-place for the insatiable desires and unlimited capacities of the human mind, and that, without him, our noblest sentiments, admiration, veneration, hope, and love, would wither and decay. We believe, too, that the love of God is not only essential to happiness, but to the strength and perfection of all the virtues; that conscience, without the sanction of God's authority and retributive justice, would be a weak director; that benevolence, unless nourished by communion with his goodness, and encouraged by his smile, could not thrive amidst the selfishness and thanklessness of the world; and that self-government, without a sense of the divine inspection, would hardly extend beyond an outward and partial purity. God, as he is essentially goodness, holiness, justice, and virtue, so he is the life, motive, and sustainer of virtue in the human soul.

But, whilst we earnestly inculcate the love of God, we believe that great care is necessary to distinguish it from counterfeits. We think that much which is called piety is worthless. Many have fallen into the error, that there can be no excess in feelings which have God for their object; and, distrusting as coldness that self-possession, without which virtue and devotion lose all their dignity, they have abandoned themselves to extravagances, which have brought contempt on piety. Most certainly, if the love of God be that which often bears its name, the less we have of it the better. If religion be the shipwreck of understanding, we cannot keep too far from it. On this subject, we always speak plainly. We cannot sacrifice our reason to the reputation of zeal. We owe it to truth and religion to maintain, that fanaticism, partial insanity, sudden impressions, and ungovernable transports, are any thing rather than piety.

We conceive, that the true love of God is a moral sentiment, founded on a clear perception, and consisting in a high esteem and veneration, of his moral perfections. Thus, it perfectly coincides, and is in fact the same thing, with the love of virtue, rectitude, and goodness. You will easily judge, then, what we esteem the surest and only decisive signs of piety. We lay no stress on strong excitements. We esteem him, and him only a pious man, who practically conforms to God's moral perfections and government; who shows his delight in God's benevolence, by loving and serving his neighbour; his delight in God's justice, by being resolutely upright; his sense of God's purity, by regulating his thoughts, imagination, and desires; and whose conversation, business, and domestic life are swayed by a regard to God's presence and authority. In all things else men may deceive themselves. Disordered nerves may give them strange sights, and sounds, and impressions. Texts of Scripture may come to them as from Heaven. Their whole souls may be moved, and their confidence in God's favor be undoubting. But in all this there is no religion. The question is, Do they love God's commands, in which his character is fully expressed, and give up to these their habits and passions? Without this, ecstasy is a mockery. One surrender of desire to God's will, is worth a thousand transports. We do not judge of the bent of men's minds by their raptures, any more than we judge of the natural direction of a tree during a storm. We rather suspect loud profession, for we have observed, that deep feeling is generally noiseless, and least seeks display.

We would not, by these remarks, be understood as wishing to exclude from religion warmth, and even transport. We honor, and highly value, true religious sensibility. We believe, that Christianity is intended to act powerfully on our whole nature, on the heart as well as the understanding and the conscience. We conceive of heaven as a state where the love of God will be exalted into an unbounded fervor and joy, and we desire, in our pilgrimage here, to drink into the spirit of that better world. But we think, that religious warmth is only to be valued, when it springs naturally from an improved character, when it comes unforced, when it is the recompense of obedience, when it is the warmth of a mind which understands God by being like him, and when, instead of disordering, it exalts the understanding, invigorates conscience, gives a pleasure to common duties, and is seen to exist in connexion with cheerfulness, judiciousness, and a reasonable frame of mind. When we observe a fervor, called religious, in men whose general character expresses little refinement and elevation, and whose piety seems at war with reason, we pay it little respect. We honor religion too much to give its sacred name to a feverish, forced, fluctuating zeal, which has little power over the life.

Another important branch of virtue, we believe to be love to Christ. The greatness of the work of Jesus, the spirit with which he executed it, and the sufferings which he bore for our salvation, we feel to be strong claims on our gratitude and veneration. We see in nature no beauty to be compared with the loveliness of his character, nor do we find on earth a benefactor to whom we owe an equal debt. We read his history with delight, and learn from it the perfection of our nature. We are particularly touched by his death, which was endured for our redemption, and by that strength of charity which triumphed over his pains. His resurrection is the foundation of our hope of immortality. His intercession gives us boldness to draw nigh to the throne of grace, and we look up to heaven with new desire, when we think, that, if we follow him here, we shall there see his benignant countenance, and enjoy his friendship for ever.

I need not express to you our views on the subject of the benevolent virtues. We attach such importance to these, that we are sometimes reproached with exalting them above piety. We regard the spirit of love, charity, meekness, forgiveness, liberality, and beneficence, as the badge and distinction of Christians, as the brightest image we can bear of God, as the best proof of piety. On this subject, I need not, and cannot enlarge; but there is one branch of benevolence which I ought not to pass over in silence, because we think that we conceive of it more highly and justly than many of our brethren. I refer to the duty of candor, charitable judgment, especially towards those who differ in religious opinion. We think, that in nothing have Christians so widely departed from their religion, as in this particular. We read with astonishment and horror, the history of the church; and sometimes when we look back on the fires of persecution, and on the zeal of Christians, in building up walls of separation, and in giving up one another to perdition, we feel as if we were reading the records of an infernal, rather than a heavenly kingdom. An enemy to every religion, if asked to describe a Christian, would, with some show of reason, depict him as an idolater of his own distinguishing opinions, covered with badges of party, shutting his eyes on the virtues, and his ears on the arguments, of his opponents, arrogating all excellence to his own sect and all saving power to his own creed, sheltering under the name of pious zeal the love of domination, the conceit of infallibility, and the spirit of intolerance, and trampling on men's rights under the pretence of saving their souls.

We can hardly conceive of a plainer obligation on beings of our frail and fallible nature, who are instructed in the duty of candid judgment, than to abstain from condemning men of apparent conscientiousness and sincerity, who are chargeable with no crime but that of differing from us in the interpretation of the Scriptures, and differing, too, on topics of great and acknowledged obscurity. We are astonished at the hardihood of those, who, with Christ's warnings sounding in their ears, take on them the responsibility of making creeds for his church, and cast out professors of virtuous lives for imagined errors, for the guilt of thinking for themselves. We know that zeal for truth is the cover for this usurpation of Christ's prerogative; but we think that zeal for truth, as it is called, is very suspicious, except in men, whose capacities and advantages, whose patient deliberation, and whose improvements in humility, mildness, and candor, give them a right to hope that their views are more just than those of their neighbours. Much of what passes for a zeal for truth, we look upon with little respect, for it often appears to thrive most luxuriantly where other virtues shoot up thinly and feebly; and we have no gratitude for those reformers, who would force upon us a doctrine which has not sweetened their own tempers, or made them better men than their neighbours.

We are accustomed to think much of the difficulties attending religious inquiries; difficulties springing from the slow developement of our minds, from the power of early impressions, from the state of society, from human authority, from the general neglect of the reasoning powers, from the want of just principles of criticism and of important helps in interpreting Scripture, and from various other causes. We find, that on no subject have men, and even good men, ingrafted so many strange conceits, wild theories, and fictions of fancy, as on religion; and remembering, as we do, that we ourselves are sharers of the common frailty, we dare not assume infallibility in the treatment of our fellow-Christians, or encourage in common Christians, who have little time for investigation, the habit of denouncing and contemning other denominations, perhaps more enlightened and virtuous than their own. Charity, forbearance, a delight in the virtues of different sects, a backwardness to censure and condemn, these are virtues, which, however poorly practised by us, we admire and recommend; and we would rather join ourselves to the church in which they abound, than to any other communion, however elated with the belief of its own orthodoxy, however strict in guarding its creed, however burning with zeal against imagined error.

I have thus given the distinguishing views of those Christians in whose names I have spoken. We have embraced this system, not hastily or lightly, but after much deliberation; and we hold it fast, not merely because we believe it to be true, but because we regard it as purifying truth, as a doctrine according to godliness, as able to "work mightily" and to "bring forth fruit" in them who believe. That we wish to spread it, we have no desire to conceal; but we think, that we wish its diffusion, because we regard it as more friendly to practical piety and pure morals than the opposite doctrines, because it gives clearer and nobler views of duty, and stronger motives to its performance, because it recommends religion at once to the understanding and the heart, because it asserts the lovely and venerable attributes of God, because it tends to restore the benevolent spirit of Jesus to his divided and afflicted church, and because it cuts off every hope of God's favor, except that which springs from practical conformity to the life and precepts of Christ. We see nothing in our views to give offence, save their purity, and it is their purity, which makes us seek and hope their extension through the world.

NATHANIEL WILLIAM TAYLOR

Concio ad Clerum
(1828)

"I would rather have ten settled opinions, and nine of them wrong, than have none of them settled," Nathaniel William Taylor (1786–1858) told his students. This amalgam of boldness and dogmatism can be found in much of Taylor's writing. So too can strong traces of it in his mixed career. Besides being, like Jonathan Edwards, both the principal philosophical theologian and revivalist of his era, he was also, unlike Edwards, a lifelong academic, serving as Professor of Dogmatic Theology at Yale Divinity School, whose establishment in 1822 coincided with the founding of America's first university schools of professional theology. Intertwined with all three of these professional roles was Taylor's central preoccupation, which, more generally, was also a problem presented to all presumptively "orthodox" thinkers in this era: how to respond to both the ethical critique of "immoral" Calvinism mounted by the newly self-confident Unitarians and the ecclesiastical activism required by the new revivalism sweeping through the churches of antebellum Protestantism. His answers not only contributed significantly to the evangelical containment of Unitarianism, but they also won the enthusiastic allegiance of the largest and brightest army of graduating ministers of any theologian in antebellum America.

After several years teaching aspects of his theological system in both lectures at Yale and polemics with Unitarians, Taylor presented its central tenets with rationalizing dexterity and rhetorical panache in his sermon, *Concio ad Clerum* ("Advice to the Clergy"), delivered at the college before the annual gathering of the Connecticut Congregational clergy. At the heart of that system was his idea of God's "moral government." Against the Unitarians, he argued that humans sinned inevitably because they were, indeed, depraved "by nature." Yet, he carefully added, they did not *choose* to sin *necessarily*, as Edwards's "consistent Calvinist" followers claimed sinners did, because they had the will to the contrary, a fact proven by a "plain" examination of the scriptures and a "Common Sense" understanding of individual sinful action. Taylor's divine moral system was as balanced (and as circular) as a new nineteenth-century watch. God preserved His justice and benevolence, because He did not cause sin and because He genuinely wanted humans *not* to sin. At the same time, He ensured the justice of the universe, because the freedom that humans had made them morally accountable, while the sins they committed justly deserved punishment. Meanwhile, humans' latent goodness, as reflected in their consciousness of their sinning and their yearning to will otherwise, gave God something to work with, as he infused grace into those (elsewhere Taylor suggested the large majority) whose perverted wills made them choose to indulge their selfish desires. Taylor's liberal orthodox vision was furiously attacked as "Arminian" by conservative Calvinists, who were put off by Taylor's departures from Edwards. Although they exaggerated these deviations somewhat, they were not altogether wrong: Taylor did diminish God's terrible and absolute sovereignty, did render the universe less mysterious, and did present less vividly the indwelling spiritual sense of the converted soul. Taylor offered instead the rock-solid trinity of divinely allowed justice, utility, and a commonsense obedience to God's revealed truth. Fittingly, he would die in the centennial year of his long shadow Edwards's death.

Sidney Earl Mead's *Nathaniel William Taylor, 1786–1858: A Connecticut Liberal* (Chicago, 1942), remains a valuable biography, especially for the theological context of Taylor's ideas. But for a strongly argued counterview stressing the continuities between Taylor and the Edwardsian tradition, see Douglas A. Sweeney, *Nathaniel Taylor and the Legacy of Jonathan Edwards* (New York, 2003). Leo P. Hirrel, *Children of Wrath: New School Calvinism and Antebellum Reform* (Lexington, Ky., 1998), portrays Taylor and his allies as formulators of a Calvinist version of social reform. A helpful discussion of the scholarly community that carried on and further modernized Taylor's "New School" Calvinist tradition at Yale College may be found in Louise L. Stevenson, *Scholarly Means to Evangelical Ends: The New Haven Scholars and the Transformation of Higher Learning in America, 1830–1890* (Baltimore, 1986). For a cogent comparison of Taylor's and Channing's governmental and humanistic rational supernaturalisms, respectively, see Claude Welch, *Protestant Thought in the Nineteenth Century,* 2 vols. (New Haven, 1972–1985), vol. 1: *1799–1870* (New Haven, 1972), chap. 6.

A Sermon Delivered in the Chapel of
Yale College, September 10, 1828

And were by nature the children of wrath, even as others

EPHESIANS II. 3.

THE Bible is a plain book. It speaks, especially on the subject of sin, directly to human consciousness; and tells us beyond mistake, what sin is, and why we sin. In the text, the Apostle asserts the fact of the moral depravity of mankind, and assigns its cause. To be "the children of wrath" is to possess the character which deserves punishment; in other words, it is to be sinners, or to be entirely depraved in respect to moral character. The text then teaches; THAT THE ENTIRE MORAL DEPRAVITY OF MANKIND IS BY NATURE.

In illustrating this position, I shall attempt to show, First, In what the moral depravity of man consists; and Secondly, That this depravity is by nature.

I. By the moral depravity of mankind I intend generally, the entire sinfulness of their moral character,—that state of the mind or heart to which guilt and the desert of wrath pertain. I may say then negatively,

This depravity does not consist in any essential attribute or property of the soul—not in *any thing created* in man by his Maker. On this point, I need only ask,—does God create in men a sinful nature, and damn them for the very nature he creates? Believe this, who can.

Nor does the moral depravity of men consist in a sinful nature, which they have corrupted by being *one* with Adam, and by *acting in his act.* To believe that I am one and the same being with another who existed thousands of years before I was born, and that by virtue of this identity I truly acted in his act, and am therefore as truly guilty of his sin as himself,—to believe this, I must renounce the reason which my Maker has given me; I must believe it also, in face of the oath of God to its falsehood, entered upon the record.

Nor does the moral depravity of men consist in any *constitutional propensities* of their nature. Whoever supposed himself or others to be guilty, for being hungry or thirsty after long abstinence from food or drink; or merely for desiring knowledge, or the esteem of his fellow-men, or any other good, abstractly from any choice to gratify such desires? Who does not know that a perfectly holy man must be subject to all these propensities? The man Christ Jesus was subject to every one of them, for he "was *in all points* tempted like as we are, yet without sin."

Nor does any degree of *excitement* in these propensities or desires, not resulting in choice, constitute moral depravity. Suppose them then, in the providence of God, excited in any degree, and yet the man to prefer doing the will of God to their gratification; all will admit that it is the noblest act of obedience conceivable in a moral being. All will agree, that the man, who always triumphs over excited propensity, who duly subordinates all his desires of inferior good to the will of God is a perfect man. It is the uniform sentiment of inspired truth, that this ruling of the spirit, this government of himself, imparts unrivalled glory to his character. We add the express declaration of the Apostle; "*Blessed* is the man that *endureth* temptation."

Nor does the moral depravity of men consist in *any disposition or tendency* to sin, which is *the cause of all sin.* It is important on this point to guard against error from the

---

Source: Nathaniel W. Taylor, *Concio ad Clerum: A Sermon Delivered in the Chapel of Yale College, September 10, 1828* (New Haven: Hezekiah Howe, 1828). Notes omitted.

ambiguity of terms. There is an obvious distinction between a *disposition* or tendency to sin which is prior to *all* sin, and a *sinful* disposition. I am not saying then, that there is not, what with entire propriety may be called a disposition or tendency to sin, which is the cause of *all* sin; nor that there is not, as *a consequence* of *this* disposition or tendency, what with equal propriety may be called a *sinful* disposition, which is the true cause of all *other* sin, itself excepted. But I say, that that which is the cause of *all* sin, is not itself sin. The cause of all sin, itself sin! Whence then came the first sin? Do you say, from a previous sin as its cause? Then you say, there is a sin before the first sin. Our first parents and fallen angels were once holy. Tell us now, whence came *their* first sin? Do you still repeat, from a previous sin? And what sort of philosophy, reason or common sense, is this—a sin before the first sin—sin before all sin?—Do you say there must be *difficulties* in theology?—I ask must there be *nonsense* in theology?

The question then still recurs, what is this moral depravity for which man deserves the wrath of God? I answer—*it is man's own act, consisting in a free choice of some object rather than God, as his chief good;—or a free preference of the world and of worldly good, to the will and glory of God.*

In support of these views of the subject, I now appeal to the testimony of some of the ablest divines, of Apostles, and of common sense.

Says Calvin, speaking of our text, "our nature is there characterized, not as it was created by God, but as it was vitiated in Adam; *because* it would be unreasonable to make God the author of death." Again, "natural depravity is not a substantial property originally innate, but can be imputed to none but man himself."—He says of sin expressly, "it is voluntary."—If they are convicted of any fault, the Lord justly reproaches them with their own perverseness." "He who sins necessarily, sins no less voluntarily."

The Westminster divines say, that "every sin both original and actual being a transgression of the righteous law of God &c." I ask, is not transgression, action? is it not something done, and done knowingly and voluntarily?

Dr. Bellamy, speaking of the *sinful* propensities of man, says "they are not created by God with the essence of the soul, but result from its native choice, or rather, more strictly, are themselves its native *choice*.—They are not natural in the same sense in which the *faculties* of our souls are; for they are not the workmanship of God, but are our native *choice*, and the *voluntary, free, spontaneous* bent of our hearts."

Says President Edwards, "The inferior principles of selflove and natural appetite which were given only to serve, (and which as he also says, 'were in man in innocence') being alone and left to themselves became reigning principles. Man did set up himself (which by the way was doing something) and the objects of his private affections and appetites as *supreme,* and so they took the place of God. Man's love to his own honour, private interest and pleasure which was before wholly subordinate unto love to God and regard to his glory, (and while thus, he says also, 'all things were in excellent order and in their proper and perfect state,') now disposes him to pursue those objects without regard to God's honour or law." Thus he adds, "it is easy to give an account, how total corruption of heart should follow—without God's putting *any evil* into his heart, or implanting any *bad principle,* or infusing any *corrupt taint,* and *so* becoming the author of depravity."—Again, he says, "If the essence of virtuousness or fault does not lie in the nature of the dispositions or *acts of the mind,* then it is certain, it lies no where at all." "That which makes vice hateful—is a certain deformity in that *evil will,* which is the soul of all vice." "If a thing be from us, and not from our *choice,* it has not the nature of blame-worthiness or ill-desert."

What says St. Paul? In the context he describes the nature of human depravity, and I request you to mark the agreement between his description and that of the last named author. He says "ye, who were dead in trespasses and sins, wherein ye *walked*." You see it was a *walking—living* death. Dead as they were, they did something; "Wherein ye walked according to the course of this world." And what is the course of this world? What is it, but as Edwards says, "Men setting up themselves and the objects of their private affections as supreme, so that these things take the place of God?" What is it, but a world loving the creature more than God the Creator, and acting accordingly.—Again says this Apostle, "Among whom we all had our conversation"—our deportment and manner of life, "in the lusts of the flesh, fulfilling the desires of the flesh and the mind." Now what is this, but freely and voluntarily yielding to propensities, which men ought to restrain and govern, and to subordinate to the will of God; what is it but propensities rising into a free prefer- ence of their objects, and going out into a free purpose of self-gratification? For how can men walk in the lusts of the flesh and fulfil the desires of the flesh and of the mind without preferring the gratification of these lusts and desires to other good? How live and act thus, without choosing to do it? You see then that the sin, which the Apostle describes consists not merely in external action, nor merely in having propensities for natural good, but in acting freely, in yielding to these propensities as a matter of choice and preference.

What saith St. James?—"Let no man say when he is tempted, I am tempted of God," (and was there ever a more fatal tempter than God, if he creates sin in us?)—"for God is not tempted of evil neither tempteth he any man; but every man is tempted when he is drawn away of his own lust and enticed. *Then,* when lust, i. e. strong desire (the same word used by Paul when he says 'I have a *desire* to depart, &c.'—and by our Lord when he says 'with *desire* have I *desired* to eat this passover') *then* when lust hath conceived it bringeth forth sin." Now when does lust or strong desire conceive and bring forth sin? When it rises into a preference of its object, and goes out in action to secure its own gratification.—Or, if you say the lust is itself the sin, (though I think this is ascribing to the Apostle the absurdity of asserting sin before sin,) yet be it so. What then is the lust which is sin, but *a preference of its object*, a *stronger* affection for it than for God? Interpret then the language of the Apostle either way, and you come to the same result,—that all sin consists in freely preferring some inferior good to God. I might add to these many other passages. I only ask what is the import of the most common terms used by Apostles to describe sin in its true nature? I refer to such as these, *minding the flesh, walking in the flesh, living after the flesh, the flesh lust- ing against the Spirit,* what is this, but freely, voluntarily setting up the gratification of our natural propensities and appetites as our chief good, fixing our supreme affections upon it,—setting the heart, when the living God claims it, upon some inferior good?

I now enquire, what says Common Sense?—Take then any action which common sense in the common use of language, calls a *sinful* action,—what is the sin of it? As an example, take the act of murder. Now do we mean by this term in common usage, to denote simply the external act of killing? Clearly not. This may be by accident, or in obe- dience to a divine law.—Do we mean simply the external act, together with the specific volition to perform the act? Clearly not; for there must be such a volition, though the act were performed in obedience to a divine command. It is only when the circumstances and manner of the action evince a selfish or malicious purpose,—a state of mind in which the perpetrator of the deed shows a preference of some private selfish interest to the life of a fellow-being, and to the will of God, that we call it murder. So true is it, that we regard this state of mind as constituting the sin of the action, that could we ascertain independently of external action, the existence of such a preference, we should, as the Bible does, pronounce it murder. This preference then of some private interest, object or end, rather than God, common sense decides to be the sin of all that we call sinful action, and strictly speaking, the sum total of all sin.

But common sense decides the question in another form. And here we come to what I regard as the turning point of the whole controversy. So far as I know, the only argument in support of the opinion that sin pertains to something which is not preference, is based in a supposed decision of common sense. The decision claimed is, that all particular or specific sins, as fraud, falsehood, injustice, unbelief, envy, pride, revenge, result from a *wicked heart,*—from a *sinful disposition,* as the cause or source of such sinful acts.—To this fact, I yield unqualified assent, as "the dictate of the universal sense and reason of mankind," and by this universal judgment, I wish the present question to be decided. Let us then look at the fact in its full force and just application. There is a man then, whose course of life is wholly that of a worldling, his heart and hand shut against human woe, living without prayer, without gratitude, unmindful of God, and rejecting the Saviour of men, devising all, purposing all, doing all, for the sake of this world.—Why is it? You say, and *all* say, and say *right,* it is owing to his love of the world—to his worldly disposition—to a heart set on the world.—Now while all say this, and are right in saying it, we have one simple question to decide, viz. what do all *mean* by it? Every child can answer. Every child knows that the meaning is, that this man does freely and voluntarily fix his affections on worldly good, in preference to God; that the man has chosen the world as his chief good, his portion, his God. He knows that this is what is meant by *a worldly heart, a worldly disposition,* which leads to all *other* sins.—So when we ascribe the sins of the miser to his *avaricious disposition,* we mean his supreme love of money; or the crimes of the hero or conqueror to his *ambitious disposition,* we mean his supreme love of fame, a state of mind which involves *preference* for its object. And whatever previous tendency, or if you will previous disposition, there is to this state of mind; this state of mind itself and not any previous thing as the cause of it, is the *wicked heart*—the sinful disposition of men. They love the creature more than the Creator, when they can and ought to love the Creator most. This forbidden choice of worldly good, this preference of the low and sordid pleasures of earth to God and his glory—this love of the world which excludes the love of the Father,—*this*—*this* is man's depravity. This is that evil treasure of the heart, from which proceed evil things; this is the fountain, the source of all *other* abominations—man's free, voluntary preference of the world as his chief good, amid the revealed glories of a perfect God.

Having attempted to show in what the moral depravity of man consists, I now proceed to show

II. That this depravity is by nature. This I understand the Apostle to assert when he says, "and were by nature the children of wrath."

What then are we to understand, when it is said that mankind are depraved *by nature?*—I answer—*that such is their nature, that they will sin and only sin in all the appropriate circumstances of their being.*

To bring this part of the subject distinctly before the mind, it may be well to remark, that the question between the Calvinists and the Arminians on the point is this—whether the depravity or sinfulness of mankind is truly and properly ascribed to their *nature* or to their *circumstances of temptation?* And since, as it must be confessed, there can no more be sin without circumstances of temptation, than there can be sin without a nature to be tempted, why ascribe sin exclusively to nature?—I answer, it is truly and properly ascribed to *nature,* and *not* to circumstances, because all mankind sin in all the appropriate circumstances of their being. For all the world ascribe an effect to the nature of a thing, when no possible change in its appropriate circumstances will change the effect: or when the effect is uniformly the same in all its appropriate circumstances. To illustrate this by an example: Suppose a tree, which in one soil bears only bad fruit. Change its circumstances, transplant it to another soil, and it bears very good fruit. Now we say, and all would say, the fact that it bore bad fruit was owing to its situation,—to its circumstances; for by changing its circumstances, you have changed its fruit. Suppose now another tree, which bears bad fruit place it where you will;—change its situation from one soil to another, dig about it and dung it, cultivate it to perfection—do what you will, it still bears bad fruit only. Now every one says, the fact is owing to *the nature* of the tree,—the cause is in the tree, in its nature and *not* in its circumstances. So of mankind, change their circumstances as you may; place them where you will within the limits of their being; do what you will to prevent the consequence, you have one uniform result, entire moral depravity. No change of condition, no increase of light nor of motives, no instructions nor warnings, no any thing, within the appropriate circumstances of their being, changes the result. Unless there be some interposition, which is not included in these circumstances, unless something be done which is above nature, the case is hopeless. Place a human being any where within the appropriate limits and scenes of his immortal existence, and such is his nature, that he will be a depraved sinner.

When therefore I say that mankind are entirely depraved *by nature,* I do not mean that their nature is *itself* sinful, nor that their nature is the *physical* or *efficient* cause of their sinning; but I mean that their nature is the occasion, or reason of their sinning;—that *such is their nature, that in all the appropriate circumstances of their being, they will sin and only sin.*

Of this fact, I now proceed to offer some of the proofs.

1. I allege the text. It is here to be remarked, that the Apostle does not say, nor can he mean, that the nature of man is itself sinful. He is assigning the cause of all sin, and says it is *by nature.* If you say that he teaches that the *nature* itself is *sinful,* then as the cause must precede its effect, you charge him with the absurdity of asserting that there is sin, before sin.

The Apostle doubtless conforms his phraseology to common usage, and must mean just what every plain man, using the same language in any similar case would mean. His language too, must be understood with such restrictions as the nature of the subject and correct usage require. How then do we understand one another when using such language? We say the lion by nature eats flesh; the ox by nature eats grass; the tree by nature bears bad fruit; and so in a thousand cases. Now we mean by this, that the *nature* of the thing is such, that uniformly in all its circumstances, it will be the cause or occasion of that which we assert;—that the lion, for example, is of such a nature that he will eat flesh. So when the Apostle asserts, that mankind are by nature sinners, he must mean simply that such is their nature that uniformly in all the appropriate circumstances of their being, they will sin. He can no more mean that the nature itself is sinful, than we can mean in the example, that the nature of the lion is the same thing as the act of eating flesh, of which it is the cause. Still less can we suppose him to authorise the inference that the act of man in sinning, is not in some most important respects widely different from the act of a lion in eating flesh; so different that the one is sin, and the other not. This difference, the known nature of sin obliges us to suppose, it is intended not to deny, but to assume. The resemblance is simply in the *certainty* of the two things, and that which occasions this certainty; though in every other respect, especially in regard to the moral freedom and moral relations of man, the very nature of the acts spoken of, and the *mode* in which the certainty of them is occasioned, they are so diverse that the one is a moral act and has all the requisites of a moral act; the other cannot be a moral act. The Apostle then, using language as all other men use it, traces the universal depravity of men to *their nature,* and thus most explicitly teaches, contrary to the Arminian view, that it is *not* owing to circumstances. If this be not his meaning he uses language as no one else uses it, and the world, critics and all, may be safely challenged to tell what he does mean.

2. The Scriptures in many forms, teach the universal sinfulness of mankind in all the appropriate circumstances of their being.

First. They declare that "the imagination of man's heart is evil from his youth." And I need not cite passages from the word of God to show in how many forms it declares, that there is none that doeth good, no not one; that all have gone out of the way; that all depart from God and yield themselves to sin from the first moment of accountable action—sinning so early, that in the figurative language of the Scriptures they are said to "go astray as soon as they be born speaking lies." Thus God in his testimony, from the beginning to the end of it, asserts this appalling fact,—the absolute uniformity of human sinfulness, throughout the world and throughout all ages. Not a solitary exception occurs. Even those who become holy through grace are not noted as exceptions, and doubtless, because the object is to describe the character which without grace, is common to all. One character then, if God's record be true, prevails with absolute unvarying uniformity, from the fall in Eden till time shall be no longer. Let the circumstances of men be what they may, the eye of God sees and the voice of God declares that "there is no difference,—all are under sin." Now I ask, why is not the exception made—why, without intimating a single exempt case through favourable circumstances, or tracing sin in a single instance to adverse circumstances, why through all the tribes of men, is *all—all sin—all* depravity, in all the circumstances of their existence, according to God's testimony?—If then the absolute uniformity of an event proves that it is *by nature,* then does this uniformity of human sinfulness prove that man is depraved by nature.

Secondly. The Scriptures teach the same thing, by asserting the universal necessity of regeneration by the Holy Spirit. "Except a man be born of water and of the Spirit, he cannot enter into the kingdom of God." Now I ask, how can the interposition of this Divine Agent be necessary to produce holiness in man, if light and truth and motives will do it? God send the Holy Ghost to perform a work, and declare the necessity of his mission for the purpose, when it might as well be done, were there no Holy Ghost? No, Brethren. Without the transforming grace of this Divine Agent, we are all "dead men" for eternity. It follows therefore that man is such a being, or has such a nature that he will sin in all circumstances of his being, if God does not interpose to save.

Thirdly. The *reason* assigned by our Lord for the necessity of the Spirit's agency, is equally decisive.—"That which is born of the flesh is flesh."—If the phrase "is flesh" is equivalent to the expression, *is sinful,* then this passage is a decisive testimony on the point under consideration. Be this however as it may, one thing is undeniable from this conversation of our Lord with Nicodemus, viz. that the first birth of a human being is an event, which involves the necessity of another birth by the divine spirit.—Say if you will, that what our Lord asserts in the passage cited is, that what is by natural birth is simply a man—a human being, thus intending to teach that none were the better for being born of Abraham; still our conclusion remains, viz. to be born once,—to become a human being, is to come under the necessity of being born again of the Spirit. As then we can be at no loss, concerning what it is to be born of the Spirit, it follows that to be born once, involves the certainty of sin—to become a human being is to become a sinner, unless there be a second birth of the Spirit.

Fourthly. I add but one more out of many other scriptural testimonies,—the express declaration of the inefficiency of all truth and motives; or of all that is called *moral suasion.* Saith the Apostle "I have planted, Apollos watered, but God gave the increase; so then neither is he that planteth any thing, nor he that watereth, but God that giveth the increase."—But who are the men that can preach better than Paul and Apollos?—Who can make the arrows of conviction thrill in the conscience, and bring the terrors of guilt and of God into the soul, as did the great Apostle of the Gentiles?—Who by telling of a Saviour's love, or of heavenly glories can do more to charm sin out of the human heart, than Apollos that "eloquent man and mighty in the Scriptures?" And yet Paul was nothing, and Apollos nothing, without God. Let then human eloquence do its best, (and it is not to be despised unless it be put in the place of the Holy Ghost)—let the powers of oratory to persuade, to allure, to awe be exhausted; such is the nature of man, that no accents of a Saviour's love, no lifting up of the everlasting doors, no rising smoke of torment, will save a human being from the character and the condemnation of a depraved sinner.

> "The transformation of apostate man
> From fool to wise, from earthly to divine,
> Is work for Him that made him."

3. I appeal to human consciousness. In making this appeal, I am aware that some may think I am not warranted. They seem to imagine, that sin in its nature and its cause, is something quite mysterious, and hidden from human discovery or comprehension. But, is this so?—God charge *sin* upon a world of accountable subjects,—provide through the blood of his Son redemption from *sin,*—summon all on pain of his wrath to repent of and to forsake *sin,*—foretell a judgment of *sin,*—award to some eternal salvation from *sin,* and to others eternal perdition for *sin*—in a word, give a law by which *is* the *knowledge of sin,* and not a soul of them be able to know or tell what *sin* is, or why he commits it!!—God surely charges sin upon the world as an intelligible reality. He charges it, in the matter and the cause of it upon human consciousness, and human consciousness must respond to the charge in a judgment going beforehand to condemnation. And if men do not know what that is, of which, if the charge of God be true, they are conscious, I beg leave to ask what do they know? What then are they conscious of? They are conscious that in all sin, they do freely and voluntarily set their hearts, their supreme affections on the world, rather than on God; they are conscious that this supreme love of the world is the fountain and source of all their *other* sins.—They are also conscious, that they are led to set their hearts on the world by those propensities for worldly good, which belong to their *nature.* They know this as well as they know why they eat when they are hungry, or drink when they are thirsty. A man choose the world as his chief good, fix his whole heart upon it, and pursue it as if God were unworthy of a thought, and not know why he does so? He knows he does so, for the good there is in it,— for the gratification of those natural propensities for this inferior good, which he ought to govern. He knows that it is not for want of knowledge; that it is not for want of motives to an opposite choice, that he thus makes light of God and everlasting glory. I say, he *knows* this, and I speak to the consciousness of all who hear me. All know, that propensities toward the good which the wealth or honour or pleasure of the world affords,—that desires of happiness from this world in some form, have led them to set their heart upon it, rather than on God. Yes, yes, we all know it, and not a man of us dares deny it.

4. I appeal to facts. And here the question is, making the proper exception in respect to those whose character has been changed by grace, what is the moral history of man since the first apostacy? It begins with a brother's imbruing his hands in a brother's blood—it terminates in the character that qualifies for companionship with the devil and his angels. What (the grace of God excepted) has ever been adequate to restrain

man from sin?—We pass by pagan nations, and merely glance at the utter inefficacy of even the miraculous interpositions of God to prevent sin and reclaim to duty. What was the character of men warned thus for a hundred and twenty years by Noah, God's commissioned servant? Its guilty millions swept to perdition by a deluge of waters, tell us. What the character of those under similar warnings, whom God destroyed by a storm of fire and brimstone on the cities of the plain? This emblem of the tempest of eternal fire, answers.—On mount Sinai God descended amid thunderings and lightnings, and with his own voice promulged his law to the hosts of Israel; and yet as it were, in this very sanctuary of his awful presence, they made a molten calf and said "these be thy Gods, O Israel." In their future history, what a course of apostacies, rebellions, idolatries, amid the warnings of indignant prophets, and a series of miracles by which God shook heaven and earth, at almost every step of his providence? When all else was in vain, when prophets and holy men had been stoned and murdered for their faithfulness in reclaiming men to allegiance to their Maker, see God sending his own Son! Him, though speaking as never man spake, doing the works of God, and proving that in him dwelt all the fulness of the Godhead—him, they nailed to the cross. Look at the persecutions that followed. See how religion doomed to the rack and the fire, stands lifting her streaming eyes to heaven, with none but God to help,—how kings and emperors like tigers, can feast as it were only on Christian blood.—See how every shrine is demolished where weakness can pray, and penitence can weep—how every thing is done, which human malice can invent, to blot out Christianity, name and memorial, from under heaven. And if you think that modern refinement and civilization have alleviated the picture, look at Paris in the French revolution—that city, the seat of art, of taste, of refinement, of every thing that can grace human nature short of religion, is converted as in a moment into a den of assassins, and her streets crowded with scaffolds raining blood on the gloomy processions of death, that pass beneath them.—But we need not look to other ages or other countries. In this land on which the Sun of Righteousnes sheds his clearest, brightest day—here where the light of salvation, with all its motives, with all the love and grace of the Saviour, with the glories of heaven and terrors of hell, is concentred and poured burning and blazing upon the human heart,—here in this assembly, what do we find? Assassins and highwaymen, murderers of fathers and murderers of mothers? No. But we do find, despisers of the Lord that bought them. We find every one whom grace has not made to differ, an enemy of God. And when the veil of eternity shall be drawn, and the light of eternity reveal the results—when the sinner's place in hell shall be fixed and the measure of his woe be full, then shall he know what that depravity is, which now tramples under foot the Son of God, and does despite unto the Spirit of grace.—These are the stubborn things, called facts; facts which show how dreadful is the depravity of man under the most perfect efforts of God to prevent it; facts which show into what depths of guilt and woe, the creature man will plunge, if the arm of grace does not hold him back; facts which show that he is depraved, not for want of light or motives, but depraved *by nature*. Especially, what other account can be given of the depravity which prevails, amid the splendours of Gospel day?

Remarks.

1. It is consistent with the doctrine of this discourse; that infants should be saved through the redemption of Christ. They belong to a race who by nature and in all the appropriate circumstances of their being, will sin. The very birth of a human being is an event which involves the certainty of entire moral depravity, without the supernatural interposition

of God to prevent it.—Do you ask, when he will begin to sin? I answer, I *do not know,* the precise instant. The Scriptures do not tell us,—and I can see no possible use, in saying that we *do* know, what it is most palpably evident we do *not* know. Is it then said, that we sin before we are born? But there is no such thing as sinning without acting; and an Apostle has told us of two infants, who, while "not yet born" had done "neither good nor evil." Do you say they begin to sin at their birth? But some knowledge of duty is requisite to sin, and we know, for the inspired historian has told us, of some children who had "no knowledge between good and evil." Do you say it must be so, for they die and death among human beings proves sin. But children die before they are born, and perhaps also some children die who have no knowledge between good and evil. Do you say they are proper subjects of baptism, and this proves sin. How do you know, that baptism is not administered to infants simply as a seal of the covenant, exhibiting and ratifying its promises of good respecting them? Do you say, the language of the Scriptures, is *universal,* that *all* have sinned. The language too is universal, that we are to "preach the Gospel to *every creature.*" Of course, if your mode of interpretation is right, we are to preach the Gospel to infants,— and to animals also!—to *every creature.*

Instead then of attempting to assign the precise instant in which men begin to sin, we choose to say they sin as soon as they become moral agents—they sin *as soon as they can;* and who will affirm that this is not soon enough? If it be asked how soon, can they sin? I answer very early; even *so early,* that they are justly represented as sinning from their youth—and in the figurative language of the scriptures, from their birth,—and even before birth; *so early* that the literal interval, if there be such an interval, between birth and the commencement of sin is either so short or unimportant, that the Spirit of inspiration has not thought it worthy of particular notice.

If then you ask, what becomes of an infant if he dies, while yet an infant?—I answer, he may be saved; in my belief he is saved, through the redemption that is in Christ Jesus. If you ask, how can this be? I reply, he belongs to a race who by nature, in all the circumstances of their immortal being without the grace of this redemption, will sin. Place an infant then from his birth under the influence of the most perfect example and instructions,—yea place him amid heaven's purity and heaven's songs, and who shall say that he will not, without the supernatural grace of God's Spirit, be a depraved sinner and fall under condemnation?—When made meet therefore for the celestial paradise and admitted there, *his* song may tell of the grace that brought him to its glories.

2. That sin or guilt pertains exclusively to voluntary action, is the true principle of orthodoxy. We have seen that the older orthodox divines assert this principle, and that they abundantly deny that God is the creator or author of sin. By some strange fatality however these writers, are not believed by many, on these points; and we are told, as the ground for discrediting these unequivocal declarations, that they also constantly affirm that men are *born* with a corrupt and sinful nature, and with guilt upon them. True, very true. But now to the real question—how in the view of these writers, does this nature with which they are born become corrupt and sinful?—By being so created? No such thing: for this they constantly and vehemently deny; and give as we have seen this reason for denying it,—that it would make God the author of sin. How then is it, that in their view each has a corrupt and sinful nature when born, and yet that God does not create it? Why, by the *real act* of each—by each one's corrupting his nature, just as Adam did his. But how can this be? They tell us how; viz. that Adam and his posterity were in God's estimation and were thus truly constituted, ONE BEING, ONE MORAL WHOLE;—so that in Adam's act of sin, all his posterity *being* ONE *with him,* also acted as truly as Adam himself; and so, each

and all corrupted their nature as freely and voluntarily as Adam corrupted his nature. The question is, not whether this is not very absurd, but what did these men believe and teach? And I say they *did* believe and *did* teach that all Adam's posterity *acted* in his act, sinned in *him* and fell with *him,* and are considered truly and properly as sinning *in manner and form,* just as Adam sinned; and every one who has read his catechism or his primer must know it.—This class of divines then never thought of predicating sin or guilt, except in cases of free voluntary action. So far as *they* are concerned therefore the doctrine of physical depravity is a theological novelty.

The history of this peculiarity, shows the same thing. The process has been this. The doctrine of imputation being rejected, as it has been in New England for many years, and with it *our personal identity with Adam,* there was no way left in which we could be viewed as the older divines viewed us; the criminal authors when born, of our own corrupt and sinful nature. Still the doctrine of a corrupt and sinful nature *as such* has been retained by *some,* and thus what the older divines made every man *as one in Adam* the author of, God must now answer for as its author by a creative act. Hence some have so professed and so preached, and have talked much of their own orthodoxy and of the heresy of others, and yet after all the outcry, not a theological writer of eminence has ventured to this hour to publish to the world such a doctrine. The entire annals of orthodoxy do not contain the doctrine that *God creates* a sinful nature in man. Those men who have fought the battles of orthodoxy from the reformation to the present day, and who have been esteemed its successful defenders, have held most firmly and asserted abundantly, that all sin or fault must belong *to the acts of the mind*—to the *evil will,* or belong to nothing at all. Brethren, were these men heretics for this? Is the man who believes and teaches the same thing, a heretic?

3. The view of sin or moral depravity maintained in this discourse, cannot be justly ascribed to mental perversion, or to any sinister or selfish design. For, what possible motive or object, can be assigned as the cause of perverting truth and evidence in such a case?—If popularity were the object, the charges of having departed from the true faith by renouncing former opinions, repeated from one end of the land to the other, show at least in respect to some of us, how ill-judged has been this expedient to gain popularity. Nor is this view of sin adopted for the sake of rejecting any one doctrine of orthodoxy, or of setting up any anti-orthodox peculiarity. For, they who adopt this view, as fully believe in the certainty of the universal and entire sinfulness of mankind—they as fully believe this sinfulness or depravity to be *by nature*—they as fully believe in the inefficacy of moral suasion and in the necessity of the Holy Spirit's agency in regeneration, as any other men. They no more deny that infants are sinners from their birth, that infants are saved through Christ, nor that they must become holy (if at all) by divine influence, than other men. And although they do deny that God creates the sin in them, and that sin pertains to any thing but voluntary action, yet the denial of either position is not an anti-orthodox peculiarity, for the ablest orthodox divines have ever denied both. The charge then of adopting this view of sin, for the purpose of opposing any doctrine of orthodoxy, is a slanderous charge.

Can any cause then of mental perversion be fairly charged? The human mind pervert truth and evidence for the sake of believing that to be sin, which as it is agreed on all hands, imparts to sin its most malignant aspect, and reveals its fullest tendencies? Men believe that to be sin, which deserves the deepest damnation which any thing can deserve, merely because they wish to believe it! You may as well suppose that for a similar reason, a man should believe his doom already fixed in hell itself. If there be any view of sin which human selfishness will resist to the last, it is this which so embodies all its guilt and all its terrors; it is this which as we all know, makes the conscience of the wicked writhe in anguish, and an ungodly world hate the servant as it hated the Master whom it crucified. Such a view of sin, is not a device to obtain popularity, nor to corrupt the Gospel of God.

4. The universal depravity of mankind is not inconsistent with the moral perfection of God. It is not uncommon to ask, (and I admit the facts on which the objection rests)— how could a God of perfect sincerity and goodness bring a race of creatures into existence, and give them such *a nature* that they will all certainly sin and incur his wrath?—It is also added, to increase the weight of the objection,—why render this universal sinfulness of a race, the consequence of one man's act—why not give to each a fair trial for himself? I answer, God does give to each a fair trial for himself. Not a human being does or can become thus sinful or depraved but by his own choice. God does not compel him to sin by the *nature* he gives him. Nor is his sin, although a consequence of Adam's sin, in such a sense its consequence, as not to be a free voluntary act of his own. He sins freely, voluntarily. There is no other way of sinning. God, (there is no irreverence in saying it,) can make nothing else sin, but the sinner's act.—Do you then say, that God gave man a nature, which He knew would lead him to sin?—What if He did?—Do you know that God could have done better, better on the whole or better, if he gave him existence at all, even for the individual himself? The error lies in the gratuitous assumption, that God could have adopted a moral system, and prevented all sin, or at least, the present degree of sin. For, no man knows this—no man can prove it. The assumption therefore is wholly unauthorised as the basis of the present objection, and the objection itself groundless. On the supposition that the evil which exists is in respect to divine prevention, incidental to the best possible system, and that notwithstanding the evil, God will secure the greatest good possible to him to secure, who can impeach either his wisdom or his goodness because evil exists? I say then that as ignorance is incompetent to make an objection, and as no one knows that this supposition is not a matter of fact, no one has a right to assert the contrary, or even to think it. Suppose then God had adopted a different system, who is competent to foretell or to conjecture the results,—or even the results of one iota of change in the present system? Suppose God had made you just like Adam or even like Lucifer, and placed you in similar circumstances, do you know that you would not have sinned as he did? How do you know that had you commenced your immortal career with such aggravated guilt, God would not have found it necessary to send you to hell without an offer of mercy, and that you would not have sunk in deeper woe than that which now awaits you?—How do you know that what might have been true respecting yourself, had not been true of any other possible system of accountable beings? How do you know, that had God ordered things otherwise than he has, this very world now cheered with the calls of mercy and brightened with the hopes of eternal life, yea that heaven itself would not now be trembling under the thunders of retributive vengeance? Man,—man in his ignorance, alter the plan and procedure of his God! How dare he think of it? Beware, ye insects of a day, ye are judging Him "whom the heaven of heavens cannot contain."

Now think of this, fellow sinner. God in adopting the present system with all the sin incidental to it, may have adopted the best possible. In giving to you the nature which he has, and in placing you in the circumstances in which he has, he may have done the best he could even for you—Say then is your existence a curse, for which your Maker is to be reproached? Is it a curse at all, unless *you* make it so? Does not his preference of holiness to sin on your part, evince toward you, perfect benevolence? Listen to his calls and intreaties and say if this is not the voice of sincerity and truth. Listen to his oath, "that he has no pleasure at all in your death," and say if he would regret your return to duty and to life? Look around you and see what proofs of love, what intimations of grace and glory provided for you, gladden every moment of your being. Think what God has done to save you; how he has laid his wrath on one for your sake, how he has cleared away the darkness and tempest around his throne and with smiles of mercy invites you to himself,—how he bade angels sing in rapturous song "good will" to the guilty and the lost—how under his commission the swift messenger bears these tidings to you and to all,—how mercy with tears points you to that crown of life—how God himself with the earnestness of a suppliant father,—with the sincerity of a God entreats you to receive his great salvation. Say now, is he not good; is he not sincere?—What "child of wrath," will not trust in such a God to save him?

5. We see the importance of this view of man's depravity, compared with any other, in its bearing on the preaching of the Gospel. To what purpose, do we preach the Gospel to men, if we cannot reach the conscience with *its charge of guilt* and *obligations to duty?* And how I ask can this be done, unless sin and duty be shown to consist simply and wholly in acts and doings which are their own? Can this be done if we tell them and they believe us, that their sin is something which God creates in them; or something done by Adam thousands of years before they existed? I care not what you call it, taste, disposition, volition, exercise, if it be that which *cannot* be unless God creates it, and cannot but be if he exerts his power to produce it, can we fasten the arrows of conviction in the conscience, and settle on the spirit the forebodings of a *merited* damnation? Can men be induced to make an effort to avoid sin which is thus produced in them, or to perform duties which must with the same passivity on their part, be produced in them? Does God charge on men, as that which deserves his endless indignation, what Himself does? Does God summon men to repentance with commands and entreaties, and at the same time tell them, that all efforts at compliance are as useless, as the muscular motions of a corpse to get life again. Does this book of God's inspiration, shock and appal the world, with the revelation of such things, respecting God and respecting man? Will the charge of *such sin* on man, touch the secret place of tears? Will the exhibition of such a God, allure the guilty to confide in his mercy? If so, preach it out—preach it consistently,—preach nothing to contradict it,—dwell on your message, that God creates men sinners and damns them for being so.—Tell them such is *their* nature and such the *mode* of his interposition, that there is no more hope from acting on the part of the sinner than from not acting; tell them they may as well sleep on, and sleep away these hours of mercy, as attempt any thing in the work of their salvation; that all is as hopeless with effort as without it. Spread over this world such a curtain of sackcloth, such a midnight of terror, and how as the appropriate effect, would each accountable immortal, either sit down in the sullenness of inaction, or take his solitary way to hell in the frenzy of despair!

But such is not the message of wrath and of mercy, by which a revolted world is to be awed and allured back to its Maker. The message we are to deliver to men is a message of wrath, because they are the perpetrators of the deed that deserves wrath.—It is a message of mercy to men who by acting, are to comply with the terms of it, and who can never hope to comply even through God's agency, without putting themselves to the doing of *the very thing* commanded of God.—And it is only by delivering such a message, that we, Brethren, can be "workers together with God." Let us then go forth with it; and clearing God, throw all the guilt of sin with its desert of wrath, upon the sinner's single self. Let us make him see and feel that he can go to hell only as a self-destroyer—that it is this fact, that will give those chains their strength to hold him, and those fires the anguish of their burning. Let us if we can, make this conviction take hold of his spirit, and ring in his conscience like the note of the second death. If he trembles at the sound in his ears, then let us point him to that mercy which a dying Jesus feels for him, and tell him with the sympathies of men who have been in the same condemnation, that he need but to love and trust HIM, and heaven is his inheritance. Without derogating from the work of God's Spirit let us urge him to his duty—*to his duty*—*to his duty,* as a point-blank direction to business now on hand and now to be done. With the authorised assurance that "peradventure God may give him repentance," let us make known to him the high command of God "*strive* to enter in at the strait gate"—and make him hear every voice of truth and mercy in heaven and on earth, echoing the mandate.

Then shall the ministers of reconciliation be clad with truth as with a garment, and delivering their message not only in its substance but in its true manner and form, shall commend themselves to every man's conscience in the sight of God. Having his strength perfected in their weakness, they shall go forth "as archangels strong," and bidding the wide earth receive God's salvation, the bands of hell shall break, and a redeemed world return to the dominion of its God.

Finally, I cannot conclude without remarking, how fearful are the condition and prospects of the sinner. His sin is his own. He yields himself by his own free act, by his own choice, to those propensities of his nature, which under the weight of God's authority he *ought to govern.* The gratification of these he makes his chief good, immortal as he is. For this he lives and acts—this he puts in the place of God—and for this, and for nothing better he tramples on God's authority and incurs his wrath. Glad would he be, to escape the guilt of it. Oh—could he persuade himself that the fault is not his own,—this would wake up peace in his guilty bosom. Could he believe that God is bound to convert and save him; or even that he could make it certain that God will do it,—this would allay his fears,—this would stamp a bow on the cloud that thickens, and darkens, and thunders damnation on his guilty path. But his guilt is all his own, and a just God may leave him to his choice. He is going on to a wretched eternity, the self-made victim of its woes. Amid sabbaths and bibles, the intercessions of saints, the songs of angels, the intreaties of God's ambassadors, the accents of redeeming love, and the blood that speaketh peace, he presses on to death. God beseeching with tenderness and terror—Jesus telling him he died once and could die again to save him—mercy weeping over him day and night—heaven lifting up its everlasting gates—hell burning, and sending up its smoke of torment, and the weeping and the wailing and the gnashing of teeth, within his hearing,—and onward still he goes.—See the infatuated immortal!—Fellow sinner,—IT IS YOU.

Bowels of divine compassion—length, breadth, height, depth of Jesus' love—Spirit of all grace, save him—Oh save him—or he dies forever.

CHARLES GRANDISON FINNEY

Selection from *Lectures on Revivals of Religion* (1835)

Charles Grandison Finney (1792–1875), evangelical preacher and later president of Oberlin College, was the most influential American revivalist of the nineteenth century. This influence was partly due to his enormous talents as a theatrical, lawyerlike persuader of souls as well as to his ingenuity in introducing to urban audiences controversial "new measures" like protracted meetings and the "anxious seat." But much of it was also due to the appeal of his systematic and thoroughly post-Calvinist revivalist theology. Finney's most famous delineation of that theology was his *Lectures on Revivals of Religion,* a compilation of discourses he delivered to audiences in New York City in the winter of 1834–35. Instead of Calvinism's deterministic and partly mystical drama of sin and salvation, Finney offered unconverted sinners a way that was at once coercive, rational, and activistic. There was only one "truth"— that of God. At the same time, absolutely critical to the conversion of "sluggish" men and women to that truth were ministers' elaborate and calculated manipulation of revivals or "excitements," which were brought about, Finney insisted, by the same sort of cause-and-effect techniques as those of any valid scientific experiment. Yet sinners' actions were also crucial. Going beyond Taylor's idea that sinners had the ability to *will* to the contrary of their sinful nature, Finney argued that men and women had the capacity to "obey" God's "truth," and, by thereby "acting right," contribute to their own salvation. Nor, once converted, could they rest. On the contrary, their subsequent sanctification required them to participate in missionary and reform crusades, which gave them opportunities to exercise their moral ability to grow in grace until they became as "perfect as God" and, in so doing, facilitate the similarly growing kingdom of Jesus Christ on earth.

William G. McLoughlin, Jr., *Modern Revivalism: Charles Grandison Finney to Billy Graham* (New York, 1959), 3–121, provides a still valuable survey of Finney's career and thought. Keith J. Hardman, *Charles Grandison Finney, 1792–1875: Revivalist and Reformer* (Syracuse, 1987); and Charles E. Hambrick-Stowe, *Charles G. Finney and the Spirit of American Evangelicalism* (Grand Rapids, 1996), are useful biographies. For a study of the legalistic dimension of Finney's theology, see David L. Weddle, *The Law as Gospel: Revival and Reform in the Theology of Charles G. Finney* (Metuchen, N.J., 1985).

I

WHAT A REVIVAL OF RELIGION IS

TEXT.—*O Lord, revive thy work in the midst of the years, in the midst of the years make known; in wrath remember mercy.*

—HAB. iii.2.

It is supposed that the prophet Habakkuk was contemporary with Jeremiah, and that this prophecy was uttered in anticipation of the Babylonish captivity. Looking at the judgments which were speedily to come upon his nation, the soul of the prophet was wrought up to an agony, and he cries out in his distress, "O Lord, revive thy work." As if he had said, "O Lord, grant that thy judgments may not make Israel desolate. In the midst of these awful years, let the judgments of God be made the means of reviving religion among us. In wrath remember mercy."

Religion is the work of man. It is something for man to do. It consists in obeying God. It is man's duty. It is true, God induces him to do it. He influences him by his Spirit, because of his great wickedness and reluctance to obey. If it were not necessary for God to influence men—if men were disposed to obey God, there would be no occasion to pray, "O Lord, revive thy work." The ground of necessity for such a prayer is, that men are wholly indisposed to obey; and unless God interpose the influence of his Spirit, not a man on earth will ever obey the commands of God.

A "Revival of Religion" presupposes a declension. Almost all the religion in the world has been produced by revivals. God has found it necessary to take advantage of the excitability there is in mankind, to produce powerful excitements among them, before he can lead them to obey. Men are so sluggish, there are so many things to lead their minds off from religion, and to oppose the influence of the gospel, that it is necessary to raise an excitement among them, till the tide rises so high as to sweep away the opposing obstacles. They must be so excited that they will break over these counteracting influences, before they will obey God.

Look back at the history of the Jews, and you will see that God used to maintain religion among *them* by special occasions, when there would be a great excitement, and people would turn to the Lord. And after they had been thus revived, it would be but a short time before there would be so many counteracting influences brought to bear upon them, that religion would decline, and keep on declining, till God could have time—so to speak—to shape the course of events so as to produce another excitement, and then pour out his Spirit again to convert sinners. Then the counteracting causes would again operate, and religion would decline, and the nation would be swept away in the vortex of luxury, idolatry, and pride.

There is so little *principle* in the church, so little firmness and stability of purpose, that unless they are greatly excited, they will not obey God. They have so little knowledge, and their principles are so weak, that unless they are excited, they will go back from the path of duty, and do nothing to promote the glory of God. The state of the world is still such, and probably will be till the millennium is fully come, that religion must be mainly

Source: Charles Grandison Finney, *Lectures on Revivals of Religion,* ed. William G. McLoughlin (Cambridge: The Belknap Press of Harvard University Press, 1960), 9–23, 403, 414–16, 419–20, 425–26. Editor's notes and some paragraph numbers omitted. Reprinted by permission of Harvard University Press © 1960 by the President and Fellows of Harvard College.

promoted by these excitements. How long and how often has the experiment been tried, to bring the church to act steadily for God, without these periodical excitements! Many good men have supposed, and still suppose, that the best way to promote, religion, to go along *uniformly,* and gather in the ungodly gradually, and without excitement. But however such reasoning may appear in the abstract, *facts* demonstrate its futility. If the church were far enough advanced in knowledge, and had stability of principle enough to *keep awake,* such a course would do; but the church is so little enlightened, and there are so many counteracting causes, that the church will not go steadily to work without a special excitement. As the millennium advances, it is probable that these periodical excitements will be unknown. Then the church will be enlightened, and the counteracting causes removed, and the entire church will be in a state of habitual and steady obedience to God. The entire church will stand and take the infant mind, and cultivate it for God. Children will be trained up in the way they should go, and there will be no such torrents of worldliness, and fashion, and covetousness, to bear away the piety of the church, as soon as the excitement of a revival is withdrawn.

It is very desirable it should be so. It is very desirable that the church should go on steadily in a course of obedience without these excitements. Such excitements are liable to injure the health. Our nervous system is so strung that any powerful excitement, if long continued, injures our health and unfits us for duty. If religion is ever to have a pervading influence in the world, it can't be so; this spasmodic religion must be done away. Then it will be uncalled for. Christians will not sleep the greater part of the time, and once in a while wake up, and rub their eyes, and bluster about, and vociferate, a little while, and then go to sleep again. Then there will be no need that ministers should wear themselves out, and kill themselves, by their efforts to roll back the flood of worldly influence that sets in upon the church. But as yet the state of the Christian world is such, that to expect to promote religion without excitements is unphilosophical and absurd. The great political, and other worldly excitements that agitate Christendom, are all unfriendly to religion, and divert the mind from the interests of the soul. Now these excitements can only be counteracted by *religious* excitements. And until there is religious principle in the world to put down irreligious excitements, it is in vain to try to promote religion, except by counteracting excitements. This is true in philosophy, and it is a historical fact.

It is altogether improbable that religion will ever make progress among *heathen* nations except through the influence of revivals. The attempt is now making to do it by education, and other cautious and gradual improvements. But so long as the laws of mind remain what they are, it cannot be done in this way. There must be excitement sufficient to wake up the dormant moral powers, and roll back the tide of degradation and sin. And precisely so far as our own land approximates to heathenism, it is impossible for God or man to promote religion in such a state of things but by powerful excitements.—This is evident from the fact that this has always been the way in which God has done it. God does not create these excitements, and choose this method to promote religion for nothing, or without reason. Where mankind are so reluctant to obey God, they will not act until they are excited. For instance, how many there are who know that they ought to be religious, but they are afraid if they become pious they shall be laughed at by their companions. Many are wedded to idols, others are procrastinating repentance, until they are settled in life, or until they have secured some favorite worldly interest. Such persons never will give up their false shame, or relinquish their ambitious schemes, till they are so excited that they cannot contain themselves any longer.

These remarks are designed only as an introduction to the discourse. I shall now proceed with the main design, to show,

I.   What a revival of religion is not;
II.   What it is; and,
III. The agencies employed in promoting it.

I. A REVIVAL OF RELIGION NOT A MIRACLE.

1. A miracle has been generally defined to be, a Divine interference, setting aside or suspending the laws of nature. It is not a miracle, in this sense. All the laws of matter and mind remain in force. They are neither suspended nor set aside in a revival.

2. It is not a miracle according to another definition of the term miracle—*something above the powers of nature*. There is nothing in religion beyond the ordinary powers of nature. It consists entirely in the *right exercise* of the powers of nature. It is just that, and nothing else. When mankind become religious, they are not *enabled* to put forth exertions which they were unable before to put forth. They only exert the powers they had before in a different way, and use them for the glory of God.

3. It is not a miracle, or dependent on a miracle, in any sense. It is a purely philosophical result of the right use of the constituted means—as much so as any other effect produced by the application of means. There may be a miracle among its antecedent causes, or there may not. The apostles employed miracles, simply as a means by which they arrested attention to their message, and established its Divine authority. But the miracle was not the revival. The miracle was one thing; the revival that followed it was quite another thing. The revivals in the apostles' days were connected with miracles, but they were not miracles.

I said that a revival is the result of the *right* use of the appropriate means. The means which God has enjoyed for the production of a revival, doubtless have a natural tendency to produce a revival. Otherwise God would not have enjoined them. But means will not produce a revival, we all know, without the blessing of God. No more will grain, when it is sowed, produce a crop without the blessing of God. It is impossible for us to say that there is not as direct an influence or agency from God, to produce a crop of grain, as there is to produce a revival. What are the laws of nature, according to which, it is supposed, that grain yields a crop? They are nothing but the constituted manner of the operations of God. In the Bible, the word of God is compared to grain, and preaching is compared to sowing seed, and the results to the springing up and growth of the crop. And the result is just as philosophical in the one case, as in the other, and is as naturally connected with the cause.

I wish this idea to be impressed on all your minds, for there has long been an idea prevalent that promoting religion has something very peculiar in it, not to be judged of by the ordinary rules of cause and effect; in short, that there is no connection of the means with the result, and no tendency in the means to produce the effect. No doctrine is more dangerous than this to the prosperity of the church, and nothing more absurd.

Suppose a man were to go and preach this doctrine among farmers, about their sowing grain. Let him tell them that God is a sovereign, and will give them a crop only when it pleases him, and that for them to plow and plant and labor as if they expected to raise a crop is very wrong, and taking the work out of the hands of God, that it interferes with his sovereignty, and is going on in their own strength; and that there is no connection between the means and the result on which they can depend. And now, suppose the farmers should believe such doctrine. Why, they would starve the world to death.

Just such results will follow from the church's being persuaded that promoting religion is somehow so mysteriously a subject of Divine sovereignty, that there is no natural connection between the means and the end. What *are* the results? Why, generation after generation have gone down to hell. No doubt more than five thousand millions have gone down to hell, while the church has been dreaming, and waiting for God to save them without the use of means. It has been the devil's most successful means of destroying souls. The connection is as clear in religion as it is when the farmer sows his grain.

There is one fact under the government of God, worthy of universal notice, and of everlasting remembrance; which is, that the most useful and important things are most easily and certainly obtained by the use of the appropriate means. This is evidently a principle in the Divine administration. Hence, all the *necessaries* of life are obtained with great *certainty* by the use of the simplest means. The luxuries are more difficult to obtain; the means to procure them are more intricate and less certain in their results; while things absolutely hurtful and poisonous, such as alcohol and the like, are often obtained only by torturing nature, and making use of a kind of infernal sorcery to procure the death-dealing abomination. This principle holds true in moral government, and as spiritual blessings are of surpassing importance, we should expect their attainment to be connected with *great certainty* with the use of the appropriate means; and such we find to be the fact; and I fully believe that could facts be known, it would be found that when the appointed means have been *rightly* used, spiritual blessings have been obtained with greater uniformity than temporal ones.

II. I AM TO SHOW WHAT A REVIVAL IS.

It presupposes that the church is sunk down in a backslidden state, and a revival consists in the return of the church from her backslidings, and in the conversion of sinners.

1. A revival always includes conviction of sin on the part of the church. Backslidden professors cannot wake up and begin right away in the service of God, without deep searchings of heart. The fountains of sin need to be broken up. In a true revival, Christians are always brought under such convictions; they see their sins in such a light, that often they find it impossible to maintain a hope of their acceptance with God. It does not always go to that extent; but there are always, in a genuine revival, deep convictions of sin, and often cases of abandoning all hope.

2. Backslidden Christians will be brought to repentance. A revival is nothing else than a new beginning of obedience to God. Just as in the case of a converted sinner, the first step is a deep repentance, a breaking down of heart, a getting down into the dust before God, with deep humility, and forsaking of sin.

3. Christians will have their faith renewed. While they are in their backslidden state they are blind to the state of sinners. Their hearts are as hard as marble. The truths of the Bible only appear like a dream. They admit it to be all true; their conscience and their judgment assent to it; but their faith does not see it standing out in bold relief, in all the burning realities of eternity. But when they enter into a revival, they no longer see men as trees walking, but they see things in that strong light which will renew the love of God in their hearts. This will lead them to labor zealously to bring others to him. They will feel grieved that others do not love God, when they love him so much. And they will set themselves feelingly to persuade their neighbors to give him their hearts. So their love to men will be renewed. They will be filled with a tender and burning love for souls. They will have a longing desire for the salvation of the whole world. They will be in agony for individuals whom they want to have saved; their friends, relations, enemies. They will not only be urging them to give their hearts to God, but they will carry them to God in the arms of faith, and with strong crying and tears beseech God to have mercy on them, and save their souls from endless burnings.

4. A revival breaks the power of the world and of sin over Christians. It brings them to such vantage ground that they get a fresh impulse towards heaven. They have a new foretaste of heaven, and new desires after union to God; and the charm of the world is broken, and the power of sin overcome.

5. When the churches are thus awakened and reformed, the reformation and salvation of sinners will follow, going through the same stages of conviction, repentance, and reformation. Their hearts will be broken down and changed. Very often the most abandoned profligates are among the subjects. Harlots, and drunkards, and infidels, and all sorts of abandoned characters, are awakened and converted. The worst part of human society are softened, and reclaimed, and made to appear as lovely specimens of the beauty of holiness.

III. I AM TO CONSIDER THE AGENCIES EMPLOYED IN CARRYING FORWARD A REVIVAL OF RELIGION.

Ordinarily, there are three agents employed in the work of conversion, and one instrument. The agents are God,—some person who brings the truth to bear on the mind,—and the sinner himself. The instrument is the truth. There are *always two* agents, God and the sinner, employed and active in every case of genuine conversion.

1. The agency of God is two-fold; by his Providence and by his Spirit.

(1.) By his providential government, he so arranges events as to bring the sinner's mind and the truth in contact. He brings the sinner where the truth reaches his ears or his eyes. It is often interesting to trace the manner in which God arranges events so as to bring this about, and how he sometimes makes every thing seem to favor a revival. The state of the weather, and of the public health, and other circumstances concur to make every thing just right to favor the application of truth with the greatest possible efficacy. How he sometimes sends a minister along, just at the time he is wanted! How he brings out a particular truth, just at the particular time when the individual it is fitted to reach is in the way to hear!

(2.) God's special agency by his Holy Spirit. Having direct access to the mind, and knowing infinitely well the whole history and state of each individual sinner, he employs that truth which is best adapted to his particular case, and then sets it home with Divine power. He gives it such vividness, strength, and power, that the sinner quails, and throws down his weapons of rebellion, and turns to the Lord. Under his influence, the truth burns and cuts its way like fire. He makes the truth stand out in such aspects, that it crushes the proudest man down with the weight of a mountain. If men were *disposed* to obey God, the truth is given with sufficient clearness in the Bible; and from preaching they could learn all that is necessary for them to know. But because they are wholly *disinclined* to obey it, God clears it up before their minds, and pours in a blaze of convincing light upon their souls, which they cannot withstand, and they yield to it, and obey God, and are saved.

2. The agency of men is commonly employed. Men are not mere *instruments* in the hands of God. Truth is the instrument. The preacher is a moral agent in the work; he acts; he is not a mere passive instrument; he is voluntary in promoting the conversion of sinners.

3. The agency of the sinner himself. The conversion of a sinner consists in his obeying the truth. It is therefore impossible it should take place without his agency, for it consists in *his* acting right. He is influenced to this by the agency of God, and by the agency of men. Men act on their fellow-men, not only by language, but by their looks, their tears, their daily deportment. See that impenitent man there, who has a pious wife. Her very looks, her tenderness, her solemn, compassionate dignity, softened and moulded into the image

of Christ, are a sermon to him all the time. He has to turn his mind away, because it is such a reproach to him. He feels a sermon ringing in his ears all day long.

Mankind are accustomed to read the countenances of their neighbors. Sinners often read the state of a Christian's mind in his eyes. If his eyes are full of levity, or worldly anxiety and contrivance, sinners read it. If they are full of the Spirit of God, sinners read it; and they are often led to conviction by barely seeing the countenance of Christians.

An individual once went into a manufactory to see the machinery. His mind was solemn, as he had been where there was a revival. The people who labored there all knew him by sight, and knew who he was. A young lady who was at work saw him, and whispered some foolish remark to her companion, and laughed. The person stopped and looked at her with a feeling of grief. She stopped, her thread broke, and she was so much agitated she could not join it. She looked out at the window to compose herself, and then tried again; again and again she strove to recover her self-command. At length she sat down, overcome with her feelings. The person then approached and spoke with her; she soon manifested a deep sense of sin. The feeling spread through the establishment like fire, and in a few hours almost every person employed there was under conviction, so much so, that the owners, though worldly men, were astounded, and requested to have the works stop and have a prayer meeting; for they said it was a great deal more important to have these people converted than to have the works go on. And in a few days, the owners and nearly every person employed in the establishment were hopefully converted. The eye of this individual, his solemn countenance, his compassionate feeling, rebuked the levity of the young woman, and brought her under conviction of sin; and this whole revival followed, probably in a great measure, from so small an incident.

If Christians have deep feeling on the subject of religion themselves, they will produce deep feeling wherever they go. And if they are cold, or light and trifling, they inevitably destroy all deep feeling, even in awakened sinners.

I knew a case, once, of an individual who was very anxious, but one day I was grieved to find that her convictions seemed to be all gone. I asked her what she had been doing. She told me she had been spending the afternoon at such a place, among some professors of religion, not thinking that it would dissipate her convictions to spend an afternoon with professors of religion. But they were trifling and vain, and thus her convictions were lost. And no doubt those professors of religion, by their folly, destroyed a soul, for her convictions did not return.

The church is required to use the means for the conversion of sinners. Sinners cannot properly be said to use the means for their own conversion. The church uses the means. What sinners do is to submit to the truth, or to resist it. It is a mistake of sinners, to think they are using means for their own conversion. The whole drift of a revival, and every thing about it, is designed to present the truth *to* your mind, for your obedience or resistance.

REMARKS.

1. Revivals were formerly regarded as miracles. And it has been so by some even in our day. And others have ideas on the subject so loose and unsatisfactory, that if they would only *think,* they would see their absurdity. For a long time, it was supposed by the church, that a revival was a miracle, an interposition of Divine power which they had nothing to do with, and which they had no more agency in producing, than they had in producing thunder, or a storm of hail, or an earthquake. It is only within a few years that ministers generally have supposed revivals were to be *promoted,* by the use of means designed and adapted specially to that object. Even in New England, it has been supposed that revivals came just

as showers do, sometimes in one town, and sometimes in another, and that ministers and churches could do nothing more to produce them, than they could to make showers of rain come on their own town, when they are falling on a neighboring town.

It used to be supposed that a revival would come about once in fifteen years, and all would be converted that God intended to save, and then they must wait until another crop came forward on the stage of life. Finally, the time got shortened down to five years, and they supposed there might be a revival about as often as that.

I have heard a fact in relation to one of these pastors, who supposed revivals might come about once in five years. There had been a revival in his congregation. The next year, there was a revival in a neighboring town, and he went there to preach, and staid several days, till he got his soul all engaged in the work. He returned home on Saturday, and went into his study to prepare for the Sabbath. And his soul was in an agony. He thought how many adult persons there were in his congregation at enmity with God—so many still unconverted—so many persons *die* yearly—such a portion of them unconverted—if a revival does not come under five years, so many adult heads of families will be in hell. He put down his calculations on paper, and embodied them in his sermon for the next day, with his heart bleeding at the dreadful picture. As I understood it, he did not do this with any expectation of a revival, but he felt deeply, and poured out his heart to his people. And that sermon awakened *forty heads of families,* and a powerful revival followed; and so his theory about a revival once in five years was all exploded.

Thus God has overthrown, generally, the theory that revivals are miracles.

2. Mistaken notions concerning the sovereignty of God, have greatly hindered revivals.

Many people have supposed God's sovereignty to be something very different from what it is. They have supposed it to be such an arbitrary disposal of events, and particularly of the gift of his Spirit, as precluded a rational employment of means for promoting a revival of religion. But there is no evidence from the Bible, that God exercises any such sovereignty as that. There are no facts to prove it. But every thing goes to show, that God has connected means with the end through all the departments of his government—in nature and in grace. There is no *natural* event in which his own agency is not concerned. He has not built the creation like a vast machine, that will go on alone without his further care. He has not retired from the universe, to let it work for itself. This is mere atheism. He exercises a universal superintendence and control. And yet every event in nature has been brought about by means. He neither administers providence nor grace with that sort of sovereignty, that dispenses with the use of means. There is no more sovereignty in one than in the other.

And yet some people are terribly alarmed at all direct efforts to promote a revival, and they cry out, "You are trying to get up a revival in your own strength. Take care, you are interfering with the sovereignty of God. Better keep along in the usual course, and let God give a revival when he thinks it is best. God is a sovereign, and it is very wrong for you to attempt to get up a revival, just because *you think* a revival is needed." This is just such preaching as the devil wants. And men cannot do the devil's work more effectually, than by preaching up the sovereignty of God, as a reason why we should not put forth efforts to produce a revival.

3. You see the error of those who are beginning to think that religion can be better promoted in the world without revivals, and who are disposed to give up all efforts to produce religious excitements. Because there are evils arising in some instances out of great excitements on the subject of religion, they are of opinion that it is best to dispense with them altogether. This cannot, and must not be. True, there is danger of abuses. In cases of great *religious* as well as all other excitements, more or less incidental evils may

be expected of course. But this is no reason why they should be given up. The best things are always liable to abuses. Great and manifold evils have originated in the providential and moral governments of God. But these *foreseen* perversions and evils were not considered a sufficient reason for giving them up. For the establishment of these governments was on the whole the best that could be done for the production of the greatest amount of happiness. So in revivals of religion, it is found by experience, that in the present state of the world, religion cannot be promoted to any considerable extent without them. The evils which are sometimes complained of, when they are real, are incidental, and of small importance when compared with the amount of good produced by revivals. The sentiment should not be admitted by the church for a moment, that revivals may be given up. It is fraught with all that is dangerous to the interests of Zion, is death to the cause of missions, and brings in its train the damnation of the world.

FINALLY—I have a proposal to make to you who are here present. I have not commenced this course of Lectures on Revivals to get up a curious theory of my own on the subject. I would not spend my time and strength merely to give you instructions, to gratify your curiosity, and furnish you something to talk about. I have no idea of preaching *about* revivals. It is not my design to preach so as to have you able to say at the close, "We *understand* all about revivals now," while you do *nothing*. But I wish to ask you a question. What do you hear lectures on revivals for? Do you mean that whenever you are convinced what your duty is in promoting a revival, you will go to work and practice it?

Will you follow the instructions I shall give you from the word of God, and put them in practice in your own hearts? Will you bring them to bear upon your families, your acquaintances, neighbors, and through the city? Or will you spend the winter in learning *about* revivals, and do nothing *for* them? I want you, as fast as you learn anything of the subject of revivals, to put it in practice, and go to work and see if you cannot promote a revival among sinners here. If you will not do this, I wish you to let me know at the beginning, so that I need not waste my strength. You ought to decide *now* whether you will do this or not. You know that we call sinners to decide on the spot whether *they* will obey the gospel. And we have no more authority to let you take time to deliberate whether *you* will obey God, than we have to let sinners do so. We call on you to unite now in a solemn pledge to God, that you will do your duty as fast as you learn what it is, and to pray that He will pour out his Spirit upon this church and upon all the city this winter....

XIX

INSTRUCTIONS TO CONVERTS

...Young converts should be faithfully warned against adopting a *false standard in religion*. They should not be left to fall in behind old professors, and keep them before their minds as a standard of holy living. They should always look at Christ as their model. Not aim at being as good Christians as the old church members, and not think they are doing pretty well because they are as much awake as the old members of the church. But they should aim at being holy, and not rest satisfied till they are as perfect as God. The church has been greatly injured for the want of attention to this matter. Young converts have come forward, and their hearts were warm and their zeal ardent enough to aim at a high standard, but they were not directed properly, and so they soon settle down into the notion that what is good enough for others is good enough for them, and therefore they never aim higher than those who are before them. And in this way the church instead of rising with every revival higher and higher in holiness, is kept nearly stationary.

Young converts should be taught *to do all their duty*. They should never make a compromise with duty, nor think of saying "I will do *this* as an offset for neglecting *that*." They should never rest satisfied till they have done their duty of every kind, in relation to their families, the church, Sabbath Schools, the impenitent around them, the disposal of their property, the conversion of the world. Let them do their duty, as they feel it when their hearts are warm; and never attempt to pick and choose among the commandments of God.

They should be made to feel that *they have no separate interest*. It is time Christians were made actually to feel that they have no interest whatever, separate from the interest of Jesus Christ and his kingdom. They should understand that they are incorporated into the family of Jesus Christ, as members in full, so that their whole interest is identified with his. They are embarked with him, they have gone on board, and taken their all. And henceforth they have nothing to do, or nothing to say, except as it is connected with this interest and bearing on the cause and kingdom of Christ....

XX

INSTRUCTIONS OF YOUNG CONVERTS

They must be taught *what sanctification is.* "What!" you will say, "do not all who are Christians know what sanctification is?" No, many do not. Multitudes would be as much at a loss to tell intelligibly what sanctification is, as they would be to tell what religion is. If the question were asked of every professor of religion in this city, What is sanctification? I doubt if one in ten would give a right answer. They would blunder just as they do when they undertake to tell what religion is, and speak of it as something dormant in the soul, something that is put in, and lies there, something that may be practised or not, and still be in them. So they speak of sanctification as if it were a sort of washing off of some defilement, or a purging out of some physical impurity. Or they will speak of it as if the faculties were steeped in sin, and sanctification is taking out the stains. This is the reason why some people will pray for sanctification, and practise sin, evidently supposing that sanctification is something that *precedes* obedience. They should be taught that sanctification is not something that precedes obedience, some change in the nature or the constitution of the soul. But sanctification *is obedience,* and, as a progressive thing, consists in obeying God more and more perfectly.

Young converts should be taught so as to understand *what perseverance is.* It is astonishing how people talk about perseverance. As if the doctrine of perseverance was "Once in grace, always in grace," or "Once converted, sure to go to heaven." This is not the idea of perseverance. The true idea is, that if a man is truly converted, HE WILL CONTINUE TO OBEY GOD. And as a *consequence,* he will surely go to heaven. But if a person gets the idea, that because he is converted, *therefore* he will assuredly go to heaven, that man will almost assuredly go to hell.

Young converts should be taught *to be religious in every thing.* They should aim to be religious in every department of life and in all that they do. If they do not *aim* at this, they should understand that they have no religion at all. If they do not intend and aim to keep all the commandments of God, what pretence can they make to piety? Whosoever shall keep the whole law and yet offend in one point, he is guilty of all. He is justly subject to the whole penalty. If he disobeys God habitually in one particular, he does not in fact obey him in any particular. Obedience to God *consists* in the state of the heart. It is being willing to obey God; willing that God should rule in all things. But if a man habitually disobeys God, in any one particular, he is in a state of mind, that renders obedience in any thing else impossible. To say that in some things a man obeys God, out of respect to his authority, and that in some other things he refuses obedience, is absurd. The fact is, that obedience to God consists in an obedient state of heart, a preference of God's authority and commandments to every thing else. If, therefore, an individual *appears* to obey in some things, and yet perseveringly and knowingly disobeys in any one thing, he is deceived. He offends in one point, and this proves that he is guilty of all; in other words, that he does not, *from the heart,* obey at all. A man may pray half of the time and have no religion; if he does not keep the commandments of God, his very prayer will be hateful to God. "He that turneth away his ear from hearing the law, even *his prayer* shall be abomination." Do you hear that? If a man refuses to obey God's law, if he refuses to comply with any one duty, he cannot pray, he has no religion, his very devotions are hateful....

They should *aim at being perfect.* Every young convert should be taught, that if it is not his *purpose* to live without sin, he has not yet begun to be religious. What is religion, but a supreme purpose of heart or disposition to obey God? If there is not this, there is no religion at all. It is one thing to *profess to be perfect,* and another thing to profess and feel that you *ought to be* perfect. It is one thing to say, that men ought to be perfect, and can be if they are so disposed, and another thing to say that *they are* perfect. If any are prepared to say that they are perfect, all I have to say is, Let them prove it. If they are so, I hope they will show it by their actions, otherwise we can never believe they are perfect.

But it is the duty of all to *aim* at being perfect. It should be their constant purpose, to live wholly to God, and obey all his commandments. They should live so, that if they should sin it would be an inconsistency, an exception, an individual case, in which they act contrary to the fixed and general purpose and tenor of their lives. They *ought not* to sin at all, they are bound to be as holy as God is, and young converts should be taught to set out in the right course, or they will never be right....

If young converts are rightly instructed and trained, it will generally be seen that they will take the right side on all great subjects that come before the church. Subjects are continually coming up before the churches, on which they have to take ground, and on many of them there is often no little difficulty to make all the church take right ground. Take the subject of Tracts, or Missions, or Sabbath schools, or Temperance, for instance, and what cavils, and objections, and resistance, and opposition, have been encountered from members of the church in different places. Go through the churches, and where you find young converts have been well taught, you never find *them* making difficulty, or raising objections, or putting forth cavils. I do not hesitate to charge it upon pastors and older members of churches, that there are so many who have to be dragged up to the right ground on all such subjects. If they had grounded them well in the principles of the gospel at the outset, when they were first converted, they would have seen the application of their principles to all these things. It is curious to see, and I have had great opportunity to see, how ready young converts are to take right ground, on any subject that may be proposed. See what they are willing to do for the education of ministers, for missions, for moral reform, for the slaves. If the great body of young converts from the late revivals had been well grounded in gospel principles, you would have found in them, throughout the church, but one heart and one soul in regard to every question of duty that occurs. Let their early education be right, and you have got a body of Christians that you can depend on. If it had been general in the church, O, how much more strength there would have been in all her great movements for the salvation of the world.

JOHN HUMPHREY NOYES

Selection from *The Berean*
(1847)

"Be ye therefore perfect, even as your Father which is in Heaven is perfect." Upon this injunction of Matthew, Finney built his doctrine of perfect holiness, which posited that the converted were capable of receiving a "second blessing" that made them able to commit sinless acts of disinterested benevolence and, by this means, help bring about the coming millennium. A moderate version of this doctrine, stressing (as did Finney) only potential and temporary sinlessness, had been a staple of Methodist preaching since John Wesley's time. Meanwhile other antebellum evangelicals utilized similar ideas as a justification for antislavery activism and other kinds of radical reform.

The most extreme version of this evangelical perfectionism was espoused by John Humphrey Noyes (1811–1886). A graduate of Dartmouth and a student of theology at Yale, the center of the post-Calvinist "new divinity," Noyes went on to found the Oneida Community, which put into practice, in line with Noyes's theories, a Bible-based communist economy and a highly regulated system of multiple sexual partnerships. These activities earned him nearly universal condemnation by his evangelical associates, but he always regarded them as logical deductions from the basic premise of evangelical perfectionism, which abjured selfishness and promised perfect holiness. Furthermore, the security of this perfect holiness, Noyes argued in the two articles printed herein, was no mere subjective fancy or external moral law, but faith in the marvelous character of the Bible itself and the reality of Christ's crucifixion and resurrection. Because men and women had already been redeemed through Christ and the millennium already begun with this second coming (which Noyes dated at A.D. 70), individuals had only to receive the grace that made possible complete salvation from sin in this world.

Robert David Thomas, *The Man Who Would Be Perfect: John Humphrey Noyes and the Utopian Impulse* (Philadelphia, 1977), is a psychobiographical study. But the best approach to Noyes's thought is still through the fascinating, if discursive, collections of his writings and papers edited by Noyes's nephew, George Wallingford Noyes, *Religious Experience of John Humphrey Noyes: Founder of the Oneida Community* (New York, 1923), and *John Humphrey Noyes: The Putney Community* (Oneida, N.Y., 1931). For a helpful discussion of the theological basis of Noyes's radical sexual ideas, see Timothy B. Spears, "Circles of Grace: Passion and Control in the Thought of John Humphrey Noyes," *New York History,* 70 (January 1989), 79–103. Spencer Klaw, *Without Sin: The Life and Death of the Oneida Community* (New York, 1993), is a readable study that brings alive the communitarian context of Noyes's ideology.

The Faith Once Delivered to the Saints

It is apparent to the most superficial inspection of the scriptures, that the religion even of the Old Testament saints, and much more that of the primitive church, was one which placed man in direct communication with God. Not a saint can be found among all whose names are enrolled on the inspired record—from Abel to the last of the apostles—whose biography does not savor strongly of that marvelousness which necessarily waits upon the open manifestations of Divinity. Dreams, visions, oracles, angelic visitations, conversations with God, inspirations, infusions of superhuman power, &c., are profusely scattered through the history of Judaism. And yet the glory of New Testament Christianity as far exceeds that of the preceding dispensation, in respect to all these and many other manifestations of God's presence, as sun-light exceeds star-light.[1]

---

1. Phrenologists define marvelousness to be "credulity—disposition to believe what is not proved, or what are considered supernatural manifestations." (*Fowler & Kirkham, p.* 141.) Spurzheim says it is "a tendency to believe in inspirations, presentiments, phantoms," &c. Combe says the organ of marvelousness" is uniformly large in fanatics. It predominates in the Rev. Edward Irving, and in all his followers whom I have seen." (*Combe's Phrenology,* p.79.) By the marvelousness of the Bible, we mean that characteristics of the Bible which requires "marvelousness" in those who receive it. The following statistics give the result of a running examination of the whole Bible with reference to this point:

MARVELOUS EVENTS RECORDED IN THE BIBLE.

Supernatural omens,..14
Significant dreams,..23
Appearances of angels and other supernatural beings,..51
Supernatural visions,...66
Miracles specifically mentioned, (not including the vast number
alluded to in Mat. 8: 16, and like passages,)...175
Inspired prophecies, revelations, and other direct communications from the Lord.....................449

Total, 778

The items here enumerated, by no means embrace all the matter in the Bible that might be classed under the head of marvelousness. Special providences, religious exercises like those described in many of the psalms, and in short every recognition of the presence and direct agency of God or any other invisible being, might be placed in the same category. But the statistics already given are sufficient for our purpose. It is manifest that marvelousness is a very prominent characteristic of the Bible; and any one who will take the trouble to examine, may see that it pervades every part, we might almost say, every page of the book. It is not confined to those portions which were written in the earlier and darker ages of Judaism. Modern philosophy teaches that supernatural wonders diminish, as light increases. But we find the contrary of this true of the Bible. The character and history of Jesus Christ is surrounded with more of the materials of marvelousness, than that of Moses and the prophets. The new dispensation which he introduced, with all its increase of light, was accompanied by dreams, visions, appearances of angels, miracles, revelations and wonders of every kind, in greater abundance than ever was known before. The New Testament begins with the record of the supernatural conception of Jesus Christ, and ends with a gorgeous vision of the spiritual world.

Thus it is manifest that the Bible is fitted to feed and perpetuate what the sages of these philosophical times call *fanaticism.* A book, filled with excellent stories of special providences, miraculous deliverances, angelic visions, spiritual ecstasies, &c. &c.,—and especially a book which is so implicitly credited as the Bible—cannot be generally read without begetting in many minds the image of its own spirit. Such men as Swedenborg and Irving, however false and pernicious may have been their views in other respects, were certainly more

---

Source: John Humphrey Noyes, The Berean: A Manual for the Help of Those Who Seek the Faith of the Primitive Church (Putney, Vt.: Spiritual Magazine, 1847), 47–51, 178–81.

The main difference between the two dispensations, was this: In accordance with the general character of the introductory dispensation, God manifested himself to the Jewish saints in an *external* manner; i.e., by visions, vocal oracles, angels, or at the most by those external influences of the Spirit which affect, as it were, only the outer surface of the soul, as in the case of prophetic inspiration. Whereas he manifested himself to Christian believers in the deep sanctuary of their hearts, making them radically new creatures, taking away their sins, and giving them full and permanent fellowship with his own vitality. The *indwelling* of God was a mystery which was "hid from the ages and generations" of Judaism, but was manifested to the primitive church. There was also this further difference. God manifested himself, even externally, only to a *few* under the Jewish dispensation. Whereas the promise of Christianity was, "I will pour out my spirit upon *all flesh*: and your sons and your daughters shall prophesy, and your young men shall see visions, and your old men shall dream dreams." This promise was fulfilled. The special manifestations which had before been confined to a few individuals in every age, were given, on the day of Pentecost and afterwards, to the whole church of God.

These differences, however, do not destroy the identity of faith under the two dispensations. The religion of both—i.e. the religion of the whole Bible—was based on immediate communication with God. The later manifestations were more complete, spiritual and universal, and of course produced greater changes of character, than the earlier; but the faith which invited and apprehended those manifestations, was the same in all ages. Hence Paul, in the 11th of Hebrews, traces the history of one and the same faith, by a continuous line, from the beginning of the world till the advent of perfection by Christianity. The generic element in all the instances of faith which he adduces—and in the faith of Christianity as well as Judaism,—is an apprehension of, and confidence in the living God, as actually present, manifesting himself by signs and wonders, communicating superhuman wisdom and power, overruling, for the believer's comfort and protection, the powers of the spiritual and natural worlds.

We must distinctly mark the difference between this faith, and several counterfeits which have been extensively substituted for it.

1. Many talk about "contending earnestly for the faith once delivered to the saints," as though this were to be referred to *theological controversy,* and as though the faith of the saints were belief in a mere scheme of doctrine. But was it by belief in an orthodox creed that the saints "stopped the mouths of lions, quenched the violence of fire, escaped the edge of the sword, out of weakness were made strong?" Nothing can be plainer than that "the faith once delivered to the saints," as exemplified by Paul in the 11th of Hebrews, was directed, not toward doctrines, but *toward the living God.*

2. Philosophers and poets have an apprehension of God as manifested in *"the works of nature,"* which they call faith. But this implies no personal acquaintance with God. Believers of this kind sustain no nearer relation to God than one man would to another, in case the parties had never seen each other or had any communication—but only had seen each other's productions. Whereas the faith exhibited in the Bible, manifestly introduced

---

nearly in spiritual concord with the Bible, in respect to marvelousness, than the philosophers and theologians who deride them. And while marvelousness remains a part of human nature, and the Bible is allowed to feed it, we may assuredly look for the appearance of such "fanatics" *ad infinitum* Those conservators therefore, of the public morals, whose business it is to put down "pestilent heresies," must either return to the policy of Popery, and forbid the reading of the Bible by any but the clergy, (and even then some *clerical* enthusiast like Luther will break forth,) or they must give up their business, and seek the welfare of mankind by endeavoring to *enlighten* and *purify the* fanatical propensities, which they can neither smother nor control. [J. H. N. note]

the saints to personal fellowship with God, so that they walked with him, conversed with him, received messages and messengers from him, and lived under his immediate protection and superintendence.

3. The faith of many religious persons consists in receiving the Bible as the word of God. They apprehend God as revealed *through the scriptures.*—This kind of faith is like that last mentioned—only the believer in this case has not merely seen the works of the unknown being, but has received a letter from him, which he reveres and believes. The letter however is not addressed to him individually, but is a circular sent "to all whom it may concern." So that there is still no personal acquaintance.

4. Another class of religionists, a little in advance of the former, by systematizing the legal developments of the Bible, build up in their minds what they call a *moral government,* and place God at the head of it as king over moral beings. Their faith apprehends God in his *official* capacity. The relation between him and them is that of king and subject. Their king, like the kings of this world, is high and lifted up, far above his common subjects, distant and reserved. They see him only through his laws and state transactions. In all this there is no personal acquaintance, no vital union. God thus apprehended, is not *in* the believer, ruling by spiritual power, but ["]*over* him" ruling by written laws. This is not "the faith once delivered to the saints."

5. Many of those already mentioned, and others, go so far as to admit certain measures of God's *personal* influence. They conceive of him not only as manifested through his works, his word, and his moral government, but as operating by his spirit on the mind. But they are careful to disclaim any thing like revelation, inspiration, and supernatural power. They regard the operations of the Spirit as only imperceptible auxiliaries to the truth, influences which never manifest themselves directly to the consciousness, or in any other way; and which never would be recognized at all, if the Bible did not testify of their existence. This is the worst counterfeit of all; for while it appropriates to itself much of the language of the ancient saints, and so makes itself the most respectable substitute for Bible faith, it as effectually excludes the living God from his proper place in the heart, and in the church, as any of the grosser forms of unbelief. It is this kind of faith which, while pretending to honor the spiritual power of God as the chief agent of salvation, yet dares not trust it, but thrusts the law into its place as the great presiding influence; and makes the Spirit its secondary adjunct. It is this kind of faith which daubs over the apostasy of Christendom from the standard of the primitive saints, by teaching that "the age of miracles is past"—an assumption, or rather a presumptuous falsehood, which is better fitted to destroy the legitimate influence of the Bible than all the enactments of Popery; since the Bible relates only to an age of miracles—its entire religion and morality is indissolubly interwoven with supernatural manifestations: it is therefore adapted only to an age of miracles, and if it were true that the age of miracles is past, men of the present day would have little more practical interest in it than they have in the Arabian Nights' Entertainment. It is this kind of faith, which, while it loudly praises the prophets and apostles, derides as visionary enthusiasm every approach toward that direct communication with God which was the glory of prophets and apostles; and thus covertly, but really casts infamy on the entire religion of the Bible, and on all the saints of God.

The true faith, of which the foregoing are counterfeits, while it recognizes the reflection of diving radiance in the works of nature, in the Bible, and in the moral government of the universe, still turns with chief interest to the direct manifestations of God by his Spirit; and it limits not the Holy One to imperceptible and dubious influences, but gives him room to reveal himself now, as in past ages, by all the appropriate operations of his infinite energy.

There is an intrinsic and palpable absurdity in the idea of admitting the Spirit of God into the world, and yet curtailing its appropriate and formerly actual manifestations, under the plea that the age of miracles is past. The age of miracles certainly is not past with God. He is as mighty as ever; and wherever his Spirit comes at all, there is super-human, i.e., miraculous power; and if miraculous power is admitted into the world in the smallest degree, it cannot be said that the age of miracles is past with reference to man; and the way is therefore open for all the primitive manifestations of divine power. And then, how irrational it is to suppose that the same agent which once gave to man gifts of superhuman wisdom and power, is still present, *but only as a latent auxiliary of the clergy!* What a blasphemous descent is this, from the sublime to the ridiculous! As well might a purblind dotard say that the sun still shines, but the age of daylight is past, and only one of the seven colors which were the elements of ancient sunlight,—and that the dimmest—is now given to the world!

We repeat it—the great central idea of "the faith once delivered to the saints," was that of *the living God present in individual believers and in the church, and manifest by manifold tokens of superhuman wisdom and power.* And let it be observed that the rela-tion between God and man which this idea involves, is not, as unbelief would suggest, unnatural, and foreign from the original design of man's constitution. God made man in his own image, with the very intent that this relation should exist between them—that man should be the temple, or, we may say, the *complement* of God. Adam at the beginning lived in open companionship with his Maker. As woman was married to man, so man was married to God. And it was to restore this union, which sin had severed, that the Son of God was made flesh, and suffered death. The renewal and everlasting confirmation of the *at-one-ment* which existed between God and the first Adam, was the great achievement of the second Adam. Moreover, it is plainly predicted in scripture that the human race in its final glory, shall return to open companionship with God—that "his tabernacle shall be with men, and he shall dwell with them, and shall be their God." A relation which existed at the beginning—which Christ came and died to establish—which will exist in the final state of man, cannot be unnatural. On the contrary, the present ordinary condition of mankind, living without God, is unnatural—at variance utterly with their original consti-tution. Man without his original spiritual Head, is as much out of the order of nature, as woman without a husband. The apostasy is the widowhood of the human race.

As the manifest indwelling of God is the essence of Bible religion, so it is the corner stone of Bible morality, education, social order, and physical well-being. All schemes of reform and improvement for soul and body, which have not this for their starting point and their end, however popular and promising they may be, are as certainly impostures as the Bible is a book of truth, and man was made to be the temple of his Maker. Who but a madman can expect to check the spiritual and physical disorders of social life, and restore mankind to harmony and happiness, while the first great wheel of the whole machinery by which the result is to be attained, is wanting? Trees without roots will as soon bud and blossom and bring forth fruit, as man will attain holiness of heart, virtue of action, wis-dom of thought and health of body, without the indwelling of God.

The true reason why the great Reformation by Luther has failed, is that it turned the faith of the world to the Bible, rather than to God. Protestants are learning by sore experi-ence that the Bible is *not* a "sufficient rule of faith and practice." The numberless and still multiplying schisms of the reformed churches, are making it more and more manifest that the balance-wheel of original Christianity is not yet recovered—that the Bible, without *inspiration* as the regulator of interpretation, is but an "apple of discord." In like manner all the subordinate reforms of more recent date which have any thing but the living God for their centre and propelling power, will sooner or later fail.

On the other hand, let the foundation of Bible faith be laid,—let God be invited by believing hearts to make his tabernacle with men, and reveal all the glory of his wisdom and power as he revealed it to the primitive church; let Him be installed and acknowledged as the ever-present and presiding Genius of Reform, and speedily sin and death will flee away, and the earth become as Eden.

Let all, then, who seek salvation for themselves, or long for the regeneration of the world—"*contend earnestly for the* FAITH ONCE DELIVERED TO THE SAINTS."

Perfectionism

Perceiving nothing in the sound or form of the word Perfectionist, essentially odious, and assuredly anticipating the time of its redemption from infamy, we will take the liberty to explain the meaning of it, as used by those who consent to bear it.

We will not attempt to state what a Perfectionist is *not;*—for this would require us to dissect and disclaim all the varying and incongruous images of perfection conjured up by the word in the various fancies of men, from a picture of a monk in sackcloth and ashes, to that of a seraph with six wings. If it is sufficient to say, that in the minds of those who consent to bear the name, so far as we know, perfection is predicated of only a single attribute, viz., holiness; and of that only in a limited sense. We find in the Bible, as well as in the nature of the case, three modifications of *perfect holiness:*—perfection of obedience; perfection of security of obedience; and perfection of holiness by experience or suffering. These distinctions may be easily understood by a simple illustration. The success of a general on a battlefield, may be perfect in a threefold manner. 1. He may be simply successful at the outset. 2. He may be successful at the outset, with an assurance of final victory. 3. He may be successful by the actual accomplishment of the victory.

1. The holiness of Adam, and of the angels that left their first estate, was perfect, considered simply as obedience to law, but destitute of prospective security, as was proved by their apostacy.

2. The holiness of Christ, the second Adam, was perfect, both as present obedience to law, and as prospectively secure. Yet in another sense it was imperfect, during his residence on earth. For "though he were a *son,* yet *learned he obedience* by the things which he suffered; and *being made perfect,* he became the author of eternal salvation to all them that obey him."—"For it became him, by whom are all things, and for whom are all things, in bringing many sons unto glory to make the captain of their salvation *perfect through sufferings."* Previous to his crucifixion, this captain of our salvation was perfectly successful in his conflict with sin, both presently and prospectively; yet the battle was before him. So Paul, while counting all things but loss, that he might overcome death by knowing the fellowship of the sufferings of Christ, denied that he had already attained the victory, or was already perfect; and yet in the next breath, falling back upon an inferior meaning of the word, he could say, "Let us therefore, as many as be perfect be thus minded."

3. The present holiness of Christ, on the throne of his glory, and of those who, having overcome by his blood, have attained that likeness of his resurrection toward which Paul was urging his way, is perfected in the highest sense. The battle is fought; the victory won; their holiness is perfect as obedience—perfect in security—and perfect by victory over suffering. Perfectionists, then, if they may be allowed to designate the place which they suppose they hold on the scale of perfection, universally disclaim the profession of

attainments above those of the *suffering* Son of God. They covet not the premature glory of victory before battle. They stand with Paul on the middle ground, between the perfection of Adam and of Christ, saved from sin—eternally saved—yet "saved by hope, waiting for the adoption, to wit, the redemption of their bodies."

We acknowledge that the phrase *perfect holiness* is almost a solecism in the first of the three senses above mentioned; for any thing short of perfect *present* obedience, is perfect disobedience; and we might as well speak of the imperfect success of a general who never began to conquer, as to speak of the imperfect holiness of one who has not yet obeyed God. The truth is too simple to need expansion, that every individual action is either wholly sinful or wholly righteous; and that every being in the universe, at any given time, is either entirely wicked or entirely holy, i.e. either conformed to law or not conformed to law: yet the prevailing modes of thought and speech force us to recognize a quality of action and character, called *imperfect holiness,* which takes rank somewhere indefinitely below what may seem the lowest possible or conceivable modification of holiness. So that, with reference to this, we must name *mere* holiness, *perfect* holiness—consigning the censure due to the impropriety of our language, to those who maintain the possibility of serving God and mammon, i.e. of being holy and sinful, at the same time. A profession, then of *perfect* holiness, thus understood, is in truth merely a profession of holiness, without which, confessedly, none can claim the name of sons or servants of God; and instead of deserving the charge of arrogance, should rather be censured, if at all, for conveying, in the language of it, the implication that men may be less than perfectly holy, and yet not perfectly sinful. But we take higher ground. The first Adam was holy; the second Adam was, in a more proper sense, perfectly holy—his holiness was secure. The gospel platform is as much above the ground of mere holiness, as a deed in fee simple is above mere possession.

As obedience is the test of all holiness, so we believe, under the gospel, *perpetuity of obedience* is the test of all holiness, Here we may speak, without solecism, of perfect holiness; and here we are exposed to a more plausible charge of arrogance. Let us examine the ground of this charge. Without entering the wide field of scripture argument, it is sufficient for our purpose to notice a single fact in relation to the views of those who most freely stigmatize the supposed self-righteousness of Perfectionists. These very persons universally and confessedly expect, at death, to become Perfectionists, and that not merely of the second, but of the third degree: in other words, while earthly Perfectionists claim only secure deliverance from sin, their accusers anticipate, within a brief space, secure deliverance from sin and all evil. What is the consideration which exempts their anticipation from the charge of self-righteous presumption, and yet leaves the burden upon our claim? Their answer assuredly must be—We anticipate, at death, secure redemption from sin and evil, as the *gift of the grace of God."* But the self-same apology relieves our claim. We *receive* present redemption from sin as the gift of the grace of God; we only enter, "by a new and living way," upon the possession of a portion of that gratuitous inheritance which they expect to receive at death. We must be permitted, then, to say boldly, that the same rule which allows men to *hope* for heaven without presumption, allows us to *receive* heaven here without self-righteousness: and the charge of arrogance is due to those who hope for the gift, while they daily displease the Giver. The same Christ who will be the believer's portion in heaven, is our righteousness and sanctification here. While, therefore, we shrink not from the odium connected with the name *Perfectionist,* we cannot despair of disabusing all honest men, ere long, of a portion of their prejudices against it, by convincing them that we join in the testimony of our living head, that "there is none good but one, that is God," and believe that by the energy of his goodness alone we are delivered from sin.

The standard by which every man judges of the nature of true humility, and of its opposite, spiritual pride, is determined by the answer which his heart gives to the question—["]Who is the author of righteousness?["] If the credit of holiness is due to him who professes it, then his profession exalts himself at the expense of God, and justly exposes him to the charge of spiritual arrogance, however high or low may be his claim. But if God alone is acknowledged as the author of righteousness, a profession of holiness is only the acknowledgment of a gift—and not only consistent with, but necessary to, the exercise of true humility. The man who has no conception of any righteousness other than his own, may well count the confession of imperfection—genuine modesty. From such we expect no mercy. But if there are any who ascribe all righteousness to God, we hope to convince them that the arrogance which boasts of the "Lord our righteousness" is the perfection of humility; and that the profession of humility which delights in the confession of sin and in the expectation of a continued commission of it, is only a modest way of robbing Christ of the crown of his glory.

Is it imagined that the man to whom God in truth has given perfect holiness, has done some great thing? He has done nothing. The great achievement of his will which, be it remembered, the grace of God has secured, is the cessation from his own works, and the commencement of an everlasting repose on the energy of the living God, as the basis and hope of his righteousness. He has simply died—and with his dying breath bequeathed his body, soul and spirit to his Maker, rolling the responsibility of his future and eternal obedience upon the everlasting arm.

We believe it is incomparably easier to receive deliverance from all sins, than to conquer one. Paul clearly presents the principle in Rom. 1:21–32, which accounts for the difficulty men find in obtaining freedom from sin.—Because they refuse to glorify God, he *gives them up* to vile affections. The affections of men are rightfully under the perfect control of God. When he is dethroned, he abandons his kingdom, and anarchy ensues; every effort to quell the rebellion of desires, which falls short of a reinstatement of God in his sovereignty over the heart, must result in disheartening failure. But why should it be difficult for Him who "stands at the door," if his petition for entrance is heard, and his claim for dominion admitted, to restore peace and security to the ruined kingdom? Why should it be thought an incredible thing, that God should raise the dead? Pride, envy, anger, sensuality, &c., are but limbs of the tree of sin, the stock of which is that *unbelief which rejects the righteousness of God.* The man who commences the work of exterminating sin at the top of the tree, or among any of the branches will soon be disheartened by the discovery that the branches he has once lopped off, soon grow again, or send their juice into other limbs. We say, therefore, it is easier to lay the ax at the root and fell the whole tree at once, than to exterminate effectually a single limb. In view of these considerations, though we object not to the name, Perfectionist—and though we verily believe and unblushingly maintain that we are free from sin—we beg to be relieved of the glory, and of the shame of the achievement; as we have been taught with the scourge, that the day has come when "all the haughtiness of men shall be brought low, and the Lord alone exalted."

WILLIAM LLOYD GARRISON

Selection from *Thoughts on African Colonization* (1832)

"Prospectus of *The Liberator*" (1837)

Few luminaries in American history have been as controversial both in their own time and since as William Lloyd Garrison (1805–1879). Some of that controversy stemmed from the harshly denunciatory style of the assaults that he habitually marshaled in his newspaper, the *Liberator,* against not only slaveholders but also his political opponents within and without the antislavery movement. But most of it was provoked by the persuasively radical arguments contained in his polemics. Of these none had so major a historical impact as his widely read *Thoughts on African Colonization.* With this book, which Garrison published the year after he started the *Liberator,* he accomplished two crucial political objectives: He launched a blistering attack on the antislavery credentials of the country's heretofore leading antislavery society, the American Colonization Society, which favored gradual, compensated emancipation and the colonization of freed slaves in Africa; and he put forward his recently embraced counter-program of uncompensated, immediate abolition and the eventual full integration of African-Americans into middle-class American society. Beyond these programmatic breakthroughs, Garrison also occupied important new theoretical ground. First, he linked the key concept of "immediate abolition" to the entire evangelical-perfectionist trinity of individual sin, willed regeneration, and the coming millennial day. Second, he advanced the first significant critique by an American white author of white racism, which he saw as both a creature of slavery and one of its major sustainers.

After helping to create a militant and widely vilified movement in the North around the program of immediate abolition, Garrison by the end of the 1830s had come to espouse a panoply of additional radical ideas. These included women's rights, pacifist "non-resistance," and the rejection of the authority of all governments resting on physical force. These positions seemed horrific even to most abolitionists, but Garrison saw them as logical derivations from both his consistent antislavery philosophy and his deep belief that not the churches but the abolition movement itself would be the spiritual vanguard of the biblically prophesied millennium. A few years later, with the threat looming of slavery's expansion into the annexed territory of Texas, Garrison extended his "come-outer" philosophy into a call for the North's secession from the union. Disunion eventually came, of course, although, ironically, through the very impure process of partisan violence that Garrison for thirty years had forsworn but, once war broke out, came himself to zealously support.

Henry Mayer, *All on Fire: William Lloyd Garrison and the Abolition of Slavery* (New York, 1998), is an excellent appreciative biography. For a more skeptical view, see John L. Thomas, *The Liberator: William Lloyd Garrison* (Boston, 1963). Aileen S. Kraditor provides a vigorously argued historical defense of Garrison's politics in her *Means and Ends in American Abolitionism: Garrison and His Critics on Strategy and Tactics, 1834–1850* (New York, 1969). For a still highly valuable study of the larger strain of radical perfectionist "come-outerism" that Garrison espoused, see Lewis Perry, *Radical Abolitionism: Anarchy and the Government of God in Antislavery Thought* (Ithaca, 1973). W. Caleb McDaniel, *The Problem of Democracy in the Age of Slavery: Garrisonian Abolitionists and Transatlantic Reform* (Baton Rouge, 2013), convincingly portrays Garrison and his comrades as a politically sophisticated group integrally connected to a transatlantic network of radical reformers. For a sympathetic treatment of Garrison's "political abolitionist" opponents, see Bruce Laurie, *Beyond Garrison: Antislavery and Social Reform* (Cambridge, 2005).

Selection from *Thoughts on African Colonization* (1832)

Section V.

THE AMERICAN COLONIZATION SOCIETY IS THE ENEMY OF IMMEDIATE ABOLITION.

It follows, as a necessary consequence, that a Society which is not hostile to slavery, which apologises for the system and for slaveholders, which recognises slaves as rightful property, and which confessedly increases their value, is *the enemy of immediate abolition.* This, I am aware, in the present corrupt state of public sentiment, will not generally be deemed an objectionable feature; but I regard it with inexpressible abhorence and dismay.

Since the deception practised upon our first parents by the old serpent, there has not been a more fatal delusion in the minds of men than that of the gradual abolition of slavery. *Gradual* abolition! do its supporters really know what they talk about? Gradually abstaining from what? From sins the most flagrant, from conduct the most cruel, from acts the most oppressive! Do colonizationists mean, that slave-dealers shall purchase or sell a few victims less this year than they did the last? that slave-owners shall liberate one, two or three out of every hundred slaves during the same period? that slave-drivers shall apply the lash to the scarred and bleeding backs of their victims somewhat less frequently? Surely not—I respect their intelligence too much to believe that they mean any such thing. But if any of the slaves should be exempted from sale or purchase, why not all? if justice require the liberation of the few, why not of the many? if it be right for a driver to inflict a number of lashes, how many shall be given? Do colonizationists mean that the practice of separating the husband from the wife, the wife from the husband, or children from their parents, shall come to an end by an almost imperceptible process? or that the slaves shall be defrauded of their just remuneration, less and less every month or every year? or that they shall be under the absolute, irresponsible control of their masters? Oh no! I place a higher value upon their good sense, humanity and morality than this! Well, then, they would immediately break up the slave traffic—they would put aside the whip—they would have the marriage relations preserved inviolate—they would not separate families—they would not steal the wages of the slaves, nor deprive them of personal liberty! This is abolition—*immediate abolition.* It is simply declaring that slave owners are bound to fulfil—now, without any reluctance or delay—the golden rule, namely, to do as they would be done by; and that, as the right to be free is inherent and inalienable in the slaves, there ought now to be a disposition on the part of the people to break their fetters. All the horrid spectres which are conjured up, on this subject, arise from a confusion of the brain, as much as from a corruption of the heart.

I utterly reject, as delusive and dangerous in the extreme, every plea which justifies a procrastinated and an indefinite emancipation, or which concedes to a slave owner the right to hold his slaves as *property* for any limited period, or which contends for the gradual preparation of the slaves for freedom; believing all such pretexts to be a fatal departure from the high road of justice into the bogs of expediency, a surrender of the

Source: William Lloyd Garrison, *Thoughts on Colonization: Or an Impartial Exhibition of the Doctrines, Principles and Purposes of the American Colonization Society* (Boston: Garrison and Knapp, 1832), 78–81, 85–86, 90,91–92, 93–94, 134, 141–47, 149–50.

great principles of equity, an indefensible prolongation of the curse of slavery, a concession which places the guilt upon any but those who incur it, and directly calculated to perpetuate the thraldom of our species.

Immediate abolition does not mean that the slaves shall immediately exercise the right of suffrage, or be eligible to any office, or be emancipated from law, or be free from the benevolent restraints of guardianship. We contend for the immediate personal freedom of the slaves, for their exemption from punishment except where law has been violated, for their employment and reward as free laborers, for their exclusive right to their own bodies and those of their own children, for their instruction and subsequent admission to all the trusts, offices, honors and emoluments of intelligent freemen. Emancipation will increase and not destroy the value of their labor; it will also increase the demand for it. Holding out the stimulus of good treatment and an adequate reward, it will induce the slaves to toil with a hundred fold more assiduity and faithfulness. Who is so blind as not to perceive the peaceful and beneficial results of such a change? The slaves, if freed, will come under the watchful cognizance of law; they will not be idle, but *avariciously* industrious; they will not rush through the country, firing dwellings and murdering the inhabitants; for freedom is all they ask—all they desire—the obtainment of which will transform them from enemies into friends, from nuisances into blessings, from a corrupt, suffering and degraded, into a comparatively virtuous, happy and elevated population.

Nor does immediate abolition mean that any compulsory power, other than moral, should be used in breaking the fetters of slavery. It calls for no bloodshed, or physical interference; it jealously regards the welfare of the planters; it simply demands an entire revolution in public sentiment, which will lead to better conduct, to contrition for past crimes, to a love instead of a fear of justice, to a reparation of wrongs, to a healing of breaches, to a suppression of revengeful feelings, to a quiet, improving, prosperous state of society! [Here follow five pages of extracts from colonizationist writings opposing immediate emancipation.]

The miserable sophistry contained in the foregoing extracts scarcely needs a serious refutation. "To say that immediate emancipation will only increase the wretchedness of the slaves, and that we must pursue a system of *gradual* abolition, is to present to us the double paradox, that we must continue to do evil, in order to cure the evil which we are doing; and that we must continue to be unjust, and to do evil, that good may come." The fatal error of *gradualists* lies here: They talk as if the friends of abolition contended only for the emancipation of the slaves, without specifying or caring what should be done with or for them! as if the planters were invoked to cease from one kind of villany, only to practise another! as if the manumitted slaves must necessarily be driven out from society into the wilderness, like wild beasts! This is talking nonsense: it is a gross perversion of reason and common sense. Abolitionists have never said, that mere manumission would be doing justice to the slaves: they insist upon a remuneration for years of unrequited toil, upon their employment as free laborers, upon their immediate and coefficient instruction, and upon the exercise of a benevolent supervision over them on the part of their employers. They declare, in the first place, that to break the fetters of the slaves, and turn them loose upon the country, without the preservative restraints of law, and destitute of occupation, would leave the work of justice only half done; and, secondly, that it is absurd to suppose that the planters would be wholly independent of the labor of the blacks—for they could no more dispense with it next week, were emancipation to take place, than they can to-day. The very ground which they assume for their opposition to slavery,—that it necessarily prevents the improvement of its victims,—shows that they contemplate the establishment of schools for the education of the slaves, and the furnishing of productive employment, immediately upon their liberation. If this were done, none of the horrors which are now so feelingly depicted, as the attendants of a sudden abolition, would ensue.

But we are gravely told that education must *precede* emancipation. The logic of this plea is, that intellectual superiority justly gives one man an oppressive control over another! Where would such a detestable principle lead but to practices the most atrocious, and results the most disastrous, if carried out among ourselves? Tell us, ye hairsplitting sophists, the exact quantum of knowledge which is necessary to constitute a freeman. If every dunce should be a slave, your servitude is inevitable; and richly do you deserve the lash for your obtuseness. Our white population, too, would furnish blockheads enough to satisfy all the classical kidnappers in the lands....

It is said, by way of extenuation, that the present owners of slaves are not responsible for the origin of this system. I do not arraign them for the crimes *of their ancestors,* but for the constant perpetration and extension of similar crimes. The plea that the evil of slavery was entailed upon them, shall avail them nothing: in its length and breadth it means that the robberies of one generation justify the robberies of another! that the inheritance of stolen property converts it into an honest acquisition! that the atrocious conduct of their fathers exonerates them from all accountability, thus presenting the strange anomaly of a race of men incapable of incurring guilt, though daily practising the vilest deeds! Scarcely any one denies that blame attaches somewhere: the present generation throws it upon the past—the past, upon its predecessor—and thus it is cast, like a ball, from one to another, down to the first importers of the Africans! "Can that be *innocence* in the temperate zone, which is the *acme of all guilt* near the equator? Can that be *honesty* in one meridian of longitude, which, at one hundred degrees east, is the *climax of injustice?*" Sixty thousand infants, the offspring of slave-parents, are annually born in this country, and doomed to remediless bondage. Is it not as atrocious a crime to kidnap these, as to kidnap a similar number on the coast of Africa?...

We are told that "it is not right that men should be free, when their freedom will prove injurious to themselves and others." This has been the plea of tyrants in all ages. If the immediate emancipation of the slaves would prove a curse, it follows that slavery is a blessing; and that it cannot be unjust, but benevolent, to defraud the laborer of his hire, to rank him as a beast, and to deprive him of his liberty. But this, every one must see, is at war with common sense, and avowedly doing evil that good may come. This plea must mean, either that a state of slavery is more favorable to the growth of virtue and the dispensation of knowledge than a state of freedom—(a glaring absurdity)—or that an immediate compliance with the demands of justice would be most unjust—(a gross contradiction).

It is boldly asserted by some colonizationists, that "*the negroes are happier when kept in bondage,*" and that "the condition of the great mass of emancipated Africans is one in comparison with which the condition of the slaves is *enviable.*" What is the inference? Why, either that slavery is not oppression—(another paradox)—or that real benevolence demands the return of the free people of color to their former state of servitude. Every kidnapper, therefore, is a true philanthropist! Our legislature should immediately offer a bounty for the body of every free colored person! The colored population of Massachusetts, at $200 for each man, woman and child, would bring at least *one million three hundred thousand dollars.* This sum would seasonably replenish our exhausted treasury. The whole free colored population of the United States, at the same price, (which is a low estimate,) would be worth *sixty-five millions of dollars!!* Think how many churches this would build, schools and colleges establish, beneficiaries educate, missionaries support, bibles and tracts circulate, railroads and canals complete, &c. &c. &c.!!!...

Those who prophesy evil, and only evil, concerning immediate abolition, absolutely disregard the nature and constitution of man, as also his inalienable rights, and annihilate or reverse the causes and effects of human action. They are continually fearful lest the slaves, in consequence of their grievous wrongs and intolerable sufferings, should attempt to gain their freedom by revolution; and yet they affect to be equally fearful lest a general emancipation should produce the same disastrous consequences. How absurd! They *know* that oppression must cause rebellion; and yet they pretend that a removal of the cause will produce a bloody effect! This is to suppose an effect without a cause, and, of course, is a contradiction in terms. Bestow upon the slaves personal freedom, and all motives for insurrection are destroyed. Treat them like rational beings, and you may surely expect rational treatment in return: treat them like beasts, and they will behave in a beastly manner.

Section IX.

THE AMERICAN COLONIZATION SOCIETY DENIES
THE POSSIBILITY OF ELEVATING THE BLACKS IN THIS COUNTRY.

THE detestation of feeling, the fire of moral indignation, and the agony of soul which I have felt kindling and swelling within me, in the progress of this review, under this section reach the acme of intensity. It is impossible for the mind to conceive, or the tongue to utter, or the pen to record, sentiments more derogatory to the character of a republican and christian people than the following. [Here follow eight pages of extracts from colonizationist authors arguing for the ineradicability of white prejudice and discrimination against blacks and therefore the wisdom and justice of encouraging their removal to Africa as their only hope for enjoying freedom and social progress.]

"My bowels, my bowels! I am pained at my very heart; my heart maketh a noise in me." Are we pagans, are we savages, are we devils? Can pagans, or savages, or devils, exhibit a more implacable spirit, than is seen in the foregoing extracts? It is enough to cause the very stones to cry out, and the beasts of the field to rebuke us.

Of this I am sure: no man, who is truly willing to admit the people of color to an equality with himself, can see any insuperable difficulty in effecting their elevation. When, therefore, I hear an individual—especially a professor of christianity—strenuously contending that there can be no fellowship with them, I cannot help suspecting the sincerity of his own republicanism or piety, or thinking that the beam is in his own eye. My bible assures me that the day is coming when even the "wolf shall dwell with the lamb, and the leopard shall lie down with the kid, and the wolf and the young lion and the fatling together;" and, if this be possible, I see no cause why those of the same species—God's rational creatures—fellow countrymen, in truth, cannot dwell in harmony together.

How abominably hypocritical, how consummately despicable, how incorrigibly tyrannical must this whole nation appear in the eyes of the people of Europe!—professing to be the *friends* of the free blacks, actuated by the purest motives of benevolence toward them, desirous to make atonement for past wrongs, challenging the admiration of the world for their patriotism, philanthropy and piety—and yet (hear, O heaven! and be astonished, O earth!) shamelessly proclaiming, with a voice louder than thunder, and an aspect malignant as sin, that while their colored countrymen remain among them, they must be trampled beneath their feet, treated as inferior beings, deprived of all the invaluable privileges of freemen, separated by the brand of indelible ignominy, and debased to a level with the beasts that perish! Yea, that they may as soon change their complexion as rise from their degradation! that no device of philanthropy can benefit them here! that they constitute a class out of which *no individual can be elevated,* and below which, *none can be depressed!*

that no talents however great, no piety however pure and devoted, no patriotism however ardent, no industry however great, no wealth however abundant, can raise them to a footing of equality with the whites! That "let them toil from youth to old age in the honorable pursuit of wisdom—let them store their minds with the most valuable researches of science and literature—and let them add to a highly gifted and cultivated intellect, a piety pure, undefiled, and unspotted from the world, *it is all nothing*—they would not be received into the *very lowest walks of society*—admiration of such uncommon beings would mingle with *disgust!*" Yea, that "there is a broad and impassible line of demarcation between every man who has *one drop* of African blood in his veins and every other class in the community"! Yea, that "the habits, the feelings, all the prejudices of society—prejudices which neither *refinement,* nor *argument,* nor *education,* nor RELIGION itself can subdue—mark the people of color, whether bond or free, as the subjects of a degradation *inevitable* and *incurable*"! Yea, that "Christianity cannot do for them here, what it will do for them in Africa"! Yea, that "this is not the fault of the colored man, NOR OF THE WHITE MAN, nor of Christianity; but AN ORDINATION OF PROVIDENCE, *and no more to be changed than the* LAWS OF NATURE"!!!

Again I ask, are we pagans, are we savages, are we devils? Search the records of heathenism, and sentiments more hostile to the spirit of the gospel, or of a more black and blasphemous complexion than these, cannot be found. I believe that they are libels upon the character of my countrymen, which time will wipe off. I call upon the spirits of the just made perfect in heaven, upon all who have experienced the love of God in their souls here below, upon the christian converts in India and the islands of the sea, to sustain me in the assertion that there *is* power enough in the religion of Jesus Christ to melt down the most stubborn prejudices, to overthrow the highest walls of partition, to break the strongest caste, to improve and elevate the most degraded, to unite in fellowship the most hostile, and to equalize and bless all its recipients. Make me *sure* that there is not, and I will give it up, now and for ever. "In Christ Jesus, all are one: there is neither Jew nor Greek, there is neither bond nor free, there is neither male nor female."

These sentiments were not uttered by infidels, nor by worthless wretches, but in many instances by professors of religion and *ministers of the gospel!* and in almost every instance by reputedly the most enlightened, patriotic and benevolent men in the land! Tell it not abroad! publish it not in the streets of Calcutta! Even the eminent President of Union College, (Rev. Dr. Nott,) could so far depart, unguardedly I hope, from christian love and integrity, as to utter this language in an address in behalf of the Colonization Society:—"With us they [the free people of color] have been degraded by slavery, and *still further degraded by the mockery of nominal freedom.*" Were this true, it would imply that we of the free States are more barbarous and neglectful than even the traffickers in souls and men stealers at the south. We have not, it is certain, treated our colored brethren as the law of kindness and the ties of brotherhood demand; but have we outdone slaveholders in cruelty? Were it true, to forge new fetters for the limbs of these degraded beings would be an act of benevolence. But their condition is as much superior to that of the slaves, as happiness is to misery. The second portion of this work, containing their proceedings in a collective capacity, shows whether they have made any progress in intelligence, in virtue, in piety, and in happiness, since their liberation. Again he says: "*We have endeavored,* but endeavored in vain, *to restore them either to self-respect, or to the respect of others.*" It is painful to contradict so worthy an individual; but nothing is more certain than that this statement is altogether erroneous. We have derided, we have shunned, we have neglected them, in every possible manner. They have had to rise not only under the mountainous weight of their own ignorance and vice, but with the additional and constant pressure of our contempt and injustice. In despite of us, they have done well. Again: *"It is not our fault that we have failed; it is not theirs."* We *are* wholly and exclusively in fault. What have we done to raise them up from the earth? What have we *not* done to keep them down? Once more: "It has resulted from a cause over which neither they, nor we, can ever have control." In other words, they have been made with skins "not colored like our own," and *therefore* we cannot recognise them as fellow-countrymen, or treat them like rational beings! One sixth of our whole population *must*, FOR EVER, in this land, remain a wretched, ignorant and degraded race,—and yet nobody be culpable—*none but the Creator* who has made us *incapable* of doing unto others as we would have them do unto us! Horrible—horrible! If this be not an impeachment of Infinite Goodness,—I do not say intentionally but *really,*— I cannot define it. The same sentiment is reiterated by a writer in the Southern Religious Telegraph, who says—"The exclusion of the free black from the civil and literary privileges of our country, depends on another circumstance than that of character—a circumstance, which, as it was entirely beyond his control, so it is unchangeable, and will for ever oper- ate. This circumstance is—*he is a black man*"!! And the Board of Managers of the Parent Society, in their Fifteenth Annual Report, declare than *"an ordination of Providence"* pre- vents the general improvement of the people of color in this land! How are God and our country dishonored, and the requirements of the gospel contemned, by this ungodly plea! Having satisfied himself that the Creator is alone blameable for the past and present deg- radation of the free blacks, Dr. Nott draws the natural and unavoidable inference that "here, therefore, they must be *forever debased, forever useless, forever a nuisance, forever a calamity,*" and then gravely declares (mark the climax!) "any yet THEY, [these ignorant, helpless, miserable creatures!] AND THEY ONLY, are qualified for colonizing Africa"!! "Why then," he asks, *"in the name of God,"*—(the abrupt appeal, in this connexion, seems almost profane,)—"should we hesitate to encourage their departure?"

Nature, we are positively assured, has raised up impassable barriers between the races. I understand by this expression, that the blacks are of a different species from our- selves, so that all attempts to generate offspring between us and them must prove as abor- tive, as between a man and a beast. It is a law of Nature that the lion shall not beget the lamb, or the leopard the bear. Now the planters at the south have clearly demonstrated, that an amalgamation with their slaves is not only possible, but a matter of course, and eminently productive. It neither ends in abortion nor produces monsters. In truth, it is often so difficult in the slave States to distinguish between the fruits of this intercourse and the children of white parents, that witnesses are summoned at court to solve the prob- lem! Talk of the barriers of Nature, when the land swarms with living refutations of the statement! Happy indeed would it be for many a female slave, if such a barrier could exist during the period of her servitude to protect her from the lust of her master!

In France, England, Spain, and other countries, persons of color maintain as high a rank and are treated as honorably as any other class of the inhabitants, in despite of the "impassable barriers of Nature," Yet it is proclaimed to the world by the Colonization Society, that the American people can never be as republican in their feelings and prac- tices as Frenchmen, Spaniards or Englishmen! Nay, that *religion* itself cannot subdue their malignant prejudices, or induce them to treat their dark-skinned brethren in accordance with their professions of republicanism! My countrymen! Is it so? Are you willing thus to be held up as tyrants and hypocrites for ever? as less magnanimous and just than the popu- lace of Europe? No—no! I cannot give you up as incorrigibly wicked, nor my country as sealed over to destruction. My confidence remains, like the oak—like the Alps—unshaken, storm proof. I am not discouraged—I am not distrustful. I still place an unwavering reliance upon the omnipotence of truth. I still believe that the demands of justice will be satisfied; that the voice of bleeding humanity will melt the most obdurate hearts; and that the land will be redeemed and regenerated by an enlightened and energetic public opinion. As long as there remains among us a single copy of the Declaration of Independence, or of the New Testament, I will not despair of the social and political elevation of my sable countrymen. Already a rallying-cry is heard from the East and the West, from the North and the South; towns and cities and states are in commotion; volunteers are trooping to the field; the spirit of freedom and the fiend of oppression are in mortal conflict, and all neutrality is at an end. Already the line of division is drawn: on one side are the friends of truth and liberty, with their banner floating high in the air, on which are inscribed in letters of light, "IMMEDIATE ABOLITION"—"NO COMPROMISE WITH OPPRESSORS"—"EQUAL RIGHTS"—"NO EXPATRIATION"—"DUTY, AND NOT CONSEQUENCES"—"LET JUSTICE BE DONE, THOUGH THE HEAVENS SHOULD FALL!"—On the opposite side stand the supporters and apologists of slavery in mighty array, with a black flag on which are seen in bloody characters, "AFRICAN COLONIZATION"—"GRADUAL ABOLITION"—"RIGHTS OF PROPERTY"—"POLITICAL EXPEDIENCY" "NO EQUALITY"—"NO REPENTANCE"—"EXPULSION OF THE BLACKS"—"PROTECTION TO TYRANTS!"—Who can doubt the issue of this controversy, or which side has the approbation of the Lord of Hosts?...

In a critical examination of the pages of the African Repository, and of the reports and addresses of the Parent Society and its auxiliaries, I cannot find in a single instance any impeachment of the conduct and feelings of society toward the people of color, or any hint that the prejudice which is so prevalent against them is unmanly and sinful, or any evidence of contrition for past injustice, or any remonstrance or entreaty with a view to a change of public sentiment, or any symptoms of moral indignation at such unchristian and anti-republican treatment. On the contrary, I find the doctrine every where inculcated that this hatred and contempt, this abuse and proscription, are not only excusable, but the natural, inevitable and incurable effects of constitutional dissimilitude, growing out of an ordination of Providence, for which there is no remedy but a separation between the two races. If the free blacks, then, have been "still further degraded by the mockery of nominal freedom," if they "must always be a separate and degraded race," if "degradation must and will press them to the earth," if from their present station "they can never rise, be their talents, their enterprise, their virtues what they may," if "in Africa alone, they can enjoy the motives for honorable ambition," the American Colonization Society is responsible for their debasement and misery; for as it numbers among its supporters the most influential men in our country, and boasts of having the approbation of an overwhelming majority of the wise and good whose examples are laws, it is able, were it willing, to effect a radical change in public sentiment—nay, it is at the present time public sentiment itself. But though it has done much, and may do more, (all that it can it will do,) to depress, impoverish and dispirit the free people of color, and to strengthen and influence mutual antipathies, it is the purpose of God, I am fully persuaded, to humble the pride of the American people by rendering the expulsion of our colored countrymen utterly impracticable, and the necessity for their admission to equal rights imperative. As neither mountains of prejudice, nor the massy shackles of law and of public opinion, have been able to keep them down to a level with slaves, I confidently anticipate their exaltation among ourselves. Through the vista of time—a short distance only,—I see them here, not in Africa, not bowed to the earth, or derided and persecuted as at present, not with a downcast air or an irresolute step, but standing erect as men destined heavenward, unembarrassed, untrammeled, with none to molest or make them afraid.

"Prospectus of *The Liberator*"
(1837)

The termination of the present year will complete the seventh volume of the Liberator: we have served, therefore, a regular apprenticeship in the cause of LIBERTY, and are now prepared to advocate it upon a more extended scale.

In commencing this publication, we had but a single object in view—the total abolition of American slavery, and, as a just consequence, the complete enfranchisement of our colored countrymen. As the first step toward this sublime result, we found the overthrow of the American Colonization Society to be indispensable,—containing, as it did, in its organization, all the elements of prejudice, caste and slavery.

In entering upon our eighth volume, the abolition of slavery will still be the grand object of our labors, though not, perhaps, so exclusively as heretofore. There are other topics, which, in our opinion, are intimately connected with the great doctrine of inalienable human rights; and which, while they conflict with no religious sect, or political party, such, are pregnant with momentous consequences to the freedom, equality and happiness of mankind. These we shall discuss as time and opportunity may permit.

The motto upon our banner has been, from the commencement of our moral warfare, "OUR COUNTRY IS THE WORLD—OUR COUNTRYMEN ARE ALL MANKIND." We trust that it will be our only epitaph. Another motto we have chosen is, UNIVERSAL EMANCIPATION. Up to this time, we have limited its application to those who are held in this country, by southern taskmasters, as marketable commodities, goods and chattels, and implements of husbandry. Henceforth, we shall use it in its widest latitude: the emancipation of our whole race from the dominion of man, from the thraldom of self, from the government of brute force, from the bondage of sin—and bringing them under the dominion of God, the control of an inward spirit, the government of the law of love, and into the obedience and liberty of Christ, who is *"the same,* yesterday, TO-DAY, and forever."

It has never been our design, in conducting the Liberator, to require of the friends of emancipation, any political or sectarian shibboleth; though, in consequence of the general corruption of all political parties and religious sects, and of the obstacles which they have thrown into the path of emancipation, we have been necessitated to reprove them all. Nor have we any intention,—at least, not while ours professes to be an anti-slavery publication, distinctively and eminently,—to assail or give the preference to any sect or party. We are bound by no denominational trammels; we are not political partizans; we have taken upon our lips no human creed; we are guided by no human authority; we cannot consent to wear the livery of any fallible body. The abolition of American slavery we hold to be COMMON GROUND, upon which men of all creeds, complexions and parties, if they have true humanity in their hearts, may meet on amicable and equal terms to effect a common object; but whoever marches on to that ground, loving his creed, or sect, or party, or any worldly interest, or personal reputation, or property, or friends, or wife, or children, or life itself, more than the cause of bleeding humanity,—expecting to promote his political designs, or to enforce his sectarian dogmas, or to drive others from the ranks on account of their modes of faith,—will assuredly prove himself to be unworthy of his

Source: Liberator, 7 (December 15, 1837), 203.

abolition profession, and his real character will be made manifest to all—for severe and unerring tests will be applied frequently: it will not be possible for him to make those sacrifices, or to endure those trials, which unbending integrity to the cause will require. For ourselves, we care not who is found upon this broad platform of our common nature: if he will join hands with us, in good faith, to undo the heavy burdens and break the yokes of our enslaved countrymen, we shall not stop to inquire, whether he is a Trinitarian or Unitarian, Baptist or Methodist, Catholic or Covenanter, Presbyterian or Quaker, Swedenborgian or Perfectionist. However, widely we may differ in our views on other subjects, we shall not refuse to labor with him against slavery, in the same phalanx, if he refuse not to labor with us. Certainly, no man can truly affirm that we have sought to bring any other religious or political tests into this philanthropic enterprise than these:—"Thou shalt love thy neighbor as thyself"—"Whatsoever ye would that men should do to you, do ye even so to them"—"Remember those in bonds as bound with them."

Intending, therefore, in the Liberator, not to conflict with any sect or party, any further than it opposes the immediate abolition of American slavery, or those moral obligations which are not less general than fundamental, we make our appeal for support to the honest-hearted—the pure-minded—the seekers after truth—those who do *not* tithe mint, anise, and cummin, nor omit the weightier matters of the law—those "who despise fraud, and loathe rapine, and abhor blood"—those who love Christ in the person of his bleeding representative at the South, above all worldly considerations—those who are not afraid to think and act independently, among *all* sects and *all* parties.

To the bigoted, the pharisaical, the time-serving, the selfish, the worshippers of expediency, the advocates of caste, the lovers of power, the enemies of liberty and equality, we make no appeal. It shall be our constant endeavor to make the Liberator so liberal in its spirit, so straight-forward in its character, so disinterested in its object, so uncompromising in its principles, and so hostile to every form of prejudice and slavery, as to render it intolerable to them.

That we shall be faultless in the manner of conducting our publication—or suit the taste of a single reader in *all* that we may select or originate—or avoid giving offence on each and every topic that may be discussed in our columns—we do not expect: it is, perhaps, utterly impracticable. If, however, we should err beyond endurance, the remedy is in the hand of every subscriber: he can stop his subscription instantly. Besides, all who dissent from us, or who wish to rebuke us, shall always find a place for their articles in the Liberator.

Next to the overthrow of slavery, the cause of PEACE will command our attention. The doctrine of non-resistance, as commonly received and practised by Friends, and certain members of other religious denominations, we conceive to be utterly indefensible in its application to national wars;—not that it "goes too far," but that it does not go far enough. If a nation may not redress its wrongs by physical force—if it may not repel or punish a foreign enemy who comes to plunder, enslave or murder its inhabitants—then it may not resort to arms to quell an insurrection, or send to prison or suspend upon a gibbet any transgressors upon its soil. If the slaves of the South have not an undoubted right to resist their masters in the last resort, then no man, or body of men, may appeal to the law of violence in self-defence—for none have ever suffered, or can suffer, more than they. If, when men are robbed of their earnings, their liberties, their personal ownership, their wives and children, they may not resist, in no case can physical resistance be allowable, either in an individual or collective capacity. Now, the doctrine we shall endeavor to inculcate is, that the kingdoms of this world are to become the kingdoms of our Lord and of his

Christ; consequently, that they are all to be supplanted, whether they are called despotic, monarchical or republican, and he only who is King of kings, and Lord of lords, is to rule in righteousness. The kingdom of God is to be established IN ALL THE EARTH, and it shall never be destroyed, but it shall "BREAK IN PIECES AND CONSUME ALL OTHERS:" its elements are righteousness, and peace, and joy in the Holy Ghost: without are dogs, and sorcerers, and whoremongers, and murderers, and idolators, and whatsoever loveth and maketh a lie. Its government is one of love, not of military coercion or physical restraint: its laws are not written upon parchment, but upon the hearts of its subjects—they are not conceived in the wisdom of man, but framed by the Spirit of God: its weapons are not carnal, but spiritual: its soldiers are clad in the whole armor of God, having their loins girt about with truth, and having on the breast-plate of righteousness—their feet are shod with the preparation of the gospel of peace—with the shield of faith they are able to quench all the fiery darts of the wicked—and they wear the helmet of salvation, and wield the sword of the Spirit, which is the word of God. Hence, when smitten on the one cheek, they turn the other also; being defamed, they entreat; being reviled, they bless; being persecuted, they suffer it; they take joyfully the spoiling of their goods; they rejoice, inasmuch as they are partakers of Christ's sufferings; they arc sheep in the midst of wolves; in no extremity whatever, even if their enemies are determined to nail them to the cross with Jesus, and if they like him could summon lesions of angels to their rescue, will they resort to the law of violence.

As to the governments of this world, whatever their titles or forms, we shall endeavor to prove, that in their essential elements, and as at present administered, they are all Anti-Christ; that they can never, by human wisdom, be brought into conformity to the will of God; that they cannot be maintained, except by naval and military power; that all their penal enactments being a dead letter without an army to carry them into effect, are virtually written in human blood; and that the followers of Jesus should instinctively shun their stations of honor, power and emolument—at the same time "submitting to every ordinance of man, for the Lord's sake," and offering no *physical* resistance to any of their mandates, however unjust or tyrannical. The language of Jesus is "My Kingdom is not of this world, else would my servants light." Calling his disciples to him, he said to them, "Ye know that they which are accounted to rule over the Gentiles, exercise lordship over them; and their great ones exercise authority upon them. *But so it* SHALL NOT *be among* YOU: but whosoever will be great among you, shall be your minister: and whosoever of you will be the chiefest, shall be servant of all. For even the Son of man came not to be ministered unto, but to minister, and to give his life a ransom for many."

Human governments are to be viewed as judicial punishments. If a people turn the grace of God into lasciviousness, or make their liberty an occasion for anarchy,—or if they refuse to belong to the "one fold and one Shepherd,"—they shall be scourged by governments of their own choosing, and burdened with taxation, and subjected to physical control, and torn by factions, and made to eat the fruit of their evil doings, until they are prepared to receive the liberty and the rest which remain, on earth as well as in heaven, for THE PEOPLE OF GOD. This is in strict accordance with the arrangement of Divine Providence.

So long as men condemn the perfect government of the Most High, and will not fill up the measure of Christ's sufferings in their own persons, just so long will they desire to usurp authority over each other—just so long will they pertinaciously cling to human governments, *fashioned in the likeness and administered in the spirit of their own disobedience.* Now, if the prayer of our Lord be not a mockery; if the kingdom of God is to come universally, and his will to be done ON EARTH As it is IN HEAVEN; and if, in that kingdom, no carnal weapon can be wielded, and swords are beaten into ploughshares, and spears into pruning hooks, and there is none to molest or make afraid, and no statute-book but the bible, and no judge but Christ; then why are not Christians obligated to come out NOW, and be separate from "the kingdoms of this world," which are all based upon THE PRINCIPLE OF VIOLENCE, and which require their officers and servants to govern and be governed by that principle? How, then, is the wickedness of men to be overcome? Not by lacerating their bodies, or incarcerating them in dungeons, or putting them upon tread-mills, or exiling them from their native country, or suspending them upon gibbets—O no!—but simply by returning good for evil, and blessing for cursing; by using those spiri-tual weapons which are "mighty, through God, to the pulling down of strong holds"; by the power of that faith which overcomes the world; by ceasing to look to man for a redress of injuries, however grievous, but committing the soul in well-doing, as unto a faithful Creator, and leaving it with God to bestow recompense—"for it is written, Vengeance is mine; I will repay, saith the Lord."

These are among the views we shall offer in connection with the heaven-originated cause of PEACE,—views which any person is at liberty to controvert in our columns, and for which no man or body of men is responsible but ourselves. If any man shall affirm that the anti-slavery cause, as such, or any anti-slavery society, is answerable for our sentiments on this subject, to him may be justly applied the apostolic declaration, "the truth is not in him." We regret, indeed, that the principles of abolitionists seem to be quite unsettled upon a question of such vast importance, and so vitally connected with the bloodless overthrow of slavery. It is time for all our friends to know where they stand. If those, whose yokes they are endeavoring to break by the fire and hammer of God's word, would not, in their opinion, be justified in appealing to physical force, how can they justify others of a different complexion in doing the same thing? And if they conscientiously believe that the slaves would be guiltless in shedding the blood of their merciless oppressors, let them say so unequivocally—for there is no neutral ground in this matter, and the time is near at hand when they will be compelled to take sides.

As our object is *universal* emancipation,—redeem woman as well as man from a servile to an equal condition,—we shall go for the RIGHTS OF WOMAN to their utmost extent....

To that little, but well-tried band of coadjutors, who, from the first moment they saw the standard of the Liberator floating in the breeze of heaven, rallied around it, and have stood by it unflinchingly, though it has been carried into the hottest of the battle; to those kind benefactors, both colored and white, who, from time to time during our seven years' strife for liberty and equal rights, have helped in many a trying exigency to sustain our publication by reasonable donations, without which it must have been discontinued, to the joy and rejoicing of every southern tyrant and every northern apologist for slavery—dona-tions made not to be trumpeted in the ear of the world, but to be expended by us in good faith, and as God's stewards, for the advancement of the common cause; to those who love FREE DISCUSSION and an independent press which no party can bribe, and no sect intimi-date; to those who are willing to renew with us another campaign against the giant crimes of this guilty land; and, especially, to our warm-hearted, true-hearted, tender-hearted col-ored friends and associates in the good work of breaking human yokes and fetters, who have given to us their confidence, affection, gratitude, the right hand of fellowship, the blessings of many ready to perish,—who have never once faltered in their attachment or support, no, not even for a moment, though others of a different complexion have turned against us,—and whose complete enfranchisement, both of soul and body, for time and eternity, is dearer to us than reputation, property, or life;—to each and all, we return our thanks for their inspiring countenance, and pledge ourselves anew to be faithful unto death—knowing full well that He who is for us, is more than they who are against us—that the battle is the Lord's, and the victory sure. Our grand object is, to hasten that glorious day when the song of the heavenly host, at the birth of Jesus, shall rise in a chorus to heaven, like the voice of many waters, from the lips of people of every tribe and tongue and nation, at the universal conquest and reign of that same JESUS THE CRUCIFIED—*"Glory to God in the highest; on earth peace, good will toward men!"*

SARAH GRIMKÉ

Selection from *Letters on the Equality of the Sexes, and the Condition of Woman* (1838)

Sarah Grimké (1792–1873) and her younger sister Angelina, the converted Quaker daughters of a wealthy and politically prominent South Carolina slaveholding family, gained notoriety by lecturing before thousands of men and women in New England in 1837 and early 1838 on behalf of the antislavery cause. They were excoriated in the press and in pulpits as well as rebuked, though not by name, in a "Pastoral Letter" issued in July 1837 by the Congregational ministerial association of Massachusetts, which denounced as antibiblical the practice of women speaking out publicly for the abolition cause. The women thus suddenly found themselves waging a two-front war: on behalf of antislavery and in defense of (against the wishes of even many abolitionists) women's right to speak and participate as equals in the country's reform crusades. In defending themselves, the sisters boldly drew out the analogy between slavery and the subordination of women.

Sarah, the less outgoing and heretofore more circumspect of the sisters, went further. Two weeks before the ministerial association issued its pastoral letter, she began writing a series of letters of her own that were first published in Boston newspapers. When it came out as a book the following year, it became the first American feminist treatise on women's rights. Actually, as its title suggests, the book was even broader than that: In chapters that ranged from the hair-raising and derivative to the astute and original, Grimké chronicled the various forms of legal and economic disabilities suffered by women throughout the world. But it was in her discussion of the theological and ethical basis of women's rights that she was the most original and incisive. Rejecting the popular "two-spheres" notion of women's and men's radically different natures and roles, she based her alternative theory of the moral identity of the two genders on the very foundation that their clerical opponents had invoked to bury the sisters: a Bible-based, rationalistic, evangelical schema of human sin and redemption. Few antebellum reformers offered such a challenging subversion of America's reigning conservative religious philosophy.

The best introduction to Grimké's gender ideas is Gerda Lerner's *The Feminist Thought of Sarah Grimké* (New York, 1998). Lerner has also written a fine biography, *The Grimké Sisters from South Carolina: Pioneers for Woman's Rights and Abolition* (New York, 1971). An instructive discussion of Grimké's feminist Christianity may be found in Rosemary Radford Ruether, "The Subordination and Liberation of Women in Christian Theology: St. Paul and Sarah Grimké," *Soundings: An Interdisciplinary Journal,* 61 (Summer 1978), 168–81. For interpretations of the female slave motif in antislavery feminist thought and writing, see Karen Sánchez-Eppler, "Bodily Bonds: The Intersecting Rhetorics of Feminism and Abolition," *Representations,* 24 (Fall 1988), 28–59; and Jean Fagan Yellin, *Women and Sisters: The Antislavery Feminists in American Culture* (New Haven, 1989).

Letters Addressed to Mary S. Parker, President
of the Boston Female Anti-Slavery Society

Letter I.

THE ORIGINAL EQUALITY OF WOMAN.

Amesbury, 7th Mo. 11th, 1837.

MY DEAR FRIEND—In attempting to comply with thy request to give my views on the Province of Woman, I feel that I am venturing on nearly untrodden ground, and that I shall advance arguments in opposition to a corrupt public opinion, and to the perverted interpretation of Holy Writ, which has so universally obtained. But I am in search of truth; and no obstacle shall prevent my prosecuting that search, because I believe the welfare of the world will be materially advanced by every new discovery we make of the designs of Jehovah in the creation of woman. It is impossible that we can answer the purpose of our being, unless we understand that purpose. It is impossible that we should fulfil our duties, unless we comprehend them; or live up to our privileges, unless we know what they are.

In examining this important subject, I shall depend solely on the Bible to designate the sphere of woman, because I believe almost every thing that has been written on this subject, has been the result of a misconception of the simple truths revealed in the Scriptures, in consequence of the false translation of many passages of Holy Writ. My mind is entirely delivered from the superstitious reverence which is attached to the English version of the Bible. King James's translators certainly were not inspired. I therefore claim the original as my standard, *believing that to have been inspired*, and I also claim to judge for myself what is the meaning of the inspired writers, because I believe it to be the solemn duty of every individual to search the Scriptures for themselves, with the aid of the Holy Spirit, and not be governed by the views of any man, or set of men.

We must first view woman at the period of her creation. "And God said, Let us make man in our own image, after our likeness; and let them have dominion over the fish of the sea, and over the fowl of the air, and over the cattle, and over all the earth, and over every creeping thing that creepeth upon the earth. So God created man in his own image, in the image of God created he him, male and female created he them." In all this sublime description of the creation of man, (which is a generic term including man and woman,) there is not one particle of difference intimated as existing between them. They were both made in the image of God; dominion was given to both over every other creature, but not over each other. Created in perfect equality, they were expected to exercise the vicegerence intrusted to them by their Maker, in harmony and love.

Let us pass on now to the recapitulation of the creation of man—"The Lord God formed man of the dust of the ground, and breathed into his nostrils the breath of life; and man became a living soul. And the Lord God said, it is not good that man should be alone, I will make him an help meet for him." All creation swarmed with animated beings capable of natural affection, as we know they still are; it was not, therefore, merely to give man a creature susceptible of loving, obeying, and looking up to him, for all that the animals could do and did do. It was to give him a companion, *in all respects* his equal;

Source: Sarah M. Grimké, *Letters on the Equality of the Sexes, and the Condition of Woman* (Boston: Isaac Knapp, 1838), 3–12, 14–21, 46–55, 115–28.

one who was like himself *a free agent,* gifted with intellect and endowed with immortality; not a partaker merely of his animal gratifications, but able to enter into all his feelings as a moral and responsible being. If this had not been the case, how could she have been an help meet for him? I understand this as applying not only to the parties entering into the marriage contract, but to all men and women, because I believe God designed woman to be an help meet for man in every good and perfect work. She was a part of himself, as if Jehovah designed to make the oneness and identity of man and woman perfect and complete; and when the glorious work of their creation was finished, "the morning stars sang together, and all the sons of God shouted for joy."

This blissful condition was not long enjoyed by our first parents. Eve, it would seem from the history, was wandering alone amid the bowers of Paradise, when the serpent met with her. From her reply to Satan, it is evident that the command not to eat "of the tree that is in the midst of the garden," was given to both, although the term man was used when the prohibition was issued by God. "And the woman said unto the serpent, WE may eat of the fruit of the trees of the garden, but of the fruit of the tree which is in the midst of the garden, God hath said, YE shall not eat of it, neither shall YE touch it, lest YE die." Here the woman was exposed to temptation from a being with whom she was unacquainted. She had been accustomed to associate with her beloved partner, and to hold communion with God and with angels; but of satanic intelligence, she was in all probability entirely ignorant. Through the subtlety of the serpent, she was beguiled. And "when she saw that the tree was good for food, and that it was pleasant to the eyes, and a tree to be desired to make one wise, she took of the fruit thereof and did eat."

We next find Adam involved in the same sin, not through the instrumentality of a supernatural agent, but through that of his equal, a being whom he must have known was liable to transgress the divine command, because he must have felt that he was himself a free agent, and that he was restrained from disobedience only by the exercise of faith and love towards his Creator. Had Adam tenderly reproved his wife, and endeavored to lead her to repentance instead of sharing in her guilt, I should be much more ready to accord to man that superiority which he claims; but as the facts stand disclosed by the sacred historian, it appears to me that to say the least, there was as much weakness exhibited by Adam as by Eve. They both fell from innocence, and consequently from happiness, *but not from equality.*

Let us next examine the conduct of this fallen pair, when Jehovah interrogated them respecting their fault. Thy both frankly confessed their guilt. "The man said, the woman whom thou gavest to be with me, she gave me of the tree and I did eat. And the woman said, the serpent beguiled me and I did eat." And the Lord God said unto the woman, "Thou wilt be subject unto thy husband, and he will rule over thee." That this did not allude to the subjection of woman to man is manifest, because the same mode of expression is used in speaking to Cain of Abel. The truth is that the curse, as it is termed, which was pronounced by Jehovah upon woman, is a simple prophecy. The Hebrew, like the French language, uses the same word to express shall and will. Our translators having been accustomed to exercise lordship over their wives, and seeing only through the medium of a perverted judgment, very naturally, though I think not very learnedly or very kindly, translated it *shall* instead of *will,* and thus converted a prediction to Eve into a command to Adam; for observe, it is addressed to the woman and not to the man. The consequence of the fall was an immediate struggle for dominion, and Jehovah foretold which would gain the ascendency; but as he created them in his image, as that image manifestly was not lost by the fall, because it is urged in Gen. 9:6, as an argument why the life of man should not be taken by his fellow man, there is no reason to suppose that sin produced any distinction between them as moral, intellectual and responsible beings. Man might just as well have endeavored by hard labor to fulfil the prophecy, thorns and thistles will the earth bring forth to thee, as to pretend to accomplish the other, "he will rule over thee," by asserting dominion over his wife.

> "Authority usurped from God, not given.
> He gave him only over beast, flesh, fowl,
> Dominion absolute: that right he holds
> By God's donation: but man o'er woman
> He made not Lord, such title to himself
> Reserving, human left from human free."

Here then I plant myself. God created us equal;—he created us free agents;—he is our Lawgiver, our King and our Judge, and to him alone is woman bound to be in subjection, and to him alone is she accountable for the use of those talents with which her Heavenly Father has entrusted her. One is her Master even Christ.

Thine for the oppressed in the bonds of womanhood

Sarah M. Grimké.

Letter II.

WOMAN SUBJECT ONLY TO GOD.

Newburyport, 7th mo. 17, 1837.

My Dear Sister,—In my last, I traced the creation and the fall of man and woman from that state of purity and happiness which their beneficent Creator designed them to enjoy. As they were one in transgression, their chastisement was the same. "So God drove out *the man,* and he placed at the East of the garden of Eden a cherubim and a flaming sword, which turned every way to keep the way of the tree of life." We now behold them expelled from Paradise, fallen from their original loveliness, but still bearing on their foreheads the image and superscription of Jehovah; still invested with high moral responsibilities, intellectual powers, and immortal souls. They had incurred the penalty of sin, they were shorn of their innocence, but they stood on the same platform side by side, acknowledging *no superior* but their God. Notwithstanding what has been urged, woman I am aware stands charged to the present day with having brought sin into the world. I shall not repel the charge by any counter assertions, although, as was before hinted, Adam's ready acquiescence with his wife's proposal, does not savor much of that superiority *in strength of mind,* which is arrogated by man. Even admitting that Eve was the greater sinner, it seems to me man might be satisfied with the dominion he has claimed and exercised for nearly six thousand years, and that more true nobility would be manifested by endeavoring to raise the fallen and invigorate the weak, than by keeping woman in subjection. But I ask no favors for my sex. I surrender not our claim to equality. All I ask of our brethren is, that they will take their feet from off our necks, and permit us to stand upright on that ground which God designed us to occupy. If he has not given us the rights which have, as I conceive, been wrested from us, we shall soon give evidence of our inferiority, and shrink back into that obscurity, which the high souled magnanimity of man has assigned us as our appropriate sphere.

As I am unable to learn from sacred writ when woman was deprived by God of her equality with man, I shall touch upon a few points in the Scriptures, which demonstrate that no supremacy was granted to man. When God had destroyed the world, except Noah and his family, by the deluge, he renewed the grant formerly made to man, and again gave him dominion over every beast of the earth, every fowl of the air, over all that moveth upon the earth, and over all the fishes of the sea; into his hands they were delivered. But was woman, bearing the image of her God, placed under the dominion of her fellow man? Never! Jehovah could not surrender his authority to govern his own immortal creatures into the hands of a being, whom he knew, and whom his whole history proved, to be unworthy of a trust so sacred and important. God could not do it, because it is a direct contravention of his law, "Thou shalt worship the Lord thy God, and *him only* shalt thou serve." If Jehovah. had appointed man as the guardian, or teacher of woman, he would certainly have given some intimation of this surrender of his own prerogative. But so far from it, we find the commands of God invariably the same to man and woman; and not the slightest intimation is given in a single passage of the Bible, that God designed to point woman to man as her instructor. The tenor of his language always is, "Look unto ME, and be ye saved, all the ends of the earth, for I am God, and there is none else."

The lust of dominion was probably the first effect of the fall; and as there was no other intelligent being over whom to exercise it, woman was the first victim of this unhallowed passion. We afterwards see it exhibited by Cain in the murder of his brother, by Nimrod in his becoming a mighty hunter of men, and setting up a kingdom over which to reign. Here we see the origin of that Upas of slavery, which sprang up immediately after the fall, and has spread its pestilential branches over the whole face of the known world. All history attests that man has subjected woman to his will, used her as a means to promote his selfish gratification, to minister to his sensual pleasures, to be instrumental in promoting his comfort; but never has he desired to elevate her to that rank she was created to fill. He has done all he could to debase and enslave her mind; and now he looks triumphantly on the ruin he has wrought, and says, the being he has thus deeply injured is his inferior.

Woman has been placed by John Quincy Adams, side by side with the slave, whilst he was contending for the right side of petition. I thank him for ranking us with the oppressed; for I shall not find it difficult to show, that in all ages and countries, not even excepting enlightened republican America, woman has more or less been made a *means* to promote the welfare of man, without due regard to her own happiness, and the glory of God as the end of her creation....

Letter III.

THE PASTORAL LETTER OF THE GENERAL ASSOCIATION OF
CONGREGATIONAL MINISTERS OF MASSACHUSETTS.

Haverhill, 7th Mo. 1837.

DEAR FRIEND,—When I last addressed thee, I had not seen the Pastoral Letter of the General Association. It has since fallen into my hands, and I must digress from my intention of exhibiting the condition of women in different parts of the world, in order to make some remarks on this extraordinary document. I am persuaded that when the minds of men and women become emancipated from the thraldom of superstition and "traditions of men," the sentiments contained in the Pastoral Letter will be recurred to with as much astonishment as the opinions of Cotton Mather and other distinguished men of his day, on the subject of witchcraft; nor will it be deemed less wonderful, that a body of divines should gravely assemble and endeavor to prove that woman has no right to "open her mouth for the dumb," than it now is that judges should have sat on the trials of witches, and solemnly condemned nineteen persons and one dog to death for witchcraft.

But to the letter. It says, "We invite your attention to the dangers which at present seem to threaten the FEMALE CHARACTER with wide-spread and permanent injury." I rejoice that they have called the attention of my sex to this subject, because I believe if woman investigates it, she will soon discover that danger is impending, though from a totally different source from that which the Association apprehends,—danger from those who, having long held the reins of *usurped* authority, are unwilling to permit us to fill that sphere which God created us to move in, and who have entered into league to crush the immortal mind of woman. I rejoice, because I am persuaded that the rights of woman, like the rights of slaves, need only be examined to be understood and asserted, even by some of those, who are now endeavoring to smother the irrepressible desire for mental and spiritual freedom which glows in the breast of many, who hardly dare to speak their sentiments.

"The appropriate duties and influence of women are clearly stated in the New Testament. Those duties are unobtrusive and private, but the sources of *mighty power.* When the mild, *dependent,* softening influence of woman upon the sternness of man's opinions is fully exercised, society feels the effects of it in a thousand ways." No one can desire more earnestly than I do, that woman may move exactly in the sphere which her Creator has assigned her; and I believe her having been displaced from that sphere has introduced confusion into the world. It is, therefore, of vast importance to herself and to all the rational creation, that she should ascertain what are her duties and her privileges as a responsible and immortal being. The New Testament has been referred to, and I am willing to abide by its decisions, but must enter my protest against the false translation of some passages by the MEN who did that work, and against the perverted interpretation by the MEN who undertook to write commentaries thereon. I am inclined to think, when we are admitted to the honor of studying Greek and Hebrew, we shall produce some various readings of the Bible a little different from those we now have.

The Lord Jesus defines the duties of his followers in his Sermon on the Mount. He lays down grand principles by which they should be governed, without any reference to sex or condition.—"Ye are the light of the world. A city that is set on a hill cannot be hid. Neither do men light a candle and put it under a bushel, but on a candlestick, and it giveth light unto all that are in the house. Let your light so shine before men, that they may see your good works, and glorify your Father which is in Heaven." I follow him through all his precepts, and find him giving the same directions to women as to men, never even referring to the distinction now so strenuously insisted upon between masculine and feminine virtues: this is one of the anti-christian "traditions of men" which are taught instead of the "commandments of God." Men and women were CREATED EQUAL; they are both moral and accountable beings, and whatever is *right* for man to do, is *right* for woman.

But the influence of woman, says the Association, is to be private and unobtrusive; her light is not to shine before man like that of her brethren; but she is passively to let the lords of the creation, as they call themselves, put the bushel over it, lest peradventure it might appear that the world has been benefitted by the rays of *her* candle. So that her quenched light, according to their judgment, will be of more use than if it were set on the candlestick. "Her influence is the source of mighty power." This has ever been the flattering language of man since he laid aside the whip as a means to keep woman in subjection. He spares her body; but the war he has waged against her mind, her heart, and her soul, has been no less destructive to her as a moral being. How monstrous, how anti-christian, is the doctrine that woman is to be dependent on man! Where, in all the sacred Scriptures, is this taught? Alas! she has too well learned the lesson, which MAN has labored to teach her. She has surrendered her dearest RIGHTS, and been satisfied with the privileges which man has assumed to grant her; she has been amused with the show of power, whilst man has absorbed all the reality into himself. He has adorned the creature whom God gave him as a companion, with baubles and gewgaws, turned her attention to personal attractions, offered incense to her vanity, and made her the instrument of his selfish gratification, a plaything to please his eye and amuse his hours of leisure. "Rule by obedience and by submission sway," or in other words, study to be a hypocrite, pretend to submit, but gain your point, has been the code of household morality which woman has been taught. The poet has sung, in sickly strains, the loveliness of woman's dependence upon man, and now we find it reechoed by those who profess to teach the religion of the Bible. God says, "Cease ye from man whose breath is in his nostrils, for wherein is he to be accounted of?" Man says, depend upon me. God says, "HE will teach us of his ways." Man says, believe it not, I am to be your teacher. This doctrine of dependence upon man is utterly at variance with the doctrine of the Bible. In that book I find nothing like the softness of woman, nor the sternness of man: both are equally commanded to bring forth the fruits of the Spirit, love, meekness, gentleness, &c.

But we are told, "the power of woman is in her dependence, flowing from a consciousness of that weakness which God has given her for her protection." If physical weakness is alluded to, I cheerfully concede the superiority; if brute force is what my brethren are claiming, I am willing to let them have all the honor they desire; but if they mean to intimate, that mental or moral weakness belongs to woman, more than to man, I utterly disclaim the charge. Our powers of mind have been crushed, as far as man could do it, our sense of morality has been impaired by his interpretation of our duties; but no where does God say that he made any distinction between us, as moral and intelligent beings.

"We appreciate," say the Association, "the *unostentatious* prayers and efforts of woman in advancing the cause of religion at home and abroad, in leading religious inquirers to THE PASTOR for instruction." Several points here demand attention. If public prayers and public efforts are necessarily ostentatious, then "Anna the prophetess, (or preacher,) who departed not from the temple, but served God with fastings and prayers night and day," "and spake of Christ to all them that looked for redemption in Israel," was ostentatious in her efforts. Then, the apostle Paul encourages women to be ostentatious in their efforts to spread the gospel, when he gives them directions how they should appear, when engaged in praying, or preaching in the public assemblies. Then, the whole association of Congregational ministers are ostentatious, in the efforts they are making in preaching and praying to convert souls.

But woman may be permitted to lead religious inquirers to the PASTORS for instruction. Now this is assuming that all pastors are better qualified to give instruction than woman. This I utterly deny. I have suffered too keenly from the teaching of man, to lead any one to him for instruction. The Lord Jesus says,—"Come unto me . . . and learn of me." He points his followers to no man; and when woman is made the favored instrument of rousing a sinner to his lost and helpless condition, she has no right to substitute any teacher for Christ; all she has to do is, to turn the contrite inquirer to the "Lamb of God which taketh away the sins of the world." More souls have probably been lost by going down to Egypt for help, and by trusting in man in the early stages of religious experience, than by any other error. Instead of the petition being offered to God,—"Lead me in thy truth, and TEACH me, for thou art the God of my salvation,"—instead of relying on the precious promises—"What man is he that feareth the Lord? him shall HE TEACH in the way that he shall choose"—"I will instruct thee and TEACH thee in the way which thou shalt go—I will guide thee with mine eye"—the young convert is directed to go to man, as if he were in the place of God, and his instructions essential to an advancement in the path of righteousness. That woman can have but a poor conception of the privilege of being taught of God, what he alone can teach, who would turn the "religious inquirer aside" from the fountain of living waters, where he might slake his thirst for spiritual instruction, to those broken cisterns which can hold no water, and therefore cannot satisfy the panting spirit. The business of men and women, who are ORDAINED OF GOD to preach the unsearchable riches of Christ to a lost and perishing world, is to lead souls to Christ, and not to Pastors for instruction.

The General Association say, that "when woman assumes the place and tone of man as a public reformer, our care and protection of her seem unnecessary; we put ourselves in self-defence against her, and her character becomes unnatural." Here again the unscriptural notion is held up, that there is a distinction between the duties of men and women as moral beings; that what is virtue in man, is vice in woman; and women who dare to obey the command of Jehovah, "Cry aloud, spare not, lift up thy voice like a trumpet, and show my people their transgression," are threatened with having the protection of the brethren withdrawn. If this is all they do, we shall not even know the time when our chastisement is inflicted; our trust is in the Lord Jehovah, and in him is everlasting strength. The motto of woman, when she is engaged in the great work of public reformation should be,—"The Lord is my light and my salvation; whom shall I fear? The Lord is the strength of my life; of whom shall I be afraid?" She must feel, if she feels rightly, that she is fulfilling one of the important duties laid upon her as an accountable being, and that her character, instead of being "unnatural," is in exact accordance with the will of Him to whom, and to no other, she is responsible for the talents and the gifts confided to her. As to the pretty simile, introduced into the "Pastoral Letter," "If the vine whose strength and beauty is to lean upon the trellis work, and half conceal its clusters, thinks to assume the independence and the overshadowing nature of the elm," &c. I shall only remark that it might well suit the poet's fancy, who sings of sparkling eyes and coral lips, and knights in armor clad; but it seems to me utterly inconsistent with the dignity of a Christian body, to endeavor to draw such an anti-scriptural distinction between men and women. Ah! how many of my sex feel in the dominion, thus unrighteously exercised over them, under the gentle appellation of *protection,* that what they have leaned upon has proved a broken reed at best, and oft a spear.

Thine in the bonds of womanhood,

SARAH M. GRIMKÉ.

Letter VIII.

ON THE CONDITION OF WOMEN IN THE UNITED STATES.

Brookline, 1837.

MY DEAR SISTER,—I have now taken a brief survey of the condition of woman in various parts of the world. I regret that my time has been so much occupied by other things, that I have been unable to bestow that attention upon the subject which it merits, and that my constant change of place has prevented me from having access to books, which might probably have assisted me in this part of my work. I hope that the principles I have asserted will claim the attention of some of my sex, who may be able to bring into view, more thoroughly than I have done, the situation and degradation of woman. I shall now proceed to make a few remarks on the condition of women in my own country.

During the early part of my life, my lot was cast among the butterflies of the *fashionable* world; and of this class of women, I am constrained to say, both from experience and observation, that their education is miserably deficient; that they are taught to regard marriage as the one thing needful, the only avenue to distinction; hence to attract the notice and win the attentions of men, by their external charms, is the chief business of fashionable girls. They seldom think that men will be allured by intellectual acquirements, because they find, that where any mental superiority exists, a woman is generally shunned and regarded as stepping out of her "appropriate sphere," which, in their view, is to dress, to dance, to set out to the best possible advantage her person, to read the novels which inundate the press, and which do more to destroy her character as a rational creature, than any thing else. Fashionable women regard themselves, and are regarded by men, as pretty toys or as mere instruments of pleasure; and the vacuity of mind, the heartlessness, the frivolity which is the necessary result of this false and debasing estimate of women, can only be fully understood by those who have mingled in the folly and wickedness of fashionable life; and who have been called from such pursuits by the voice of the Lord Jesus, inviting their weary and heavy laden souls to come unto Him and learn of Him, that they may find something worthy of their immortal spirit, and their intellectual powers; that they may learn the high and holy purposes of their creation, and consecrate themselves unto the service of God; and not, as is now the case, to the pleasure of man.

There is another and much more numerous class in this country, who are withdrawn by education or circumstances from the circle of fashionable amusements, but who are brought up with the dangerous and absurd idea, that *marriage* is a kind of preferment; and that to be able to keep their husband's house, and render his situation comfortable, is the end of her being. Much that she does and says and thinks is done in reference to this situation; and to be married is too often held up to the view of girls as the sine qua non of human happiness and human existence. For this purpose more than for any other, I verily believe the majority of girls are trained. This is demonstrated by the imperfect education which is bestowed upon them, and the little pains taken to cultivate their minds, after they leave school, by the little time allowed them for reading, and by the idea being constantly inculcated, that although all household concerns should be attended to with scrupulous punctuality at particular seasons, the improvement of their intellectual capacities is only a secondary consideration, and may serve as an occupation to fill up the odds and ends of time. In most families, it is considered a matter of far more consequence to call a girl off from making a pie, or a pudding, than to interrupt her whilst engaged in her studies. This mode of training necessarily exalts, in their view, the animal above the intellectual and spiritual nature, and teaches women to regard themselves as a kind of machinery, necessary to keep the domestic engine in order, but of little value as the *intelligent* companions of men.

Let no one think, from these remarks, that I regard a knowledge of housewifery as beneath the acquisition of women. Far from it: I believe that a complete knowledge of household affairs is an indispensable requisite in a woman's education,—that by the mistress of a family, whether married or single, doing her duty thoroughly and *understandingly,* the happiness of the family is increased to an incalculable degree, as well as a vast amount of time and money saved. All I complain of is, that our education consists so almost exclusively in culinary and other manual operations. I do long to see the time, when it will no longer be necessary for women to expend so many precious hours in furnishing "a well spread table," but that their husbands will forego some of their accustomed indulgences in this way, and encourage their wives to devote some portion of their time to mental cultivation, even at the expense of having to dine sometimes on baked potatoes, or bread and butter....

The influence of women over the minds and character of *children* of both sexes, is allowed to be far greater than that of men. This being the case by the very ordering of nature, women should be prepared by education for the performance of their sacred duties as mothers and as sisters....

There is another way in which the general opinion, that women are inferior to men, is manifested, that bears with tremendous effect on the laboring class, and indeed on almost all who are obliged to earn a subsistence, whether it be by mental or physical exertion—I allude to the disproportionate value set on the time and labor of men and of women. A man who is engaged in teaching, can always, I believe, command a higher price for tuition than a woman—even when he teaches the same branches, and is not in any respect superior to the woman. This I know is the case in boarding and other schools with which I have been acquainted, and it is so in every occupation in which the sexes engage indiscriminately. As for example, in tailoring, a man has twice, or three times as much for making a waistcoat or pantaloons as a woman, although the work done by each may be equally good. In those employments which are peculiar to women, their time is estimated at only half the value of that of men. A woman who goes out to wash, works as hard in proportion as a wood sawyer, or a coal heaver, but she is not generally able to make more than half as much by a day's work. The low remuneration which women receive for their work, has claimed the attention of a few philanthropists, and I hope it will continue to do so until some remedy is applied for this enormous evil. I have known a widow, left with four or five children, to provide for, unable to leave home because her helpless babes demand her attention, compelled to earn a scanty subsistence, by making coarse shirts at 12 1–2 cents a piece, or by taking in washing, for which she was paid by some wealthy persons 12 1–2 cents per dozen. All these things evince the low estimation in which woman is held. There is yet another and more disastrous consequence arising from this unscriptural notion—women being educated, from the earliest childhood, to regard themselves as inferior creatures, have not that self-respect which conscious equality would engender, and hence when their virtue is assailed, they yield to temptation with facility, under the idea that it rather exalts than debases them, to be connected with a superior being.

There is another class of women in this country, to whom I cannot refer, without feelings of the deepest shame and sorrow. I allude to our female slaves. Our southern cities are whelmed beneath a tide of pollution; the virtue of female slaves is wholly at the mercy of irresponsible tyrants, and women are bought and sold in our slave markets, to gratify the brutal lust of those who bear the name of Christians. In our slave States, if amid all her degradation and ignorance, a woman desires to preserve her virtue unsullied, she is either bribed or whipped into compliance, or if she dares resist her seducer, her life by the laws of some of the slave States may be, and has actually been sacrificed to the fury of disappointed passion. Where such laws do not exist, the power which is necessarily vested in the master over his property, leaves the defenceless slave entirely at his mercy, and the sufferings of some females on this account, both physical and mental, are intense....

...Nor does the colored woman suffer alone: the moral purity of the white woman is deeply contaminated. In the daily habit of seeing the virtue of her enslaved sister sacrificed without hesitancy or remorse, she looks upon the crimes of seduction and illicit intercourse without horror, and although not personally involved in the guilt, she loses that value for innocence in her own, as well as the other sex, which is one of the strongest safeguards to virtue. She lives in habitual intercourse with men, whom she knows to be polluted by licentiousness, and often is she compelled to witness in her own domestic circle, those disgusting and heart-sickening jealousies and strifes which disgraced and distracted the family of Abraham. In addition to all this, the female slaves suffer every species of degradation and cruelty, which the most wanton barbarity can inflict; they are indecently divested of their clothing, sometimes tied up and severely whipped, sometimes prostrated on the earth, while their naked bodies are torn by the scorpion lash.

"The whip on woman's shrinking flesh!
Our soil yet reddening with the stains
Caught from her scourging warm and fresh."

Can any American woman look at these scenes of shocking licentiousness and cruelty, and fold her hands in apathy, and say, "I have nothing to do with slavery"? *She cannot and be guiltless.*

I cannot close this letter, without saying a few words on the benefits to be derived by men, as well as women, from the opinions I advocate relative to the equality of the sexes. Many women are now supported, in idleness and extravagance, by the industry of their husbands, fathers, or brothers, who are compelled to toil out their existence, at the counting house, or in the printing office, or some other laborious occupation, while the wife and daughters and sisters take no part in the support of the family, and appear to think that their sole business is to spend the hard bought earnings of their male friends. I deeply regret such a state of things, because I believe that if women felt their responsibility, for the support of themselves, or their families it would add strength and dignity to their characters, and teach them more true sympathy for their husbands, than is now generally manifested,—a sympathy which would be exhibited by actions as well as words. Our brethren may reject my doctrine, because it runs counter to common opinions, and because it wounds their pride; but I believe they would be "partakers of the benefit" resulting from the Equality of the Sexes, and would find that woman, as their equal, was unspeakably more valuable than woman as their inferior, both as a moral and an intellectual being.

Thine in the bonds of womanhood,

SARAH M. GRIMKÉ.

Letter XV.

MAN EQUALLY GUILTY WITH WOMAN IN THE FALL.

Uxbridge, 10*th Mo.* 20*th,* 1837.

MY DEAR SISTER,—It is said that "modern Jewish women light a lamp every Friday evening, half an hour before sunset, which is the beginning of their Sabbath, in remembrance of their original mother, who first extinguished the lamp of righteousness,—to remind them of their obligation to rekindle it." I am one of those who always admit, to its fullest extent, the popular charge, that woman brought sin into the world. I accept it as a powerful reason, why woman is bound to labor with double diligence, for the regeneration of that world she has been instrumental in ruining.

But, although I do not repel the imputation, I shall notice some passages in the sacred Scriptures, where this transaction is mentioned, which prove, I think, the identity and equality of man and woman, and that there is no difference in their guilt in the view of that God who searcheth the heart and trieth the reins of the children of men. In Is. 43: 27, we find the following passage—"Thy first father hath sinned, and thy teachers have transgressed against me"—which is synonymous with Rom. 5: 12. "Wherefore, as by ONE MAN sin entered into the world, and death by sin, &c." Here man and woman are included under one term, and no distinction is made in their criminality. The circumstances of the fall are again referred to in 2 Cor. 11: 3—"But I fear lest, by any means, as the serpent *beguiled* Eve through his subtility, so your mind should be beguiled from the simplicity that is in Christ." Again, 1st Tim. 2: 14—"Adam *was not deceived;* but the woman being *deceived,* was in the transgression." Now, whether the fact, that Eve was beguiled and deceived, is a proof that her crime was of deeper dye than Adam's, who was not deceived, but was fully aware of the consequences of sharing in her transgression, I shall leave the candid reader to determine.

My present object is to show, that, as woman is charged with all the sin that exists in the world, it is her solemn duty to labor for its extinction; and that this she can never do effectually and extensively, until her mind is disenthralled of those shackles which have been riveted upon her by a *"corrupt public opinion, and a perverted interpretation of the holy Scriptures."* Woman must feel that she is the equal, and is designed to be the fellow laborer of her brother, or she will be studying to find out the *imaginary* line which separates the sexes, and divides the duties of men and women into two distinct classes, a separation not even hinted at in the Bible, where we are expressly told, "there is neither male nor female, for ye are all one in Christ Jesus"....

To perform our duties, we must comprehend our rights and responsibilities; and it is because we do not understand, that we now fall so far short in the discharge of our obligations. Unaccustomed to think for ourselves, and to search the sacred volume, to see how far we are living up to the design of Jehovah in our creation, we have rested satisfied with the sphere marked out for us by man, never detecting the fallacy of that reasoning which forbids woman to exercise some of her noblest faculties, and stamps with the reproach of indelicacy those actions by which women were formerly dignified and exalted in the church.

I should not mention this subject again, if it were not to point out to my sisters what seems to me an irresistible conclusion from the literal interpretation of St. Paul, without reference to the context, and the peculiar circumstances and abuses which drew forth the expressions, "I suffer not a woman to teach"—"Let your women keep silence in the church," i. e. congregation. It is manifest, that if the apostle meant what his words imply, when taken in the strictest sense, then women have no right to *teach* Sabbath or day schools, or to open their lips to sing in the assemblies of the people; yet young and delicate women are engaged in all these offices; they are expressly trained to exhibit themselves, and raise their voices to a high pitch in the choirs of our places of worship. I do not intend to sit in judgment on my sisters for doing these things; I only want them to see, that they are as really infringing a *supposed* divine command, by instructing their pupils in the Sabbath or day schools, and by singing in the congregation, as if they were engaged in preaching the unsearchable riches of Christ to a lost and perishing world. Why, then, are we permitted to break this injunction in some points, and so seduously warned not to overstep the bounds set for us by our *brethren* in another? Simply, as I believe, because in the one case we subserve *their* views and *their* interests, and act in *subordination to them;* whilst in the other, we come in contact with their interests, and claim to be on an equality with them in the highest and most important trust ever committed to man, namely, the ministry of the word. It is manifest, that if women were permitted to be ministers of the gospel, as they unquestionably were in the primitive ages of the Christian church, it would interfere materially with the present organized system of spiritual power and ecclesiastical authority, which is now vested solely in the hands of men. It would either show that all the paraphernalia of theological seminaries, &c. &c. to prepare men to become evangelists, is wholly unnecessary, or it would create a necessity for similar institutions in order to prepare women for the same office; and this would be an encroachment on that learning, which our kind brethren have so ungenerously monopolized. I do not ask any one to believe my statements, or adopt my conclusions, because they are mine; but I do earnestly entreat my sisters to lay aside their prejudices, and examine these subjects *for themselves,* regardless of the "traditions of men," because they are intimately connected with their duty and their usefulness in the present important crisis....

DUTIES OF WOMEN.

One of the duties which devolve upon women in the present interesting crisis, is to prepare themselves for more extensive usefulness, by making use of those religious and literary privileges and advantages that are within their reach, if they will only stretch out their hands and possess them. By doing this, they will become better acquainted with their rights as moral beings, and with their responsibilities growing out of those rights: they will regard themselves, as they really are, FREE AGENTS, immortal beings, amenable to no tribunal but that of Jehovah, and bound not to submit to any restriction imposed for self-ish purposes, or to gratify that love of power which has reigned in the heart of man from Adam down to the present time. In contemplating the great moral reformations of the day, and the part which they are bound to take in them, instead of puzzling themselves with the harassing, because unnecessary inquiry, how far they may go without overstepping the bounds of propriety, which separate male and female duties, they will only inquire, "Lord, what wilt thou have us to do?" They will be enabled to see the simple truth, that God has made no distinction between men and women as moral beings; that the distinction now so much insisted upon between male and female virtues is as absurd as it is unscriptural, and has been the fruitful source of much mischief—granting to man a license for the exhibition of brute force and conflict on the battle field; for sternness, selfishness, and the exercise of irresponsible power in the circle of home—and to woman a permit to rest on an arm of flesh, and to regard modesty and delicacy, and all the kindred virtues, as peculiarly appropriate to her. Now to me it is perfectly clear, that WHATSOEVER IT IS MORALLY RIGHT FOR A MAN TO DO, IT IS MORALLY RIGHT FOR A WOMAN TO DO; and that confusion must exist in the moral world, until woman takes her stand on the same platform with man, and feels that she is clothed by her Maker with the *same rights,* and, of course, that upon her devolve the *same duties.*

It is not my intention, nor indeed do I think it is in my power, to point out the precise duties of women. To him who still teacheth by his Holy Spirit as never man taught, I refer my beloved sisters. There is a vast field of usefulness before them. The signs of the times give portentous evidence, that a day of deep trial is approaching; and I urge them, by every consideration of a Savior's dying love, by the millions of heathen in our midst, by the sufferings of woman in almost every portion of the world, by the fearful ravages which slavery, intemperance, licentiousness and other iniquities are making of the happiness of our fellow creatures, to come to the rescue of a ruined world, and to be found co-workers with Jesus Christ....

CONCLUSION.

I have now, my dear sister, completed my series of letters. I am aware, they contain some new views; but I believe they are based on the immutable truths of the Bible. All I ask for them is, the candid and prayerful consideration of Christians. If they strike at some of our bosom sins, our deep-rooted prejudices, our long cherished opinions, let us not condemn them on that account, but investigate them fearlessly and prayerfully, and not shrink from the examination; because, if they are true, they place heavy responsibilities upon women. In throwing them before the public, I have been actuated solely by the belief, that if they are acted upon, they will exalt the character and enlarge the usefulness of my own sex, and contribute greatly to the happiness and virtue of the other. That there is a root of bitterness continually springing up in families and troubling the repose of both men and women, must be manifest to even a superficial observer; and I believe it is the mistaken notion of the inequality of the sexes. As there is an assumption of superiority on the one part, which is not sanctioned by Jehovah, there is an incessant struggle on the other to rise to that degree of dignity, which God designed women to possess in common with men, and to maintain those rights and exercise those privileges which every woman's common sense, apart from the prejudices of education, tells her are inalienable; they are a part of her moral nature, and can only cease when her immortal mind is extinguished.

One word more. I feel that I am calling upon my sex to sacrifice what has been, what is still dear to their hearts, the adulation, the flattery, the attentions of trifling men. I am asking them to repel these insidious enemies whenever they approach them; to manifest by their conduct, that, although they value highly the society of pious and intelligent men, they have no taste for idle conversation, and for that silly preference which is manifested for their personal accommodation, often at the expense of great inconvenience to their male companions. As an illustration of what I mean, I will state a fact.

I was traveling lately in a stage coach. A gentleman, who was also a passenger, was made sick by riding with his back to the horses. I offered to exchange seats, assuring him it did not affect me at all unpleasantly; but he was too polite to permit a lady to run the risk of being discommoded. I am sure he meant to be very civil, but I really thought it was a foolish piece of civility. This kind of attention encourages selfishness in woman, and is only accorded as a sort of quietus, in exchange for those *rights* of which we are deprived. Men and women are equally bound to cultivate a spirit of accommodation; but I exceedingly deprecate her being treated like a spoiled child, and sacrifices made to her selfishness and vanity. In lieu of these flattering but injurious attentions, yielded to her as an inferior, as a mark of benevolence and courtesy, I want my sex to claim nothing from their brethren but what their brethren may justly claim from them, in their intercourse as Christians. I am persuaded woman can do much in this way to elevate her own character. And that we may become duly sensible of the dignity of our nature, only a little lower than the angels, and bring forth fruit to the glory and honor of Emanuel's name, is the fervent prayer of

Thine in the bonds of womanhood,

Sarah M. Grimké.

GEORGE BANCROFT

"The Office of the People in Art, Government, and Religion" (1835)

The man of letters as politician was a recognizable type in antebellum America. What made George Bancroft (1800–1891) unusual was the fact that, despite his Harvard education and Whig- and banker-connected family interests, he was a Democrat—indeed, for some years the Democratic boss of Massachusetts. Furthermore, although he was one of the first Americans to be awarded a Ph.D. degree at a European university, he was also a highly popular professional author. His best-selling ten-volume *History of the United States* boasted the largest readership of any historical work published in America in the nineteenth century.

One key to understanding both his unexpected embrace of the Democratic party and his success as an author lay in his knack for formulating an idea of democracy that was at once idealistic, populistic, and—despite the overlay of Romantic philosophy—deeply conservative. In Bancroft's oration, which follows, "reason" or truth is the product, not of an active mind, but of a ready and passive assent to the universal or common opinions of men and women. Bancroft admitted the existence of conflicting sects, but only those aspects of their outlook that comported easily with other or past opinions were "received into the common inheritance." History moved, in Bancroft's view, but only slowly and ineluctably toward the very present that middle-class Christian democracy had already achieved. The future, happily, could only bring more of the same.

Russell B. Nye's *George Bancroft: Brahmin Rebel* (New York, 1944), is still useful on Bancroft's literary career. For a severe but discerning study of Bancroft's intellectual and political career, see Lilian Handlin, *George Bancroft: The Intellectual as Democrat* (New York, 1984). Sacvan Bercovitch provides an appraisal of Bancroft's theory of American history in his *Rites of Assent: Transformations in the Symbolic Construction of America* (New York, 1993), 168–93.

An Oration Delivered Before the Adelphi Society of Williamstown College in August, 1835.

I.

The material world does not change in its masses or in its powers. The stars shine with no more lustre than when they first sang together in the glory of their birth. The flowers that gemmed the fields and the forests, before America was discovered, now bloom around us in their season. The sun that shone on Homer shines on us in unchanging lustre. The bow that beamed on the patriarch still glitters in the clouds. Nature is the same. For her no new forces are generated; no new capacities are discovered. The earth turns on its axis, and perfects its revolutions, and renews its seasons, without increase or advancement.

But a like passive destiny does not attach to the inhabitants of the earth. For them the expectations of social improvement are no delusion; the hopes of philanthropy are more than a dream. The five senses do not constitute the whole inventory of our sources of knowledge. They are the organs by which thought connects itself with the external universe; but the power of thought is not merged in the exercise of its instruments. We have functions which connect us with heaven, as well as organs which set us in relation with earth. We have not merely the senses opening to us the external world, but an internal sense, which places us in connexion with the world of intelligence and the decrees of God.

There is a *spirit in man:* not in the privileged few; not in those of us only who by the favor of Providence have been nursed in public schools: IT IS IN MAN: it is the attribute of the race. The spirit, which is the guide to truth, is the gracious gift to each member of the human family.

Reason exists within every breast. I mean not that faculty which deduces inferences from the experience of the senses, but that higher faculty, which from the infinite treasures of its own consciousness, originates truth, and assents to it by the force of intuitive evidence; that faculty which raises us beyond the control of time and space, and gives us faith in things eternal and invisible. There is not the difference between one mind and another, which the pride of philosophers might conceive. To them no faculty is conceded, which does not belong to the meanest of their countrymen. In them there can not spring up a truth which does not equally have its germ in every mind. They have not the power of creation; they can but reveal what God has implanted in every breast.

The intellectual functions, by which relations are perceived, are the common endowments of the race. The differences are apparent, not real. The eye in one person may be dull, in another quick, in one distorted, and in another tranquil and clear; yet the relation of the eye to light is in all men the same. Just so judgment may be liable in individual minds to the bias of passion, and yet its relation to truth is immutable, and is universal.

In questions of practical duty, conscience is God's umpire, whose light illumines every heart. There is nothing in books, which had not first, and has not still its life within us. Religion itself is a dead letter, wherever its truths are not renewed in the soul. Individual conscience may be corrupted by interest, or debauched by pride, yet the rule of morality is

Source: George Bancroft, *Literary and Historical Miscellanies* (New York: Harper & Bros., 1855), 408–11, 413–16, 417–29, 430–32, 433–35.

distinctly marked; its harmonies are to the mind like music to the ear; and the moral judgment, when carefully analyzed and referred to its principles, is always founded in right.
The eastern superstition, which bids its victims prostrate themselves before the advancing
car of their idols, springs from a noble root, and is but a melancholy perversion of that
self-devotion, which enables the Christian to bear the cross, and subject his personal passions to the will of God. Immorality of itself never won to its support the inward voice;
conscience if questioned, never forgets to curse the guilty with the memory of sin, to cheer
the upright with the meek tranquillity of approval. And this admirable power, which is the
instinct of Deity, is the attribute of every man; it knocks at the palace gate, it dwells in the
meanest hovel. Duty, like death, enters every abode, and delivers its message. Conscience,
like reason and judgment, is universal....

But I am asked if I despise learning? Shall one who has spent much of his life in
schools and universities plead the equality of uneducated nature? Is there no difference
between the man of refinement and the savage?

"I am a man," said Black Hawk nobly to the chief of the first republic in the world; "I
am a man," said the barbarous chieftain, "and you are another."

I speak for the universal diffusion of human powers, not of human attainments; for
the capacity for progress, not for the perfection of undisciplined instincts. The fellowship
which we should cherish with the race, receives the Comanche warrior and the Caffre
within the pale of equality. Their functions may not have been exercised, but they exist.
Immure a person in a dungeon; as he comes to the light of day, his vision seems incapable
of performing its office. Does that destroy your conviction in the relation between the eye
and light? The rioter over his cups resolves to eat and drink and be merry; he forgets his
spiritual nature in his obedience to the senses; but does that destroy the relation between
conscience and eternity? "What ransom shall we give?" exclaimed the senators of Rome to
the savage Attila. "Give," said the barbarian, "all your gold and jewels, your costly furniture and treasures, and set free every slave." "Ah," replied the degenerate Romans, "what
then will be left to us?" "I leave you your souls," replied the unlettered invader from the
steppes of Asia, who had learnt in the wilderness to value the immortal mind, and to
despise the servile herd, that esteemed only their fortunes, and had no true respect for
themselves. You cannot discover a tribe of men, but you also find the charities of life,
and the proofs of spiritual existence. Behold the ignorant Algonquin deposit a bow and
quiver by the side of the departed warrior; and recognise his faith in immortality. See the
Comanche chieftain, in the heart of our continent, inflict on himself severest penance; and
reverence his confession of the needed atonement for sin. The Barbarian who roams our
western prairies has like passions and like endowments with ourselves. He bears within
him the instinct of Deity; the consciousness of a spiritual nature; the love of beauty; the
rule of morality.

And shall we reverence the dark-skinned Caffre? Shall we respect the brutal
Hottentot? You may read the right answer written on every heart. It bids me not despise
the sable hunter, that gathers a livelihood in the forests of Southern Africa. All are men.
When we know the Hottentot better, we shall despise him less.

II.

If it be true, that the gifts of mind and heart are universally diffused, if the sentiment of
truth, justice, love, and beauty exists in every one, then it follows, as a necessary consequence, that the common judgment in taste, politics, and religion, is the highest authority

on earth, and the nearest possible approach to an infallible decision. From the consideration of individual powers I turn to the action of the human mind in masses.

If reason is a universal faculty, the universal decision is the nearest criterion of truth. The common mind winnows opinions; it is the sieve which separates error from certainty. The exercise by many of the same faculty on the same subject would naturally lead to the same conclusions. But if not, the very differences of opinion that arise prove the supreme judgment of the general mind. Truth is one. It never contradicts itself. One truth cannot contradict another truth. Hence truth is a bond of union. But error not only contradicts truth, but may contradict itself; so that there may be many errors, and each at variance with the rest. Truth is therefore of necessity an element of harmony; error as necessarily an element of discord. Thus there can be no continuing universal judgment but a right one. Men cannot agree in an absurdity; neither can they agree in a falsehood.

If wrong opinions have often been cherished by the masses, the cause always lies in the complexity of the ideas presented. Error finds its way into the soul of a nation, only through the channel of truth. It is to a truth that men listen; and if they accept error also, it is only because the error is for the time so closely interwoven with the truth, that the one cannot readily be separated from the other.

Unmixed error can have no existence in the public mind. Wherever you see men clustering together to form a party, you may be sure that however much error may be there, truth is there also. Apply this principle boldly; for it contains a lesson of candor, and a voice of encouragement. There never was a school of philosophy, nor a clan in the realm of opinion, but carried along with it some important truth. And therefore every sect that has ever flourished has benefited Humanity; for the errors of a sect pass away and are forgotten; its truths are received into the common inheritance. To know the seminal thought of every prophet and leader of a sect, is to gather all the wisdom of mankind....

The sentiment of beauty, as it exists in the human mind, is the criterion in works of art, inspires the conceptions of genius, and exercises a final judgment on its productions. For who are the best judges in matters of taste? Do you think the cultivated individual? Undoubtedly not; but the collective mind. The public is wiser than the wisest critic. In Athens, the arts were carried to perfection, when "the fierce democracie" was in the ascendant; the temple of Minerva and the works of Phidias were planned and perfected to please the common people. When Greece yielded to tyrants, her genius for excellence in art expired; or rather, the purity of taste disappeared; because the artist then endeavored to gratify a patron, and therefore, humored his caprice; while before he had endeavored to delight the race.

When, after a long eclipse, the arts again burst into a splendid existence, it was equally under a popular influence. During the rough contests and feudal tyrannies of the middle age, religion had opened in the church an asylum for the people. There the serf and the beggar could kneel; there the pilgrim and the laborer were shrived; and the children of misfortune not less than the prosperous were welcomed to the house of prayer. The church was, consequently, at once the guardian of equality, and the nurse of the arts; and the souls of Giotto, and Perugino, and Raphael, moved by an infinite sympathy with the crowd, kindled into divine conceptions of beautiful forms. Appealing to the sentiment of devotion in the common mind, they dipped their pencils in living colors, to decorate the altars where man adored. By degrees the wealthy nobility desired in like manner to adorn their palaces; but at the attempt, the quick familiarity of the artist with the beautiful declined. Instead of the brilliant works which spoke to the soul, a school arose, who appealed to the senses; and in the land which had produced the most moving pictures, addressed to the religious feeling, and instinct with the purest beauty, the banquet halls were covered with grotesque forms, such as float before the imagination, when excited and bewildered by sensual indulgence. Instead of holy families, the ideal representations of the virgin mother and the godlike child, of the enduring faith of martyrs, of the blessed benevolence of evangelic love, there came the motley group of fawns and satyrs, of Diana stooping to Endymion, of voluptuous beauty, and the forms of licentiousness. Humanity frowned on the desecration of the arts; and painting, no longer vivified by a fellow-feeling with the multitude, lost its greatness in the attempt to adapt itself to personal humors.

If with us the arts are destined to a brilliant career, the inspiration must spring from the vigor of the people. Genius will not create, to flatter patrons or decorate saloons. It yearns for larger influences; it feeds on wider sympathies; and its perfect display can never exist, except in an appeal to the general sentiment for the beautiful.

Again. Italy is famed for its musical compositions, its inimitable operas. It is a well-known fact, that the best critics are often deceived in their judgment of them; while the pit, composed of the throng, does, without fail, render a true verdict.

But the taste for music, it may be said, is favored by natural organization. Precisely a statement that sets in a clearer light the natural capacity of the race; for taste is then not an acquisition, but in part a gift. But let us pass to works of literature.

Who are by way of eminence the poets of all mankind? Surely Homer and Shakspeare. Now Homer formed his taste, as he wandered from door to door, a vagrant minstrel, paying for hospitality by a song; and Shakspeare wrote for an audience, composed in a great measure of the common people.

The little story of Paul and Virginia is a universal favorite. When it was first written, the author read it aloud to a circle in Paris, composed of the wife of the prime minister, and the choicest critics of France. They condemned it, as dull and insipid. The author appealed to the public; and the children of all Europe reversed the decree of the Parisians. The judgment of children, that is, the judgment of the common mind under its most innocent and least imposing form, was more trustworthy than the criticism of the select refinement of the most polished city in the world.

Demosthenes of old formed himself to the perfection of eloquence by means of addresses to the crowd. The great comic poet of Greece, emphatically the poet of the vulgar mob, is distinguished above all others for the incomparable graces of his diction; and it is related of one of the most skilful writers in the Italian, that when inquired of where he had learned the purity and nationality of his style, he replied, from listening to the country people, as they brought their produce to market.

At the revival of letters a distinguishing feature of the rising literature was the employment of the dialect of the vulgar. Dante used the language of the populace and won immortality; Wickliffe, Luther, and at a later day Descartes, each employed his mother tongue, and carried truth directly to all who were familiar with its accents. Every beneficent revolution in letters has the character of popularity; every great reform among authors has sprung from the power of the people in its influence on the development and activity of mind.

The same influence continues unimpaired. Scott, in spite of his reverence for the aristocracy, spurned a drawing-room reputation; the secret of Byron's superiority lay in part in the agreement which existed between his muse and the democratic tendency of the age.

German literature is almost entirely a popular creation. It was fostered by no monarch; it was dandled by no aristocracy. It was plebeian in its origin, and therefore manly in its results.

III.

In like manner the best government rests on the people and not on the few, on persons and not on property, on the free development of public opinion and not on authority; because the munificent Author of our being has conferred the gifts of mind upon every member of the human race without distinction of outward circumstances. Whatever of other possessions may be engrossed, mind asserts its own independence. Lands, estates, the produce of mines, the prolific abundance of the seas, may be usurped by a privileged class. Avarice, assuming the form of ambitious power, may grasp realm after realm, subdue continents, compass the earth in its schemes of aggrandizement, and sigh after other worlds; but mind eludes the power of appropriation; it exists only in its own individuality, it is a property which cannot be confiscated and cannot be torn away; it laughs at chains; it bursts from imprisonment; it defies monopoly. A government of equal rights must, therefore, rest upon mind; not wealth, not brute force, the sum of the moral intelligence of the community should rule the State. Prescription can no more assume to be a valid plea for political injustice; society studies to eradicate established abuses, and to bring social institutions and laws into harmony with moral right; not dismayed by the natural and necessary imperfections of all human effort, and not giving way to despair, because every hope does not at once ripen into fruit.

The public happiness is the true object of legislation, and can be secured only by the masses of mankind themselves awakening to the knowledge and the care of their own interests. Our free institutions have reversed the false and ignoble distinctions between men; and refusing to gratify the pride of caste, have acknowledged the common mind to be the true material for a commonwealth. Every thing has hitherto been done for the happy few. It is not possible to endow an aristocracy with greater benefits than they have already enjoyed; there is no room to hope that individuals will be more highly gifted or more fully developed than the greatest sages of past times. The world can advance only through the culture of the moral and intellectual powers of the people. To accomplish this end by means of the people themselves, is the highest purpose of government. If it be the duty of the individual to strive after a perfection like the perfection of God, how much more ought a nation to be the image of Deity. The common mind is the true Parian marble, fit to be wrought into likeness to a God. The duty of America is to secure the culture and the happiness of the masses by their reliance on themselves.

The absence of the prejudices of the old world leaves us here the opportunity of consulting independent truth; and man is left to apply the instinct of freedom to every social relation and public interest. We have approached so near to nature, that we can hear her gentlest whispers; we have made Humanity our lawgiver and our oracle; and, therefore, the nation receives, vivifies and applies principles, which in Europe the wisest accept with distrust. Freedom of mind and of conscience, freedom of the seas, freedom of industry, equality of franchises, each great truth is firmly grasped, comprehended and enforced; for the multitude is neither rash nor fickle. In truth, it is less fickle than those who profess to be its guides. Its natural dialectics surpass the logic of the schools. Political action has never been so consistent and so unwavering, as when it results from a feeling or a principle, diffused through society. The people is firm and tranquil in its movements, and necessarily acts with moderation, because it becomes but slowly impregnated with new ideas; and effects no changes, except in harmony with the knowledge which it has acquired. Besides, where it is permanently possessed of power, there exists neither the occasion nor the desire for frequent change. It is not the parent of tumult; sedition is bred in the lap of luxury, and its chosen emissaries are the beggared spendthrift and the impoverished libertine. The government by the people is in very truth the strongest government in the world. Discarding the implements of terror, it dares to rule by moral force, and has its citadel in the heart.

Such is the political system which rests on reason, reflection, and the free expression of deliberate choice. There may be those who scoff at the suggestion, that the decision of the whole is to be preferred to the judgement of the enlightened few. They say in their hearts that the masses are ignorant; that farmers know nothing of legislation; that mechanics should not quit their workshops to join in forming public opinion. But true political science does indeed venerate the masses. It maintains, not as has been perversely asserted, that "the people can make right," but that the people can DISCERN right. Individuals are but shadows, too often engrossed by the pursuit of shadows; the race is immortal: individuals are of limited sagacity; the common mind is infinite in its experience: individuals are languid and blind; the many are ever wakeful: individuals are corrupt; the race has been redeemed: individuals are time-serving; the masses are fearless: individuals may be false, the masses are ingenuous and sincere: individuals claim the divine sanction of truth for the deceitful conceptions of their own fancies; the Spirit of God breathes through the combined intelligence of the people. Truth is not to be ascertained by the impulses of an individual; it emerges from the contradictions of personal opinion; it raises itself in majestic serenity above the strifes of parties and the conflict of sects; it acknowledges neither the solitary mind, nor the separate faction as its oracle; but owns as its only faithful interpreter the dictates of pure reason itself, proclaimed by the general voice of mankind. The decrees of the universal conscience are the nearest approach to the presence of God in the soul of man.

Thus the opinion which we respect is, indeed, not the opinion of one or of a few, but the sagacity of the many. It is hard for the pride of cultivated philosophy to put its ear to the ground, and listen reverently to the voice of lowly humanity; yet the people collectively are wiser than the most gifted individual, for all his wisdom constitutes but a part of theirs. When the great sculptor of Greece was endeavoring to fashion the perfect model of beauty, he did not passively imitate the form of the loveliest woman of his age; but he gleaned the several lineaments of his faultless work from the many. And so it is that a perfect judgment is the result of comparison, when error eliminates error, and truth is established by concurring witnesses. The organ of truth is the invisible decision of the unbiased world; she pleads before no tribunal but public opinion; she owns no safe interpreter but the common mind; she knows no court of appeals but the soul of humanity. It is when the multitude give counsel, that right purposes find safety; theirs is the fixedness that cannot be shaken; theirs is the understanding which exceeds in wisdom; theirs is the heart, of which the largeness is as the sand on the seashore.

It is not by vast armies, by immense natural resources, by accumulations of treasure, that the greatest results in modern civilization have been accomplished. The traces of the career of conquest pass away, hardly leaving a scar on the national intelligence. The famous battle grounds of victory are, most of them, comparatively indifferent to the human race; barren fields of blood, the scourges of their times, but affecting the social condition as little as the raging of a pestilence. Not one benevolent institution, not one ameliorating principle in the Roman state, was a voluntary concession of the aristocracy; each useful element was borrowed from the Democracies of Greece, or was a reluctant concession to the demands of the people. The same is true in modern political life. It is the confession of an enemy to Democracy, that "ALL THE GREAT AND NOBLE INSTITUTIONS OF THE WORLD HAVE COME FROM POPULAR EFFORTS."

It is the uniform tendency of the popular element to elevate and bless Humanity. The exact measure of the progress of civilization is the degree in which the intelligence of the common mind has prevailed over wealth and brute force; in other words, the measure of the progress of civilization is the progress of the people. Every great object, connected with the benevolent exertions of the day, has reference to the culture of those powers which are alone the common inheritance. For this the envoys of religion cross seas, and visit remotest isles; for this the press in its freedom teems with the production of maturest thought; for this the philanthropist plans new schemes of education; for this halls in every city and village are open to the public instructor. Not that we view with indifference the glorious efforts of material industry; the increase in the facility of internal intercourse; the accumulations of thrifty labor; the varied results of concentrated action. But even there it is mind that achieves the triumph. It is the genius of the architect that gives beauty to the work of human hands, and makes the temple, the dwelling, or the public edifice, an outward representation of the spirit of propriety and order. It is science that guides the blind zeal of cupidity to the construction of the vast channels of communication, which are fast binding the world into one family. And it is as a method of moral improvement, that these swifter means of intercourse derive their greatest value. Mind becomes universal property; the poem that is published on the soil of England, finds its response on the shores of lake Erie and the banks of the Missouri, and is admired near the sources of the Ganges. The defence of public liberty in our own halls of legislation penetrates the plains of Poland, is echoed along the mountains of Greece, and pierces the darkest night of eastern despotism.

The universality of the intellectual and moral powers, and the necessity of their development for the progress of the race, proclaim the great doctrine of the natural right of every human being to moral and intellectual culture. It is the glory of our fathers to have established in their laws the equal claims of every child to the public care of its morals and its mind. From this principle we may deduce the universal right to leisure; that is, to time not appropriated to material purposes, but reserved for the culture of the moral affections and the mind. It does not tolerate the exclusive enjoyment of leisure by a privileged class; but defending the rights of labor, would suffer none to sacrifice the higher purposes of existence in unceasing toil for that which is not life. Such is the voice of nature; such the conscious claim of the human mind. The universe opens its pages to every eye; the music of creation resounds in every ear; the glorious lessons of immortal truth, that are written in the sky and on the earth, address themselves to every mind, and claim attention from every human being. God has made man upright, that he might look before and after; and he calls upon every one not merely to labor, but to reflect; not merely to practise the revelations of divine will, but to contemplate the displays of divine power. Nature claims for every man leisure, for she claims every man as a witness to the divine glory, manifested in the created world....

The right to universal education being thus acknowledged by our conscience, not less than by our laws, it follows, that the people is the true recipient of truth. Do not seek to conciliate individuals; do not dread the frowns of a sect; do not yield to the proscriptions of a party; but pour out truth into the common mind. Let the waters of intelligence, like the rains of heaven, descend on the whole earth. And be not discouraged by the dread of encountering ignorance. The *prejudices of ignorance are more easily removed than the prejudices of interest; the first are blindly adopted; the second wilfully preferred.* Intelligence must be diffused among the whole people; truth must be scatted among those who have no interest to suppress its growth. The seeds that fall on the exchange, or in the hum of business, may be choked by the thorns that spring up in the hotbed of avarice; the seeds that are let fall in the saloon, may be like those dropped by the wayside, which take no root. Let the young aspirant after glory scatter the seeds of truth broadcast on the wide bosom of Humanity; in the deep, fertile soil of the public mind. There it will strike deep root and spring up, and bear an hundredfold, and bloom for ages, and ripen fruit through remote generations.

It is alone by infusing great principles into the common mind, that revolutions in human society are brought about. They never have been, they never can be, effected by superior individual excellence. The age of the Antonines is the age of the greatest glory of the roman empire. Men distinguished by every accomplishment of culture and science, for a century in succession, possessed undisputed sway over more than a hundred millions of men; till at last, in the person of Mark Aurelian, philosophy herself seemed to mount the throne. And did she stay the downward tendencies of the Roman empire? Did she infuse new elements of life into the decaying constitution? Did she commence one great, beneficent reform? Not one permanent amelioration was effected; philosophy was clothed with absolute power; and yet absolute power accomplished nothing for Humanity. It could accomplish nothing. Had it been possible, Aurelian would have wrought a change. Society can be regenerated, the human race can be advanced, only by moral principles diffused through the multitude.

And now let us take an opposite instance; let us see, if amelioration follows, when in despite of tyranny truth finds access to the common people; and Christianity itself shall furnish my example.

When Christianity first made its way into Rome, the imperial city was the seat of wealth, philosophy, and luxury. Absolute government was already established; and had the will of Claudius been gained, or the conscience of Messalina been roused, or the heart of Narcissus, once a slave, then prime minister, been touched by the recollections of his misfortunes, the aid of the sovereign of the civilized world would have been engaged. And did the messenger of divine truth make his appeal to them? Was his mission to the emperor and his millions? to the empress and her flatterers? to servile senators? to wealthy favorites? Paul preserves for us the names of the first converts; the Roman Mary and Junia; Julia and Nerea; and the beloved brethren; all plebeian names, unknown to history....

Yes, reforms in society are only effected through the masses of the people, and through them have continually taken place. New truths have been successively developed, and, becoming the common property of the human family, have improved its condition. This progress is advanced by every sect, precisely because each sect, to obtain vitality, does of necessity embody a truth; by every political party, for the conflicts of party are the war of ideas; by every nationality, for a nation cannot exist as such, till humanity makes it a special trustee of some part of its wealth for the ultimate benefit of all. The irresistible tendency of the human race is therefore to advancement, for absolute power has never succeeded, and can never succeed, in suppressing a single truth. An idea once revealed may find its admission into every living breast and live there. Like God it becomes immortal and omnipresent. The movement of the species is upward, irresistibly upward. The individual is often lost; Providence never disowns the race. No principle once promulgated, has ever been forgotten. No "timely tramp" of a despot's foot ever trod out one idea. The world cannot retrograde; the dark ages cannot return. Dynasties perish; cities are buried; nations have been victims to error, or martyrs for right; Humanity has always been on the advance; gaining maturity, universality, and power.

Yes, truth is immortal; it cannot be destroyed; it is invincible, it cannot long be resisted. Not every great principle has yet been generated; but when once proclaimed and diffused, it lives without end, in the safe custody of the race. States may pass away; every just principle of legislation which has been once established will endure. Philosophy has sometimes forgotten God; a great people never did. The skepticism of the last century could not uproot Christianity, because it lived in the hearts of the millions. Do you think that infidelity is spreading? Christianity never lived in the hearts of so many millions as at this moment. The forms under which it is professed may decay, for they, like all that is the work of man's hands, are subject to the changes and chances of mortal being; but the spirit of truth is incorruptible; it may be developed, illustrated, and applied; it never can die; it never can decline.

No truth can perish; no truth can pass away. The flame is undying, though generations disappear. Wherever moral truth has started into being, Humanity claims and guards the bequest. Each generation gathers together the imperishable children of the past, and increases them by new sons of light, alike radiant with immortality.

ORESTES BROWNSON

"The Laboring Classes"
(1840)

If the evangelical age encouraged an ethos of perpetual conversions, Orestes Brownson (1803–1876) was its *ne plus ultra*. Growing up as an impoverished adopted orphan in rural Vermont and later the "burned-over district" of upstate New York, over the course of two decades he progressed through, successively, Presbyterianism, Universalism, skepticism, Unitarianism, and Transcendentalism. He finally rested in 1844, to the shock of his former reform colleagues, with Roman Catholicism, after which he reigned for three more decades as America's most famous and formidable Catholic intellectual. Yet for Brownson these twists and turns were perfectly logical dialectical movements as he made his way, albeit in public, through progressively higher understandings of the truth. Moreover, in these later years he retained the same polemical ardor, philosophical acumen, and (to many vexed Church officers) headstrong independence that had characterized his early years as a political and religious radical. He also retained his rage for authoritative order in the service of two goals: the reconciliation of the material and spiritual in the cosmos, and of society and the state in the "church."

He displayed both concerns in a two-part article "The Laboring Classes," which he published in his *Boston Quarterly Review* four years before his conversion to Roman Catholicism, during the depth of the nation's first industrial depression. Beginning as a review of Thomas Carlyle's furiously anti-laissez-faire *Chartism* (1839), it quickly transmogrified into the most radically anti-capitalist tract ever before penned by an American writer. First, eight years before Marx and Engels' *Communist Manifesto,* he transformed the Jacksonians' promiscuous populist impulse into a class-struggle vision of modern capitalism. In Brownson's view the real "people" in modern society were increasingly the "laboring classes" arrayed against a capitalist class whose monopoly of capital and industrial production subjected their (a term he also used) "proletaries" to exploitation and an abject dependency. Second, he proposed, not only the traditional Jacksonian restrictions on the federal government's powers to provide special "privileges" to the rich, but also the wholesale dismantling of the banking and credit system and the abolition of inheritance. Third, he frankly predicted all of this would come as a result of a violent war "the like of which the world as yet has never witnessed." Finally, as a necessary by-product, that war would result in the total overthrow of organized religion—or, as he put it, virulently mixing Transcendentalist "come-outer" and French Revolutionary-like vitriolic rhetoric, the "final destruction of the priestly order." Only through such means could the democratic state guarantee the dignified proprietorships of ordinary people and the social gospel of Jesus Christ. With his article greeted by (as he would later put it) "one universal scream of horror" from both the Whigs he despised and the Democrats he supported, Brownson hastily began exploring alternate "conservative" means by which to protect the body and spirit of "the people" even against themselves.

By doing justice to both Brownson's politics and his theology, Patrick W. Carey has given us the best biography to date in his *Orestes A. Brownson: American Religious Weathervane* (Grand Rapids, Mich., 2004). Carey has also provided an invaluable annotated listing of Brownson's published writings in *Orestes A. Brownson: A Bibliography, 1826–1876* (Milwaukee, 1997). For a provocative treatment of Brownson's Christian radical "populist" thought, see Christopher Lasch, *The True and Only Heaven: Progress and Its Critics* (New York, 1991), chap. 5. Two valuable readings of Brownson's turn to Catholicism may be found in Jenny Franchot, *Roads to Rome: The Antebellum Protestant Encounter with Catholicism* (Berkeley, 1994), chap. 17; and Patrick Allitt, *Catholic Converts: British and American Intellectuals Turn to Rome* (Ithaca, 1997), chap. 4.

[I.]

...No one can observe the signs of the times with much care, without perceiving that a crisis as to the relation of wealth and labor is approaching. It is useless to shut our eyes to the fact, and like the ostrich fancy ourselves secure because we have so concealed our heads that we see not the danger. We or our children will have to meet this crisis. The old war between the King and the Barons is well nigh ended, and so is that between the Barons and the Merchants and Manufacturers,—landed capital and commercial capital. The business man has become the peer of my Lord. And now commences the new struggle between the operative and his employer, between wealth and labor. Every day does this struggle extend further and wax stronger and fiercer; what or when the end will be God only knows....

What we would ask is, throughout the Christian world, the actual condition of the laboring classes, viewed simply and exclusively in their capacity of laborers? They constitute at least a moiety of the human race. We exclude the nobility, we exclude also the middle class, and include only actual laborers, who are laborers and not proprietors, owners of none of the funds of production, neither houses, shops, nor lands, nor implements of labor, being therefore solely dependent on their hands. We have no means of ascertaining their precise proportion to the whole number of the race; but we think we may estimate them at one half. In any contest they will be as two to one, because the large class of proprietors who are not employers, but laborers on their own lands or in their own shops will make common cause with them.

Now we will not so belie our acquaintance with political economy, as to allege that these alone perform all that is necessary to the production of wealth. We are not ignorant of the fact, that the merchant, who is literally the common carrier and exchange dealer, performs a useful service, and is therefore entitled to a portion of the proceeds of labor. But make all necessary deductions on his account, and then ask what portion of the remainder is retained, either in kind or in its equivalent, in the hands of the original producer, the workingman? All over the world this fact stares us in the face, the workingman is poor and depressed, while a large portion of the non-workingmen, in the sense we now use the term, are wealthy. It may be laid down as a general rule, with but few exceptions, that men are rewarded in an inverse ratio to the amount of actual service they perform. Under every government on earth the largest salaries are annexed to those offices, which demand of their incumbents the least amount of actual labor either mental or manual. And this is in perfect harmony with the whole system of repartition of the fruits of industry, which obtains in every department of society. Now here is the system which prevails, and here is its result. The whole class of simple laborers are poor, and in general unable to procure anything beyond the bare necessaries of life.

In regard to labor two systems obtain; one that of slave labor, the other that of free labor. Of the two, the first is, in our judgment, except so far as the feelings are concerned, decidedly the least oppressive. If the slave has never been a free man, we think, as a general rule, his sufferings are less than those of the free laborer at wages. As to actual freedom one has just about as much as the other. The laborer at wages has all the disadvantages of

Source: Boston Quarterly Review, 3 (July 1840), 366, 367–68, 369–70, 371–76, 376–77, 378–80, 381–82, 383–84, 385–86, 388, 388–89, 391–92, 393–95; and 3 (October 1840), 436, 436–38, 472–77, 478, 478–79, 480–81. Notes omitted.

freedom and none of its blessings, while the slave, if denied the blessings, is freed from the disadvantages. We are no advocates of slavery, we are as heartily opposed to it as any modern abolitionist can be; but we say frankly that, if there must always be a laboring population distinct from proprietors and employers, we regard the slave system as decidedly preferable to the system at wages. It is no pleasant thing to go days without food, to lie idle for weeks, seeking work and finding none, to rise in the morning with a wife and children you love, and know not where to procure them a breakfast, and to see constantly before you no brighter prospect than the almshouse. Yet these are no unfrequent incidents in the lives of our laboring population....

We pass through our manufacturing villages, most of them appear neat and flourishing. The operatives are well dressed, and we are told, well paid. They are said to be healthy, contented, and happy. This is the fair side of the picture; the side exhibited to distinguished visitors. There is a dark side, moral as well as physical. Of the common operatives, few, if any, by their wages, acquire a competence. A few of what Carlyle terms not inaptly the *body-servants* are well paid, and now and then an agent or an overseer rides in his coach. But the great mass wear out their health, spirits, and morals, without becoming one whit better off than when they commenced labor. The bills of mortality in these factory villages are not striking, we admit, for the poor girls when they can toil no longer go home to die. The average life, working life we mean, of the girls that come to Lowell, for instance, from Maine, New Hampshire, and Vermont, we have been assured, is only about three years. What becomes of them then? Few of them ever marry; fewer still ever return to their native places with reputations unimpaired. "She has worked in a Factory," is almost enough to damn to infamy the most worthy and virtuous girl. We know no sadder sight on earth than one of our factory villages presents, when the bell at break of day, or at the hour of breakfast, or dinner, calls out its hundreds or thousands of operatives. We stand and look at these hard working men and women hurrying in all directions, and ask ourselves, where go the proceeds of their labors? The man who employs them, and for whom they are toiling as so many slaves, is one of our city nabobs, revelling in luxury; or he is a member of our legislature, enacting laws to put money in his own pocket; or he is a member of Congress, contending for a high Tariff to tax the poor for the benefit of the rich; or in these times he is shedding crocodile tears over the deplorable condition of the poor laborer, while he docks his wages twenty-five per cent; building miniature log cabins, shouting Harrison and "hard cider." And this man too would fain pass for a Christian and a republican. He shouts for liberty, stickles for equality, and is horrified at a Southern planter who keeps slaves.

One thing is certain; that of the amount actually produced by the operative, he retains a less proportion than it costs the master to feed, clothe, and lodge his slave. Wages is a cunning device of the devil, for the benefit of tender consciences, who would retain all the advantages of the slave system, without the expense, trouble, and odium of being slaveholders....

Now, what is the prospect of those who fall under the operation of this system? We ask, is there a reasonable chance that any considerable portion of the present generation of laborers, shall ever become owners of a sufficient portion of the funds of production, to be able to sustain themselves by laboring on their own capital, that is, as independent laborers? We need not ask this question, for everybody knows there is not. Well, is the condition of a laborer at wages the best that the great mass of the working people ought to be able to aspire to? Is it a condition,—nay can it be made a condition,—with which a man should be satisfied; in which he should be contented to live and die?

In our own country this condition has existed under its most favorable aspects, and has been made as good as it can be. It has reached all the excellence of which it is susceptible. It is now not improving but growing worse. The actual condition of the working-man to-day, viewed in all its bearings, is not so good as it was fifty years ago. If we have not been altogether misinformed, fifty years ago, health and industrious habits, constituted no mean stock in trade, and with them almost any man might aspire to competence and independence. But it is so no longer. The wilderness has receded, and already the new lands are beyond the reach of the mere laborer, and the employer has him at his mercy. If the present relation subsist, we see nothing better for him in reserve than what he now possesses, but something altogether worse.

We are not ignorant of the fact that men born poor become wealthy, and that men born to wealth become poor; but this fact does not necessarily diminish the numbers of the poor, nor augment the numbers of the rich. The relative numbers of the two classes remain, or may remain, the same. But be this as it may; one fact is certain, no man born poor has ever, by his wages, as a simple operative, risen to the class of the wealthy. Rich he may have become, but it has not been by his own manual labor. He has in some way contrived to tax for his benefit the labor of others. He may have accumulated a few dollars which he has placed at usury, or invested in trade; or he may, as a master workman, obtain a premium on his journeymen; or he may have from a clerk passed to a partner, or from a workman to an overseer. The simple market wages for ordinary labor, has never been adequate to raise him from poverty to wealth. This fact is decisive of the whole controversy, and proves that the system of wages must be supplanted by some other system, or else one half of the human race must for ever be the virtual slaves of the other.

Now the great work for this age and the coming, is to raise up the laborer, and to realize in our own social arrangements and in the actual condition of all men, that equality between man and man, which God has established between the rights of one and those of another. In other words, our business is to emancipate the proletaries, as the past has emancipated the slaves. This is our work. There must be no class of our fellow men doomed to toil through life as mere workmen at wages. If wages are tolerated it must be, in the case of the individual operative, only under such conditions that by the time he is of a proper age to settle in life, he shall have accumulated enough to be an independent laborer on his own capital,—on his own farm or in his own shop. Here is our work. How is it to be done?

Reformers in general answer this question, or what they deem its equivalent, in a manner which we cannot but regard as very unsatisfactory. They would have all men wise, good, and happy; but in order to make them so, they tell us that we want not external changes, but internal; and therefore instead of declaiming against society and seeking to disturb existing social arrangements, we should confine ourselves to the individual reason and conscience; seek merely to lead the individual to repentance, and to reformation of life; make the individual a practical, a truly religious man, and all evils will either disappear, or be sanctified to the spiritual growth of the soul.

This is doubtless a capital theory, and has the advantage that kings, hierarchies, nobilities,—in a word, all who fatten on the toil and blood of their fellows, will feel no difficulty in supporting it. Nicholas of Russia, the Grand Turk, his Holiness the Pope, will hold us their especial friends for advocating a theory, which secures to them the odor of sanctity even while they are sustaining by their anathemas or their armed legions, a system of things of which the great mass are and must be the victims. If you will only allow me to keep thousands toiling for my pleasure or my profit, I will even aid you in your pious efforts to convert their souls. I am not cruel; I do not wish either to cause, or to see suffering; I am therefore disposed to encourage your labors for the souls of the working-man, providing you will secure to me the products of his bodily toil. So far as the salvation of his soul will not interfere with my income, I hold it worthy of being sought; and if a few thousand dollars will aid you, Mr. Priest, in reconciling him to God, and making fair weather for him hereafter, they are at your service. I shall not want him to work for me in the world to come, and I can indemnify myself for what your salary costs me, by paying him less wages. A capital theory this, which one may advocate without incurring the reproach of a disorganizer, a jacobin, a leveller, and without losing the friendship of the rankest aristocrat in the land.

This theory, however, is exposed to one slight objection, that of being condemned by something like six thousand years' experience. For six thousand years its beauty has been extolled, its praises sung and its blessings sought, under every advantage which learning, fashion, wealth, and power can secure; and yet under its practical operations, we are assured, that mankind, though totally depraved at first, have been growing worse and worse ever since.

For our part, we yield to none in our reverence for science and religion; but we confess that we look not for the regeneration of the race from priests and pedagogues. They have had a fair trial. They cannot construct the temple of God. They cannot conceive its plan, and they know not how to build. They daub with untempered mortar, and the walls they erect tumble down if so much as a fox attempt to go up thereon. In a word they always league with the people's masters, and seek to reform without disturbing the social arrangements which render reform necessary. They would change the consequents without changing the antecedents, secure to men the rewards of holiness, while they continue their allegiance to the devil. We have no faith in priests and pedagogues. They merely cry peace, peace, and that too when there is no peace, and can be none.

We admit the importance of what Dr. Channing in his lectures on the subject we are treating recommends as "self-culture." Self-culture is a good thing, but it cannot abolish inequality, nor restore men to their rights. As a means of quickening moral and intellectual energy, exalting the sentiments, and preparing the laborer to contend manfully for his rights, we admit its importance, and insist as strenuously as any one on making it as universal as possible; but as constituting in itself a remedy for the vices of the social state, we have no faith in it. As a means it is well, as the end it is nothing.

The truth is, the evil we have pointed out is not merely individual in its character. It is not, in the case of any single individual, of any one man's procuring, nor can the efforts of any one man, directed solely to his own moral and religious perfection, do aught to remove it. What is purely individual in its nature, efforts of individuals to perfect themselves, may remove. But the evil we speak of is inherent in all our social arrangements, and cannot be cured without a radical change of those arrangements. Could we convert all men to Christianity in both theory and practice, as held by the most enlightened sect of Christians among us, the evils of the social state would remain untouched. Continue our present system of trade, and all its present evil consequences will follow, whether it be carried on by your best men or your worst. Put your best men, your wisest, most moral, and most religious men, at the head of your paper money banks, and the evils of the present banking system will remain scarcely diminished. The only way to get rid of its evils is to change the system, not its managers. The evils of slavery do not result from the personal characters of slave masters. They are inseparable from the system, let who will be masters. Make all your rich men good Christians, and you have lessened not the evils of existing inequality in wealth. The mischievous effects of this inequality do not result from the personal characters of either rich or poor, but from itself, and they will continue, just so long as there are rich men and poor men in the same community. You must abolish the system or accept its consequences. No man can serve both God and Mammon. If you will serve the devil, you must look to the devil for your wages; we know no other way....

The evil we have pointed out, we have said, is not of individual creation, and it is not to be removed by individual effort, saving so far as individual effort induces the combined effort of the mass. But whence has this evil originated? How comes it that all over the world the working classes are depressed, are the low and vulgar, and virtually the slaves of the non-working classes? This is an inquiry which has not yet received the attention it deserves. It is not enough to answer, that it has originated entirely in the inferiority by nature of the working classes; that they have less skill and foresight, and are less able than the upper classes, to provide for themselves, or less susceptible of the highest moral and intellectual cultivation. Nor is it sufficient for our purpose to be told, that Providence has decreed that some shall be poor and wretched, ignorant and vulgar; and that others shall be rich and vicious, learned and polite, oppressive and miserable. We do not choose to charge this matter to the will of God. "The foolishness of man per-verteth his way, and his heart fretteth against the Lord." God has made of one blood all the nations of men to dwell on all the face of the earth, and to dwell there as brothers, as members of one and the same family; and although he has made them with a diversity of powers, it would perhaps, after all, be a bold assertion to say that he has made them with an inequality of powers. There is nothing in the actual difference of the powers of individuals, which accounts for the striking inequalities we everywhere discover in their condition. The child of the plebeian, if placed early in the proper circumstances, grows up not less beautiful, active, intelligent, and refined, than the child of the patrician; and the child of the patrician may become as coarse, as brutish as the child of any slave. So far as observation on the original capacities of individuals goes nothing is discovered to throw much light on social inequalities.

The cause of the inequality, we speak of, must be sought in history, and be regarded as having its root in Providence, or in human nature, only in that sense in which all his-torical facts have their origin in these. We may perhaps trace it in the first instance to conquest, but not to conquest as the ultimate cause....For our part we are disposed to seek the cause of the inequality of conditions of which we speak, in religion, and to charge it to the priesthood. And we are confirmed in this, by what appears to be the instinctive tendency of every, or almost every, social reformer. Men's instincts, in a matter of this kind, are worthier of reliance than their reasonings. Rarely do we find in any age or coun-try, a man feeling himself commissioned to labor for a social reform, who does not feel that he must begin it by making war upon the priesthood. This was the case with the old Hebrew reformers, who are to us the prophets of God; with Jesus, the Apostles, and the early Fathers of the Church; with the French democrats of the last century; and is the case with the Young Germans, and the Socialists, as they call themselves in England, at the present moment. Indeed it is felt at once that no reform can be effected without resisting the priests and emancipating the people from their power.

Historical research, we apprehend, will be found to justify this instinct, and to autho-rize the eternal hostility of the reformer, the advocate of social progress, to the priesthood. How is it, we ask, that man comes out of the savage state? In the savage state, properly so called, there is no inequality of the kind of which we speak. The individual system obtains there. Each man is his own centre, and is a whole in himself. There is no community, there are no members of society; for society is not. This individuality, which, if combined with the highest possible moral and intellectual cultivation, would be the perfection of man's earthly condition, must be broken down before the human race can enter into the path of civilization, or commence its career of progress. But it cannot be broken down by material force. It resists by its own nature the combination of individuals necessary to subdue it. It can be successfully attacked only by a spiritual power and subjugated only by the representatives of that power, that is to say, the priests.

Man is naturally a religious being, and disposed to stand in awe of invisible powers. This makes, undoubtedly, under certain relations, his glory; but when coupled with his ignorance, it becomes the chief source of his degradation and misery. He feels within the workings of a mysterious nature, and is conscious that hidden and superior powers are at work all around him, and perpetually influencing his destiny; now wafting him onward with a prosperous gale, or now resisting his course, driving him back; defeating his plans, blasting his hopes, and wounding his heart. What are his relations to these hidden, mysterious, and yet all-influencing forces? Can their anger be appeased? Can their favor be secured? Thus he asks himself. Unable to answer, he goes to the more aged and experienced of his tribe, and asks them the same questions. They answer as best they can. What is done by one is done by another, and what is done once is done again. The necessity of instruction, which each one feels in consequence of his own feebleness and inexperience, renders the recurrence to those best capable of giving it, or supposed to be the best capable of giving it, frequent and uniform. Hence the priest. He who is consulted prepares himself to answer, and therefore devotes himself to the study of man's relations to these invisible powers, and the nature of these invisible powers themselves. Hence religion becomes a special object of study, and the study of it a profession. Individuals whom a thunderstorm, an earthquake, an eruption of a volcano, an eclipse of the sun or moon, any unusual appearance in the heavens or earth, has frightened, or whom some unforeseen disaster has afflicted, go to the wise-man for explanation, to know what it means, or what they shall do in order to appease the offended powers. When reassured they naturally feel grateful to this wise-man, they load him with honors, and in the access of their gratitude raise him far above the common level, and spare him the common burdens of life. Once thus distinguished, he becomes an object of envy. His condition is looked upon as superior to that of the mass. Hence a multitude aspire to possess themselves of it. When once the class has become somewhat numerous, it labors to secure to itself the distinction it has received, its honors and its emoluments, and to increase them. Hence the establishment of priesthoods or sacerdotal corporations, such as the Egyptian, the Braminical, the Ethiopian, the Jewish, the Scandinavian, the Druidical, the Mexican, and Peruvian....

Now if we glance over the history of the world, we shall find, that at the epoch of coming out of the savage state, these corporations are universally instituted. We find them among every people; and among every people, at this epoch, they are the dominant power, ruling with an iron despotism. The real idea at the bottom of these institutions, is the control of individual freedom by moral laws, the assertion of the supremacy of moral power over physical force,—a great truth, and one which can never be too strenuously insisted on; but a truth which at this epoch can only enslave the mass of the people to its professed representatives, the priests. Through awe of the gods, through fear of divine displeasure, and dread of the unforeseen chastisements that displeasure may inflict, and by pretending, honestly or not, to possess the secret of averting it, and of rendering the gods propitious, the priests are able to reduce the people to the most wretched subjection, and to keep them there; at least for a time.

But these institutions must naturally be jealous of power, and ambitious of confining it to as few hands as possible. If the sacerdotal corporations were thrown open to all the world, all the world would rush into them, and then there would be no advantage in being a priest. Hence the number who may be priests must be limited. Hence again a distinction of clean and unclean is introduced. Men can be admitted into these corporations only as they descend from the priestly race. As in India, no man can aspire to the priesthood unless of Braminical descent, and among the Jews unless he be of the tribe of Levi. The priestly race was the ruling race; it dealt with science, it held communion with the Gods, and therefore was the purer race. The races excluded from the priesthood were not only regarded as inferior, but as unclean. The Gibeonite to a Jew was both an inferior and an impure. The operation of the principles involved in these considerations, has, in our judgment, begun and effected the slavery of the great mass of the people. It has introduced distinctions of blood or race, founded privileged orders, and secured the rewards of industry to the few, while it has reduced the mass to the most degrading and hopeless bondage....

Mankind came out of the savage state by means of the priests. Priests are the first civilizers of the race. For the wild freedom of the savage, they substitute the iron despotism of the theocrat. This is the first step in civilization, in man's career of progress. It is not strange then that some should prefer the savage state to the civilized. Who would not rather roam the forest with a free step and unshackled limb, though exposed to hunger, cold, and nakedness, than crouch an abject slave beneath the whip of a master? As yet civilization has done little but break and subdue man's natural love of freedom; but tame his wild and eagle spirit. In what a world does man even now find himself, when he first awakes and feels some of the workings of his manly nature? He is in a cold, damp, dark dungeon, and loaded all over with chains, with the iron entering into his very soul. He cannot make one single free movement. The priest holds his conscience, fashion controls his tastes, and society with her forces invades the very sanctuary of his heart, and takes command of his love, that which is purest and best in his nature, which alone gives reality to his existence, and from which proceeds the only ray which pierces the gloom of his prison-house. Even that he cannot enjoy in peace and quietness, nor scarcely at all. He is wounded on every side, in every part of his being, in every relation in life, in every idea of his mind, in every sentiment of his heart. O, it is a sad world, a sad world to the young soul just awakening to its diviner instincts! A sad world to him who is not gifted with the only blessing which seems compatible with life as it is—absolute insensibility. But no matter. A wise man never murmurs. He never kicks against the pricks. What is is, and there is an end of it; what can be may be, and we will do what we can to make life what it ought to be. Though man's first step in civilization is slavery, his last step shall be freedom. The free soul can never be wholly subdued; the etherial fire in man's nature may be smothered, but it cannot be extinguished. Down, down deep in the centre of his heart it burns inextinguishable and forever, glowing intenser with the accumulating heat of centuries; and one day the whole mass of Humanity shall become ignited, and be full of fire within and all over, as a live coal; and then—slavery, and whatever is foreign to the soul itself, shall be consumed.

But, having traced the inequality we complain of to its origin, we proceed to ask again what is the remedy? The remedy is first to be sought in the destruction of the priest. We are not mere destructives. We delight not in pulling down; but the bad must be removed before the good can be introduced. Conviction and repentance precede regeneration. Moreover we are Christians, and it is only by following out the Christian law, and the example of the early Christians, that we can hope to effect anything. Christianity is the sublimest protest against the priesthood ever uttered, and a protest uttered by both God and man; for he who uttered it was God-Man. In the person of Jesus both God and Man protest against the priesthood. What was the mission of Jesus but a solemn summons of every priesthood on earth to judgment, and of the human race to freedom? He discomfited the learned doctors, and with whips of small cords drove the priests, degenerated into mere money changers, from the temple of God. He instituted himself no priesthood, no form of religious worship. He recognised no priest but a holy life, and commanded the construction of no temple but that of the pure heart. He preached no formal religion, enjoined no creed, set apart no day for religious worship. He preached fraternal love, peace on earth, and good will to men. He came to the soul enslaved, "cabined, cribbed, confined," to the poor child of mortality, bound hand and foot, unable to move, and said in the tones of a God, "Be free; be enlarged; be there room for thee to grow, expand, and overflow with the love thou wast made to overflow with.".…

We object not to religious instruction; we object not to the gathering together of the people on one day in seven, to sing and pray, and listen to a discourse from a religious teacher; but we object to everything like an outward, visible church; to everything that in the remotest degree partakes of the priest. A priest is one who stands as a sort of mediator between God and man; but we have one mediator, Jesus Christ, who gave himself a ransom for all, and that is enough. It may be supposed that we, protestants, have no priests; but for ourselves we know no fundamental difference between a catholic priest and a protestant clergyman, as we know no difference of any magnitude, in relation to the principles on which they are based, between a protestant church and the catholic church. Both are based on the principle of authority; both deny in fact, however it may be in manner, the authority of reason, and war against freedom of mind; both substitute dead works for true righteousness, a vain show for the reality of piety, and are sustained as the means of reconciling us to God without requiring us to become godlike. Both therefore ought to go by the board.…

The next step in this work of elevating the working classes will be to resuscitate the Christianity of Christ.…

According to the Christianity of Christ no man can enter the kingdom of God, who does not labor with all zeal and diligence to establish the kingdom of God on the earth; who does not labor to bring down the high, and bring up the low; to break the fetters of the bound and set the captive free; to destroy all oppression, establish the reign of justice, which is the reign of equality, between man and man; to introduce new heavens and a new earth, wherein dwelleth righteousness, wherein all shall be as brothers, loving one another, and no one possessing what another lacketh. No man can be a Christian who does not labor to reform society, to mould it according to the will of God and the nature of man; so that free scope shall be given to every man to unfold himself in all beauty and power, and to grow up into the stature of a perfect man in Christ Jesus. No man can be a Christian who does not refrain from all practices by which the rich grow richer and the poor poorer, and who does not do all in his power to elevate the laboring classes, so that one man shall not be doomed to toil while another enjoys the fruits; so that each man shall be free and independent, sitting under "his own vine and figtree with none to molest or to make afraid.".…

Having, by breaking down the power of the priesthood and the Christianity of the priests, obtained an open field and freedom for our operations, and by preaching the true Gospel of Jesus, directed all minds to the great social reform needed, and quickened in all souls the moral power to live for it or to die for it; our next resort must be to government, to legislative enactments. Government is instituted to be the agent of society, or more properly the organ through which society may perform its legitimate functions. It is not the master of society; its business is not to control society, but to be the organ through which society effects its will. Society has never to petition government; government is its servant, and subject to its commands.

Now the evils of which we have complained are of a social nature. That is, they have their root in the constitution of society as it is, and they have attained to their present growth by means of social influences, the action of government, of laws, and of systems and institutions upheld by society, and of which individuals are the slaves. This being the case, it is evident that they are to be removed only by the action of society, that is, by government, for the action of society is government.

But what shall government do? Its first doing must be an *undoing*. There has been thus far quite too much government, as well as government of the wrong kind. The first act of government we want, is a still further limitation of itself. It must begin by circumscribing within narrower limits its powers. And then it must proceed to repeal all laws which bear against the laboring classes, and then to enact such laws as are necessary to enable them to maintain their equality. We have no faith in those systems of elevating the working classes, which propose to elevate them without calling in the aid of the government. We must have government, and legislation expressly directed to this end.

But again what legislation do we want so far as this country is concerned? We want first the legislation which shall free the government, whether State or Federal, from the control of the Banks. The Banks represent the interest of the employer, and therefore of necessity interests adverse to those of the employed; that is, they represent the interests of the business community in opposition to the laboring community. So long as the government remains under the control of the Banks, so long it must be in the hands of the natural enemies of the laboring classes, and may be made, nay, will be made, an instrument of depressing them yet lower....

Following the destruction of the Banks, must come that of all monopolies, of all PRIVILEGE. There are many of these. We cannot specify them all; we therefore select only one, the greatest of them all, the privilege which some have of being born rich while others are born poor. It will be seen at once that we allude to the hereditary descent of property, an anomaly in our American system, which must be removed, or the system itself will be destroyed. We cannot now go into a discussion of this subject, but we promise to resume it at our earliest opportunity. We only say now, that as we have abolished hereditary monarchy and hereditary nobility, we must complete the work by abolishing hereditary property. A man shall have all he honestly acquires, so long as he himself belongs to the world in which he acquires it. But his power over his property must cease with his life, and his property must then become the property of the state, to be disposed of by some equitable law for the use of the generation which takes his place. Here is the principle without any of its details, and this is the grand legislative measure to which we look forward. We see no means of elevating the laboring classes which can be effectual without this. And is this a measure to be easily carried? Not at all. It will cost infinitely more than it cost to abolish either hereditary monarchy or hereditary nobility. It is a great measure, and a startling. The rich, the business community, will never voluntarily consent to it, and we think we know too much of human nature to believe that it will ever be effected peaceably. It will be effected only by the strong arm of physical force. It will come, if it ever come at all, only at the conclusion of war, the like of which the world as yet has never witnessed, and from which, however inevitable it may seem to the eye of philosophy, the heart of Humanity recoils with horror.

[II.]

A[n] objection, which we have heard urged against our views, is that we would abolish the priesthood, and dispense with all religious instruction, and all religious worship. To this objection we reply, that the inference drawn from what we have said against priests, is unwarranted....

But what are our views of the priesthood? To what did we in reality object, when we objected to the priesthood? These questions we can answer only by giving at some length our views of Christianity, as an outward, visible institution.

The mission of Jesus was twofold. One purpose of his mission was to atone for sin, and prepare the soul for heaven in the world to come. The other purpose was to found a holy kingdom on the earth, under the dominion of which all men should finally be brought. This last purpose is the only one which concerns us in our present inquiry.

This holy kingdom, which Christ came to found on the earth, has been mistaken for the outward, visible Church; and the Church has therefore been held to be a spiritual body, a body corporate, independent in itself, and distinct from the body politic civil society, or the State. This has given rise to a double organization of mankind; one for material interests called the State, and under the control of the civil government proper; the other for spiritual purposes, called the Church, and governed by laws and officers of its own, distinct from those of the State.

Now to this we strenuously object. We would establish the kingdom of God on the earth; but we would not have a *double* organization of mankind. We would have but a single organization; and this organization we would call not the Church, but the State. This organization should be based on the principles of the Gospel, and realize them as perfectly, as finite man can realize them.

The kingdom of God is an inward, spiritual kingdom. In plain language, it is the dominion of truth, justice, and love. Now, we would build up this kingdom not by founding an outward visible Church, but by cultivating the principles of truth, justice, and love, in the soul of the individual, and by bringing society and all its acts into perfect harmony with them. Our views, if carried out, would realize not a union, but the unity, the identity, of Church and State. They would indeed destroy the Church as a *separate* body, as a distinct organization; but they would do it by transferring to the State the moral ideas on which the Church was professedly founded, and which it has failed to realize. They would realize that idea of a "Christian Commonwealth," after which our Puritan fathers so earnestly and perseveringly struggled. They are nothing but the views of the first settlers of this state, developed and systematized, and freed from the theological phraseology in which they were then expressed. We are true to their idea, to their spirit, and are laboring to realize that which they most desired. We therefore remind those who profess to reverence our Puritan ancestors, that they would do well to study the history and opinions of those ancestors, and forbear to censure us, till they are prepared to condemn them....

The great evil of all modern society, in relation to the material order, is the separation of the capitalist from the laborer,—the division of the community into two classes, one of which owns the funds, and the other of which performs the labor, of production.

This division obtains throughout the civilized world, but is less clearly marked with us, than anywhere else. To a considerable extent, our agricultural population combines the proprietor and laborer in the same individual; and where this is not the case, the condition of the proletaries, or hired men, as we call them, presents its most favorable aspect,—at least so far as the non-slaveholding states are concerned. The hired men in the agricultural districts are hardly distinguished from their employers. They are as well dressed, as well educated, work no harder, and mingle with them very nearly on terms of equality in the general intercourse of society.

But this is not universally true, and is becoming less and less so every year. It is said that our agricultural population is rising in wealth, intelligence, and refinement, and this is unquestionably true of landed proprietors. The proportion of what we term gentlemen farmers is, no doubt, rapidly increasing. But this, while it speaks well for the proprietor, tells a mournful tale for the proletary. Where the man who owns the plough holds it, there can be no great disparity between the employer and employed; but this disparity necessarily increases just in proportion as the owner of the plough employs another to hold it. The distance between the owner of the farm, and the men who cultivate it, is, therefore, becoming every day greater and greater.

But it is in our cities, large towns, and manufacturing villages, that the condition of the laboring population is the most unfavorable. The distinction between the capitalist and the proletary, in these, is as strongly marked as it is in the old world. The distance between the wife and daughters of an Abbot Lawrence, and the poor factory girl employed in his mills, is as great as that between the wife and daughters of an English nobleman, and the daughter of one of his tenants, and the intercourse less frequent. Intermarriage between the families of the wealthy factory owners, and those of the operatives, is as much an outrage on the public sense of propriety, as it was in ancient Rome between the patricians and plebeians,—almost as much as it would be at the south between the family of a planter and that of one of his slaves.

Still, taking our country throughout, the condition of the proletary population has been, and is altogether superior here to what it is in any other part of the civilized world. We do not, however, attribute this fact to our democratic institutions, nor to the adoption of more enlightened systems of social, political, or domestic economy, than are adopted elsewhere. It is owing to causes purely accidental, and which are rapidly disappearing. The first of these accidental causes may be traced to the original equality of the first settlers of this country. But this equality no longer exists. Fortunes are said to be more unequal with us than they are in France. The second cause, and the main one, has consisted in the low price of land. The ease with which individuals have been able to procure them farms, and pass from the class of proletaries to that of proprietors, has had a constant tendency to diminish the number of proletaries, and to raise the price of labor. But this cause becomes less and less powerful. Few, comparatively speaking, of the proletaries, in any of the old states, can ever become land-owners. Land there, is already too high for that. The new lands are rapidly receding to the west, and can even now be reached only by the those who have some little capital in advance. Moreover, these new lands are not inexhaustible. Fifty years to come, if emigration go on at the rate it has for fifty years past, will leave very little for the new emigrant.

The causes removed, which have hitherto favored the working-man, and lessened the distance between him and the proprietor, what is to prevent the reproduction here, in our land of boasted equality, of the order of things which now exists in the old world? As yet, that order does not exist here in all its revolting details; but who can fail to see that there is a strong tendency to it? Our economical systems are virtually those of England; our passions, our views, and feelings are similar; and what is to prevent the reproduction of the same state of things in relation to our laboring population with that which gangrenes English society? We confess, we cannot see any causes at work among us likely to prevent it.

The remedies relied on by the political reformers are free trade, and universal suffrage; by the moral reformers, universal education, and religious culture. We agree with both, and sustain them as far as they go; but they are insufficient. These measures are all good and necessary; but inadequate, unless something more radical still be adopted along with them. Alone they are mere palliatives. They may serve to conceal the sore, perhaps assuage its pain; but they cannot cure it.

Universal suffrage is little better than a mockery, where the voters are not socially equal. No matter what party you support, no matter what men you elect, property is always the basis of your governmental action. No policy has ever yet been pursued by our government, state or federal, under one party or another, notwithstanding our system of universal suffrage, which has had for its aim the elevation of man, independent of his relation as a possessor of property. In no instance have the rights of the proletary prevailed over the interests of the proprietor. To separate power from property, we hold to be impossible under our present system. Its interests will always predominate in the measures of government, though they may sometimes be defeated in elections. The interests of property may now and then be divided, as they were under General Jackson's administration. The interests of the state banks, and particularly of those of New York, were then opposed to those of the United States Bank. The interests of landed property combined with those of labor are now arrayed against the banks generally; and if they are successful, it will not be because the interests of labor count for anything; but because the farming and planting interests are stronger than the mercantile and manufacturing interests. The proletaries, though voters in this contest, serve merely to swell the forces of one or the other party. They gain nothing by the fact that they are voters; they will gain, however, if the landed interests triumph; because, in the actual condition of our country, the interest of the laborer is mainly identified with those of land. But, let which interest will triumph, the laborer will gain nothing directly. He will only gain so far as it is impossible to separate his interest from the interest which triumphs. Still, universal suffrage is a right, and is worth something. All we mean to say is, that in itself, it by no means constitutes a sovereign remedy for the evils under which the laboring classes suffer. It by no means gives them that degree of political power, which theorists imagine. To be rendered efficient, it must be coupled with something like equality of fortunes. The proprietors may indeed sometimes be outvoted in an election, but their interests will invariably triumph in the legislative halls, and at the tribunals of justice. At least, this has been the experience of this country thus far. We will hope that the future will furnish a different experience.

The system of free trade, so far as it has as yet been advocated in this country, we approve, as a means of social amelioration; but we cannot rely on it, as alone sufficient. Because, to amount to much, the competitors must start even, and with nearly equal chances of success, which cannot be, with our present constitution of property, nor, indeed, with our present constitution of human nature. Moreover, if the system of free trade be pushed to its last results, it becomes the introduction of a system of universal competition, a system of universal strife, where each man is for himself, and no man for another. It would be a return to the pure individuality of the savage state, the abolition of all government, and the adoption, as the practical rule of conduct, of the maxim, "save who can." We have not yet advanced far enough in moral or social science to adopt this rule. We would indeed restrict as much as possible the sphere of government, and enlarge that of the individual; but government, as the organ and agent of society, is a positive good, and can never be dispensed with. We have, moreover, no faith in bringing about the social order we desire, by the agency of selfishness and strife. True democracy can never rest permanently on the maxim, "I am as good as you;" but it must resort to this other maxim, "You are as good as I." The spirit, by which it must ultimately be sustained, is not the spirit that will not submit to tyranny, but the spirit that will not tyrannize.

In universal education and religious culture, we have faith indeed; but not as final measures. Their office is to generate the moral force needed; but the generation of that force is not the reform. Mind is undoubtedly superior to matter, and all reforms must come from within; but the mental and moral reform, effected in the interior of man, will prove insufficient, unless it come out of the interior, and remodel the exterior. What we contend is not, that free trade, universal suffrage, universal education, and religious culture, are not essential, indispensable means to the social regeneration we are in pursuit of; but that, if we stop with them, and leave the material order of society untouched, they will prove inadequate. We make no war on the political reformer, nor on the moral reformer. Our plan includes all they propose, and more too. Ours includes that, without which theirs would accomplish little.

With this view of the case, it becomes necessary to seek something more ultimate, more radical than our most approved reformers have as yet ventured upon. This something we have professed to find in the abolition of hereditary property, a measure foreshadowed in the first number of this Journal, and implied, at least in our own mind, by almost every article we have ever written on the subject of social reform. We have long been thoroughly convinced that, without resorting to some such measure, it would be useless to talk of social progress, or to speak in behalf of the laborer.

The doctrine we have long labored to maintain is, that the work of this country is to emancipate labor, by raising up the laborer from a mere workman, without capital, to be a proprietor, and a workman on his own farm, or in his own shop....

Now we would ask, how is it possible to gain the end here implied, without a change in the present constitution of property?... Hereditary property, unless the amount inherited by each individual could be rendered equal, is unquestionably a privilege. It gives, and always must give, to one portion of the community an advantage over the rest, to which they are entitled by no natural superiority of intellect, or of virtue. Will the public conscience, then, of the American people tolerate it? Will it sanction privilege?...

The American people may be mistaken as to men and measures, but we are confident that in principle, they will all assent to the doctrine of equality. We feel confident of their unanimous support, when we say that all the members of the community should have, so far as society is concerned, equal chances. But equal chances imply equal starting points. Nobody, it would seem, could pretend that where the points of departure were unequal the chances could be equal. Do the young man inheriting ten thousand pounds, and the one whose inheritance is merely the gutter, start even? Have they equal chances? It may be said both are free to rise as high as they can,—one starting with ten thousand pounds in advance, and the other starting with the gutter. But it might as well be said the chances of the eldest son of the Duke of Newcastle, and those of the eldest son of one of the lowest of the Duke's tenants, are equal, since both unquestionably are free to rise as high as they can,—one starting with a dukedom in advance, and the other with nothing. But to pretend this is mere jesting....

The proposition, for the abolition of hereditary property, it follows from these considerations, is merely a logical conclusion from the admitted premises of the American people, and, *a fortiori*, of the democratic party. We have merely followed the invincible law of logic in putting it forth. We are compelled, either to abandon the American theory of government and society, or else contend for the abolition of hereditary properly, and they who censure us as a rash innovator, and call us "infamous" for choosing the latter alternative, are either false in their professions of attachment to American principles, or from two given ideas incapable of inferring a third.

Are we wrong? What in one word is this American system? Is it not the abolition of all artificial distinctions, all social advantages founded on birth or any other accident, and leaving every man to stand on his own feet, for precisely what God and nature have made him? Does not this system declare that society should make no distinction between the child of the rich man and the child of the poor man; that she shall neither reward the child for the virtues, nor punish him for the vices of the parent? Is this the American system, yes or no? If it be not, what mean all our boasts of equality, all our Fourth of July oratory, all our patriotic songs and national glorifications? What else is it that we are constantly throwing in the face of the old world? and on what else do we profess to found our claims to admiration and imitation? Everybody knows that this is the system, which the American people profess, and to which they stand committed before the world. We pray them, then, to tell us how with this system, which repudiates all distinctions founded on birth, they can reconcile hereditary property, which has no other basis than the accident of birth on which to rest? The logic by which they can do it is above, or below, our comprehension....

CATHARINE BEECHER

Selection from *A Treatise on Domestic Economy* (1841)

As the sister of the novelist Harriet Beecher Stowe and the daughter and sister, respectively, of two of America's most illustrious preachers, Lyman and Henry Ward Beecher, Catharine Beecher (1800–1878) was born to the evangelical purple. Nonetheless, by her own right and in her own sphere (to borrow one of her favored terms), she was fully as influential as they in theirs. That sphere was American middle-class female culture. An indefatigable organizer of women's schools and colleges and a resourceful battler for the advancement of women teachers in public education, Beecher was the antebellum era's leader in the takeoff of American female education. Equally important was her role in intellectually reconciling, for the many women who read her books, existing patterns of female subordination with the values of American democracy.

In the opening chapters of her popular *Treatise on Domestic Economy,* she managed this feat in three main ways. She showed that a Christian and liberal idea of democracy was perfectly consistent with social hierarchies. She argued that women's domestic and teaching sphere, properly defined, was not only the basis of women's social advancement, but was central to the very functioning of American democracy and the evangelical regeneration of the world. Finally, by proposing a new scheme of professionalized domestic work and female schooling, she sought to show that women's activities as well as their mental health necessitated autonomous and utilitarian rationalistic thinking skills—or the very same skills that had often been considered by educational reformers since Locke the primary ingredients of *masculine* success in school and work.

Kathryn Kish Sklar's *Catharine Beecher: A Study in American Domesticity* (New Haven, 1973) is a first-rate biographical study that gives full attention to Beecher's social thought. Although it focuses primarily on Catharine's feminist younger sister Isabella Beecher Hooker, Barbara A. White's collective biography *The Beecher Sisters* (New Haven, 2003) sheds much light on the familial context of all the famous sisters' careers. Jane Roland Martin, *Reclaiming a Conversation: The Ideal of the Educated Woman* (New Haven, 1985), 103–83, provides a stimulating interpretation of Beecher's educational theories. For studies of the antebellum ideology of domesticity in, respectively, economic thought and imaginative literature, see Jeanne Boydston, *Home and Work: Housework, Wages, and the Ideology of Labor in the Early Republic* (New York, 1990); and Gillian Brown, *Domestic Individualism: Imagining Self in Nineteenth-Century America* (Berkeley, 1990).

Chapter I.

THE PECULIAR RESPONSIBILITIES OF AMERICAN WOMEN.

There are some reasons, why American women should feel an interest in the support of the democratic institutions of their Country, which it is important that they should consider. The great maxim, which is the basis of all our civil and political institutions, is, that "all men are created equal," and that they are equally entitled to "life, liberty, and the pursuit of happiness."

But it can readily be seen, that this is only another mode of expressing the fundamental principle which the Great Ruler of the Universe has established, as the law of His eternal government. "Thou shalt love thy neighbor as thyself;" and "Whatsoever ye would that men should do to you, do ye even so to them," are the Scripture forms, by which the Supreme Lawgiver requires that each individual of our race shall regard the happiness of others, as of the same value as his own; and which forbid any institution, in private or civil life, which secures advantages to one class, by sacrificing the interests of another.

The principles of democracy, then, are identical with the principles of Christianity.

But, in order that each individual may pursue and secure the highest degree of happiness within his reach, unimpeded by the selfish interests of others, a system of laws must be established, which sustain certain relations and dependencies in social and civil life. What these relations and their attending obligations shall be, are to be determined, not with reference to the wishes and interests of a few, but solely with reference to the general good of all; so that each individual shall have his own interest, as well as the public benefit, secured by them.

For this purpose, it is needful that certain relations be sustained, which involve the duties of subordination. There must be the magistrate and the subject, one of whom is the superior, and the other the inferior. There must be the relations of husband and wife, parent and child, teacher and pupil, employer and employed, each involving the relative duties of subordination. The superior, in certain particulars, is to direct, and the inferior is to yield obedience. Society could never go forward, harmoniously, nor could any craft or profession be successfully pursued, unless these superior and subordinate relations be instituted and sustained.

But who shall take the higher, and who the subordinate, stations in social and civil life? This matter, in the case of parents and children, is decided by the Creator. He has given children to the control of parents, as their superiors, and to them they remain subordinate, to a certain age, or as long as they are members of their household. And parents can delegate such a portion of their authority to teachers and employers, as the interests of their children require.

In most other cases, in a truly democratic state, each individual is allowed to choose for himself, who shall take the position of his superior. No woman is forced to obey any husband but the one she chooses for herself; nor is she obliged to take a husband, if she prefers to remain single. So every domestic, and every artisan or laborer, after passing from parental control, can choose the employer to whom he is to accord obedience, or, if he prefers to relinquish certain advantages, he can remain without taking a subordinate place to any employer.

Source: Catharine E. Beecher, *A Treatise on Domestic Economy, for the Use of Young Ladies at Home, at School,* rev. ed. (New York: Harper & Bros., 1846), 25–28, 32–34, 35–41, 43–44, 45–46, 47–49, 50–53, 53–54, 54–62.

Each subject, also, has equal power with every other, to decide who shall be his superior as a ruler. The weakest, the poorest, the most illiterate, has the same opportunity to determine this question, as the richest, the most learned, and the most exalted.

And the various privileges that wealth secures, are equally open to all classes. Every man may aim at riches, unimpeded by any law or institution which secures peculiar privileges to a favored class, at the expense of another. Every law, and every institution, is tested by examining whether it secures equal advantages to all; and, if the people become convinced that any regulation sacrifices the good of the majority to the interests of the smaller number, they have power to abolish it.

The institutions of monarchical and aristocratic nations are based on precisely opposite principles. They secure, to certain small and favored classes, advantages, which can be maintained, only by sacrificing the interests of the great mass of the people. Thus, the throne and aristocracy of England are supported by laws and customs, which burden the lower classes with taxes, so enormous, as to deprive them of all the luxuries, and of most of the comforts, of life. Poor dwellings, scanty food, unhealthy employments, excessive labor, and entire destitution of the means and time for education, are appointed for the lower classes, that a few may live in palaces, and riot in every indulgence.

The tendencies of democratic institutions, in reference to the rights and interests of the female sex, have been fully developed in the United States; and it is in this aspect, that the subject is one of peculiar interest to American women. In this Country, it is established, both by opinion and by practice, that woman has an equal interest in all social and civil concerns; and that no domestic, civil, or political, institution, is right, which sacrifices her interest to promote that of the other sex. But in order to secure her the more firmly in all these privileges, it is decided, that, in the domestic relation, she take a subordinate station, and that, in civil and political concerns, her interests be intrusted to the other sex, without her taking any part in voting, or in making and administering laws....

It appears...that it is in America, alone, that women are raised to equality with the other sex; and that, both in theory and practice, their interests are regarded as of equal value. They are made subordinate in station, only where a regard to their best interests demands it, while, as if in compensation for this, by custom and courtesy, they are always treated as superiors. Universally, in this Country, through every class of society, precedence is given to woman, in all the comforts, conveniences, and courtesies, of life.

In civil and political affairs, American women take no interest or concern, except so far as they sympathize with their family and personal friends; but in all cases, in which they do feel a concern, their opinions and feelings have a consideration, equal, or even superior, to that of the other sex.

In matters pertaining to the education of their children, in the selection and support of a clergyman, in all benevolent enterprises, and in all questions relating to morals or manners, they have a superior influence. In such concerns, it would be impossible to carry a point, contrary to their judgment and feelings; while an enterprise, sustained by them, will seldom fail of success.

If those who are bewailing themselves over the fancied wrongs and injuries of women in this Nation, could only see things as they are, they would know, that, whatever remnants of a barbarous or aristocratic age may remain in our civil institutions, in reference to the interests of women, it is only because they are ignorant of them, or do not use their influence to have them rectified; for it is very certain that there is nothing reasonable, which American women would unite in asking, that would not readily be bestowed.

The preceding remarks, then, illustrate the position, that the democratic institutions of this Country are in reality no other than the principles of Christianity carried into operation, and that they tend to place woman in her true position in society, as having equal rights with the other sex; and that, in fact, they have secured to American women a lofty and fortunate position, which, as yet, has been attained by the women of no other nation....

It...appears, that the sublime and elevating anticipations which have filled the mind and heart of the religious world, have become so far developed, that philosophers and statesmen are perceiving the signs, and are predicting the approach, of the same grand consummation. There is a day advancing, "by seers predicted, and by poets sung," when the curse of selfishness shall be removed; when "scenes surpassing fable, and yet true," shall be realized; when all nations shall rejoice and be made blessed, under those benevolent influences, which the Messiah came to establish on earth.

And this is the Country, which the Disposer of events designs shall go forth as the cynosure of nations, to guide them to the light and blessedness of that day. To us is committed the grand, the responsible privilege, of exhibiting to the world, the beneficent influences of Christianity, when carried into every social, civil, and political institution; and, though we have, as yet, made such imperfect advances, already the light is streaming into the dark prison-house of despotic lands, while startled kings and sages, philosophers and statesmen, are watching us with that interest, which a career so illustrious, and so involving their own destiny, is calculated to excite. They are studying our institutions, scrutinizing our experience, and watching for our mistakes, that they may learn whether "a social revolution, so irresistible, be advantageous or prejudicial to mankind."

There are persons, who regard these interesting truths merely as food for national vanity; but every reflecting and Christian mind, must consider it as an occasion for solemn and anxious reflection. Are we, then, a spectacle to the world? Has the Eternal Lawgiver appointed us to work out a problem, involving the destiny of the whole earth? Are such momentous interests to be advanced or retarded, just in proportion as we are faithful to our high trust? "What manner of persons, then, ought we to be," in attempting to sustain so solemn, so glorious a responsibility?

But the part to be enacted by American women, in this great moral enterprise, is the point to which special attention should here be directed.

The success of democratic institutions, as is conceded by all, depends upon the intellectual and moral character of the mass of the people. If they are intelligent and virtuous, democracy is a blessing; but if they are ignorant and wicked, it is only a curse, and as much more dreadful than any other form of civil government, as a thousand tyrants are more to be dreaded than one. It is equally conceded, that the formation of the moral and intellectual character of the young is committed mainly to the female hand. The mother forms the character of the future man; the sister bends the fibers that are hereafter to be the forest tree; the wife sways the heart, whose energies may turn for good or for evil the destinies of a nation. Let the women of a country be made virtuous and intelligent, and the men will certainly be the same. The proper education of a man decides the welfare of an individual; but educate a woman, and the interests of a whole family are secured.

If this be so, as none will deny, then to American women, more than to any others on earth, is committed the exalted privilege of extending over the world those blessed influences, which are to renovate degraded man, and "clothe all climes with beauty."

No American woman, then, has any occasion for feeling that hers is an humble or insignificant lot. The value of what an individual accomplishes, is to be estimated by the importance of the enterprise achieved, and not by the particular position of the laborer. The drops of heaven which freshen the earth, are each of equal value, whether they fall in the lowland meadow, or the princely parterre. The builders of a temple are of equal importance, whether they labor on the foundations, or toil upon the dome.

Thus, also, with those labors which are to be made effectual in the regeneration of the Earth. And it is by forming a habit of regarding the apparently insignificant efforts of each isolated laborer, in a comprehensive manner, as indispensible portions of a grand result, that the minds of all, however humble their sphere of service, can be invigorated and cheered. The woman, who is rearing a family of children; the woman, who labors in the schoolroom; the woman, who, in her retired chamber, earns, with her needle, the mite, which contributes to the intellectual and moral elevation of her Country; even the humble domestic, whose example and influence may be moulding and forming young minds, while her faithful services sustain a prosperous domestic state;—each and all may be animated by the consciousness, that they are agents in accomplishing the greatest work that ever was committed to human responsibility. It is the building of a glorious temple, whose base shall be coextensive with the bounds of the earth, whose summit shall pierce the skies, whose splendor shall beam on all lands; and those who hew the lowliest stone, as much as those who carve the highest capital, will be equally honored, when its top-stone shall be laid, with new rejoicings of the morning stars, and shoutings of the sons of God.

Chapter II.

DIFFICULTIES PECULIAR TO AMERICAN WOMEN.

In the preceding chapter, were presented those views, which are calculated to inspire American women with a sense of their high responsibilities to their Country, and to the world; and of the excellence and grandeur of the object to which their energies may be consecrated.

But it will be found to be the law of moral action, that whatever involves great results and great benefits, is always attended with great hazards and difficulties. And as it has been shown, that American women have a loftier position, and a more elevated object of enterprise, than the females of any other nation, so it will appear, that they have greater trials and difficulties to overcome, than any other women are called to encounter.

Properly to appreciate the nature of these trials, it must be borne in mind, that the estimate of evils and privations depends, not so much on their positive nature, as on the character and habits of the person who meets them. A woman, educated in the savage state, finds it no trial to be destitute of many conveniences, which a woman, even of the lowest condition, in this Country, would deem indispensable to existence. So a woman, educated with the tastes and habits of the best New England or Virginia housekeepers, would encounter many deprivations and trials, which would never occur to one reared in the log cabin of a new settlement. So, also, a woman, who has been accustomed to carry forward her arrangements with well-trained domestics, would meet a thousand trials to her feelings and temper, by the substitution of ignorant foreigners, or shiftless slaves, which would be of little account to one who had never enjoyed any better service.

Now, the larger portion of American women are the descendants of English progenitors, who, as a nation, are distinguished for systematic housekeeping, and for a great love of order, cleanliness, and comfort. And American women, to a greater or less extent, have inherited similar tastes and habits. But the prosperity and democratic tendencies of this Country produce results, materially affecting the comfort of housekeepers, which the females of monarchical and aristocratic lands are not called to meet. In such countries, all ranks and classes are fixed in a given position, and each person is educated for a particular sphere and style of living. And the dwellings, conveniences, and customs of life, remain very nearly the same, from generation to generation. This secures the preparation of all classes for their particular station, and makes the lower orders more dependent, and more subservient to employers.

But how different is the state of things in this Country. Every thing is moving and changing. Persons in poverty, arc rising to opulence, and persons of wealth, are sinking to poverty. The children of common laborers, by their talents and enterprise, are becoming nobles in intellect, or wealth, or office; while the children of the wealthy, enervated by indulgence, are sinking to humbler stations. The sons of the wealthy are leaving the rich mansions of their fathers, to dwell in the log cabins of the forest, where very soon they bear away the daughters of ease and refinement, to share the privations of a new settlement. Meantime, even in the more stationary portions of the community, there is a mingling of all grades of wealth, intellect, and education. There are no distinct classes, as in aristocratic lands, whose bounds are protected by distinct and impassable lines, but all are thrown into promiscuous masses. Thus, persons of humble means are brought into contact with those of vast wealth, while all intervening grades are placed side by side. Thus, too, there is a constant comparison of conditions, among equals, and a constant temptation presented to imitate the customs, and to strive for the enjoyments, of those who possess larger means.

In addition to this, the flow of wealth, among all classes, is constantly increasing the number of those who live in a style demanding much hired service, while the number of those, who are compelled to go to service, is constantly diminishing. Our manufactories, also, are making increased demands for female labor, and offering larger compensation. In consequence of these things, there is such a disproportion between those who wish to hire, and those who are willing to go to domestic service, that, in the non-slaveholding States, were it not for the supply of poverty-stricken foreigners, there would not be a domestic for each family who demands one. And this resort to foreigners, poor as it is, scarcely meets the demand; while the disproportion must every year increase, especially if our prosperity increases. For, just in proportion as wealth rolls in upon us, the number of those, who will give up their own independent homes to serve strangers, will be diminished.

The difficulties and sufferings, which have accrued to American women, from this cause, are almost incalculable. There is nothing, which so much demands system and regularity, as the affairs of a housekeeper, made up, as they are, of ten thousand desultory and minute items; and yet, this perpetually fluctuating state of society seems forever to bar any such system and regularity. The anxieties, vexations, perplexities, and even hard labor, which come upon American women, from this state of domestic service, are endless; and many a woman has, in consequence, been disheartened, discouraged, and ruined in health. The only wonder is, that, amid so many real difficulties, American women are still able to maintain such a character for energy, fortitude, and amiableness, as is universally allowed to be their due.

But the second, and still greater difficulty, peculiar to American women, is, a delicacy of constitution, which renders them early victims to disease and decay....

A perfectly healthy woman, especially a perfectly healthy mother, is so infrequent, in some of the wealthier classes, that those, who are so, may be regarded as the exceptions, and not as the general rule. The writer has heard some of her friends declare, that they would ride fifty miles, to see a perfectly healthy and vigorous woman, out of the laboring classes. This, although somewhat jocose, was not an entirely unfair picture of the true state of female health in the wealthier classes.

There are many causes operating, which serve to perpetuate and increase this evil. It is a well-known fact, that mental excitement tends to weaken the physical system, unless it is counterbalanced by a corresponding increase of exercise and fresh air. Now, the people of this Country are under the influence of high commercial, political, and religious stimulus, altogether greater than was ever known by any other nation; and in all this, women are made the sympathizing companions of the other sex. At the same time, young girls, in pursuing an education, have ten times greater an amount of intellectual taxation demanded, than was ever before exacted. Let any daughter, educated in our best schools at this day, compare the course of her study with that pursued in her mother's early life, and it will be seen that this estimate of the increase of mental taxation probably falls below the truth. Though, in some countries, there are small classes of females, in the higher circles, who pursue literature and science to a far greater extent than in any corresponding circles in this Country, yet, in no nation in the world are the advantages of a good intellectual education enjoyed, by so large a proportion of the females. And this education has consisted far less of accomplishments, and far more of those solid studies which demand the exercise of the various powers of mind, than the education of the women of other lands.

And when American women are called to the responsibilities of domestic life, the degree in which their minds and feelings are taxed, is altogether greater than it is in any other nation.

No women on earth have a higher sense of their moral and religious responsibilities, or better understand, not only what is demanded of them, as housekeepers, but all the claims that rest upon them as wives, mothers, and members of a social community. An American woman, who is the mistress of a family, feels her obligations, in reference to her influence over her husband, and a still greater responsibility in rearing and educating her children. She feels, too, the claims which the moral interests of her domestics have on her watchful care. In social life, she recognises the claims of hospitality, and the demands of friendly visiting. Her responsibility, in reference to the institutions of benevolence and religion, is deeply realized. The regular worship of the Lord's Day, and all the various religious meetings and benevolent societies which place so much dependence on female influence and example, she feels obligated to sustain. Add to these multiplied responsibilities, the perplexities and evils which have been pointed out, resulting from the fluctuating state of society, and the deficiency of domestic service, and no one can deny that American women are exposed to a far greater amount of intellectual and moral excitement, than those of any other land. Of course, in order to escape the danger resulting from this, a greater amount of exercise in the fresh air, and all those methods which strengthen the constitution, are imperiously required.

But, instead of this, it will be found, that, owing to the climate and customs of this Nation, there are no women who secure so little of this healthful and protecting regimen, as ours. Walking and riding and gardening, in the open air, are practised by the women of other lands, to a far greater extent, than by American females....

But there is one peculiarity of situation, in regard to American women, which makes this delicacy of constitution still more disastrous. It is the liability to the exposures and hardships of a newly-settled country....

...If the American women of the East merit the palm, for their skill and success as accomplished housekeepers, still more is due to the heroines of the West, who, with such unyielding fortitude and cheerful endurance, attempt similar duties, amid so many disadvantages and deprivations.

But, though American women have those elevated principles and feelings, which enable them to meet such trials in so exemplary a manner, their physical energies are not equal to the exertions demanded. Though the mind may be bright and firm, the casket is shivered; though the spirit may be willing, the flesh is weak. A woman of firm health, with the hope and elasticity of youth, may be envied rather than pitied, as she shares with her young husband the hopes and enterprises of pioneer life. But, when the body fails, then the eye of hope grows dim, the heart sickens, the courage dies; and, in solitude, weariness, and suffering, the wanderer pines for the dear voices and the tender sympathies of a far distant home. Then it is, that the darkest shade is presented, which marks the peculiar trials and liabilities of American women, and which exhibits still more forcibly the disastrous results of that delicacy of constitution which has been pointed out. For, though all American women, or even the greater part of them, are not called to encounter such trials, yet no mother, who rears a family of daughters, can say, that such a lot will not fall to one of her flock; nor can she know which will escape. The reverses of fortune, and the chances of matrimony, expose every woman in the Nation to such liabilities, for which she needs to be prepared.

Chapter III.

REMEDIES FOR THE PRECEDING DIFFICULTIES.

Having pointed out the peculiar responsibilities of American women, and the peculiar embarrassments which they are called to encounter, the following suggestions are offered, as remedies for such difficulties.

In the first place, the physical and domestic education of daughters should occupy the principal attention of mothers, in childhood; and the stimulation of the intellect should be very much reduced. As a general rule, daughters should not be sent to school before they are six years old; and, when they are sent, far more attention should be paid to their physical development, than is usually done. They should never be confined, at any employment, more than an hour at a time; and this confinement should be followed by sports in the open air. Such accommodations should be secured, that, at all seasons, and in all weathers, the teacher can every half hour send out a portion of her school, for sports. And still more care should be given to preserve pure air in the schoolroom. The close stoves, crowded condition, and poisonous air, of most schoolrooms, act as constant drains on the health and strength of young children.

In addition to this, much less time should be given to school, and much more to domestic employments, especially in the wealthier classes. A little girl may begin, at five or six years of age, to assist her mother; and, if properly trained, by the time she is ten, she can render essential aid. From this time, until she is fourteen or fifteen, it should be the principal object of her education to secure a strong and healthy constitution, and a thorough practical knowledge of all kinds of domestic employments....

It is in this point of view, that the dearth of good domestics in this Country may, in its results, prove a substantial blessing. If all housekeepers, who have the means, could secure good servants, there would be little hope that so important a revolution, in the domestic customs of the wealthy classes, could be effected. And so great is the natural indolence of mankind, that the amount of exercise, needful for health, will never be secured by those who are led to it through no necessity, but merely from rational considerations. Yet the pressure of domestic troubles, from the want of good domestics, has already determined many a mother, in the wealthy classes, to train her daughters to aid her in domestic service; and thus necessity is compelling mothers to do what abstract principles of expediency could never secure.

A second method of promoting the same object, is, to raise the science and practice of Domestic Economy to its appropriate place, as a regular study in female seminaries.... But it is to the mothers of our Country, that the community must look for this change. It cannot be expected, that teachers, who have their attention chiefly absorbed by the intellectual and moral interests of their pupils, should properly realize the importance of this department of education. But if mothers generally become convinced of this, their judgement and wishes will meet the respectful consideration they deserve, and the object will be accomplished.

The third method of securing a remedy for the evils pointed out, is, the endowment of female institutions, under the care of suitable trustees, who shall secure a proper course of education. The importance of this measure cannot be realized by those, who have not turned their attention to this subject; and for such, the following considerations are presented.

The endowment of colleges, and of law, medical, and divinity, schools, for the other sex, is designed to secure a thorough and proper education, for those who have the most important duties of society to perform. The men who are to expound the laws, the men who have the care of the public health, and the men who are to communicate religious instruction, should have well-disciplined and well-informed minds; and it is mainly for this object that collegiate and professional institutions are established. Liberal and wealthy individuals contribute funds, and the legislatures of the States also lend assistance, so that every State in this Nation has from one to twenty such endowed institutions, supplied with buildings, apparatus, a library, and a faculty of learned men to carry forward a superior course of instruction. And the use of all these advantages is secured, in many cases, at an expense, no greater than is required to send a boy to a common school and pay his board there. No private school could offer these advantages, without charging such a sum, as would forbid all but the rich from securing its benefits. By furnishing such superior advantages, on low terms, multitudes are properly educated, who would otherwise remain in ignorance; and thus the professions are supplied, by men properly qualified for them.

Were there no such institutions, and no regular and appropriate course of study demanded for admission to the bar, the pulpit, and to medical practice, the education of most professional men would be desultory, imperfect, and deficient. Parents and children would regulate the course of study according to their own crude notions; and, instead of having institutions which agree in carrying on a similar course of study, each school would have its own peculiar system, and compete and conflict with every other. Meantime, the public would have no means of deciding which was best, nor any opportunity for learning when a professional man was properly qualified for his duties. But as it is, the diploma of a college, and the license of an appointed body of judges, must both be secured, before a young man feels that he has entered the most promising path to success in his profession.

Our Country, then, is most abundantly supplied with endowed institutions, which secure a liberal education, on such low terms as make them accessible to all classes, and in which the interests of education are watched over, sustained, and made permanent, by an appropriate board of trustees.

But are not the most responsible of all duties committed to the charge of woman? Is it not her profession to take care of mind, body, and soul? and that, too, at the most critical of all periods of existence? And is it not as much a matter of public concern that she should be properly qualified for her duties, as that ministers, lawyers, and physicians, should be prepared for theirs? And is it not as important to endow institutions which shall make a superior education accessible to all classes,—for females, as for the other sex? And is it not equally important, that institutions for females be under the supervision of intelligent and responsible trustees, whose duty it shall be to secure a uniform and appropriate education for one sex as much as for the other? It would seem as if every mind must accord an affirmative reply, as soon as the matter is fairly considered....

In attempting a sketch of the kind of institutions which are demanded, it is very fortunate that there is no necessity for presenting a theory, which may, or may not, be approved by experience. It is the greatest honor of one of our newest Western States that it can boast of such an Institution, endowed, too, wholly by the munificence of a single individual. A slight sketch of this Institution, which the writer has examined in all its details, will give an idea of what can be done, by showing what has actually been accomplished....

To secure adequate exercise for the pupils, two methods are adopted. By the first, each young lady is required to spend a certain portion of time in domestic employments, either in sweeping, dusting, setting and clearing tables, washing and ironing, or other household concerns.

Let not the aristocratic mother and daughter express their dislike of such an arrangement, till they can learn how well it succeeds. Let them walk, as the writer has done, through the large airy halls, kept clean and in order by their fair occupants, to the washing and ironing-rooms. There they will see a long hall, conveniently fitted up with some thirty neatly-painted tubs, with a clean floor, and water conducted so as to save both labor and slopping. Let them see some thirty or forty merry girls, superintended by a motherly lady, chatting and singing, washing and starching, while every convenience is at hand, and every thing around is clean and comfortable. Two hours, thus employed, enable each young lady to wash the articles she used during the previous week, which is all that is demanded, while thus they are all practically initiated into the arts and mysteries of the wash-tub. The Superintendent remarked to the writer, that, after a few weeks of probation, most of her young washers succeeded quite as well as those whom she could hire, and who made it their business. Adjacent to the washing-room, is the ironing establishment; where another class is arranged, on the ironing-day, around long, extended tables, with heating-furnaces, clothes-frames, and all needful appliances.

By as systematic arrangement of school and domestic duties, a moderate portion of time, usually not exceeding two hours a day, from each of the pupils, accomplished all the domestic labor of a family of ninety, except the cooking, which was done by two hired domestics. This part of domestic labor it was deemed inexpedient to incorporate as a portion of the business of the pupils, inasmuch as it could not be accommodated to the arrangements of the school, and was in other respects objectionable.

Is it asked, how can young ladies paint, play the piano, and study, when their hands and dresses must be unfitted by such drudgery? The woman who asks this question, has yet to learn that a pure and delicate skin is better secured by healthful exercise, than by any other method; and that a young lady, who will spend two hours a day at the wash-tub, or with a broom, is far more likely to have rosy cheeks, a finely-moulded form, and a delicate skin, than one who lolls all day in her parlor or chamber, or only leaves it, girt in tight dresses, to make fashionable calls. It is true, that long-protracted daily labor hardens the hand, and unfits it for delicate employments; but the amount of labor needful for health produces no such effect. As to dress, and appearance, if neat and convenient accommodations are furnished, there is no occasion for the exposures which demand shabby dresses. A dark calico, genteelly made, with an oiled-silk apron, and wide cuffs of the same material, secures both good looks and good service. This plan of domestic employments for the pupils in this Institution, not only secures regular healthful exercise, but also aids to reduce the expenses of education, so that, with the help of the endowments, it is brought within the reach of many, who otherwise could never gain such advantages.

In addition to this, a system of Calisthenic exercises is introduced, which secures all the advantages which dancing is supposed to effect, and which is free from the dangerous tendencies of that fascinating and fashionable amusement. This system is so combined with music, and constantly varying evolutions, as to serve as an amusement, and also as a mode of curing distortions, particularly all tendencies to curvature of the spine; while, at the same time, it tends to promote grace of movement, and easy manners.

Another advantage of this Institution, is, an elevated and invigorating course of mental discipline. Many persons seem to suppose, that the chief object of an intellectual education is the acquisition of knowledge. But it will be found, that this is only a secondary object. The formation of habits of investigation, of correct reasoning, of persevering attention, of regular system, of accurate analysis, and of vigorous mental action, is the primary object to be sought in preparing American women for their arduous duties; duties which will demand not only quickness of perception, but steadiness of purpose, regularity of system, and perseverance in action.

It is for such purposes, that the discipline of the Mathematics is so important an element in female education; and it is in this aspect, that the mere acquisition of facts, and the attainment of accomplishments, should be made of altogether secondary account.

In the Institution here described, a systematic course of study is adopted, as in our colleges; designed to occupy three years. The following slight outline of the course, will exhibit the liberal plan adopted in this respect.

In Mathematics, the whole of Arithmetic contained in the larger works used in schools, the whole of Euclid, and such portions from Day's Mathematics as are requisite to enable the pupils to demonstrate the various problems in Olmsted's larger work on Natural Philosophy. In Language, besides English Grammar, a short course in Latin is required, sufficient to secure an understanding of the philosophy of the language, and that kind of mental discipline which the exercise of translating affords. In Philosophy, Chemistry, Astronomy, Botany, Geology and Mineralogy, Intellectual and Moral Philosophy, Political Economy, and the Evidences of Christianity, the same textbooks are used as are required at our best colleges. In Geography, the most thorough course is adopted; and in History, a more complete knowledge is secured, by means of charts and textbooks, than most of our colleges offer. To these branches, are added Griscom's Physiology, Bigelow's Technology, and Jahn's Archaeology, together with a course of instruction in polite literature, for which Chamber's English Literature is employed as the textbook, each recitation being attended with selections and criticisms, from teacher or pupils, on the various authors brought into notice. Vocal Music, on the plan of the Boston Academy, is a part of the daily instructions. Linear drawing, and penciling, are designed also to be a part of the course. Instrumental Music is taught, but not as a part of the regular course of study.

To secure the proper instruction in all these branches, the division of labor, adopted in colleges, is pursued. Each teacher has distinct branches as her department, for which she is responsible, and in which she is independent. One teacher performs the duties of a *governess,* in maintaining rules, and attending to the habits and manners of the pupils. By this method, the teachers have sufficient time, both to prepare themselves, and to impart instruction and illustration in the classroom. In this Institution it is made a direct object of effort *to cure defects of character and habits.* At the frequent meetings of the Principal and teachers, the peculiarities of each pupil are made the subjects of inquiry; and methods are devised for remedying defects through the personal influence of the several teachers. This, when thus made a direct object of combined effort, often secures results most gratifying and encouraging.

One peculiarity of this Institution demands consideration. By the method adopted here, the exclusive business of educating their own sex is, as it ever ought to be, confined to females. The Principal of the Institution, indeed, is a gentleman; but, while he takes the position of a father of the family, and responsible head of the whole concern, the entire charge of instruction, and most of the responsibilities in regard to health, morals, and manners, rest upon the female teachers, in their several departments. The Principal is the chaplain and religious teacher; and is a member of the board of instructors, so far as to have a right to advise, and an equal vote, in every question pertaining to the concerns of the School; and thus he acts as a sort of regulator and mainspring in all the various departments. But no one person in the Institution is loaded with the excessive responsibilities, which rest upon one, where a large institution of this kind has a Principal, who employs and directs all the subordinate assistants. The writer has never before seen the principle of the division of labor and responsibility so perfectly carried out in any female institution; and she believes that experience will prove that this is the true model for combining, in appropriate proportions, the agency of both sexes in carrying forward such an institution. There are cases where females are well qualified, and feel willing to take the place occupied by the Principal but such cases are rare.

One thing more should be noticed, to the credit of the rising State where this Institution is located. A female association has been formed, embracing a large portion of the ladies of standing and wealth, the design of which, is, to educate, gratuitously, at this, and other similar, institutions, such females as are anxious to obtain a good education, and are destitute of the means. If this enterprise is continued, with the same energy and perseverance as has been manifested during the last few years, that State will take the lead of her sister States in well-educated women; and if the views in the preceding pages are correct, this will give her precedence in every intellectual and moral advantage.

Many, who are not aware of the great economy secured by a proper division of labor, will not understand how so extensive a course can be properly completed in three years. But in this Institution, none are received under fourteen; and a certain amount of previous acquisition is required, in order to admission, as is done in our colleges. This secures a diminution of classes, so that but few studies are pursued at one time; while the number of well-qualified teachers is so adequate, that full time is afforded for all needful instruction and illustration. Where teachers have so many classes, that they merely have time to find out what the pupils learn from books, without any aid from their teachers, the acquisitions of the pupils are vague and imperfect, and soon pass away; so that an immense amount of expense, time, and labor, is spent in acquiring or recalling what is lost about as fast as it is gained.

Parents are little aware of the immense waste incurred by the present mode of conducting female education. In the wealthy classes, young girls are sent to school, as a matter of course, year after year, confined, for six hours a day, to the schoolhouse, and required to add some time out of school to learning their lessons. Thus, during the most critical period of life, they are for a long time immured in a room, filled with an atmosphere vitiated by many breaths, and are constantly kept under some sort of responsibility in regard to mental effort. Their studies are pursued at random, often changed with changing schools, while book after book (heavily taxing the parent's purse) is conned awhile, and then supplanted by others. Teachers have usually so many pupils, and such a variety of branches to teach, that little time can be afforded to each pupil; while scholars, at this thoughtless period of life, feeling sure of going to school as long as they please, manifest little interest in their pursuits.

The writer believes that the actual amount of education, permanently secured by most young ladies from the age of ten to fourteen, could all be acquired in one year, at the Institution described, by a young lady at the age of fifteen or sixteen.

Instead of such a course as the common one, if mothers would keep their daughters as their domestic assistants, until they are fourteen, requiring them to study one lesson, and go out, once a day, to recite it to a teacher, it would abundantly prepare them, after their constitutions are firmly established, to enter such an institution, where, in three years, they could secure more, than almost any young lady in the Country now gains by giving the whole of her youth to school pursuits.

In the early years of female life, reading, writing, needlework, drawing, and music, should alternate with domestic duties; and one hour a day, devoted to some study, in addition to the above pursuits, would be all that is needful to prepare them for a thorough education after growth is attained, and the constitution established. This is the time when young women would feel the value of an education, and pursue their studies with that maturity of mind, and vividness of interest, which would double the perpetuity and value of all their acquisitions.

The great difficulty, which opposes such a plan, is, the want of institutions that would enable a young lady to complete, in three years, the liberal course of study, here described. But if American mothers become convinced of the importance of such advantages for their daughters, and will use their influence appropriately and efficiently, they will certainly be furnished. There are other men of liberality and wealth, besides the individual referred to, who can be made to feel that a fortune, expended in securing an appropriate education to American women, is as wisely bestowed, as in founding colleges for the other sex, who are already so abundantly supplied. We ought to have institutions, similar to the one described, in every part of this Nation; and funds should be provided, for educating young women destitute of means: and if American women think and feel, that, by such a method, their own trials will be lightened, and their daughters will secure a healthful constitution and a thorough domestic and intellectual education, the appropriate expression of their wishes will secure the necessary funds. The tide of charity, which has been so long flowing from the female hand to provide a liberal education for young men, will flow back with abundant remuneration.

The last method suggested for lessening the evils peculiar to American women, is, a decided effort to oppose the aristocratic feeling, that labor is degrading; and to bring about the impression, that it is refined and lady-like to engage in domestic pursuits. In past ages, and in aristocratic countries, leisure and indolence and frivolous pursuits have been deemed lady-like and refined, because those classes, which were most refined, countenanced such an opinion. But whenever ladies of refinement, as a general custom, patronise domestic pursuits, then these employments will be deemed lady-like. It may be urged, however, that it is impossible for a woman who cooks, washes, and sweeps, to appear in the dress, or acquire the habits and manners, of a lady; that the drudgery of the kitchen is dirty work, and that no one can appear delicate and refined, while engaged in it. Now all this depends on circumstances. If a woman has a house, destitute of neat and convenient facilities; if she has no habits of order and system; if she is remiss and careless in person and dress;—then all this may be true. But, if a woman will make some sacrifices of costly ornaments in her parlor, in order to make her kitchen neat and tasteful; if she will sacrifice expensive dishes, in order to secure such conveniences for labor as protect from exposures; if she will take pains to have the dresses, in which she works, made of suitable materials, and in good taste; if she will rise early, and systematize and oversee the work of her family, so as to have it done thoroughly, neatly, and in the early part of the day; she will find no necessity for any such apprehensions. It is because such work has generally been done by vulgar people, and in a vulgar way, that we have such associations; and when ladies manage such things, as ladies should, then such associations will be removed. There are pursuits, deemed very refined and genteel, which involve quite as much exposure as kitchen employments. For example, to draw a large landscape, in colored crayons, would be deemed very lady-like; but the writer can testify, from sad experience, that no cooking, washing, sweeping, or any other domestic duty, ever left such deplorable traces on hands, face, and dress, as this same lady-like pursuit. Such things depend entirely on custom and associations; and every American woman, who values the institutions of her Country, and wishes to lend her influence in extending and perpetuating such blessings, may feel that she is doing this, whenever, by her example and influence, she destroys the aristocratic association, which would render domestic labor degrading.

HENRY C. CAREY

Selection from *The Harmony of Interests* (1851)

The "harmony of interests" was a cliché among Whig intellectuals and politicians, but none of them strove harder to put that idea on firm theoretical ground than Henry C. Carey (1793–1879). The son of the Irish immigrant and Philadelphia publisher Matthew Carey—and himself a publisher and successful investor and the doyen of a large and admiring circle of journalists, entrepreneurs, and politicians—Carey was the incarnation of the era's ideal of the civically active, enterprising, and upwardly mobile citizen. But his greatest fame in America and Europe came from his series of multivolume treatises on political economy. In each of them he made—often with an array of statistical evidence—the same central argument: The pessimistic conclusions of classical economists about the inevitability of poverty caused by increasing population pressing on limited land and resources were wrong because labor's value and, therefore, share of wealth, could be increased by the application of capital, technology, and locally based but nationally connected "associations" of production and exchange.

In his polemical book, *The Harmony of Interests,* Carey spelled out the political implications of this analysis. Democrats' pseudo free-trade policies forced vulnerable farmers and laborers to exchange their products on unfavorable terms with distant, monopolistic urban (and especially English) capitalists. By contrast, government-supported schemes of "protection," such as tariffs and subsidized transportation networks, facilitated the laboring classes' participation in mixed farming and manufacturing centers, which, in turn, stimulated equality-engendering wealth. And not only wealth: In the chapters that follow, Carey argued that such government-protected associations were integral to the maintenance and speedy extension of America's democratic, domestic-minded, and non-imperialistic Christian "empire."

For an overview of Carey's theories, see Rodney J. Morrison, *Henry C. Carey and American Economic Development* (Philadelphia, 1986). For an excellent discussion of Carey's social thought in the context of American Whiggery, see Daniel Walker Howe, *The Political Culture of the American Whigs* (Chicago, 1979), 108–22. Paul K. Conkin analyzes Carey's economic ideas as part of a nineteenth-century tradition of American political economy in *Prophets of Prosperity: America's First Political Economists* (Bloomington, Ind., 1980), 261–307. Jeffrey Sklansky, *The Soul's Economy: Market Society and Selfhood in American Thought. 1820–1920* (Chapel Hill, 2002), 73–103, provides provocative interpretation of Carey and leading proslavery Southern social critics as comparable producers of a new American sociology.

Chapter XXI.

HOW PROTECTION AFFECTS MORALS.

THE moral man is sensible of the duties he owes to his wife, his children, society, and himself. He frequents neither taverns nor gaming-houses. His place is home.

The more perfect the morality the more productive will be the labour of a community, and the greater will be the power of its members to improve their moral and intellectual condition. If protection be "a war upon labour and capital," it must tend to the deterioration of morality and the diminution of the reward of labour.

The more equal the division of a community between the sexes, the greater will be the power to contract matrimony, and the higher will be morality. The monopoly system tends to expel the men and produce inequality in the number of the sexes, and thus to diminish the power to contract matrimony, thereby producing a tendency to immorality. The object of protection is to enable men to remain at home, and thus bring about equality, which cannot exist where the tendency to dispersion exists.

The more men can remain at home, the better they can perform their duties to their children. The monopoly system tends to compel them to perform their exchanges in distant markets and to separate themselves from wives and children. The object of protection is to bring the consumer to take his place by the side of the producer, and enable them to effect their exchanges at home.

The more directly the consumer exchanges with the producer, the less will be the disposition and the power to commit frauds. The farmer of Illinois has no object in adulterating his corn, because corn is cheap; but the miller of England mixes beans with the corn, because corn is dear. The planter of Alabama would gain nothing by substituting flour for cotton, because the latter is cheap; but the manufacturer of England does so because cotton is dear. The coffee planter delivers coffee. The English shopkeeper substitutes chicory for coffee, because the latter is dear. The inducement to fraud in these cases results from the distance between the producer and the consumer, which it is the object of protection to diminish. The shoemaker makes good shoes for his customers; but he makes indifferent ones for the traders who deal with persons that are distant. The gunsmith furnishes to his neighbours guns that will stand the proof; but when he makes others to be sold in Africa, he cares little if they burst at the first fire. The necessity for maintaining the monopoly of machinery now enjoyed by England leads to frauds and forgeries of every description, with a view to displace the foreign produce and deceive the foreign producer. The *power* to commit frauds thus results from the distance between the consumer and the producer. Protection looks to bringing them near together, and thus diminishing that power....

The man who makes his exchanges in distant markets spends much time on the road and in taverns, and is liable to be led into dissipation. The more he can effect his exchanges at home, the less is the danger of any such result. The object of the monopoly system is that of compelling him to effect all his exchanges at a distance, and to employ for that purpose numerous wagoners, porters, sailors, and other persons, most of whom have scarcely any home except the tavern.

The more uniform the standard of value, the less does trade resemble gambling. The object of the monopoly system is to subject the produce of the world to a standard of

Source: Henry C. Carey, *The Harmony of Interests: Agricultural, Manufacturing, and Commercial* (Philadelphia: J. S. Skinner, 1851), 202–3, 203–4, 204–6, 206–7, 208, 208–9, 213–14, 215–16, 216–17, 227, 227–29.

the most variable kind, and to render agriculture, manufactures, and trade, mere gambling. The object of protection is to withdraw the produce of the world from that standard, enabling every community to measure the products of its labour by its own standard, giving labour for labour.

The object of the English system is to promote *centralization,* and its necessary consequence is that of compelling the dispersion of man in search of food. London and Liverpool, Manchester and Birmingham, have grown with vast rapidity by the same system which has exhausted Ireland, India, and the West Indies. The same journal informs us of the construction of a new town opposite Liverpool, of the great additions to London, and of the absolute necessity for promoting emigration from Ireland, Scotland, and even from England. As each successive province is exhausted, there arises a desire, and even a necessity for adding to the list. Bengal and Bombay having ceased to be productive, Affghanistan is attempted, and the Punjaub is conquered. The ruin of the West Indies is followed by an invasion of China, for the purpose of compelling the Chinese to perfect freedom of trade. The Highlands are depopulated, and Australia is colonized.

Mr. Jefferson held great cities to be "great sores." He desired that the manufacturer should take his place by the side of the agriculturist—that the loom and the anvil should be in close proximity to the plough and the harrow. Mr. Jefferson looked and thought for himself. He had studied political economy before it became necessary for Mr. Malthus to invent a theory of population that should satisfactorily account for the scarcity of food under the unnatural policy of England, and thus relieve the law-makers of that country from all charge of mis-government. He studied, too, before Mr. Ricardo had invented a theory of rent, for the maintenance of which it was necessary to prove that the poor cultivator, beginning the work of settlement, always commenced upon the rich soils—the swamps and river-bottoms—and that with the progress of population he had recourse to the poor soils of the hills, yielding a constantly diminishing return to labour—and therefore it was that he thought for himself. Modern financiers have blindly adopted the English system, based on the theories of Malthus and Ricardo, and the perfection of civilization is now held to be found in that system which shall most rapidly build up great cities, and most widely separate the manufacturer from the agriculturist. The more perfect the centralization, the greater, according to them, will be the tendency towards improvement.

Mr. Jefferson was in favour of combined action, as being that which would most tend to promote human improvement, physical, moral, intellectual, and political. That it does so, would seem to be obvious, as it is where combination of action most exists that men live best and are best instructed—commit least crimes, and think most for themselves. There, too, there exists the strongest desire to have protection....

It is here supposed that the desire for protection results from a selfish desire to tax others, but the persons exclusively devoted to manufactures of any kind are too few in number to affect the elections, and yet wherever mills or furnaces are established, the majority of the people become advocates of the doctrine of protection, and that majority mainly consists of agriculturists,—farmers and planters. Why it is so, may be found in the fact that they experience the benefits resulting from making a market on the land for the products of the land, and desire that their neighbours may do the same. Ignorant selfishness would induce them to desire to retain for themselves the advantage they had gained. Enlightened selfishness would induce them to teach others that which they themselves had learned.

Ignorant selfishness is the characteristic of the savage. It disappears as men acquire the habit of association with their neighbour men. The proclaimed object of the monopoly system is that of producing a necessity for scattering ourselves over large surfaces, and thus increasing the difficulty of association, and the object is attained. "The prospect of heaven itself," says Cooper, in one of his novels, "would have no charm for an American of the backwoods, if he thought there was any place further west."

Such is the common impression. It is believed that men separate from each other because of something in their composition that tends to produce a desire for flying to wild lands, there probably to perish of fever, brought on by exposure, and certainly to leave behind them all that tends to make life desirable. Such is not the character of man anywhere. He is everywhere disposed to remain at home, when he can, and if the farmers and planters of the Union can be brought to understand their true interests, at home he will remain, and doing so, his condition and that of all around him, will be improved. The habit of association is necessary to the improvement of man. With it comes the love of the good and the beautiful. "I wish," says the author of a recent agricultural address, "that we could create a general passion for gardening and horticulture. We want," he continues, "more beauty about our houses. The scenes of childhood are the memories of our future years. Let our dwellings be beautified with plants and flowers. Flowers are, in the language of a late cultivator, 'the playthings of childhood and the ornaments of the grave; they raise smiling looks to man and grateful ones to God.'"

We do want more beauty about our houses, and not only about our houses but about our minds, and that it may be obtained, we must rid ourselves of a system which makes the producer the servant of the exchanger. Such is the object of protection.

It is most truly said that "there is no friendship in trade." As now carried on, it certainly does not tend to promote kindly feelings among the human race, nor can it do so while the system remains unchanged. The great object of traders appears to be the production of discord. By so doing, England has obtained the supreme control of India. Her journals are unceasingly engaged in sowing discord among the various portions of this Union, and the effort would be successful were it not that there is no real discordance in their true interests.

It is time that the people of Great Britain should open their eyes to the fact that their progress is in the same direction in which have gone the communities of Athens, and Rome, and every other that has desired to support itself by the labour of others. It is time that they should awake to the fact that the numerous and splendid gin-shops, the perpetual recurrence of child-murder for the purpose of plundering burial societies, and the enormous increase of crime and pauperism, are but the natural consequence of a system that tends to drive capital from the land, to be employed in spindles and ships, and labour from the healthful and inspiring pursuits of the country, to seek employment in Liverpool and Manchester, where severe labour in the effort of under-work the poor Hindoo, and drive him from his loom, is rewarded with just sufficient to keep the labourer from starving in the lanes and cellars with which those cities so much abound.

That "there is no friendship in trade," is most true, and yet trade is the deity worshipped in this school. In it "commerce is king," and yet to commerce we owe much of the existing demoralization of the world. The anxiety to sell cheap induces the manufacturer to substitute cotton for silk, and flour for cotton, and leads to frauds and adulterations of every description. Bankruptcy and loss of honour follow in the train of its perpetual revulsions. To obtain intelligence an hour beforehand of an approaching famine, and thus to be enabled to buy corn at less than it is worth, or to hear in advance of the prospect of good harvests, and to sell it at more than it is worth, is but an evidence of superior sagacity. To buy your coat in the cheapest market, careless what are the sufferings of the poor tailor, and sell your grain in the dearest, though your neighbour may be starving, is the cardinal principle of this school....

The whole tendency of the system is to the production of a gambling spirit. In England, it makes railroad kings, ending in railroad bankrupts, like Henry Hudson. If we could trace the effect of the great speculation of which this man was the father, we should find thousands and tens of thousand of husbands and wives, parents and children, utterly beggared to build up the fortunes of the few, and thus increase the inequality of social condition which lies at the root of all evil. If we examine it here, we see it sending tens of thousands to California, eager for gold, there to lose both health and life. It is sending thousands of boys and girls to our cities—the former to become shopmen, and the latter prostitutes, while hundreds of thousands are at the same time making their way to the West, there to begin the work of cultivation, while millions upon millions of acres in the old States remain untouched. With every step of our progress in that direction, social inequality tends to increase. The skilful speculator realizes a fortune by the same opera- tion that ruins hundreds around him, and adds to his fortune by buying their property under the hammer of the sheriff. The wealthy manufacturer is unmoved by revulsions in the British market which sweep away his competitors, and, when the storm blows over, he is enabled to double, treble, or quadruple, his already overgrown fortune. The conse- quence is, that great manufacturing towns spring up in one quarter of the Union, while almost every effort to *localize* manufactures (thus bringing the loom and the anvil really to the side of the plough and the harrow) is followed by ruin. The system tends to make the rich richer and the poor poorer. The coal miner of the present year works for half wages, but the coal speculator obtains double profits, and thus is it ever—the producer is sacrificed to the exchanger. With the growth of the exchanging class, great cities rise up, filled with shops, at which men can cheaply become intoxicated. New York has 4567 places at which liquor is sold, and the *Five-Points* are peopled with the men who make Astor- place riots. Single merchants employ 160 clerks, while thousands of those who are forced into our cities and seek to obtain a living by trade are ruined. Opera singers receive large salaries paid by the contributions of men whose shirts are made by women whose wages scarcely enable them to live.

The whole system of trade, as at present conducted, and as it must continue to be con- ducted if the colonial system be permitted longer to exist, is one of mere gambling, and of all qualities, that which most distinguishes the gambler is ignorant selfishness. He ruins his friends and wastes his winnings on a running-horse, or on a prostitute....

As a necessary consequence of the system, money becomes more and more an object of consideration in the contraction of the important engagement of matrimony, and mar- riage settlements begin to appear among us. The newspapers of the day inform us of the recent execution of one for $200,000.

If we look westward, it is the same. Centralization produces depopulation, and that is followed by poverty and crime. London grows upon the system that ruins India and fills it with bands of plunderers. The West and South-west are filled with gamblers, and land-pirates abound. The late war has brought into existence a new species of fraud, in the counterfeiting of land warrants, and this is but one of the many evils resulting from that measure....

The object of protection is the establishment of perfect free trade, by the annexation of men and of nations. Every man brought here increases the domain of free trade, and diminishes the necessity for custom-houses. Every man brought here consumes four, six, ten, or twelve pounds of cotton for one that he could consume at home, and every one is a customer to the farmer for bushels instead of gills. Between the honest and intelligent man who desires to see the establishment of *real* free-trade, the Christian who desires to see an improvement in the standard of morality, the planter who desires an increased market for his cotton, the farmer who desires larger returns to his labour, the landowner who desires to see an increase in the value of his land, and the labourer who desires to sell his labour at the highest price, there is perfect harmony of interest....

Chapter XXIII.

HOW PROTECTION AFFECTS THE POLITICAL CONDITION OF MAN.

THE larger the return to labour, the greater will be the power to accumulate capital. The larger the proportion which capital seeking to be employed bears to the labourers who are to employ it, the larger will be the wages of labour, the greater the power of the labourer to accumulate for himself, and the more perfect will be his control over the disposition of his labour and the application of its proceeds, whether to private or to public purposes.

The freeman chooses his employer, sells his labour, and disposes of the proceeds at his pleasure. The slave does none of these things. His master takes the produce of his labour, and returns him such portion as suits his pleasure.

Throughout the world, and in all ages, freedom has advanced with every increase in the ratio of wealth to population. When the people of England were poor, they were enslaved, but with growing wealth they have become more free. So has it been in Belgium and in France. So is it now in Russia and Germany, and so must it everywhere be. India is poor, and the many are slaves to the few. So is it in Ireland. Freedom is there unknown. The poor Irishman, limited to the labours of agriculture, desires a bit of land, and he gives the chief part of the product of his year's labour for permission to starve upon the balance, happy to be permitted to remain on payment of this enormous rent. He is the slave of the land-owner, without even the slave's right to claim of him support in case of sickness, or if, escaping from famine, he should survive to an age that deprives him of the power of labouring for his support. England employs fleets, paid for out of taxes imposed on starving Irishmen, to prevent the people of Brazil from *buying* black men, and women, and children, on the coast of Africa, while holding herself ready to *give* white men, and women, and children, to any who will carry them from her shores, and even to add thereto a portion of the cost of their transportation; and this she does without requiring the transporter to produce even the slightest evidence that they have been delivered at their destined port in "good order and well-conditioned." When Ireland shall become rich, labour will become valuable, and man will become free. When Italy was filled with prosperous communities, labour was productive, and it was in demand; and then men who had it to sell fixed the price at which it should be sold. With growing poverty, labour ceased to be in demand, and the buyer fixed the price. The labourer then became a slave. If we follow the history of Tuscany, we can find men becoming enslaved as poverty succeeded wealth; and again may we trace them becoming more and more free, as wealth has grown with continued peace. So has it been in Egypt, and Sicily, and Spain. Everywhere poverty, or a deficiency of those aids to labour which constitute wealth, is, and has invariably been, the companion of slavery; and everywhere wealth, or an abundance of ploughs, and harrows, and horses, and cows, and oxen, and cultivated lands, and houses, and mills, is, and has invariably been, the companion, and the cause, of freedom.

If protection be a "war upon labour and capital," it must tend to prevent the growth of wealth, and thus to deteriorate the political condition of man.

The farmer who exchanges his food with the man, who produces iron by means of horses, wagons, canal-boats, merchants, ships, and sailors, gives much food for little iron. The iron man, who exchanges his products for food through the instrumentality of the same machinery, gives much iron for little food. The chief part of the product is swallowed up by the men who stand between, and grow rich while the producers remain poor. The growth of wealth is thus prevented, and inequality of political condition is maintained.

The farmer who exchanges directly with the producer of iron gives labour for labour. Both thus grow rich, because the class that desires to stand between has no opportunity of enriching themselves at their expense. Equality of condition is thus promoted.

The object of protection is that of bringing the consumer of food to take his place by the side of the producer of food, and thus promoting the growth of wealth and the improvement of political condition. That it does produce that effect, is obvious from the fact that, in periods of protection, such vast numbers seek our shores, and that immigration becomes stationary, or diminishes, with every approach towards that system which is usually denominated free trade.

The colonial system is based upon cheap labour. Protection seeks to increase the reward of labour. The one fills factories with children of tender years, and expels men to Canada and Australia; the other unites the men and sends the children to school....

Protection looks to the improvement of the political condition of the human race. To accomplish that object, it is needed that the value of man be raised, and that men should everywhere be placed in a condition to sell their labour to the highest bidder—to the man who will give in return the largest quantity of food, clothing, shelter, and other of the comforts of life. To enable the Hindoo to sell his labour and to fix its price, it is necessary to raise the price of his chief product, cotton. That is to be done by increasing the consumption, and that object is to be attained by diminishing the waste of labour attendant upon its transit between the producer and the consumer. Fill this country with furnaces and mills, and railroads will be made in every direction, and the consumption of cotton will speedily rise to twenty pounds per head, while millions of European labourers, mechanics, farmers, and capitalists will cross the Atlantic, and every million will be a customer for one-fourth as much as was consumed by the people of Great Britain and Ireland in 1847. The harmony of the interests of the cotton-growers throughout the world is perfect, and all the discord comes from the power of the exchangers to produce apparent discord.

It is asserted, however, that protection tends to build up a body of capitalists at the expense of the consumer, and thus produce inequality of condition. That such is the effect of *inadequate* protection is not to be doubted. So long as we continue under a necessity for seeking in England a market for our surplus products, her markets will fix the price for the world, and so long as we shall continue to be under a *necessity* for seeking there a small supply of cloth or iron, so long will the prices in her markets fix the price of all, and the domestic producer of cloth and iron will profit by the difference of freight both out and home. With this profit he takes the risk of ruin, which is of perpetual occurrence among the men of small capitals. Those who are already wealthy have but to stop their furnaces or mills until prices rise, and then they have the markets to themselves, for their poorer competitors have been ruined. Such is the history of many of the large fortunes accumulated by the manufacture of cloth and iron in this country, and such the almost universal history of every effort to establish manufactures south and west of New England.

Inadequate and uncertain protection benefits the farmer and planter little, while the uncertainty attending it tends to make the rich richer and the poor poorer, thus producing social and political inequality.

Adequate and certain protection, on the contrary, tends to the production of equality—first, because by its aid the *necessity* for depending on foreign markets for the sale of our products, or the supply of our wants, will be brought to an end, and thenceforth the prices, being fixed at home, will be steady, and then the smaller capitalist will be enabled to maintain competition with the larger one, with great advantage to the consumers—farmers, planters, and labourers; and, second, because its benefits will be, as they always have been, felt chiefly by the many with whom the price of labour constitutes the sole fund out of which they are to be maintained.

If we take the labour that is employed in the factories of the country, from one extremity to the other, it will be found that nearly the whole of it would be waste, if not so employed. If we take that which is employed in getting out the timber and the stone for building factories and furnaces, it will be found that a large portion of it would otherwise be waste. If we inquire into the operations of the farmer, we find that the vicinity of a factory, or furnace, enables him to save much of the labour of transportation, and to sell many things that would otherwise be waste. Thus far, the advantage would seem to be all on the side of the employed, and not on that of the employer.

The object of protection is that of securing a demand for labour, and its tendency is to produce equality of condition. The jealousy of "overgrown capitalists" has caused many changes of policy; but, so far as they have tended to the abolition of protection, they have invariably tended to the production of inequality. The wealthy capitalist suffers some loss; but he is not ruined. A change takes place, and he is ready to avail himself of it, and at once regains all that had been lost, with vast increase. The small capitalist has been swept away, and his mill is in a state of ruin. By the time he can prepare himself to recommence his business, the chance being past, he is swept away again, and perhaps for the last time.

For months past, the rate of interest on a certain species of securities has been very low. The wealthy man could borrow at four per cent.; the poor man, requiring a small loan on a second-rate security, could scarcely obtain it at any price. The man who has coal to sell, or iron to sell, must have the aid of middlemen to act as endorsers upon the paper received from his customers, and their commissions absorb the profits. The wages of the miner have been greatly reduced, while the profits of the speculator have been increased. The reason of all this is, that, throughout the nation, there prevails no confidence in the future. It is seen that we are consuming more than we produce; that our exports do not pay for our imports; that we are running in debt; that furnaces and mills are being closed; and every one knows what must be the end of such a system. Re-enact the tariff of 1842, and the trade of the middleman would be at an end, because confidence in the future would be felt from one extremity of the land to the other. Should we not find in this some evidence of the soundness of the principle upon which it was based? The system which gives confidence must be right; that which destroys it must be wrong.

Confidence in the future—Hope—gives power to individuals and communities. It is that which enables the poor man to become rich, and the character of all legislative action is to be judged by its greater or less tendency to produce this effect. A review of the measures urged upon the nation by the advocates of the system miscalled free trade, shows, almost without an exception, they have tended to the destruction of confidence, and therefore to the production of the political revolutions referred to in the first chapter.

The direct effect of the insecurity that has existed has been to centralize the business of manufacture in one part of the Union and in the hands of a comparatively limited number of persons—such as could afford to take large risks in hope of realizing large profits. Had the tariff of 1828 been made the settled law of the land, the Middle and Southern States would now be studded with factories and furnaces, and while the North and East would not have been less rich, they would be far richer, and the present inequality of condition would not now exist.

The power of the North, as compared with that of the South, is due to the jealousy of the former entertained by the latter, which has prevented the establishment of a decided system, having for its object the destruction of the English monopoly, and the ultimate establishment of perfect freedom of trade.

The object of the colonial system was that of taxing the world for the maintenance of a great mercantile, manufacturing, and landed aristocracy, and the mode of accomplishment was that of securing a monopoly of machinery. The object of protection is to break down that monopoly, and with it the aristocracy that collects for the people of Great Britain and the world those immense taxes, to be appropriated to the payment of fleets and armies officered by younger sons, and kept on foot for the maintenance of the existing inequality in Great Britain, Ireland, and India. All, therefore, who desire to see improvement in the political condition of the people of the world, should advocate the system which tends to break down monopoly and establish perfect freedom of trade.

Conclusion.

Much is said of "the mission" of the people of these United States, and most of it is said by persons who appear to limit themselves to the consideration of the *powers* of the nation, and rarely to think of its *duties*. By such men the grandeur of the national position is held to be greatly increased by having expended sixty or eighty millions upon a war with a weak neighbour, and having thus acquired the power to purchase, at a high price, a vast body of wild land that would, in the natural course of events, have been brought within the Union, in reasonable time, without the cost of a dollar or a life. By such men, the fitting out of expeditions for the purpose of producing civil war among our neighbours of Cuba, is held to be another evidence of grandeur. Others would have us to mix ourselves up with all the revolutionists of Europe; while a fourth and last set sigh at the reflection that our fleets and armies are too small for the magnificence of our position.

By some it is supposed that our "mission" is that of monopolizing the commerce of the world, and the time is anxiously looked for when we shall have "diplomatic relations" with "vast regions of the East," Persia, Corea, Cochin-China, Burmah and Japan, with whom "nothing but the steam-ship can successfully introduce our commerce." By "persevering and successful efforts," it is thought we may secure the "commerce of Japan.". . .

The cost of a mission to Japan would build half a dozen furnaces that would add more to the wealth of the nation in five years than the commerce of that country would do in half a century. The amount we have expended on the mission to Austria, in search of a market for tobacco, would bring here as many Germans as would consume almost as much of our tobacco as is now consumed in the empire, and those tobacco consumers would do more for the growth of New York than either Japan or Austria.

The English doctrine of "ships, colonies, and commerce" is thus reproduced on this side of the Atlantic, and its adoption by the nation would be followed by effects similar to those which have been already described as existing in England. There, for a time, it gave the power to tax the world for the maintenance of fleets and armies, as had before been done by Athens and by Rome, and there it is now producing the same results that have elsewhere resulted from the same system, poverty, depopulation, exhaustion, and weakness.

But little study of our history is required to satisfy the inquirer that the power of the Union, and its magnificent position among the nations of the earth, are due to the fact that we have to so great an extent abstained from measures requiring the maintenance of fleets and armies. The consequence has been that taxes have been light, capital has accumulated rapidly, labour has been productive, and the labourer has received wages that have enabled him to feed, clothe, and educate his children, and the nation has thus performed its true "mission" in elevating the condition of man. If we desire to find exceptions to this, we must look to those periods in which the policy of Washington, Jefferson, Madison, Monroe, and Jackson, was departed from, and when the government adopted measures tending to the maintenance of the English monopoly of machinery, and there we shall find taxes more heavy, capital accumulating more slowly, labour more unproductive, and the wages of labour so much depressed that the labourer finds it difficult to feed or clothe his children, and still more difficult to educate them.

Two systems are before the world; the one looks to increasing the proportion of persons and of capital engaged in trade and transportation, and therefore to diminishing the proportion engaged in producing commodities with which to trade, with *necessarily* diminished return to the labour of all; while the other looks to increasing the proportion engaged in the work of production, and diminishing that engaged in trade and transportation, with increased return to all, giving to the labourer good wages, and to the owner of capital good profits. One looks to increasing the quantity of raw materials to be exported, and diminishing the inducements to the import of men, thus impoverishing both farmer and planter by throwing on them the burden of freight; while the other looks to increasing the import of men, and diminishing the export of raw materials, thereby enriching both planter and farmer by relieving them from the payment of freight. One looks to giving the *products* of millions of acres of land and of the labour of millions of men for the *services* of hundreds of thousands of distant men; the other to bringing the distant men to consume on the land the products of the land, exchanging day's labour for day's labour. One looks to compelling the farmers and planters of the Union to continue their contributions for the support of the fleets and the armies, the paupers, the nobles, and the sovereigns of Europe; the other to enabling ourselves to apply the same means to the moral and intellectual improvement of the sovereigns of America. One looks to the continuance of that *bastard* freedom of trade which denies the principle of protection, yet doles it out as revenue duties; the other to extending the area of *legitimate* free trade by the establishment of perfect protection, followed by the annexation of individuals and communities, and ultimately by the abolition of custom-houses. One looks to exporting men to occupy desert tracts, the sovereignty of which is obtained by aid of diplomacy or war; the other to increasing the value of an immense extent of vacant land by importing men by millions for their occupation. One looks to the *centralization* of wealth and power in a great commercial city that shall rival the great cities of modern times, which have been and are being supported by aid of contributions which have exhausted every nation subjected to them; the other to *concentration*, by aid of which a market shall be made upon the land for the products of the land, and the farmer and planter be enriched. One looks to increasing the necessity for commerce; the other to increasing the power to maintain it. One looks to underworking the Hindoo, and sinking the rest of the world to his level; the other to raising the standard of man throughout the world to our level. One looks to pauperism, ignorance, depopulation, and barbarism; the other to increasing wealth, comfort, intelligence, combination of action, and civilization. One looks towards universal war; the other towards universal peace. One is the English system; the other we may be proud to call the American system, for it is the only one ever devised the tendency of which was that of ELEVATING while EQUALIZING the condition of man throughout the world.

SUCH is the true MISSION of the people of these United States. To them has been granted a privilege never before granted to man, that of the exercise of the right of perfect self-government; but, as rights and duties are inseparable, with the grant of the former came the obligation to perform the latter. Happily their performance is pleasant and profitable, and involves no sacrifice. To raise the value of labour throughout the world, we need only to raise the value of our own. To raise the value of land throughout the world, it is needed only that we adopt measures that shall raise the value of our own. To diffuse intelligence and to promote the cause of morality throughout the world, we are required only to pursue the course that shall diffuse education throughout our own land, and shall enable every man more readily to acquire property, and with it respect for the rights of property. To improve the political condition of man throughout the world, it is needed that we ourselves should remain at peace, avoid taxation for the maintenance of fleets and armies, and become rich and prosperous. To raise the condition of woman throughout the world, it is required of us only that we pursue that course that enables men to remain at home and marry, that they may surround themselves with happy children and grand-children. To substitute true Christianity for the detestable system known as the Malthusian, it is needed that we prove to the world that it is population that makes the food come from the rich soils, and that food tends to increase more rapidly than population, thus vindicating the policy of God to man. Doing these things, the addition to our population by immigration will speedily rise to millions, and with each and every year the desire for that perfect freedom of trade which results from incorporation within the Union, will be seen to spread and to increase in its intensity, leading gradually to the establishment of an empire the most extensive and magnificent the world has yet seen, based upon the principles of maintaining peace itself, and strong enough to insist upon the maintenance of peace by others, yet carried on without the aid of fleets, or armies, or taxes, the sales of public lands alone sufficing to pay the expenses of government.

To establish such an empire—to prove that among the people of the world, whether agriculturists, manufacturers, or merchants, there is perfect harmony of interests, and that the happiness of individuals, as well as the grandeur of nations, is to be promoted by perfect obedience to that greatest of all commands, "Do unto others as ye would that others should do unto you,"—is the object and will be the result of that mission. Whether that result shall be speedily attained, or whether it shall be postponed to a distant period, will depend greatly upon the men who are charged with the performance of the duties of government. If their movements be governed by that enlightened self-interest which induces man to seek his happiness in the promotion of that of his fellowman, it will come soon. If, on the contrary, they be governed by that ignorant selfishness which leads to the belief that individuals, party, or national interests, are to be promoted by measures tending to the deterioration of the condition of others, it will be late.

Part Four

Romantic Intellect and Cultural Reform

Introduction

"The key to the period appeared to be that the mind had become aware of itself." So Ralph Waldo Emerson characterized, fifty years afterward, the spirit of that enthusiastic circle of young ministers, teachers, writers, and their followers, who from Boston, Cambridge, Concord, and other New England outposts disseminated America's most important philosophy of Romanticism. At the heart of their Romanticism—or Transcendentalism, as their outlook came to be known—lay a gigantic paradox. On one hand, the young Transcendentalists, "born [as Ralph Waldo Emerson wrote] with knives in their brain," turned to the mind itself as an object of inquiry independent of the external world of commonsense perceptions their rationalist Unitarian elders had taught them were the proper objects of thought. On the other hand, they often went beyond these transcendental dialectics to conclude, as did the post-Kantian writers they generally followed, that the self-reflexive mind not only provides substantive enabling conditions for our experience of the world but can also constitute that world or an ideal version of it. Reinforcing this last tendency was their religious commitment; like their European Romantic counterparts, they sought not just to understand the world but to bring it in line with qualities they believed authentic religion promoted—principally the capacity for wonder and a sense of wholeness. Vibrating among these three poles, but rarely reconciling them, the Transcendentalists produced a body of cultural criticism as trenchant, buoyant, and innocent as any in American intellectual history.

No Transcendentalist text captures so fully both the critical and the visionary sides of the movement as Emerson's "Divinity School Address." In startling imagery and prophetic language, he disparaged all Christian sects, whether orthodox or liberal, that based their claims to authority on evidence external to human consciousness. In place of these dead faiths, Emerson preached "the God within" and a nature vibrant with symbolic meaning. Emerson also wrote a good deal of social criticism along similar lines, criticizing modern society's deadening mechanism and fragmentation and advocating as antidotes ways of seeing that facilitated organic wholeness and spiritual vitality. But for Emerson the greatest cultural threat to the divine self came from the tendency of America's business civilization to breed a stifling conformity. In his essay "Self-Reliance," Emerson argued that this debilitating self-alienation could be overcome by fashioning an "aboriginal Self" whose very rootlessness guaranteed its power and security.

Emerson's essay is printed here also because it demonstrates so well the theoretical ambiguities of Transcendentalism's relation to the practice of reform. Although Emerson in his essays frequently pitted the "active soul" *against* social reformers, other Transcendentalists were (as Emerson himself was at times) more sympathetic toward at least certain kinds of organized reform. These included educators such as Bronson Alcott, who organized schools and discussion groups that stressed intuitive learning through the medium of "Conversations." The most famous of these was the Temple School, where Alcott coaxed his elementary pupils into interpreting the Gospel texts in light of their own inward promptings, which he afterward published in *Conversations with Children on the Gospels,* an excerpt from which is printed herein. The Transcendentalists also encompassed socialists who sought to achieve self-sufficiency through collective associations of work in their community of Brook Farm. In her essay "Plan of the West Roxbury Community," Elizabeth Peabody, looking at their designs through the lens of her liberal Christian Transcendentalism, detected in them both happy portents and worrisome dangers.

Finally, there were those ambiguously reform-minded, individualistic Transcendentalists who wrote densely packed, metaphor-laden, personal-critico-prophetic essays designed (as Henry David Thoreau said of his *Walden)* "to wake my neighbors up." Of these discursive odes Margaret Fuller's *Woman in the Nineteenth Century* startled many because of both its subject matter and its point of view. In her book Fuller presented a scheme of female self-culture that aimed at achieving transcendental wholeness through the transcendence of conventional "masculine" and "feminine" roles and identities. Even more than women, American slaves were obviously denied opportunities for self-development and as a consequence won the sympathy of Transcendentalist adherents. Still, the most elaborate Transcendentalist statement on the slavery question, Thoreau's famous essay on civil resistance, was primarily concerned not with slaves but with the moral and political slavishness that he saw as endemic in the free democratic North. As a corrective Thoreau offered one of the most complete theories of principled social activism ever written.

Although of great historical importance, the Transcendentalists did not have a monopoly on loosely defined "Romantic" cultural mind-sets in America. On the contrary, by the 1840s Romantic concepts were beginning to permeate the thinking of many intellectuals distant from or even hostile to the Transcendentalists' liberal religion and radical social ideas. Some embraced "sentimentalist" outlooks that touted melting emotions of love, spirituality, and sympathy, especially with the "lowly," including women, children, African-Americans, and the poor. Others, in both the North and the South, tried to use Romantic and sentimental ideas to justify traditional institutions and values. Still others charted a middle course in favor of conservative cultural reform. One of the most famous of these was the Congregational minister Horace Bushnell. In his discourse "Christian Nurture," he provided a striking example of how Romantic ideas could be used to shore up a liberalized version of post-Calvinist Protestantism, the family, and, by extension, the primary social institutions of antebellum America.

In the end, both Transcendentalism and Romanticism had their greatest long-range cultural impact in America in literature and literary theory. The Transcendentalist call for "new demands on literature" to be realized by the symbol-making powers of independent American writers has been heeded repeatedly in literary and academic circles down to our own time. Yet the Romantic era's greatest imaginative prose writers wrote in a vein that was certainly inward-turned but by no means wholly Transcendentalist. For writers like Nathaniel Hawthorne and Herman Melville, the mind disclosed demonic impulses rarely turned up by Emerson's young psychic probers. Curiously, though, their fascination with dissonances in the Romantic mind made them more, not less, concerned with America's *collective* destiny. In his essay on Hawthorne that concludes Part Four, Melville not only argued for the recognition of these "powers of darkness," but also daringly insisted that thinkers like Hawthorne who exposed them ought to be embraced as the true exponents of American democratic culture. Only Melville's fellow New Yorker Walt Whitman was more sanguine about the prospects for America's comradely hug of the delinquent Romantic self.

Recommendations for Further Reading

Vernon Louis Parrington, *Main Currents in American Thought,* vol. 2: *1800–1860, The Romantic Revolution in America* (New York, 1927); F. O. Matthiessen, *American Renaissance: Art and Expression in the Age of Emerson and Whitman* (New York, 1941); Perry Miller, ed., *The Transcendentalists: An Anthology* (Cambridge, Mass., 1950); Daniel Aaron, *Men of Good Hope: A Story of American Progressives* (New York, 1951); R. W. B. Lewis, *The American Adam: Innocence, Tragedy, and Tradition in the Nineteenth Century* (Chicago, 1955); William R. Hutchison, *The Transcendentalist Ministers: Church Reform in the New England Renaissance* (New Haven, 1959); David Levin, *History as Romantic Art: Bancroft, Prescott, Motley, and Parkman* (Stanford, 1959); James Hastings Nichols, *Romanticism in American Theology: Nevin and Schaff at Mercersburg* (Chicago, 1961); Leo Marx, *The Machine in the Garden: Technology and the Pastoral Ideal in America* (New York, 1964); Neil Harris, *The Artist in American Society: The Formative Years, 1790–1860* (Chicago, 1966); Lawrence Buell, *Literary Transcendentalism: Style and Vision in the American Renaissance* (Ithaca, 1973); Susan P. Conrad, *Perish the Thought: Intellectual Women in Romantic America, 1830–1860* (New York, 1976); Ann Douglas, *The Feminization of American Culture* (New York, 1977); Taylor Stoehr, *Nay-Saying in Concord: Emerson, Alcott, and Thoreau* (Hamden, Conn., 1979); Anne C. Rose, *Transcendentalism as a Social Movement, 1830–1850* (New Haven, 1981); Peter Carafiol, *Transcendent Reason: James Marsh and the Forms of Romantic Thought* (Tallahassee, Fla. 1982); Michael T. Gilmore, *American Romanticism and the Marketplace* (Chicago, 1985); Irving Howe, *The American Newness: Culture and Politics in the Age of Emerson* (Cambridge, Mass., 1986); Leon Chai, *The Romantic Foundations of the American Renaissance* (Ithaca, 1987); Stanley Cavell, *In Quest of the Ordinary: Lines of Skepticism and Romanticism* (Chicago, 1988); David S. Reynolds, *Beneath the American Renaissance: The Subversive Imagination in America in the Age of Emerson and Melville* (New York, 1988); Richard A. Grusin, *Transcendentalist Hermenuetics: Institutional Authority and the Higher Criticism* (Durham, N.C., 1991); Carl J. Guarneri, *The Utopian Alternative: Fourierism in Nineteenth-Century America* (Ithaca, 1991); Michael Broyles, *"Music of the Highest Class": Elitism and Populism in Antebellum Boston* (New Haven, 1992); George Kateb, *The inner Ocean: Individualism and Democratic Culture* (Ithaca, 1992); Walter H. Conser, Jr., *God and the Natural World: Religion and Science in Antebellum America* (Columbia, S.C., 1993); Lewis Perry, *Boats Against the Current: American Culture Between Revolution and Modernity, 1820–1860* (New York, 1993); Arthur Versluis, *American Transcendentalism and Asian Religions* (New York, 1993); Barbara Novak, *Nature and Culture: American Landscape and Painting, 1825–1875,* rev. ed. (New York, 1995); Richard F. Teichgraeber III, *Sublime Thoughts/ Penny Wisdom: Situating Emerson and Thoreau in the American Market* (Baltimore, 1995); Charles Capper and Conrad Edick Wright, eds., *Transient and Permanent: The Transcendentalist Movement and Its Contexts* (Boston, 1999); Catherine L. Albanese, *A Republic of Mind and Spirit: A Cultural History of American Metaphysical Religion* (New Haven, 2007); Philip F. Gura, *American Transcendentalism: A History* (New York, 2007); Elisabeth Hurth, *Between Faith and Unbelief: American Transcendentalists and the Challenge of Atheism* (Leiden, 2007); Barbara L. Packer, *The Transcendentalists* (Athens, Ga., 2007); Carl J. Richard, *The Golden Age of the Classics in America: Greece, Rome, and the Antebellum United States* (Cambridge, Mass., 2009); Laura Dassow Walls, *The Passage to Cosmos: Alexander von Humboldt and the Shaping of America* (Chicago, 2009); Joel Myerson, Sandra Harbert Petrulionis, and Laura Dassow Walls, eds., *The Oxford Handbook of Transcendentalism* (New York, 2010); Thomas Albert Howard, *God and the Atlantic: America, Europe, and the Religious Divide* (New York, 2011); Ethan J. Kytle, *Romantic Reformers and the Antislavery Struggle in the Civil War Era* (Cambridge, 2014).

A. BRONSON ALCOTT

Selection from *Conversations with Children on the Gospels* (1836–37)

From a hardscrabble Connecticut farm family, Amos Bronson Alcott (1799–1888), who started out in life peddling wares to Southern planters and teaching in makeshift schools in rural New England, possessed a pedigree considerably humbler than that of his mostly Harvard-trained, ministerial comrades. Moreover, his sometimes grandiloquently disembodied writing frequently brought forth a cascade of ridicule from conservative newspaper editors eager to discredit the burgeoning outré movement. Yet in his later life, culturally ambitious middle-class Midwesterners flocked to his "conversations" on religion and philosophy. Ironically, Emerson, who tried with little success to get Alcott to inject some grit and "go" into his writing, nonetheless admired him tremendously for his uncompromising philosophical idealism, which Alcott principally took from Plato and the Neoplatonists rather than from the protomodern German post-Kantians who inspired many in the Transcendentalist circle. "He has more of the godlike than any man I have ever seen," Emerson wrote after the collapse of one of Alcott's reform ventures. "I can never doubt him. His ideal is beheld with such unrivalled distinctness, that he is not only justified but necessitated to condemn & to seek to upheave the vast Actual and cleanse the world." Actually, a gifted teacher, Alcott was the circle's first institution-builder in his Temple School in Boston, where he dispensed with rote memorization and minimized the use of corporal punishment. (Occasionally, to dramatize the suffering caused to the innocent by others' transgressions, he required a misbehaving pupil to strike *him!*) Pedagogically, he emphasized both inductive learning and Socratic teaching. His philosophical goal was to lead his students to the discovery of the reality of a spiritual world that lay behind the outward one they perceived through their senses. And although these leadings might sometimes sound to a modern reader irritatingly heavy-handed, records of his classroom teaching, including those printed below, suggest that he was conscious of those dangers and tried to forestall or minimize them, often aided by his pupils, who sometimes resisted giving answers that he seems to have wanted. More important, these records show that he did succeed, often ingeniously, in activating his pupils' minds, most impressively by getting them to attach thoughts to words they were heretofore taught to parrot. In short, the Temple School served as a dialogical vehicle for creating the self-reflexive "Man Thinking" that Emerson aimed to inspire on the public lecture circuit.

In 1834 Alcott arrived in Boston with great hopes for the patronage of the highly educated and often wealthy families of the city's Unitarian elite attracted to liberal educational reform. In fact, his school initially met with enormous success. However, as the heated controversy set off by the young Transcendentalists, who attacked their rationalist Unitarian elders for insisting that Jesus' recorded miracles empirically warranted the truth of Christianity,

Alcott eagerly stepped forth as a fellow combatant. Rather than scriptural exegeses, though, his chosen weapon was his students' discussions of the Gospels, which once they became publicly known were widely seen as striking at virtually every foundation of established Unitarianism. Taking Plato's idea of preexistence as his anchor and William Wordsworth's Immortality Ode as his motto ("Our birth is but a sleep and a forgetting:/. . . But trailing clouds of glory do we come/From God, who is our home:/Heaven lies about us in our infancy!"), Alcott reasoned that children, being near in time to that prenatal state, would be better able to intuit (or remember) the spiritual meanings of scriptural passages than adults blinded by their pride in their knowledge of outward things. To Harvard theologians who had devoted their careers to patiently gathering and testing textual and historical evidence to support their biblical interpretations, Alcott's appeal to the intuitions of mostly five- to eight-year-old children to interrogate sacred texts, including passages thought to be of questionable character for children, such as the virgin birth and circumcision, was (as one eminent Harvard divine reportedly said) nothing more than absurd, blasphemous, and obscene confirmations of the Calvinists' longtime prediction that Unitarianism would sooner or later devolve into infidelity if not atheism. Almost immediately after Alcott published the meetings' transcripts in his *Conversations with Children on the Gospels,* the school's parents began removing their children, soon reducing his charges to his three daughters and one African American girl whom Alcott refused to expel despite the entreaties of the last of his patrons. None could have guessed that his failed experiment anticipated by nearly a century the progressive schooling, championed most famously by the philosophically anti-idealist John Dewey, that would put student thinking at the center of teaching pedagogy.

The selections below are taken from transcripts of the conversations as recorded by Alcott's head teacher, Elizabeth Peabody. (For more on Peabody, see the headnote to her essay "Plan of the West Roxbury Community" in this sourcebook). By Transcendentalist standards, comparatively moderate both theologically and socially, Peabody nonetheless published numerous forthright, if often qualified, defenses of Alcott's teaching practices and philosophical premises. However, nervous about her reputation among Boston's elite Unitarian families who employed her as a tutor and teacher and accurately predicting the storm likely to ensue once the conversations were published, she insisted he censor all recorded remarks of hers that would show her as a participant in the conversations rather than the "passive recorder" she wanted to appear as. She also begged him to omit the more daring remarks of the children, mostly about sex, birth, and other "bodily" facts, which Alcott encouraged them to see as symbolic of spiritual "facts." Either knowingly or naively, he restored her omissions and made some into footnotes while retaining even more provocative fare in the appendix, thus affording hostile readers and newspaper editors an easy way to locate and quote from these sensational extracts without bothering to read the rest of the book. All the excerpts in the appendix were taken from later conversations in which Alcott read passages from the earlier ones and asked if the children had anything to add. Consequently, these later responses appear here in numbered endnotes to these original passages. The children's remarks that Alcott restored in the book are printed as footnotes marked by asterisks.

The "Recorder" is Peabody and the "Editor" is Alcott. Two notably active participants in these Conversations are Lemuel Shaw, Jr., the eight-year-old son of Lemuel Shaw, the Chief Justice of the Massachusetts Supreme Judicial Court, and seven-year-old Josiah Phillips Quincy, the grandson of Josiah Quincy, Boston's former mayor and then current president of Harvard University. F. B. Sanborn and William T. Harris, *A. Bronson Alcott: His Life and Philosophy,* 2 vols. (Boston, 1893) is a dated but comprehensive study of Alcott's thought and career. For a more technically rigorous account of Alcott's philosophy, see Murray G. Murphey, "Amos Bronson Alcott: The Origin and Development of His Philosophy," undergraduate honors thesis, Harvard University, 1949. The best modern biography is Frederick C. Dahlstrand's *Amos Bronson Alcott: An Intellectual Biography* (Rutherford, N.J., 1982). A helpful discussion of of Alcott's educational ideas and practices may be found in Dorothy McCuskey, *Bronson Alcott, Teacher* (New York, 1940).

EDITOR'S PREFACE

THE work now presented to the reader, forms the introduction to a course of conversations with children, on the Life of Christ, as recorded in the Gospels. It is the Record of an attempt to unfold the Idea of Spirit from the Consciousness of Childhood; and to trace its Intellectual and Corporeal Relations; its Temptations and Disciplines; its Struggles and Conquests, while in the Flesh. To this end, the character of Jesus has been presented to the consideration of children, as the brightest Symbol of Spirit; and they have been encouraged to express their views regarding it. The Conductor of these conversations has reverently explored their consciousness, for the testimony which it might furnish in favor of the truth of Christianity.

Assuming as a fact the spiritual integrity of the young mind, he was desirous of placing under the inspection of children, a character so much in conformity with their own, as that of Jesus of Nazareth. He believed that children would as readily apprehend the divine beauty of this character, when rightly presented, as adults. He even hoped that, through their simple consciousness, the Divine Idea of a Man, as Imaged in Jesus, yet almost lost to the world, might be revived in the mind of adults, who might thus be recalled into the spiritual kingdom. These views, confirmed by long intimacy with the young, as well as by the tendency of his own mind to regard the bright visions of childhood, as the promise of the soul's future blessedness; as the loadstar to conduct it through this terrestrial Life, led him to undertake this enterprise, and to prosecute it with a deep and kindling interest, which he feels will continue unabated to its close.

The Editor will not, meanwhile, conceal the fact, that it is with no little solicitude that he ventures these documents before the eyes of others. He feels that his book should be studied in Simplicity. It is, in no small measure, the production of children. It is a record of their consciousness; a natural history of the undepraved spirit. It is the testimony of unspoiled natures to the spiritual purity of Jesus. It is a revelation of the Divinity in the soul of childhood. Like the Sacred volume—on which it is, indeed, a juvenile commentary—of which it is an interpretation, it cannot be at once, apprehended in all its bearings, and find its true value.

There may be those, however, who, unconscious of its worth, shall avail themselves of the statements, views, and speculations, which it contains, to the detriment of religion and humanity; not perceiving, that it is a work, intended rather to awaken thought; enkindle feeling; and quicken to duty; than to settle opinions, or promulgate sentiments of any kind. Whoever shall find its significance, will scarce treat with disrespect these products of the sacred being of childhood. For childhood utters sage things, worthy of all note; and he who scoffs at its improvisations, or perverts its simple sayings, proves the corruption of his own being, and his want of reverence for the Good, the Beautiful, the True, and the Holy. He beholds not the Face of the Heavenly Father.

It has been a main purpose of the Conductor of these conversations, to tempt forth, by appropriate questions, the cherished sentiments of the children on the subjects presented to their consideration. It was no part of his intention to bring forward, except by necessary implication, his own favorite opinions as a means of biassing, in the smallest degree, the judgments and decisions of the children. He wished to inculcate only what was the universal product of our common nature. He endeavoured to avoid dogmatizing. He

Source: A. Bronson Alcott, *Conversations with Children on the Gospels,* 2 vols. (Boston: James Munroe and Company, 1836–37), I, xi–xviii, 60–66, 228–31; II, 10–18. Notes altered.

was desirous of gathering the sentiments of the little circle, in which it is his pleasure and privilege to move as teacher and friend. He believed that Christianity was in Childhood, and he sought the readiest and simplest means to unfold it, and bring it into the light of day.

That he has withheld his own sentiments from the children in all instances, he can scarce hope. It was next to impossible. He has doubtless led them, in some instances, by the tenor of his questions, and his manner of disposing of replies, to the adoption or rejection of sentiments, foreign to their nature. But he believes that he has seldom erred in this way. He preferred to become the simple Analyst of the consciousness of the children, and, having no opinions of his own to establish against their common convictions, he treated with reverence whatever he found within it, deeming it, when spontaneous, a revelation of the same Divinity, as was Jesus.

He is aware that the work which he has assumed is one of great difficulty. He feels that it is not easy to ascertain the precise state of a child's mind. He knows that much of what a child utters has been received from others; that language is an uncertain organ in his use; that he often endows words with his own significance; that he is liable to mistake the phenomena of his own consciousness; and, moreover, that his scanty vocabulary often leaves him without the means of revealing himself. Still some certainty is attainable. For a child can be trusted when urged to ingenuous expression; and when all temptations to deceive are withdrawn. A wise and sympathizing observer will readily distinguish the real from the assumed; penetrate through all the varying phases of expression, and do him justice.

Yet, while so little is done to guard children against servile imitation, by a wise training of their minds to original thought, we are in danger of not giving them credit for what is their own. So little confidence, indeed, do we place in their statements, and so imitative do we deem them, that, when a wise saying chances to drop from their lips, instead of regarding it, as it of right should be, the product of their own minds, we seek its origin among adults, as if it must of necessity spring from this source alone. We greatly underrate the genius of children. We do not apprehend the inward power, that but awaits the genial touch, to be quickened into life. The art of tempting this forth we have scarce attained. We have outlived our own simple consciousness, and have thus lost our power of apprehending them. We have yet to learn, that Wisdom and Holiness are of no Age; that they preëxist, separate from time, and are the possession of Childhood, not less than of later years; that they, indeed, often appear in fresher features, in the earlier seasons of life, than in physical maturity. In Man they are often quenched by the vulgar aims of the corporeal life.

To a child, all questions touching the Soul are deeply interesting. He loves his own consciousness. It is a charmed world to him. As yet he has not been drawn out of it by the seductions of the propensities; nor is he beguiled by the illusions of his external senses. And were he assisted in the study and discipline of it, by those who could meet his wants, and on whom he could rely, his spiritual acquirements would keep pace with his years, and he would grow up wise in the mysteries of the spiritual kingdom. The Divine Idea of a Man, the vision of Self-Perfection, would live in his consciousness; instead of being, as now, pushed aside by the intrusive images, and vulgar claims, of unhallowed appetite and desire. Christ would be formed in the Soul the Hope of Immortality. . . .

CONVERSATION VIII.

NATIVITY OF SPIRIT.

FAMILY RELATION.

Review.

Mr. Alcott	began by asking, What was our conversation upon the last time?
CHARLES and OTHERS.	The journey of Mary. The visit to her cousin Elisabeth. Their conversation.
Mr. Alcott	then read

THE BIRTH AND NAMING OF JOHN THE BAPTIST.

Birth and Naming

LUKE i. 57 to the end

57 Now Elisabeth's full time came that she should be delivered: and she brought forth a son.

58 And her neighbours and her cousins heard how the Lord had showed great mercy upon her; and they rejoiced with her.

59 And it came to pass, that on the eighth day they came to circumcise the child; and they called him Zacharias, after the name of his father.

60 And his mother answered and said, Not *so;* but he shall be called John.

61 And they said unto her, There is none of thy kindred that is called by this name.

62 And they made signs to his father, how he would have him called.

63 And he asked for a writing-table, and wrote, saying, His name is John. And they marvelled all.

64 And his mouth was opened immediately, and his tongue *loosed,* and he spake and praised God.

65 And fear came on all that dwelt round about them: and all these sayings were noised abroad throughout all the hill country of Judea.

66 And all they that heard *them* laid *them* up in their hearts, saying, What manner of child shall this be! And the hand of the Lord was with him.

67 And his father Zacharias was filled with the Holy Ghost, and prophesied, saying,

68 Blessed *be* the Lord God of Israel;
For he hath visited and redeemed his people,

69 And hath raised up an horn of salvation for us,
In the house of his servant David;

70 As he spake by the mouth of his holy prophets,
Which have been since the world began:

71 That we should be saved from our enemies,
And from the hand of all that hate us:

72 To perform the mercy *promised* to our fathers,
And to remember his holy covenant;

73 The oath which he sware to our father Abraham,
74 That he would grant unto us,
      That we, being delivered out of the hand of our enemies, Might serve him without fear,
75 In holiness and righteousness before him, All the days of our life.
76 And thou, child, shalt be called the prophet of the Highest,
      For thou shalt go before the face of the Lord to prepare his ways;
77 To give knowledge of salvation unto his people,
      By the remission of their sins,
78 Through the tender mercy of our God;
      Whereby the day-spring from on high hath visited us,
79 To give light to them that sit in darkness and *in* the shadow of death;
      To guide our feet into the way of peace.
80 And the child grew, and waxed strong in spirit, and was in the deserts till the day of his showing unto Israel.

Idea of Birth-place and Birth.

Now what came into your minds while I was reading?

JOSIAH.	The deserts seemed to me a great space covered with sand, like that in the hour-glass. The sun was shining on it, and making it sparkle. There were no trees. John was there alone.
EDWARD J.	I thought the deserts meant woods, with paths here and there.
LUCY.	I thought of a space covered with grass and some wild flowers, and John walking about.
CHARLES.	I thought of a prairie.
ALEXANDER.	I thought of a rocky country.
AUGUSTINE.	I thought of a few trees scattered over the country, with bees in the trunks.
GEORGE K.	I thought of a place without houses, excepting John's; and flowers, trees, and bee-hives.

Birth.

MR. ALCOTT.	I should like to hear all your pictures, but as I have not time, you may tell me now what interested you most? [1]
CHARLES.	The prophecy of Zacharias.
LUCIA.	Elisabeth's saying the child's name must be John.
LUCY.	Zacharias finding his speech again.
ANDREW.	The birth of the child.
MR. ALCOTT.	How was it?
ANDREW.	I thought, one night, as Elisabeth was sleeping, an angel brought her a child, and made her dream she had one, and she awoke and it was lying at her side.
WILLIAM B.	I think he was born like other children except that Elisabeth had visions. [2]

GEORGE K.	I thought God sent an angel to give her a child. It cried as soon as it came and waked up its mother to give it something to eat.
LUCIA.	When John was first born, his mother did not know it, for he was born in the night; but she found it by her side in the morning.
CHARLES.	Elisabeth must have had some vision as well as Zacharias, or how could she know the child was theirs? Zacharias could not speak.
NATHAN.	I don't see why John came in the night. All other children come in the day.

Sacredness of Birth.

MR. ALCOTT.	No; more frequently in the night. God draws a veil over these sacred events, and they ought never to be thought of except with reverence. The coming of a spirit is a great event. It is greater than death. It should free us from all wrong thoughts.[3]

Travail of Body with Spirit.

What is meant by "delivered"?

WILLIAM B.	She delivered her child to Zacharias.
OTHERS.	No; God delivered the child to Elisabeth.
CHARLES.	Elisabeth's thoughts made the child's soul, and when it was fairly born she was delivered from the anxiety of the thought.*

Emblems of Birth.

MR. ALCOTT.	You may give me some emblems of birth.
ALEXANDER.	Birth is like the rain. It comes from heaven.
LUCIA.	I think it is like a small stream coming from a great sea; and it runs back every night, and so becomes larger and larger every day, till at last it is large enough to send out other streams.
LEMUEL.	Lives streamed from the ocean first; now smaller streams from the larger ones, and so on.
SAMUEL R.	Birth is like the rising light of the sun; the setting is death.
ANDREW.	God's wind came upon the ocean of life, and washed up the waters a little into a channel, and that is birth. They run up farther, and that is living.
MR. ALCOTT.	I should like to have all your emblems but have not time. There is no adequate sign of birth in the outward world, except the physiological facts that attend it, with which you are not acquainted.

Naming of Spirit Incarnate.

Why did they call the child John?

SEVERAL.	Because the angel told them to.

---

* MR. ALCOTT. Yes, the deliverance of the spirit is the first thing. And I am glad to find, that you have so strong an impression of that. The physiological facts, sometimes referred to, are only a sign of the spiritual birth. You have seen the rose opening from the seed with the assistance of the atmosphere; this is the birth of the rose. It typifies the bringing forth of the spirit, by pain, and labor, and patience.[4] [Restored by the Editor.]

RECORDER.	The Hebrew word *John* means gift of God. They felt he was so kindly given that they called him Gift.
MR. ALCOTT.	Why did the people marvel?
FRANKLIN and OTHERS.	Because it was the custom to name children from relations.
JOSEPH.	And the people did not know that the angel had told them to name him John.
MR. ALCOTT.	What loosed Zacharias' tongue?
EDWARD J.	The power of God.
ANOTHER.	His faith.
LUCIA.	The child was born, and it was said that he should speak then.
CHARLES.	It was promised that he should speak.
FRANK.	Because God did not want to make the angel tell a lie.
FRANKLIN.	It was a reward of his obedience.
WILLIAM B.	He gave up a natural desire to name him from himself.

Influence of Nature on Imagination.

MR. ALCOTT.	Why was it "noised abroad"?
SEVERAL.	It was a great event to have a child, born from such old parents.
MR. ALCOTT.	And in the country, especially a hilly country, the people being imaginative, seem quite disposed to look beyond external things. They are apt to think singular events typify, or are a sign of, something supernatural. They wondered what kind of child this would be.

Analysis of the Prophecy of Zacharias.

How had the Lord "visited his people"? [5]

LEMUEL.	He had visited their spirits.
FRANKLIN.	By sending John to tell that Jesus was coming.
MR. ALCOTT.	What is it to redeem a people?
LUCIA.	To make them good.
EDWARD B.	To save them from sin.
MR. ALCOTT.	A man who loves to eat and drink, an intemperate man, a passionate man, is a slave to the body; and when his spirit is released from his body, by renewing thoughts, that withdraw his attention from his body, he is redeemed, just as a prisoner taken out of a dungeon is said to be redeemed from captivity.[6] What is meant by "horn of salvation"?
CHARLES.	A great deal of mercy.
MR. ALCOTT.	What is meant by "house of David"?
FRANKLIN.	Jesus was a descendant of David.
MR. ALCOTT.	What enemies are mentioned here?
CHARLES.	Spiritual enemies.
MR. ALCOTT.	What fathers are meant here?
CHARLES.	All good people who went before.
MR. ALCOTT.	What is "holy covenant"?
(*No answer.*)	

It is a promise, on condition of holiness, of giving blessings. And the oath?
(*Here it was found necessary to discriminate between profane swearing and judicial oaths, which they had confounded.*)[7]
Is there any such promise to us, as was made by that covenant?

CHARLES.	It is made to all good people.
MR. ALCOTT.	What is meant by "prophet of the highest"?
CHARLES.	Announcer of Jesus Christ.
MR. ALCOTT.	What is it to "give knowledge of salvation"?
CHARLES.	To tell us how to be good, and forgive our sins that are repented of.
MR. ALCOTT.	What is "day-spring"?
CHARLES.	Righteousness, wisdom.
MR. ALCOTT.	What is it to "sit in darkness"?[8]
CHARLES.	To be wicked.

Emblems of John and Jesus.

MR. ALCOTT.	If John was the day-spring, who was the risen sun?
ALL.	Jesus.
MR. ALCOTT.	What is it to "wax strong in spirit"?
CHARLES.	To stand fast by God.
FRANKLIN.	To grow better and better.
MR. ALCOTT. reads	"And he was in the deserts."
CHARLES.	In the country; at his father's house.

Prejudice.

EDWARD B.	Why are Jews held in such contempt, when Jesus was born a Jew.
FRANKLIN.	Because they killed Jesus, and said, "his blood be on us and our children."
EDWARD B.	And Jews are mean, avaricious, (*Mr. Alcott explained the last characteristics by the oppressions they had suffered.*)
MR. ALCOTT.	Who think it is a wicked prejudice?
WELLES.	It is a right prejudice.
ALL.	There are no right prejudices.

Subject.

MR. ALCOTT.	What has been the subject of this conversation?
NATHAN.	Putting spirits into bodies.
MR. ALCOTT.	And the nativity, or birth of spirit in the flesh.

Endnotes

1. (*Here Charles changed his picture, and supposed John dressed in a camel's hairy hide, with his tail for a belt.*)

MR. ALCOTT.	You make him quite a savage. Who was John the Baptist like?
CHARLES.	Dr. Graham. [Graham was a health and diet reformer whose controversial lectures on human physiology and anatomy influenced Alcott's ideas about the relation between the body and spirit.

Just that year one of Graham's lectures "for married women
only" stirred up a mob from which he narrowly escaped.]
2. Mr. Alcott. Do any of you think your mothers had visions of you?
(*Several.*)*

---

* *Restored by the Editor.*

3. Mr. Alcott. And now I don't want you to speak; but to hold up your hands, if you
have ever heard any disagreeable or vulgar things about birth.
(*None raised hands.*)
Men have been brought before Courts of Justice for saying vulgar things about the birth
of Christ; and all birth is sacred as Jesus Christ's. And I have heard of children
saying very profane things about it; and have heard fathers and mothers do so. I
hope that none of us will ever violate the sacredness of this subject.
4. Mr. Alcott. Edward B., it seems, had some profane notions of birth, connected with
some physiological facts; but they were corrected here. Did you
ever hear this line,

"The throe of suffering is the birth of bliss"?

George K.   Yes; it means that Love, and Joy, and Faith, lead you to have suffering,
which makes more happiness for you.
Mr. Alcott.   Yes; you have the thought. And a mother suffers when she has a child.
When she is going to have a child, she gives up her body to God,
and he works upon it, in a mysterious way, and with her aid,
brings forth the Child's Spirit in a little Body of its own, and
when it has come, she is blissful. But I have known some mothers who are so timid that they are not willing to bear the pain;
they fight against God, and suffer much more.
Charles.   I should think it ought to be the father, he is so much stronger.
Mr. Alcott.   He suffers because it is his part to see the suffering in order to relieve it.
But it is thought, and with good reason, that if there were no
wrong doing there would be no suffering attending this mysterious act. When Adam and Eve did wrong, it was said that Adam
should earn bread by the sweat of his brow, and Eve have pain
in bringing her children into the world. We never hear of trees
groaning to put forth their leaves.
Charles.   They have no power to do wrong.
Mr. Alcott.   True; God only gives them power to put forth, and they do it without
pain. A rose has no pain in being born. . . .

---

5. Mr. Alcott. Does the Lord visit his people now?
Charles.   Yes; in little babies.
Mr. Alcott.   Every one is a visiter on the Earth from the Lord. I hope you will all be
pleasant visiters. Some visiters are very unpleasant; they do not
like what is given them to eat and drink; they do not like the
beds they lie on. Do you think a drunkard is a pleasant visiter?
Is he doing what he is sent to do?
(*They all laughed.*)

EMMA.   I am not a very pleasant visiter, but I have a very pleasant visit.

6. MR. ALCOTT. How many of you are redeemed?

NATHAN.   I am not quite, but almost.

7. (*Here Mr. Alcott repeated that to speak of God without having a holy feeling was profanity; but an oath in a Court of Justice was sacred. It was speaking of God seriously, with a holy feeling.*)

8. Mr. Alcott.   Tell me what the shadow of death means. Would there be any shadow without light?

Which was made first, light or darkness?

CHARLES.   It seems to me that there was darkness first; I can't think otherwise.
Darkness.

MR. ALCOTT.   Is darkness real, positive? I thought darkness was the shadow of light. What if the sun should be put out?

ANDREW.   Then there would be darkness.

NATHAN.   When there is darkness we would not know it if light had not been first.

MR. ALCOTT.   Which of you think light came first? If light made the darkness, then if there had been no light there would have been no darkness. When the light goes out of this room does any thing come in?

CHARLES.   Yes; darkness comes in.

MR. ALCOTT.   Nothing comes in; and I cannot conceive of there not being light. Darkness is the absence of light to our external senses.

CONVERSATION XXIV

SPIRITUAL REFINEMENT

CHASTITY

Review.

MR. ALCOTT.   Where did we leave Jesus?

SEVERAL.   In Galilee, with John, and Andrew, and Peter.

MR. ALCOTT.   Do you remember the last words?

GEORGE K.   "Hereafter ye shall see heaven open, and the angels of God ascending and descending upon the Son of man."

FREDERIC.   And we said, that meant good thoughts entering in and proceeding from the Spirit of man.

Mr. Alcott   then read the

MARRIAGE FESTIVAL, AT CANA, IN GALILEE

JOHN ii. 1–12

Affability.

1   And the third day there was a marriage in Cana of Galilce; and the mother of Jesus was there.

2   And both Jesus was called, and his disciples, to the marriage.

3   And when they wanted wine, the mother of Jesus saith unto him, They have no wine.

4 Jesus saith unto her, Woman, what have I to do with thee? mine hour is not yet come.

5 His mother saith unto the servants, Whatsoever he saith unto you, do *it*.

6 And there were set there six water-pots of stone, after the manner of the purifying of the Jews, containing two or three firkins apiece.

7 Jesus saith unto them, Fill the water-pots with water. And they filled them up to the brim.

8 And he saith unto them, Draw out now, and bear unto the Governor of the feast. And they bare *it*.

9 When the ruler of the feast had tasted the water that was made wine, and knew not whence it was: (but the servants which drew the water knew;) the governor of the feast called the bridegroom,

10 And saith unto him, Every man at the beginning doth set forth good wine; and when men have well drunk, then that which is worse: *but* thou hast kept the good wine until now.

11 This beginning of miracles did Jesus in Cana of Galilee, and manifested forth his glory; and his disciples believed on him.

12 After this he went down to Capernaum, he, and his mother, and his brethren, and his disciples: and they continued there not many days: and asked the usual question.

Human Supremacy

JOSIAH.	The changing of the water into wine interested me most. If we had faith, and were as good as Jesus, we could change water into wine.
MR.	ALCOTT. Do all think so?

(*Most held up hands.*)

Views of Phenomena.

NATHAN.	I liked the water changing into wine. He had more spirit than we have, but I don't see how he did it.
EDWARD J.	I liked his mother telling him there was no wine.
MARTHA.	I was most interested in his answer. I thought it meant that his time to do the miracle would come. I was rather surprised that his mother told him they had no wine. It seemed as if she believed he could make some, and yet he had worked no miracles before.
GEORGE K.	I thought, when he said, "My hour is not yet come," that he meant his hour to die was not yet come, so he would do this miracle.
ANDREW.	I cannot express my thoughts about his turning water into wine.
JOHN B.	And I cannot express my thought about his saying, "Woman, what have I to do with thee?" and yet I think I know what it means.
MR. ALCOTT.	Do you often have thoughts which you cannot express?
JOHN and ANDREW.	Yes.
AUGUSTINE.	I had some thoughts I could not express about the angels of God ascending and descending upon the Son of man.
FRANKLIN.	I thought in this place, that Mary had faith that Jesus would do the miracle, and his answer meant that he would, bye and bye. It is plain she expected it, from what she said to the servants.

FREDERIC.	I think as George said.

(*He repeated it.*)

LEMUEL.	I thought "mine hour is not yet come," meant the hour to do the miracle.
GEORGE B.	I saw the stone watering pots in the court.
ALEXANDER.	I do not think we could turn water into wine, even if we were as good as Jesus.
SAMUEL R.	I think his answer meant, that there was no need of making the wine quite yet.
MR. ALCOTT.	Was it such wine as we have in our decanters?
SAMUEL R.	No; it tasted like wine, but it was like water. It would not intoxicate.
GEORGE K.	I think it was a mysterious medicinal wine.
LEMUEL.	I think they were made to think it was wine.
MR. ALCOTT.	Was the miracle worked in their minds or upon the water?

(*Half thought one way, half the other.*)

EMMA.	I think his mother telling him there was no wine, shows her faith in him.
LUCIA.	I have nothing to say, but I was interested.
MR. ALCOTT.	I like to have you say freely, that you have nothing to say, when you have nothing.

But now can you tell me what is the significance of this?

(*None answered.*)

Idea and Emblem of Purity.

What does marriage mean?

GEORGE K.	Deep love.
CHARLES.	Union of Spirit.
MR. ALCOTT.	What did Jesus mean to teach by this miracle?
HALES.	What he could do.
EMMA.	His faith and power.
NATHAN.	For us to believe in God as he did.
CHARLES.	It was to teach temperance.
FREDERIC.	Faith in God.

(*The rest said they did not know.*)

MR. ALCOTT.	Do you think that you see all the meaning of this miracle?

(*All.*)

When you were talking of the Temptation, you were somewhat puzzled, as you are now, for you were thinking altogether of outward things. The mountain, the pinnacle of the temple, troubled you. Can you not turn your thoughts inward, as you did then, and ask yourselves, what these things may be emblems of?

CHARLES.	Water is an emblem of purity.
MR. ALCOTT.	And wine?

(*There was no answer.*)

And the change?

LEMUEL.	Of growing better; making good better.
ONE.	The bride was purity.
MR. ALCOTT.	Charles said marriage was spiritual union. Can you work up these emblems into something?
NATHAN.	The water meant purity, the wine goodness.
MR. ALCOTT.	And did Christ's presence sanctify the union?

View of Phenomena.

AUGUSTINE.	There must have been real wine made, for the governor of the feast tasted it.
MR. ALCOTT.	Do you think that to view it all as an outward fact, would be more interesting and wonderful, than to view it as emblematic?
AUGUSTINE.	No; not more wonderful; but that is the way it really was.
MR. ALCOTT.	Did he do this to gratify their appetites?
AUGUSTINE.	No; but to supply their wants.
MR. ALCOTT.	Do you think that the whole matter was simply that there was a wedding, and there was not wine enough, and Jesus being there, kindly made them some wine?
AUGUSTINE and OTHERS.	Yes.
MR. ALCOTT.	Do any of you think that it means more?

(*Some rose.*)

Now all who think Jesus turned water into wine, literally and actually, may rise.

(*All rose.*)

And as an emblem of a beautiful truth?

(*They still stood up.*)

Intermission.

(*Here there was an intermission, and when they assembled again, Mr. Alcott again read the passage, paraphrasing the fourth verse,—"Woman, my thoughts are not like yours; you are thinking of making wine; I am thinking what wine signifies."*)

MR. ALCOTT.	What does this whole story signify?

(*No answer.*)

Which do you think was the greatest miracle, to change water into wine, or to open the minds of men into the real meaning of marriage?

(*No answer.*)

Origin and Cause of Miracles in Spirit.

Where do miracles begin?

(*No answer.*)

Do they begin in the Spirit, and flow out into things, or begin in things?

SEVERAL.	In the Spirit.
MR. ALCOTT.	Where is the cause of miracles?
SEVERAL.	In the Spirit.
MR. ALCOTT.	Where is the Life that causes a seed to spring out and seek the light?
LUCIA.	In God.
MR. ALCOTT.	Where is God?
LUCIA.	In the seed.
MR. ALCOTT.	How is spiritual "glory" shown forth?
LUCIA.	By being good.

Types of Miraculous Agency.

MR. ALCOTT.	Give me some fact of Nature, by which spiritual glory is shown forth
AUGUSTINE.	In the oak coming out of the acorn.

ANDREW.	In the rose coming out of the bud, for there is power.
FRANKLIN.	Dr. Channing shows forth spiritual glory in his thoughts and feelings, when he preaches and tries to make people good.
EMMA.	God shows forth glory in Nature, and in the Soul of man.
SAMUEL T.	A little baby shows forth spiritual glory.
MARTHA.	A dove shows forth God's glory.
ALEXANDER.	An elephant shows forth patience and nobleness.
GEORGE K.	A lion shows forth the power of God.
OTHERS.	The sun. The moon. The stars, &c.
MR. ALCOTT.	The glory is not of things themselves; but things shadow forth the glory of God.

Does any outward thing show it forth completely? Lions, flowers, stars?
(*They signified dissent while he remained in the Outward creation; but when he said,*)
In Human Nature?

| ALL. | Yes; in Jesus Christ. |
| MR. ALCOTT. | Do you think that Jesus showed forth all the glory of God; that nothing at all was withheld? |

(*Some said yes, some no.*)

Apprehension of Phenomena.

Now tell me, do you think the change of water into wine was actually made in the outward world?
(*All held up hands but Francis and Franklin.*)
Was that all the miracle?
(*All said no, but Alexander and Augustine.*)

| AUGUSTINE. | I think he had no other meaning than to show that he was willing to supply their needs. |
| MR. ALCOTT. | Had Jesus never performed any other miracle, should you have regarded this as something very great? |

(*Most held up hands.*)

| WELLES. | If he had not done any other miracle, I should have thought that Jesus brought the wine himself. |

Type of Marriage and Chastity.

FRANKLIN.	I think the miracle was emblematic.
MR. ALCOTT.	Do others think so? and of what?
JOHN B.	It was emblematic of power.
FRANKLIN.	I think it was emblematic of purity, united to greater purity—to faith and love.
EMMA.	And that is marriage.
MR. ALCOTT.	Is marriage an emblem?
EMMA.	Yes; it is an emblem of two spirits united in purity and love.
SAMUEL R.	I think the whole story is an emblem of changing good into better.
GEORGE K.	I think water was pure, and wine was purer, and it signified that they must purify their spirits.
MARTHA.	The wine was purer than the water.
AUGUSTINE.	Wine is not so pure as water—water represents truth.

ANDREW.	I think the wine was the Spirit of Jesus.
WELLES.	Water represents purity, but wine means more things, love, faith, &c.
MR. ALCOTT.	Did you ever hear the word Chastity? That word represents something more than purity, for it implies self-restraint. This story may represent deep love, as one of you said at the beginning of the Conversation, and when deep love is restrained by principles, it is chastity.

Recorder's Remark.

RECORDER.	I think you have led the children into an allegorical interpretation of this passage, when their own minds did not tend towards it. In no conversation has it been so difficult to keep them to the subject, nor have you suggested so much. I cannot help being gratified at this, myself; because I do not believe the Evangelist had any idea of setting forth any thing but the kind sanction of Jesus to the innocent festivities which celebrate marriage.
MR. ALCOTT.	It is remarkable, that this is the only instance in which I have premeditated one of these Conversations. I studied this passage beforehand, and in no instance have we succeeded so ill. It is better to give the subject up to the children, and let them lead us where they will. The course pursued in this, is in violation of the plan proposed at the beginning of the Conversations, and confirms the naturalness of that plan, by the want of success which has attended this effort. I think this worthy of remark.

RALPH WALDO EMERSON

"The Divinity School Address" (1838)

"Self-Reliance" (1841)

"A believer in Unity, a seer of Unity, I yet behold two." This self-described ruling characteristic of Ralph Waldo Emerson (1803–1882)—which both epitomized his position as a Transcendentalist and defined his power as a writer and thinker—is well displayed in the two works presented herein.

The first was his severe critique of the Unitarian church delivered in 1838 before a mixed audience of sympathetic graduating Harvard Divinity School students and their mostly perplexed and exasperated teachers. Historians have long recognized that Emerson's portrayal of his inherited faith as "corpse-cold" was something of a caricature. Yet in reading this address, it is easy to see why for Emerson this was no hyperbole. *Any* religion that put God "outside of me" vitiated itself, Emerson thought, and to Emerson, Unitarianism did just that in a doubly deadening way—first, by asserting that the intellectual authority of its faith rested on a certain class of supernatural events (Christ's miracles); second, by claiming that the truthfulness of such events could be demonstrated on entirely empirical grounds. Emerson, on the contrary, sought to demonstrate, both poetically and discursively, that a religious faith became living only when submerged in nature, which, in turn, was brought to life by men and women perceiving, through their godlike "Reason," both its physical and symbolic character.

Such divine double vision obviously required expunging not only an external god but external society as well, a subject Emerson explored in his essay "Self-Reliance" published three years later. Now he struck a new note of defiance: He no longer offered himself as a "new Teacher" in a renewed church but as a seer-sayer imparting to his readers "truth and health in rough electric shocks." The truth they needed to know was that in order to be self-reliant, they had to be nonconforming. Yet his social vision was neither anarchic nor hermetic. What he desired—and what tied him to the bustling democracy for which he would soon become a national spokesman—was a society so fluid that all of its parts would be capable of constantly moving and changing and therefore feeling their "power." Meanwhile, the "Self-reliance" that such a society facilitated was for Emerson ultimately God-reliance: In a culture so freed of external fixity and so stripped of psychic relations with family and property, individuals had only one source of secure and unchanging "Principles"—the God within. No one in nineteenth-century Western thought, not even Nietzsche (who admired Emerson greatly), offered a more exhilaratingly—or chillingly—transvalued vision of emerging modern culture.

Robert D. Richardson Jr., *Emerson: The Mind on Fire* (Berkeley, 1995), is a superb biography that delivers what its subtitle promises. One of the most profound studies of Emerson's thought remains Stephen E. Whicher's *Freedom and Fate: An Inner Life of Ralph Waldo Emerson* (Philadelphia, 1953). For an excellent up-to-date appraisal that stresses the cosmopolitan cast of Emerson's mind, see Lawrence Buell, *Emerson* (Cambridge, Mass., 2003). Contrasting discussions of Emerson's early intellectual career may be found in David M. Robinson, *Apostle of Culture: Emerson as Preacher and Lecturer* (Philadelphia, 1982); Mary Kupiec Cayton, *Emerson's Emergence: Self and Society in the Transformation of New England, 1800–1845* (Chapel Hill, 1989); and Kenneth S. Sacks, *Understanding Emerson: "The American Scholar" and His Struggle for Self-Reliance* (Princeton, 2003). For a probing revisionary case for the "pragmatist" core of Emerson's mature thinking, see David M. Robinson, *Emerson and the Conduct of Life: Pragmatism and Ethical Purpose in the Later Work* (Cambridge, 1993). George Kateb, *Emerson and Self-Reliance* (Thousand Oaks, Calif., 1995), is a powerful analysis of Emerson's politics by a contemporary political theorist. For two strong recent books that situate Emerson's political thought within the context of transatlantic liberalism, see Neal Dolan, *Emerson's Liberalism* (Madison, 2009); and Alex Zakaras, *Individuality and Mass Democracy: Mill, Emerson, and the Burden of Citizenship* (New York, 2009).

"The Divinity School Address"
(1838)

An Address Delivered Before the Senior Class
in Divinity College, Cambridge, Sunday Evening, 15 July, 1838

In this refulgent summer it has been a luxury to draw the breath of life. The grass grows, the buds burst, the meadow is spotted with fire and gold in the tint of flowers. The air is full of birds, and sweet with the breath of the pine, the balm-of-Gilead, and the new hay. Night brings no gloom to the heart with its welcome shade. Through the transparent darkness the stars pour their almost spiritual rays. Man under them seems a young child, and his huge globe a toy. The cool night bathes the world as with a river, and prepares his eyes again for the crimson dawn. The mystery of nature was never displayed more happily. The corn and the wine have been freely dealt to all creatures, and the never-broken silence with which the old bounty goes forward, has not yielded yet one word of explanation. One is constrained to respect the perfection of this world, in which our senses converse. How wide; how rich; what invitation from every property it gives to every faculty of man! In its fruitful soils; in its navigable sea; in its mountains of metal and stone; in its forests of all woods; in its animals; in its chemical ingredients; in the powers and path of light, heat, attraction, and life, it is well worth the pith and heart of great men to subdue and enjoy it. The planters, the mechanics, the inventors, the astronomers, the builders of cities, and the captains, history delights to honor.

But the moment the mind opens, and reveals the laws which traverse the universe, and make things what they are, then shrinks the great world at once into a mere illustration and fable of this mind. What am I? and What is? asks the human spirit with a curiosity new-kindled, but never to be quenched. Behold these outrunning laws, which our imperfect apprehension can see tend this way and that, but not come full circle. Behold these infinite relations, so like, so unlike; many, yet one. I would study, I would know, I would admire forever. These works of thought have been the entertainments of the human spirit in all ages.

A more secret, sweet, and overpowering beauty appears to man when his heart and mind open to the sentiment of virtue. Then instantly he is instructed in what is above him. He learns that his being is without bound; that, to the good, to the perfect, he is born, low as he now lies in evil and weakness. That which he venerates is still his own, though he has not realized it yet. He *ought*. He knows the sense of that grand word, though his analysis fails entirely to render account of it. When in innocency, or when by intellectual perception, he attains to say,—"I love the Right; Truth is beautiful within and without, forevermore. Virtue, I am thine: save me: use me: thee will I serve, day and night, in great, in small, that I may be not virtuous, but virtue;"—then is the end of the creation answered, and God is well pleased.

The sentiment of virtue is a reverence and delight in the presence of certain divine laws. It perceives that this homely game of life we play, covers, under what seem foolish details, principles that astonish. The child amidst his baubles, is learning the action of

Source: The Collected Works of Ralph Waldo Emerson, ed. Alfred R. Ferguson, vol. 1: *Nature, Addresses, and Lectures*, ed. Robert E. Spiller and Alfred R. Ferguson (Cambridge: The Belknap Press of Harvard University Press, 1971), 76–93. Reprinted by permission of Harvard University Press, Copyright © 1971 by the President and Fellows of Harvard College.

light, motion, gravity, muscular force; and in the game of human life, love, fear, justice, appetite, man, and God, interact. These laws refuse to be adequately stated. They will not by us or for us be written out on paper, or spoken by the tongue. They elude, evade our persevering thought, and yet we read them hourly in each other's faces, in each other's actions, in our own remorse. The moral traits which are all globed into every virtuous act and thought,— in speech, we must sever, and describe or suggest by painful enumeration of many particulars. Yet, as this sentiment is the essence of all religion, let me guide your eye to the precise objects of the sentiment, by an enumeration of some of those classes of facts in which this element is conspicuous.

The intuition of the moral sentiment is an insight of the perfection of the laws of the soul. These laws execute themselves. They are out of time, out of space, and not subject to circumstance. Thus; in the soul of man there is a justice whose retributions are instant and entire. He who does a good deed, is instantly ennobled himself. He who does a mean deed, is by the action itself contracted. He who puts off impurity, thereby puts on purity. If a man is at heart just, then in so far is he God; the safety of God, the immortality of God, the majesty of God do enter into that man with justice. If a man dissemble, deceive, he deceives himself, and goes out of acquaintance with his own being. A man in the view of absolute goodness, adores, with total humility. Every step so downward, is a step upward. The man who renounces himself, comes to himself by so doing.

See how this rapid intrinsic energy worketh everywhere, righting wrongs, correcting appearances, and bringing up facts to a harmony with thoughts. Its operation in life, though slow to the senses, is, at last, as sure as in the soul. By it, a man is made the Providence to himself, dispensing good to his goodness, and evil to his sin. Character is always known. Thefts never enrich; alms never impoverish; murder will speak out of stone walls. The least admixture of a lie,—for example, the smallest mixture of vanity, the least attempt to make a good impression, a favorable appearance,—will instantly vitiate the effect. But speak the truth, and all nature and all spirits help you with unexpected furtherance. Speak the truth, and all things alive or brute are vouchers, and the very roots of the grass underground there, do seem to stir and move to bear you witness. See again the perfection of the Law as it applies itself to the affections, and becomes the law of society. As we are, so we associate. The good, by affinity, seek the good; the vile, by affinity, the vile. Thus of their own volition, souls proceed into heaven, into hell.

These facts have always suggested to man the sublime creed, that the world is not the product of manifold power, but of one will, of one mind; and that one mind is everywhere active, in each ray of the star, in each wavelet of the pool; and whatever opposes that will, is everywhere baulked and baffled, because things are made so, and not otherwise. Good is positive. Evil is merely privative, not absolute. It is like cold, which is the privation of heat. All evil is so much death or nonentity. Benevolence is absolute and real. So much benevolence as a man hath, so much life hath he. For all things proceed out of this same spirit, which is differently named love, justice, temperance, in its different applications, just as the ocean receives different names on the several shores which it washes. All things proceed out of the same spirit, and all things conspire with it. Whilst a man seeks good ends, he is strong by the whole strength of nature. In so far as he roves from these ends, he bereaves himself of power, of auxiliaries; his being shrinks out of all remote channels, he becomes less and less, a mote, a point, until absolute badness is absolute death.

The perception of this law of laws always awakens in the mind a sentiment which we call the religious sentiment, and which makes our highest happiness. Wonderful is its power to charm and to command. It is a mountain air. It is the embalmer of the world. It is myrrh and storax, and chlorine and rosemary. It makes the sky and the hills sublime, and the silent song of the stars is it. By it, is the universe made safe and habitable, not by science or power. Thought may work cold and intransitive in things, and find no end or unity. But the dawn of the sentiment of virtue on the heart, gives and is the assurance that Law is sovereign over all natures; and the worlds, time, space, eternity, do seem to break out into joy.

This sentiment is divine and deifying. It is the beatitude of man. It makes him illimitable. Through it, the soul first knows itself. It corrects the capital mistake of the infant man, who seeks to be great by following the great, and hopes to derive advantages *from another,*—by showing the fountain of all good to be in himself, and that he, equally with every man, is an inlet into the deeps of Reason. When he says, "I ought;" when love warms him; when he chooses, warned from on high, the good and great deed; then, deep melodies wander through his soul from Supreme Wisdom. Then he can worship, and be enlarged by his worship; for he can never go behind this sentiment. In the sublimest flights of the soul, rectitude is never surmounted, love is never outgrown.

This sentiment lies at the foundation of society, and successively creates all forms of worship. The principle of veneration never dies out. Man fallen into superstition, into sensuality, is never wholly without the visions of the moral sentiment. In like manner, all the expressions of this sentiment are sacred and permanent in proportion to their purity. The expressions of this sentiment affect us deeper, greatlier, than all other compositions. The sentences of the oldest time, which ejaculate this piety, are still fresh and fragrant. This thought dwelled always deepest in the minds of men in the devout and contemplative East; not alone in Palestine, where it reached its purest expression, but in Egypt, in Persia, in India, in China. Europe has always owed to oriental genius, its divine impulses. What these holy bards said, all sane men found agreeable and true. And the unique impression of Jesus upon mankind, whose name is not so much written as ploughed into the history of this world, is proof of the subtle virtue of this infusion.

Meantime, whilst the doors of the temple stand open, night and day, before every man, and the oracles of this truth cease never, it is guarded by one stern condition; this, namely; It is an intuition. It cannot be received at second hand. Truly speaking, it is not instruction, but provocation, that I can receive from another soul. What he announces, I must find true in me, or wholly reject; and on his word, or as his second, be he who he may, I can accept nothing. On the contrary, the absence of this primary faith is the presence of degradation. As is the flood so is the ebb. Let this faith depart, and the very words it spake, and the things it made, become false and hurtful. Then falls the church, the state, art, letters, life. The doctrine of the divine nature being forgotten, a sickness infects and dwarfs the constitution. Once man was all; now he is an appendage, a nuisance. And because the indwelling Supreme Spirit cannot wholly be got rid of, the doctrine of it suffers this perversion, that the divine nature is attributed to one or two persons, and denied to all the rest, and denied with fury. The doctrine of inspiration is lost; the base doctrine of the majority of voices, usurps the place of the doctrine of the soul. Miracles, prophecy, poetry, the ideal life, the holy life, exist as ancient history merely; they are not in the belief, nor in the aspiration of society; but, when suggested, seem ridiculous. Life is comic or pitiful, as soon as the high ends of being fade out of sight, and man becomes near-sighted, and can only attend to what addresses the senses.

These general views, which, whilst they are general, none will contest, find abundant illustration in the history of religion, and especially in the history of the Christian church. In that, all of us have had our birth and nurture. The truth contained in that, you, my young friends, are now setting forth to teach. As the Cultus, or established worship of the civilized world, it has great historical interest for us. Of its blessed words, which have been the consolation of humanity, you need not that I should speak. I shall endeavor to discharge my duty to you, on this occasion, by pointing out two errors in its administration, which daily appear more gross from the point of view we have just now taken.

Jesus Christ belonged to the true race of prophets. He saw with open eye the mystery of the soul. Drawn by its severe harmony, ravished with its beauty, he lived in it, and had his being there. Alone in all history, he estimated the greatness of man. One man was true to what is in you and me. He saw that God incarnates himself in man, and evermore goes forth anew to take possession of his world. He said, in this jubilee of sublime emotion, "I am divine. Through me, God acts; through me, speaks. Would you see God, see me; or, see thee, when thou also thinkest as I now think." But what a distortion did his doctrine and memory suffer in the same, in the next, and the following ages! There is no doctrine of the Reason which will bear to be taught by the Understanding. The understanding caught this high chant from the poet's lips, and said, in the next age, "This was Jehovah come down out of heaven. I will kill you, if you say he was a man." The idioms of his language, and the figures of his rhetoric, have usurped the place of his truth; and churches are not built on his principles, but on his tropes. Christianity became a Mythus, as the poetic teaching of Greece and of Egypt, before. He spoke of miracles; for he felt that man's life was a miracle, and all that man doth, and he knew that this daily miracle shines, as the man is diviner. But the very word Miracle, as pronounced by Christian churches, gives a false impression; it is Monster. It is not one with the blowing clover and the falling rain.

He felt respect for Moses and the prophets; but no unfit tenderness at postponing their initial revelations, to the hour and the man that now is; to the eternal revelation in the heart. Thus was he a true man. Having seen that the law in us is commanding, he would not suffer it to be commanded. Boldly, with hand, and heart, and life, he declared it was God. Thus was he a true man. Thus is he, as I think, the only soul in history who has appreciated the worth of a man.

1. In thus contemplating Jesus, we become very sensible of the first defect of historical Christianity. Historical Christianity has fallen into the error that corrupts all attempts to communicate religion. As it appears to us, and as it has appeared for ages, it is not the doctrine of the soul, but an exaggeration of the personal, the positive, the ritual. It has dwelt, it dwells, with noxious exaggeration about the *person* of Jesus. The soul knows no persons. It invites every man to expand to the full circle of the universe, and will have no preferences but those of spontaneous love. But by this eastern monarchy of a Christianity, which indolence and fear have built, the friend of man is made the injurer of man. The manner in which his name is surrounded with expressions, which were once sallies of admiration and love, but are now petrified into official titles, kills all generous sympathy and liking. All who hear me, feel, that the language that describes Christ to Europe and America, is not the style of friendship and enthusiasm to a good and noble heart, but is appropriated and formal,—paints a demigod, as the Orientals or the Greeks would describe Osiris or Apollo. Accept the injurious impositions of our early catechetical instruction, and even honesty and self-denial were but splendid sins, if they did not wear the Christian name. One would rather by

"A pagan suckled in a creed outworn,"

than to be defrauded of his manly right in coming into nature, and finding not names and places, not land and professions, but even virtue and truth foreclosed and monopolized. You shall not be a man even. You shall not own the world; you shall not dare, and live after the infinite Law that is in you, and in company with the infinite Beauty which heaven and earth reflect to you in all lovely forms; but you must subordinate your nature to Christ's nature; you must accept our interpretations; and take his portrait as the vulgar draw it.

That is always best which gives me to myself. The sublime is excited in me by the great stoical doctrine, Obey thyself. That which shows God in me, fortifies me. That which shows God out of me, makes me a wart and a wen. There is no longer a necessary reason for my being. Already the long shadows of untimely oblivion creep over me, and I shall decease forever.

The divine bards are the friends of my virtue, of my intellect, of my strength. They admonish me, that the gleams which flash across my mind, are not mine, but God's; that they had the like, and were not disobedient to the heavenly vision. So I love them. Noble provocations go out from them, inviting me also to emancipate myself; to resist evil; to subdue the world; and to Be. And thus by his holy thoughts, Jesus serves us, and thus only. To aim to convert a man by miracles, is a profanation of the soul. A true conversion, a true Christ, is now, as always, to be made, by the reception of beautiful sentiments. It is true that a great and rich soul, like his, falling among the simple, does so preponderate, that, as his did, it names the world. The world seems to them to exist for him, and they have not yet drunk so deeply of his sense, as to see that only by coming again to themselves, or to God in themselves, can they grow forevermore. It is a low benefit to give me something; it is a high benefit to enable me to do somewhat of myself. The time is coming when all men will see, that the gift of God to the soul is not a vaunting, overpowering, excluding sanctity, but a sweet, natural goodness, a goodness like thine and mine, and that so invites thine and mine to be and to grow.

The injustice of the vulgar tone of preaching is not less flagrant to Jesus, than it is to the souls which it profanes. The preachers do not see that they make his gospel not glad, and shear him of the locks of beauty and the attributes of heaven. When I see a majestic Epaminondas, or Washington; when I see among my contemporaries, a true orator, an upright judge, a dear friend; when I vibrate to the melody and fancy of a poem; I see beauty that is to be desired. And so lovely, and with yet more entire consent of my human being, sounds in my ear the severe music of the bards that have sung of the true God in all ages. Now do not degrade the life and dialogues of Christ out of the circle of this charm, by insulation and peculiarity. Let them lie as they befel, alive and warm, part of human life, and of the landscape, and of the cheerful day.

2. The second defect of the traditionary and limited way of using the mind of Christ is a consequence of the first; this, namely; that the Moral Nature, that Law of laws, whose revelations introduce greatness,—yea, God himself, into the open soul, is not explored as the fountain of the established teaching in society. Men have come to speak of the revelation as somewhat long ago given and done, as if God were dead. The injury to faith throttles the preacher; and the goodliest of institutions becomes an uncertain and inarticulate voice.

It is very certain that it is the effect of conversation with the beauty of the soul, to beget a desire and need to impart to others the same knowledge and love. If utterance is denied, the thought lies like a burden on the man. Always the seer is a sayer. Somehow his dream is told. Somehow he publishes it with solemn joy. Sometimes with pencil on canvas; sometimes with chisel on stone; sometimes in towers and aisles of granite, his soul's worship is builded; sometimes in anthems of indefinite music; but clearest and most permanent, in words.

The man enamored of this excellency, becomes its priest or poet. The office is coeval with the world. But observe the condition, the spiritual limitation of the office. The spirit only can teach. Not any profane man, not any sensual, not any liar, not any slave can teach, but only he can give, who has; he only can create, who is. The man on whom the soul descends, through whom the soul speaks, alone can teach. Courage, piety, love, wisdom, can teach; and every man can open his door to these angels, and they shall bring him the gift of tongues. But the man who aims to speak as books enable, as synods use, as the fashion guides, and as interest commands, babbles. Let him hush.

To this holy office, you propose to devote yourselves. I wish you may feel your call in throbs of desire and hope. The office is the first in the world. It is of that reality, that it cannot suffer the deduction of any falsehood. And it is my duty to say to you, that the need was never greater of new revelation than now. From the views I have already expressed, you will infer the sad conviction, which I share, I believe, with numbers, of the universal decay and now almost death of faith in society. The soul is not preached. The Church seems to totter to its fall, almost all life extinct. On this occasion, any complaisance, would be criminal, which told you, whose hope and commission it is to preach the faith of Christ, that the faith of Christ is preached.

It is time that this ill-suppressed murmur of all thoughtful men against the famine of our churches; this moaning of the heart because it is bereaved of the consolation, the hope, the grandeur, that come alone out of the culture of the moral nature; should be heard through the sleep of indolence, and over the din of routine. This great and perpetual office of the preacher is not discharged. Preaching is the expression of the moral sentiment in application to the duties of life. In how many churches, by how many prophets, tell me, is man made sensible that he is an infinite Soul; that the earth and heavens are passing into his mind; that he is drinking forever the soul of God? Where now sounds the persuasion, that by its very melody imparadises my heart, and so affirms its own origin in heaven? Where shall I hear words such as in elder ages drew men to leave all and follow,—father and mother, house and land, wife and child? Where shall I hear these august laws of moral being so pronounced, as to fill my ear, and I feel ennobled by the offer of my uttermost action and passion? The test of the true faith, certainly, should be its power to charm and command the soul, as the laws of nature control the activity of the hands,—so commanding that we find pleasure and honor in obeying. The faith should blend with the light of rising and of setting suns, with the flying cloud, the singing bird, and the breath of flowers. But now the priest's Sabbath has lost the splendor of nature; it is unlovely; we are glad when it is done; we can make, we do make, even sitting in our pews, a far better, holier, sweeter, for ourselves.

Whenever the pulpit is usurped by a formalist, then is the worshipper defrauded and disconsolate. We shrink as soon as the prayers begin, which do not uplift, but smite and offend us. We are fain to wrap our cloaks about us, and secure, as best we can, a solitude that hears not. I once heard a preacher who sorely tempted me to say, I would go to church no more. Men go, thought I, where they are wont to go, else had no soul entered the temple in the afternoon. A snowstorm was falling around us. The snowstorm was real; the preacher merely spectral; and the eye felt the sad contrast in looking at him, and then out of the window behind him, into the beautiful meteor of the snow. He had lived in vain. He had no one word intimating that he had laughed or wept, was married or in love, had been commended, or cheated, or chagrined. If he had ever lived and acted, we were none the wiser for it. The capital secret of his profession, namely, to convert life into truth, he had not learned. Not one fact in all his experience, had he yet imported into his doctrine.

This man had ploughed, and planted, and talked, and bought, and sold; he had read books; he had eaten and drunken; his head aches; his heart throbs; he smiles and suffers; yet was there not a surmise, a hint, in all the discourse, that he had ever lived at all. Not a line did he draw out of real history. The true preacher can always be known by this, that he deals out to the people his life,—life passed through the fire of thought. But of the bad preacher, it could not be told from his sermon, what age of the world he fell in; whether he had a father or a child; whether he was a freeholder or a pauper; whether he was a citizen or a countryman; or any other fact of his biography.

It seemed strange that the people should come to church. It seemed as if their houses were very unentertaining, that they should prefer this thoughtless clamor. It shows that there is a commanding attraction in the moral sentiment, that can lend a faint tint of light to dulness and ignorance, coming in its name and place. The good hearer is sure he has been touched sometimes; is sure there is somewhat to be reached, and some word that can reach it. When he listens to these vain words, he comforts himself by their relation to his remembrance of better hours, and so they clatter and echo unchallenged.

I am not ignorant that when we preach unworthily, it is not always quite in vain. There is a good ear, in some men, that draws supplies to virtue out of very indifferent nutriment. There is poetic truth concealed in all the common-places of prayer and of sermons, and though foolishly spoken, they may be wisely heard; for, each is some select expression that broke out in a moment of piety from some stricken or jubilant soul, and its excellency made it remembered. The prayers and even the dogmas of our church, are like the zodiac of Denderah, and the astronomical monuments of the Hindoos, wholly insulated from anything now extant in the life and business of the people. They mark the height to which the waters once rose. But this docility is a check upon the mischief from the good and devout. In a large portion of the community, the religious service gives rise to quite other thoughts and emotions. We need not chide the negligent servant. We are struck with pity, rather, at the swift retribution of his sloth. Alas for the unhappy man that is called to stand in the pulpit, and *not* give bread of life. Everything that befals, accuses him. Would he ask contributions for the missions, foreign or domestic? Instantly his face is suffused with shame, to propose to his parish, that they should send money a hundred or a thousand miles, to furnish such poor fare as they have at home, and would do well to go the hundred or the thousand miles, to escape. Would he urge people to a godly way of living;—and can he ask a fellow creature to come to Sabbath meetings, when he and they all know what is the poor uttermost they can hope for therein? Will he invite them privately to the Lord's Supper? He dares not. If no heart warm this rite, the hollow, dry, creaking formality is too plain, than that he can face a man of wit and energy, and put the invitation without terror. In the street, what has he to say to the bold village blasphemer? The village blasphemer sees fear in the face, form, and gait of the minister.

Let me not taint the sincerity of this plea by any oversight of the claims of good men. I know and honor the purity and strict conscience of numbers of the clergy. What life the public worship retains, it owes to the scattered company of pious men, who minister here and there in the churches, and who, sometimes accepting with too great tenderness the tenet of the elders, have not accepted from others, but from their own heart, the genuine impulses of virtue, and so still command our love and awe, to the sanctity of character. Moreover, the exceptions are not so much to be found in a few eminent preachers, as in the better hours, the truer inspirations of all,—nay, in the sincere moments of every man. But with whatever exception, it is still true, that tradition characterizes the preaching of this country; that it comes out of the memory, and not out of the soul; that it aims at what is usual, and not at what is necessary and eternal; that thus, historical Christianity destroys the power of preaching, by withdrawing it from the exploration of the moral nature of man, where the sublime is, where are the resources of astonishment and power. What a cruel injustice it is to that Law, the joy of the whole earth, which alone can make thought dear and rich; that Law whose fatal sureness the astronomical orbits poorly emulate, that it is travestied and depreciated, that it is behooted and behowled, and not a trait, not a word of it articulated. The pulpit in losing sight of this Law, loses all its inspiration, and gropes after it knows not what. And for want of this culture, the soul of the community is sick and faithless. It wants nothing so much as a stern, high, stoical, Christian discipline, to make it know itself and the divinity that speaks through it. Now man is ashamed of himself; he skulks and sneaks through the world, to be tolerated, to be pitied, and scarcely in a thousand years does any man dare to be wise and good, and so draw after him the tears and blessings of his kind.

Certainly there have been periods when, from the inactivity of the intellect on certain truths, a greater faith was possible in names and persons. The Puritans in England and America, found in the Christ of the Catholic Church, and in the dogmas inherited from Rome, scope for their austere piety, and their longings for civil freedom. But their creed is passing away, and none arises in its room. I think no man can go with his thoughts about him, into one of our churches, without feeling that what hold the public worship had on men, is gone or going. It has lost its grasp on the affection of the good, and the fear of the bad. In the country,—neighborhoods, half parishes are *signing off,*—to use the local term. It is already beginning to indicate character and religion to withdraw from the religious meetings. I have heard a devout person, who prized the Sabbath, say in bitterness of heart, "On Sundays, it seems wicked to go to church." And the motive, that holds the best there, is now only a hope and a waiting. What was once a mere circumstance, that the best and the worst men in the parish, the poor and the rich, the learned and the ignorant, young and old, should meet one day as fellows in one house, in sign of an equal right in the soul,—has come to be a paramount motive for going thither.

My friends, in these two errors, I think, I find the causes of that calamity of a decaying church and a wasting unbelief, which are casting malignant influences around us, and making the hearts of good men sad. And what greater calamity can fall upon a nation, than the loss of worship? Then all things go to decay. Genius leaves the temple, to haunt the senate, or the market. Literature becomes frivolous. Science is cold. The eye of youth is not lighted by the hope of other worlds, and age is without honor. Society lives to trifles, and when men die, we do not mention them.

And now, my brothers, you will ask, What in these desponding days can be done by us? The remedy is already declared in the ground of our complaint of the Church. We have contrasted the Church with the Soul. In the soul, then, let the redemption be sought. In one soul, in your soul, there are resources for the world. Wherever a man comes, there comes revolution. The old is for slaves. When a man comes, all books are legible, all things transparent, all religions are forms. He is religious. Man is the wonderworker. He is seen amid miracles. All men bless and curse. He saith yea and nay, only. The stationariness of religion; the assumption that the age of inspiration is past, that the Bible is closed; the fear of degrading the character of Jesus by representing him as a man; indicate with sufficient clearness the falsehood of our theology. It is the office of a true teacher to show us that God is, not was; that He speaketh, not spake. The true Christianity,—a faith like Christ's in the infinitude of man,—is lost. None believeth in the soul of man, but only in some man or person old and departed. Ah me! no man goeth alone. All men go in flocks to this saint or that poet, avoiding the God who seeth in secret. They cannot see in secret; they love to be blind in public. They think society wiser than their soul, and know not that one soul, and their soul, is wiser than the whole world. See how nations and races flit by on the sea of time, and leave no ripple to tell where they floated or sunk, and one good soul shall make the name of Moses, or of Zeno, or of Zoroaster, reverend forever. None assayeth the stern ambition to be the Self of the nation, and of nature, but each would be an easy secondary to some Christian scheme, or sectarian connexion, or some eminent man. Once leave your own knowledge of God, your own sentiment, and take secondary knowledge, as St. Paul's, or George Fox's, or Swedenborg's, and you get wide from God with every year this secondary form lasts, and if, as now, for centuries,—the chasm yawns to that breadth, that men can scarcely be convinced there is in them anything divine.

Let me admonish you, first of all, to go alone; to refuse the good models, even those most sacred in the imagination of men, and dare to love God without mediator or veil. Friends enough you shall find who will hold up to your emulation Wesleys and Oberlins, Saints and Prophets. Thank God for these good men, but say, " I also am a man." Imitation cannot go above its model. The imitator dooms himself to hopeless mediocrity. The inventor did it, because it was natural to him, and so in him it has a charm. In the imitator, something else is natural, and he bereaves himself of his own beauty, to come short of another man's.

Yourself a newborn bard of the Holy Ghost,—cast behind you all conformity, and acquaint men at first hand with Deity. Be to them a man. Look to it first and only, that you are such; that fashion, custom, authority, pleasure, and money are nothing to you,—are not bandages over your eyes, that you cannot see,—but live with the privilege of the immeasurable mind. Not too anxious to visit periodically all families and each family in your parish connexion,—when you meet one of these men or women, be to them a divine man; be to them thought and virtue; let their timid aspirations find in you a friend; let their trampled instincts be genially tempted out in your atmosphere; let their doubts know that you have doubted, and their wonder feel that you have wondered. By trusting your own soul, you shall gain a greater confidence in other men. For all our penny-wisdom, for all our soul-destroying slavery to habit, it is not to be doubted, that all men have sublime thoughts; that all men do value the few real hours of life; they love to be heard; they love to be caught up into the vision of principles. We mark with light in the memory the few interviews, we have had in the dreary years of routine and of sin, with souls that made our souls wiser; that spoke what we thought; that told us what we knew; that gave us leave to be what we inly were. Discharge to men the priestly office, and, present or absent, you shall be followed with their love as by an angel.

And, to this end, let us not aim at common degrees of merit. Can we not leave, to such as love it, the virtue that glitters for the commendation of society, and ourselves pierce the deep solitudes of absolute ability and worth? We easily come up to the standard of goodness in society. Society's praise can be cheaply secured, and almost all men are content with those easy merits; but the instant effect of conversing with God, will be, to put them away. There are sublime merits; persons who are not actors, not speakers, but influences; persons too great for fame, for display, who disdain eloquence; to whom all we call art and artist, seems too nearly allied to show and by-ends, to the exaggeration of the finite and selfish, and loss of the universal. The orators, the poets, the commanders encroach on us only as fair women do, by our allowance and homage. Slight them by preoccupation of mind, slight them, as you can well afford to do, by high and universal aims, and they instantly feel that you have right, and that it is in lower places that they must shine. They also feel your right; for they with you are open to the influx of the all-knowing Spirit, which annihilates before its broad noon the little shades and gradations of intelligence in the compositions we call wiser and wisest.

In such high communion, let us study the grand strokes of rectitude: a bold benevolence, an independence of friends, so that not the unjust wishes of those who love us, shall impair our freedom, but we shall resist for truth's sake the freest flow of kindness, and appeal to sympathies far in advance; and,—what is the highest form in which we know this beautiful element,—a certain solidity of merit, that has nothing to do with opinion, and which is so essentially and manifestly virtue, that it is taken for granted, that the right, the brave, the generous step will be taken by it, and nobody thinks of commending it. You would compliment a coxcomb doing a good act, but you would not praise an angel. The silence that accepts merit as the most natural thing in the world, is the highest applause. Such souls, when they appear, are the Imperial Guard of Virtue, the perpetual reserve, the dictators of fortune. One needs not praise their courage,—they are the heart and soul of nature. O my friends, there are resources in us on which we have not drawn. There are men who rise refreshed on hearing a threat; men to whom a crisis which intimidates and paralyzes the majority—demanding not the faculties of prudence and thrift, but comprehension, immovableness, the readiness of sacrifice,—comes graceful and beloved as a bride. Napoleon said of Massena, that he was not himself until the battle began to go against him; then, when the dead began to fall in ranks around him, awoke his powers of combination, and he put on terror and victory as a robe. So it is in rugged crises, in unweariable endurance, and in aims which put sympathy out of question, that the angel is shown. But these are heights that we can scarce remember and look up to, without contrition and shame. Let us thank God that such things exist.

And now let us do what we can to rekindle the smouldering, nigh quenched fire on the altar. The evils of the church that now is, are manifest. The question returns, What shall we do? I confess, all attempts to project and establish a Cultus with new rites and forms, seem to me vain. Faith makes us, and not we it, and faith makes its own forms. All attempts to contrive a system, are as cold as the new worship introduced by the French to the goddess of Reason,—to-day, pasteboard and fillagree, and ending to-morrow in madness and murder. Rather let the breath of new life be breathed by you through the forms already existing. For, if once you are alive, you shall find they shall become plastic and new. The remedy to their deformity is, first, soul, and second, soul, and evermore, soul. A whole popedom of forms, one pulsation of virtue can uplift and vivify. Two inestimable advantages Christianity has given us; first; the Sabbath, the jubilee of the whole world; whose light dawns welcome alike into the closet of the philosopher, into the garret of toil, and into prison cells, and everywhere suggests, even to the vile, a thought of the dignity of spiritual being. Let it stand forevermore, a temple, which new love, new faith, new sight shall restore to more than its first splendor to mankind. And secondly, the institution of preaching,—the speech of man to men,—essentially the most flexible of all organs, of all forms. What hinders that now, everywhere, in pulpits, in lecture-rooms, in houses, in fields, wherever the invitation of men or your own occasions lead you, you speak the very truth, as your life and conscience teach it, and cheer the waiting, fainting hearts of men with new hope and new revelation?

I look for the hour when that supreme Beauty, which ravished the souls of those Eastern men, and chiefly of those Hebrews, and through their lips spoke oracles to all time, shall speak in the West also. The Hebrew and Greek Scriptures contain immortal sentences, that have been bread of life to millions. But they have no epical integrity; are fragmentary; are not shown in their order to the intellect. I look for the new Teacher, that shall follow so far those shining laws, that he shall see them come full circle; shall see their rounding complete grace; shall see the world to be the mirror of the soul; shall see the identity of the law of gravitation with purity of heart; and shall show that the Ought, that Duty, is one thing with Science, with Beauty, and with Joy.

"Self-Reliance"
(1841)

"Ne te quæsiveris extra."[1]

"Man is his own star; and the soul that can
Render an honest and a perfect man,
Commands all light, all influence, all fate;
Nothing to him falls early or too late
Our acts our angels are, or good or ill,
Our fatal shadows that walk by us still."

*Epilogue to Beaumont and Fletcher's
Honest Man's Fortune.*

Cast the bantling on the rocks,
Suckle him with the she-wolf's teat;
Wintered with the hawk and fox,
Power and speed be hands and feet.

I read the other day some verses written by an eminent painter which were original and not conventional. The soul always hears an admonition in such lines, let the subject be what it may. The sentiment they instil is of more value than any thought they may contain. To believe your own thought, to believe that what is true for you in your private heart, is true for all men,—that is genius. Speak your latent conviction and it shall be the universal sense; for the inmost in due time becomes the outmost,—and our first thought is rendered back to us by the trumpets of the Last Judgment. Familiar as the voice of the mind is to each, the highest merit we ascribe to Moses, Plato, and Milton, is that they set at naught books and traditions, and spoke not what men but what they thought. A man should learn to detect and watch that gleam of light which flashes across his mind from within, more than the lustre of the firmament of bards and sages. Yet he dismisses without notice his thought, because it is his. In every work of genius we recognize our own rejected thoughts: they come back to us with a certain alienated majesty. Great works of art have no more affecting lesson for us than this. They teach us to abide by our spontaneous impression with good-humored inflexibility then most when the whole cry of voices is on the other side. Else, tomorrow a stranger will say with masterly good sense precisely what we have thought and felt all the time, and we shall be forced to take with shame our own opinion from another.

There is a time in every man's education when he arrives at the conviction that envy is ignorance; that imitation is suicide; that he must take himself for better, for worse, as his portion; that though the wide universe is full of good, no kernel of nourishing corn can

---

1. "Look to no one outside yourself." Persius, Satires, 1.7.

Source: The Collected Works of Ralph Waldo Emerson, ed. Joseph Slater and Douglas Emory Wilson, vol. 2: *Essays: First Series,* ed. Joseph Slater, Alfred R. Ferguson, and Jean Ferguson Carr (Cambridge: The Belknap Press of Harvard University Press, 1979), 25–51. Reprinted by permission of Harvard University Press, Copyright © 1979 by the President and Fellows of Harvard College.

come to him but through his toil bestowed on that plot of ground which is given to him to till. The power which resides in him is new in nature, and none but he knows what that is which he can do, nor does he know until he has tried. Not for nothing one face, one character, one fact makes much impression on him, and another none. This sculpture in the memory is not without preestablished harmony. The eye was placed where one ray should fall, that it might testify of that particular ray. We but half express ourselves, and are ashamed of that divine idea which each of us represents. It may be safely trusted as proportionate and of good issues, so it be faithfully imparted, but God will not have his work made manifest by cowards. A man is relieved and gay when he has put his heart into his work and done his best; but what he has said or done otherwise, shall give him no peace. It is a deliverance which does not deliver. In the attempt his genius deserts him; no muse befriends; no invention, no hope.

Trust thyself: every heart vibrates to that iron string. Accept the place the divine Providence has found for you; the society of your contemporaries, the connexion of events. Great men have always done so and confided themselves childlike to the genius of their age, betraying their perception that the absolutely trustworthy was seated at their heart, working through their hands, predominating in all their being. And we are now men, and must accept in the highest mind the same transcendent destiny; and not minors and invalids in a protected corner, not cowards fleeing before a revolution, but guides, redeemers, and benefactors, obeying the Almighty effort, and advancing on Chaos and the Dark.

What pretty oracles nature yields us on this text in the face and behavior of children, babes and even brutes. That divided and rebel mind, that distrust of a sentiment because our arithmetic has computed the strength and means opposed to our purpose, these have not. Their mind being whole, their eye is as yet unconquered, and when we look in their faces, we are disconcerted. Infancy conforms to nobody: all conform to it, so that one babe commonly makes four or five out of the adults who prattle and play to it. So God has armed youth and puberty and manhood no less with its own piquancy and charm, and made it enviable and gracious and its claims not to be put by, if it will stand by itself. Do not think the youth has no force because he cannot speak to you and me. Hark! in the next room his voice is sufficiently clear and emphatic. It seems he knows how to speak to his contemporaries. Bashful or bold, then, he will know how to make us seniors very unnecessary.

The nonchalance of boys who are sure of a dinner, and would disdain as much as a lord to do or say aught to conciliate one, is the healthy attitude of human nature. A boy is in the parlour what the pit is in the playhouse; independent, irresponsible, looking out from his corner on such people and facts as pass by, he tries and sentences them on their merits, in the swift summary way of boys, as good, bad, interesting, silly, eloquent, troublesome. He cumbers himself never about consequences, about interests: he gives an independent, genuine verdict. You must court him: he does not court you. But the man is, as it were, clapped into jail by his consciousness. As soon as he has once acted or spoken with eclat, he is a committed person, watched by the sympathy or the hatred of hundreds whose affections must now enter into his account. There is no Lethe for this. Ah, that he could pass again into his neutrality! Who can thus avoid all pledges, and having observed, observe again from the same unaffected, unbiassed, unbribable, unaffrighted innocence, must always be formidable. He would utter opinions on all passing affairs, which being seen to be not private but necessary, would sink like darts into the ear of men, and put them in fear.

These are the voices which we hear in solitude, but they grow faint and inaudible as we enter into the world. Society everywhere is in conspiracy against the manhood of every one of its members. Society is a joint-stock company in which the members agree for the better securing of his bread to each shareholder, to surrender the liberty and culture of the eater. The virtue in most request is conformity. Self-reliance is its aversion. It loves not realities and creators, but names and customs.

Whoso would be a man must be a nonconformist. He who would gather immortal palms must not be hindered by the name of goodness, but must explore if it be goodness. Nothing is at last sacred but the integrity of your own mind. Absolve you to yourself, and you shall have the suffrage of the world. I remember an answer which when quite young I was prompted to make to a valued adviser who was wont to importune me with the dear old doctrines of the church. On my saying, What have I to do with the sacredness of traditions, if I live wholly from within? my friend suggested—"But these impulses may be from below, not from above." I replied, "They do not seem to me to be such; but if I am the Devil's child, I will live then from the Devil." No law can be sacred to me but that of my nature. Good and bad are but names very readily transferable to that or this; the only right is what is after my constitution, the only wrong what is against it. A man is to carry himself in the presence of all opposition as if every thing were titular and ephemeral but he. I am ashamed to think how easily we capitulate to badges and names, to large societies and dead institutions. Every decent and well-spoken individual affects and sways me more than is right. I ought to go upright and vital, and speak the rude truth in all ways. If malice and vanity wear the coat of philanthropy, shall that pass? If an angry bigot assumes this bountiful cause of Abolition, and comes to me with his last news from Barbadoes, why should I not say to him, "Go love thy infant; love thy wood-chopper: be good-natured and modest: have that grace; and never varnish your hard, uncharitable ambition with this incredible tenderness for black folk a thousand miles off. Thy love afar is spite at home." Rough and graceless would be such greeting, but truth is handsomer than the affectation of love. Your goodness must have some edge to it—else it is none. The doctrine of hatred must be preached as the counteraction of the doctrine of love when that pules and whines. I shun father and mother and wife and brother, when my genius calls me. I would write on the lintels of the door-post, *Whim.* I hope it is somewhat better than whim at last, but we cannot spend the day in explanation. Expect me not to show cause why I seek or why I exclude company. Then, again, do not tell me, as a good man did to-day, of my obligation to put all poor men in good situations. Are they *my* poor? I tell thee, though foolish philanthropist, that I grudge the dollar, the dime, the cent I give to such men as do not belong to me and to whom I do not belong. There is a class of persons to whom by all spiritual affinity I am bought and sold; for them I will go to prison, if need be; but your miscellaneous popular charities; the education at college of fools; the building of meeting-houses to the vain end to which many now stand; alms to sots; and the thousand-fold Relief Societies;—though I confess with shame I sometimes succumb and give the dollar, it is a wicked dollar which by and by I shall have the manhood to withhold.

Virtues are in the popular estimate rather the exception than the rule. There is the man *and* his virtues. Men do what is called a good action, as some piece of courage or charity, much as they would pay a fine in expiation of daily non-appearance on parade. Their works are done as an apology or extenuation of their living in the world,—as invalids and the insane pay a high board. Their virtues are penances. I do not wish to expiate, but to live. My life is for itself and not for a spectacle. I much prefer that it should be of a lower strain, so it be genuine and equal, than that it should be glittering and unsteady. I wish it to be sound and sweet, and not to need diet and bleeding. I ask primary evidence that you are a man, and refuse this appeal from the man to his actions. I know that for myself it makes no difference whether I do or forbear those actions which are reckoned excellent. I cannot consent to pay for a privilege where I have intrinsic right. Few and mean as my gifts may be, I actually am, and do not need for my own assurance or the assurance of my fellows any secondary testimony.

What I must do, is all that concerns me, not what the people think. This rule, equally arduous in actual and in intellectual life, may serve for the whole distinction between greatness and meanness. It is the harder, because you will always find those who think they know what is your duty better than you know it. It is easy in the world to live after the world's opinion; it is easy in solitude to live after our own; but the great man is he who in the midst of the crowd keeps with perfect sweetness the independence of solitude.

The objection to conforming to usages that have become dead to you, is, that it scatters your force. It loses your time and blurs the impression of your character. If you maintain a dead church, contribute to a dead Bible-Society, vote with a great party either for the Government or against it, spread your table like base housekeepers,—under all these screens, I have difficulty to detect the precise man you are. And, of course, so much force is withdrawn from your proper life. But do your work, and I shall know you. Do your work, and you shall reinforce yourself. A man must consider what a blindman's buff is this game of conformity. If I know your sect, I anticipate your argument. I hear a preacher announce for his text and topic the expediency of one of the institutions of his church. Do I not know beforehand that not possibly can he say a new and spontaneous word? Do I not know that with all this ostentation of examining the grounds of the institution, he will do no such thing? Do I not know that he is pledged to himself not to look but at one side,—the permitted side, not as a man, but as a parish minister? He is a retained attorney, and these airs of the bench are the emptiest affectation. Well, most men have bound their eyes with one or another handkerchief, and attached themselves to some one of these communities of opinion. This conformity makes them not false in a few particulars, authors of a few lies, but false in all particulars. Their every truth is not quite true. Their two is not the real two, their four not the real four: so that every word they say chagrins us, and we know not where to begin to set them right. Meantime nature is not slow to equip us in the prison-uniform of the party to which we adhere. We come to wear one cut of face and figure, and acquire by degrees the gentlest asinine expression. There is a mortifying experience in particular which does not fail to wreak itself also in the general history; I mean "the foolish face of praise," the forced smile which we put on in company where we do not feel at ease in answer to conversation which does not interest us. The muscles, not spontaneously moved, but moved by a low usurping wilfulness, grow tight about the outline of the face with the most disagreeable sensation.

For nonconformity the world whips you with its displeasure. And therefore a man must know how to estimate a sour face. The bystanders look askance on him in the public street or in the friend's parlor. If this aversation had its origin in contempt and resistance like his own, he might well go home with a sad countenance; but the sour faces of the multitude, like their sweet faces, have no deep cause, but are put on and off as the wind blows, and a newspaper directs. Yet is the discontent of the multitude more formidable than that of the senate and the college. It is easy enough for a firm man who knows the world to brook the rage of the cultivated classes. Their rage is decorous and prudent, for they are timid as being very vulnerable themselves. But when to their feminine rage the indignation of the people is added, when the ignorant and the poor are aroused, when the unintelligent brute force that lies at the bottom of society is made to growl and mow, it needs the habit of magnanimity and religion to treat it godlike as a trifle of no concernment.

The other terror that scares us from self-trust is our consistency; a reverence for our past act or word, because the eyes of others have no other data for computing our orbit than our past acts, and we are loath to disappoint them.

But why should you keep your head over your shoulder? Why drag about this corpse of your memory, lest you contradict somewhat you have stated in this or that public place? Suppose you should contradict yourself; what then? It seems to be a rule of wisdom never to rely on your memory alone, scarcely even in acts of pure memory, but to bring the past for judgment into the thousand-eyed present, and live ever in a new day. In your metaphysics you have denied personality to the Deity: yet when the devout motions of the soul come, yield to them heart and life, though they should clothe God with shape and color. Leave your theory as Joseph his coat in the hand of the harlot, and flee.

A foolish consistency is the hobgoblin of little minds, adored by little statesmen and philosophers and divines. With consistency a great soul has simply nothing to do. He may as well concern himself with his shadow on the wall. Speak what you think now in hard words, and to-morrow speak what to-morrow thinks in hard words again, though it contradict every thing you said to-day.—"Ah, so you shall be sure to be misunderstood."—Is it so bad then to be misunderstood? Pythagoras was misunderstood, and Socrates, and Jesus, and Luther, and Copernicus, and Galileo, and Newton, and every pure and wise spirit that ever took flesh. To be great is to be misunderstood.

I suppose no man can violate his nature. All the sallies of his will are rounded in by the law of his being as the inequalities of Andes and Himmaleh are insignificant in the curve of the sphere. Nor does it matter how you gauge and try him. A character is like an acrostic or Alexandrian stanza;—read it forward, backward, or across, it still spells the same thing. In this pleasing contrite wood-life which God allows me, let me record day by day my honest thought without prospect or retrospect, and, I cannot doubt, it will be found symmetrical, though I mean it not, and see it not. My book should smell of pines and resound with the hum of insects. The swallow over my window should interweave that thread or straw he carries in his bill into my web also. We pass for what we are. Character teaches above our wills. Men imagine that they communicate their virtue or vice only by overt actions and do not see that virtue or vice emit a breath every moment.

There will be an agreement in whatever variety of actions, so they be each honest and natural in their hour. For of one will, the actions will be harmonious, however unlike they seem. These varieties are lost sight of at a little distance, at a little height of thought. One tendency unites them all. The voyage of the best ship is a zigzag line of a hundred tacks. See the line from a sufficient distance, and it straightens itself to the average tendency. Your genuine action will explain itself and will explain your other genuine actions. Your conformity explains nothing. Act singly, and what you have already done singly, will justify you now. Greatness appeals to the future. If I can be firm enough to-day to do right and scorn eyes, I must have done so much right before, as to defend me now. Be it how it will, do right now. Always scorn appearances, and you always may. The force of character is cumulative. All the foregone days of virtue work their health into this. What makes the majesty of the heroes of the senate and the field, which so fills the imagination? The consciousness of a train of great days and victories behind. They shed an united light on the advancing actor. He is attended as by a visible escort of angels. That is it which throws thunder into Chatham's voice, and dignity into Washington's port, and America into Adams's eye. Honor is venerable to us because it is no ephemeris. It is always ancient virtue. We worship it to-day, because it is not of to-day. We love it and pay it homage, because it is not a trap for our love and homage, but is self-dependent, self-derived, and therefore of an old immaculate pedigree, even if shown in a young person.

I hope in these days we have heard the last of conformity and consistency. Let the words be gazetted and ridiculous henceforward. Instead of the gong for dinner, let us hear a whistle from the Spartan fife. Let us never bow and apologize more. A great man is coming to eat at my house. I do not wish to please him: I wish that he should wish to please me. I will stand here for humanity, and though I would make it kind, I would make it true. Let us affront and reprimand the smooth mediocrity and squalid contentment of the times, and hurl in the face of custom, and trade, and office, the fact which is the upshot of all history, that there is a great responsible Thinker and Actor working wherever a man works; that a true man belongs to no other time or place, but is the centre of things. Where he is, there is nature. He measures you, and all men, and all events. Ordinarily every body in society reminds us of somewhat else or of some other person. Character, reality, reminds you of nothing else; it takes place of the whole creation. The man must be so much that he must make all circumstances indifferent. Every true man is a cause, a country, and an age; requires infinite spaces and numbers and time fully to accomplish his design;—and posterity seem to follow his steps as a train of clients. A man Cæsar is born, and for ages after, we have a Roman Empire. Christ is born, and millions of minds so grow and cleave to his genius, that he is confounded with virtue and the possible of man. An institution is the lengthened shadow of one man; as, Monachism, of the Hermit Antony, the Reformation, of Luther; Quakerism, of Fox; Methodism, of Wesley; Abolition, of Clarkson. Scipio, Milton called "the height of Rome;" and all history resolves itself very easily into the biography of a few stout and earnest persons.

Let a man then know his worth, and keep things under his feet. Let him not peep or steal, or skulk up and down with the air of a charity-boy, a bastard, or an interloper, in the world which exists for him. But the man in the street finding no worth in himself which corresponds to the force which built a tower or sculptured a marble god, feels poor when he looks on these. To him a palace, a statue, or a costly book have an alien and forbidding air, much like a gay equipage, and seem to say like that, "Who are you, sir?" Yet they all are his, suitors for his notice, petitioners to his faculties that they will come out and take possession. The picture waits for my verdict: it is not to command me, but I am to settle its claims to praise. That popular fable of the sot who was picked up dead drunk in the street, carried to the duke's house, washed and dressed and laid in the duke's bed, and, on his waking, treated with all obsequious ceremony like the duke, and assured that he had been insane, owes its popularity to the fact, that it symbolizes so well the state of man, who is in the world a sort of sot, but now and then wakes up, exercises his reason, and finds himself a true prince.

Our reading is mendicant and sycophantic. In history, our imagination plays us false. Kingdom and lordship, power and estate are a gaudier vocabulary than private John and Edward in a small house and common day's work: but the things of life are the same to both: the sum total of both is the same. Why all this deference to Alfred, and Scanderbeg, and Gustavus? Suppose they were virtuous: did they wear out virtue? As great a stake depends on your private act to-day, as followed their public and renowned steps. When private men shall act with original views, the lustre will be transferred from the actions of kings to those of gentlemen.

The world has been instructed by its kings, who have so magnetized the eyes of nations. It has been taught by this colossal symbol the mutual reverence that is due from man to man. The joyful loyalty with which men have everywhere suffered the king, the noble, or the great proprietor to walk among them by a law of his own, make his own scale of men and things, and reverse theirs, pay for benefits not with money but with honor, and represent the Law in his person, was the hieroglyphic by which they obscurely signified their consciousness of their own right and comeliness, the right of every man.

The magnetism which all original action exerts is explained when we inquire the reason of self-trust. Who is the Trustee? What is the aboriginal Self on which a universal reliance may be grounded? What is the nature and power of that science-baffling star, without parallax, without calculable elements, which shoots a ray of beauty even into trivial and impure actions, if the least mark of independence appear? The inquiry leads us to that source, at once the essence of genius, of virtue, and of life, which we call Spontaneity or Instinct. We denote this primary wisdom as Intuition, whilst all later teachings are tuitions. In that deep force, the last fact behind which analysis cannot go, all things find their common origin. For the sense of being which in calm hours rises, we know not how, in the soul, is not diverse from things, from space, from light, from time, from man, but one with them, and proceeds obviously from the same source whence their life and being also proceed. We first share the life by which things exist, and afterwards see them as appearances in nature, and forget that we have shared their cause. Here is the fountain of action and of thought. Here are the lungs of that inspiration which giveth man wisdom, and which cannot be denied without impiety and atheism. We lie in the lap of immense intelligence, which makes us receivers of its truth and organs of its activity. When we discern justice, when we discern truth, we do nothing of ourselves, but allow a passage to its beams. If we ask whence this comes, if we seek to pry into the soul that causes, all philosophy is at fault. Its presence or its absence is all we can affirm. Every man discriminates between the voluntary acts of his mind, and his involuntary perceptions, and knows that to his involuntary perceptions a perfect faith is due. He may err in the expression of them, but he knows that these things are so, like day and night, not to be disputed. My wilful actions and acquisitions are but roving;—the idlest reverie, the faintest native emotion, command my curiosity and respect. Thoughtless people contradict as readily the statement of perceptions as of opinions, or rather much more readily; for, they do not distinguish between perception and notion. They fancy that I choose to see this or that thing. But perception is not whimsical, but fatal. If I see a trait, my children will see it after me, and in course of time, all mankind,—although it may chance that no one has seen it before me. For my perception of it is as much a fact as the sun.

The relations of the soul to the divine spirit are so pure that it is profane to seek to interpose helps. It must be that when God speaketh, he should communicate not one thing, but all things; should fill the world with his voice; should scatter forth light, nature, time, souls, from the centre of the present thought; and new date and new create the whole. Whenever a mind is simple, and receives a divine wisdom, old things pass away,—means, teachers, texts, temples fall; it lives now and absorbs past and future into the present hour. All things are made sacred by relation to it,—one as much as another. All things are dissolved to their centre by their cause, and in the universal miracle petty and particular miracles disappear. If, therefore, a man claims to know and speak of God, and carries you backward to the phraseology of some old mouldered nation in another country, in another world, believe him not. Is the acorn better than the oak which is its fulness and completion? Is the parent better than the child into whom he has cast his ripened being? Whence then this worship of the past? The centuries are conspirators against the sanity and authority of the soul. Time and space are but physiological colors which the eye makes, but the soul is light; where it is, is day; where it was, is night; and history is an impertinence and an injury, if it be anything more than a cheerful apologue or parable of my being and becoming.

Man is timid and apologetic; he is no longer upright; he dares not say "I think," "I am," but quotes some saint or sage. He is ashamed before the blade of grass or the blowing rose. These roses under my window make no reference to former roses or to better ones; they are for what they are; they exist with God to-day. There is no time to them. There is simply the rose; it is perfect in every moment of its existence. Before a leaf-bud has burst, its whole life acts; in the full-blown flower, there is no more; in the leafless root, there is no less. Its nature is satisfied, and it satisfies nature, in all moments alike. But man postpones or remembers; he does not live in the present, but with reverted eye laments the past, or, heedless of the riches that surround him, stands on tiptoe to foresee the future. He cannot be happy and strong until he too lives with nature in the present, above time.

This should be plain enough. Yet see what strong intellects dare not yet hear God himself, unless he speak the phraseology of I know not what David, or Jeremiah, or Paul. We shall not always set so great a price on a few texts, on a few lives. We are like children who repeat by rote the sentences of grandames and tutors, and, as they grow older, of the men of talents and character they chance to see,—painfully recollecting the exact words they spoke; afterwards, when they come into the point of view which those had who uttered these sayings, they understand them, and are willing to let the words go; for, at any time, they can use words as good, when occasion comes. If we live truly, we shall see truly. It is as easy for the strong man to be strong, as it is for the weak to be weak. When we have new perception, we shall gladly disburden the memory of its hoarded treasures as old rubbish. When a man lives with God, his voice shall be as sweet as the murmur of the brook and the rustle of the corn.

And now at last the highest truth on this subject remains unsaid; probably, cannot be said; for all that we say is the far off remembering of the intuition. That thought, by what I can now nearest approach to say it, is this. When good is near you, when you have life in yourself, it is not by any known or accustomed way; you shall not discern the foot-prints of any other; you shall not see the face of man; you shall not hear any name;—the way, the thought, the good shall be wholly strange and new. It shall exclude example and experience. You take the way from man, not to man. All persons that ever existed are its forgotten ministers. Fear and hope are alike beneath it. There is somewhat low even in hope. In the hour of vision, there is nothing that can be called gratitude, nor properly joy. The soul raised over passion beholds identity and eternal causation, perceives the self-existence of Truth and Right, and calms itself with knowing that all things go well. Vast spaces of nature, the Atlantic Ocean, the South Sea,—long intervals of time, years, centuries,—are of no account. This which I think and feel underlay every former state of life and circumstances, as it does underlie my present, and what is called life, and what is called death.

Life only avails, not the having lived. Power ceases in the instant of repose; it resides in the moment of transition from a past to a new state, in the shooting of the gulf, in the darting to an aim. This one fact the world hates, that the soul *becomes;* for, that forever degrades the past, turns all riches to poverty, all reputation to a shame, confounds the saint with the rogue, shoves Jesus and Judas equally aside. Why then do we prate of self-reliance? Inasmuch as the soul is present, there will be power not confident but agent. To talk of reliance, is a poor external way of speaking. Speak rather of that which relies, because it works and is. Who has more obedience than I, masters me, though he should not raise his finger. Round him I must revolve by the gravitation of spirits. We fancy it rhetoric when we speak of eminent virtue. We do not yet see that virtue is Height, and that a man or a company of men plastic and permeable to principles, by the law of nature must overpower and ride all cities, nations, kings, rich men, poets, who are not.

This is the ultimate fact which we so quickly reach on this as on every topic, the resolution of all into the ever blessed ONE. Self-existence is the attribute of the Supreme Cause, and it constitutes the measure of good by the degree in which it enters into all lower forms. All things real are so by so much virtue as they contain. Commerce, husbandry, hunting, whaling, war, eloquence, personal weight, are somewhat, and engage my respect as examples of its presence and impure action. I see the same law working in nature for conservation and growth. Power is in nature the essential measure of right. Nature suffers nothing to remain in her kingdom which cannot help itself. The genesis and maturation of a planet, its poise and orbit, the bended tree recovering itself from the strong wind, the vital resources of every animal and vegetable, are demonstrations of the self-sufficing, and therefore self-relying soul.

Thus all concentrates; let us not rove; let us sit at home with the cause. Let us stun and astonish the intruding rabble of men and books and institutions by a simple declaration of the divine fact. Bid the invaders take the shoes from off their feet, for God is here within. Let our simplicity judge them, and our docility to our own law demonstrate the poverty of nature and fortune beside our native riches.

But now we are a mob. Man does not stand in awe of man, nor is his genius admonished to stay at home, to put itself in communication with the internal ocean, but it goes abroad to beg a cup of water of the urns of other men. We must go alone. I like the silent church before the service begins, better than any preaching. How far off, how cool, how chaste the persons look, begirt each one with a precinct or sanctuary. So let us always sit. Why should we assume the faults of our friend, or wife, or father, or child, because they sit around our hearth, or are said to have the same blood? All men have my blood, and I have all men's. Not for that will I adopt their petulance or folly, even to the extent of being ashamed of it. But your isolation must not be mechanical, but spiritual, that is, must be elevation. At times the whole world seems to be in conspiracy to importune you with emphatic trifles. Friend, client, child, sickness, fear, want, charity, all knock at once at thy closet door and say,—"Come out unto us." But keep thy state; come not into their confusion. The power men possess to annoy me, I give them by a weak curiosity. No man can come near me but through my act. "What we love that we have, but by desire we bereave ourselves of the love."

If we cannot at once rise to the sanctities of obedience and faith, let us at least resist our temptations; let us enter into the state of war, and wake Thor and Woden, courage and constancy, in our Saxon breasts. This is to be done in our smooth times by speaking the truth. Check this lying hospitality and lying affection. Live no longer to the expectation of these deceived and deceiving people with whom we converse. Say to them, O father, O mother, wife, O brother, O friend, I have lived with you after appearances hitherto. Henceforward I am the truth's. Be it known unto you that henceforward I obey no law less than the eternal law. I will have no covenants but proximities. I shall endeavor to nourish my parents, to support my family, to be the chaste husband of one wife,—but these relations I must fill after a new and unprecedented way. I appeal from your customs. I must be myself. I cannot break myself any longer for you, or you. If you can love me for what I am, we shall be the happier. If you cannot, I will still seek to deserve that you should. I will not hide my tastes or aversions. I will so trust that what is deep is holy, that I will do strongly before the sun and moon whatever inly rejoices me, and the heart appoints. If you are noble, I will love you; if you are not, I will not hurt you and myself by hypocritical attentions. If you are true, but not in the same truth with me, cleave to your companions; I will seek my own. I do this not selfishly, but humbly and truly. It is alike your interest and mine and all men's, however long we have dwelt in lies, to live in truth. Does this sound harsh to-day? You will soon love what is dictated by your nature as well as mine, and if we follow the truth, it will bring us out safe at last.—But so you may give these friends pain. Yes, but I cannot sell my liberty and my power, to save their sensibility. Besides, all persons have their moments of reason when they look out into the region of absolute truth; then will they justify me and do the same thing.

The populace think that your rejection of popular standards is a rejection of all standard, and mere antinomianism; and the bold sensualist will use the name of philosophy to gild his crimes. But the law of consciousness abides. There are two confessionals, in one or the other of which we must be shriven. You may fulfil your round of duties by clearing yourself in the *direct*, or, in the *reflex* way. Consider whether you have satisfied your relations to father, mother, cousin, neighbor, town, cat, and dog; whether any of these can upbraid you. But I may also neglect this reflex standard, and absolve me to myself. I have my own stern claims and perfect circle. It denies the name of duty to many offices that are called duties. But if I can discharge its debts, it enables me to dispense with the popular code. If any one imagines that this law is lax, let him keep its commandment one day.

And truly it demands something godlike in him who has cast off the common motives of humanity, and has ventured to trust himself for a taskmaster. High be his heart, faithful his will, clear his sight, that he may in good earnest be doctrine, society, law to himself, that a simple purpose may be to him as strong as iron necessity is to others.

If any man consider the present aspects of what is called by distinction society, he will see the need of these ethics. The sinew and heart of man seem to be drawn out, and we are become timorous desponding whimperers. We are afraid of truth, afraid of fortune, afraid of death, and afraid of each other. Our age yields no great and perfect persons. We want men and women who shall renovate life and our social state, but we see that most natures are insolvent, cannot satisfy their own wants, have an ambition out of all proportion to their practical force, and do lean and beg day and night continually. Our housekeeping is mendicant, our arts, our occupations, our marriages, our religion we have not chosen, but society has chosen for us. We are parlor soldiers. We shun the rugged battle of fate, where strength is born.

If our young men miscarry in their first enterprizes, they lose all heart. If the young merchant fails, men say he is *ruined*. If the finest genius studies at one of our colleges, and is not installed in an office within one year afterwards in the cities or suburbs of Boston or New York, it seems to his friends and to himself that he is right in being disheartened and in complaining the rest of his life. A sturdy lad from New Hampshire or Vermont, who in turn tries all the professions, who *teams it, farms it, peddles,* keeps a school, preaches, edits a newspaper, goes to Congress, buys a township, and so forth, in successive years, and always, like a cat, falls on his feet, is worth a hundred of these city dolls. He walks abreast with his days, and feels no shame in not "studying a profession," for he does not postpone his life, but lives already. He has not one chance, but a hundred chances. Let a Stoic open the resources of man, and tell men they are not leaning willows, but can and must detach themselves; that with the exercise of self-trust, new powers shall appear; that a man is the word made flesh, born to shed healing to the nations, that he should be ashamed of our compassion, and that the moment he acts from himself, tossing the laws, the books, idolatries, and customs out of the window, we pity him no more but thank and revere him,—and that teacher shall restore the life of man to splendor, and make his name dear to all History.

It is easy to see that a greater self-reliance must work a revolution in all the offices and relations of men; in their religion; in their education; in their pursuits; their modes of living; their association; in their property, in their speculative views.

1. In what prayers do men allow themselves! That which they call a holy office, is not so much as brave and manly. Prayer looks abroad and asks for some foreign addition to come through some foreign virtue, and loses itself in endless mazes of natural and supernatural, and mediatorial and miraculous. Prayer that craves a particular commodity,—any thing less than all good,—is vicious. Prayer is the contemplation of the facts of life from the highest point of view. It is the soliloquy of a beholding and jubilant soul. It is the spirit of God pronouncing his works good. But prayer as a means to effect a private end, is meanness and theft. It supposes dualism and not unity in nature and consciousness. As soon as the man is at one with God, he will not beg. He will then see prayer in all action. The prayer of the farmer kneeling in his field to weed it, the prayer of the rower kneeling with the stroke of his oar, are true prayers heard throughout nature, though for cheap ends. Caratach, in Fletcher's Bonduca, when admonished to inquire the mind of the god Audate, replies,—

> "His hidden meaning lies in our endeavors,
> Our valors are our best gods."

Another sort of false prayers are our regrets. Discontent is the want of self-reliance: it is infirmity of will. Regret calamities, if you can thereby help the sufferer; if not, attend your own work, and already the evil begins to be repaired. Our sympathy is just as base. We come to them who weep foolishly, and sit down and cry for company, instead of imparting to them truth and health in rough electric shocks, putting them once more in communication with their own reason. The secret of fortune is joy in our hands. Welcome evermore to gods and men is the self-helping man. For him all doors are flung wide: him all tongues greet, all honors crown, all eyes follow with desire. Our love goes out to him and embraces him, because he did not need it. We solicitously and apologetically caress and celebrate him, because he held on his way and scorned our disapprobation. The gods love him because men hated him. "To the persevering mortal," said Zoroaster, "the blessed Immortals are swift."

As men's prayers are a disease of the will, so are their creeds a disease of the intellect. They say with those foolish Israelites, "Let not God speak to us, lest we die. Speak thou, speak any man with us, and we will obey." Everywhere I am hindered of meeting God in my brother, because he has shut his own temple doors, and recites fables merely of his brother's, or his brother's brother's God. Every new mind is a new classification. If it prove a mind of uncommon activity and power, a Locke, a Lavoisier, a Hutton, a Bentham, a Fourier, it imposes its classification on other men, and lo! a new system. In proportion to the depth of the thought, and so to the number of the objects it touches and brings within reach of the pupil, is his complacency. But chiefly is this apparent in creeds and churches, which are also classifications of some powerful mind acting on the elemental thought of Duty, and man's relation to the Highest. Such is Calvinism, Quakerism, Swedenborgianism. The pupil takes the same delight in subordinating every thing to the new terminology, as a girl who has just learned botany in seeing a new earth and new seasons thereby. It will happen for a time, that the pupil will find his intellectual power has grown by the study of his master's mind. But in all unbalanced minds, the classification is idolized, passes for the end, and not for a speedily exhaustible means, so that the walls of the system blend to their eye in the remote horizon with the walls of the universe; the luminaries of heaven seem to them hung on the arch their master built. They cannot imagine how you aliens have any right to see,—how you can see; "It must be somehow that you stole the light from us." They do not yet perceive, that light, unsystematic, indomitable, will break into any cabin, even into theirs. Let them chirp awhile and call it their own. If they are honest and do well, presently their neat new pinfold will be too strait and low, will crack, will lean, will rot and vanish, and the immortal light, all young and joyful, million-orbed, million-colored, will beam over the universe as on the first morning.

2. It is for want of self-culture that the superstition of Travelling, whose idols are Italy, England, Egypt, retains its fascination for all educated Americans. They who made England, Italy, or Greece venerable in the imagination, did so by sticking fast where they were, like an axis of the earth. In manly hours, we feel that duty is our place. The soul is no traveller: the wise man stays at home, and when his necessities, his duties, on any occasion call him from his house, or into foreign lands, he is at home still, and shall make men sensible by the expression of his countenance, that he goes the missionary of wisdom and virtue, and visits cities and men like a sovereign, and not like an interloper or a valet.

I have no churlish objection to the circumnavigation of the globe, for the purposes of art, of study, and benevolence, so that the man is first domesticated, or does not go abroad with the hope of finding somewhat greater than he knows. He who travels to be amused, or to get somewhat which he does not carry, travels away from himself, and grows old even in youth among old things. In Thebes, in Palmyra, his will and mind have become old and dilapidated as they. He carries ruins to ruins.

Travelling is a fool's paradise. Our first journeys discover to us the indifference of places. At home I dream that at Naples, at Rome, I can be intoxicated with beauty, and lose my sadness. I pack my trunk, embrace my friends, embark on the sea, and at last wake up in Naples, and there beside me is the stern Fact, the sad self, unrelenting, identical, that I fled from. I seek the Vatican, and the palaces. I affect to be intoxicated with sights and suggestions, but I am not intoxicated. My giant goes with me wherever I go.

3. But the rage of travelling is a symptom of a deeper unsoundness affecting the whole intellectual action. The intellect is vagabond, and our system of education fosters restlessness. Our minds travel when our bodies are forced to stay at home. We imitate; and what is imitation but the travelling of the mind? Our houses are built with foreign taste; our shelves are garnished with foreign ornaments; our opinions, our tastes, our faculties, lean, and follow the Past and the Distant. The soul created the arts wherever they have flourished. It was in his own mind that the artist sought his model. It was an application of his own thought to the thing to be done and the conditions to be observed. And why need we copy the Doric or the Gothic model? Beauty, convenience, grandeur of thought, and quaint expression are as near to us as to any, and if the American artist will study with hope and love the precise thing to be done by him, considering the climate, the soil, the length of the day, the wants of the people, the habit and form of the government, he will create a house in which all these will find themselves fitted, and taste and sentiment will be satisfied also.

Insist on yourself; never imitate. Your own gift you can present every moment with the cumulative force of a whole life's cultivation; but of the adopted talent of another, you have only an extemporaneous, half possession. That which each can do best, none but his Maker can teach him. No man yet knows what it is, nor can, till that person has exhibited it. Where is the master who could have taught Shakspeare? Where is the master who could have instructed Franklin, or Washington, or Bacon, or Newton? Every great man is a unique. The Scipionism of Scipio is precisely that part he could not borrow. Shakspeare will never be made by the study of Shakspeare. Do that which is assigned you, and you cannot hope too much or dare too much. There is at this moment for you an utterance brave and grand as that of the colossal chisel of Phidias, or trowel of the Egyptians, or the pen of Moses, or Dante, but different from all these. Not possibly will the soul all rich, all eloquent, with thousand-cloven tongue, deign to repeat itself; but if you can hear what these patriarchs say, surely you can reply to them in the same pitch of voice: for the ear and the tongue are two organs of one nature. Abide in the simple and noble regions of thy life, obey thy heart, and thou shalt reproduce the Foreworld again.

4. As our Religion, our Education, our Art look abroad, so does our spirit of society. All men plume themselves on the improvement of society, and no man improves.

Society never advances. It recedes as fast on one side as it gains on the other. It undergoes continual changes: it is barbarous, it is civilized, it is christianized, it is rich, it is scientific; but this change is not amelioration. For every thing that is given, something is taken. Society acquires new arts and loses old instincts. What a contrast between the well-clad, reading, writing, thinking American, with a watch, a pencil, and a bill of exchange in his pocket, and the naked New Zealander, whose property is a club, a spear, a mat, and an undivided twentieth of a shed to sleep under. But compare the health of the two men, and you shall see that the white man has lost his aboriginal strength. If the traveller tell us truly, strike the savage with a broad axe, and in a day or two the flesh shall unite and heal as if you struck the blow into soft pitch, and the same blow shall send the white to his grave.

The civilized man has built a coach, but has lost the use of his feet. He is supported on crutches, but lacks so much support of muscle. He has a fine Geneva watch, but he fails of the skill to tell the hour by the sun. A Greenwich nautical almanac he has, and so being sure of the information when he wants it, the man in the street does not know a star in the sky. The solstice he does not observe; the equinox he knows as little; and the whole bright calendar of the year is without a dial in his mind. His note-books impair his memory; his libraries overload his wit; the insurance office increases the number of accidents; and it may be a question whether machinery does not encumber; whether we have not lost by refinement some energy, by a Christianity entrenched in establishments and forms, some vigor of wild virtue. For every stoic was a stoic; but in Christendom where is the Christian?

There is no more deviation in the moral standard than in the standard of height or bulk. No greater men are now than ever were. A singular equality may be observed between the great men of the first and of the last ages; nor can all the science, art, religion and philosophy of the nineteenth century avail to educate greater men than Plutarch's heroes, three or four and twenty centuries ago. Not in time is the race progressive. Phocion, Socrates, Anaxagoras, Diogenes, are great men, but they leave no class. He who is really of their class will not be called by their name, but will be his own man, and, in his turn the founder of a sect. The arts and inventions of each period are only its costume, and do not invigorate men. The harm of the improved machinery may compensate its good. Hudson and Behring accomplished so much in their fishing-boats, as to astonish Parry and Franklin, whose equipment exhausted the resources of science and art. Galileo, with an opera-glass, discovered a more splendid series of celestial phenomena than any one since. Columbus found the New World in an undecked boat. It is curious to see the periodical disuse and perishing of means and machinery which were introduced with loud laudation, a few years or centuries before. The great genius returns to essential man.

We reckoned the improvements of the art of war among the triumphs of science, and yet Napoleon conquered Europe by the Bivouac, which consisted of falling back on naked valor, and disencumbering it of all aids. The Emperor held it impossible to make a perfect army, says Las Cases, "without abolishing our arms, magazines, commissaries, and carriages, until in imitation of the Roman custom, the soldier should receive his supply of corn, grind it in his hand-mill, and bake his bread himself."

Society is a wave. The wave moves onward, but the water of which it is composed, does not. The same particle does not rise from the valley to the ridge. Its unity is only phenomenal. The persons who make up a nation to-day, next year die, and their experience with them.

And so the reliance on Property, including the reliance on governments which protect it, is the want of self-reliance. Men have looked away from themselves and at things so long, that they have come to esteem the religious, learned, and civil institutions, as guards of property, and they deprecate assaults on these, because they feel them to be assaults on property. They measure their esteem of each other, by what each has, and not by what each is. But a cultivated man becomes ashamed of his property, out of new respect for his nature. Especially he hates what he has, if he see that it is accidental,—came to him by inheritance, or gift, or crime; then he feels that it is not having; it does not belong to him, has no root in him, and merely lies there, because no revolution or no robber takes it away. But that which a man is, does always by necessity acquire, and what the man acquires is living property, which does not wait the beck of rulers, or mobs, or revolutions, or fire, or storm, or bankruptcies, but perpetually renews itself wherever the man breathes. "Thy lot or portion of life," said the Caliph Ali, "is seeking after thee; therefore be at rest from seeking after it." Our dependence on these foreign goods leads us to our slavish respect for numbers. The political parties meet in numerous conventions; the greater the concourse, and with each new uproar of announcement, The delegation from Essex! The Democrats from New Hampshire! The Whigs of Maine! the young patriot feels himself stronger than before by a new thousand of eyes and arms. In like manner the reformers summon conventions, and vote and resolve in multitude. Not so, O friends! will the God deign to enter and inhabit you, but by a method precisely the reverse. It is only as a man puts off all foreign support, and stands alone, that I see him to be strong and to prevail. He is weaker by every recruit to his banner. Is not a man better than a town? Ask nothing of men, and in the endless mutation, thou only firm column must presently appear the upholder of all that surrounds thee. He who knows that power is inborn, that he is weak because he has looked for good out of him and elsewhere, and so perceiving, throws himself unhesitatingly on his thought, instantly rights himself, stands in the erect position, commands his limbs, works miracles; just as a man who stands on his feet is stronger than a man who stands on his head.

So use all that is called Fortune. Most men gamble with her, and gain all, and lose all, as her wheel rolls. But do thou leave as unlawful these winnings, and deal with Cause and Effect, the chancellors of God. In the Will work and acquire, and thou hast chained the wheel of Chance, and shalt sit hereafter out of fear from her rotations. A political victory, a rise of rents, the recovery of your sick, or the return of your absent friend, or some other favorable event, raises your spirits, and you think good days are preparing for you. Do not believe it. Nothing can bring you peace but yourself. Nothing can bring you peace but the triumph of principles.

ELIZABETH PALMER PEABODY

"Plan of the West Roxbury Community" (1842)

If there was one figure who defied the stereotype of the self-centered Transcendentalist intellectual, it was surely Elizabeth Palmer Peabody (1804–1894). Unfortunately her bountiful promotion of causes and careers—from those of Unitarianism's leader William Ellery Channing and Transcendentalism's philosopher-reformer Bronson Alcott to that of her brother-in-law Nathaniel Hawthorne—has largely obscured her own distinctive achievements. Highly enterprising, she was the first American woman to establish her own publishing company. She also owned a bookstore on Boston's West Street, which served as a major intellectual resource and chief gathering point for her Transcendentalist colleagues, and in later years founded the American kindergarten movement. But most important intellectually, in her many religious and educational writings, she carefully tempered her Transcendentalist intuitionism with two Unitarian-like qualifiers: a strong devotion to Christian ethics and a constant concern for balancing the claims of the individual with those of society.

These ethical commitments were much in view in two articles Peabody published in the Transcendentalists' journal the *Dial*. In the first, "A Glimpse of Christ's Idea of Society," she urged replacing the traditional church-based Christian faith with a capaciously "social" Christianity based on the benevolent communitarian ethics of Jesus and the millennialist vision she claimed inspired the ongoing socialist and welfare reform movements in Europe and America. Both the ethics and the vision would have a long afterlife beginning a half-century later in the liberal Protestant ideas and organizations associated with the "Social Gospel." In Peabody's follow-up "Postscript" printed below, she offered a sympathetic sketch of the plans of the Brook Farmers led by George Ripley to implement these ideas by introducing in a pastoral setting libertarian work rules, egalitarian rewards, and uplifting cultural practices. For Peabody the result was mixed. The community promised to become the highest embodiment so far of Christ's idea of a "University." Yet this was only a promise, and meanwhile it threatened to become entangled on the horns of the very dilemma of ideological selectivity and open discourse that had bedeviled the Transcendentalists' Puritan utopian ancestors.

The best biography of Peabody is Bruce A. Ronda, *Elizabeth Peabody: A Reformer on Her Own Terms* (Cambridge, Mass., 1999). Ronda has also edited an excellent collection, *Letters of Elizabeth Palmer Peabody: American Renaissance Woman* (Middletown, Conn., 1984). For the family context of Peabody's life and career, see Megan Marshall's collective biography of Elizabeth and her sisters Sophia (Hawthorne) and Mary (Mann): *The Peabody Sisters: Three Women Who Ignited American Romanticism* (Boston, 2006). For a good discussion of Peabody's religious and historical thought and its moderately gender-conscious cast, see Nina Baym, "The Ann Sisters: Elizabeth Peabody's Gendered Millennialism," in Baym's *Feminism and American Literary History* (New Brunswick, N.J., 1992), 136–50, 249–52. Sterling F. Delano, *Brook Farm: The Dark Side of Utopia* (Cambridge, Mass., 2004), is the best study to date of the community.

"Plan of the West Roxbury Community" (1842)

In the last number of the Dial were some remarks, under the perhaps ambitious title, of "A Glimpse of Christ's Idea of Society;" in a note to which, it was intimated, that in this number, would be given an account of an attempt to realize in some degree this great Ideal, by a little company in the midst of us, as yet without name or visible existence. The attempt is made on a very small scale. A few individuals, who, unknown to each other, under different disciplines of life, reacting from different social evils, but aiming at the same object,— of being wholly true to their natures as men and women; have been made acquainted with one another, and have determined to become the Faculty of the Embryo University.

In order to live a religious and moral life worthy the name, they feel it is necessary to come out in some degree from the world, and to form themselves into a community of property, so far as to exclude competition and the ordinary rules of trade;—while they reserve sufficient private property, or the means of obtaining it, for all purposes of independence, and isolation at will. They have bought a farm, in order to make agriculture the basis of their life, it being the most direct and simple in relation to nature.

A true life, although it aims beyond the highest star, is redolent of the healthy earth. The perfume of clover lingers about it. The lowing of cattle is the natural bass to the melody of human voices.

On the other hand, what absurdity can be imagined greater than the institution of cities? They originated not in love, but in war. It was war that drove men together in multitudes, and compelled them to stand so close, and build walls around them. This crowded condition produces wants of an unnatural character, which resulted in occupations that regenerated the evil, by creating artificial wants. Even when that thought of grief,

> "I know, where'er I go
> That there hath passed away a glory from the Earth,"

came to our first parents, as they saw the angel, with the flaming sword of self-consciousness, standing between them and the recovery of spontaneous Life and Joy, we cannot believe they could have anticipated a time would come, when the sensuous apprehension of Creation—the great symbol of God—would be taken away from their unfortunate children,—crowded together in such a manner as to shut out the free breath and he Universal Dome of Heaven, some opening their eyes in the dark cellars of the narrow, crowded streets of walled cities. How could they have believed in such a conspiracy against the soul, as to deprive it of the sun and sky, and glorious apparelled Earth!—The growth of cities, which were the embryo of nations hostile to each other, is a subject worthy the thoughts and pen of the philosophic historian. Perhaps nothing would stimulate courage to seek, and hope to attain social good, so much, as a profound history of the origin, in the mixed nature of man, and the exasperation by society, of the various organized Evils under which humanity groans. Is there anything, which exists in social or political life,

Source: Dial, 2 (January 1842), 361–68, 368–69,369–70, 371–72, 372.

contrary to the soul's Ideal? That thing is not eternal, but finite, saith the Pure Reason. It has a beginning, and so a history. What man has done, man may *undo.* "By man came death; by man also cometh the resurrection from the dead."

The plan of the Community, as an Economy, is in brief this; for all who have property to take stock, and receive a fixed interest thereon; then to keep house or board in commons, as they shall severally desire, at the cost of provisions purchased at wholesale, or raised on the farm; and for all to labor in community, and be paid at a certain rate an hour, choosing their own number of hours, and their own kind of work. With the results of this labor, and their interest, they are to pay their board, and also purchase whatever else they require at cost, at the warehouses of the Community, which are to be filled by the Community as such. To perfect this economy, in the course of time they must have all trades, and all modes of business carried on among themselves, from the lowest mechanical trade, which contributes to the health and comfort of life, to the finest art which adorns it with food or drapery for the mind.

All labor, whether bodily or intellectual, is to be paid at the same rate of wages; on the principle, that as the labor becomes merely bodily, it is a greater sacrifice to the individual laborer, to give his time to it; because time is desirable for the cultivation of the intellect, in exact proportion to ignorance. Besides, intellect labor involves in itself higher pleasures, and is more its own reward, than bodily labor.

Another reason, for setting the same pecuniary value on every kind of labor, is, to give outward expression to the great truth, that all labor is sacred, when done for a common interest. Saints and philosophers already know this, but the childish world does not; and very decided measures must be taken to equalize labors, in the eyes of the young of the community, who are not beyond the moral influences of the world without them. The community will have nothing done within its precincts, but what is done by its own members, who stand all in social equality;—that the children may not "learn to expect one kind of service from Love and Goodwill, and another from the obligation of others to render it,"—a grievance of the common society stated, by one of the associated mothers, as destructive of the soul's simplicity. Consequently, as the Universal Education will involve all kinds of operation, necessary to the comforts and elegances of life, every associate, even if he be the digger of a ditch as his highest accomplishment, will be an instructor in that to the young members. Nor will this elevation of bodily labor be liable to lower the tone of manners and refinement in the community. The "children of light" are not altogether unwise in their generation. They have an invisible but all-powerful guard of principles. Minds incapable of refinement, will not be attracted into this association. It is an Ideal community, and only to the ideally inclined will it be attractive; but these are to be found in every rank of life, under every shadow of circumstance. Even among the diggers in the ditch are to be found some, who through religious cultivation, can look down, in meek superiority, upon the outwardly refined, and the book-learned.

Besides, after becoming members of this community, none will be engaged merely in bodily labor. The hours of labor for the Association will be limited by a general law, and can be curtailed at the will of the individual still more; and means will be given to all for intellectual improvement and for social intercourse, calculated to refine and expand. The hours redeemed from labor by community, will not be reapplied to the acquisition of wealth, but to the production of intellectual goods. This community aims to be rich, not in the metallic representative of wealth, but in the wealth itself, which money should represent; namely, LEISURE TO LIVE IN ALL THE FACULTIES OF THE SOUL. As a community, it will traffic with the world at large, in the products of Agricultural labor; and it will sell education to as many young persons as can be domesticated in the families, and enter into the common life with their own children. In the end, it hopes to be enabled to provide—not only all the necessaries, but all the elegances desirable for bodily and for spiritual health; books, apparatus, collections for science, works of art, means of beautiful amusement. These things are to be common to all; and thus that object, which alone gilds and refines the passion for individual accumulation, will no longer exist for desire, and whenever the Sordid passion appears, it will be seen in its naked selfishness. In its ultimate success, the community will realize all the ends which selfishness seeks, but involved in spiritual blessings, which only greatness of soul can aspire after.

And the requisitions on the individuals, it is believed, will make this the order forever. The spiritual good will always be the condition of the temporal. Every one must labor for the community in a reasonable degree, or not taste its benefits. The principles of the organization therefore, and not its probable results in future time, will determine its members. These principles are coöperation in social matters, instead of competition or balance of interests; and individual self-unfolding, in the faith that the whole soul of humanity is in each man and woman. The former is the application of the love of man; the latter of the love of God, to life. Whoever is satisfied with society, as it is; whose sense of justice is not wounded by its common action, institutions, spirit of commerce, has no business with this community; neither has any one who is willing to have other men (needing more time for intellectual cultivation than himself) give their best hours and strength to bodily labor, to secure himself immunity therefrom. And whoever does not measure what society owes to its members of cherishing and instruction, by the needs of the individuals that compose it, has no lot in this new society. Whoever is willing to receive from his fellow men that, for which he gives no equivalent, will stay away from its precincts forever.

But whoever shall surrender himself to its principles, shall find that its yoke is easy and its burden light. Everything can be said of it, in a degree, which Christ said of his kingdom, and therefore it is believed that in some measure it does embody his Idea. For its Gate of entrance is strait and narrow. It is literally a pearl *hidden in a field*. Those only who are willing to lose their life for its sake shall find it. Its voice is that which sent the young man sorrowing away. "Go sell all thy goods and give to the poor, and then come and follow me." "Seek first the kingdom of Heaven, and its righteousness, and all other things shall be added to you."

This principle, with regard to labor, lies at the root of moral and religious life; for it is not more true that "money is the root of all evil," than that *labor is the germ of all good.*

All the work is to be offered for the free choice of the members of the community, at stated seasons, and such as is not chosen, will be hired. But it is not anticipated that any work will be set aside to be hired, for which there is actual ability in the community. It is so desirable that the hired labor should be avoided, that it is believed the work will all be done freely, even though at voluntary sacrifice. If there is some exception at first, it is because the material means are inadequate to the reception of all who desire to go. They cannot go, unless they have shelter; and in this climate, they cannot have shelter unless they can build houses; and they cannot build houses unless they have money. It is not here as in Robinson Crusoe's Island, or in the prairies and rocky mountains of the far west, where the land and the wood are not appropriated. A single farm, in the midst of Massachusetts, does not afford range enough for men to create out of the Earth a living, with no other means; as the wild Indians, or the United States Army in Florida may do.

This plan, of letting all persons choose their own departments of action, will immediately place the Genius of Instruction on its throne. Communication is the life of spiritual life. Knowledge pours itself out upon ignorance by a native impulse. All the arts crave response. "WISDOM CRIES." If every man and woman taught only what they loved, and so many hours as they could naturally communicate, instruction would cease to be a drudgery, and we may add, learning would be no longer a task. The known accomplishments of many of the members of this association have already secured it an interest in the public mind, as a school of literary advantages quite superior. Most of the associates have had long practical experience in the details of teaching, and have groaned under the necessity of taking their method and law from custom and caprice, when they would rather have found it in the nature of the thing taught, and the condition of the pupil to be instructed. Each instructer appoints his hours of study or recitation, and the scholars, or the parents of the children, or the educational committee, choose the studies, for the time, and the pupils submit, as long as they pursue their studies with any teacher, to his regulations.

As agriculture is the basis of their external life, scientific agriculture, connected with practice, will be a prominent part of the instruction from the first. This obviously involves the natural sciences, mathematics, and accounts. But to classical learning justice is also to be done. Boys may be fitted for our colleges there, and even be carried through the college course. The particular studies of the individual pupils, whether old or young, male or female, are to be strictly regulated, according to their inward needs. As the children of the community can remain in the community after they become of age, as associates, if they will; there will not be an entire subserviency to the end of preparing the means of earning a material subsistence, as is frequently the case now. Nevertheless, as they will have had an opportunity, in the course of their minority, to earn three or four hundred dollars, they can leave the community at twenty years of age, if they will, with that sufficient capital, which, together with their extensive education, will gain *a subsistence* anywhere, in the best society of the world. It is this feature of the plan, which may preclude from parents any question as to their right to go into this community, and forego forever all hope of great individual accumulation *for their children;* a customary plea for spending life in making money. Their children will be supported at free board, until they are ten years of age; educated gratuitously; taken care of in case of their parents' sickness and death; and they themselves will be supported, after seventy years of age, by the community, unless their accumulated capital supports them.

There are some persons who have entered the community without money. It is believed that these will be able to support themselves and dependents, by less work, more completely, and with more ease than elsewhere; while their labor will be of advantage to the community. It is in no sense an eleemosynary establishment, but it is hoped that in the end it will be able to receive all who have the spiritual qualifications.

It seems impossible that the little organization can be looked on with any unkindness by the world without it. Those, who have not the faith that the principles of Christ's kingdom are applicable to real life in the world, will smile at it, as a visionary attempt. But even they must acknowledge it can do no harm, in any event. If it realizes the hope of its founders, it will immediately become a manifold blessing. Its moral *aura* must be salutary. As long as it lasts, it will be an example of the beauty of brotherly love. If it succeeds in uniting successful labor with improvement in mind and manners, it will teach a noble lesson to the agricultural population, and do something to check that rush from the country to the city, which is now stimulated by ambition, and by something better, even a desire for learning. Many a young man leaves the farmer's life, because only by so doing can he have intellectual companionship and opportunity; and yet, did he but know it, professional life is ordinarily more unfavorable to the perfection of the mind, than the farmer's life; if the latter is lived with wisdom and moderation, and the labor mingled as it might be with study. This community will be a school for young agriculturalists, who may learn within its precincts, not only the skilful practice, but the scientific reasons of their work, and be enabled afterwards to improve their art continuously. It will also prove the best of normal schools, and as such, may claim the interest of those, who mourn over the inefficiency of our common school system, with its present ill-instructed teachers.

It should be understood also, that after all the working and teaching, which individuals of the community may do, they will still have leisure, and in that leisure can employ themselves in connexion with the world around them. Some will not teach at all; and those especially can write books, pursue the Fine Arts, for private emolument if they will, and exercise various functions of men.—From this community might go forth preachers of the gospel of Christ, who would not have upon them the odium, or the burthen, that now diminishes the power of the clergy. And even if *pastors* were to go from this community, to reside among congregations as now, for a salary given, the fact that they would have something to retreat upon, at any moment, would save them from that virtual dependence on their congregations, which now corrupts the relation. There are doubtless beautiful instances of the old true relation of pastor and people, even of teacher and taught, in the decaying churches around us, but it is in vain to attempt to conceal the ghastly fact, that many a taper is burning dimly in the candlestick, no longer silver or golden, because compassion forbids to put it quite out. But let the spirit again blow "where it listeth," and not circumscribe itself by salary and other commodity,—and the Preached word might reassume the awful Dignity which is its appropriate garment; and though it sit down with publicans and sinners, again speak "with authority and not as the scribes."

We write, as is evident perhaps, not as members, which we are not, but interested spectators of the growth of this little community.... We shall now proceed to make some observations that may sound like criticism, but this we do without apology, for earnest seekers of a true life are not liable to be petulant.

The very liberality, and truth to nature of the plan, is a legitimate reason for fearing it will not succeed as a special community in any given time....

To be a little more explicit. The men and women of the world, as they rise, are not at the present moment wise enough, in the Hebrew sense of the word wisdom, even if they are good-intentioned enough, to enter into a plan of so great mutual confidence. To all the evils arising from constitutional infirmity and perversion they must, especially at first, be exposed. There will always be natures too cold too satisfy the warm-hearted, too narrow for the enjoyment of the wide-visioned, some will be deficient in reason, and some in sensibility, and there will be many who, from defect of personal power, will let run to waste beautiful hearts, and not turn to account great insight of natural wisdom. Love, justice, patience, forbearance, every virtue under heaven, are always necessary in order to do the social duties. There is no knot that magnanimity cannot untie; but the Almighty Wisdom and Goodness will not allow any tower to be builded by the children of men, where they can understand one another *without* this solvent magnanimity. There must ever be sincerity of good design, and organic truth, for the evolution of Beauty.

Now there can be only one way of selecting and winnowing their company. The power to do this must be inherent in their constitution; they must keep sternly true to their principles.

In the first place, they must not compromise their principle of labor, in receiving members. Every one, who has any personal power, whether bodily or mental, must bring the contribution of personal service, no matter how much money he brings besides. This personal service is not to amount to drudgery in any instance, but in every able-bodied or sound-minded person, it should be at least equivalent to the care of their own persons.

Exchange, or barter of labor, so as to distribute to each according to his genius, is to be the means of ease, indefinitely, but no absolute dispensation should be given, except for actual infirmity. "My Father worketh hitherto, and I work," is always the word of the divine humanity.

But granting that they keep the gate of entrance narrow, as the gate of life, which is being as liberal as the moral Law, a subtle temptation assails them from the side of their Organization. Woe be unto them if they lean upon it; if they ever forget that it is only what they have made it, and what they sustain it to be. It not only must be ever instinct with spirit, but it must never be thought, even then, to circumscribe the spirit. It can do nothing more, even if it work miracles, than make bread out of stones, and after all, man liveth not by bread alone, but by *every word that proceedeth out of the mouth of God....*

Another danger which should be largely treated is the spirit of coterie. The breadth of their platform, which admits all sects; and the generality of their plan, which demands all degrees of intellectual culture to begin with, is some security against this. But the ultimate security must be in numbers. Some may say, "already this taint has come upon them, for they are doubtless *transcendentalists.*" But to mass a few protestants together and call them transcendentalists, is a popular cant. Transcendentalism belongs to no sect of religion, and no social party. It is the common ground to which all sects may rise, and be purified of their narrowness; for it consists in seeking the spiritual ground of all manifestations. As already in the pages of this periodical, Calvinist, and Unitarian, and Episcopalian, and Baptist, and Quaker, and Swedenborgian, have met and spoken in love and freedom, on this common basis; so it would be seen, if the word were understood, that transcendentalism, notwithstanding its name is taken in vain by many moonshiny youths and misses who assume it, would be the best of all guards against the spirit of coterie. Much as we respect our friends of the community, we dare not hope for them quite so much, as to aver that they *transcend,* as yet, all the limitations that separate men from love and mutual trust....

There may be some persons, at a distance, who will ask, to what degree has this community gone into operation? We cannot answer this with precision, for we do not write as organs of this association, and have reason to feel, that if we applied to them for information, they would refuse it, out of their dislike to appear in public. We desire this to be distinctly understood. But we can see, and think we have a right to say, that it has purchased the Farm, which some of its members cultivated for a year with success, by way of trying their love and skill for agricultural labor;—that in the only house they are as yet rich enough to own, is collected a large family, including several boarding scholars, and that all work and study together. They seem to be glad to know of all, who desire to join them in the spirit, that at any moment, when they are able to enlarge their habitations, they may call together those that belong to them.

MARGARET FULLER

Selection from *Woman in the Nineteenth Century* (1845)

As the editor of the Transcendentalists' journal the *Dial,* the literary editor of Horace Greeley's *New-York Tribune,* a strong defender of both avant-garde literature and democratic cultural values, and a leading foreign correspondent and revolutionary activist in Italy, Margaret Fuller (1810–1850) was well known for crossing boundaries. But the boundaries she was most famous for crossing were those of gender, especially in her book, *Woman in the Nineteenth Century.* The first major philosophical American work on the woman question, Fuller's volume would remain a seminal text for feminist intellectuals into the twenty-first century.

In her book she applied to the problem of gender roles the Romantic concepts of natural diversity, divine incarnation, and transcendental self-culture, or the self-conscious cultivation of the mind in the direction of wholeness of being. For Fuller these concepts dictated, on one hand, an acknowledgment of the "great radical dualism" of male and female, yet, on the other hand, the denial that most individuals of either gender embodied exclusively "masculine" or "feminine" characteristics. At the same time, without defining women's specific economic roles that followed from her androgynous schema, she made it clear that women's self-cultivation, if it was to be organic, had to give rise to an expansion of employment opportunities unlimited by laws and conventions. Although the ends she proposed for female emancipation were thus individualistic, the *means* she suggested were at least partly social. They were also conflict ridden. In order to break women's psychic dependency on men and achieve soul dependency, she proposed that women for the time being look to themselves as teachers. Her hope, however, was thoroughly Romantic humanist: If women lived truly "self-centered," and therefore God-centered, lives, they would stimulate a new race of men to do likewise and so usher in a new harmony between the sexes.

Charles Capper, *Margaret Fuller: An American Romantic Life,* vol. 1: *The Private Years* (New York, 1992); and vol. 2: *The Public Years* (New York, 2007), is a comprehensive biography that focuses on Fuller's career as an intellectual. For stimulating contrasting discussions of the contexts and trajectory of Fuller's gender thought, see Daniel Walker Howe, "Margaret Fuller's Heroic Ideal of Womanhood," in Howe's *Making the American Self: Jonathan Edwards to Abraham Lincoln* (Cambridge, Mass., 1997), 212–34; and the Norton Critical Edition of Fuller's *Woman in the Nineteenth Century,* ed. Larry J. Reynolds (New York, 1998), 235–97. A provocative comparison of Fuller's and Emerson's ideas on women's rights may be found in Phyllis Cole, "Woman Questions: Emerson, Fuller, and New England Reform," in Charles Capper and Conrad Edick Wright, eds., *Transient and Permanent: The Transcendentalist Movement and Its Contexts* (Boston, 1999), 408–46.

...So great has been, from time to time, the promise, that in all ages, men have said the gods themselves came down to dwell with them; that the All-Creating wandered on the earth to taste, in a limited nature, the sweetness of virtue; that the All-Sustaining incarnated himself to guard, in space and time, the destinies of this world; that heavenly genius dwelt among the shepherds, to sing to them and teach them how to sing. Indeed

> "Der stets den Hirten gnadig sich bewies."

"He has constantly shown himself favorable to shepherds."

And the dwellers in green pastures and natural students of the stars were selected to hail, first among men, the holy child, whose life and death were to present the type of excellence, which has sustained the heart of so large a portion of mankind in these later generations.

Such marks have been made by the footsteps of *man*, (still alas! to be spoken of as the *ideal* man,) wherever he has passed through the wilderness of *men*, and whenever the pigmies stepped in one of those they felt dilate within the breast somewhat that promised nobler stature and purer blood. They were impelled to forsake their evil ways of decrepit scepticism, and covetousness of corruptible possessions. Conviction flowed in upon them. They, too, raised the cry; God is living, now, to-day; and all beings are brothers, for they are his children. Simple words enough, yet which only angelic nature, can use or hear in their full free sense.

These were the triumphant moments, but soon the lower nature took its turn, and the era of a truly human life was postponed.

Thus is man still a stranger to his inheritance, still a pleader, still a pilgrim. Yet his happiness is secure in the end. And now, no more a glimmering consciousness, but assurance begins to be felt and spoken, that the highest ideal man can form of his own powers, is that which he is destined to attain. Whatever the soul knows how to seek, it cannot fail to obtain. This is the law and the prophets. Knock and it shall be opened, seek and ye shall find. It is demonstrated; it is a maxim. Man no longer paints his proper nature in some form and says, "Prometheus had it; it is God-like;" but "Man must have it; it is human." However disputed by many, however ignorantly used, or falsified by those who do receive it, the fact of an universal, unceasing revelation has been too clearly stated in words to be lost sight of in thought, and sermons preached from the text, "Be ye perfect," are the only sermons of a pervasive and deep-searching influence....

Could we indeed say what we want, could we give a description of the child that is lost, he would be found. As soon as the soul can affirm clearly that a certain demonstration is wanted, it is at hand. When the Jewish prophet described the Lamb, as the expression of what was required by the coming era, the time drew nigh. But we say not, see not as yet, clearly, what we would. Those who call for a more triumphant expression of love, a love that cannot be crucified, show not a perfect sense of what has already been given. Love has already been expressed, that made all things new, that gave the worm its place and ministry as well as the eagle; a love to which it was alike to descend into the depths of hell, or to sit at the right hand of the Father.

Yet, no doubt, a new manifestation is at hand, a new hour in the day of man....

Source: S. Margaret Fuller, *Woman in the Nineteenth Century* (New York: Greeley & McElrath, 1845), 7–9, 10, 13–16, 16–19, 20–21, 22–30, 31–32, 33, 35, 36–38, 49–51, 90–93, 102–4, 105, 106–8, 154–64. Notes omitted.

Meanwhile not a few believe, and men themselves have expressed the opinion, that the time is come when Eurydice is to call for an Orpheus, rather than Orpheus for Eurydice: that the idea of Man, however imperfectly brought out, has been far more so than that of Woman, that she, the other half of the same thought, the other chamber of the heart of life, needs now to take her turn in the full pulsation, and that improvement in the daughters will best aid in the reformation of the sons of this age.

It should be remarked that, as the principle of liberty is better understood, and more nobly interpreted, a broader protest is made in behalf of Woman. As men become aware that few men have had a fair chance, they are inclined to say that no women have had a fair chance. The French Revolution, that strangely disguised angel, bore witness in favor of woman, but interpreted her claims no less ignorantly than those of man. Its idea of happiness did not rise beyond outward enjoyment, unobstructed by the tyranny of others. The title it gave was citoyen, citoyenne, and it is not unimportant to woman that even this species of equality was awarded her. Before, she could be condemned to perish on the scaffold for treason, not as a citizen, but as a subject. The right with which this title then invested a human being, was that of bloodshed and license. The Goddess of Liberty was impure. As we read the poem addressed to her not long since, by Beranger, we can scarcely refrain from tears as painful as the tears of blood that flowed when "such crimes were committed in her name." Yes! man, born to purify and animate the unintelligent and the cold, can, in his madness, degrade and pollute no less the fair and the chaste. Yet truth was prophesied in the ravings of that hideous fever, caused by long ignorance and abuse. Europe is conning a valued lesson from the blood-stained page. The same tendencies, farther unfolded, will bear good fruit in this country.

Yet, by men in this country, as by the Jews, when Moses was leading them to the promised land, everything has been done that inherited depravity could do, to hinder the promise of heaven from its fulfillment. The cross here as elsewhere, has been planted only to be blasphemed by cruelty and fraud. The name of the Prince of Peace has been profaned by all kinds of injustice toward the Gentile whom he said he came to save. But I need not speak of what has been done towards the red man, the black man. Those deeds, are the scoff of the world; and they have been accompanied by such pious words that the gentlest would not dare to intercede with "Father, forgive them, for they know not what they do."

Here, as elsewhere, the gain of creation consists always in the growth of individual minds, which live and aspire, as flowers bloom and birds sing, in the midst of morasses; and in the continual development of that thought, the thought of human destiny, which is given to eternity adequately to express, and which ages of failure only seemingly impede. Only seemingly, and whatever seems to the contrary, this country is as surely destined to elucidate a great moral law, as Europe was to promote the mental culture of man.

Though the national independence be blurred by the servility of individuals, though freedom and equality have been proclaimed only to leave room for a monstrous display of slave-dealing and slave-keeping; though the free American so often feels himself free, like the Roman, only to pamper his appetites and his indolence through the misery of his fellow beings, still it is not in vain, that the verbal statement has been made, "All men are born free and equal." There it stands, a golden certainty wherewith to encourage the good, to shame the bad. The new world may be called clearly to perceive that it incurs the utmost penalty, if it reject or oppress the sorrowful brother. And, if men are deaf, the angels hear. But men cannot be deaf. It is inevitable that an external freedom, an independence of the encroachments of other men, such as has been achieved for the nation, should be so also for every member of it. That which has once been clearly conceived in the intelligence cannot fail sooner or later to be acted out....

We sicken no less at the pomp than the strife of words. We feel that never were lungs so puffed with the wind of declamation, on moral and religious subjects, as now. We are tempted to implore these "word-heroes," these word-Catos, word-Christs, to beware of cant above all things; to remember that hypocrisy is the most hopeless as well as the meanest of crimes, and that those must surely be polluted by it, who do not reserve a part of their morality and religion for private use. Landor says that he cannot have a great deal of mind who cannot afford to let the larger part of it lie fallow, and what is true of genius is not less so of virtue. The tongue is a valuable member, but should appropriate but a small part of the vital juices that are needful all over the body. We feel that the mind may "grow black and rancid in the smoke" even "of altars." We start up from the harangue to go into our closet and shut the door. There inquires the spirit, "Is this rhetoric the bloom of healthy blood or a false pigment artfully laid on?" And yet again we know where is so much smoke, must be some fire; with so much talk about virtue and freedom, must be mingled some desire for them; that it cannot be in vain that such have become the common topics of conversation among men, rather than schemes for tyranny and plunder, that the very newspapers see it best to proclaim themselves Pilgrims, Puritans, Heralds of Holiness. The king that maintains so costly a retinue cannot be a mere boast, or Carabbas fiction. We have waited here long in the dust; we are tired and hungry, but the triumphal procession must appear at last.

Of all its banners, none has been more steadily upheld, and under none have more valor and willingness for real sacrifices been shown, than that of the champions of the enslaved African. And this band it is, which, partly from a natural following out of principles, partly because many women have been prominent in that cause, makes, just now, the warmest appeal in behalf of woman.

Though there has been a growing liberality on this subject, yet society at large is not so prepared for the demands of this party, but that they are and will be for some time, coldly regarded as the Jacobins of their day.

"Is it not enough," cries the irritated trader, "that you have done all you could to break up the national union, and thus destroy the prosperity of our country, but now you must be trying to break up family union, to take my wife away from the cradle and the kitchen hearth to vote at polls, and preach from a pulpit? Of course, if she does such things, she cannot attend to those of her own sphere. She is happy enough as she is. She has more leisure than I have, every means of improvement, every indulgence."

"Have you asked her whether she was satisfied with these *indulgences?*"

"No, but I know she is. She is too amiable to wish what would make me unhappy, and too judicious to wish to step beyond the sphere of her sex. I will never consent to have our peace disturbed by any such discussions."

"'Consent—you?' it is not consent from you that is in question, it is assent from your wife."

"Am not I the head of my house?"

"You are not the head of your wife. God has given her a mind of her own."

"I am the head and she the heart."

"God grant you play true to one another then. I suppose I am to be grateful that you did not say she was only the hand. If the head represses no natural pulse of the heart, there can be no question as to your giving your consent. Both will be of one accord, and there needs but to present any question to get a full and true answer. There is no need of precaution, of indulgence, or consent. But our doubt is whether the heart does consent with the head, or only obeys its decrees with a passiveness that precludes the exercise of its natural powers, or a repugnance that turns sweet qualities to bitter, or a doubt that lays waste the fair occasions of life. It is to ascertain the truth, that we propose some liberating measures."

Thus vaguely are these questions proposed and discussed at present. But their being proposed at all implies much thought and suggests more. Many women are considering within themselves, what they need that they have not, and what they can have, if they find they need it. Many men are considering whether women are capable of being and having more than they are and have, *and,* whether, if so, it will be best to consent to improvement in their condition....

The numerous party, whose opinions are already labelled and adjusted too much to their mind to admit of any new light, strive, by lectures on some model-woman of bride-like beauty and gentleness, by writing and lending little treatises, intended to mark out with precision the limits of woman's sphere, and woman's mission, to prevent other than the rightful shepherd from climbing the wall, or the flock from using any chance to go astray.

Without enrolling ourselves at once on either side, let us look upon the subject from the best point of view which to-day offers. No better, it is to be feared, than a high house-top. A high hill-top, or at least a cathedral spire, would be desirable.

It may well be an Anti-Slavery party that pleads for woman, if we consider merely that she does not hold property on equal terms with men; so that, if a husband dies, without making a will, the wife, instead of taking at once his place as head of the family, inherits only a part of his fortune, often brought him by herself, as if she were a child, or ward only, not an equal partner.

We will not speak of the innumerable instances in which profligate and idle men live upon the earnings of industrious wives; or if the wives leave them, and take with them the children, to perform the double duty of mother and father, follow from place to place, and threaten to rob them of the children, if deprived of the rights of a husband, as they call them, planting themselves in their poor lodgings, frightening them into paying tribute by taking from them the children, running into debt at the expense of these otherwise so overtasked helots....

...Knowing that there exists in the minds of men a tone of feeling towards women as towards slaves, such as is expressed in the common phrase, "Tell that to women and children," that the infinite soul can only work through them in already ascertained limits; that the gift of reason, man's highest, prerogative, is allotted to them in much lower degree; that they must be kept from mischief and melancholy by being constantly engaged in active labor, which is to be furnished and directed by those better able to think, &c. &c.; we need not multiply instances, for who can review the experience of last week without recalling words which imply, whether in jest or earnest, these views or views like these; knowing this, can we wonder that many reformers think that measures are not likely to be taken in behalf of women, unless their wishes could be publicly represented by women?

That can never be necessary, cry the other side. All men are privately influenced by women; each has his wife, sister, or female friends, and is too much biased by these relations to fail of representing their interests, and, if this is not enough, let them propose and enforce their wishes with the pen. The beauty of home would be destroyed, the delicacy of the sex be violated, the dignity of halls of legislation degraded by an attempt to introduce them there. Such duties are inconsistent with those of a mother; and then we have ludicrous pictures of ladies in hysterics at the polls, and senate chambers filled with cradles.

But if in reply, we admit as truth that woman seems destined by nature rather for the inner circle, we must add that the arrangements of civilized life have not been as, yet, such as to secure it to her. Her circle, if the duller, is not the quieter. If kept from "excitement," she is not from drudgery. Not only the Indian squaw carries the burdens of the Camp, but the favorites of Louis the Fourteenth accompany him in his journeys, and the washer-woman stands at her tub and carries home her work at all seasons, and in all states of health. Those who think the physical circumstances of woman would make a part in the affairs of national government unsuitable, are by no means those who think it impossible for the negresses to endure field work, even during pregnancy, or the sempstresses to go through their killing labors.

As to the use of the pen, there was quite as much opposition to woman's possessing herself of that help to free agency, as there is now to her seizing on the rostrum or the desk; and she is likely to draw, from a permission to plead her cause that way, opposite inferences to what might be wished by those who now grant it.

As to the possibility of her filling with grace and dignity, any such position, we should think those who had seen the great actresses, and heard the Quaker preachers, of modern times, would not doubt, that woman can express publicly the fulness of thought and creation, without losing any of the peculiar beauty of her sex. What can pollute and tarnish is to act thus from any motive except that something needs to be said or done. Women could take part in the processions, the songs, the dances of old religion; no one fancied their delicacy was impaired by appearing in public for such a cause.

As to her home, she is not likely to leave it more than she now does for balls, theatres, meetings for promoting missions, revival meetings, and others to which she flies, in hope of an animation for her existence, commensurate with what she sees enjoyed by men. Governors of ladies' fairs are no less engrossed by such a change, than the Governor of the state by his; presidents of Washingtonian societies no less away from home than presidents of conventions. If men look straitly to it, they will find that, unless their lives are domestic, those of the women will not be. A house is no home unless it contains food and fire for the mind as well as for the body. The female Greek, of our day, is as much in the street as the male to cry, What news? We doubt not it was the same in Athens of old. The women, shut out from the market place, made up for it at the religious festivals. For human beings are not so constituted that they can live without expansion. If they do not get it one way, they must another, or perish.

As to men's representing women fairly at present, while we hear from men who owe to their wives not only all that is comfortable or graceful, but all that is wise in the arrangement of their lives, the frequent remark, "You cannot reason with a woman," when from those of delicacy, nobleness, and poetic culture, the contemptuous phrase "women and children," and that in no light sally of the hour, but in works intended to give a permanent statement of the best experiences, when not one man, in the million, shall I say? no, not in the hundred million, can rise above the belief that woman was made *for man*, when such traits as these are daily forced upon the attention, can we feel that man will always do justice to the interests of woman? Can we think that he takes a sufficiently discerning and religious view of her office and destiny, *ever* to do her justice, except when prompted by sentiment, accidentally or transiently, that is, for the sentiment will vary according to the relations in which he is placed. The lover, the poet, the artist, are likely to view her nobly.

The father and the philosopher have some chance of liberality; the man of the world, the legislator for expediency, none.

Under these circumstances, without attaching importance, in themselves, to the changes demanded by the champions of woman, we hail them as signs of the times. We would have every arbitrary barrier thrown down. We would have every path laid open to woman as freely as to man. Were this done and a slight temporary fermentation allowed to subside, we should see crystallizations more pure and of more various beauty. We believe the divine energy would pervade nature to a degree unknown in the history of former ages, and that no discordant collision, but a ravishing harmony of the spheres would ensue.

Yet, then and only then, will mankind be ripe for this, when inward and outward freedom for woman as much as for man shall be acknowledged as a right, not yielded as a concession. As the friend of the negro assumes that one man cannot by right, hold another in bondage, so should the friend of woman assume that man cannot, by right, lay even well-meant restrictions on woman. If the negro be a soul, if the woman be a soul, appareled in flesh, to one Master only are they accountable. There is but one law for souls, and if there is to be an interpreter of it, he must come not as man, or son of man, but as son of God.

Were thought and feeling once so far elevated that man should esteem himself the brother and friend, but nowise the lord and tutor of woman, were he really bound with her in equal worship, arrangements as to function and employment would be of no consequence. What woman needs is not as a woman to act or rule, but as a nature to grow, as an intellect to discern, as a soul to live freely and unimpeded, to unfold such powers as were given her when we left our common home. If fewer talents were given her, yet if allowed the free and full employment of these, so that she may render back to the giver his own with usury, she will not complain; nay I dare to say she will bless and rejoice in her earthly birthplace, her earthly lot. Let us consider what obstructions impede this good era, and what signs give reason to hope that it draws near.

I was talking on this subject with Miranda, a woman, who, if any in the world could, might speak without heat and bitterness of the position of her sex. Her father was a man who cherished no sentimental reverence for woman, but a firm belief in the equality of the sexes. She was his eldest child, and came to him at an age when he needed a companion. From the time she could speak and go alone, he addressed her not as a plaything, but as a living mind. Among the few verses he ever wrote was a copy addressed to this child, when the first locks were cut from her head, and the reverence expressed on this occasion for that cherished head, he never belied. It was to him the temple of immortal intellect. He respected his child, however, too much to be an indulgent parent. He called on her for clear judgment, for courage, for honor and fidelity; in short, for such virtues as he knew. In so far as he possessed the keys to the wonders of this universe, he allowed free use of them to her, and by the incentive of a high expectation, he forbade, as far as possible, that she should let the privilege lie idle.

Thus this child was early led to feel herself a child of the spirit. She took her place easily, not only in the world of organized being, but in the world of mind. A dignified sense of self-dependence was given as all her portion, and she found it a sure anchor. Herself securely anchored, her relations with others were established with equal security. She was fortunate in a total absence of those charms which might have drawn to her bewildering flatteries, and in a strong electric nature, which repelled those who did not belong to her, and attracted those who did. With men and women her relations were noble, affectionate without passion, intellectual without coldness. The world was free to her, and she lived freely in it. Outward adversity came, and inward conflict, but that faith and self-respect had early been awakened which must always lead at last, to an outward serenity and an inward peace.

Of Miranda I had always thought as an example, that the restraints upon the sex were insuperable only to those who think them so, or who noisily strive to break them. She had taken a course of her own, and no man stood in her way. Many of her acts had been unusual, but excited no uproar. Few helped, but none checked her, and the many men, who knew her mind and her life, showed to her confidence, as to a brother, gentleness as to a sister. And not only refined, but very coarse men approved and aided one in whom they saw resolution and clearness of design. Her mind was often the leading one, always effective.

When I talked with her upon these matters, and had said very much what I have written, she smilingly replied: "and yet we must admit that I have been fortunate, and this should not be. My good father's early trust gave the first bias, and the rest followed of course. It is true that I have had less outward aid, in after years, than most women, but that is of little consequence. Religion was early awakened in my soul, a sense that what the soul is capable to ask it must attain, and that, though I might be aided and instructed by others, I must depend on myself as the only constant friend. This self dependence, which was honored in me, is deprecated as a fault in most women. They are taught to learn their rule from without, not to unfold it from within.

"This is the fault of man, who is still vain, and wishes to be more important to woman than, by right, he should be."

"Men have not shown this disposition toward you," I said.

"No! because the position I early was enabled to take was one of self-reliance. And were all women as sure of their wants as I was, the result would be the same. But they are so overloaded with precepts by guardians, who think that nothing is so much to be dreaded for a woman as originality of thought or character, that their minds are impeded by doubts till they lose their chance of fair free proportions. The difficulty is to get them to the point from which they shall naturally develop self-respect, and learn self-help.

"Once I thought that men would help to forward this state of things more than I do now. I saw so many of them wretched in the connections they had formed in weakness and vanity. They seemed so glad to esteem women whenever they could.

"The soft arms of affection," said one of the most discerning spirits, "will not suffice for me, unless on them I see the steel bracelets of strength."

But early I perceived that men never, in any extreme of despair, wished to be women. On the contrary they were ever ready to taunt one another at any sign of weakness, with,

"Art thou not like the women, who"—

The passage ends various ways, according to the occasion and rhetoric of the speaker. When they admired any woman they were inclined to speak of her as "above her sex." Silently I observed this, and feared it argued a rooted scepticism, which for ages had been fastening on the heart, and which only an age of miracles could eradicate. Ever I have been treated with great sincerity; and I look upon it as a signal instance of this, that an intimate friend of the other sex said, in a fervent moment, that I "deserved in some star to be a man." He was much surprised when I disclosed my view of my position and hopes, when I declared my faith that the feminine side, the side of love, of beauty, of holiness, was now to have its full chance, and that, if either were better, it was better now to be a woman, for even the slightest achievement of good was furthering an especial work of our time. He smiled incredulous. "She makes the best she can of it," thought he. "Let Jews believe the pride of Jewry, but I am of the better sort, and know better."...

This by no means argues a willing want of generosity toward woman. Man is as generous toward her, as he knows how to be.

Wherever she has herself arisen in national or private history, and nobly shone forth in any form of excellence, men have received her, not only willingly, but with triumph. Their encomiums indeed, are always, in some sense, mortifying; they show too much surprise. Can this be you? he cries to the transfigured Cinderella; well I should never have thought it, but I am very glad. We will tell every one that you have *"surpassed your sex."*

In every-day life the feelings of the many are stained with vanity. Each wishes to be lord in a little world, to be superior at least over one; and he does not feel strong enough to retain a life-long ascendancy over a strong nature. Only a Theseus could conquer before he wed the Amazonian Queen. Hercules wished rather to rest with Dejanira, and received the poisoned robe, as a fit guerdon. The tale should be interpreted to all those who seek repose with the weak.

But not only is man vain and fond of power, but the same want of development, which thus affects him morally, prevents his intellectually discerning the destiny of woman. The boy wants no woman, but only a girl to play ball with him, and mark his pocket handkerchief....

The sexes should not only correspond to and appreciate, but prophesy to one another. In individual instances this happens. Two persons love in one another the future good which they aid one another to unfold. This is imperfectly or rarely done in the general life. Man has gone but little way; now he is waiting to see whether woman can keep step with him, but instead of calling out, like a good brother, "you can do it, if you only think so," or impersonally; "anyone can do what he tries to do;" he often discourages with schoolboy brag: "Girls can't do that; girls can't play ball." But let any one defy their taunts, break through and be brave and secure they rend the air with shouts....

No! man is not willingly ungenerous. He wants faith and love, because he is not yet himself an elevated being. He cries, with sneering skepticism, Give us a sign. But if the sign appears, his eyes glisten, and he offers not merely approval, but homage....

The man habitually most narrow towards women will be flushed, as by the worst assault on Christianity, if you say it has made no improvement in her condition. Indeed, those most opposed to new acts in her favor, are jealous of the reputation of those which have been done.

We will not speak of the enthusiasm excited by actresses, improvisatrici, female singers, for here mingles the charm of beauty and grace; but female authors, even learned women, if not insufferably ugly and slovenly, from the Italian professor's daughter, who taught behind the curtain, down to Mrs. Carter and Madame Dacier, are sure of an admiring audience, and what is far better, chance to use what they have learned, and to learn more, if they can once get a platform on which to stand.

But how to get this platform, or how to make it of reasonably easy access is the difficulty. Plants of great vigor will almost always struggle into blossom, despite impediments. But there should be encouragement, and a free genial atmosphere for those of more timid sort, fair play for each in its own kind. Some are like the little, delicate flowers which love to hide in the dripping mosses, by the sides of mountain torrents, or in the shade of tall trees. But others require an open field, a rich and loosened soil, or they never show their proper hues.

It may be said that man does not have his fair play either; his energies are repressed and distorted by the interposition of artificial obstacles. Ay, but he himself has put them there; they have grown out of his own imperfections. If there *is* a misfortune in woman's lot, it is in obstacles being interposed by men, which do *not* mark her state; and, if they express her past ignorance, do not her present needs. As every man is of woman born, she has slow but sure means of redress, yet the sooner a general justness of thought makes smooth the path, the better.

Man is of woman born, and her face bends over him in infancy with an expression he can never quite forget. Eminent men have delighted to pay tribute to this image, and it is an hacknied observation, that most men of genius boast some remarkable development in the mother. The rudest tar brushes off a tear with his coat-sleeve at the hallowed name. The other day, I met a decrepit old man of seventy, on a journey, who challenged the stage-company to guess where he was going. They guessed aright, "To see your mother." "Yes," said he, "she is ninety-two, but has good eye-sight still, they say. I have not seen her these forty years, and I thought I could not die in peace without." I should have liked his picture painted as a companion piece to that of a boisterous little boy, whom I saw attempt to declaim at a school exhibition—

> "O that those lips had language. Life has passed
> With me but roughly since I heard thee last."

He got but very little way before sudden tears shamed him from the stage....

[T]hough there has been great disparity betwixt the nations as between individuals in their culture on this point, yet the idea of woman has always cast some rays and often been forcibly represented.

Far less has woman to complain that she has not had her share of power. This, in all ranks of society, except the lowest, has been hers to the extent that vanity would crave, far beyond what wisdom would accept. In the very lowest, where man, pressed by poverty, sees in woman only the partner of toils and cares, and cannot hope, scarcely has an idea of a comfortable home, he often maltreats her, and is less influenced by her. In all ranks, those who are gentle and uncomplaining, too candid to intrigue, too delicate to encroach, suffer much. They suffer long, and are kind; verily, they have their reward. But wherever man is sufficiently raised above extreme poverty or brutal stupidity, to care for the comforts of the fireside, or the bloom and ornament of life, woman has always power enough, if she choose to exert it; and is usually disposed to do so, in proportion to her ignorance and childish vanity. Unacquainted with the importance of life and its purposes, trained to a selfish coquetry and love of petty power, she does not look beyond the pleasure of making herself felt at the moment, and governments are shaken and commerce broken up to gratify the pique of a female favorite. The English shopkeeper's wife does not vote, but it is for her interest that the politician canvasses by the coarsest flattery. France suffers no woman on her throne, but her proud nobles kiss the dust at the feet of Pompadour and Dubarry; for such flare in the lighted foreground where in Roland would modestly aid in the closet. Spain, (that same Spain which sang of Ximena and the Lady Teresa,) shuts up her women in the care of duennas, and allows them no book but the Breviary, but the ruin follows only the more surely from the worthless favorite of a worthless queen. Relying on mean precautions, men indeed cry peace, peace, where there is no peace.

It is not the transient breath of poetic incense that women want; each can receive that from a lover. It is not life-long, sway; it needs but to become a coquette, a shrew, or a good cook, to be sure of that. It is not money, nor notoriety, nor the badges of authority that men have appropriated to themselves. If demands, made in their behalf, lay stress on any of these particulars, those who make them have not searched deeply into the need. It is for that which at once includes these and precludes them; which would not be forbidden power, lest there be temptation to steal and misuse it; which would not have the mind perverted by flattery from a worthiness of esteem. It is for that which is the birthright of every being capable to receive it,—the freedom, the religious the intelligent freedom of the universe, to use its means to learn its secret as far as nature has enabled them, with God alone for their guide and their judge.

Ye cannot believe it, men; but the only reason why women ever assume what is more appropriate to you, is because you prevent them from finding out what is fit for themselves. Were they free, were they wise fully to develop the strength and beauty of woman; they would never wish to be men, or manlike. The well-instructed moon flies not from her orbit to seize on the glories of her partner. No; for she knows that one law rules, one heaven contains, one universe replies to them alike. It is with women as with the slave.

> "Vor dem Sklaven, wenn er die Kette bricht,
> Vor dem freien Menschen erzittert nicht."

Tremble not before the free man, but before the slave who has chains to break.

In slavery, acknowledged slavery, women are on a par with men. Each is a work-tool, an article of property, no more! In perfect freedom, such as is painted in Olympus, in Swedenborg's angelic state, in the heaven where is there is no marrying nor giving in marriage, each is a purified intelligence, an enfranchised soul,—no less!...

Mysticism, which may be defined as the brooding-soul of the world, cannot fail of its oracular promise as to woman. "The mothers"—"The mother of all things," are expressions of thought which lead the mind towards this side of universal growth. Whenever a mystical whisper was heard, from Behmen down to St. Simon, sprang up the thought, that, if it be true, as the legend says, that humanity withers through a fault committed by and a curse laid upon woman, through her pure child, or influence, shall the new Adam, the redemption, arise. Innocence is to be replaced by virtue, dependence by a willing submission, in the heart of the Virgin Mother of the new race.

The spiritual tendency is towards the elevation of woman, but the intellectual by itself is not so. Plato sometimes seems penetrated by that high idea of love, which considers man and woman as the two-fold expression of one thought. This is the angel of Swedenborg, the angel of the coming age, cannot surpass, but only explain more fully. But then again Plato, the man of intellect, treats woman in the Republic as property, and, in the Timæus, says that man, if he misuse the privileges of one life, shall be degraded into the form of woman, and then, if he do not redeem himself, into that of a bird. This, as I said above, expresses most happily how anti-poetical is this state of mind. For the poet, contemplating the world of things, selects various birds as the symbols of his most gracious and ethereal thoughts, just as he calls upon his genius, as muse, rather than as God. But the intellect, cold, is ever more masculine than feminine; warmed by emotion, it rushes towards mother earth, and puts on the forms of beauty.

The electrical, the magnetic element in woman has not been fairly brought out at any period. Every thing might be expected from it; she has far more of it than man. This is commonly expressed by saying that her intuitions are more rapid and more correct. You will often see men of high intellect absolutely stupid in regard to the atmospheric changes, the fine invisible links which connect the forms of life around them, while common women, if pure and modest, so that a vulgar self do not overshadow the mental eye, will seize and delineate these with unerring discrimination.

Women who combine this organization with creative genius, are very commonly unhappy at present. They see too much to act in conformity with those around them, and their quick impulses seem folly to those who do not discern the motives. This is an usual effect of the apparition of genius, whether in man or woman, but is more frequent with regard to the latter, because a harmony, an obvious order and self-restraining decorum, is most expected from her.

Then women of genius, even more than men, are likely to be enslaved by an impassioned sensibility. The world repels them more rudely, and they are of weaker bodily frame.

Those, who seem overladen with electricity, frighten those around them. "When she merely enters the room, I am what the French call *herissé*," said a man of petty feelings and worldly character of such a woman, whose depth of eye and powerful motion announced the conductor of the mysterious fluid.

Woe to such a woman who finds herself linked to such a man in bonds too close. It is the cruelest of errors. He will detest her with all the bitterness of wounded self-love. He will take the whole prejudice of manhood upon himself, and to the utmost of his power imprison and torture her by its imperious rigors.

Yet, allow room enough, and the electric fluid will be found to invigorate and embellish, not destroy life. Such women are the great actresses, the songsters. Such traits we read in a late searching, though too French analysis of the character of Mademoiselle Rachel, by a modern La Rochefoucoult. The Greeks thus represent the muses; they have not the golden serenity of Apollo; they are *over*-flowed with thought; there is something tragic in their air. Such are the Sibyls of Guercino, the eye is over-full of expression, dilated and lustrous; it seems to have drawn the whole being into it.

Sickness is the frequent result of this over-charged existence. To this region, however misunderstood, or interpreted with presumptuous carelessness, belong the phenomena of magnetism, or mesmerism, as it is now often called, where the trance of the Ecstatica purports to be produced by the agency of one human being on another, instead of, as in her case, direct from the spirit.

The worldling has his sneer at this as at the services of religion. "The churches can always be filled with women." "Show me a man in one of your magnetic states, and I will believe."

Women are, indeed, the easy victims both of priest-craft and self-delusion, but this would not be, if the intellect was developed in proportion to the other powers. They would, then, have a regulator, and be more in equipoise, yet must retain the same nervous susceptibility, while their physical structure is such as it is.

It is with just that hope, that we welcome every thing that tends to strengthen the fibre and develop the nature on more sides. When the intellect and affections are in harmony; when intellectual consciousness is calm and deep; inspiration wilt not be confounded with fancy....

The especial genius of woman I believe to be electrical in movement, intuitive in function, spiritual in tendency. She excels not so easily in classification, or re-creation, as in an instinctive seizure of causes, and a simple breathing out of what she receives that has the singleness of life, rather than the selecting and energizing of art.

More native is it to her to be the living model of the artist than to set apart from herself any one form in objective reality; more native to inspire and receive the poem, than to create it. In so far as soul is in her completely developed, all soul is the same; but as far as it is modified in her as woman, it flows, it breathes, it sings, rather than deposits soil, or finishes, work, and that which is especially feminine flushes, in blossom, the face of earth, and pervades, like air and water, all this seeming solid globe, daily renewing and purifying its life. Such may be the especially feminine element, spoken of as Femality. But it is no more the order of nature that it should be incarnated pure in any form, than that the masculine energy should exist unmingled with it in any form.

Male and female represent the two sides of the great radical dualism. But, in fact, they are perpetually passing into one another. Fluid hardens to solid, solid rushes to fluid. There is no wholly masculine man, no purely feminine woman.

History jeers at the attempts of physiologists to bind great original laws by the forms which flow from them. They make a rule; they say from observation, what can and cannot be. In vain! Nature provides exceptions to every rule. She sends women to battle, and sets Hercules spinning; she enables women to bear immense burdens, cold, and frost; she enables the man, who feels maternal love, to nourish his infant like a mother. Of late she plays still gayer pranks. Not only she deprives organizations, but organs, of a necessary end. She enables people to read with the top of the head, and see with the pit of the stomach. Presently she will make a female Newton, and a male Syren.

Man partakes of the feminine in the Apollo, woman of the masculine as Minerva....

Let us be wise and not impede the soul. Let her work as she will. Let us have one creative energy, one incessant revelation. Let it take what form it will, and let us not bind it by the past to man or woman, black or white. Jove sprang from Rhea, Pallas from Jove. So let it be.

If it has been the tendency of these remarks to call woman rather to the Minerva side,—if I, unlike the more generous writer, have spoken from society no less than the soul,—let it be pardoned! It is love that has caused this, love for many incarcerated souls, that might be freed, could the idea of religious self-dependence be established in them, could the weakening habit of dependence on others be broken up....

It is, therefore, only in the present crisis that the preference is given to Minerva. The power of continence must establish the legitimacy of freedom, the power of self-poise the perfection of motion.

Every relation, every gradation of nature is incalculably precious, but only to the soul which is poised upon itself, and to whom no loss, no change, can bring dull discord, for it is in harmony with the central soul.

If any individual live too much in relations, so that he becomes a stranger to the resources of his own nature, he falls, after a while, into a distraction, or imbecility, from which he can only be cured by a time of isolation, which gives the renovating fountains time to rise up. With a society it is the same. Many minds, deprived of the traditionary or instinctive means of passing a cheerful existence, must find help in self-impulse, or perish. It is therefore that, while any elevation, in the view of union, is to be hailed with joy, we shall not decline celibacy as the great fact of the time. It is one from which no vow, no arrangement, can at present save a thinking mind. For now the rowers are pausing on their oars; they wait a change before they can pull together. All tends to illustrate the thought of a wise contemporary. Union is only possible to those who are units. To be fit for relations in time, souls, whether of man or woman, must be able to do without them in the spirit.

It is therefore that I would have woman lay aside all thought, such as she habitually cherishes, of being taught and led by men. I would have her, like the Indian girl, dedicate herself to the Sun, the Sun of Truth, and go no where if his beams did not make clear the path. I would have her free from compromise, from complaisance, from helplessness, because I would have her good enough and strong enough to love one and all beings, from the fulness, not the poverty of being.

Men, as at present instructed, will not help this work, because they also are under the slavery of habit. I have seen with delight their poetic impulses. A sister is the fairest ideal, and how nobly Wordsworth, and even Byron, have written of a sister.

There is no sweeter sight than to see a father with his little daughter. Very vulgar men become refined to the eye when leading a little girl by the hand. At that moment the right relation between the sexes seems established, and you feel as if the man would aid in the noblest purpose, if you ask him in behalf of his little daughter. Once two fine figures stood before me, thus. The father of very intellectual aspect, his falcon eye softened by affection as he looked down on his fair child, she the image of himself, only more graceful and brilliant in expression. I was reminded of Southey's Kehama; when lo, the dream was rudely broken. They were talking of education, and he said,

"I shall not have Maria brought too forward. If she knows too much, she will never find a husband; superior women hardly ever can."

"Surely," said his wife, with a blush, "you wish Maria to be as good and wise as she can, whether it will help her to marriage or not."

"No," he persisted, "I want her to have a sphere and a home, and some one to protect her when I am gone."

It was a trifling incident, but made a deep impression. I felt that the holiest relations fail to instruct the unprepared and perverted mind. If this man, indeed, could have looked at it on the other side, he was the last that would have been willing to have been taken himself for the home and protection he could give, but would have been much more likely to repeat the tale of Alcibiades with his phials.

But men do *not* look at both sides, and women must leave off asking them and being influenced by them, but retire within themselves, and explore the groundwork of life till they find their peculiar secret. Then, when they come forth again, renovated and baptized, they will know how to turn all dross to gold, and will be rich and free though they live in a hut, tranquil, if in a crowd. Then their sweet singing shall not be from passionate impulse, but the lyrical overflow of a divine rapture, and a new music shall be evolved from this many-chorded world.

Grant her, then, for a while, the armor and the javelin. Let her put from her the press of other minds and meditate in virgin loneliness. The same idea shall re-appear in due time as Muse, or Ceres, the all-kindly patient Earth-Spirit....

And now I have designated in outline, if not in fullness, the stream which is ever flowing from the heights of my thought.

In the earlier tract, I was told, I did not make my meaning sufficiently clear. In this I have consequently tried to illustrate it in various ways, and may have been guilty of much repetition. Yet, as I am anxious to leave no room for doubt, I shall venture to retrace, once more, the scope of my design in points, as was done in old-fashioned sermons.

Man is a being of two-fold relations, to nature beneath, and intelligences above him. The earth is his school, if not his birth-place: God his object: life and thought, his means of interpreting nature, and aspiring to God.

Only a fraction of this purpose is accomplished in the life of any one man. Its entire accomplishment is to be hoped only from the sum of the lives of men, or man considered as a whole.

As this whole has one soul and one body, any injury or obstruction to a part, or to the meanest member, affects the whole. Man can never be perfectly happy or virtuous, till all men are so.

To address man wisely, you must not forget that his life is partly animal, subject to the same laws with nature.

But you cannot address him wisely unless you consider him still more as soul, and appreciate the conditions and destiny of soul.

The growth of man is two-fold, masculine and feminine.

As far as these two methods can be distinguished they are so as

Energy and Harmony.

Power and Beauty.

Intellect and Love.

Or by some such rude classification, for we have not language primitive and pure enough to express such ideas with precision.

These two sides are supposed to be expressed in man and woman, that is, as the more and less, for the faculties have not been given pure to either, but only in preponderance. There are also exceptions in great number, such as men of far more beauty than power, and the reverse. But as a general rule, it seems to have been the intention to give a preponderance on the one side, that is called masculine, and on the other, one that is called feminine.

There cannot be a doubt that, if these two developments were in perfect harmony, they would correspond to and fulfil one another, like hemispheres, or the tenor and bass in music.

But there is no perfect harmony in human nature; and the two parts answer one another only now and then, or, if there be a persistent consonance, it can only be traced, at long intervals, instead of discoursing an obvious melody.

What is the cause of this?

Man, in the order of time, was developed first; as energy comes before harmony; power before beauty.

Woman was therefore under his care as an elder. He might have been her guardian and teacher.

But as human nature goes not straight forward, but by excessive action and then reaction in an undulated course, he misunderstood and abused his advantages, and became her temporal master instead of her spiritual sire.

On himself came the punishment. He educated woman more as a servant than a daughter, and found himself a king without a queen.

The children of this unequal union showed unequal natures, and, more and more, men seemed sons of the hand-maid, rather than princes.

At last there were so many Ishmaelites that the rest grew frightened and indignant. They laid the blame on Hagar, and drove her forth into the wilderness.

But there were none the fewer Ishmaelites for that.

At last men became a little wiser, and saw that the infant Moses was, in every case, saved by the pure instincts of woman's breast. For, as too much adversity is better for the moral nature than too much prosperity, woman, in this respect, dwindled less than man, though in other respects, still a child in leading strings.

So man did her more and more justice, and grew more and more kind.

But yet, his habits and his will corrupted by the past, he did not clearly see that woman was half himself, that her interests were identical with his, and that, by the law of their common being, he could never reach his true proportions while she remained in any wise shorn of hers.

And so it has gone on to our day; both ideas developing, but more slowly than they would under a clearer recognition of truth and justice, which would have permitted the sexes their due influence on one another, and mutual improvement from more dignified relations.

Wherever there was pure love, the natural influences were, for the time, restored.

Wherever the poet or artist gave free course to his genius, he saw the truth, and expressed it in worthy forms, for these men especially share and need the feminine principle. The divine birds need to be brooded into life and song by mothers.

Wherever religion (I mean the thirst for truth and good, not the love of sect and dogma,) had its course, the original design was apprehended in its simplicity, and the dove presaged sweetly from Dodona's oak.

I have aimed to show that no age was left entirely without a witness of the equality of the sexes in function, duty and hope.

Also that, when there was unwillingness or ignorance, which prevented this being acted upon, women had not the less power for their want of light and noble freedom. But it was power which hurt alike them and those against whom they made use of the arms of the servile; cunning, blandishment, and unreasonable emotion.

That now the time has come when a clearer vision and better action are possible. When man and woman may regard one another as brother and sister, the pillars of one porch, the priests of one worship.

I have believed and intimated that this hope would receive an ampler fruition, than ever before, in our own land.

And it will do so if this land carry out the principles from which sprang our national life.

I believe that, at present, women are the best helpers of one another.

Let them think; let them act; till they know what they need.

We only ask of men to remove arbitrary barriers. Some would like to do more. But I believe it needs for woman to show herself in her native dignity, to teach them how to aid her; their minds are so encumbered by tradition.

When Lord Edward Fitzgerald travelled with the Indians, his manly heart obliged him at once, to take the packs from the squaws and carry them. But we do not read that the red men followed his example, though they are ready enough to carry the pack of the white woman, because she seems to them a superior being.

Let woman appear in the mild majesty of Ceres, and rudest churls will be willing to learn from her.

You ask, what use will she make of liberty, when she has so long been sustained and restrained?

I answer; in the first place, this will not be suddenly given. I read yesterday a debate of this year on the subject of enlarging women's rights over property. It was a leaf from the class-book that is preparing for the needed instruction. The men learned visibly as they spoke. The champions of woman saw the fallacy of arguments, on the opposite side, and were startled by their own convictions. With their wives at home, and the readers of the paper, it was the same. And so the stream flows on; thought urging action, and action leading to the evolution of still better thought.

But, were this freedom to come suddenly, I have no fear of the consequences. Individuals might commit excesses, but there is not only in the sex a reverence for decorums and limits inherited and enhanced from generation to generation, which many years of other life could not efface, but a native love, in woman as woman, of proportion, of "the simple art of not too much," a Greek moderation, which would create immediately a restraining party, the natural legislators and instructors of the rest, and would gradually establish such rules as are needed to guard, without impeding, life.

The Graces would lead the choral dance, and teach the rest to regulate their steps to the measure of beauty.

But if you ask me what offices they may fill; I reply—any. I do not care what case you put; let them be sea-captains, if you will. I do not doubt there are women well fitted for such an office, and, if so, I should be glad to see them in it, as to welcome the maid of Saragossa, or the maid of Missolonghi, or the Suliote heroine, or Emily Plater.

I think women need, especially at this juncture, a much greater range of occupation than they have, to rouse their latent powers. A party of travelers lately visited a lonely hut on a mountain. There they found an old woman that told them she and her husband had lived there forty years. "Why," they said, "did you choose so barren a spot? She "did not know; *it was the man's notion.*"

And, during forty years, she had been content to act, without knowing why, upon "the man's notion." I would not have it so.

In families that I know, some little girls like to saw wood, others to use carpenters' tools. Where these tastes are indulged, cheerfulness and good humor are promoted. Where they are forbidden, because "such things are not proper for girls," they grow sullen and mischievous.

Fourier had observed these wants of women, as no one can fail to do who watches the desires of little girls, or knows the ennui that haunts grown women, except where they make to themselves a serene little world by art of some kind. He, therefore, in proposing a great variety of employments, in manufactures or the care of plants and animals, allows for one third of woman, as likely to have a taste for masculine pursuits, one third of men for feminine.

Who does not observe the immediate glow and serenity that is diffused over the life of women, before restless or fretful, by engaging in gardening, building, or the lowest department of art. Here is something that is not routine, something that draws forth life toward the infinite.

I have no doubt, however, that a large proportion of women would give themselves to the same employments as now, because there are circumstances that must lead them. Mothers will delight to make the nest soft and warm. Nature would take care of that; no need to clip the wings of any bird that wants to soar and sing, or finds in itself the strength of pinion for a migratory flight unusual to its kind. The difference would be that *all* need not be constrained to employments, for which *some* are unfit.

I have urged upon the sex self-subsistence in its two forms of self-reliance and self-impulse, because I believe them to be the needed means of the present juncture.

I have urged on woman independence of man, not that I do not think the sexes mutually needed by one another, but because in woman this fact has led to an excessive devotion, which has cooled love, degraded marriage, and prevented either sex from being what it should be to itself or the other.

I wish woman to live, *first* for God's sake. Then she will not make an imperfect man her god, and thus sink to idolatry. Then she will not take what is not fit for her from a sense of weakness and poverty. Then, if she finds what she needs in man embodied, she will know how to love, and be worthy of being loved.

By being more a soul, she will not be less woman, for nature is perfected through spirit.

Now there is no woman, only an overgrown child.

That her hand may be given with dignity, she must be able to stand alone. I wish to see men and women capable of such relations as are depicted by Landor in his Pericles and Aspasia, where grace is the natural garb of strength, and the affections are calm, because deep. The softness is that of a firm tissue, as when

> "The gods approve
> The depth, but not the tumult of the soul,
> A fervent, not ungovernable love."

A profound thinker has said, "no married woman can represent the female world, for she belongs to her husband. The idea of woman must be represented by a virgin."

But that is the very fault of marriage, and of the present relation between the sexes, that the woman does belong to the man, instead of forming a whole with him. Were it otherwise, there would be no such limitation to the thought.

Woman, self-centred, would never be absorbed by any relation; it would be only an experience to her as to man. It is a vulgar error that love, *a* love to woman is her whole existence; she also is born for Truth and Love in their universal energy. Would she but assume her inheritance, Mary would not be the only virgin mother. Not Manzoni alone would celebrate in his wife the virgin mind with the maternal wisdom and conjugal affections. The soul is ever young, ever virgin.

And will not she soon appear? The woman who shall vindicate their birthright for all women; who shall teach them what to claim, and how to use what they obtain? Shall not her name be for her era Victoria, for her country and life Virginia? Yet predictions are rash; she herself must teach us to give her the fitting name.

An idea not unknown to ancient times has of late been revived, that, in the metamorphoses of life, the soul assumes the form, first of man, then of woman, and takes the chances, and reaps the benefits of either lot. Why then, say some, lay such emphasis on the rights or needs of woman? What she wins not, as woman, will come to her as man.

That makes no difference. It is not woman, but the law of right, the law of growth, that speaks in us, and demands the perfection of each being in its kind, apple as apple, woman as woman. Without adopting your theory I know that I, a daughter, live through the life of man; but what concerns me now is, that my life be a beautiful, powerful, in a word, a complete life in its kind. Had I but one more moment to live, I must wish the same.

Suppose, at the end of your cycle, your great world-year, all will be completed, whether I exert myself or not (and the supposition is *false,*) but suppose it true, am I to be indifferent about it? Not so! I must beat my own pulse true in the heart of the world; for *that* is virtue, excellence, health.

Thou, Lord of Day! didst leave us to-night so calmly glorious, not dismayed that cold winter is coming, not postponing thy beneficence to the fruitful summer! Thou didst smile on thy day's work when it was done, and adorn thy down-going as thy up-rising, for thou art loyal, and it is thy nature to give life, if thou canst, and shine at all events!

I stand in the sunny noon of life. Objects no longer glitter in the dews of morning, neither are yet softened by the shadows of evening. Every spot is seen, every chasm revealed. Climbing the dusty hill, some fair effigies that once stood for symbols of human destiny have been broken: those I still have with me, show defects in this broad light. Yet enough is left, even by experience, to point distinctly to the glories of that destiny; faint, but not to be mistaken streaks of the future day. I can say with the bard,

"Though many have suffered shipwreck, still beat noble hearts."

Always the soul says to us all: Cherish your best hopes as a faith, and abide by them in action. Such shall be the effectual fervent means to their fulfilment.

> For the Power to whom we bow
> Has given its pledge that, if not now,
> They of pure and steadfast mind,
> By faith exalted, truth refined,
> *Shall* hear all music loud and clear,
> Whose first notes they ventured here.
> Then fear not thou to wind the horn,
> Though elf and gnome thy courage scorn;
> Ask for the Castle's King and Queen;
> Though rabble rout may rush between,
> Beat thee senseless to the ground,
> In the dark beset thee round;
> Persist to ask and it will come,
> Seek not for rest in humbler home;
> So shalt thou see what few have seen,
> The palace home of King and Queen.

HENRY DAVID THOREAU

"Resistance to Civil Government" (1849)

No major American writer is so thoroughly identified with his own acts as Henry David Thoreau (1817–1862). A little over a year after Independence Day of 1845, when Thoreau moved into his hut off Concord's Walden Pond so that he could live simply in order to "live deep and suck out all the marrow of life," he was arrested by the town's sheriff for refusing to pay the poll tax. His reason for noncompliance was his belief that the money raised by the tax went to a government that supported slavery and was just then prosecuting, in Thoreau's view and that of many other Northerners, an imperialistic and slavery-expansionist war with Mexico.

But his subsequently published essay justifying his stance was more than an agitational antislavery tract; it was also an imaginative work of political thought that was to inspire reformers as disparate in their causes as Tolstoy, Gandhi, and Martin Luther King, Jr. As a theoretical work it can be read on four levels: first, as a rationale for the priority of individual "conscience" over political "expediency"; second, as a cluster of differing governmental models for realizing that priority; third, as an argument for the practical power of symbolic actions of nonviolent resistance in a morally confused democratic society; and finally, as a dramatization of psychic rewards granted to the Transcendentalist thinker willing to convert his revulsion from "a cheap and superficial life" into a struggle against his "underbred" townsmen and that "half-witted...timid" entity known to Thoreau as the democratic state.

Sherman Paul, *The Shores of America: Thoreau's Inward Exploration* (Urbana, Ill., 1958); and Robert D. Richardson, Jr., *Henry Thoreau: A Life of the Mind* (Berkeley, 1986), are two good intellectual biographies. For a fine study of Thoreau's "naturalist" ethics, see David M. Robinson, *Natural Life: Thoreau's Worldly Transcendentalism* (Ithaca, 2004). For a somewhat tendentious but still fresh appreciation of Thoreau's politics, see Bob Pepperman Taylor, *America's Bachelor Uncle: Thoreau and the American Polity* (Lawrence, Kans., 1996). Valuable historical accounts of Thoreau's antislavery ideas may be found in Daniel Walker Howe, "The Constructed Self Against the State," in Howe's *Making the American Self: Jonathan Edwards to Abraham Lincoln* (Cambridge, Mass., 1997); and Robert A. Gross, "Quiet War with the State: Henry David Thoreau and Civil Disobedience, *Yale Review*, 93 (2005), 1–17. For recent discussions of Thoreau's politics by two political theorists, see Jack Turner, ed., *A Political Companion to Henry David Thoreau* (Lexington, Ky., 2009); and Shannon L. Mariotti, *Thoreau's Democratic Withdrawal: Alienation, Participation, and Modernity* (Madison, Wis., 2010).

I heartily accept the motto,—"That government is best which governs least;" and I should like to see it acted up to more rapidly and systematically. Carried out, it finally amounts to this, which also I believe,—"That government is best which governs not at all;" and when men are prepared for it, that will be the kind of government which they will have. Government is at best but an expedient; but most governments are usually, and all governments are sometimes, inexpedient. The objections which have been brought against a standing army, and they are many and weighty, and deserve to prevail, may also at last be brought against a standing government. The standing army is only an arm of the standing government. The government itself, which is only the mode which the people have chosen to execute their will, is equally liable to be abused and perverted before the people can act through it. Witness the present Mexican war, the work of comparatively a few individuals using the standing government as their tool; for, in the outset, the people would not have consented to this measure.

This American government,—what is it but a tradition, though a recent one, endeavoring to transmit itself unimpaired to posterity, but each instant losing some of its integrity? It has not the vitality and force of a single living man; for a single man can bend it to his will. It is a sort of wooden gun to the people themselves; and, if ever they should use it in earnest as a real one against each other, it will surely split. But it is not the less necessary for this; for the people must have some complicated machinery or other, and hear its din, to satisfy that idea of government which they have. Governments show thus how successfully men can be imposed on, even impose on themselves, for their own advantage. It is excellent, we must all allow; yet this government never of itself furthered any enterprise, but by the alacrity with which it got out of its way. *It* does not keep the country free. *It* does not settle the West. *It* does not educate. The character inherent in the American people has done all that has been accomplished; and it would have done somewhat more, if the government had not sometimes got in its way. For government is an expedient by which men would fain succeed in letting one another alone; and, as has been said, when it is most expedient, the governed are most let alone by it. Trade and commerce, if they were not made of India rubber, would never manage to bounce over the obstacles which legislators are continually putting in their way; and, if one were to judge these men wholly by the effects of their actions, and not partly by their intentions, they would deserve to be classed and punished with those mischievous persons who put obstructions on the railroads.

But, to speak practically and as a citizen, unlike those who call themselves no-government men, I ask for, not at once no government, but *at once* a better government. Let every man make known what kind of government would command his respect, and that will be one step toward obtaining it.

After all, the practical reason why, when the power is once in the hands of the people, a majority are permitted, and for a long period continue, to rule, is not because they are most likely to be in the right, nor because this seems fairest to the minority, but because they are physically the strongest. But a government in which the majority rule in all cases cannot be based on justice, even as far as men understand it. Can there

Source: The Writings of Henry D. Thoreau, ed. William L. Howarth et al., *Reform Papers,* ed. Wendell Glick (Princeton: Princeton University Press, 1973), 63–90. Reprinted by permission of Princeton University Press, Copyright © 1973.

not be a government in which majorities do not virtually decide right and wrong, but conscience?—in which majorities decide only those questions to which the rule of expediency is applicable? Must the citizen ever for a moment, or in the least degree, resign his conscience to the legislator? Why has every man a conscience, then? I think that we should be men first, and subjects afterward. It is not desirable to cultivate a respect for the law, so much as for the right. The only obligation which I have a right to assume, is to do at any time what I think right. It is truly enough said, that a corporation has no conscience; but a corporation of conscientious men is a corporation *with* a conscience. Law never made men a whit more just; and, by means of their respect for it, even the well-disposed are daily made the agents of injustice. A common and natural result of an undue respect for law is, that you may see a file of soldiers, colonel, captain, corporal, privates, powder-monkeys and all, marching in admirable order over hill and dale to the wars, against their wills, aye, against their common sense and consciences, which makes it very steep marching indeed, and produces a palpitation of the heart. They have no doubt that it is a damnable business in which they are concerned; they are all peaceably inclined. Now, what are they? Men at all? or small moveable forts and magazines, at the service of some unscrupulous man in power? Visit the Navy Yard, and behold a marine, such a man as an American government can make, or such as it can make a man with its black arts, a mere shadow and reminiscence of humanity, a man laid out alive and standing, and already, as one may say, buried under arms with funeral accompaniments, though it may be

> "Not a drum was heard, not a funeral note,
>   As his corse to the rampart we hurried;
> Not a soldier discharged his farewell shot
>   O'er the grave where our hero we buried."

The mass of men serve the State thus, not as men mainly, but as machines, with their bodies. They are the standing army, and the militia, jailers, constables, *posse comitatus,* &. In most cases there is no free exercise whatever of the judgment or of the moral sense; but they put themselves on a level with wood and earth and stones, and wooden men can perhaps be manufactured that will serve the purpose as well. Such command no more respect than men of straw, or a lump of dirt. They have the same sort of worth only as horses and dogs. Yet such as these even are commonly esteemed good citizens. Others, as most legislators, politicians, lawyers, ministers, and officeholders, serve the State chiefly with their heads; and, as they rarely make any moral distinctions, they are as likely to serve the devil, without intending it, as God. A very few, as heroes, patriots, martyrs, reformers in the great sense, and *men,* serve the State with their consciences also, and so necessarily resist it for the most part; and they are commonly treated by it as enemies. A wise man will only be useful as a man, and will not submit to be "clay," and "stop a hole to keep the wind away," but leave that office to his dust at least:—

> "I am too high-born to be propertied,
>   To be a secondary at control,
> Or useful serving-man and instrument
>   To any sovereign state throughout the world."

He who gives himself entirely to his fellow-men appears to them useless and selfish; but he who gives himself partially to them is pronounced a benefactor and philanthropist.

How does it become a man to behave toward this American government to-day? I answer that he cannot without disgrace be associated with it. I cannot for an instant recognize that political organization as *my* government which is the *slave's* government also.

All men recognize the right of revolution; that is, the right to refuse allegiance to and to resist the government, when its tyranny or its inefficiency are great and unendurable. But almost all say that such is not the case now. But such was the case, they think, in the Revolution of '75. If one were to tell me that this was a bad government because it taxed certain foreign commodities brought to its ports, it is most probable that I should not make an ado about it, for I can do without them: all machines have their friction; and possibly this does enough good to counterbalance the evil. At any rate, it is a great evil to make a stir about it. But when the friction comes to have its machine, and oppression and robbery are organized, I say, let us not have such a machine any longer. In other words, when a sixth of the population of a nation which has undertaken to be the refuge of liberty are slaves, and a whole country is unjustly overrun and conquered by a foreign army, and subjected to military law, I think that it is not too soon for honest men to rebel and revolutionize. What makes this duty the more urgent is the fact, that the country so overrun is not our own, but ours is the invading army.

Paley, a common authority with many on moral questions, in his chapter on the "Duty of Submission to Civil Government," resolves all civil obligation into expediency; and he proceeds to say, "that so long as the interest of the whole society requires it, that is, so long as the established government cannot be resisted or changed without public inconveniency, it is the will of God that the established government be obeyed, and no longer." ... "This principle being admitted, the justice of every particular case of resistance is reduced to a computation of the quantity of the danger and grievance on the one side, and of the probability and expense of redressing it on the other." Of this, he says, every man shall judge for himself. But Paley appears never to have contemplated those cases to which the rule of expediency does not apply, in which a people, as well as an individual, must do justice, cost what it may. If I have unjustly wrested a plank from a drowning man, I must restore it to him though I drown myself. This, according to Paley, would be inconvenient. But he that would save his life, in such a case, shall lose it. This people must cease to hold slaves, and to make war on Mexico, though it cost them their existence as a people.

In their practice, nations agree with Paley; but does any one think that Massachusetts does exactly what is right at the present crisis?

> "A drab of state, a cloth-o'-silver slut,
> To have her train borne up, and her soul trail in the dirt."

Practically speaking, the opponents to a reform in Massachusetts are not a hundred thousand politicians at the South, but a hundred thousand merchants and farmers here, who are more interested in commerce and agriculture than they are in humanity, and are not prepared to do justice to the slave and to Mexico, *cost what it may.* I quarrel not with far-off foes, but with those who, near at home, co-operate with, and do the bidding of those far away, and without whom the latter would be harmless. We are accustomed to say, that the mass of men are unprepared; but improvement is slow, because the few are not materially wiser or better than the many. It is not so important that many should be as good as you, as that there be some absolute goodness somewhere; for that will leaven the whole lump. There are thousands who are in *opinion* opposed to slavery and to the war, who yet in effect do nothing to put an end to them; who, esteeming themselves children of Washington and Franklin, sit down with their hands in their pockets, and say that they know not what to do, and do nothing; who even postpone the question of freedom to the question of free-trade, and quietly read the prices-current along with the latest advices from Mexico, after dinner, and, it may be, fall asleep over them both. What is the price-current of an honest man and patriot to-day? They hesitate, and they regret, and sometimes they petition; but they do nothing in earnest and with effect. They will wait, well-disposed, for others to remedy the evil, that they may no longer have it to regret. At most, they give only a cheap vote, and a feeble countenance and God-speed, to the right, as it goes by them. There are nine hundred and ninety-nine patrons of virtue to one virtuous man; but it is easier to deal with the real possessor of a thing than with the temporary guardian of it.

All voting is a sort of gaming, like chequers or backgammon, with a slight moral tinge to it, a playing with right and wrong, with moral questions; and betting naturally accompanies it. The character of the voters is not staked. I cast my vote, perchance, as I think right; but I am not vitally concerned that that right should prevail. I am willing to leave it to the majority. Its obligation, therefore, never exceeds that of expediency. Even voting *for the right* is *doing* nothing for it. It is only expressing to men feebly your desire that it should prevail. A wise man will not leave the right to the mercy of chance, nor wish it to prevail through the power of the majority. There is but little virtue in the action of masses of men. When the majority shall at length vote for the abolition of slavery, it will be because they are indifferent to slavery, or because there is but little slavery left to be abolished by their vote. *They* will then be the only slaves. Only *his* vote can hasten the abolition of slavery who asserts his own freedom by his vote.

I hear of a convention to be held at Baltimore, or elsewhere, for the selection of a candidate for the Presidency, made up chiefly of editors, and men who are politicians by profession; but I think, what is it to any independent, intelligent, and respectable man what decision they may come to, shall we not have the advantage of his wisdom and honesty, nevertheless? Can we not count upon some independent votes? Are there not many individuals in the country who do not attend conventions? But no: I find that the respectable man, so called, has immediately drifted from his position, and despairs of his country, when his country has more reason to despair of him. He forthwith adopts one of the candidates thus selected as the only *available* one, thus proving that he is himself *available* for any purposes of the demagogue. His vote is of no more worth than that of any unprincipled foreigner or hireling native, who may have been bought. Oh for a man who is a *man,* and, as my neighbor says, has a bone in his back which you cannot pass your hand through! Our statistics are at fault: the population has been returned too large. How many *men* are there to a square thousand miles in this country? Hardly one. Does not America offer any inducement for men to settle here? The American has dwindled into an Odd Fellow,—one who may be known by the development of his organ of gregariousness, and a manifest lack of intellect and cheerful self-reliance; whose first and chief concern, on coming into the world, is to see that the alms-houses are in good repair; and, before yet he has lawfully donned the virile garb, to collect a fund for the support of the widows and orphans that may be; who, in short, ventures to live only by the aid of the mutual insurance company, which has promised to bury him decently.

It is not a man's duty, as a matter of course, to devote himself to the eradication of any, even the most enormous wrong; he may still properly have other concerns to engage him; but it is his duty, at least, to wash his hands of it, and, if he gives it no thought longer, not to give it practically his support. If I devote myself to other pursuits and contemplations, I must first see, at least, that I do not pursue them sitting upon another man's shoulders.

I must get off him first, that he may pursue his contemplations too. See what gross inconsistency is tolerated. I have heard some of my townsmen say, "I should like to have them order me out to help put down an insurrection of the slaves, or to march to Mexico,—see if I would go;" and yet these very men have each, directly by their allegiance, and so indirectly, at least, by their money, furnished a substitute. The soldier is applauded who refuses to serve in an unjust war by those who do not refuse to sustain the unjust government which makes the war; is applauded by those whose own act and authority he disregards and sets at nought; as if the State were penitent to that degree that it hired one to scourge it while it sinned, but not to that degree that it left off sinning for a moment. Thus, under the name of order and civil government, we are all made at last to pay homage to and support our own meanness. After the first blush of sin, comes its indifference; and from immoral it becomes, as it were, *un*moral, and not quite unnecessary to that life which we have made.

The broadest and most prevalent error requires the most disinterested virtue to sustain it. The slight reproach to which the virtue of patriotism is commonly liable, the noble are most likely to incur. Those who, while they disapprove of the character and measures of a government, yield to it their allegiance and support, are undoubtedly its most conscientious supporters, and so frequently the most serious obstacles to reform. Some are petitioning the State to dissolve the Union, to disregard the requisitions of the President. Why do they not dissolve it themselves,—the union between themselves and the State,—and refuse to pay their quota into its treasury? Do not they stand in the same relation to the State, that the State does to the Union? And have not the same reasons prevented the State from resisting the Union, which have prevented them from resisting the State?

How can a man be satisfied to entertain an opinion merely, and enjoy *it?* Is there any enjoyment in it, if his opinion is that he is aggrieved? If you are cheated out of a single dollar by your neighbor, you do not rest satisfied with knowing that you are cheated, or with saying that you are cheated, or even with petitioning him to pay you your due; but you take effectual steps at once to obtain the full amount, and see that you are never cheated again. Action from principle,—the perception and the performance of right,—changes things and relations; it is essentially revolutionary, and does not consist wholly with any thing which was. It not only divides states and churches, it divides families; aye, it divides the *individual,* separating the diabolical in him from the divine.

Unjust laws exist; shall we be content to obey them, or shall we endeavor to amend them, and obey them until we have succeeded, or shall we transgress them at once? Men generally, under such a government as this, think that they ought to wait until they have persuaded the majority to alter them. They think that, if they should resist, the remedy would be worse than the evil. But it is the fault of the government itself that the remedy is worse than the evil. *It* makes it worse. Why is it not more apt to anticipate and provide for reform? Why does it not cherish its wise minority. Why does it cry and resist before it is hurt? Why does it not encourage its citizens to be on the alert to point out its faults, and *do* better than it would have them? Why does it always crucify Christ, and excommunicate Copernicus and Luther, and pronounce Washington and Franklin rebels?

One would think, that a deliberate and practical denial of its authority was the only offence never contemplated by government; else, why has it not assigned its definite, its suitable and proportionate penalty? If a man who has no property refuses but once to earn nine shillings for the State, he is put in prison for a period unlimited by any law that I know, and determined only by the discretion of those who placed him there; but if he should steal ninety times nine shillings from the State, he is soon permitted to go at large again.

If the injustice is part of the necessary friction of the machine of government, let it go, let it go: perchance it will wear smooth,—certainly the machine will wear out. If the injustice has a spring, or a pulley, or a rope, or a crank, exclusively for itself, then perhaps you may consider whether the remedy will not be worse than the evil; but if it is of such a nature that it requires you to be the agent of injustice to another, then, I say, break the law. Let your life be a counter friction to stop the machine. What I have to do is to see, at any rate, that I do not lend myself to the wrong which I condemn.

As for adopting the ways which the State has provided for remedying the evil, I know not of such ways. They take too much time, and a man's life will be gone. I have other affairs to attend to. I came into this world, not chiefly to make this a good place to live in, but to live in it, be it good or bad. A man has not every thing to do, but something; and because he cannot do *every thing*, it is not necessary that he should do *something* wrong. It is not my business to be petitioning the governor or the legislature any more than it is theirs to petition me; and, if they should not hear my petition, what should I do then? But in this case the State has provided no way: its very Constitution is the evil. This may seem to be harsh and stubborn and unconcilliatory; but it is to treat with the utmost kindness and consideration the only spirit that can appreciate or deserves it. So is all change for the better, like birth and death which convulse the body.

I do not hesitate to say, that those who call themselves abolitionists should at once effectually withdraw their support, both in person and property, from the government of Massachusetts, and not wait till they constitute a majority of one, before they suffer the right to prevail through them. I think that it is enough if they have God on their side, without waiting for that other one. Moreover, any man more right than his neighbors, constitutes a majority of one already.

I meet this American government, or its representative the State government, directly, and face to face, once a year, no more, in the person of its tax-gatherer; this is the only mode in which a man situated as I am necessarily meets it; and it then says distinctly, Recognize me; and the simplest, the most effectual, and, in the present posture of affairs, the indispensablest mode of treating with it on this head, of expressing your little satisfaction with and love for it, is to deny it then. My civil neighbor, the tax-gatherer, is the very man I have to deal with,—for it is, after all, with men and not with parchment that I quarrel,—and he has voluntarily chosen to be an agent of the government. How shall he ever know well what he is and does as an officer of the government, or as a man, until he is obliged to consider whether he shall treat me, his neighbor, for whom he has respect, as a neighbor and well-disposed man, or as a maniac and disturber of the peace, and see if he can get over this obstruction to his neighborliness without a ruder and more impetuous thought or speech corresponding with his action? I know this well, that if one thousand, if one hundred, if ten men whom I could name,— if ten *honest* men only,—aye, if *one* HONEST man, in this State of Massachusetts, *ceasing to hold slaves,* were actually to withdraw from this copartnership, and be locked up in the county jail therefor, it would be the abolition of slavery in America. For it matters not how small the beginning may seem to be: what is once well done is done for ever. But we love better to talk about it: that we say is our mission. Reform keeps many scores of newspapers in its service, but not one man. If my esteemed neighbor, the State's ambassador, who will devote his days to the settlement of the question of human rights in the Council Chamber, instead of being threatened with the prisons of Carolina, were to sit down the prisoner of Massachusetts, that State which is so anxious to foist the sin of slavery upon her sister,—though at present she can discover only an act of inhospitality to be the ground of a quarrel with her,—the Legislature would not wholly waive the subject the following winter.

Under a government which imprisons any unjustly, the true place for a just man is also a prison. The proper place to-day, the only place which Massachusetts has provided for her freer and less desponding spirits, is in her prisons, to be put out and locked out of the State by her own act, as they have already put themselves out by their principles. It is there that the fugitive slave, and the Mexican prisoner on parole, and the Indian come to plead the wrongs of his race, should find them; on that separate, but more free and honorable ground, where the State places those who are not *with* her but *against* her,—the only house in a slave-state in which a free man can abide with honor. If any think that their influence would be lost there, and their voices no longer afflict the ear of the State, that they would not be as an enemy within its walls, they do not know by how much truth is stronger than error, nor how much more eloquently and effectively he can combat injustice who has experienced a little in his own person. Cast your whole vote, not a strip of paper merely, but your whole influence. A minority is powerless while it conforms to the majority; it is not even a minority then; but it is irresistible when it clogs by its whole weight. If the alternative is to keep all just men in prison, or give up war and slavery, the State will not hesitate which to choose. If a thousand men were not to pay their tax-bills this year, that would not be a violent and bloody measure, as it would be to pay them, and enable the State to commit violence and shed innocent blood. This is, in fact, the definition of a peaceable revolution, if any such is possible. If the tax-gatherer, or any other public officer, asks me, as one has done, "But what shall I do?" my answer is, "If you really wish to do any thing, resign your office." When the subject has refused allegiance, and the officer has resigned his office, then the revolution is accomplished. But even suppose blood should flow. Is there not a sort of blood shed when the conscience is wounded? Through this wound a man's real manhood and immortality flow out, and he bleeds to an everlasting death. I see this blood flowing now.

I have contemplated the imprisonment of the offender, rather than the seizure of his goods,—though both will serve the same purpose,—because they who assert the purest right, and consequently are most dangerous to a corrupt State, commonly have not spent much time in accumulating property. To such the State renders comparatively small service, and a slight tax is wont to appear exorbitant, particularly if they are obliged to earn it by special labor with their hands. If there were one who lived wholly with-out the use of money, the State itself would hesitate to demand it of him. But the rich man—not to make any invidious comparison—is always sold to the institution which makes him rich. Absolutely speaking, the more money, the less virtue; for money comes between a man and his objects, and obtains them for him; and it was certainly no great virtue to obtain it. It puts to rest many questions which he would otherwise be taxed to answer; while the only new question which it puts is the hard but superfluous one, how to spend it. Thus his moral ground is taken from under his feet. The opportunities of living are diminished in proportion as what are called the "means" are increased. The best thing a man can do for his culture when he is rich is to endeavour to carry out those schemes which he entertained when he was poor. Christ answered the Herodians according to their condition. "Show me the tribute-money," said he;—and one took a penny out his pocket;—If you use money which has the image of Caesar on it, and which he has made current and valuable, that is, *if you are men of the State,* and gladly enjoy the advantages of Caesar's government, then pay him back some of his own when he demands it; "Render therefore to Caesar that which is Caesar's, and to God those things which are God's,"—leaving them no wiser than before as to which was which; for they did not wish to know.

When I converse with the freest of my neighbors, I perceive that, whatever they may say about the magnitude and seriousness of the question, and their regard for the public tranquility, the long and the short of the matter is, that they cannot spare the protection of the existing government, and they dread the consequences of disobedience to it to their property and families. For my own part, I should not like to think that I ever rely on the protection of the State. But, if I deny the authority of the State when it presents its tax-bill, it will soon take and waste all my property, and so harass me and my children without end. This is hard. This makes it impossible for a man to live honestly and at the same time comfortably in outward respects. It will not be worth the while to accumulate property; that would be sure to go again. You must hire or squat somewhere, and raise but a small crop, and eat that soon. You must live within yourself, and depend upon yourself, always tucked up and ready for a start, and not have many affairs. A man may grow rich in Turkey even, if he will be in all respects a good subject of the Turkish government. Confucius said,—"If a State is governed by the principles of reason, poverty and misery are subjects of shame; if a State is not governed by the principles of reason, riches and honors are the subjects of shame." No: until I want the protection of Massachusetts to be extended to me in some distant southern port, where my liberty is endangered, or until I am bent solely on building up an estate at home by peaceful enterprise, I can afford to refuse allegiance to Massachusetts, and her right to my property and life. It costs me less in every sense to incur the penalty of disobedience to the State, than it would to obey. I should feel as if I were worth less in that case.

Some years ago, the State met me in behalf of the church, and commanded me to pay a certain sum toward the support of a clergyman whose preaching my father attended, but never I myself. "Pay it," it said, "or be locked up in the jail." I declined to pay. But, unfortunately, another man saw fit to pay it. I did not see why the schoolmaster should be taxed to support the priest, and not the priest the schoolmaster; for I was not the State's schoolmaster, but I supported myself by voluntary subscription. I did not see why the lyceum should not present its tax-bill, and have the State to back its demand, as well as the church. However, at the request of the selectmen, I condescended to make some such statement as this in writing:—"Know all men by these presents, that I, Henry Thoreau, do not wish to be regarded as a member of any incorporated society which I have not joined." This I gave to the town-clerk; and he has it. The State, having thus learned that I did not wish to be regarded as a member of that church, has never made a like demand on me since; though it said that it must adhere to its original presumption that time. If I had known how to name them, I should then have signed off in detail from all the societies which I never signed on to; but I did not know where to find a complete list.

I have paid no poll-tax for six years. I was put into a jail once on this account, for one night; and, as I stood considering the walls of solid stone, two or three feet thick, the door of wood and iron, a foot thick, and the iron grating which strained the light, I could not help being struck with the foolishness of that institution which treated me as if I were mere flesh and blood and bones, to be locked up. I wondered that it should have concluded at length that this was the best use it could put me to, and had never thought to avail itself of my services in some way. I saw that, if there was a wall of stone between me and my townsmen, there was a still more difficult one to climb or break through, before they could get to be as free as I was. I did not for a moment feel confined, and the walls seemed a great waste of stone and mortar. I felt as if I alone of all my townsmen had paid my tax. They plainly did not know how to treat me, but behaved like persons who are underbred. In every threat and in every compliment there was a blunder; for they thought that my chief desire was to stand the other side of that stone wall. I could not but smile to see how industriously they locked the door on my meditations, which followed them out again without let or hinderance, and *they* were really all that was dangerous. As they could not reach me, they had resolved to punish my body; just as boys, if they cannot come at some person against whom they have a spite, will abuse his dog. I saw that the State was half-witted, that it was timid as a lone woman with her silver spoons, and that it did not know its friends from its foes, and I lost all my remaining respect for it, and pitied it.

Thus the State never intentionally confronts a man's sense, intellectual or moral, but only his body, his senses. It is not armed with superior wit or honesty, but with superior physical strength. I was not born to be forced. I will breathe after my own fashion. Let us see who is the strongest. What force has a multitude? They only can force me who obey a higher law than I. They force me to become like themselves. I do not hear of *men* being *forced* to live this way or that by masses of men. What sort of life were that to live? When I meet a government which says to me, "Your money or your life," why should I be in haste to give it my money? It may be in a great strait, and not know what to do: I cannot help that. It must help itself; do as I do. It is not worth the while to snivel about it. I am not responsible for the successful working of the machinery of society. I am not the son of the engineer. I perceive that, when an acorn and a chestnut fall side by side, the one does not remain inert to make way for the other, but both obey their own laws, and spring and grow and flourish as best they can, till one, perchance, overshadows and destroys the other. If a plant cannot live according to its nature, it dies; and so a man.

The night in prison was novel and interesting enough. The prisoners in their shirt-sleeves were enjoying a chat and the evening air in the door-way, when I entered. But the jailer said, "Come, boys, it is time to lock up;" and so they dispersed, and I heard the sound of their steps returning into the hollow apartments. My roommate was introduced to me by the jailer, as "a first-rate fellow and a clever man." When the door was locked, he showed me where to hang my hat, and how he managed matters there. The rooms were whitewashed once a month; and this one, at least, was the whitest, most simply furnished, and probably the neatest apartment in the town. He naturally wanted to know where I came from, and what brought me there; and, when I had told him, I asked him in my turn how he came there, presuming him to be an honest man, of course; and, as the world goes, I believe he was. "Why," said he, "they accuse me of burning a barn; but I never did it." As near as I could discover, he had probably gone to bed in a barn when drunk, and smoked his pipe there; and so a barn was burnt. He had the reputation of being a clever man, had been there some three months waiting for his trial to come on, and would have to wait as much longer; but he was quite domesticated and contented, since he got his board for nothing, and thought that he was well treated.

He occupied one window, and I the other; and I saw, that, if one stayed there long, his principal business would be to look out the window. I had soon read all the tracts that were left there, and examined where former prisoners had broken out, and where a grate had been sawed off, and heard the history of the various occupants of that room; for I found that even here there was a history and a gossip which never circulated beyond the walls of the jail. Probably this is the only house in the town where verses are composed, which are afterward printed in a circular form, but not published. I was shown quite a long list of verses which were composed by some young men who had been detected in an attempt to escape, who avenged themselves by singing them.

I pumped my fellow-prisoner as dry as I could, for fear I should never see him again; but at length he showed me which was my bed, and left me to blow out the lamp.

It was like travelling into a far country, such as I had never expected to behold, to lie there for one night. It seemed to me that I never had heard the town-clock strike before, nor the evening sounds of the village; for we slept with the windows open, which were inside the grating. It was to see my native village in the light of the middle ages, and our Concord was turned into a Rhine stream, and visions of knights and castles passed before me. They were the voices of old burghers that I heard in the streets. I was an involuntary spectator and auditor of whatever was done and said in the kitchen of the adjacent village-inn,—a wholly new and rare experience to me. It was a closer view of my native town. I was fairly inside of it. I never had seen its institutions before. This is one of its peculiar institutions; for it is a shire town. I began to comprehend what its inhabitants were about.

In the morning, our breakfasts were put through the hole in the door, in small oblong-square tin pans, made to fit, and holding a pint of chocolate, with brown bread, and an iron spoon. When they called for the vessels again, I was green enough to return what bread I had left; but my comrade seized it, and said that I should lay that up for lunch or dinner. Soon after, he was let out to work at haying in a neighboring field, whither he went every day, and would not be back till noon; so he bade me good-day, saying that he doubted if he should see me again.

When I came out of prison,—for some one interfered, and paid the tax,—I did not perceive that great changes had taken place on the common, such as he observed who went in a youth, and emerged a tottering and gray-headed man; and yet a change had to my eyes come over the scene,—the town, and State, and country,—greater than any that mere time could effect. I saw yet more distinctly the State in which I lived. I saw to what extent the people among whom I lived could be trusted as good neighbors and friends; that their friendship was for summer weather only, that they did not greatly purpose to do right; that they were a distinct race from me by their prejudices and superstitions, as the Chinamen and Malays are; that, in their sacrifices to humanity, they ran no risks, not even to their property; that, after all, they were not so noble but they treated the thief as he had treated them, and hoped, by a certain outward observance and a few prayers, and by walking in a particular straight though useless path from time to time, to save their souls. This may be to judge my neighbors harshly; for I believe that most of them are not aware that they have such an institution as the jail in their village.

It was formerly the custom in our village, when a poor debtor came out of jail, for his acquaintances to salute him, looking through their fingers, which were crossed to represent the grating of a jail window, "How do ye do?" My neighbors did not thus salute me, but first looked at me, and then at one another, as if I had returned from a long journey. I was put into jail as I was going to the shoemaker's to get a shoe which was mended. When I was let out the next morning,

I proceeded to finish my errand, and, having put on my mended shoe, joined a huckleberry party, who were impatient to put themselves under my conduct; and in half an hour,—for the horse was soon tackled,—was in the midst of a huckleberry field, on one of our highest hills, two miles off; and then the State was nowhere to be seen.

This is the whole history of "My Prisons."

I have never declined paying the highway tax, because I am as desirous of being a good neighbor as I am of being a bad subject; and, as for supporting schools, I am doing my part to educate my fellow-countrymen now. It is for no particular item in the tax-bill that I refuse to pay it. I simply wish to refuse allegiance to the State, to withdraw and stand aloof from it effectually. I do not care to trace the course of my dollar, if I could, till it buys a man, or a musket to shoot one with,—the dollar is innocent,—but I am concerned to trace the effects of my allegiance. In fact, I quietly declare war with the State, after my fashion, though I will still make what use and get what advantage of her I can, as is usual in such cases.

If others pay the tax which is demanded of me, from a sympathy with the State, they do but what they have already done in their own case, or rather they abet injustice to a greater extent than the State requires. If they pay the tax from a mistaken interest in the individual taxed, to save his property or prevent his going to jail, it is because they have not considered wisely how far they let their private feelings interfere with the public good.

This, then, is my position at present. But one cannot be too much on his guard in such a case, lest his action be biased by obstinacy, or an undue regard for the opinions of men. Let him see that he does only what belongs to himself and to the hour.

I think sometimes, Why, this people mean well; they are only ignorant; they would do better if they knew how: why give your neighbors this pain to treat you as they are not inclined to? But I think, again, this is no reason why I should do as they do, or permit others to suffer much greater pain of a different kind. Again, I sometimes say to myself, When many millions of men, without heat, without ill-will, without personal feeling of any kind, demand of you a few shillings only, without the possibility, such is their constitution, of retracting or altering their present demand, and without the possibility, on your side, of appeal to any other millions, why expose yourself to this overwhelming brute force? You do not resist cold and hunger, the winds and the waves, thus obstinately; you quietly submit to a thousand similar necessities. You do not put your head into the fire. But just in proportion as I regard this as not wholly a brute force, but partly a human force, and consider that I have relations to those millions as to so many millions of men, and not of mere brute or inanimate things, I see that appeal is possible, first and instantaneously, from them to the Maker of them, and, secondly, from them to themselves. But, if I put my head deliberately into the fire, there is no appeal to fire or to the Maker of fire, and I have only myself to blame. If I could convince myself that I have any right to be satisfied with men as they are, and to treat them accordingly, and not according, in some respects, to my requisitions and expectations of what they and I ought to be, then, like a good Mussulman and fatalist, I should endeavor to be satisfied with things as they are, and say it is the will of God. And, above all, there is this difference between resisting this and a purely brute or natural force, that I can resist this with some effect; but I cannot expect, like Orpheus, to change the nature of the rocks and trees and beasts.

I do not wish to quarrel with any man or nation. I do not wish to split hairs, to make fine distinctions, or set myself up as better than my neighbors. I seek rather, I may say, even an excuse for conforming to the laws of the land. I am but too ready to conform to them. Indeed I have reason to suspect myself on this head; and each year, as the tax-gatherer comes round, I find myself disposed to review the acts and position of the general and state governments, and the spirit of the people, to discover a pretext for conformity. I believe that the State will soon be able to take all my work of this sort out of my hands, and then I shall be no better a patriot than my fellow-countrymen. Seen from a lower point of view, the Constitution, with all its faults, is very good; the law and the courts are very respectable; even this State and this American government are, in many respects, very admirable and rare things, to be thankful for, such as a great many have described them; but seen from a point of view a little higher, they are what I have described them; seen from a higher still, and the highest, who shall say what they are, or that they are worth looking at or thinking of at all?

However, the government does not concern me much, and I shall bestow the fewest possible thoughts on it. It is not many moments that I live under a government, even in this world. If a man is thought-free, fancy-free, imagination-free, that which *is not* never for a long time appearing *to be to* him, unwise rulers or reformers cannot fatally interrupt him.

I know that most men think differently from myself; but those whose lives are by profession devoted to the study of these or kindred subjects, content me as little as any. Statesmen and legislators, standing so completely within the institution, never distinctly and nakedly behold it. They speak of moving society, but have no resting-place without it. They may be men of a certain experience and discrimination, and have no doubt invented ingenious and even useful systems, for which we sincerely thank them; but all their wit and usefulness lie within certain not very wide limits. They are wont to forget that the world is not governed by policy and expediency. Webster never goes behind government, and so cannot speak with authority about it. His words are wisdom to those legislators who contemplate no essential reform in the existing government; but for thinkers, and those who legislate for all time, he never once glances at the subject. I know of those whose serene and wise speculations on this theme would soon reveal the limits of his mind's range and hospitality. Yet, compared with the cheap professions of most reformers, and the still cheaper wisdom and eloquence of politicians in general, his are almost the only sensible and valuable words, and we thank Heaven for him. Comparatively, he is always strong, original, and, above all, practical. Still his quality is not wisdom, but prudence. The lawyer's truth is not Truth, but consistency, or a consistent expediency. Truth is always in harmony with herself, and is not concerned chiefly to reveal the justice that may consist with wrong-doing. He well deserves to be called, as he has been called, the Defender of the Constitution. There are really no blows to be given by him but defensive ones. He is not a leader, but a follower. His leaders are the men of '87. "I have never made an effort," he says, "and never propose to make an effort; I have never countenanced an effort, and never mean to countenance an effort, to disturb the arrangement as originally made, by which the various States came into the Union." Still thinking of the sanction which the Constitution gives to slavery, he says, "Because it was a part of the original compact,—let it stand." Notwithstanding his special acuteness and ability, he is unable to take a fact out of its merely political relations, and behold it as it lies absolutely to be disposed of by the intellect,—what, for instance, it behooves a man to do here in America to-day with regard to slavery,—but ventures, or is driven, to make some such desperate answer as the following, while professing to speak absolutely, and as a private man,—from which what new and singular code of social duties might be inferred?—"The manner," says he, "in which the governments of those States where slavery exists are to regulate it, is for their own consideration, under their responsibility to their constituents, to the general laws of propriety, humanity, and justice, and to God. Associations formed elsewhere, springing from a feeling of humanity, or any other cause, have nothing whatever to do with it. They have never received any encouragement from me, and they never will.[1]

They who know of no purer sources of truth, who have traced up its stream no higher, stand, and wisely stand, by the Bible and the Constitution, and drink at it there with reverence and humility; but they who behold where it comes trickling into this lake or that pool, gird up their loins once more, and continue their pilgrimage toward its fountain-head.

No man with a genius for legislation has appeared in America. They are rare in the history of the world. There are orators, politicians, and eloquent men, by the thousand; but the speaker has not yet opened his mouth to speak, who is capable of settling the much-vexed questions of the day. We love eloquence for its own sake, and not for any truth which it may utter, or any heroism it may inspire. Our legislators have not yet learned the comparative value of free-trade and of freedom, of union, and of rectitude, to a nation. They have no genius or talent for comparatively humble questions of taxation and finance, commerce and manufactures and agriculture. If we were left solely to the wordy wit of legislators in Congress for our guidance, uncorrected by the seasonable experience and the effectual complaints of the people, America would not long retain her mark among the nations. For eighteen hundred years, though perchance I have no right to say it, the New Testament has been written; yet where is the legislator who has wisdom and practical talent enough to avail himself of the light which it sheds on the science of legislation?

The authority of government, even such as I am willing to submit to,—for I will cheerfully obey those who know and can do better than I, and in many things even those who neither know nor can do so well,—is still an impure one: to be strictly just, it must have the sanction and consent of the governed. It can have no pure right over my person and property but what I concede to it. The progress from an absolute to a limited monarchy, from a limited monarchy to a democracy, is a progress toward a true respect for the individual. Is a democracy, such as we know it, the last improvement possible in government? Is it not possible to take a step further towards recognizing and organizing the rights of man? There will never be a really free and enlightened State, until the State comes to recognize the individual as a higher and independent power, from which all its own power and authority are derived, and treats him accordingly. I please myself with imagining a State at last which can afford to be just to all men, and to treat the individual with respect as a neighbor; which even would not think it inconsistent with its own repose, if a few were to live aloof from it, not meddling with it, nor embraced by it, who fulfilled all the duties of neighbors and fellow-men. A State which bore this kind of fruit, and suffered it to drop off as fast as it ripened, would prepare the way for a still more perfect and glorious State, which also I have imagined, but not yet anywhere seen.

---

1. These extracts have been inserted since the Lecture was read. [H.D.T. note]

HORACE BUSHNELL

"Christian Nurture"
(1847)

Throughout much of his long pastorate at the North Congregational Church in Hartford, Connecticut, Horace Bushnell (1802–1876) was embroiled in theological controversy. (In 1852 he avoided a heresy trial before the General Assembly of the Congregational Church only because his loyal, well-to-do parishioners withdrew their church's affiliation with the body.) Yet Bushnell was probably the most influential American religious thinker of the nineteenth century. What principally gave him that influence was his ingenuity in eloquently synthesizing—in his many sermons, lectures, and treatises—the inherited post-Calvinist strains of supernatural governance and original sin with newer naturalistic and Romantic notions of psychology and culture. One seminal argument that Bushnell pursued, in works like *God in Christ* and *Nature and the Supernatural,* was the idea that biblical events and commandments must be understood not as baldly literal statements but as faded social, emotive, and therefore figurative symbols nonetheless true for that fact. Another was the notion that God's spiritual authority is an immanent yet transcendent organic presence animating all of nature. This last idea was also at the foundation of Bushnell's liberalizing yet fundamentally conservative social thought.

Nowhere can this hybrid be better seen than in his famous discourse on child rearing. In it he disparaged not only the orthodox Calvinists' belief in children's unmixed depravity of heart but also the evangelicals' self-defeating and corrupting dependence on "rude" and hyperindividualistic adult conversions. On the other hand, the moral growth of experientially sinning yet "ductile" children could not be looked for in purely natural developments or lonely, Transcendendentalist introspections. Rather, the social-minded Bushnell argued, it came through children's "organic" imbibing of loving, God-infused parental influences that flowed in their unconscious wills in such subtle, powerful, and totalistic ways that they grew up to be Christians without ever knowing when they had not been such. Few texts in American thought have presented such a seductively authoritative model of moral acculturation as did "Christian Nurture."

Robert Bruce Mullin, *The Puritan as Yankee: A Life of Horace Bushnell* (Grand Rapids, 2002), is a solid biography that places due emphasis on Bushnell's ideas. The best introduction to Bushnell's thought remains H. Shelton Smith, ed., *Horace Bushnell* (New York, 1965). For two helpful studies of the social and cultural implications of Bushnell's theology, see Conrad Cherry, *Nature and Religious Imagination: From Edwards to Bushnell* (Philadelphia, 1980), 157–238; and David L. Smith, *Symbolism and Growth: The Religious Thought of Horace Bushnell* (Chico, Calif., 1981). An appreciative discussion of the strikingly modern character of Bushnell's social thought may be found in Daniel Walker Howe, "The Social Science of Horace Bushnell," *Journal of American History*, 70 (September 1983), 305–22.

Ephesians 6: 4. *Bring Them Up in the Nurture and Admonition of the Lord.*

THERE is then some kind of nurture which is of the Lord, deriving a quality and a power from Him, and communicating the same. Being instituted by Him, it will of necessity have a method and a character peculiar to itself, or rather to Him. It will be the Lord's way of education, having aims appropriate to Him, and if realized in its full intent, terminating in results impossible to be reached by any merely human method.

What then is the true idea of Christian, or divine nurture, as distinguished from that which is not Christian? What is its aim? What its method of working? What its powers and instruments? What its contemplated results? Few questions have greater moment, and it is one of the pleasant signs of the times, that the subject involved is beginning to attract new interest, and excite a spirit of inquiry which heretofore has not prevailed in our churches.

In ordinary cases, the better and more instructive way of handling this subject, would be to go directly into the practical methods of parental discipline, and show by what modes of government and instruction we may hope to realize the best results. But unhappily the public mind is pre-occupied extensively by a view of the whole subject, which I must regard as a theoretical mistake, and one which must involve, as long as it continues, practical results systematically injurious. This mistaken view it is necessary, if possible, to remove. And accordingly what I have to say will take the form of an argument on the question thus put in issue; though I design to gather round the subject, as I proceed, as much of practical instruction as the mode of the argument will suffer. Assuming then the question above stated, What is the true idea of Christian education?—I answer in the following proposition, which it will be the aim of my argument to establish, viz:

THAT THE CHILD IS TO GROW UP A CHRISTIAN. In other words, the aim, effort and expectation should be, not, as is commonly assumed, that the child is to grow up in sin, to be converted after he comes to a mature age; but that he is to open on the world as one that is spiritually renewed, not remembering the time when he went through a technical experience, but seeming rather to have loved what is good from his earliest years. I do not affirm that every child may, in fact and without exception, be so trained that he certainly will grow up a Christian. The qualifications it may be necessary to add, will be given in another place, where they can be stated more intelligibly.

This doctrine is not a novelty, now rashly and for the first time propounded, as some of you may be tempted to suppose. I shall show you, before I have done with the argument, that it is as old as the Christian church, and prevails extensively at the present day, in other parts of the world. Neither let your own experience raise a prejudice against it. If you have endeavored to realize the very truth I here affirm, but find that your children do not exhibit the character you have looked for; if they seem to be intractable to religious influences, and sometimes to display an apparent aversion to the very subject of religion itself, you are not, of course, to conclude that the doctrine I here maintain is untrue or impracticable. You may be unreasonable in your expectations of your children. Possibly, there may be seeds of holy principle in them, which you do not discover. A child acts out his present feelings, the feelings of the moment, without qualification or disguise. And how, many times, would you all appear, if you were to do the same? Will you expect of them to be better and more constant

Source: Horace Bushnell, *Views of Christian Nurture, and of Subjects Adjacent Thereto* (Hartford: Edwin Hunt, 1847), 5–22.

and consistent than yourselves; or will you rather expect them to be children, human children still, living a mixed life, trying out the good and evil of the world, and preparing, as older Christians do, when they have taken a lesson of sorrow and emptiness, to turn again to the true good? Perhaps they will go through a rough mental struggle, at some future day, and seem, to others and to themselves, there to have entered on a Christian life. And yet it may be true that there was still some root of right principle established in their childhood, which is here only quickened and developed, as when Christians of a mature age are revived in their piety, after a period of spiritual lethargy; for it is conceivable that regenerate character may exist, long before it is fully and formally developed. But suppose there is really no trace or seed of holy principle in your children, has there been no fault of piety and constancy in your church, no want of Christian sensibility and love to God, no carnal spirit visible to them and to all, and imparting its noxious and poisonous quality to the Christian atmosphere in which they have had their nurture? For it is not for you alone to realize all that is included in the idea of Christian education. It belongs to the church of God, according to the degree of its social power over you and in you and around your children, to bear a part of the responsibility with you. Then, again, have you nothing to blame in yourselves, no lack of faithfulness, no indiscretion of manner, or of temper, no mistake of duty, which, with a better and more cultivated piety, you would have been able to avoid? Have you been so nearly even with your privilege and duty, that you can find no relief but to lay some charge upon God, or comfort yourselves in the conviction that he has appointed the failure you deplore? When God marks out a plan of education, or sets up an aim to direct its efforts, you will see, at once, that he could not base it on a want of piety in you, or on any imperfections that flow from a want of piety. It must be a plan measured by Himself and the fullness of his own gracious intentions. Besides, you must not assume that we, in this age, are the best Christians that have ever lived, or most likely to produce all the fruits of piety. An assumption so pleasing to our vanity is more easily made than verified, but vanity is the weakest as it is the cheapest of all arguments. We have some good points, in which we compare favorably with other Christians, and Christians of other times, but our style of piety is sadly deficient, in many respects, and that to such a degree that we have little cause for self-congratulation. With all our activity and boldness of movement, there is a certain hardness and rudeness, a want of sensibility to things that do not lie in action, which cannot be too much deplored, or too soon rectified. We hold a piety of conquest rather than of love. A kind of public piety that is strenuous and fiery on great occasions, but wants the beauty of holiness, wants constancy, singleness of aim, loveliness, purity, richness, blamelessness, and—if I may add another term not so immediately religious, but one that carries, by association, a thousand religious qualities—wants domesticity of character; wants them, I mean, not as compared with the perfect standard of Christ, but as compared with other examples of piety that have been given in former times, and others that are given now.

For some reason, we do not make a Christian atmosphere about us,—do not produce the conviction that we are living unto God. There is a marvelous want of savor in our piety. It is a flower of autumn, colored as highly as it need be to the eye, but destitute of fragrance. It is too much to hope that, with such an instrument, we can fulfill the true idea of Christian education. Any such hope were even presumptuous. At the same time, there is no so ready way of removing the deficiencies just described, as to recall our churches to their duties in domestic life; those humble, daily, hourly duties, where the spirit we breathe shall be a perpetual element of power and love bathing the life of childhood.

Thus much it was necessary to say, for the removal of prejudices, that are likely to rise up in your minds, and make you inaccessible to the arguments I may offer. Let all such prejudices be removed, or, if this be too much, let them, at least, be suspended till you have heard what I have to advance; for it cannot be desired of you to believe any thing more than what is shown you by adequate proofs. Which also it is right to ask, that you will hear, if offered, in a spirit of mind, such as becomes our wretched and low attainments, and with a willingness to let God be exalted, though at the expense of some abasement in ourselves. In pursuing the argument, I shall

I. Collect some considerations which occur to us, viewing the subject on the human side, and then—

II. Show how far and by what methods God has justified, on his part, the doctrine we maintain.

There is then, as the subject appears to us—

1. No absurdity in supposing that children are to grow up in Christ. On the other hand, if there is no absurdity, there is a very clear moral incongruity in setting up a contrary supposition, to be the aim of a system of Christian education. There could not be a worse or more baleful implication given to a child, than that he is to reject God and all holy principle, till he has come to a mature age. What authority have you from the Scriptures to tell your child, or, by any sign, to show him that you do not expect him truly to love and obey God, till after he has spent whole years in hatred and wrong? What authority to make him feel that he is the most unprivileged of all human beings, capable of sin, but incapable of repentance; old enough to resist all good, but too young to receive any good whatever? It is reasonable to suppose that you have some express authority for a lesson so manifestly cruel and hurtful, else you would shudder to give it. I ask you for the chapter and verse, out of which it is derived. Meantime, wherein would it be less incongruous for you to teach your child that he is to lie and steal, and go the whole round of the vices and then, after he comes to mature age, reform his conduct by the rules of virtue? Perhaps you do not give your child to expect that he is to grow up in sin, you only expect that he will yourself. That is scarcely better, for that which is your expectation, will assuredly be his; and what is more, any attempt to maintain a discipline at war with your own secret expectations, will only make a hollow and worthless figment of that which should be an open earnest reality. You will never practically aim at what you practically despair of, and if you do not practically aim to unite your child to God, you will aim at something less, that is, something unchristian, wrong, sinful.

But my child is a sinner, you will say, and how can I expect him to begin a right life, until God gives him a new heart? This is the common way of speaking, and I state the objection in its own phraseology, that it may recognize itself. Who then has told you that a child cannot have the new heart of which you speak? Whence do you learn that if you live the life of Christ, before him and with him, the law of the Spirit of Life may not be such as to include and quicken him also? And why should it be thought incredible that there should be some really good principle awakened in the mind of a child? For this is all that is implied in a Christian state. The Christian is one who has simply *begun* to love what is good for its own sake, and why should it be thought impossible for a child to have this love begotten in him? Take any scheme of depravity you please, there is yet nothing in it to forbid the possibility that a child should be led, in his first moral act, to cleave unto what is good and right, any more than in the first of his twentieth year. He is, in that case, only a child converted to good, leading a mixed life as all Christians do. The good in him goes into combat with the evil, and holds a qualified sovereignty. And why may not this internal conflict of goodness cover the whole life from its dawn, as well as any part of it? And what more appropriate to the doctrine of spiritual influence itself, than to believe that as the Spirit of Jehovah fills all the worlds of matter, and holds a presence of power and government in all objects, so all human souls, the infantile as well as the adult, have a nurture of the Spirit appropriate to their age and their wants? What opinion is more essentially monstrous, in fact, than that which regards the Holy Spirit as having no agency in the immature souls of children, who are growing up helpless and unconscious into the perils of time?

2. It is to be expected that Christian education will radically differ from that which is not Christian. Now it is the very character and mark of all unchristian education, that it brings up the child for future conversion. No effort is made, save to form a habit of outward virtue, and, if God please to convert the family to something higher and better, after they come to the age of maturity, it is well. Is then Christian education, or the nurture of the Lord, no way different from this? Or is it rather to be supposed that it will have a higher aim and a more sacred character.

And, since it is the distinction of Christian parents, that they are themselves in the nurture of the Lord, since Christ and the Divine Love, communicated through him, are become the food of their life, what will they so naturally seek as to have their children partakers with them, heirs together with them in the grace of life? I am well aware of the common impression that Christian education is sufficiently distinguished by the endeavor of Christian parents to teach their children the lessons of scripture history, and the doctrines or dogmas of scripture theology. But if they are given to understand, at the same time, that these lessons can be expected to produce no fruit till they are come to a mature age, that they are to grow up still in the same character as other children do, who have no such instruction, what is this but to enforce the practical rejection of all the lessons taught them? And which, in truth, is better for them, to grow up in sin under scripture light, with a heart hardened by so many religious lessons; or to grow up in sin unvexed and unannoyed, by the wearisome drill of lectures that only discourage all practical benefit? Which is better, to be piously brought up to sin, or to be allowed quietly to vegetate in it? These are questions that I know not how to decide, but the doubt in which they leave us, will at least suffice to show that Christian education has, in this view, no such eminent advantages over that which is unchristian, as to raise any broad and dignified distinction between them. We certainly know that much of what is called Christian nurture, only serves to make the subject of religion odious, and that, as nearly as we can discover, in exact proportion to the amount of religious teaching received. And no small share of the difficulty to be overcome afterwards, in the struggle of conversion, is created in just this way. On the other hand, you will hear, for example, of cases like the following. A young man, correctly but not religiously brought up, light and gay in his manners and thoughtless hitherto in regard to any thing of a serious nature, happens accidentally one Sunday, while his friends are gone to ride, to take down a book on the evidences of Christianity. His eye, floating over one of the pages, becomes fixed, and he is surprised to find his feelings flowing out strangely into its holy truths. He is conscious of no struggle of hostility, but a new joy dawns in his being. Henceforth, to the end of a long and useful life, he is a Christian man. The love into which he was surprised continues to flow, and he is remarkable, in the churches, all his life long, as one of the most beautiful, healthful and dignified examples of Christian piety. Now a very little mis-education, called Christian, discouraging the piety it teaches, and making enmity itself a necessary ingredient in the struggle of conversion, conversion no reality without a struggle, might have sufficed to close the mind of this man against every thought of religion to the end of life. Such facts, (for the case above given is a fact and not a fancy) compel us to suspect the value of much that is called Christian education. They suggest the possibility also that Christian piety should begin in other and milder forms of exercise, than those which commonly distinguish the conversion of adults—that Christ himself, by that renewing Spirit who can sanctify from the womb, should be practically infused into the childish mind; in other words, that the house, having a domestic Spirit of grace dwelling in it, should become the church of childhood, the table and hearth a holy rite, and life an element of saving power. Something is wanted that is better than teaching, something that transcends mere effort and will-work—the loveliness of a good life, the repose of faith, the confidence of righteous expectation, the sacred and cheerful liberty of the Spirit—all glowing about the young soul, as a warm and genial nurture, and forming in it, by methods that are silent and imperceptible, a spirit of duty and religious obedience to God. This only is Christian nurture, the nurture of the Lord.

3. It is a fact that all Christian parents would like to see their children grow up in piety; and, the better Christians they are, the more earnestly they desire it; and, the more lovely and constant the Christian spirit they manifest, the more likely is it, in general, that their children will early display the Christian character. This is current opinion. But why should a Christian parent, the deeper his piety and the more closely he is drawn to God, be led to desire, the more earnestly, what, in God's view, is even absurd or impossible. And, if it be generally seen that the children of such are the more likely to become Christians early, what forbids the hope that, if they were better Christians still, living a more single and Christ-like life, and more cultivated in their views of family nurture, they might not see their children grow up in piety towards God. Or if they may not always see it as clearly as they desire, might they not still be able to implant some holy principle, which shall be the seed of a Christian character in their children, though not developed fully and visibly till a later period in life?

4. Assuming the corruption of human nature, when should we think it wisest to undertake or expect a remedy? When evil is young and pliant to good, or when it is confirmed by years of sinful habit? And when, in fact, is the human heart found to be so ductile to the motives of religion, as in the simple, ingenuous age of childhood? How easy it is then, as compared with the stubbornness of adult years, to make all wrong seem odious, all good lovely and desirable. If not discouraged by some ill-temper, which bruises all the gentle sensibilities, or repelled by some technical view of religious character, which puts it beyond his age; how ready is the child to be taken by good, as it were, beforehand, and yield his ductile nature to the truth and Spirit of God, and to a fixed prejudice against all that God forbids. He cannot understand, of course, in the earliest stage of childhood, the philosophy of religion as a renovated experience, and that is not the form of the first lessons he is to receive. He is not to be told that he must have a new heart and exercise faith in Christ's atonement. We are to understand, that a right spirit may be virtually exercised in children, when, as yet, it is not intellectually received, or as a form of doctrine. Thus if they are put upon an effort to be good, connecting the fact that God desires it and will help them in the endeavor, that is all which, in a very early age, they can receive, and that includes every thing—repentance, love, duty, dependence, faith. Nay, the operative truth necessary to a new life, may possibly be communicated through and from the parent, being revealed in his looks, manners and ways of life, before they are of an age to understand the teaching of words; for the Christian scheme, the gospel, is really wrapped up in the life of every Christian parent and beams out from him as a living epistle, before it escapes from the lips, or is taught in words. And the Spirit of truth may as well make this living truth effectual, as the preaching of the gospel itself. Never is it too early for good to be communicated. Infancy and childhood are the ages most pliant to good. And who can think it necessary that the plastic nature of childhood must first be hardened into stone, and stiffened into enmity towards God and all duty, before it can become a candidate for Christian character! There could not be a more unnecessary mistake, and it is as unnatural and pernicious, I fear, as it is unnecessary.

There are many who assume the radical goodness of human nature, and the work of Christian education is, in their view, only to educate, or educe the good that is in us. Let no one be disturbed by the suspicion of a coincidence between what I have here said and such a theory. The natural pravity of man is plainly asserted in the scriptures, and, if it were not, the familiar laws of physiology would require us to believe, what amounts to the same thing. And if neither scripture nor physiology taught us the doctrine, if the child was born as clear of natural prejudice or damage, as Adam before his sin, spiritual education, or, what is the same, probation, that which trains a being for a stable, intelligent virtue hereafter, would still involve an experiment of evil, therefore a fall and bondage under the laws of evil; so that, view the matter as we will, there is no so unreasonable assumption, none so wide of all just philosophy, as that which proposes to form a child to virtue, by simply educing or drawing out what is in him. The growth of Christian virtue is no vegetable process, no mere onward development. It involves a struggle with evil, a fall and rescue. The soul becomes established in holy virtue, as a free exercise, only as it is passed round the corner of fall and redemption, ascending thus unto God through a double experience, in which it learns the bitterness of evil and the worth of good, fighting its way out of one and achieving the other as a victory. The child, therefore, may as well begin life under a law of hereditary damage, as to plunge himself into evil by his own experiment, which he will as naturally do from the simple impulse of curiosity, or the instinct of knowledge, as from any noxious quality in his mold derived by descent. For it is not sin which he derives from his parents; at least not sin in any sense which imports blame, but only some prejudice to the perfect harmony of his mold, some kind of pravity or obliquity which inclines him to evil. These suggestions are offered, not as necessary to be received in every particular, but simply to show that the scheme of education proposed, is not to be identified with another, which assumes the radical goodness of human nature, and according to which, if it be true, Christian education is insignificant.

5. It is implied in all our religious philosophy, that if a child ever does any thing in a right spirit, ever loves any thing because it is good and right, it involves the dawn of a new life. This we cannot deny or doubt, without bringing in question our whole scheme of doctrine. Is it then incredible that some really good feeling should be called into exercise in a child? In all the discipline of the house, quickened as it should be by the Spirit of God, is it true that he can never once be brought to submit to parental authority lovingly and because it is right? Must we even hold the absurdity of the scripture counsel—"Children, obey your parents in the Lord, for this is right"? When we speak thus of a love to what is right and good, we must of course discriminate between the mere excitement of a natural sensibility to pleasure in the contemplation of what is good, (of which the worst minds are more or less capable) and a practical subordination of the soul to its power, a practical embrace of its law. The child must not only be touched with some gentle emotions towards what is right, but he must love it with a fixed love, love it for the sake of its principle, receive it as a vital and formative power. Nor is there any age, which offers itself to God's truth and love, and to that quickening spirit whence all good proceeds, with so much of ductile feeling and susceptibilities so tender. The child is under parental authority too for the very purpose, it would seem, of having the otherwise abstract principle of all duty impersonated in his parents and thus brought home to his practical embrace; so that, learning to obey his parents in the Lord because it is right, he may thus receive, before he can receive it intellectually, the principle of all piety and holy obedience. And when he is brought to exercise a spirit of true and loving submission to the good law of his parents, what will you see, many times, but a look of childish joy and a happy sweetness of manner and a ready delight in authority, as like to all the demonstrations of Christian experience, as any thing childish can be to what is mature?

6. Children have been so trained as never to remember the time when they began to be religious. Baxter was, at one time, greatly troubled concerning himself, because he could recollect no time, when there was a gracious change in his character. But he discovered, at length, that "education is as properly a means of grace as preaching," and thus found a sweeter comfort in his love to God, that he learned to love him so early. The European churches, generally, regard Christian piety more as a habit of life, formed under the training of childhood, and less as a marked spiritual change in experience. In Germany, for example, the church includes all the people, and it is remarkable that, under a scheme so loose, and with so much of pernicious error taught in the pulpit, there is yet so much of deep religious feeling, so much of lovely and simple character, and a savor of Christian piety so generally prevalent in the community. So true is this, that the German people are every day spoken of as a people religious by nature; no other way being observed of accounting for the strong religious bent they manifest. Whereas it is due, beyond any reasonable question, to the fact that children are placed under a form of treatment which expects them to be religious, and are not discouraged by the demand of an experience above their years. Again, the Moravian Brethren, it is agreed by all, give as ripe and graceful an exhibition of piety, as any body of Christians living on the earth, and it is the radical distinction of their system that it rests its power on Christian education. They make their churches schools of holy nurture to childhood, and expect their children to grow up there, as plants in the house of the Lord. Accordingly it is affirmed that not one in ten of the members of that church, recollects any time, when he began to be religious. Is it then incredible that what has been can be? Would it not be wiser and more modest, when facts are against us, to admit that there is certainly some bad error, either in our life, or in our doctrine, or in both, which it becomes us to amend?

Once more, if we narrowly examine the relation of parent and child, we shall not fail to discover something like a law of organic connection,[1] as regards character, subsisting between them. Such a connection as makes it easy to believe, and natural to expect that the faith of the one will be propagated in the other. Perhaps I should rather say, such a connection as induces the conviction that the character of one is actually included in that of the other, as a seed is formed in the capsule; and being there matured, by a nutriment derived from the stem, is gradually separated from it. It is a singular fact, that many believe substantially the same thing, in regard to evil character, but have no thought of any such possibility in regard to good. There has been much speculation, of late, as to whether a child is born in depravity, or whether the depraved character is superinduced afterwards. But, like many other great questions, it determines much less than is commonly supposed; for, according to the most proper view of the subject, a child is really not born till he emerges from the infantile state, and never before that time can be said to receive a separate and properly individual nature. The declaration of scripture, and the laws of physiology, I have already intimated, compel the belief that a child's nature is somehow depravated by descent from parents, who are under the corrupting effects of sin. But this, taken as a

---

1. Some persons have blamed the use here made of the term "organic," as a singularity of mine. So far from that, it is a term in common philosophic use in connection with all the great questions of government and society. The days of the "social compact" theory, for example, are gone by, and it is now held by almost all the late writers, that we naturally exist as organic bodies, just as we do as individuals, and that civil government is born with us, in virtue of our organic unity in bodies or States—that the State must legislate for itself in some way, just as the conscience legislates for the individual. Government is, in this view, the organic conscience of the State— no matter what may be the form, or who presides. [H.B. note]

question relating to the mere *punctum temporis,* or precise point of birth, is not a question of any so grave import, as is generally supposed; for the child, after birth, is still within the matrix of the parental life, and will be more or less, for many years. And the parental life will be flowing into him all that time, just as naturally, and by a law as truly organic, as when the sap of the trunk flows into a limb. We must not govern our thoughts, in such a matter, by our eyes; and because the physical separation has taken place, conclude that no organic relation remains. Even the physical being of the child is dependent still for nutrition on organic processes not in itself. Meantime, the mental being and character have scarcely begun to have a proper individual life. Will, in connection with conscience, is the basis of personality, or individuality, and these exist as yet only in their rudimental type, as when the form of a seed is beginning to be unfolded at the root of a flower. At first, the child is held as a mere passive lump in the arms, and he opens into conscious life under the soul of the parent streaming into his eyes and ears, through the manners and tones of the nursery. The kind and degree of passivity are gradually changed as life advances. A little farther on it is observed that a smile wakens a smile—any kind of sentiment or passion, playing in the face of the parent, wakens a responsive sentiment or passion. Irritation irritates, a frown withers, love expands a look congenial to itself, and why not holy love? Next the ear is opened to the understanding of words, but what words the child shall hear, he cannot choose, and has as little capacity to select the sentiments that are poured into his soul. Farther on, the parents begin to govern him by appeals to will, expressed in commands, and whatever their requirement may be, he can as little withstand it, as the violet can cool the scorching sun, or the tattered leaf can tame the hurricane. Next they appoint his school, choose his books, regulate his company, decide what form of religion, and what religious opinions he shall be taught, by taking him to a church of their own selection. In all this, they infringe upon no right of the child, they only fulfill an office which belongs to them. Their will and character are designed to be the matrix of the child's will and character. Meantime he approaches more and more closely, and by a gradual process, to the proper rank and responsibility of an individual creature, during all which process of separation, he is having their exercises and ways translated into him. Then, at last, he comes forth to act his part in such color of evil, (and why not of good?) as he has derived from them. The tendency of all our modern speculations is to an extreme individualism, and we carry out doctrines of free will so far as to make little or nothing of organic laws; not observing that character may be, to a great extent, only the free development of exercises previously wrought in us, or extended to us, when other wills had us within their sphere. All the Baptist theories of religion are based in this error. They assume as a first truth, that no such thing is possible as an organic connection of character, an assumption which is plainly refuted by what we see with our eyes, and, as I shall by and by show, by the declarations of scripture. We have much to say also, in common with the Baptists, about the beginning of moral agency, and we seem to fancy that there is some definite moment when a child becomes a moral agent, passing out of a condition where he is a moral nullity, and where no moral agency touches his being. Whereas he is rather to be regarded at the first, as lying within the moral agency of the parent and passing out by degrees through a course of mixed agency, to a proper independency and self-possession. The supposition that he becomes, at some certain moment, a complete moral agent, which a moment before he was not, is clumsy and has no agreement with observation. The separation is gradual. He is never, at any moment after birth, to be regarded as perfectly beyond the sphere of good and bad exercises; for the parent exercises himself in the child, playing his emotions and sentiments, and working a character in him, by virtue of an organic power. And this is the very idea of Christian education, that it begins with nurture or cultivation. And the intention is that the Christian life and spirit of the parents shall flow into the mind of the child, to blend with his incipient and half-formed exercises; that they shall thus beget their own good within him, their thoughts, opinions, faith and love, which are to become a little more, and yet a little more, his own separate exercise, but still the same in character. The contrary assumption, that virtue must be the product of separate and absolutely independent choice, is pure assumption. As regards the measure of personal merit and demerit, it is doubtless true that every subject of God is to be responsible only for what is his own. But virtue still is rather a *state* of being than an act or series of acts; and if we look at the causes which induce or prepare such a state, the will of the person himself may have a part among those causes more or less important, and it works no absurdity to suppose that one may be even prepared to such a state, by causes prior to his own will; so that, when he sets off to act for himself, his struggle and duty may be rather to sustain and perfect the state begun, than to produce a new one. Certain it is that we are never, at any age, so independent as to be wholly out of the reach of organic laws which affect our character. All society is organic—the church, the state, the school, the family,—and there is a spirit in each of these organisms, peculiar to itself, and more or less hostile, more or less favorable to religious character, and to some extent, at least, sovereign over the individual man. A very great share of the power in what is called a revival of religion, is organic power; nor is it any the less divine on that account. The child is only more within the power of organic laws than we all are. We possess only a mixed individuality all our life long. A pure, separate, individual man, living *wholly* within, and from him-self, is a mere fiction. No such person ever existed, or ever can. I need not say that this view of an organic connection of character subsisting between parent and child, lays a basis for notions of Christian education, far different from those which now prevail, under the cover of a merely fictitious and mischievous individualism.

Perhaps it may be necessary to add, that, in the strong language I have used concerning the organic connection of character between the parent and the child, it is not designed to assert a power in the parent to renew the child, or that the child can be renewed by any agency of the Spirit less immediate, than that which renews the parent himself. When a germ is formed on the stem of any plant, the formative instinct of the plant may be said in one view to produce it; but the same solar heat which quickens the plant, must quicken also the germ and sustain the internal action of growth, by a common presence in both. So if there be an organic power of character in the parent, such as that of which I have spoken, it is not a complete power in itself, but only such a power as demands the realizing presence of the Spirit of God, both in the parent and the child, to give it effect. As Paul said, "I have begotten you through the gospel," so may we say of the parent, who having a living gospel enveloped in his life, brings it into organic connection with the soul of childhood. But the declaration excludes the necessity of a divine influence, not more in one case than in the other.

Such are some of the considerations that offer themselves, viewing our subject on the human side, or as it appears in the light of human evidence—all concurring to produce the conviction, that it is the only true idea of Christian education, that the child is to grow up in the life of the parent, and be a Christian, in principle, from his earliest years.

HERMAN MELVILLE

"Hawthorne and His Mosses"
(1850)

"I love all men who dive." In announcing this preference Herman Melville (1819–1891) could have been holding a mirror up to himself. Certainly no writer in America—indeed in modern literature—has sought to plunge more deeply into the philosophical and psychological depths of human consciousness in his fiction than Melville. The tour de force of this sort of plunging was, of course, *Moby-Dick*. But it was also much in evidence in his extraordinary review of a collection of short stories by Nathaniel Hawthorne (1804–1864), whom he had just opportunely met. Hawthorne was then most admired, despite the recent publication of his *Scarlet Letter,* as a genteel writer of brightly idealized tales and sketches. In his review Melville exuberantly exploded this comforting stereotype by calling attention, as twentieth-century critics later would also, to the "blackness" he found displayed everywhere in Hawthorne's best stories.

But the most interesting aspect of this essay was Melville's assimilation of Hawthorne to his powerful, if tension-filled, call for the integration of the Romantic intellect with American democratic culture. Thus, through his hot-souled Virginian persona, Melville thundered for the end to "literary flunkeyism towards England" and for a new collective, democratic literature to match America's new and future political greatness. Yet in other places Melville also argued that such a democratic literature, if it was to be truly great, could only be constituted, as Hawthorne's was, by *both* a sensibility of all-embracing "love and humor" and a deep intellectual vision too disturbing and profound to be easily accessible to the multitude. Herein, according to Melville, lay the genius of writers like Shakespeare and now Hawthorne: They contrived genial masks to soothe the complacent and cowardly while flashing forth in "cunning glimpses" the fearful but vital truths that would be "all but madness for any good man, in his own proper character, to utter, or even hint of." With his prescription for genius *and* popularity announced, Melville turned to completing the novel that would prove him right by half.

Andrew Delbanco's *Melville: His World and Work* (New York, 2005), is a splendid critical biography. For two differing interpretations of Hawthorne and Melville's "highbrow" Romanticism, see Henry Nash Smith, *Democracy and the Novel: Popular Resistance to Classic American Writers* (New York, 1978), 3–55; and Michael T. Gilmore, *American Romanticism and the Marketplace* (Chicago, 1985), 52–153. The cultural background of Melville's critical outlook are helpfully illuminated in Perry Miller, *The Raven and the Whale: The War of Words and Wits in the Era of Poe and Melville* (New York, 1956); and Thomas Bender, *New York Intellect: A History of Intellectual Life in New York City, from 1750 to the Beginnings of Our Own Time* (New York, 1987), 119–68. For an excellent study that emphasizes the affinities between Melville's thought and that of leading European Romantics, see Robert Milder, *Exiled Royalties: Melville and the Life We Imagine* (New York, 2006).

By a Virginian Spending July in Vermont

A papered chamber in a fine old farm-house—a mile from any other dwelling, and dipped to the eaves in foliage—surrounded by mountains, old woods, and Indian ponds,—this, surely, is the place to write of Hawthorne. Some charm is in this northern air, for love and duty seem both impelling to the task. A man of a deep and noble nature has seized me in this seclusion. His wild, witch voice rings through me; or, in softer cadences, I seem to hear it in the songs of the hill-side birds, that sing in the larch trees at my window.

Would that all excellent books were foundlings, without father or mother, that so it might be, we could glorify them, without including their ostensible authors. Nor would any true man take exception to this;—least of all, he who writes,—"When the Artist rises high enough to achieve the Beautiful, the symbol by which he makes it perceptible to mortal senses becomes of little value in his eyes, while his spirit possesses itself in the enjoyment of the reality."

But more than this. I know not what would be the right name to put on the title-page of an excellent book, but this I feel, that the names of all fine authors are fictitious ones, far more so than that of Junius,—simply standing, as they do, for the mystical, ever-eluding Spirit of all Beauty, which ubiquitously possesses men of genius. Purely imaginative as this fancy may appear, it nevertheless seems to receive some warranty from the fact, that on a personal interview no great author has ever come up to the idea of his reader. But that dust of which our bodies are composed, how can it fitly express the nobler intelligences among us? With reverence be it spoken, that not even in the case of one deemed more than man, not even in our Saviour, did his visible frame betoken any-thing of the augustness of the nature within. Else, how could those Jewish eyewitnesses fail to see heaven in his glance.

It is curious, how a man may travel along a country road, and yet miss the grandest, or sweetest of prospects, by reason of an intervening hedge, so like all other hedges, as in no way to hint of the wide landscape beyond. So has it been with me concerning the enchant-ing landscape in the soul of this Hawthorne, this most excellent Man of Mosses. His "Old Manse" has been written now four years, but I never read it till a day or two since. I had seen it in the book-stores—heard of it often—even had it recommended to me by a tasteful friend, as a rare, quiet book, perhaps too deserving of popularity to be popular. But there are so many books called "excellent," and so much unpopular merit, that amid the thick stir of other things, the hint of my tasteful friend was disregarded; and for four years the Mosses on the old Manse never refreshed me with their perennial green. It may be, how-ever, that all this while, the book, like wine, was only improving in flavor and body. At any rate, it so chanced that this long procrastination eventuated in a happy result. At breakfast the other day, a mountain girl, a cousin of mine, who for the last two weeks has every morning helped me to strawberries and raspberries,—which, like the roses and pearls in the fairy-tale, seemed to fall into the saucer from those strawberry-beds her cheeks,—this delightful creature, this charming Cherry says to me—"I see you spend your mornings in the hay-mow; and yesterday I found there 'Dwight's Travels in New England.' Now I have something far better than that,—something more congenial to our summer on these hills.

Source: *The Writings of Herman Melville: The Northwestern-Newberry Edition*, ed. Harrison Hayford, Hershel Parker, and G. Thomas Tanselle, vol. 9: *The Piazza Tales and Other Prose Pieces, 1839–1860*, ed. Harrison Hayford et al. (Evanston, Ill.: Northwestern University Press; Chicago: Newberry Library, 1987), 239–53. Reprinted by permission of Northwestern University Press, Copyright © 1987.

Take these raspberries, and then I will give you some moss."—"Moss!" said I.—"Yes, and you must take it to the barn with you, and good-bye to 'Dwight.'"

With that she left me, and soon returned with a volume, verdantly bound, and garnished with a curious frontispiece in green,—nothing less, than a fragment of real moss cunningly pressed to a fly-leaf.—"Why this," said I spilling my raspberries, "this is the 'Mosses from an Old Manse.'" "Yes" said cousin Cherry "yes, it is that flowery Hawthorne."—"Hawthorne and Mosses" said I "no more: it is morning: it is July in the country: and I am off for the barn."

Stretched on that new mown clover, the hill-side breeze blowing over me through the wide barn door, and soothed by the hum of the bees in the meadows around, how magically stole over me this Mossy Man! and how amply, how bountifully, did he redeem that delicious promise to his guests in the Old Manse, of whom it is written—"Others could give them pleasure, or amusement, or instruction—these could be picked up anywhere—but it was for me to give them rest. Rest, in a life of trouble! What better could be done for weary and world-worn spirits? what better could be done for anybody, who came within our magic circle, than to throw the spell of a magic spirit over him?"—So all that day, half-buried in the new clover, I watched this Hawthorne's "Assyrian dawn, and Paphian sunset and moonrise, from the summit of our Eastern Hill."

The soft ravishments of the man spun me round about in a web of dreams, and when the book was closed, when the spell was over, this wizard "dismissed me with but misty reminiscences, as if I had been dreaming of him."

What a mild moonlight of contemplative humor bathes that Old Manse!—the rich and rare distilment of a spicy and slowly-oozing heart. No rollicking rudeness, no gross fun fed on fat dinners, and bred in the lees of wine,—but a humor so spiritually gentle, so high, so deep, and yet so richly relishable, that it were hardly inappropriate in an angel. It is the very religion of mirth; for nothing so human but it may be advanced to that. The orchard of the Old Manse seems the visible type of the fine mind that has described it. Those twisted, and contorted old trees, "that stretch out their crooked branches, and take such hold of the imagination, that we remember them as humorists, and odd-fellows." And then, as surrounded by these grotesque forms, and hushed in the noon-day repose of this Hawthorne's spell, how aptly might the still fall of his ruddy thoughts into your soul be symbolized by "the thump of a great apple, in the stillest afternoon, falling without a breath of wind, from the mere necessity of perfect ripeness"! For no less ripe than ruddy are the apples of the thoughts and fancies in this sweet Man of Mosses.

"Buds and Bird-voices"—What a delicious thing is that!—"Will the world ever be so decayed, that Spring may not renew its greenness?"—And the "Fire-Worship." Was ever the hearth so glorified into an altar before? The mere title of that piece is better than any common work in fifty folio volumes. How exquisite is this:—"Nor did it lessen the charm of his soft, familiar courtesy and helpfulness, that the mighty spirit, were opportunity offered him, would run riot through the peaceful house, wrap its inmates in his terrible embrace, and leave nothing of them save their whitened bones. This possibility of mad destruction only made his domestic kindness the more beautiful and touching. It was so sweet of him, being endowed with such power, to dwell, day after day, and one long, lonesome night after another, on the dusky hearth, only now and then betraying his wild nature, by thrusting his red tongue out of the chimney-top! True, he had done much mischief in the world, and was pretty certain to do more, but his warm heart atoned for all. He was kindly to the race of man."

But he has still other apples, not quite so ruddy, though full as ripe;—apples, that have been left to wither on the tree, after the pleasant autumn gathering is past. The sketch of "The Old Apple Dealer" is conceived in the subtlest spirit of sadness; he whose "subdued and nerveless boyhood prefigured his abortive prime, which, likewise, contained within itself the prophecy and image of his lean and torpid age." Such touches as are in this piece can not proceed from any common heart. They argue such a depth of tenderness, such a boundless sympathy with all forms of being, such an omnipresent love, that we must needs say, that this Hawthorne is here almost alone in his generation,—at least, in the artistic manifestation of these things. Still more. Such touches as these,—and many, very many similar ones, all through his chapters—furnish clews, whereby we enter a little way into the intricate, profound heart where they originated. And we see, that suffering, some time or other and in some shape or other,—this only can enable any man to depict it in others. All over him, Hawthorne's melancholy rests like an Indian Summer, which though bathing a whole country in one softness, still reveals the distinctive hue of every towering hill, and each far-winding vale.

But it is the least part of genius that attracts admiration. Where Hawthorne is known, he seems to be deemed a pleasant writer, with a pleasant style,—a sequestered, harmless man, from whom any deep and weighty thing would hardly be anticipated:—a man who means no meanings. But there is no man, in whom humor and love, like mountain peaks, soar to such a rapt height, as to receive the irradiations of the upper skies;—there is no man in whom humor and love are developed in that high form called genius; no such man can exist without also possessing, as the indispensable complement of these, a great, deep intellect, which drops down into the universe like a plummet. Or, love and humor are only the eyes, through which such an intellect views this world. The great beauty in such a mind is but the product of its strength. What, to all readers, can be more charming than the piece entitled "Monsieur du Miroir"; and to a reader at all capable of fully fathoming it, what, at the same time, can possess more mystical depth of meaning?—Yes, there he sits, and looks at me,—this "shape of mystery," this "identical Monsieur du Miroir."—Methinks I should tremble now, were his wizard power of gliding through all impediments in search of me, to place him suddenly before my eyes."

How profound, nay appalling, is the moral evolved by the "Earth's Holocaust"; where—beginning with the hollow follies and affectations of the world,—all vanities and empty theories and forms, are, one after another, and by an admirably graduated, growing comprehensiveness, thrown into the allegorical fire, till, at length, nothing is left but the all-engendering heart of man; which remaining still unconsumed, the great conflagration is nought.

Of a piece with this, is the "Intelligence Office," a wondrous symbolizing of the secret workings in men's souls. There are other sketches, still more charged with ponderous import.

"The Christmas Banquet," and "The Bosom Serpent" would be fine subjects for a curious and elaborate analysis, touching the conjectural parts of the mind that produced them. For spite of all the Indian-summer sunlight on the hither side of Hawthorne's soul, the other side—like the dark half of the physical sphere—is shrouded in a blackness, ten times black. But this darkness but gives more effect to the ever-moving dawn, that forever advances through it, and circumnavigates his world. Whether Hawthorne has simply availed himself of this mystical blackness as a means to the wondrous effects he makes it to produce in his lights and shades; or whether there really lurks in him, perhaps unknown to himself, a touch of Puritanic gloom,—this, I cannot altogether tell. Certain it is, however, that this great power of blackness in him derives its force from its appeals to that Calvinistic sense of Innate Depravity and Original Sin, from whose visitations, in some shape or other, no deeply thinking mind is always and wholly free. For, in certain moods, no man can weigh this world, without throwing in something, somehow like Original Sin, to strike the uneven balance. At all events, perhaps no writer has ever wielded this terrific thought with greater terror than this same harmless Hawthorne. Still more: this black conceit pervades him, through and through. You may be witched by his sunlight,—transported by the bright gildings in the skies he builds over you;—but there is the blackness of darkness beyond; and even his bright gildings but fringe, and play upon the edges of thunder-clouds.—In one word, the world is mistaken in this Nathaniel Hawthorne. He himself must often have smiled at its absurd misconception of him. He is immeasurably deeper than the plummet of the mere critic. For it is not the brain that can test such a man; it is only the heart. You cannot come to know greatness by inspecting it; there is no glimpse to be caught of it, except by intuition; you need not ring it, you but touch it, and you find it is gold.

Now it is that blackness in Hawthorne, of which I have spoken, that so fixes and fascinates me. It may be, nevertheless, that it is too largely developed in him. Perhaps he does not give us a ray of his light for every shade of his dark. But however this may be, this blackness it is that furnishes the infinite obscure of his back-ground,—that back-ground, against which Shakespeare plays his grandest conceits, the things that have made for Shakespeare his loftiest, but most circumscribed renown, as the profoundest of thinkers. For by philosophers Shakespeare is not adored as the great man of tragedy and comedy.—"Off with his head! so much for Buckingham!" this sort of rant, interlined by another hand, brings down the house,—those mistaken souls, who dream of Shakespeare as a mere man of Richard-the-Third humps, and Macbeth daggers. But it is those deep far-away things in him; those occasional flashings-forth of the intuitive Truth in him; those short, quick probings at the very axis of reality;—these are the things that make Shakespeare, Shakespeare. Through the mouths of the dark characters of Hamlet, Timon, Lear, and Iago, he craftily says, or sometimes insinuates the things, which we feel to be so terrifically true, that it were all but madness for any good man, in his own proper character, to utter, or even hint of them. Tormented into desperation, Lear the frantic King tears off the mask, and speaks the sane madness of vital truth. But, as I before said, it is the least part of genius that attracts admiration. And so, much of the blind, unbridled admiration that has been heaped upon Shakespeare, has been lavished upon the least part of him. And few of his endless commentators and critics seem to have remembered, or even perceived, that the immediate products of a great mind are not so great, as that undeveloped, (and sometimes undevelopable) yet dimly-discernable greatness, to which these immediate products are but the infallible indices. In Shakespeare's tomb lies infinitely more than Shakespeare ever wrote. And if I magnify Shakespeare, it is not so much for what he did do, as for what he did not do, or refrained from doing. For in this world of lies, Truth is forced to fly like a scared white doe in the woodlands; and only by cunning glimpses will she reveal herself, as in Shakespeare and other masters of the great Art of Telling the Truth,—even though it be covertly, and by snatches.

But if this view of the all-popular Shakespeare be seldom taken by his readers, and if very few who extol him, have ever read him deeply, or, perhaps, only have seen him on the tricky stage, (which alone made, and is still making him his mere mob renown)—if few men have time, or patience, or palate, for the spiritual truth as it is in that great genius;—it is, then, no matter of surprise that in a contemporaneous age, Nathaniel Hawthorne is a man, as yet, almost utterly mistaken among men. Here and there, in some quiet arm-chair in the noisy town, or some deep nook among the noiseless mountains, he may be appreciated for something of what he is. But unlike Shakespeare, who was forced to the contrary course by circumstances, Hawthorne (either from simple disinclination, or else from inaptitude) refrains from all the popularizing noise and show of broad farce, and blood-besmeared tragedy; content with the still, rich utterances of a great intellect in repose, and which sends few thoughts into circulation, except they be arterialized at his large warm lungs, and expanded in his honest heart.

Nor need you fix upon that blackness in him, if it suit you not. Nor, indeed, will all readers discern it, for it is, mostly, insinuated to those who may best understand it, and account for it; it is not obtruded upon every one alike.

Some may start to read of Shakespeare and Hawthorne on the same page. They may say, that if an illustration were needed, a lesser light might have sufficed to elucidate this Hawthorne, this small man of yesterday. But I am not, willingly, one of those, who, as touching Shakespeare at least, exemplify the maxim of Rochefoucault, that "we exalt the reputation of some, in order to depress that of others";—who, to teach all noble-souled aspirants that there is no hope for them, pronounce Shakespeare absolutely unapproachable. But Shakespeare has been approached. There are minds that have gone as far as Shakespeare into the universe. And hardly a mortal man, who, at some time or other, has not felt as great thoughts in him as any you will find in Hamlet. We must not inferentially malign mankind for the sake of any one man, whoever he may be. This is too cheap a purchase of contentment for conscious mediocrity to make. Besides, this absolute and unconditional adoration of Shakespeare has grown to be a part of our Anglo Saxon superstitions. The Thirty Nine articles are now Forty. Intolerance has come to exist in this matter. You must believe in Shakespeare's unapproachability, or quit the country. But what sort of a belief is this for an American, a man who is bound to carry republican progressiveness into Literature, as well as into Life? Believe me, my friends, that Shakespeares are this day being born on the banks of the Ohio. And the day will come, when you shall say who reads a book by an Englishman that is a modern? The great mistake seems to be, that even with those Americans who look forward to the coming of a great literary genius among us, they somehow fancy he will come in the costume of Queen Elizabeth's day,—be a writer of dramas founded upon old English history, or the tales of Boccaccio. Whereas, great geniuses are parts of the times; they themselves are the times; and possess a correspondent coloring. It is of a piece with the Jews, who while their Shiloh was meekly walking in their streets, were still praying for his magnificent coming; looking for him in a chariot, who was already among them on an ass. Nor must we forget, that, in his own life-time, Shakespeare was not Shakespeare, but only Master William Shakespeare of the shrewd, thriving, business firm of Condell, Shakespeare & Co., proprietors of the Globe Theatre in London; and by a courtly author, of the name of Greene, was hooted at, as an "upstart crow" beautified "with other birds' feathers." For, mark it well, imitation is often the first charge brought against real originality. Why this is so, there is not space to set forth here. You must have plenty of sea-room to tell the Truth in; especially, when it seems to have an aspect of newness, as America did in 1492, though it was then just as old, and perhaps older than Asia, only those sagacious philosophers, the common sailors, had never seen it before; swearing it was all water and moonshine there.

Now, I do not say that Nathaniel of Salem is a greater than William of Avon, or as great. But the difference between the two men is by no means immeasurable. Not a very great deal more, and Nathaniel were verily William.

This, too, I mean, that if Shakespeare has not been equalled, he is sure to be surpassed, and surpassed by an American born now or yet to be born. For it will never do for us who in most other things out-do as well as out-brag the world, it will not do for us to fold our hands and say, In the highest department advance there is none. Nor will it at all do to say, that the world is getting grey and grizzled now, and has lost that fresh charm which she wore of old, and by virtue of which the great poets of past times made themselves what we esteem them to be. Not so. The world is as young today, as when it was created; and this Vermont morning dew is as wet to my feet, as Eden's dew to Adam's. Nor has Nature been all over ransacked by our progenitors, so that no new charms and mysteries remain for this latter generation to find. Far from it. The trillionth part has not yet been said; and all that has been said, but multiplies the avenues to what remains to be said. It is not so much paucity, as superabundance of material that seems to incapacitate modern authors.

Let America then prize and cherish her writers; yea, let her glorify them. They are not so many in number, as to exhaust her good-will. And while she has good kith and kin of her own, to take to her bosom, let her not lavish her embraces upon the household of an alien. For believe it or not England, after all, is, in many things, an alien to us. China has more bowels of real love for us than she. But even were there no Hawthorne, no Emerson, no Whittier, no Irving, no Bryant, no Dana, no Cooper, no Willis (not the author of the "Dashes," but the author of the "Belfry Pigeon")—were there none of these, and others of like calibre among us, nevertheless, let America first praise mediocrity even, in her own children, before she praises (for everywhere, merit demands acknowledgment from every one) the best excellence in the children of any other land. Let her own authors, I say, have the priority of appreciation. I was much pleased with a hot-headed Carolina cousin of mine, who once said,—"If there were no other American to stand by, in Literature,—why, then I would stand by Pop Emmons and his 'Fredoniad,' and till a better epic came along, swear it was not very far behind the Iliad." Take away the words, and in spirit he was sound.

Not that American genius needs patronage in order to expand. For that explosive sort of stuff will expand though screwed up in a vice, and burst it, though it were triple steel. It is for the nation's sake, and not for her authors' sake, that I would have America be heedful of the increasing greatness among her writers. For how great the shame, if other nations should be before her, in crowning her heroes of the pen. But this is almost the case now. American authors have received more just and discriminating praise (however loftily and ridiculously given, in certain cases) even from some Englishmen, then from their own countrymen. There are hardly five critics in America; and several of them are asleep. As for patronage, it is the American author who now patronizes his country, and not his country him. And if at times some among them appeal to the people for more recognition, it is not always with selfish motives, but patriotic ones.

It is true, that but few of them as yet have evinced that decided originality which merits great praise. But that graceful writer, who perhaps of all Americans has received the most plaudits from his own country for his production,—that very popular and amiable writer, however good, and self-reliant in many things, perhaps owes his chief reputation to the self-acknowledged imitation of a foreign model, and to the studied avoidance of all topics but smooth ones. But it is better to fail in originality, than to succeed in imitation. He who has never failed somewhere, that man can not be great. Failure is the true test of greatness. And if it be said, that continual success is a proof that a man wisely knows his powers,—it is only to be added, that, in that case, he knows them to be small. Let us believe it, then, once for all, that there is no hope for us in these smooth pleasing writers that know their powers. Without malice, but to speak the plain fact, they but furnish an appendix to Goldsmith, and other English authors. And we want no American Goldsmiths; nay, we want no American Miltons. It were the vilest thing you could say of a true American author, that he were an American Tompkins. Call him an American, and have done; for you can not say a nobler thing of him.—But it is not meant that all American writers should studiously cleave to nationality in their writings; only this, no American writer should write like an Englishman, or a Frenchman; let him write like a man, for then he will be sure to write like an American. Let us away with this Bostonian leaven of literary flunkeyism towards England. If either must play the flunkey in this thing, let England do it, not us. And the time is not far off when circumstances may force her to it. While we are rapidly preparing for that political supremacy among the nations, which prophetically awaits us at the close of the present century; in a literary point of view, we are deplorably unprepared for it; and we seem studious to remain so. Hitherto, reasons might have existed why this should be; but no good reason exists now. And all that is requisite to amendment in this matter, is simply this: that, while freely acknowledging all excellence, everywhere, we should refrain from unduly lauding foreign writers and, at the same time, duly recognize the meritorious writers that are our own;—those writers, who breathe that unshackled, democratic spirit of Christianity in all things, which now takes the practical lead in this world, though at the same time led by ourselves—us Americans. Let us boldly contemn all imitation, though it comes to us graceful and fragrant as the morning; and foster all originality, though, at first, it be crabbed and ugly as our own pine knots. And if any of our authors fail, or seem to fail, then, in the words of my enthusiastic Carolina cousin, let us clap him on the shoulder, and back him against all Europe for his second round. The truth is, that in our point of view, this matter of a national literature has come to such a pass with us, that in some sense we must turn bullies, else the day is lost, or superiority so far beyond us, that we can hardly say it will ever be ours.

And now, my countrymen, as an excellent author, of your own flesh and blood,—an unimitating, and, perhaps, in his way, an inimitable man—whom better can I commend to you, in the first place, than Nathaniel Hawthorne. He is one of the new, and far better generation of your writers. The smell of your beeches and hemlocks is upon him; your own broad praries are in his soul; and if you travel away inland into his deep and noble nature, you will hear the far roar of his Niagara. Give not over to future generations the glad duty of acknowledging him for what he is. Take that joy to your self, in your own generation; and so shall he feel those grateful impulses in him, that may possibly prompt him to the full flower of some still greater achievement in your eyes. And by confessing him, you thereby confess others; you brace the whole brotherhood. For genius, all over the world, stands hand in hand, and one shock of recognition runs the whole circle round.

In treating of Hawthorne, or rather of Hawthorne in his writings (for I never saw the man; and in the chances of a quiet plantation life, remote from his haunts, perhaps never shall) in treating of his works, I say, I have thus far omitted all mention of his "Twice Told Tales," and "Scarlet Letter." Both are excellent; but full of such manifold, strange and diffusive beauties, that time would all but fail me, to point the half of them out. But there are things in those two books, which, had they been written in England a century ago, Nathaniel Hawthorne had utterly displaced many of the bright names we now revere on authority. But I am content to leave Hawthorne to himself, and to the infallible finding of posterity; and however great may be the praise I have bestowed upon him, I feel, that in so doing, I have more served and honored myself, than him. For, at bottom, great excellence is praise enough to itself; but the feeling of a sincere and appreciative love and admiration towards it, this is relieved by utterance; and warm, honest praise ever leaves a pleasant flavor in the mouth; and it is an honorable thing to confess to what is honorable in others.

But I cannot leave my subject yet. No man can read a fine author, and relish him to his very bones, while he reads, without subsequently fancying to himself some ideal image of the man and his mind. And if you rightly look for it, you will almost always find that the author himself has somewhere furnished you with his own picture.—For poets (whether in prose or verse), being painters of Nature, are like their brethren of the pencil, the true portrait-painters, who, in the multitude of likenesses to be sketched, do not invariably omit their own; and in all high instances, they paint them without any vanity, though, at times, with a lurking something, that would take several pages to properly define.

I submit it, then, to those best acquainted with the man personally, whether the following is not Nathaniel Hawthorne;—and to himself, whether something involved in it does not express the temper of his mind,—that lasting temper of all true, candid men—a seeker, not a finder yet:—

"A man now entered, in neglected attire, with the aspect of a thinker, but somewhat too rough-hewn and brawny for a scholar. His face was full of sturdy vigor, with some finer and keener attribute beneath; though harsh at first, it was tempered with the glow of a large, warm heart, which had force enough to heat his powerful intellect through and through. He advanced to the Intelligencer, and looked at him with a glance of such stern sincerity, that perhaps few secrets were beyond its scope.

"'I seek for Truth,' said he."

* * * * *

Twenty four hours have elapsed since writing the foregoing. I have just returned from the hay mow, charged more and more with love and admiration of Hawthorne. For I have just been gleaning through the Mosses, picking up many things here and there that had previously escaped me. And I found that but to glean after this man, is better than to be in at the harvest of others. To be frank (though, perhaps, rather foolish) notwithstanding what I wrote yesterday of these Mosses, I had not then culled them all; but had, nevertheless, been sufficiently sensible of the subtle essence, in them, as to write as I did. To what infinite height of loving wonder and admiration I may yet be borne, when by repeatedly banquetting on these Mosses, I shall have thoroughly incorporated their whole stuff into my being,—that, I can not tell. But already I feel that this Hawthorne has dropped germinous seeds into my soul. He expands and deepens down, the more I contemplate him; and further, and further, shoots his strong New-England roots into the hot soil of my Southern soul.

By careful reference to the "Table of Contents," I now find, that I have gone through all the sketches; but that when I yesterday wrote, I had not at all read two particular pieces, to which I now desire to call special attention,—"A Select Party," and "Young Goodman Brown." Here, be it said to all those whom this poor fugitive scrawl of mine may tempt to the perusal of the "Mosses," that they must on no account suffer themselves to be trifled with, disappointed, or deceived by the triviality of many of the titles to these Sketches. For in more than one instance, the title utterly belies the piece. It is as if rustic demijohns containing the very best and costliest of Falernian and Tokay, were labelled "Cider," "Perry," and "Elderberry wine." The truth seems to be, that like many other geniuses, this Man of Mosses takes great delight in hoodwinking the world,—at least, with respect to himself. Personally, I doubt not, that he rather prefers to be generally esteemed but a so-so sort of author; being willing to reserve the thorough and acute appreciation of what he is, to that party most qualified to judge—that is, to himself. Besides, at the bottom of their natures, men like Hawthorne, in many things, deem the plaudits of the public such strong presumptive evidence of mediocrity in the object of them, that it would in some degree render them doubtful of their own powers, did they hear much and vociferous braying concerning them in the public pastures. True, I have been braying myself (if you please to be witty enough, to have it so) but then I claim to be the first that has so brayed in this particular matter; and therefore, while pleading guilty to the charge still claim all the merit due to originality.

But with whatever motive, playful or profound, Nathaniel Hawthorne has chosen to entitle his pieces in the manner he has, it is certain, that some of them are directly calculated to deceive—egregiously deceive, the superficial skimmer of pages. To be downright and candid once more, let me cheerfully say, that two of these titles did dolefully dupe no less an eagle-eyed reader than myself; and that, too, after I had been impressed with a sense of the great depth and breadth of this American man. "Who in the name of thunder" (as the country-people say in this neighborhood) "who in the name of thunder," would anticipate any marvel in a piece entitled "Young Goodman Brown"? You would of course suppose that it was a simple little tale, intended as a supplement to "Goody Two Shoes." Whereas, it is deep as Dante; nor can you finish it, without addressing the author in his own words—"It is yours to penetrate, in every bosom, the deep mystery of sin." And with Young Goodman, too, in allegorical pursuit of his Puritan wife, you cry out in your anguish,—

> "'Faith!' shouted Goodman Brown, in a voice of agony and desperation; and the echoes of the forest mocked him, crying—'Faith! Faith!' as if bewildered wretches were seeking her all through the wilderness."

Now this same piece, entitled "Young Goodman Brown," is one of the two that I had not all read yesterday; and I allude to it now, because it is, in itself, such a strong positive illustration of that blackness in Hawthorne, which I had assumed from the mere occasional shadows of it, as revealed in several of the other sketches. But had I previously perused "Young Goodman Brown," I should have been at no pains to draw the conclusion, which I came to, at a time, when I was ignorant that the book contained one such direct and unqualified manifestation of it.

The other piece of the two referred to, is entitled "A Select Party," which, in my first simplicity upon originally taking hold of the book, I fancied must treat of some pumpkin-pie party in Old Salem, or some chowder party on Cape Cod. Whereas, by all the gods of Peedee! it is the sweetest and sublimest thing that has been written since Spencer wrote. Nay, there is nothing in Spencer that surpasses it, perhaps, nothing that equals it. And the test is this: read any canto in "The Faery Queen," and then read "A Select Party," and decide which pleases you the most,—that is, if you are qualified to judge. Do not be frightened at this; for when Spencer was alive, he was thought of very much as Hawthorne is now,—was generally accounted just such a "gentle" harmless man. It may be, that to common eyes, the sublimity of Hawthorne seems lost in his sweetness,—as perhaps in this same "Select Party" of his; for whom, he has builded so august a dome of sunset clouds, and served them on richer plate, than Belshazzar's when he banquetted his lords in Babylon.

But my chief business now, is to point out a particular page in this piece, having reference to an honored guest, who under the name of "The Master Genius" but in the guise of "a young man of poor attire, with no insignia of rank or acknowledged eminence," is introduced to the Man of Fancy, who is the giver of the feast. Now the page having reference to this "Master Genius," so happily expresses much of what I yesterday wrote, touching the coming of the literary Shiloh of America, that I cannot but be charmed by the coincidence; especially, when it shows such a parity of ideas, at least in this one point, between a man like Hawthorne and a man like me.

And here, let me throw out another conceit of mine touching this American Shiloh, or "Master Genius," as Hawthorne calls him. May it not be, that this commanding mind has not been, is not, and never will be, individually developed in any one man? And would it, indeed, appear so unreasonable to suppose, that this great fullness and overflowing may be, or may be destined to be, shared by a plurality of men of genius? Surely, to take the very greatest example on record, Shakespeare cannot be regarded as in himself the concretion of all the genius of his time; nor as so immeasurably beyond Marlow, Webster, Ford, Beaumont, Jonson, that those great men can be said to share none of his power? For one, I conceive that there were dramatists in Elizabeth's day, between whom and Shakespeare the distance was by no means great. Let anyone, hitherto little acquainted with those neglected old authors, for the first time read them thoroughly, or even read Charles Lamb's Specimens of them, and he will be amazed at the wondrous ability of those Anaks of men, and shocked at this renewed example of the fact, that Fortune has more to do with fame than merit,—though, without merit, lasting fame there can be none.

Nevertheless, it would argue too illy of my country were this maxim to hold good concerning Nathaniel Hawthorne, a man, who already, in some few minds, has shed "such a light, as never illuminates the earth, save when a great heart burns as the household fire of a grand intellect."

The words are his,—in the "Select Party"; and they are a magnificent setting to a coincident sentiment of my own, but ramblingly expressed yesterday, in reference to himself. Gainsay it who will, as I now write, I am Posterity speaking by proxy—and after times will make it more than good, when I declare—that the American, who up to the present day, has evinced, in Literature, the largest brain with the largest heart, that man is Nathaniel Hawthorne. Moreover, that whatever Nathaniel Hawthorne may hereafter write, "The Mosses from an Old Manse" will be ultimately accounted his masterpiece. For there is a sure, though a secret sign in some works which prove the culmination of the powers (only the developable ones, however) that produced them. But I am by no means desirous of the glory of a prophet. I pray Heaven that Hawthorne may *yet* prove me an impostor in this prediction. Especially, as I somehow cling to the strange fancy, that, in all men, hiddenly reside certain wondrous, occult properties—as in some plants and minerals—which by some happy but very rare accident (as bronze was discovered by the melting of the iron and brass in the burning of Corinth) may chance to be called forth here on earth; not entirely waiting for their better discovery in the more congenial, blessed atmosphere of heaven.

Once more—for it is hard to be finite upon an infinite subject, and all subjects are infinite. By some people, this entire scrawl of mine may be esteemed altogether unnecessary, inasmuch, "as years ago" (they may say) "we found out the rich and rare stuff in this Hawthorne, whom you now parade forth, as if only *yourself* were the discoverer of this Portuguese diamond in our Literature."—But even granting all this; and adding to it, the assumption that the books of Hawthorne have sold by the five-thousand,—what does that signify?—They should be sold by the hundred-thousand; and read by the million; and admired by every one who is capable of admiration.

Part Five

The Quest for Union and Renewal

Introduction

The fervent calls by American writers and critics for a new national literature mingled in the antebellum period with a swelling national chorus for strengthening and expanding the union. This is not surprising. The antebellum North and South shared many of the same intellectual and cultural values derived from both their Protestant and Enlightenment past and their Romantic present. In fact, so strong was this nationalist sentiment that Democrats and Whigs each put forward their own ideology of either majoritarian democracy or state-supported economic growth as the key to sustaining it. Yet, no more for political intellectuals than for literary ones was the idea of an American union absolute. Inherited and, to some extent, competing republican ideas of liberty, federalism, and moral law dictated modifications. The most difficult modifications were those required by the question of slavery. It was not just that the issue was divisive, or even that with the emergence of the controversy over the extension of slavery in the territories it had become so all-engrossing. Rather, the intellectual problem was much more basic: In contesting the issue of slavery, ideologists and intellectuals advanced such radically counterposed notions of society and government as to call into question, even while supporting union in the abstract, the substance of American nationhood.

Southern writers were particularly insistent in claiming that Northern paeans to a strong union masked schemes subversive of a national polity. For many Southerners the greatest of these schemes was the common Northern assertion of the supremacy of the federal government in matters that affected vital Southern minority interests, of which slavery was the most important. The Southern thinker who was among the earliest to sound this alarm, and who subsequently constructed the most elaborate countertheory of federal-state relations, was John C. Calhoun. In his *Disquisition on Government,* he argued that only a national government based on a concurrence of "interests" as represented by the various states could protect minorities from oppression by majorities and foster political leaders dedicated to the good of the whole.

In his *Disquisition* Calhoun made it clear that the good he sought depended on restricting the sphere of liberty to the "intelligent" and "deserving." This fact should remind us that Southern intellectual apologists for slavery were hardly mere ideologists of the popular sentiments of their section. It is true many proslavery intellectuals defended slavery by appealing to the very source that inspired most Northerners *and* Southerners—the Bible. Also many Southern political leaders claimed that slavery guaranteed a *white* democratic society by providing opportunities for small slaveholders and obviating the need for a white proletariat. But by the 1840s some Southern writers were also beginning to turn to heterodox racist science to justify their system. Moreover, by the 1850s most leading antebellum Southern intellectuals preferred to portray slavery as a system *at odds* with important aspects of democratic capitalism for whites as well as for blacks. Louisa McCord, who embraced both free-trade capitalism and slavery, exploited this very tension between these two systems in her stoically reactionary assault on Northern feminism and concomitant defense of the two-spheres ideology of gender relations. By contrast, George Fitzhugh, in his defense of Southern slavery, dispensed with both the harsh realism and procapitalist economics accepted by McCord. Indeed, in his *Sociology for the South*, Fitzhugh not only delineated the organic social solidarity he claimed Southern slavery fostered, but he also went one step further: He proposed that the entire anarchical Northern "free trade" social system be supplanted by some version of "slavery."

Like Southern proslavery writers, Northern antislavery intellectuals and ideologues also articulated visions of an ideal American polity. But because Northern writers enjoyed the benefit of a popular culture that was, however nonabolitionist, still freer and more sophisticated than that of the South, their visions were correspondingly wider. This difference became especially obvious in the decade following the Compromise of 1850, when anxious Northerners faced the moral and political challenge of responding to both the Compromise's fugitive slave provision and the subsequent, and increasingly violent, controversy about slavery's status in the Western territories. At one extreme, heretofore moderate evangelical-minded antislavery writers indicted the slave system because of its corruption of national and communal ideals. (In *Uncle Tom's Cabin* Harriet Beecher Stowe portrayed Southern slavery as, contra Fitzhugh, predatory and mammon-enthralled and thus just the opposite of the Christian, familial, and altruistic culture she hoped somehow her *own* capitalistic society could become.) By contrast, William Lloyd Garrison and his followers continued to promote their perfectionist antislavery philosophy, which made the individual sacrosanct and necessitated the withdrawal of the North from its union with the newly expansionist slave South. Finally, Northern African-Americans, reacting to both the dangerous new federal "slave"-catching measures and the heightened racist and nationalistic character of the debates over slavery, began to put forward their own schemes for protecting their rights. One of the most far-reaching of these was Martin Delany's proposal and rationale, in his *Condition of the Colored People of the United States*, for the emigration of African-Americans and the establishment of a black nation of their own somewhere in the world.

Most white and black abolitionists and antislavery advocates, however, grappled with the intertwined problems of slavery and nationhood in terms that were not primarily evangelical, antinomian, *or* black nationalist. Among these "mainstream" abolitionists, few were so influential and resourceful as Frederick Douglass. In his July Fourth oration, Douglass mixed Enlightenment, republican, and humanized Christian ideals to produce an extraordinarily damning yet hopeful view of the democratic possibilities of American middle-class civilization. The Northern thinker who went the furthest, though, in trying to integrate an antislavery perspective with a moral vision of the American union was Abraham Lincoln. Eschewing in his antislavery and prolabor speeches both abolitionism and complete racial equality, Lincoln nonetheless imbued his Whiggishly nationalist solutions of self-government and upward mobility with an intense moral-egalitarian fervor. But it was in his two greatest Civil War addresses that he disclosed his view of the ultimate forces behind the union's moral redemption—namely, righteousness actualized through divine vengeance, human suffering, and human forgiveness. No public statement, discursive or poetic, has synthesized so many strands in the American intellectual tradition while seeming to express something beyond it. But Lincoln's complex nationalism was not the only vision of the future Union to emerge out of the Civil war. Of these prospective manifestos few were so hubris-filled and farsighted as Franis Lieber's. Three years, after the Union had consolidated in bloodshed under the hostile eyes of the great European powers, the Prussian emigré, in his influential address "Nationalism and Internationalism," confidently spied a not-too-distant time when an "exceptional" United States would assume its leading place in a new "Cis-Caucasian" order of international law and commercial and cultural interdependency.

Recommendations for Further Reading

William Stanton, *The Leopard's Spots: Scientific Attitudes toward Race in America, 1815–59* (Chicago, 1960); William R. Taylor, *Cavalier and Yankee: The Old South and American National Character* (New York, 1961); Edmund Wilson, *Patriotic Gore: Studies in the Literature of the American Civil War* (New York, 1962); Paul C. Nagel, *One Nation Indivisible: The Union in American Thought, 1776–1861* (New York, 1964); George M. Fredrickson, *The Inner Civil War: Northern Intellectuals and the Crisis of the Union* (New York, 1965); Clement Eaton, *The Mind of the Old South* (Baton Rouge, 1967); John Higham, *From Boundlessness to Consolidation: The Transformation of American Culture, 1848–1860* (Ann Arbor, 1969); Eric Foner, *Free Soil, Free Labor, Free Men: The Ideology of the Republican Party Before the Civil War* (New York, 1970); George M. Fredrickson, *The Black Image in the White Mind: The Debate on Afro-American Character and Destiny, 1817–1914* (New York, 1971); Major Eugene D. Genovese, *Roll, Jordan, Roll* (New York, 1974); Major L. Wilson, *Space, Time, and Freedom: The Quest for Nationality and the Irrepressible Conflict, 1815–1861* (Westport, Conn., 1974); Stanley M. Elkins, *Slavery: A Problem in American Institutional and Intellectual Life*, rev. ed. (Chicago, 1976); Drew Gilpin Faust, *A Sacred Circle: The Dilemma of the Intellectual in the Old South, 1840–1860* (Baltimore, 1977); Lawrence W. Levine, *Black Culture and Black Consciousness: Afro-American Folk Thought from Slavery to Freedom* (New York, 1977); James H. Moorhead, *American Apocalypse: Yankee Protestants and the Civil War, 1860–1869* (New Haven, 1978); Reginald Horsman, *Race and Manifest Destiny: Origins of American Racial Anglo-Saxonism* (New York, 1981); Bertram Wyatt-Brown, *Southern Honor: Ethics and Behavior in the Old South* (New York, 1982); David Brion Davis, *Slavery and Human Progress* (New York, 1984); Louis S. Gerteis, *Morality and Utility in American Antislavery Reform* (Chapel Hill, 1987); Sterling Stuckey, *Slave Culture: Nationalist Theory and the Foundations of Black America* (New York, 1987); Drew Gilpin Faust, *The Creation of Confederate Nationalism: Ideology and Identity in the Civil War South* (Baton Rouge, 1988); Larry E. Tise, *Proslavery: A History of the Defense of Slavery in America, 1701–1840* (Athens, Ga., 1988); Louis D. Rubin, Jr., *The Edge of the Swamp: A Study in the Literature and Society of the Old South* (Baton Rouge, 1989); Anne C. Rose, *Victorian America and the Civil War* (Cambridge, 1992); Mitchell Snay, *Gospel of Disunion: Religion and Separatism in the Antebellum South* (Cambridge, 1993); Eric J. Sundquist, *To Wake the Nations: Race in the Making of American Literature* (Cambridge, Mass., 1993); Wilson Jeremiah Moses, *Afrotopia: The Roots of African American Popular History* (Cambridge, 1998); Mia Bay, *The White Image in the Black Mind: African-American Ideas about White People, 1830–1925* (New York, 2000); Bruce Dain, *A Hideous Monster of the Mind: American Race Theory in the Early Republic* (Cambridge, Mass., 2002); Patrick Rael, *Black Identity and Black Protest in the Antebellum North* (Chapel Hill, 2002); Michael O'Brien, *Conjectures of Order: Intellectual Life and the American South, 1810–1860*, 2 vols. (Chapel Hill, 2004); Elizabeth Fox-Genovese and Eugene D. Genovese, *The Mind of the Master Class: History and Faith in the Southern Slaveholders' Worldview* (Cambridge, 2005); Mark A. Noll, *The Civil War as a Theological Crisis* (Chapel Hill, 2006); Robert E. Bonner, *Mastering America: Southern Slaveholders and the Crisis of American Nationhood* (New York, 2009); Lacy K. Ford, *Deliver Us from Evil: The Slavery Question in the Old South* (New York, 2009); Stephen G. Hall, *A Faithful Account of the Race: African American Historical Writing in Nineteenth-Century America* (Chapel Hill, 2009); Michael T. Bernath, *Confederate Minds: The Struggle for Intellectual Independence in the Civil War South* (Chapel Hill, 2010); Laurie Maffly-Kipp, *Setting Down the Sacred Past: African American Race Histories* (Cambridge, Mass., 2010); Margaret Abruzzo, *Polemical Pain: Slavery, Cruelty, and the Rise of Humanitarianism* (Baltimore, 2011); Justin Buckley Dyer, *Natural Law and the Antislavery Constitutional Tradition* (New York, 2012); Lewis Perry, *Civil Disobedience: An American Tradition* (New Haven, 2013); David Brion Davis, *The Problem of Slavery in the Age of Emancipation* (New York, 2014).

JOHN C. CALHOUN

Selection from *A Disquisition on Government* (c. late 1840s)

Throughout most of his long career as, among other roles, secretary of war, vice president, senator, secretary of state, and persistent presidential aspirant, John C. Calhoun (1782–1850) devoted himself overwhelmingly to two efforts—an unflagging defense of slavery and slaveholder political interests and the contrivance of a governmental structure that would protect those interests while, if possible, preserving the American union. Yet Calhoun's intellectual concerns transcended to some extent the proslavery interests that drove them. One concern looked backward: his Southern republican preoccupation with preserving "honor" and "virtue" in the increasingly competitive democratic capitalist culture in which he participated. The other looked forward: his advanced awareness of the problem of preserving minority interests in an increasingly centralized national economy and polity.

His most complete answer to all these problems, which he formulated in his posthumously published *Disquisition on Government,* was the "concurrent majority," or government by the majority of each of the interests in a community considered separately and concurring unanimously. By thus providing an absolute veto to each interest, Calhoun argued, oppressive majorities—the hobgoblin of classical republican theory—would be prevented. But Calhoun's scheme was not just negative. Interests that under the democratic system of numerical majorities warred against each other, egged on by demagogic spoils-men, would be converted into cooperative communities, although of a very special sort. Monolithic and elite-dominated, they would guarantee rule and even relative "liberty" only to those virtuous and intelligent enough to contribute to "the march of progress" and the improvement of the race. For democrats North and South, the price of Calhoun's utopian union was high indeed. This historical fact, however, has not prevented twentieth-century political theorists from trying to appropriate Calhoun's block "pluralist" solutions to modern problems as diverse as the corporate state and the divisions of a multicultural society.

Irving H. Bartlett's *John C. Calhoun: A Biography* (New York, 1993), emphasizes both the cultural contexts and the ideological significance of Calhoun's life and thought. For excellent discussions of Calhoun's thought in the contexts of, respectively, white republicanism in the Lower South and a long discourse about majority rule and minority interests, see Lacy K. Ford, "Republican Ideology in a Slave Society: The Political Economy of John C. Calhoun," *Journal of Southern History,* 54 (August 1988), 405–24; and Ford's "Inventing the Concurrent Majority: Madison, Calhoun, and the Problem of Majoritarianism in American Political Thought," 60 (February 1994), 19–58. Interpretations of Calhoun's text may be found in Guy Story Brown, *Calhoun's Philosophy of Politics: A Study of* A Disquisition on

[G]overnment, although intended to protect and preserve society, has itself a strong tendency to disorder and abuse of its powers, as all experience and almost every page of history testify. The cause is to be found in the same constitution of our nature which makes government indispensable. The powers which it is necessary for government to possess, in order to repress violence and preserve order, cannot execute themselves. They must be administered by men in whom, like others, the individual are stronger than the social feelings. And hence, the powers vested in them to prevent injustice and oppression on the part of others, will, if left unguarded, be by them converted into instruments to oppress the rest of the community. That, by which this is prevented, by whatever name called, is what is meant by CONSTITUTION, in its most comprehensive sense, when applied to GOVERNMENT.

Having its origin in the same principle of our nature, *constitution* stands to *government, as government* stands to *society;* and, as the end for which society is ordained, would be defeated without government, so that for which government is ordained would, in a great measure, be defeated without constitution. But they differ in this striking particular. There is no difficulty in forming government. It is not even a matter of choice, whether there shall be one or not. Like breathing, it is not permitted to depend on our volition. Necessity will force it on all communities in some one form or another. Very different is the case as to constitution. Instead of a matter of necessity, it is one of the most difficult tasks imposed on man to form a constitution worthy of the name; while, to form a perfect one,— one that would completely counteract the tendency of government to oppression and abuse, and hold it strictly to the great ends for which it is ordained,—has thus far exceeded human wisdom, and possibly ever will. From this, another striking difference results. Constitution is the contrivance of man, while government is of Divine ordination. Man is left to perfect what the wisdom of the Infinite ordained, as necessary to preserve the race....

How government, then, must be constructed, in order to counteract, through its organism, this tendency on the part of those who make and execute the laws to oppress those subject to their operation,...next...claims attention.

There is but one way in which this can possibly be done; and that is, by such an organism as will furnish the ruled with the means of resisting successfully this tendency on the part of the rulers to oppression and abuse. Power can only be resisted by power,—and tendency by tendency. Those who exercise power and those subject to its exercise,—the rulers and the ruled,—stand in antagonistic relations to each other. The same constitution of our nature which leads rulers to oppress the ruled,—regardless of the object for which government is ordained,—will, with equal strength, lead the ruled to resist, when possessed of the means of making peaceable and effective resistance. Such an organism, then, as will furnish the means by which resistance may be systematically and peaceably made on the part of the ruled, to oppression and abuse of power on the part of the rulers, is the first and indispensable step towards *forming* a constitutional government. And as this can only be effected by or through the right of suffrage,—(the right on the part of the ruled to choose their rulers at proper intervals, and to hold them there-by responsible for their conduct,)—the responsibility of the rulers to the ruled, through the right of suffrage, is the indispensable and primary principle in the *foundation* of a constitutional government. When this right is properly guarded, and the people sufficiently enlightened to understand

Source: The Works of John C. Calhoun, vol. 1: *A Disquisition on Government and a Discourse on the Constitution and Government of the United States,* ed. Richard K. Crallé (Charleston, S.C.: Steam Power-Press of Walker & James, 1851), 7–8, 12–17, 24–31, 35–36, 45–49, 55–59.

their own rights and the interests of the community, and duly to appreciate the motives and conduct of those appointed to make and execute the laws, it is all-sufficient to give to those who elect, effective control over those they have elected.

I call the right of suffrage the indispensable and primary principle; for it would be a great and dangerous mistake to suppose, as many do, that it is, of itself, sufficient to form constitutional governments. To this erroneous opinion may be traced one of the causes, why so few attempts to form constitutional governments have succeeded; and why, of the few which have, so small a number have had durable existence. It has led, not only to mistakes in the attempts to form such governments, but to their overthrow, when they have, by some good fortune, been correctly formed. So far from being, of itself, sufficient,—however well guarded it might be, and however enlightened the people,—it would, unaided by other provisions, leave the government as absolute, as it would be in the hands of irresponsible rulers; and with a tendency, at least as strong, towards oppression and abuse of its powers; as I shall next proceed to explain.

The right of suffrage, of itself, can do no more than give complete control to those who elect, over the conduct of those they have elected. In doing this, it accomplishes all it possibly can accomplish. This is its aim,—and when this is attained, its end is fulfilled. It can do no more, however enlightened the people, or however widely extended or well guarded the right may be. The sum total, then, of its effects, when most successful, is, to make those elected, the true and faithful representatives of those who elected them,—instead of irresponsible rulers,—as they would be without it; and thus, by converting it into an agency, and the rulers into agents, to divest government of all claims to sovereignty, and to retain it unimpaired to the community. But it is manifest that the right of suffrage, in making these changes, transfers, in reality, the actual control over the government, from those who make and execute the laws, to the body of the community; and, thereby, places the powers of the government as fully in the mass of the community, as they would be if they, in fact, had assembled, made, and executed the laws themselves, without the intervention of representatives or agents. The more perfectly it does this, the more perfectly it accomplishes its ends; but in doing so, it only changes the seat of authority, without counteracting, in the least, the tendency of the government to oppression and abuse of its powers.

If the whole community had the same interests, so that the interests of each and every portion would be so affected by the action of the government, that the laws which oppressed or impoverished one portion, would necessarily oppress and impoverish all others,—or the reverse,—then the right of suffrage, of itself, would be all-sufficient to counteract the tendency of the government to oppression and abuse of its powers; and, of course, would form, of itself, a perfect constitutional government. The interest of all being the same, by supposition, as far as the action of the government was concerned, all would have like interests as to what laws should be made, and how they should be executed. All strife and struggle would cease as to who should be elected to make and execute them. The only question would be, who was most fit; who the wisest and most capable of understanding the common interest of the whole. This decided, the election would pass off quietly, and without party discord; as no one portion could advance its own peculiar interest without regard to the rest, by electing a favorite candidate.

But such is not the case. On the contrary, nothing is more difficult than to equalize the action of the government, in reference to the various and diversified interests of the community; and nothing more easy than to pervert its powers into instruments to aggrandize and enrich one or more interests by oppressing and impoverishing the others; and this too, under the operation of laws, couched in general terms;—and which, on their face, appear fair and equal. Nor is this the case in some particular communities only. It is so in all; the small and the great,—the poor and the rich,—irrespective of pursuits, productions, or degrees of civilization;—with, however, this difference, that the more extensive and populous the country, the more diversified the condition and pursuits of its population, and the richer, more luxurious, and dissimilar the people, the more difficult is it to equalize the action of the government,—and the more easy for one portion of the community to pervert its powers to oppress, and plunder the other.

Such being the case, it necessarily results, that the right of suffrage, by placing the control of the government in the community must, from the same constitution of our nature which makes government necessary to preserve society, lead to conflict among its different interests,—each striving to obtain possession of its powers, as the means of protecting itself against the others;—or of advancing its respective interests, regardless of the interests of others. For this purpose, a struggle will take place between the various interests to obtain a majority, in order to control the government. If no one interest be strong enough, of itself, to obtain it, a combination will be formed between those whose interests are most alike;—each conceding something to the others, until a sufficient number is obtained to make a majority. The process may be slow, and much time may be required before a compact, organized majority can be thus formed; but formed it will be in time, even without preconcert or design, by the sure workings of that principle or constitution of our nature in which government itself originates. When once formed, the community will be divided into two great parties,—a major and minor,—between which there will be incessant struggles on the one side to retain, and on the other to obtain the majority,—and, thereby, the control of the government and the advantages it confers.

So deeply seated, indeed, is this tendency to conflict between the different interests or portions of the community, that it would result from the action of the government itself, even though it were possible to find a community, where the people were all of the same pursuits, placed in the same condition of life, and in every respect, so situated, as to be without inequality of condition or diversity of interests. The advantages of possessing the control of the powers of the government, and, thereby, of its honors and emoluments, are, of themselves, exclusive of all other considerations, ample to divide even such a community into two great hostile parties....

As, then, the right of suffrage, without some other provision, cannot counteract this tendency of government, the next question for consideration is—What is that other provision? This demands the most serious consideration; for of all the questions embraced in the science of government, it involves a principle, the most important, and the least understood; and when understood, the most difficult of application in practice. It is, indeed, emphatically, that principle which *makes* the constitution, in its strict and limited sense.

From what has been said, it is manifest, that this provision must be of a character calculated to prevent any one interest, or combination of interests, from using the powers of government to aggrandize itself at the expense of the others. Here lies the evil: and just in proportion as it shall prevent, or fail to prevent it, in the same degree it will effect, or fail to effect the end intended to be accomplished. There is but one certain mode in which this result can be secured; and that is, by the adoption of some restriction or limitation, which shall so effectually prevent any one interest, or combination of interests, from obtaining the exclusive control of the government, as to render hopeless all attempts directed to that end. There is, again, but one mode in which this can be effected; and that is, by taking the sense of each interest or portion of the community, which may be unequally and injuriously affected by the action of the government, separately, through its own majority, or in some other way by which its voice may be fairly expressed; and to require the consent of each interest, either to put or to keep the government in action. This, too, can be accomplished only in one way,—and that is, by such an organism of the government,—and, if necessary for the purpose, of the community also,—as will, by dividing and distributing the powers of government, give to each division or interest, through its appropriate organ, either a concurrent voice in making and executing the laws, or a veto on their execution. It is only by such an organism, that the assent of each can be made necessary to put the government in motion; or the power made effectual to arrest its action, when put in motion;—and it is only by the one or the other that the different interests, orders, classes, or portions, into which the community may be divided, can be protected, and all conflict and struggle between them prevented,—by rendering it impossible to put or to keep it in action, without the concurrent consent of all.

Such an organism as this, combined with the right of suffrage, constitutes, in fact, the elements of constitutional government. The one, by rendering those who make and execute the laws responsible to those on whom they operate, prevents the rulers from oppressing the ruled; and the other, by making it impossible for any one interest or combination of interests or class, or order, or portion of the community, to obtain exclusive control, prevents any one of them from oppressing the other. It is clear, that oppression and abuse of power must come, if at all, from the one or the other quarter. From no other can they come. It follows, that the two, suffrage and proper organism combined, are sufficient to counter-act the tendency of government to oppression and abuse of power; and to restrict it to the fulfilment of the great ends for which it is ordained.

In coming to this conclusion, I have assumed the organism to be perfect, and the different interests, portions, or classes of the community, to be sufficiently enlightened to understand its character and object, and to exercise, with due intelligence, the right of suffrage. To the extent that either may be defective, to the same extent the government would fall short of fulfilling its end. But this does not impeach the truth of the principles on which it rests. In reducing them to proper form, in applying them to practical uses, all elementary principles are liable to difficulties; but they are not, on this account, the less true, or valuable. Where the organism is perfect, every interest will be truly and fully represented, and of course the whole community must be so. It maybe difficult, or even impossible, to make a perfect organism,—but, although this be true, yet even when, instead of the sense of each and of all, it takes that of a few great and prominent interests only, it would still, in a great measure, if not altogether, fulfil the end intended by a constitution. For, in such case, it would require so large a portion of the community, compared with the whole, to concur, or acquiesce in the action of the government, that the number to be plundered would be too few, and the number to be aggrandized too many, to afford adequate motives to oppression and the abuse of its powers. Indeed, however imperfect the organism, it must have more or less effect in diminishing such tendency.

It may be readily inferred, from what has been stated, that the effect of organism is neither to supersede nor diminish the importance of the right of suffrage; but to aid and perfect it. The object of the latter is, to collect the sense of the community. The more fully and perfectly it accomplishes this, the more fully and perfectly it fulfils its end. But the most it can do, of itself, is to collect the sense of the greater number; that is, of the stronger interests, or combination of interests; and to assume this to be the sense of the community. It is only when aided by a proper organism, that it can collect the sense of the entire community,—of each and all its interests; of each, through its appropriate organ, and of the whole, through all of them united. This would truly be the sense of the entire community;

for whatever diversity each interest might have within itself,—as all would have the same interest in reference to the action of the government, the individuals composing each would be fully and truly represented by its own majority or appropriate organ, regarded in reference to the other interests. In brief, every individual of every interest might trust, with confidence, its majority or appropriate organ, against that of every other interest.

It results, from what has been said, that there are two different modes in which the sense of the community may be taken; one, simply by the right of suffrage, unaided; the other, by the right through a proper organism. Each collects the sense of the majority. But one regards numbers only, and considers the whole community as a unit, having but one common interest throughout; and collects the sense of the greater number of the whole, as that of the community. The other, on the contrary, regards interests as well as numbers,— considering the community as made up of different and conflicting interests, as far as the action of the government is concerned; and takes the sense of each, through its majority or appropriate organ, and the united sense of all, as the sense of the entire community. The former of these I shall call the numerical, or absolute majority, and the latter, the concurrent, or constitutional majority. I call it the constitutional majority, because it is an essential element in every constitutional government,—be its form what it may. So great is the difference, politically speaking, between the two majorities, that they cannot be confounded, without leading to great and fatal errors; and yet the distinction between them has been so entirely overlooked, that when the term majority is used in political discussions, it is applied exclusively to designate the numerical,—as if there were no other. Until this distinction is recognized, and better understood, there will continue to be great liability to error in properly constructing constitutional governments, especially of the popular form, and of preserving them when properly constructed. Until then, the latter will have a strong tendency to slide, first, into the government of the numerical majority, and, finally, into absolute government of some other form. To show that such must be the case, and at the same time to mark more strongly the difference between the two, in order to guard against the danger of overlooking it, I propose to consider the subject more at length.

The first and leading error which naturally arises from overlooking the distinction referred to, is, to confound the numerical majority with the people; and this so completely as to regard them as identical. This is a consequence that necessarily results from considering the numerical as the only majority. All admit, that a popular government, or democracy, is the government of the people; for the terms imply this. A perfect government of the kind would be one which would embrace the consent of every citizen or member of the community; but as this is impracticable, in the opinion of those who regard the numerical as the only majority, and who can perceive no other way by which the sense of the people can be taken,—they are compelled to adopt this as the only true basis of popular government, in contradistinction to governments of the aristocratical or monarchical form. Being thus constrained, they are, in the next place, forced to regard the numerical majority, as, in effect, the entire people; that is, the greater part as the whole; and the government of the greater part as the government of the whole. It is thus the two come to be confounded, and a part made identical with the whole. And it is thus, also, that all the rights, powers, and immunities of the whole people come to be attributed to the numerical majority; and, among others, the supreme, sovereign authority of establishing and abolishing governments at pleasure.

This radical error, the consequence of confounding the two, and of regarding the numerical as the only majority, has contributed more than any other cause, to prevent the formation of popular constitutional governments,—and to destroy them even when they have been formed. It leads to the conclusion that, in their formation and establishment nothing more is necessary than the right of suffrage,—and the allotment to each division of the community a representation in the government, in proportion to numbers. If the numerical majority were really the people; and if, to take its sense truly, were to take the sense of the people truly, a government so constituted would be a true and perfect model of a popular constitutional government; and every departure from it would detract from its excellence. But, as such is not the case,—as the numerical majority, instead of being the people, is only a portion of them,—such a government, instead of being a true and perfect model of the people's government, that is, a people self-governed, is but the government of a part, over a part,—the major over the minor portion.

But this misconception of the true elements of constitutional government does not stop here. It leads to others equally false and fatal, in reference to the best means of preserving and perpetuating them, when, from some fortunate combination of circumstances, they are correctly formed. For they who fall into these errors regard the restrictions which organism imposes on the will of the numerical majority as restrictions on the will of the people, and, therefore, as not only useless, but wrongful and mischievous. And hence they endeavor to destroy organism, under the delusive hope of making government more democratic.

Such are some of the consequences of confounding the two, and of regarding the numerical as the only majority. And in this may be found the reason why so few popular governments have been properly constructed, and why, of these few, so small a number have proved durable. Such must continue to be the result, so long as these errors continue to be prevalent....

The necessary consequence of taking the sense of the community by the concurrent majority is, as has been explained, to give to each interest or portion of the community a negative on the others. It is this mutual negative among its various conflicting interests, which invests each with the power of protecting itself;—and places the right and safety of each, where only they can be securely placed, under its own guardianship. Without this there can be no systematic, peaceful, or effective resistance to the natural tendency of each to come into conflict with the others: and without this there can be no constitution. It is this negative power,—the power of preventing or arresting the action of the government,—be it called by what term it may,—veto, interposition, nullification, check, or balance of power,—which, in fact, forms the constitution. They are all but different names for the negative power. In all its forms, and under all its names, it results from the concurrent majority. Without this there can be no negative and, without a negative, no constitution. The assertion is true in reference to all constitutional governments, be their forms what they may. It is, indeed, the negative power which makes the constitution,—and the positive which makes the government. The one is the power of acting;—and the other the power of preventing or arresting action. The two, combined, make constitutional governments.

But, as there can be no constitution without the negative power, and no negative power without the concurrent majority;—it follows, necessarily, that where the numerical majority has the sole control of the government, there can be no constitution; as constitution implies limitation or restriction,—and, of course, is inconsistent with the idea of sole or exclusive power. And hence, the numerical, unmixed with the concurrent majority, necessarily forms, in all cases, absolute government....

Among the other advantages which governments of the concurrent have over those of the numerical majority,—and which strongly illustrates their more popular character, is,— that they admit, with safety, a much greater extension of the right of suffrage. It may be safely extended in such governments to universal suffrage: that is,—to every male citizen of mature age, with few ordinary exceptions; but it cannot be so far extended in those of the numerical majority, without placing them ultimately under the control of the more ignorant and dependent portions of the community. For, as the community becomes populous, wealthy, refined, and highly civilized, the difference between the rich and the poor will become more strongly marked; and the number of the ignorant and dependent greater in proportion to the rest of the community. With the increase of this difference, the tendency to conflict between them will become stronger; and, as the poor and dependent become more numerous in proportion, there will be, in governments of the numerical majority, no want of leaders among the wealthy and ambitious, to excite and direct them in their efforts to obtain the control.

The case is different in governments of the concurrent majority. There, mere numbers have not the absolute control; and the wealthy and intelligent being identified in interest with the poor and ignorant of their respective portions or interests of the community, become their leaders and protectors. And hence, as the latter would have neither hope nor inducement to rally the former in order to obtain the control, the right of suffrage, under such a government, may be safely enlarged to the extent stated, without incurring the hazard to which such enlargement would expose governments of the numerical majority.

In another particular, governments of the concurrent majority have greatly the advantage. I allude to the difference in their respective tendency, in reference to dividing or uniting the community. That of the concurrent...is to unite the community, let its interests be ever so diversified or opposed; while that of the numerical is to divide it into two conflicting portions, let its interests be, naturally, ever so united and identified.

That the numerical majority will divide the community, let it be ever so homogeneous, into two great parties, which will be engaged in perpetual struggles to obtain the control of the government, has already been established. The great importance of the object at stake, must necessarily form strong party attachments and party antipathies;— attachments on the part of the members of each to their respective parties, through whose efforts they hope to accomplish an object dear to all; and antipathies to the opposite party, as presenting the only obstacle to success.

In order to have a just conception of their force, it must be taken into consideration, that the object to be won or lost appeals to the strongest passions of the human heart,— avarice, ambition, and rivalry. It is not then wonderful, that a form of government, which periodically stakes all its honors and emoluments, as prizes to be contended for, should divide the community into two great hostile parties; or that party attachments, in the progress of the strife, should become so strong among the members of each respectively, as to absorb almost every feeling of our nature, both social and individual; or that their mutual antipathies should be carried to such an excess as to destroy, almost entirely, all sympathy between them, and to substitute in its place the strongest aversion. Nor is it surprising, that under their joint influence, the community should cease to be the common centre of attachment, or that each party should find that centre only in itself. It is thus, that, in such governments, devotion to party becomes stronger than devotion to country,—the promotion of the interests of party more important than the promotion of the common good of the whole, and its triumph and ascendency, objects of far greater solicitude, than the safety and prosperity of the community. It is thus, also, that the numerical majority, by regarding the community as a unit, and having, as such, the same interests throughout all its parts, must, by its necessary operation, divide it into two hostile parts, waging, under the forms of law, incessant hostilities against each other.

The concurrent majority, on the other hand, tends to unite the most opposite and conflicting interests, and to blend the whole in one common attachment to the country. By giving to each interest, or portion, the power of self-protection, all strife and struggle between them for ascendency, is prevented; and, thereby, not only every feeling calculated to weaken the attachment to the whole is suppressed, but the individual and the social feelings are made to unite in one common devotion to country. Each sees and feels that it can best promote its own prosperity by conciliating the good-will, and promoting the prosperity of the others. And hence, there will be diffused throughout the whole community kind feelings between its different portions; and, instead of antipathy, a rivalry amongst them to promote the interests of each other, as far as this can be done consistently with the interest of all. Under the combined influence of these causes, the interests of each would be merged in the common interests of the whole; and thus, the community would become a unit, by becoming the common centre of attachment of all its parts. And hence, instead of faction, strife, and struggle for party ascendency, there would be patriotism, nationality, harmony, and a struggle only for supremacy in promoting the common good of the whole.

… [I]t is a great and dangerous error to suppose that all people are equally entitled to liberty. It is a reward to be earned, not a blessing to be gratuitously lavished on all alike;—a reward reserved for the intelligent, the patriotic, the virtuous and deserving;—and not a boon to be bestowed on a people too ignorant, degraded and vicious, to be capable either of appreciating or of enjoying it. Nor is it any disparagement to liberty, that such is, and ought to be the case. On the contrary, its greatest praise,—its proudest distinction is, that an all-wise Providence has reserved it, as the noblest and highest reward for the development of our faculties, moral and intellectual. A reward more appropriate than liberty could not be conferred on the deserving;—nor a punishment inflicted on the undeserving more just, than to be subject to lawless and despotic rule. This dispensation seems to be the result of some fixed law;—and every effort to disturb or defeat it, by attempting to elevate a people in the scale of liberty, above the point to which they are entitled to rise, must ever prove abortive, and end in disappointment. The progress of a people rising from a lower to a higher point in the scale of liberty, is necessarily slow,—and by attempting to precipitate, we either retard, or permanently defeat it.

There is another error, not less great and dangerous, usually associated with the one which has just been considered. I refer to the opinion, that liberty and equality are so intimately united, that liberty cannot be perfect without perfect equality.

That they are united to a certain extent,—and that equality of citizens, in the eyes of the law, is essential to liberty in a popular government, is conceded. But to go further, and make equality of *condition* essential to liberty, would be to destroy both liberty and progress. The reason is, that inequality of condition, while it is a necessary consequence of liberty, is, at the same time, indispensable to progress. In order to understand why this is so, it is necessary to bear in mind, that the main spring to progress is, the desire of individuals to better their condition; and that the strongest impulse which can be given to it is, to leave individuals free to exert themselves in the manner they may deem best for that purpose, as far at least as it can be done consistently with the ends for which government is ordained,—and to secure to all the fruits of their exertions. Now, as individuals differ greatly from each other, in intelligence, sagacity, energy, perseverance, skill, habits of industry and economy, physical power, position and opportunity,—the necessary effect of leaving all free to exert themselves to better their condition, must be a corresponding inequality between those who may possess these qualities and advantages in a high degree, and those who may be deficient in them. The only means by which this result can be prevented are, either to impose such restrictions on the exertions of those who may possess them in a high degree, as will place them on a level with those who do not; or to deprive them of the fruits of their exertions. But to impose such restrictions on them would be destructive of liberty,—while, to deprive them of the fruits of their exertions, would be to destroy the desire of bettering their condition. It is, indeed, this inequality of condition between the front and rear ranks, in the march of progress, which gives so strong an impulse to the former to maintain their position, and to the latter to press forward into their files. This gives to progress its greatest impulse. To force the front rank back to the rear, or attempt to push forward the rear into line with the front, by the interposition of the government, would put an end to the impulse, and effectually arrest the march of progress.

These great and dangerous errors have their origin in the prevalent opinion that all men are born free and equal;—than which nothing can be more unfounded and false. It rests upon the assumption of a fact, which is contrary to universal observation, in whatever light it may be regarded. It is, indeed, difficult to explain how an opinion so destitute of all sound reason, ever could have been so extensively entertained, unless we regard it as being confounded with another, which has some semblance of truth;—but which, when properly understood, is not less false and dangerous. I refer to the assertion, that all men are equal in the state of nature; meaning, by a state of nature, a state of individuality, supposed to have existed prior to the social and political state; and in which men lived apart and independent of each other. If such a state ever did exist, all men would have been, indeed, free and equal in it; that is, free to do as they pleased, and exempt from the authority or control of others— as, by supposition, it existed anterior to society and government. But such a state is purely hypothetical. It never did, nor can exist; as it is inconsistent with the preservation and perpetuation of the race. It is, therefore, a great misnomer to call it *the state of nature*. Instead of being the natural state of man, it is, of all conceivable states, the most opposed to his nature—most repugnant to his feelings, and most incompatible with his wants. His natural state is, the social and political—the one for which his Creator made him, and the only one in which he can preserve and perfect his race. As, then, there never was such a state as the, so called, state of nature, and never can be, it follows, that men, instead of being born in it, are born in the social and political state; and of course, instead of being born free and equal, are born subject, not only to parental authority, but to the laws and institutions of the country where born, and under whose protection they draw their first breath.

LOUISA McCORD

"Enfranchisement of Woman"
(1852)

As a manager, before her marriage, of an inherited cotton plantation of some two hundred slaves and, during the Civil War, an efficient organizer of nursing at the makeshift military hospital at South Carolina College, Louisa McCord (1810–1879), the classically educated daughter of the president of the United States Bank, Langdon Cheves, was not a stereotypical Southern belle. (In a bust by the sculptor Hiram Powers, McCord appears in a draped toga, looking very much the strong and handsome Roman matron Cornelia that she portrayed in her verse drama, *Caius Gracchus*.) This same strength drove her writings as well. The most intellectually influential female author in the Old South and the only woman in ante-bellum America to write extensively about political economy, McCord vigorously defended in articles in the leading Southern journals both free-trade policies and the Southern slave system. The latter, she argued, guaranteed both the economically profitable exploitation of a biologically inferior race and its protection from a competitive system that would otherwise bring about its extinction.

This fiercely sober, bipolar vision was also the basis of her searing anti–women's rights essay that she published in her region's premiere intellectual journal, the *Southern Quarterly Review*. She aimed her article at two targets: the reported proceedings of the second "National Woman's Rights Convention" held in 1851 in Worcester, Massachusetts, and that same year's anonymous review in the liberal British quarterly, the *Westminster Review*, of the previous year's first convention at Worcester, which had given a formidable and widely noted defense of the new movement's principles. (The *"third* sex" author who McCord mistakenly supposed was the unmarried English utilitarian and pro–women's rights writer Harriet Martineau was, in fact, the liberal philosopher John Stuart Mill's new wife, Harriet Taylor.) McCord's bull's-eye was a negative version of the same argument linking antislavery ideology and women's political activism that radical abolitionists like Garrison and Grimké had put up a decade and a half earlier (and reproduced by Taylor in her article). Specifically, McCord argued that men's politics was the marketplace of a coarse sort of heroism, cunning, and force. It would be nothing short of disastrous, she insisted, for women to enter such a field. Rather, women needed to exploit their equal (if unequally used) intellect and their tough-minded moral superiority within their domestic sphere, "bearing and forbearing" and thereby "softening and civilizing this hard world." Although she was hopeful that such an ideal, if earnestly sought, would bring progress for both women and society, its Stoic, almost tragic (not to speak of brutally racist) cast separates it from the sentimental pieties of both antifeminists and proslavery apologists, North and South. Ironically, only a woman who knew (and perhaps coveted) the intellectual birthright and myths of Southern slaveholding men and their culture could have imagined it.

Louisa S. McCord: Political and Social Essays (Charlottesville, 1995), and *Louisa S. McCord: Poems, Drama, Biography, Letters* (Charlottesville, 1996), ed. Richard C.

Lounsbury, provide a comprehensive scholarly edition of McCord's writings. Leigh Fought, *Southern Womanhood and Slavery: A Biography of Louisa S. McCord* (Columbia, Mo., 2003), is a recent biographical study. A good analysis of McCord's economic theories may be found in Eugene D. Genovese and Elizabeth Fox-Genovese, "Slavery, Economic Development, and the Law: The Dilemma of the Southern Political Economists, 1800–1860," *Washington and Lee Law Review,* 41 (Winter 1984), 1–29. For a fine discussion of McCord's social views, see Elizabeth Fox-Genovese, *Within the Plantation Household: Black and White Women of the Old South* (Chapel Hill, 1988), 242–89. A more gender-conscious evaluation may be found in Susan A. Eacker, "A 'Dangerous Inmate' of the South: Louisa McCord on Gender and Slavery," in Christopher Morris and Steven G. Reinhardt, eds., *Southern Writers and Their Worlds* (College Station, Tex., 1996), 27–40.

…Universal equality! *Fraternité* extended even to womanhood! And why not Up for your rights, ladies! What is the worth of a civilization which condemns one half of mankind to Helot submissiveness? Call ye this civilization, with such a stained and blurred blot upon it? "Out, damned spot! Out, I say! One; two; why then 'tis time to do it!" The knell of injustice has sounded! The world is awake! All men (and women too) are born free and equal. Every man shall have his rights, according to his own reading of them. Let A knock down B, and B trip up C. *Vogue la galère!* Reform! Reform! If the world should be turned somewhat topsy-turvy thereby, and chance, hi the hustle, to be kicked back to barbarism and the dark ages, or even to something worse, perchance, than man has yet the memory of—never mind. *Fiat Justicia ruat Cælum.* Capital motto that, by the way. Like the prince's tent of the fairy-tale, it is capable of limitless extension, and all can find shelter under its interpretations. Justicia, says the communist beggar—*Justicia* means, whip me down those rich fellows and let me revel in their luxuries. Why should not I too ride in the king's carriages? *Justicia,* says Louis Napoleon, means, that I shall do what I please in this realm of France. Shoot down the beggarly rascal who disputes it. *Justicia,* says Austria, means that Hungary shall not breathe without my permit. *Justicia,* growls the Russian bear, means imperial might. *Justicia,* answers Kossuth, means democratic might. *Justicia,* shouts Cuffee, means that I am a sun-burned white man. *Justicia,* responds Harriet Martineau, means that I may discard decency and my petticoats at my own convenience; and, *Justicia,* echo her Worcester Convention sisters, means extinction to all law, human and divine. God is a bugbear—decency a dream. *Fiat Justicia ruat Cælum.* The beggar shall have his *patés de foie gras;* the negro shall be christened a white man; and woman—surely she, too, shall profit by this general revolution! Stand to your colours, ladies! Take for your flag the whole animal, in *extenso,* from snout to tail, with the motto, *ab actu ad posse valet consecutio;* i.e.—if a man swallows the head, surely he may take in the tail also. Follow close, ladies. The door of privilege is open pretty wide for the admission of Cuffee. Should *he* get in, surely *you* might follow. Woman is awake. "You see her eyes are open." "Ay, but their sense is shut." Forgive us, you true women; you, the noblest of practical philosophers; you, who bear and forbear, humbling yourselves, that others may rise upon your efforts, and yet ceasing those efforts, never; you, who see with love and without envy, husband, brother, or son, too often in the pride of manhood, with slight and sneer contemning his "womankind," and holding her even in his love, as

"Something better than his dog—a little dearer than his horse;"

you, who can see this, feel it, and yet strive on; you, whose heart may ache, and yet labour still, seeking no reward, knowing no reward, save the fulfilment of that high duty, of that great mission of love, which is woman's mission on earth. *Your* eyes are indeed open, nor is their sense shut. A true woman, fulfilling a woman's duties, (and do not let our masculine readers suppose that we would *confine* these to shirt-making, pudding-mixing, and other such household gear, nor yet even to the adornment of her own fair person,) a high-minded, intellectual woman, disdaining not her position, nor, because the world calls it humble, seeking to put aside God's and Nature's law, to *her* pleasure; an earnest woman, striving, as all earnest minds *can* strive, to do and to work, even as the Almighty laws of Nature teach her that God would have her to do and to work, is, perhaps, the highest personification of Christian self-denial, love and charity, which the world can see. God, who

Source: Southern Quarterly Review, 5 (April 1852), 322–41.

has made every creature to its place, has, perhaps, not given to woman the most enviable position in his creation, but a most clearly defined position he *has* given her. Let her object, then, be to raise herself *in* that position. *Out* of it, there is only failure and degradation. There be those, however, and unfortunately not a few, who look upon these old-fashioned ideas as exploded. God's and Nature's laws have nothing to do with the question. A Harriet Martineau, or a Fanny Wright, would prefer a different position in the picture, and many a weak sister is misled by them.

In every error there is its shadow of truth. Error is but truth turned awry, or looked at through a wrong medium. As the straightest rod will, in appearance, curve when one half of it is placed under water, so God's truths, leaning down to earth, are often distorted to our view. Woman's condition certainly admits of improvement, (but when have the strong forgotten to oppress the weak?) but never can any amelioration result from the guidance of her prophets in this present move. Here, as in all other improvements, the good must be brought about by working with, not against—by seconding, not opposing—Nature's laws. Woman, seeking as a woman, may raise her position,—seeking as a man, we repeat, she but degrades it. Every thing contrary to Nature, is abhorrent to Nature, and the mental aberrations of woman, which we are now discussing, excite at once pity and disgust, like those revolting physical deformities which the eye turns from with involuntary loathing, even while the hand of charity is extended to relieve them. We are no undervaluer of woman; rather we profess ourselves her advocate. Her mission is, to our seeming, even nobler than man's, and she is, in the true fulfilment of that mission, certainly the higher being. Passion governed, suffering conquered, self forgotten, how often is she called upon, as daughter, wife, sister and mother, to breathe in her half-broken but loving heart, the whispered prayer, that greatest, most beautiful, most self-forgetting of all prayers ever uttered,—"Father, forgive them, they know not what they do." Woman's duty, woman's nature, is to love, to sway by love; to govern by love, to teach by love, to civilize by love! Our reviewer may sneer,—already does sneer,—about "animal functions" and the "maternity argument." We fear not to meet him, or rather her; (for we do not hesitate to pronounce this article to be the production of one of the *third* sex; that, viz. of the Worcester Convention petticoated would-be's;) true woman's love is too beautiful a thing to be blurred by such sneers. It is a love such as man knoweth not, and Worcester Conventionists cannot imagine. Pure and holy, self-devoted and suffering, woman's love is the breath of that God of love, who, loving and pitying, has bid *her* learn to love and to suffer, implanting in her bosom the one single comfort that she is the watching spirit, the guardian angel of those she loves. We say not that all women are thus; we say not that most women are thus. Alas! no; for thus would man's vices be shamed from existence, and the world become perfect. But we do say, that such is the type of woman, such her moral formation, such her perfection, she falls short of the model type of her nature. Only in aiming at this type, is there any use for her in this world, and only in proportion as she nears it, each according to the talent which God has given her, can she contribute to bring forward the world in that glorious career of progress which Omniscience has marked out for it. Each can labour, each can strive, lovingly and earnestly, in her own sphere. "Life is real! Life is earnest!" Not less for her than for man. She has no right to bury her talent beneath silks or ribands, frippery or flowers; nor yet has she the right, because she fancies not her task, to grasp at another's, which is, or which she imagines is, easier. This is baby play. "Life is real! Life is earnest!" Let woman so read it—let woman so team it—and she has no need to make her influence felt by a stump speech, or a vote at the polls; she has no need for the exercise of her intellect (and woman, we grant, may have a great, a longing, a hungering intellect, equal to man's) to be gratified with a seat in Congress, or a scuffle for the ambiguous honour of the Presidency. Even at her own fire-side, may she find duties enough, cares enough, troubles enough, thought enough, wisdom enough, to fit a martyr for the stake, a philosopher for life, or a saint for heaven. There are, there have been, and there will be, in every age, great hero-souls in woman's form, as well as man's. It imports little whether history notes them. The hero-soul aims at its certain duty, heroically meeting it, whether glory or shame, worship or contumely, follow its accomplishment. Laud and merit is due to such performance. *Fulfil* thy destiny; *oppose* it not. Herein lies thy track. Keep it. Nature's sign-posts are within thee, and it were well for thee to learn to read them. Poor fool! canst thou not spell out thy lesson, that ever thus thou fightest against Nature? Not there! not there! Nothing is done by *that* track. Never; from the creation of the world, never. Hero-souls will not try it. It is the mock-hero, the dissatisfied, the grasping, the self-ish, the low-aspiring, who tries that track. Turn aside from it, dear friends—there is no heaven-fruit there; only hell-fruit and sorrow.

We regret to believe that this move for woman's (so called) enfranchisement, is hith-erto, entirely (at least in its modern rejuvenescence) of American growth. Thank heaven! our modest Southern sisters have held aloof from the defiling pitch, and Worcester Conventions are entirely a Yankee notion. Not a little surprised have we been to see, in so long-established and respectable a periodical as the Westminster Quarterly, a grave defence of such mad pranks as are being enacted by these petticoated despisers of their sex,—these would-be men,—these things that puzzle us to name. They should be women, but, like Macbeth's witches, they come to us in such a questionable shape, that we hesitate so to interpret them. Moral monsters they are; things which Nature disclaims. In ceasing to be women, they yet have failed to make themselves men. Unsexed things they are, we trust, like the poor bat in the fable, who complains, "neither mouse nor bird will play with me," destined to flit their twilight course, alone and unimitated.

Such is the point of view in which we have hitherto looked upon this subject, that we feel as though to attack it seriously, were scarcely less ridiculous than to defend it. But the poison is spreading; and, truly, except that the fashion of the thing is a little newer, it is but a piece with negro emancipation; a subject with which the world has been stunned for many a year, until, at last, it now seems ready, with fanatic zeal, to sacrifice all that it has gained, of good, of beautiful, and of true, at the shrine of this fearful phantom. Madness becomes, sometimes, contagious; and, to judge from the symptoms, society labours, at present, under a high state of brain-fever—delirious, decidedly—raving over one fantastic dream or another. Communism and abolitionism have been dancing their antics through its bewildered brain; and now behold the *chef d'œuvre* of folly! Mounted on Cuffee's shoul-ders, in rides the lady! The genius of communism bows them both in, mouthing over Mr. Jefferson's "free and equal" sentence, and banishing the motto, *par nobile fratrum*. Woman! woman! respect thyself and man will respect thee. Oh! cast not off thy spear and thy shield, thine Ægis, thine anchor, thy stay! Wrapped, thou art, in a magic cloud. Cast it not off to destroy thine own divinity. Man worships thee and himself; he knows not why. Ignorantly, in thee, he bows to his "Unknown God." The benevolent, the true, the holy, the just; in a word, the God of Love speaks to him through *thee*. Woman, *cherish thy mis-sion*. Fling thyself not from the high pedestal whereon God has placed thee. Cast not from thee thy moral strength—for, lo! what then art thou! Wretchedly crawling to thy shame, thy physical weakness trampled under foot by a brutal master, behold thee, thou proud mother of earth, to what art thou sunk!

We have said that this move is entirely of American growth. Our reviewer tells us, exultingly, that there are indications of the example being followed in England, and that a petition of women, agreed to by a large public meeting at Sheffield, and claiming the elective franchise, was presented to the House of Lords by the Earl of Carlisle. Heaven bless the mark!—surely our poor world is moon-struck! Let us, however, hear some of the reviewer's arguments, though we confess it is with a sickening loathing that we turn them over.

What first do these reformers ask? "Admission in law and in fact, to equality in all rights, political, civil and social, with the male citizens of the community." "Women are entitled to the right of suffrage, and to be considered eligible to office." "Civil and political rights acknowledge no sex, and therefore the word 'male' should be struck from every state constitution." "A co-equal share in the formation and administration of laws,—municipal, state and national,—through legislative assemblies, courts and executive offices." Then follows the memorable quotation from the "memorable document" about all men being created free and equal, the ladies arguing, with some reason, that "men" here, certainly stands for human beings, and thereby prove their right at least equal to Cuffee's. In fact, the reviewer remarks, that such being American principles, "the contradiction between principle and practice cannot be explained away. A like dereliction of the fundamental maxims of their political creed, has been committed by the Americans in the flagrant instance of the negroes; but of this (she charitably remarks) they are learning to recognize the turpitude. After a struggle, which, by many of its incidents, deserves the name of heroic, the abolitionists are now so strong in numbers and influence, that they hold the balance of parties in the United States. It was fitting that the men whose names will remain associated with the extirpation, from the democratic soil of America, of the aristocracy of colour, should be among the originators, for America, and for the rest of the world, of the first collective protest against the aristocracy of sex; a distinction as accidental as that of colour, and fully as irrelevant to all questions of government."

This is certainly taking a position, and we are glad to see that the advocates of this move class themselves exactly where they should be, cheek by jowl with the abolitionists. We thank them, at least, for saving us the trouble of proving this position. Of the first Worcester Convention, that of 1850, (which is, in fact, the second Woman's Rights Convention, the first having been held somewhere in Ohio,) "the president was a woman, and nearly all the chief speakers women,—numerously reinforced, however, by men, among whom were some of the most distinguished leaders in the *kindred cause* of negro emancipation." One of the resolutions of this meeting declares "that every party which claims to represent the humanity, the civilization, and the progress of the age, is bound to inscribe upon its banners, equality before the law, *without distinction of sex or colour.*" Oh! there are things so horrible that man, in sheer terror, will mock at what he hates, and think to sneer the scoffing field away. We laugh at this, but it is frightful;—frightful to think that thousands of women, in these United States, have signed, and thousands more, if these accounts be correct, are willing to sign their names to such a document. Oh! woman, thou the ministering angel of God's earth, to what devil's work art thou degrading thyself.

But, their reasoning in all this? for they have an argument. First, then, as we have just seen, they claim that the distinctions of *sex and colour are accidental and irrelevant to all questions of government.* This is certainly clinching the argument, and that by an assumption which is so extremely illogical, that we are forced to say, if this reforming sisterhood can advance no better ground for their pretensions, it shows them but ill-fitted for the reins of state which they propose taking in hand. The distinction of colour has for many years been a point in discussion, and science has now settled that, so far from being accidental, it is an immutable fact of creation, that the black skin and woolly head are distinctive marks of race, which no age, climate, nor circumstance, has ever been able to efface; and there is no more accident in a negro's not being born a white man, than there is in his not being born a baboon, a mouse, or an elephant. As to the distinction of sex being accidental, this is a remarkable discovery of the present enlightened and progressive age. Sex and colour are severally so essential to the being of a woman and a negro, that it is impossible to imagine the existence of either, without these distinctive marks. We have hitherto understood that the sex of a human being was fixed long before its entrance into this world, by rules and causes, which, entirely unknown to man, were equally beyond his reach, and that of accident. Such has, we believe, been the received opinion of the learned; but Miss Martineau (who is, we take it, our reviewer) has determined to assume the position of vice regent to Deity, (a power, by the way, which she seems inclined entirely to depose,) and, like *Sganarelle,* in Molière's witty play of the *"Medecin malgrè lui,"* she arranges things to suit her own ignorance. Sganarelle having assumed the fact that the heart was on the right side of the human system, has the suggestion made by one of his bewildered admired admirers, that the generally received opinion of science and experience has universally placed it on the left. Oh! answers the ready quack, *"celà étant autrefois ainsi: mais nous avons changé tout celà."* If Miss Martineau and her sisterhood should prove powerful enough to depose *Le Bon Dieu,* and perfect their democratic system, by reducing His influence to a *single vote,* we do not doubt that, according to the approved majority system, it will be clearly and indisputably proved that Cuffee is Sir Isaac Newton, and Mrs. Cuffee, Napoleon Buonaparte, and Miss Martineau herself may stand for Cuffee, unless, indeed, she should prefer (as some of her recent works seem to indicate) to have it decided that she is *Le Bon Dieu* himself. She could probably carry the votes, with equal ease either way, and get rid of these little accidental distinctions. We, however, must, at this point of the question, be old-fashioned enough to declare ourselves conservatives. We cannot entirely shake off old prejudices, and still, spite of Dr. Sganarelle and Miss Martineau, are inclined to look for our hearts on the left side of our bodies, and for our God in the glorious works of his creation. We prefer His rule to Miss Martineau's, and believe that He has given the distinctions of race and sex, not accidentally, (with Omniscience there is no accident,) but distinctively, to mark the unchanging order of His creation—certain beings to certain ends.

All the further arguments of our reviewer are based upon the assumption we have been discussing, and with it fall to the ground. If beings are created to different ends, it is impossible to consider in them the point of equality or inequality, except in so far as their differences are of a kind to still allow them to be cast in the same category. As, for instance, the man, as animal, is superior to the beast, whose subordinate intellect makes him, as co-labourer of the soil, or as rival candidate for its benefits, inferior to man. The white man is, for the same reason, superior to the negro. The woman, classed as man, must also be inferior, if only (we waive for the moment the question of intellect) because she is inferior in corporeal strength. A female-man must necessarily be inferior to a male-man, so long as the latter has the power to knock her down. In womanhood is her strength and her triumph. Class both as woman, and the man again becomes the inferior, inasmuch as he is incapable of fulfilling her functions. A male woman could as ill assume the place and duties of womanhood, as a female-man could those of manhood. Each is strong in his own nature. They are neither inferior, nor superior, nor equal. They are different. The air has its uses, and the fire has its uses, but these are neither equal nor unequal—they are different.

"A reason (says the reviewer) must be given why any thing should be permitted to one person and interdicted to another." A reason!—a reason why man cannot drink fire and breathe water! A scientific answer about hydrogen and oxygen will not answer the purpose. These are facts, not reasons. Why? Why? Why is anything on God's earth what it is? Can Miss Martineau tell? We cannot. God has made it so, and reason, instinct and experience teach us its uses. Woman, Nature teaches you yours.

"The speakers at the Convention in America, have (says the reviewer) done wisely and right, in refusing to entertain the question of the peculiar aptitudes, either of women or of men, or the limits within which this or that occupation may be supposed to be more adapted to the one or the other." In the name of all that is foolish, what shall we consider, if not the aptitude of a person or thing to his or its uses? It is fortunate that Miss Martineau has never descended from her high sphere, to allow herself to be burthened with the cares of a family; for had she, in that capacity, forgotten to consult the aptitudes of things to their uses, she might, in some inauspicious fit of philosophic experiment, have committed the unlucky blunder of packing her children in December ice to warm them, or, perchance, cast the little unfortunates into the fire, by way of cleansing their dirty faces. And what might the philosophical and reforming world have thus lost! The ignorant mob, who persist in judging of the uses of things by their aptitudes, might have committed the egregious mistake of taking this doubty philosopher—this Wilberforce of women—this *petit bon Dieu*—for a murderess, and hung her for the interesting little experiment of burning her brats.

We, of the conservatives, who judge of the uses of things by their aptitudes, can read woman's duties anywhere better than in an election crowd, scuffling with Cuffee for a vote. Imagine the lovely Miss Caroline, the fascinating Miss Martha, elbowing Sambo for the stump! All being equals, and no respect for persons to be expected, the natural conclusion is, that Miss Caroline or Martha, being indisputably (even the Worcester conventionalists allow that) corporeally weaker than Sambo, would be thrust into the mud. "Hello da! Miss Caroline git two teet knock out, and Miss Marta hab a black eye and bloody nose!" "Well, wha' faw I stop fa dat? Ebery man must help hisself. I git de stump anyhow, and so, fellow-citizens, Sambo will show how Miss Marta desarve what she git." Or, let us suppose them hoisted through this dirty work. The member is chaired—some fair lady, some Mrs. or Miss Paulina Davis, who, we see, figures as President of the last convention, or one of her vices, Angelina Grimké Weld, or Lucretia Mott—let us imagine the gende Paulina, Angelina, or Lucretia fairly pitted, in the Senate, against Mr. Foote, for instance, or Mr. Benton, or the valourous Houston, or any other mere patriot, whom luck and electioneering have foisted there. We do not doubt their feminine power, in the war of words—and again we beg to defer a little the question of intellect—but are the ladies ready for a boxing match? Such things happen sometimes; and though it is not impossible that the fair Paulina, Angelina and Lucretia might have the courage to face a pistol, have they the strength to resist a blow? La Fontaine tells us a fable of a wax candle, which, being ambitiously desirous of immortality, and seeing a handful of clay, that, hardened by the fire into a brick, was enabled to resist time and the elements, turned the matter over for a while in its waxen brains, and finally determined to try the experiment in its own person. A fire being conveniently near, and concluding, we presume, like the lady conventionalists, that all arguments on aptitudes and uses was quite *de trop,* in so clear a case of logical induction,

> "Par sa propre et pure folie
> Il se lança dedans. Ce fut mal raisonné.
> Ce cièrge ne savait grain de philosophie."

The fact that women have been queens and regents, and filled well these positions, cited by the reviewer in the cases of Elizabeth, Isabella, Maria Theresa, Catharine of Russia,

Blanche, etc., proves that woman, as a woman and a monarch—with the double difference, that the habits of the civilized world accord to these positions—has had the intellect to fill the position well; but it does not prove, and rather goes to disprove, her power of struggling with the masses. As woman and queen, doubly isolated from those masses, she kept her position, simply because of such isolation—because, supported by the laws and habits of society, none dared insult or resist her. But, suppose those laws and habits abrogated, what would have become of the virago, Elizabeth, when she gave the lordly Essex a blow on the ear? If ever it should happen to the fair Paulina, Angelina or Lucretia to try, under the new *regime,* a similar experiment on any of their male coadjutors or opponents, it is rather probable that they may receive, upon the subject of aptitudes and uses, a somewhat striking lesson. Of the combatant ladies, similarly cited, the same remark is to be made. Ladies of the feudal ages, they generally were petty monarchs: that is to say, defending their strongholds. These were always supported and strengthened, rather than impeded by their sex, the *prestige* of sex seconding and doubling the admiration accorded to their remarkable actions. Joan of Arc, (decidedly the most remarkable of heroines, and, strange to say, not cited by the reviewer,) was a wonderful woman; great as a woman; a phenomenon in her way, certainly, but still a woman-phenomenon. Her deeds were unusual for woman, but, nevertheless, done as a woman, and claiming, for their sanction, not the rights and habits of manhood, but divine inspiration. She never levelled herself to man, or, so doing, must have sunk to the rank of the coarse *femmes de la Halle* of the French revolution. Such, too, would of necessity be the case with the man-woman that our conventionists would manufacture. Deprived of all which has hitherto, in separating her from man, wrapped her, as it were, in a veil of deity; naked of all those observances and distinctions which have been, if not always her efficient, still her only shield; turned out upon the waste common of existence, with no distinctive mark but corporeal weakness; she becomes the inevitable victim of brutal strength. The reviewer acknowledges (or rather, remarks, for she does not seem to be conscious that it is an acknowledgment) that to account for the subjection of woman, "no other explanation is needed than physical force." Setting aside, then, for the moment, all other differences, we would be glad to have the lady explain how she would do away with the difficulty arising from this acknowledged physical inferiority? Man is corporeally stronger than woman, and because he, in the unjust use of his strength, has frequently, habitually, (we will allow her the full use of her argument,) even invariably, oppressed and misused woman, how does she propose to correct the abuse? Strangely, by pitting woman against man, in a direct state of antagonism; by throwing them into the arena together, stripped for the strife; by saying to the man, this woman is a man like yourself, your equal and similar, possessing all rights which you possess, and (of course she must allow) possessing none others. In such a strife, what becomes of corporeal weakness? Perhaps we will be told how man conquers the wild beast, and, by knowledge and intellect, holds in sway the mighty elephant and the forest's king. True, by *intellect.* He has the superiority of intellect, and he uses it. It is God's and nature's law, that he should use it. Man, generally, uses it to subdue his inferior, the beast. The white man uses it to subdue his inferior, the negro. Both are right, for both are according to God's law. The same argument has been used, to prove the necessity of woman's subjection. This, we think, is taking mistaken ground, and unnecessarily assuming a doubtfully tenable position. Woman's bodily frame is enough to account for her position. The differences of mind between the sexes, we are, ourselves, inclined to regard rather as differences than inequalities. More of this anon, however. Granting, for the moment, exact mental equality, how will the conventionists redeem corporeal deficiencies? They do not pretend that woman is the superior mind, only the equal. Still, then, man—where they are matched against each other—where woman assumes manhood, and measures herself hand to hand with him—has, of necessity, the superiority—a brutal superiority; if you please, but still the superiority—and, in proportion as it is brutal, will the triumph it gives be brutal. Woman throws away her strength, when she *brings herself down* to man's level. She throws away that moral strength, that shadow of divinity, which nature has given her to keep man's ferocity in curb. Grant her to be his equal, and instantly she sinks to his inferior, which, as yet, we maintain she has never been.

Many women—even, we grant, the majority of women—throw themselves away upon follies. So, however, do men; and this, perhaps, as a necessary consequence, for woman is the mother of the man. Woman has allowed herself to be, alternately, made the toy and the slave of man; but this rather through her folly than her nature. Not wholly *her* folly, either. *Her* folly, and *man's* folly, have made the vices and the punishment of both. Woman has certainly not her true place, and this place she as certainly should seek to gain. We have said that every error has its shadow of truth, and, so far, the conventionists are right. But, alas! how wide astray are they groping from their goal! Woman has not her true place, because she—because man—has not yet learned the full extent and importance of her mission. These innovators would seek to restore, by driving her entirely from that mission; as though some unlucky pedestrian, shoved from the security of the side-walk, should, in his consternation, seek to remedy matters, by rushing into the thickest thoroughfare of hoofs and wheels. Woman will reach the greatest height of which she is capable—the greatest, perhaps, of which humanity is capable—not by becoming man, but by becoming, more than ever, woman. By perfecting herself, she perfects mankind; and hers, we have said, is the higher mission, because, from her, must the advance towards perfection begin. The woman must raise the man, by helping, not by rivalling, him. Without woman, this world of mankind were a wrangling dog-kennel. Could woman be transformed into man, the same result would follow. She it is who softens; she it is who civilizes; and, although history acknowledges her not, she it is who, not in the meteoric brilliancy of warrior or monarch, but in the quiet, unwearied and unvarying path of duty, the home of the mother, the wife and the sister, teaching man his destiny, purifies, exalts, and guides him to his duty.

> "Under a nominal recognition of a moral code, common to both [says our reviewer] in practice, self-will and self-assertion form the type of what are designated as manly virtues; while abnegation of self, patience, resignation and submission to power, unless when resistance is demanded by other interests than their own, have been stamped, by general consent, as pre-eminently the duties and graces required of women. The meaning being merely that power makes itself the centre of moral obligation, and that a man likes to have his own will, but does not like that his domestic companion should have a will different from his."

Now, all this means, if it means anything, that woman, in the present condition of the world, is a self-denying, patient model of Christian love and charity; while man, unable to conquer his harsher passions, still benefits by her virtues. The reviewer, envying him the lordly privilege of getting into a passion, raving and ranting, would advise all womankind to disturb him in his monopoly, and to rave, rant and be selfish along with him. We confess, for ourselves, that where a poor woman, borne away by human weakness, and restive under oppression, catches the raving malady a little, we seldom feel inclined to be harsh in our judgments of her. Nature is frail—we pity her, and confess that her case is a hard one. Even Zantippe, "the famous old scold," could, no doubt, have shown cause for exasperation; and it is not unlikely that, as philosophers are men, the good dame had no little reason on her side. Still, if she had borne life meekly, although her present great renown in history and spelling-book, spreading the knowledge of her name as far as that of old crooked back Z himself, would never have been attained; even Miss Martineau, we think, must confess that, while less celebrated, Mrs. Zantippe would have been a more perfect and more amiable character; and we, while we feel a deep interest in the sorrows of this far-famed personage, would hardly deem her a desirable model for our daughters. Wrath and power are hideous and fearful; wrath and weakness are hideous and contemptible. We trust that such of our sisters as may have attained the beautiful point of perfection, which our reviewer rather contemptuously refers to, will be sufficiently rewarded by the proud consciousness of duty fulfilled, to induce them to work on, in their righteous course—if not a flashing beacon of fight to a benighted world, at least a holy ray of God's own sunlight, to purify and to bless. If ladies fear that these concessions are too great, and the pride of sex inclines them to rebel a little, let them remember that they are concessions, not to man, but to God;—not to the husband or the brother—who, if he raves too hard, it is not in human weakness not to feel a little spiteful against—but to nature and mankind. Each,—the lowliest individual woman,—is in bearing and forbearing, in earnest striving and in patient suffering, doing her share towards softening and civilizing this hard world. Such is God's task to her, and she must fulfil it, or pass away either the frivolous plaything of a day, or the scorned abortion of a misplaced and grovelling ambition.

As regards the question of intellect, it is a most difficult one to argue. We are ourselves inclined to believe that the difference of intellect in the sexes exists, as we have said, rather in kind than degree. There is much talk of the difference of education and rearing bestowed upon individuals of either sex, and we think too much stress is laid upon it. Education, no doubt, influences the intellect in each individual case; but it is as logically certain, that intellect, in its kind and degree, influences education *en masse;*—that is to say, Thomas, the individual man, may be better suited to woman's duties, than Betty, the individual woman, and *vice versa.* Thomas might make a capital child's nurse, in which Betty succeeds but badly, while Betty might be quite competent to beat Thomas hollow in a stump oration; and yet we have a fair right to argue, that Thomas and Betty are but individual exceptions to a general rule, which general rule is plainly indicated by the universal practice of mankind. The fact that such relative positions of the sexes, and such habits of mind, have existed, more or less modified, in all ages of the world, and under all systems of government, goes far to prove that these are the impulses of instinct and teachings of Nature. It is certainly a little hard upon Mrs. Betty to be forced from occupations for which she feels herself particularly well qualified, and to make way for Mr. Thomas, who, although particularly *ill*-qualified for them, will be certain to assert his right; but laws cannot be made for exceptional cases, and if Mrs. Betty has good sense, as well as talent, she will let the former curb the latter; she will teach her woman-intellect to curb her man-intellect, and will make herself the stronger woman thereby. The fact that less effort has been made to teach woman certain things, is a strong argument that she has (taking her as a class) less aptitude for being taught those certain things. It is difficult to chain down mind by any habit or any teaching, and if woman's intellect had the same turn as man's, it is most unlikely that so many myriads should have passed away and "made no sign." In the field of literature, how many women have enjoyed all the advantages which men can command, and yet how very few have distinguished themselves; and how far behind are even those few from the great and burning lights of letters! Who ever hopes to see a woman Shakspeare! And yet a greater than Shakspeare may she be. It may be doubtful whether the brilliant intellect, which, inspiring noble thoughts, leaves still the great thinker grovelling in the lowest vices and slave of his passions, without the self-command to keep them in sway, is superior to that which, knowing good and evil, grasps almost instinctively at the first. Such, in its uncorrupted nature, is woman's intellect—such her inspiration. While man *writes,* she *does;* while he imagines the hero-soul, she is often performing its task; while he is painting, she is acting. The heart, it is sometimes argued, and not the brain, is the priceless pearl of womanhood, "the oracular jewel, the Urim and Thummim, before which gross man can only inquire and adore." This is fancy and not reasoning. The heart is known to be only a part of our anatomical system, regulating the currents of the blood, and nothing more. It has, by an allegory based upon exploded error, been allowed to stand for a certain class of feelings which every body now knows to be, equally with other classes, dependant upon the brain; and, in a serious argument, not the heart and the brain, but the difference of brain; not the feeling and the intellect, but the varieties of intellect, should be discussed. We consider, therefore, the question of pre-eminence as simply idle. We have already endeavoured to prove that, whatever the intellect of woman, it would have no influence in altering the relative position of the sexes; we now go farther, and maintain that the nature of her intellect confirms this position. The higher intellect, the better is she suited to fulfil that heaviest task of life which makes her the "martyr to the pang without the palm." If she suffers,—what is this but the fate of every higher grade of humanity, which rises in suffering as it rises in dignity? for, is not all intellect suffering?

We have, throughout this article, made no reference to the biblical argument, because, with those who receive it, it is too well known and too decisive to need farther comment. To those who reject it, it is of course no argument. We have endeavoured to prove that common sense, quite independently of revelation, marks the place of woman, and that while the Scriptures confirm, they are by no means necessary to decide the question.

The resolutions of the last Worcester Convention are taken so entirely (in many sentences verbatim) from the article in the Westminster, which we have been reviewing, that very evidently the same mind has inspired both, showing thus a systematizing of the subject, that proves, we fear, some truth in the assertion of the reviewer, that this movement is a political one, and "carried on in a form which denotes an intention to persevere." A letter was read to the meeting from Miss Martineau, and putting two and two together, we conclude that Miss Martineau was the *de facto* composer of these resolutions, in which morbid vanity, "that brawl-begotten child of struggling self-conceit and self-disgust," so painfully exhibits itself. Should we prove mistaken, we can only regret that there should be two women in the world capable of such a composition. The reviewer thinks, farther, that this move "is destined to inaugurate one of the most important of those movements towards political and social reform, which are the best characteristics of the present age." When a grave periodical allows such sentiments to soil its pages, it is time for us to cease to laugh. It is time for man to open his eyes to the mischievous effects of a progressive system of reform, which allows, not illogically, such a bud to be grafted upon it. It is time for woman, in right earnest, to take up arms in her own cause, ere she be hurled by traitors of her own sex from the high pedestal where God has placed her. Let her wield those weapons of love, charity, affection, firmness, and fortitude, with which Nature arms her, and, though her path be through sorrow, even through sorrow climbs she to perfection. Richter somewhere compares a young bride to the sleeping child of *Carafola,* over which an angel holds a crown of thorns. The angel of sorrow shall indeed wake her by pressing that crown upon her brow; but let her not shrink from the waking. "Life is real! Life is earnest!" and its duties are not to be shunned because our weakness relishes them not. Let woman make herself free, in the true sense of the word, by the working out of her mission. "Liberty is duty, not license;" and woman is freest when she is the truest woman; when she finds the fewest difficulties in the way of conforming herself to her nature.

> "Not enjoyment, and not sorrow,
> Is our destined end or way,
> But to live that each to-morrow
> Find us farther than to-day.
>
> "Let us then be up and doing,
> With a heart for any fate,
> Still achieving, still pursuing,
> Learn to labour and to wait."

Woman is not what she might be, not what she ought to be. Half persuaded, as she is, that her position is one of degradation and inferiority, she becomes, as a matter of necessity, degraded to that opinion, just in so far as she is convicted of its truth; and hence, too often, folly becomes her pleasure, vanity her pride. But this is man's blotting of God's fair work. Woman is neither man's equal nor inferior, but only his different. It would indeed be well if man, convinced of this, could, in his relations with her, "throw aside his instruments of torture," and aid rather than oppress her. Thus, we firmly believe, it will be, in the perfection of time, worked out by woman's endurance and patient labouring in her own sphere; but never, certainly, by her assumption of another, equally ill-adapted to her mental and her bodily faculties. For her it is (God's apostle of love) to pass through life with "the cross, that emblem of self-sacrifice, in her hand, while her pathway across the desert is marked by the flowers which spring beneath her steps." Life's devoted martyr she may be—man's ministering angel she may be; but, for heaven's sake, mesdames, the conventionists,—not Cuffee's rival candidate for the Presidency!

GEORGE FITZHUGH

Selection from *Sociology for the South*
(1854)

The self-educated Port Royal, Virginia, lawyer-journalist George Fitzhugh (1806–1881) was a paradoxical figure among Southern intellectuals. He was often by turns parochial, naive, and hopelessly addicted to special pleading. Yet he was also the one Southern writer who more than any other tried to cast a defense of slavery that would be almost universal in its scope.

In *Sociology for the South,* Fitzhugh's first major work, he argued essentially four things. The first three were that slavery was an organic system that, therefore, could not be criticized *or* defended on any mechanistic or purely rationalistic basis; that slavery's essential feature was the master-slave relationship, which was both interdependent (as in feudalism) and protective (as in an ideal patriarchal family); and that the absence of such a feature in the North and in Europe made their capitalist systems and cultures inherently predatory and anarchic and, therefore, vastly inferior both economically and morally to the slave system and culture in the South. But what made Fitzhugh's argument unique and so radical was the soft bombshell he dropped in the closing section of his chapter "Negro Slavery": that because the essence of slavery was "protection" through "government," the system so defined ought in various ways to be applied to the North and *extended* in various ways in what Fitzhugh implicitly conceded was a less than perfectly patriarchal South. The supreme irony of Fitzhugh's position was that in advancing such protective schemes he was merely echoing, as he pointed out, many of the liberal and radical sentiments of reformers and critics in capitalist Europe and the North. As a picture of Southern slavery, Fitzhugh's critique was obviously perverse, but as a window on the contradictions of nineteenth-century capitalist culture, it was extraordinarily illuminating.

Harvey Wish, *George Fitzhugh: Propagandist of the Old South* (Baton Rouge, 1943), is a useful biography. For three provocative but divergent interpretations of the ideological significance of Fitzhugh's proslavery thought, see C. Vann Woodward's introduction, "George Fitzhugh, *Sui Generis,*" to his edition of Fitzhugh's *Cannibals All! or Slaves Without Masters* (Cambridge, Mass., 1960), vii–xxxix; Eugene D. Genovese, *The World the Slaveholders Made: Two Essays in Interpretation* (New York, 1969), 115–244, 258–65; and Drew Gilpin Faust, *A Sacred Circle: The Dilemma of the Intellectual in the Old South, 1840–1860* (Baltimore, 1977), 112–31.

Chapter I.

FREE TRADE.

Political economy is the science of free society. Its theory and its history alike establish this position. Its fundamental maxims, *Laissez-faire* and "*Pas trop gouverner,*" are at war with all kinds of slavery, for they in fact assert that individuals and peoples prosper most when governed least. It is not, therefore, wonderful that such a science should not have been believed or inculcated whilst slavery was universal. Roman and Greek masters, feudal lords and Catholic priests, if conscientious, must have deemed such maxims false and heretical, or if unconscientious, would find in their self-interest sufficient reasons to prevent their propagation....

Until now, industry had been controlled and directed by a few minds. Monopoly in its every form had been rife. Men were suddenly called on to walk alone, to act and work for themselves without guide, advice or control from superior authority. In the past, nothing like it had occurred; hence no assistance could be derived from books. The prophets themselves had overlooked or omitted to tell of the advent of this golden era, and were no better guides than the historians and philosophers. A philosophy that should guide and direct industry was equally needed with a philosophy of morals. The occasion found and made the man. For writing a one-sided philosophy, no man was better fitted than Adam Smith....

Adam Smith's philosophy is simple and comprehensive, (*teres et rotundus.*) Its leading and almost its only doctrine is, that individual well-being and social and national wealth and prosperity will be best promoted by each man's eagerly pursuing his own selfish welfare unfettered and unrestricted by legal regulations, or governmental prohibitions, farther than such regulations may be necessary to prevent positive crime. That some qualifications of this doctrine will not be found in his book, we shall not deny, but this is his system. It is obvious enough that such a governmental policy as this doctrine would result in, would stimulate energy, excite invention and industry, and bring into livelier action, genius, skill and talent. It had done so before Smith wrote, and it was no doubt the observation of those effects that suggested the theory. His friends and acquaintances were of that class, who, in the war of the wits to which free competition invited, were sure to come off victors. His country, too, England and Scotland, in the arts of trade and in manufacturing skill, was an over-match for the rest of the world. International free trade would benefit his country as much as social free trade would benefit his friends. This was his world, and had it been the only world his philosophy would have been true. But there was another and much larger world, whose misfortunes, under his system, were to make the fortunes of his friends and his country. A part of that world, far more numerous than his friends and acquaintance was at his door, they were the unemployed poor, the weak in mind or body, the simple and unsuspicious, the prodigal, the dissipated, the improvident and the vicious. *Laissez-faire* and *pas trop gouverner* suited not them; one portion of them needed support and protection; the other, much and rigorous government. Still they were fine subjects out of which the astute and designing, the provident and avaricious, the cunning, the prudent and the industrious might make fortunes in the field of free competition. Another portion of the world which Smith overlooked, were the countries with which England traded, covering a space many hundred times larger than England herself. She was daily growing richer, more

Source: George Fitzhugh, *Sociology for the South, or the Failure of Free Society* (Richmond, Va.: A. Morris, 1854), 7, 9–10, 11–14, 20–21, 22–28, 29–33, 80–84, 85–86, 88–89, 89–95.

powerful and intellectual, by her trade, and the countries with which she traded poorer, weaker, and more ignorant. Since the vast extension of trade, consequent on the discoveries of Columbus and Vasco de Gama, the civilized countries of Europe which carried on this trade had greatly prospered, but the savages and barbarians with whom they traded had become more savage and barbarous or been exterminated. Trade is a war of the wits, in which the stronger witted are as sure to succeed as the stronger armed in a war with swords. Strength of wit has this great advantage over strength of arm, that it never tires, for it gathers new strength by appropriating to itself the spoils of the vanquished. And thus, whether between nations or individuals, the war of free trade is constantly widening the relative abilities of the weak and the strong. It has been justly observed that under this system the rich are continually growing richer and the poor poorer. The remark is true as well between nations as between individuals. Free trade, when the American gives a bottle of whiskey to the Indian for valuable furs, or the Englishman exchanges with the African blue-beads for diamonds, gold and slaves, is a fair specimen of all free trade when unequals meet. Free trade between England and Ireland furnishes the latter an excellent market for her beef and potatoes, in exchange for English manufactures. The labor employed in manufacturing pays much better than that engaged in rearing beeves and potatoes. On the average, one hour of English labor pays for two of Irish. Again, manufacturing requires and encourages skill and intelligence; grazing and farming require none. But far the worst evils of this free trade remain to be told. Irish pursuits depressing education and refinement, England becomes a market for the wealth, the intellect, the talent, energy and enterprise of Ireland. All men possessing any of these advantages or qualities retreat to England to spend their incomes, to enter the church, the navy, or the army, to distinguish themselves as authors, to engage in mechanic or manufacturing pursuits. Thus is Ireland robbed of her very life's blood, and thus do our Northern States rob the Southern....

Political economy is quite as objectionable, viewed as a rule of morals, as when viewed as a system of economy. Its authors never seem to be aware that they are writing an ethical as well as an economical code; yet it is probable that no writings, since the promulgation of the Christian dispensation, have exercised so controlling an influence on human conduct as the writings of these authors. The morality which they teach is one of simple and unadulterated selfishness. The public good, the welfare of society, the prosperity of one's neighbors, is, according to them, best promoted by each man's looking solely to the advancement of his own pecuniary interests. They maintain that national wealth, happiness and prosperity being but the aggregate of individual wealth, happiness and prosperity, if each man pursues exclusively his own selfish good, he is doing the most he can to promote the general good. They seem to forget that men eager in the pursuit of wealth are never satisfied with the fair earnings of their own bodily labor, but find their wits and cunning employed in over-reaching others much more profitable than their hands. *Laissez-faire*, free competition begets a war of the wits, which these economists encourage, quite as destructive to the weak, simple, and guileless, as the war of the sword....

It begets another war in the bosom of society still more terrible than this. It arrays capital against labor. Every man is taught by political economy that it is meritorious to make the best bargains one can. In all old countries, labor is superabundant, employers less numerous than laborers; yet all the laborers must live by the wages they receive from the capitalists. The capitalist cheapens their wages; they compete with and underbid each other, for employed they must be on any terms. This war of the rich with the poor and the poor with one another, is the morality which political economy inculcates. It is the only morality, save the Bible, recognized or acknowledged in free society, and is far more efficacious in directing worldly men's conduct than the Bible, for that teaches self-denial, not self-indulgence and aggrandizement. This process of underbidding each other by the poor, which universal liberty necessarily brings about, has well been compared by the author of Alton Locke to the prisoners in the Black Hole of Calcutta strangling one another. A beautiful system of ethics this, that places all mankind in antagonistic positions, and puts all society at war. What can such a war result in but the oppression and ultimate extermination of the weak? In such society the astute capitalist, who is very skilful and cunning, gets the advantage of every one with whom he competes or deals; the sensible man with moderate means gets the advantage of most with whom he has business, but the mass of the simple and poor are outwitted and cheated by everybody.

Woman fares worst when thrown into this warfare of competition. The delicacy of her sex and her nature prevents her exercising those coarse arts which men do in the vulgar and promiscuous jostle of life, and she is reduced to the necessity of getting less than half price for her work. To the eternal disgrace of human nature, the men who employ her value themselves on the Adam Smith principle for their virtuous and sensible conduct. "Labor is worth what it will bring; they have given the poor woman more than any one else would, or she would not have taken the work." Yet she and her children are starving, and the employer is growing rich by giving her half what her work is worth. Thus does free competition, the creature of free society, throw the whole burden of the social fabric on the poor, the weak and ignorant. They produce every thing and enjoy nothing. They are "the muzzled ox that treadeth out the straw."

In free society none but the selfish virtues are in repute, because none other help a man in the race of competition. In such society virtue loses all her loveliness, because of her selfish aims. Good men and bad men have the same end in view: self-promotion, self-elevation. The good man is prudent, cautious, and cunning of fence; he knows well, the arts (the virtues, if you please) which enable him to advance his fortunes at the expense of those with whom he deals; he does not "cut too deep"; he does not cheat and swindle, he only makes good bargains and excellent profits. He gets more subjects by this course; everybody comes to him to be bled. He bides his time; takes advantage of the follies, the improvidence and vices of others, and makes his fortune out of the follies and weaknesses of his fellow-men. The bad man is rash, hasty, unskilful and impolitic. He is equally selfish, but not half so prudent and cunning. Selfishness is almost the only motive of human conduct in free society, where every man is taught that it is his first duty to change and better his pecuniary situation.

The first principles of the science of political economy inculcate separate, individual action, and are calculated to prevent that association of labor without which nothing great can be achieved; for man isolated and individualized is the most helpless of animals. We think this error of the economists proceeded from their adopting Locke's theory of the social contract. We believe no heresy in moral science has been more pregnant of mischief than this theory of Locke. It lies at the bottom of all moral speculations, and if false, must infect with falsehood all theories built on it. Some animals are by nature gregarious and associative. Of this class are men, ants and bees. An isolated man is almost as helpless and ridiculous as a bee setting up for himself. Man is born a member of society, and does not form society. Nature, as in the cases of bees and ants, has it ready formed for him. He and society are congenital. Society is the being—he one of the members of that being. He has no rights whatever, as opposed to the interests of society; and that society may very properly make any use of him that will redound to the public good. Whatever rights he has are subordinate to the good of the whole; and he has never ceded rights to it, for he was born its slave, and had no rights to cede.

Government is the creature of society, and may be said to derive its powers from the consent of the governed; but society does not owe its sovereign power to the separate consent, volition or agreement of its members. Like the hive, it is as much the work of nature as the individuals who compose it. Consequences, the very opposite of the doctrine of free trade, result from this doctrine of ours. It makes each society a band of brothers, working for the common good, instead of a bag of cats biting and worrying each other. The competitive system is a system of antagonism and war; ours of peace and fraternity. The first is the system of free society; the other that of slave society. The Greek, the Roman, Judaistic, Egyptian, and all ancient polities, were founded on our theory. The loftiest patrician in those days, valued himself not on selfish, cold individuality, but on being the most devoted servant of society and his country. In ancient times, the individual was considered nothing, the State every thing. And yet, under this system, the noblest individuality was evolved that the world has ever seen. The prevalence of the doctrines of political economy has injured Southern character, for in the South those doctrines most prevail. Wealthy men, who are patterns of virtue in the discharge of their domestic duties, value themselves on never intermeddling in public matters. They forget that property is a mere creature of law and society, and are willing to make no return for that property to the public, which by its laws gave it to them, and which guard and protect them in its possession.

All great enterprises owe their success to association of capital and labor. The North is indebted for its great wealth and prosperity to the readiness with which it forms associations for all industrial and commercial purposes. The success of Southern farming is a striking instance of the value of the association of capital and laborers, and ought to suggest to the South the necessity of it for other purposes.

The dissociation of labor and disintegration of society, which liberty and free competition occasion, is especially injurious to the poorer class; for besides the labor necessary to support the family, the poor man is burdened with the care of finding a home, and procuring employment, and attending to all domestic wants and concerns. Slavery relieves our slaves of these cares altogether, and slavery is a form, and the very best form, of socialism. In fact, the ordinary wages of common labor are insufficient to keep up separate domestic establishments for each of the poor, and association or starvation is in many cases inevitable. In free society, as well in Europe as in America, this is the accepted theory, and various schemes have been resorted to, all without success, to cure the evil. The association of labor properly carried out under a common head or ruler, would render labor more efficient, relieve the laborer of many of the cares of household affairs, and protect and support him in sickness and old age, besides preventing the too great reduction of wages by redundancy of labor and free competition. Slavery attains all these results. What else will? ...

A maxim well calculated not only to retard the progress of civilization, but to occasion its retrogression, has grown out of the science of political economy. "The world is too much governed," has become quite an axiom with many politicians. Now the need of law and government is just in proportion to man's wealth and enlightenment. Barbarians and savages need and will submit to but few and simple laws, and little of government. The love of personal liberty and freedom from all restraint, are distinguishing traits of wild men and wild beasts. Our Anglo-Saxon ancestors loved personal liberty because they were barbarians, but they did not love it half so much as North American Indians or Bengal tigers, because they were not half so savage. As civilization advances, liberty recedes; and it is fortunate for man that he loses his love of liberty just as fast as he becomes more moral and intellectual. The wealthy, virtuous and religious citizens of large towns enjoy less of liberty than any other persons whatever, and yet they are the most useful and rationally happy of all mankind. The best governed countries, and those which have prospered most, have always been distinguished for the number and stringency of their laws. Good men obey superior authority, the laws of God, of morality, and of their country; bad men love liberty and violate them. It would be difficult very often for the most ingenious casuist to distinguish between sin and liberty; for virtue consists in the performance of duty, and the obedience to that law or power that imposes duty, whilst sin is but the violation of duty and disobedience to such law and power. It is remarkable, in this connection, that sin began by the desire for liberty and the attempt to attain it in the person of Satan and his fallen angels. The world wants good government and a plenty of it—not liberty. It is deceptive in us to boast of our Democracy, to assert the capacity of the people for self-government, and then refuse to them its exercise. In New England, and in all our large cities, where the people govern most, they are governed best. If government be not too much centralized, there is little danger of too much government. The danger and evil with us is of too little. Carlyle says of our institutions, that they are "anarchy plus a street constable." We ought not to be bandaged up too closely in our infancy, it might prevent growth and development; but the time is coming when we shall need more of government, if we would secure the permanency of our institutions.

All men concur in the opinion that some government is necessary. Even the political economist would punish murder, theft, robbery, gross swindling, &c.; but they encourage men to compete with and slowly undermine and destroy one another by means quite as effective as those they forbid. We have heard a distinguished member of this school object to negro slavery, because the protection it afforded to an inferior race would perpetuate that race, which, if left free to compete with the whites, must be starved out in a few generations. Members of Congress, of the Young American party, boast that the Anglo-Saxon race is manifestly destined to eat out all other races, as the wire-grass destroys and takes the place of other grasses. Nay, they allege this competitive process is going on throughout all nature; the weak are everywhere devouring the strong; the hardier plants and animals destroying the weaker, and the superior races of man exterminating the inferior. They would challenge our admiration for this war of nature, by which they say Providence is perfecting its own work—getting rid of what is weak and indifferent, and preserving only what is strong and hardy. We see the war, but not the improvement. This competitive, destructive system has been going on from the earliest records of history; and yet the plants, the animals, and the men of to-day are not superior to those of four thousand years ago. To restrict this destructive, competitive propensity, man was endowed with reason, and enabled to pass laws to protect the weak against the strong. To encourage it, is to encourage the strong to oppress the weak, and to violate the primary object of all government. It is strange it should have entered the head of any philosopher to set the weak, who are the majority of mankind, to competing, contending and fighting with the strong, in order to improve their condition.

Hobbes maintains that "a state of nature is a state of war." This is untrue of a state of nature, because men are naturally associative; but it is true of a civilized state of universal liberty, and free competition, such as Hobbes saw around him, and which no doubt suggested his theory. The wants of man and his history alike prove that slavery has always been part of his social organization. A less degree of subjection is inadequate for the government and protection of great numbers of human beings.

An intelligent English writer, describing society as he saw it, uses this language:

"There is no disguising from the cool eye of philosophy, that all living creatures exist in a state of natural warfare; and that man (in hostility with all) is at enmity also with his own species; man is the natural enemy of man; and society, unable to change his nature, succeeds but in establishing a hollow truce by which fraud is substituted for violence."

Such is free society, fairly portrayed; such are the infidel doctrines of political economy, when candidly avowed. Slavery and Christianity bring about a lasting peace, not "a hollow truce." But we mount a step higher. We deny that there is a society in free countries. They who act each for himself, who are hostile, antagonistic and competitive, are not social and do not constitute a society. We use the term free society, for want of a better; but, like the term free government, it is an absurdity: those who are governed are not free—those who are free are not social....

Chapter IV.

THE TWO PHILOSOPHIES.

In the three preceding chapters we have shewn that the world is divided between two philosophies. The one the philosophy of free trade and universal liberty—the philosophy adapted to promote the interests of the strong, the wealthy and the wise. The other, that of socialism, intended to protect the weak, the poor and the ignorant. The latter is almost universal in free society; the former prevails in the slaveholding States of the South. Thus we see each section cherishing theories at war with existing institutions. The people of the North and of Europe are pro-slavery men in the abstract; those of the South are theoretical abolitionists. This state of opinions is readily accounted for. The people in free society feel the evils of universal liberty and free competition, and desire to get rid of those evils. They propose a remedy, which is in fact slavery; but they are wholly unconscious of what they are doing, because never having lived in the midst of slavery, they know not what slavery is. The citizens of the south, who have seen none of the evils of liberty and competition, but just enough of those agencies to operate as healthful stimulants to energy, enterprise and industry, believe free competition to be an unmixed good.

The South, quiet, contented, satisfied, looks upon all socialists and radical reformers as madmen or knaves. It is as ignorant of free society as that society is of slavery. Each section sees one side of the subject alone; each, therefore, takes partial and erroneous views of it. Social science will never take a step in advance till some Southern slaveholder, competent for the task, devotes a life-time to its study and elucidation; for slavery can only be understood by living in its midst, whilst thousands of books daily exhibit the minutest workings of free society. The knowledge of the numerous theories of radical reform proposed in Europe, and the causes that have led to their promulgation, is of vital importance to us. Yet we turn away from them with disgust, as from something unclean and vicious. We occupy high vantage ground for observing, studying and classifying the various phenomena of society, yet we do not profit by the advantages of our position. We should do so, and indignantly hurl back upon our assailants the charge, that there is something wrong and rotten in our system. From their own mouths we can show free society to be a monstrous abortion, and slavery to be the healthy, beautiful and natural being which they are trying, unconsciously, to adopt.

Chapter V.

NEGRO SLAVERY.

We have already stated that we should not attempt to introduce any new theories of government and of society, but merely try to justify old ones, so far as we could deduce such theories from ancient and almost universal practices. Now it has been the practice in all countries and in all ages, in some degree, to accommodate the amount and character of government control to the wants, intelligence, and moral capacities of the nations or individuals to be governed. A highly moral and intellectual people, like the free citizens of ancient Athens, are best governed by a democracy. For a less moral and intellectual one, a limited and constitutional monarchy will answer. For a people either very ignorant or very wicked, nothing short of military despotism will suffice. So among individuals, the most moral and well-informed members of society require no other government than law. They are capable of reading and understanding the law, and have sufficient self-control and virtuous disposition to obey it. Children cannot be governed by mere law; first, because they do not understand it, and secondly, because they are so much under the influence of impulse, passion and appetite, that they want sufficient self-control to be deterred or governed by the distant and doubtful penalties of the law. They must be constantly controlled by parents or guardians, whose will and orders shall stand in the place of law for them. Very wicked men must be put into penitentiaries; lunatics into asylums, and the most wild of them into straight jackets, just as the most wicked of the sane are manacled with irons; and idiots must have committees to govern and take care of them. Now, it is clear the Athenian democracy would not suit a negro nation, nor will the government of mere law suffice for the individual negro. He is but a grown up child, and must be governed as a child, not as a lunatic or criminal. The master occupies towards him the place of parent or guardian. We shall not dwell on this view, for no one will differ with us who thinks as we do of the negro's capacity, and we might argue till dooms-day, in vain, with those who have a high opinion of the negro's moral and intellectual capacity.

Secondly. The negro is improvident; will not lay up in summer for the wants of winter; will not accumulate in youth for the exigencies of age. He would become an insufferable burden to society. Society has the right to prevent this, and can only do so by subjecting him to domestic slavery.

In the last place, the negro race is inferior to the white race, and living in their midst, they would be far outstripped or outwitted in the chase of free competition. Gradual but certain extermination would be their fate. We presume the maddest abolitionist does not think the negro's providence of habits and money-making capacity at all to compare to those of the whites. This defect of character would alone justify enslaving him, if he is to remain here. In Africa or the West Indies, he would become idolatrous, savage and cannibal, or be devoured by savages and cannibals. At the North he would freeze or starve.

… [A]bolish negro slavery, and how much of slavery still remains. Soldiers and sailors in Europe enlist for life; here, for five years. Are they not slaves who have not only sold their liberties, but their lives also? And they are worse treated than domestic slaves. No domestic affection and self-interest extend their aegis over them. No kind mistress, like a guardian angel, provides for them in health, tends them in sickness, and soothes their dying pillow. Wellington at Waterloo was a slave. He was bound to obey, or would, like admiral Byng, have been shot for gross misconduct, and might not, like a common laborer, quit his work at any moment. He had sold his liberty, and might not resign without the consent of his master, the king. The common laborer may quit his work at any moment, whatever his contract; declare that liberty is an inalienable right, and leave his employer to redress by a useless suit for damages. The highest and most honorable position on earth was that of the slave Wellington; the lowest, that of the free man who cleaned his boots and fed his hounds. The African cannibal, caught, christianized and enslaved, is as much elevated by slavery as was Wellington. The kind of slavery is adapted to the men enslaved. Wives and apprentices are slaves; not in theory only, but often in fact. Children are slaves to their parents, guardians and teachers. Imprisoned culprits are slaves. Lunatics and idiots are slaves also. Three-fourths of free society are slaves, no better treated, when their wants and capacities are estimated, than negro slaves. The masters in free society, or slave society, if they perform properly their duties, have more cares and less liberty than the slaves themselves. "In the sweat of thy face shalt thou earn thy bread!" made all men slaves, and such all *good men* continue to be....

We have a further question to ask. If it be right and incumbent to subject children to the authority of parents and guardians, and idiots and lunatics to committees, would it not be equally right and incumbent to give the free negroes masters, until at least they arrive at years of discretion, which very few ever did or will attain? What is the difference between the authority of a parent and of a master? Neither pay wages, and each is entitled to the services of those subject to him. The father may not sell his child forever, but may hire him out till he is twenty-one. The free negro's master may also be restrained from selling. Let him stand in *loco parentis,* and call him papa instead of master. Look closely into slavery, and you will see nothing so hideous in it; or if you do, you will find plenty of it at home in its most hideous form....

It is a common remark, that the grand and lasting architectural structures of antiquity were the results of slavery. The mighty and continued association of labor requisite to their construction, when mechanic art was so little advanced, and labor-saving processes unknown, could only have been brought about by a despotic authority, like that of the master over his slaves. It is, however, very remarkable, that whilst in taste and artistic skill the world seems to have been retrograding ever since the decay and abolition of feudalism, in mechanical invention and in great utilitarian operations requiring the wielding of immense capital and much labor, its progress has been unexampled. Is it because capital is more despotic in its authority over free laborers than Roman masters and feudal lords were over their slaves and vassals?

Free society has continued long enough to justify the attempt to generalize its phenomena, and calculate its moral and intellectual influences. It is obvious that, in whatever is purely utilitarian and material, it incites invention and stimulates industry. Benjamin Franklin, as a man and a philosopher, is the best exponent of the working of the system. His sentiments and his philosophy are low, selfish, atheistic and material. They tend directly to make man a mere "featherless biped," well-fed, well-clothed and comfortable, but regardless of his soul as "the beasts that perish."

Since the Reformation the world has as regularly been retrograding in whatever belongs to the departments of genius, taste and art, as it has been progressing in physical science and its application to mechanical construction. Mediæval Italy rivalled if it did not surpass ancient Rome, in poetry, in sculpture, in painting, and many of the fine arts. Gothic architecture reared its monuments of skill and genius throughout Europe, till the 15th century, but Gothic architecture died with the Reformation. The age of Elizabeth was the Augustan age of England. The men who lived then acquired their sentiments in a world not yet deadened and vulgarized by puritanical cant and levelling demagoguism. Since then men have arisen who have been the fashion and the go for a season, but none have appeared whose names will descend to posterity. Liberty and equality made slower advances in France. The age of Louis XIV was the culminating point of French genius and art. It then shed but a flickering and lurid light. Frenchmen are servile copyists of Roman art, and Rome had no art of her own. She borrowed from Greece; distorted and deteriorated what she borrowed; and France imitates and falls below Roman distortions.

The genius of Spain disappeared with Cervantes; and now the world seems to regard nothing as desirable except what will make money and what costs money. There is not a poet, an orator, a sculptor, or painter in the world. The tedious elaboration necessary to all the productions of high art would be ridiculed in this money-making, utilitarian charlatan age. Nothing now but what is gaudy and costly excites admiration. The public taste is debased.

But far the worst feature of modern civilization, which is the civilization of free society, remains to be exposed. Whilst labor-saving processes have probably lessened by one half, in the last century, the amount of work needed for comfortable support, the free laborer is compelled by capital and competition to work more than he ever did before, and is less comfortable. The organization of society cheats him of his earnings, and those earnings go to swell the vulgar pomp and pageantry of the ignorant millionaires, who are the only great of the present day. These reflections might seem, at first view, to have little connexion with negro slavery; but it is well for us of the South not to be deceived by the tinsel glare and glitter of free society, and to employ ourselves in doing our duty at home, and studying the past, rather than in insidious rivalry of the expensive pleasures and pursuits of men whose sentiments and whose aims are low, sensual and grovelling.

Human progress, consisting in moral and intellectual improvement, and there being no agreed and conventional standard weights or measures of moral and intellectual qualities and quantities, the question of progress can never be accurately decided. We maintain that man has not improved, because in all save the mechanic arts he reverts to the distant past for models to imitate, and he never imitates what he can excel.

We need never have white slaves in the South, because we have black ones. Our citizens, like those of Rome and Athens, are a privileged class. We should train and educate them to deserve the privileges and to perform the duties which society confers on them. Instead, by a low demagoguism depressing their self-respect by discourses on the equality of man, we had better excite their pride by reminding them that they do not fulfil the menial offices which white men do in other countries. Society does not feel the burden of providing for the few helpless paupers in the South. And we should recollect that here we have but half the people to educate, for half arc negroes; whilst at the North they profess to educate all. It is in our power to spike this last gun of the abolitionists. We should educate all the poor. The abolitionists say that it is one of the necessary consequences of slavery that the poor are neglected. It was not so in Athens, and in Rome, and should not be so in the South. If we had less trade with and less dependence on the North, all our poor might be profitable and honorably employed in trades, professions and manufactures. Then we should have a rich and denser population. Yet we but marshal her in the way that she was going. The South is already aware of the necessity of a new policy, and has begun to act on it. Every day more and more is done for education, the mechanic arts, manufactures and internal improvements. We will soon be independent of the North.

We deem this peculiar question of negro slavery of very little importance. The issue is made throughout the world on the general subject of slavery in the abstract. The argument has commenced. One set of ideas will govern and control after awhile the civilized world. Slavery will every where be abolished, or every where be re-instituted. We think the opponents of practical, existing slavery, are estopped by their own admission; nay, that unconsciously, as socialists, they are the defenders and propagandists of slavery, and have furnished the only sound arguments on which its defence and justification can be rested. We have introduced the subject of negro slavery to afford us a better opportunity to disclaim the purpose of reducing the white man any where to the condition of negro slaves here. It would be very unwise and unscientific to govern white men as you would negroes. Every shade and variety of slavery has existed in the world. In some cases there has been much of legal regulation, much restraint of the master's authority; in others, none at all. The character of slavery necessary to protect the whites in Europe should be much milder than negro slavery, for slavery is only needed to protect the white man, whilst it is more necessary for the government of the negro even than for his protection. But even negro slavery should not be outlawed. We might and should have laws in Virginia, as in Louisiana, to make the master subject to presentment by the grand jury and to punishment, for any inhuman or improper treatment or neglect of his slave.

We abhor the doctrine of the "Types of Mankind;" first, because it is at war with scripture, which teaches us that the whole human race is descended from a common parentage; and, secondly, because it encourages and incites brutal masters to treat negroes, not as weak, ignorant and dependent brethren, but as wicked beasts, without the pale of humanity. The Southerner is the negro's friend, his only friend. Let no intermeddling abolitionist, no refined philosophy, dissolve this friendship.

MARTIN DELANY

Selection from *The Condition, Elevation, Emigration, and Destiny of the Colored People of the United States* (1852)

"I thank God for making me a man simply, but Delany always thanks Him for making him a black man," Frederick Douglass once remarked, speaking of his former coeditor, the free-born physician, army major, and political leader Martin Delany (1812–1885). In a like but more scholarly spirit, historians have credited Delany with being the principal founding father of "black nationalism" in America. In fact, both these personal and ideological components of Delany's African-American racialism were complex and shifting, as he showed even in his seminal *Condition of the Colored People of the United States*.

In his book Delany urged important modifications of the two cardinal dogmas of the abolitionist movement: that slavery was the abiding sin of the nation and its remedy lay in building an interracial movement to overthrow it based on a color-blind ethic of liberal egalitarianism and benevolent Christianity. For Delany, American slavery was but the most vicious part of a worldwide system of racial exploitation and disenfranchisement shackling free as well as enslaved African-descended people. The remedy required, therefore, not dependence on the doubtful benevolence of whites, but on the collective economic and political self-reliance of blacks, whose racial identity was constructed out of their common experiences of oppression and their peculiar biological and cultural condition. And the ultimate goal? Here the unsentimental Delany was ambiguous. On one level he proposed, as he announced in his title, not just the "elevation" of his race but also the free "emigration" of its American branch, probably to South America or the Caribbean, as well as (as he had proposed in his earlier plan, now reprinted in his book's appendix) to parts of Africa. Less important, though, than his specific prescriptions, which would fluctuate over the remaining three decades of his life, was his abiding commitment to his ideal of pan-African self-dependence, whether in the United States or in the world. Here he laid out versions of this ideal, ranging from entrepreneurial schemes of black economic development, colonialist fantasies of African-American settler states, and a progressive immigrant-minded vanguard community serving as both a haven and a vehicle for the independent flourishing of an oppressed and divinely chosen people. It was a vision that at least in part both his American nation's Puritan forebears and his white expansionist contemporaries would have recognized.

Victor Ullman, *Martin R. Delany: The Beginnings of Black Nationalism* (Boston, 1971), is the standard biography. For an important early revisionist analysis of Delany's "black nationalism," see Theodore Draper, "The Father of American Black Nationalism," *New York Review of Books*, 14 (March 12, 1970), 33–41. Tunde Adeleke, *Without Regard to Race: The Other Martin Robison Delany* (Jackson, Miss., 2003), makes a more detailed case along similar lines. Robert S. Levine's *Martin Delany, Frederick Douglass, and the*

Politics of Representative Identity (Chapel Hill, 1997) provide an imaginative reconstruction of the two African-American leaders' self-representations in the context of black and white antislavery writing. For a nuanced interpretation of the debates over African-American emigration and black nationalism in the decade in which Delany composed his book, see Wilson Jeremiah Moses, *The Golden Age of Black Nationalism, 1850–1925* (New York, 1978), chap. 2. For a provocative reading of Delany's pan-African diasporic vision in the context of a capacious Atlantic "counter-culture of modernity," see Paul Gilroy, *The Black Atlantic: Modernity and Double Consciousness* (Cambridge, Mass., 1993), chap. 1.

Chapter II.

COMPARATIVE CONDITION OF THE COLORED PEOPLE
OF THE UNITED STATES.

The United States, untrue to her trust and unfaithful to her professed principles of republican equality, has also pursued a policy of political degradation to a large portion of her native born countrymen, and that class is the Colored People. Denied an equality not only of political, but of natural rights, in common with the rest of our fellow citizens, there is no species of degradation to which we are not subject.

Reduced to abject slavery is not enough, the very thought of which should awaken every sensibility of our common nature; but those of their descendants who are freemen even in the non-slaveholding States, occupy the very same position politically, religiously, civilly and socially, (with but few exceptions,) as the bondman occupies in the slave States.

In those States, the bondman is disfranchised, and for the most part so are we. He is denied all civil, religious, and social privileges, except such as he gets by mere sufferance, and so are we. They have no part nor lot in the government of the country, neither have we. They are ruled and governed without representation, existing as mere nonentities among the citizens, and excrescences on the body politic—a mere dreg in community, and so are we. Where then is our political superiority to the enslaved? none, neither are we superior in any other relation to society, except that we are defacto masters of ourselves and joint rulers of our own domestic household, while the bondman's self is claimed by another, and his relation to his family denied him. What the unfortunate classes are in Europe, such are we in the United States, which is folly to deny, insanity not to understand, blindness not to see, and surely now full time that our eyes were opened to these startling truths, which for ages have stared us full in the face.

It is time that we had become politicians, we mean, to understand the political economy and domestic policy of nations; that we had become as well as moral theorists, also the practical demonstrators of equal rights and self-government. Except we do, it is idle to talk about rights, it is mere chattering for the sake of being seen and heard—like the slave, saying something because his so called "master" said it, and saying just what he told him to say. Have we not now sufficient intelligence among us to understand our true position, to realise our actual condition, and determine for ourselves what is best to be done? If we have not now, we never shall have, and should at once cease prating about our equality, capacity, and all that.

Twenty years ago, when the writer was a youth, his young and yet uncultivated mind was aroused, and his tender heart made to leap with anxiety in anticipation of the promises then held out by the prime movers in the cause of our elevation.

In 1830 the most intelligent and leading spirits among the colored men in the United States, such as James Forten, Robert Douglass, I. Bowers, A. D. Shadd, John Peck, Joseph Cassey, and John B. Vashon of Pennsylvania; John T. Hilton, Nathaniel and Thomas Paul, and James G. Barbodoes of Massachusetts; Henry Sipkins, Thomas Hamilton, Thomas L. Jennings, Thomas Downing, Samuel E. Cornish, and others of New York; R. Cooley and others of Maryland, and representatives from other States which cannot now be

Source: Martin Robison Delany, *The Condition, Elevation, Emigration, and Destiny of the Colored People of the United States* (Philadelphia: Published by the Author, 1852), 14–30, 190–96, 197–202, 202–3, 204–6, 207–8, 209–10, 212–13, 214.

recollected, the data not being at hand, assembled in the city of Philadelphia, in the capacity of a National Convention, to "devise ways and means for the bettering of our condition." These Conventions determined to assemble annually, much talent, ability, and energy of character being displayed; when in 1831 at a sitting of the Convention in September, from their previous pamphlet reports, much interest having been created throughout the country, they were favored by the presence of a number of whites, some of whom were able and distinguished men, such as Rev. R. R. Gurley, Arthur Tappan, Elliot Cresson, John Rankin, Simeon Jocelyn and others, among them William Lloyd Garrison, then quite a young man, all of whom were staunch and ardent Colonizationists, young Garrison at that time, doing his mightiest in his favorite work.

Among other great projects of interest brought before the convention at a previous sitting, was that of the expediency of a general emigration, as far as it was practicable, of the colored people to the British Provinces of North America. Another was that of raising sufficient means for the establishment and erection of a College for the proper education of the colored youth. These gentlemen long accustomed to observation and reflection on the condition of their people, saw at once, that there must necessarily be means used adequate to the end to be attained—that end being an unqualified equality with the ruling class of their fellow citizens. He saw that as a class, the colored people of the country were ignorant, degraded and oppressed, by far the greater portion of them being abject slaves in the South, the very condition of whom was almost enough, under the circumstances, to blast the remotest hope of success, and those who were freemen, whether in the South or North, occupied a subservient, servile, and menial position, considering it a favor to get into the service of the whites, and do their degrading offices. That the difference between the whites and themselves, consisted in the superior advantages of the one over the other, in point of attainments. That if a knowledge of the arts and sciences, the mechanical occupations, the industrial occupations, as farming, commerce, and all the various business enterprises, and learned professions were necessary for the superior position occupied by their rulers, it was also necessary for them. And very reasonably too, the first suggestion which occurred to them was, the advantages of a location, then the necessity of a qualification. They reasoned with themselves, that all distinctive differences made among men on account of their origin, is wicked, unrighteous, and cruel, and never shall receive countenance in any shape from us, therefore, the first acts of the measures entered into by them, was to protest, solemnly protest, against every unjust measure and policy in the country, having for its object the proscription of the colored people, whether state, national, municipal, social, civil, or religious.

But being far-sighted, reflecting, discerning men, they took a political view of the subject, and determined for the good of their people to be governed in their policy according to the facts as they presented themselves. In taking a glance at Europe, they discovered there, however unjustly, as we have shown in another part of this pamphlet, that there are and have been numerous classes proscribed and oppressed, and it was not for them to cut short their wise deliberations, and arrest their proceedings in contention, as to the cause, whether on account of language, the color of eyes, hair, skin, or their origin of country—because all this is contrary to reason, a contradiction to common sense, at war with nature herself, and at variance with facts as they stare us every day in the face, among all nations, in every country—this being made the pretext as a matter of *policy* alone—a fact worthy of observation, that wherever the objects of oppression are the most easily distinguished by any peculiar or general characteristics, these people are the more easily oppressed, because the war of oppression is the more easily waged against them. This is the case with the modern Jews and many other people who have strongly-marked, peculiar, or distinguishing characteristics.

This arises in this wise. The policy of all those who proscribe any people, induces them to select as the objects of proscription, those who differed as much as possible, in some particulars, from themselves. This is to ensure the greater success, because it engenders the greater prejudice, or in other words, elicits less interest on the part of the oppressing class, in their favor. This fact is well understood in national conflicts, as the soldier or civilian, who is distinguished by his dress, mustache, or any other peculiar appendage, would certainly prove himself a madman, if he did not take the precaution to change his dress, remove his mustache, and conceal as much as possible his peculiar characteristics, to give him access among the repelling party. This is mere policy, nature having nothing to do with it. Still, it is a fact, a great truth well worthy of remark, and as such we adduce it for the benefit of those of our readers, unaccustomed to an enquiry into the policy of nations.

In view of these truths, our fathers and leaders in our elevation, discovered that as a policy, we the colored people were selected as the subordinate class in this country, not on account of any actual or supposed inferiority on their part, but simply because, in view of all the circumstances of the case, they were the very best class that could be selected. They would have as readily had any other class as subordinates in the country, as the colored people, but the condition of society *at the time,* would not admit of it. In the struggle for American Independence, there were among those who performed the most distinguished parts, the most common-place peasantry of the Provinces. English, Danish, Irish, Scotch, and others, were among those whose names blazoned forth as heroes in the American Revolution. But a single reflection will convince us, that no course of policy could have induced the proscription of the parentage and relatives of such men as Benjamin Franklin the printer, Roger Sherman the cobbler, the tinkers, and others of the signers of the Declaration of Independence. But as they were determined to have a subservient class, it will readily be conceived, that according to the state of society at the time, the better policy on their part was, to select some class, who from their political position—however much they may have contributed their aid as we certainly did, in the general struggle for liberty by force of arms—who had the least claims upon them, or who had the *least chance,* or was the *least potent* in urging their claims. This class of course was the colored people and Indians.

The Indians who in the early settlement of the continent, before an African captive had ever been introduced thereon, were reduced to the most abject slavery, toiling day and night in the mines, under the relentless hands of heartless Spanish taskmasters, but being a race of people raised to the sports of fishing, the chase, and of war, were wholly unaccustomed to labor, and therefore sunk under the insupportable weight, two millions and a half having fallen victims to the cruelty of oppression and toil suddenly placed upon their shoulders. And it was only this that prevented their farther enslavement as a class, after the provinces were absolved from the British Crown. It is true that their general enslavement took place on the islands and in the mining districts of South America, where indeed, the Europeans continued to enslave them, until a comparatively recent period; still, the design, the feeling, and inclination from policy, was the same to do so here, in this section of the continent.

Nor was it until their influence became too great, by the political position occupied by their brethren in the new republic, that the German and Irish peasantry ceased to be sold as slaves for a term of years fixed by law, for the repayment of their passage-money, the descendants of these classes of people for a long time being held as inferiors, in the estimation of the ruling class, and it was not until they assumed the rights and privileges guaranteed to them by the established policy of the country, among the leading spirits of whom were their relatives, that the policy towards them was discovered to be a bad one, and accordingly changed. Nor was it, as is frequently very erroneously asserted, by colored as well as white persons, that it was on account of hatred to the African, or in other words, on account of hatred to his color, that the African was selected as the subject of oppression in this country. This is sheer nonsense; being based on policy and nothing else, as shown in another place. The Indians, who being the most foreign to the sympathies of the Europeans on this continent, were selected in the first place, who, being unable to withstand the hardships, gave way before them.

But the African race had long been known to Europeans, in all ages of the world's history, as a long-lived, hardy race, subject to toil and labor of various kinds, subsisting mainly by traffic, trade, and industry, and consequently being as foreign to the sympathies of the invaders of the continent as the Indians, they were selected, captured, brought here as a laboring class, and as a matter of policy held as such. Nor was the absurd idea of natural inferiority of the African ever dreamed of, until recently adduced by the slave-holders and their abettors, in justification of their policy. This, with contemptuous indignation, we fling back into their face, as a scorpion to a vulture. And so did our patriots and leaders in the cause of regeneration know better, and never for a moment yielded to the base doctrine. But they had discovered the great fact, that a cruel policy was pursued towards our people, and that they possessed distinctive characteristics which made them the objects of proscription. These characteristics being strongly marked in the colored people, as in the Indians, by color, character of hair and so on, made them the more easily distinguished from other Americans, and the policies more effectually urged against us. For this reason they introduced the subject of emigration to Canada, and a proper institution for the education of the youth.

At this important juncture of their proceedings, the afore named white gentlemen were introduced to the notice of the Convention, and after gaining permission to speak, expressed their gratification and surprise at the qualification and talent manifested by different members of the Convention, all expressing their determination to give the cause of the colored people more serious reflection. Mr. Garrison, the youngest of them all, and none the less honest on account of his youthfulness, being but 26 years of age at the time, (1831) expressed his determination to change his course of policy at once, and espouse the cause of the elevation of the colored people here in their own country. We are not at present well advised upon this point, it now having escaped our memory, but we are under the impression that Mr. Jocelyn also, at once changed his policy.

During the winter of 1832, Mr. Garrison issued his "Thoughts on African Colonization," and near about the same time or shortly after, issued the first number of the "Liberator," in both of which, his full convictions of the enormity of American slavery, and the wickedness of their policy towards the colored people, were fully expressed. At the sitting of the Convention in this year, a number, perhaps all of these gentlemen were present, and those who had denounced the Colonization scheme, and espoused the cause of the elevation of the colored people in this country, or the Anti-Slavery cause, as it was now termed, expressed themselves openly and without reserve.

Sensible of the high-handed injustice done to the colored people in the United States, and the mischief likely to emanate from the unchristian proceedings of the deceptious Colonization scheme, like all honest hearted penitents, with the ardor only known to new converts, they entreated the Convention, whatever they did, not to entertain for a moment, the idea of recommending emigration to their people, nor the establishment of separate institutions of learning. They earnestly contended, and doubtless honestly meaning what they said, that they (the whites) had been our oppressors and injurers, they had obstructed our progress to the high positions of civilization, and now, it was their bounden duty to make full amends for the injuries thus inflicted on an unoffending people. They exhorted the Convention to cease; as they had laid on the burden, they would also take it off; as they had obstructed our pathway, they would remove the hindrance. In a word, as they had oppressed and trampled down the colored people, they would now elevate them. These suggestions and promises, good enough to be sure, after they were made, were accepted by the Convention—though some gentlemen were still in favor of the first project as the best policy, Mr. A. D. Shadd of West Chester, Pa., as we learn from himself, being one among that number—ran through the country like wild-fire, no one thinking, and if he thought, daring to speak above his breath of going anywhere out of certain prescribed limits, or of sending a child to school, if it should but have the name of "colored" attached to it, without the risk of being termed a "traitor" to the cause of his people, or an enemy to the Anti-Slavery cause.

At this important point in the history of our efforts, the colored men stopped suddenly, and with their hands thrust deep in their breeches-pockets, and their mouths gaping open, stood gazing with astonishment, wonder, and surprise, at the stupendous moral colossal statues of our Anti-Slavery friends and brethren, who in the heat and zeal of honest hearts, from a desire to make atonement for the many wrongs inflicted, promised a great deal more than they have ever been able half to fulfill, in thrice the period in which they expected it. And in this, we have no fault to find with our Anti-Slavery friends, and here wish it to be understood, that we are not laying anything to their charge as blame, neither do we desire for a moment to reflect on them, because we heartily believe that all that they did at the time, they did with the purest and best of motives, and further believe that they now are, as they then were, the truest friends we have among the whites in this country. And hope, and desire, and request, that our people should always look upon *true* anti-slavery people, Abolitionists we mean, as their friends, until they have just cause for acting otherwise. It is true, that the Anti-Slavery, like all good causes, has produced some recreants, but the cause itself is no more to be blamed for that, than Christianity is for the malconduct of any professing hypocrite, nor the society of Friends, for the conduct of a broad-brimmed hat and shad-belly coated horse-thief, because he spoke *thee* and *thou* before stealing the horse. But what is our condition even amidst our Anti-Slavery friends? And here, as our sole intention is to contribute to the elevation of our people, we must be permitted to express our opinion freely, without being thought uncharitable.

In the first place, we should look at the objects for which the Anti-Slavery cause was commenced, and the promises or inducements it held out at the commencement. It should be borne in mind, that Anti-Slavery took its rise among *colored men,* just at the time they were introducing their greatest projects for their own elevation, and that our Anti-Slavery brethren were converts of the colored men, in behalf of their elevation. Of course, it would be expected that being baptized into the new doctrines, their faith would induce them to embrace the principles therein contained, with the strictest possible adherence.

The cause of dissatisfaction with our former condition, was, that we were proscribed, debarred, and shut out from every respectable position, occupying the places of inferiors and menials.

It was expected that Anti-Slavery, according to its professions, would extend to colored persons, as far as in the power of its adherents, those advantages nowhere else to be obtained among white men. That colored boys would get situations in their shops and stores, and every other advantage tending to elevate them as far as possible, would be extended to them. At least, it was expected, that in Anti-Slavery establishments, colored men would have the preference. Because, there was no other ostensible object in view, in the commencement of the Anti-Slavery enterprise, than the *elevation* of the *colored man,* by facilitating his efforts in attaining to equality with the white man. It was urged, and it was true, that the colored people were susceptible of all that the whites were, and all that was required was to give them a fair opportunity, and, they would prove their capacity. That it was unjust, wicked, and cruel, the result of an unnatural prejudice, that debarred them from places of respectability, and that public opinion could and should be corrected upon this subject. That it was only necessary to make a sacrifice of feeling, and an innovation on the customs of society, to establish a different order of things,—that as Anti-Slavery men, they were willing to make these sacrifices, and determined to take the colored man by the hand, making common cause with him in affliction, and bear a part of the odium heaped upon him. That his cause was the cause of God—that "In as much as ye did it not unto the least of these little ones, ye did it not unto me," and that as Anti-Slavery men, they would "do right if the heavens fell." Thus, was the cause espoused, and thus did we expect much. But in all this, we were doomed to disappointment, sad, sad disappointment. Instead of realising what we had hoped for, we find ourselves occupying the very same position in relation to our Anti-Slavery friends, as we do in relation to the proslavery part of the community—a mere secondary, underling position, in all our relations to them, and anything more than this, is not a matter of course affair—it comes not by established anti-slavery custom or right, but like that which emanates from the proslavery portion of the community, by mere sufferance.

It is true, that the "Liberator" office, in Boston, has got Elijah Smith, a colored youth, at the cases—the "Standard," in New York, a young colored man, and the "Freeman," in Philadelphia, William Still, another, in the publication office, as "packing clerk;" yet these are but three out of the hosts that fill these offices in their various departments, all occupying places that could have been, and as we once thought, would have been, easily enough, occupied by colored men. Indeed, we can have no other idea about anti-slavery in this country, than that the legitimate persons to fill any and every position about an anti-slavery establishment are colored persons. Nor will it do to argue in extenuation, that white men are as justly entitled to them as colored men; because white men do not from *necessity* become anti-slavery men in order to get situations; they being white men, may occupy any position they are capable of filling—in a word, their chances are endless, every avenue in the country being opened to them. They do not therefore become abolitionists, for the sake of employment—at least, it is not the song that Anti-Slavery sung, in the first love of the new faith, proclaimed by its disciples.

And if it be urged that colored men are incapable as yet to fill these positions, all that we have to say is, that the cause has fallen far short; almost equivalent to a failure, of a tithe, of what it promised to do in half the period of its existence, to this time, if it have not as yet, now a period of twenty years, raised up colored men enough, to fill the offices within its patronage. We think it is not unkind to say, if it had been half as faithful to itself, as it should have been—its professed principles we mean; it could have reared and tutored from childhood, colored men enough by this time, for its own especial purpose. These we know could have been easily obtained, because colored people in general, are favorable to the anti-slavery cause, and wherever there is an adverse manifestation, it arises from sheer ignorance; and we have now but comparatively few such among us. There is one thing certain, that no colored person, except such as would reject education altogether, would be adverse to putting their child with an anti-slavery person, for educational advantages. This then, could have been done. But it has not been done, and let the cause of it be whatever it may, and let whoever may be to blame, we are willing to let all that pass, and extend to our anti-slavery brethren the right-hand of fellowship, bidding them God-speed in the propagation of good and wholesome sentiments—for whether they are practically carried out or not, the professions are in themselves all right and good. Like Christianity, the principles are holy and of divine origin. And we believe, if ever a man started right, with pure and holy motives, Mr. Garrison did; and that, had he the power of making the cause what it should be, it would all be right, and there never would have been any cause for the remarks we have made, though in kindness, and with the purest of motives. We are nevertheless, still occupying a miserable position in the community, wherever we live; and what we most desire is, to draw the attention of our people to this fact, and point out what, in our opinion, we conceive to be a proper remedy....

Chapter XXIII.

THINGS AS THEY ARE.

"And if thou boast TRUTH to utter,
SPEAK, and leave the rest to God."

IN presenting this work, we have but a single object in view, and that is, to inform the minds of the colored people at large, upon many things pertaining to their elevation, that but few among us are acquainted with. Unfortunately for us, as a body, we have been taught to believe, that we must have some person to think for us, instead of thinking for ourselves. So accustomed are we to submission and this kind of training, that it is with difficulty, even among the most intelligent of the colored people, an audience may be elicited for any purpose whatever, if the expounder is to be a colored person; and the introduction of any subject is treated with indifference, if not contempt, when the originator is a colored person. Indeed, the most ordinary white person, is almost revered, while the most qualified colored person is totally neglected. Nothing from them is appreciated.

We have been standing comparatively still for years, following in the footsteps of our friends, believing that what they promise us can be accomplished, just because they say so, although our own knowledge should long since, have satisfied us to the contrary. Because even were it possible, with the present hate and jealousy that the whites have towards us in this country, for us to gain equality of rights with them; we never could have an equality of the exercise and enjoyment of those rights—because, the great odds of numbers are against us. We might indeed, as some at present, have the right of the elective franchise— nay, it is not the elective franchise, because the *elective franchise* makes the enfranchised, *eligible* to any position attainable; but we may exercise the right of *voting* only, which to us, is but poor satisfaction; and we by no means care to cherish the privilege of voting somebody into office, to help to make laws to degrade us.

In religion—because they are both *translators* and *commentators,* we must believe nothing, however absurd, but what our oppressors tell us. In Politics, nothing but such as they promulge; in Anti-Slavery, nothing but what our white brethren and friends say we must; in the mode and manner of our elevation, we must do nothing, but that which may be laid down to be done by our white brethren from some quarter or other; and now, even on the subject of emigration, there are some colored people to be found, so lost to their own interest and self-respect, as to be gulled by slave owners and colonizationists, who are led to believe there is no other place in which they can become elevated, but Liberia, a government of American slave-holders, as we have shown—simply, because white men have told them so.

Upon the possibility, means, mode and manner, of our Elevation in the United States—Our Original Rights and Claims as Citizens—Our Determination not to be Driven from our Native Country—the Difficulties in the Way of our Elevation—Our Position in Relation to our Anti-Slavery Brethren—the Wicked Design and Injurious Tendency of the American Colonization Society—Objections to Liberia—Objections to Canada—Preferences to South America, &c., &c., all of which we have treated without reserve; expressing our mind freely, and with candor, as we are determined that as far as we can at present do so, the minds of our readers shall be enlightened. The custom of concealing information upon vital and important subjects, in which the interest of the people is involved, we do not agree with, nor favor in the least; we have therefore, laid this cursory treatise before our readers, with the hope that it may prove instrumental in directing the attention of our people in the right way, that leads to their Elevation. Go or stay—of course each is free to do as he pleases—one thing is certain; our Elevation is the work of our own hands. And Mexico, Central America, the West Indies, and South America, all present now, opportunities for the individual enterprise of our young men, who prefer to remain in the United States, in preference to going where they can enjoy real freedom, and equality of rights. Freedom of Religion, as well as of politics, being tolerated in all of these places.

Let our young men and women, prepare themselves for usefulness and business; that the men may enter into merchandise, trading, and other things of importance; the young women may become teachers of various kinds, and otherwise fill places of usefulness. Parents must turn their attention more to the education of their children. We mean, to educate them for useful practical business purposes. Educate them for the Store and the Counting House—to do every-day practical business. Consult the children's propensities, and direct their education according to their inclinations. It may be, that there is too great a desire on the part of parents, to give their children a professional education, before the body of the people are ready for it. A people must be a business people, and have more to depend upon than mere help in people's houses and Hotels, before they are either able to support, or capable of properly appreciating the services of professional men, among them. This has been one of our great mistakes—we have gone in advance of ourselves. We have commenced at the superstructure of the building, instead of the foundation—at the top instead of the bottom. We should first be mechanics and common tradesmen, and professions as a matter of course would grow out of the wealth made thereby. Young men and women, must now prepare for usefulness—the day of our Elevation is at hand—all the world now gazes at us—and Central and South America, and the West Indies, bid us come and be men and women, protected, secure, beloved and Free.

The branches of Education most desirable for the preparation of youth, for practical useful every-day life, are Arithmetic and good Penmanship, in order to be Accountants; and a good rudimental knowledge of Geography—which has ever been neglected, and under estimated—and of Political Economy; which without the knowledge of the first, no people can ever become adventurous—nor of the second, never will be an enterprising people. Geography, teaches a knowledge of the world, and Political Economy, a knowledge of the wealth of nations; or how to make money. These are not abstruse sciences, or learning not easily acquired or understood; but simply, common School Primer learning, that everybody may get. And, although it is the very Key to prosperity and success in common life, but few know anything about it. Unfortunately for our people, so soon as their children learn to read a Chapter in the New Testament, and scribble a miserable hand, they are pronounced to have "Learning enough;" and taken away from School, no use to themselves, nor community. This is apparent in our Public Meetings, and Official Church Meetings; of the great number of men present, there are but few capable of filling a Secretaryship. Some of the large cities may be an exception to this. Of the multitudes of Merchants, and Business men throughout this country, Europe, and the world, few are qualified, beyond the branches here laid down by us as necessary for business. What did John Jacob Astor, Stephen Girard, or do the millionaires and the greater part of the merchant princes, and mariners, know about Latin and Greek, and the Classics? Precious few of them know anything. In proof of this, in 1841, during the Administration of President Tyler, when the mutiny was detected on board of the American Man of War Brig Somers, the names of the Mutineers, were recorded by young S—a Midshipman in Greek. Captain Alexander Slidell McKenzie, Commanding, was unable to read them; and in his dispatches to the Government, in justification of his policy in executing the criminals, said that he "discovered some curious characters which he was unable to read," &c.; showing thereby, that high functionary, did not understand. even the Greek Alphabet, which was only necessary, to have been able to read proper names written in Greek.

What we most need then, is a good business practical Education; because, the Classical and Professional education of so many of our young men, before their parents are able to support them, and community ready to patronize them, only serves to lull their energy, and cripple the otherwise, praiseworthy efforts they would make in life. A Classical education, is only suited to the wealthy, or those who have a prospect of gaining a livelihood by it. The writer does not wish to be understood, as underrating a Classical and Professional education; this is not his intention; he fully appreciates them, having had some such advantages himself; but he desires to give a proper guide, and put a check to the extravagant idea that is fast obtaining, among our people especially, that a Classical, or as it is termed, a "finished education," is necessary to prepare one for usefulness in life. Let us have an education, that shall practically develop our thinking faculties and manhood; and then, and not until then, shall we be able to vie with our oppressors, go where we may. We as heretofore, have been on the extreme; either no qualification at all, or a Collegiate education. We jumped too far; taking a leap from the deepest abyss to the highest summit; rising from the ridiculous to the sublime; without medium or intermission.

Let our young women have an education; let their minds be well informed; well stored with useful information and practical proficiency, rather than the light superficial acquirements, popularly and fashionably called accomplishments. We desire accomplishments, but they must be *useful*.

Our females must be qualified, because they are to be the mothers of our children. As mothers are the first nurses and instructors of children; from them children consequently, get their first impressions, which being always the most lasting, should be the most correct. Raise the mothers above the level of degradation, and the offspring is elevated with them. In a word, instead of our young men, transcribing in their blank books, recipes for *Cooking;* we desire to see them making the transfer of *Invoices of Merchandise*. Come to our aid then; the *morning* of our *Redemption* from degradation, adorns the horizon....

Chapter XXIV.

A GLANCE AT OURSELVES—CONCLUSION.

With broken hopes—sad devastation;
A race *resigned* to DEGRADATION!

WE have said much to our young men and women, about their vocation and calling; we have dwelt much upon the menial position of our people in this country. Upon this point we cannot say too much, because there is a seeming satisfaction and seeking after such positions manifested on their part, unknown to any other people. There appears to be, a want of a sense of propriety or *self-respect,* altogether inexplicable; because young men, and women among us, many of whom have good trades and homes, adequate to their support, voluntarily leave them, and seek positions, such as servants, waiting maids, coachmen, nurses, cooks in gentlemens' kitchen, or such like occupations, when they can gain a livelihood at something more respectable, or elevating in character. And the worse part of the whole matter is, that they have become so accustomed to it, it has become so "fashionable," that it seems to have become second nature, and they really become offended, when it is spoken against.

Among the German, Irish, and other European peasantry who come to this country, it matters not what they were employed at before and after they come; just so soon as they can better their condition by keeping shops, cultivating the soil, the young men and women going to night-schools, qualifying themselves for usefulness, and learning trades—they do so. Their first and last care, object and aim is, to better their condition by raising themselves above the condition that necessity places them in. We do not say too much, when we say, as an evidence of the deep degradation our race, in the United States, that there are those among us, the wives and daughters, some of the *first ladies,* (and who dare say they are not the "first," because they belong to the "first class" and associate where anybody among us can?) whose husbands are industrious, able and willing to support them, who voluntarily leave home, and become chamber-maids, and stewardesses, upon vessels and steamboats, in all probability, to enable them to obtain some more fine or costly article of dress or furniture.

We have nothing to say against those whom *necessity* compels to do these things, those who can do no better; we have only to do with those who can, and will not, or do not do better. The whites are always in the advance, and we either standing still or retrograding; as that which does not go forward, must either stand in one place or go back. The father in all probability is a farmer, mechanic, or man of some independent business; and the wife, sons and daughters, are chamber-maids, on vessels, nurses and waiting-maids, or coachmen and cooks in families. This is retrogradation. The wife, sons, and daughters should be elevated above this condition as a necessary consequence.

If we did not love our race superior to others, we would not concern ourself about their degradation; for the greatest desire of our heart is, to see them stand on a level with the most elevated of mankind. No people are ever elevated above the condition of their *females;* hence, the condition of the *mother* determines the condition of the child. To know the position of a people, it is only necessary to know the *condition* of their *females;* and despite themselves, they cannot rise above their level. Then what is our condition? Our *best ladies* being washerwomen, chamber-maids, children's traveling nurses, and common house servants, and menials, we are all a degraded, miserable people, inferior to any other people as a whole, on the face of the globe.

These great truths, however unpleasant, must be brought before the minds of our people in its true and proper light, as we have been too delicate about them, and too long concealed them for fear of giving offence. It would have been infinitely better for our race, if these facts had been presented before us half a century ago—we would have been now proportionably benefitted by it.

As an evidence of the degradation to which we have been reduced, we dare premise, that this chapter will give offence to many, very many, and why? Because they may say, "He dared to say that the occupation of a *servant* is a degradation." It is not necessarily degrading; it would not be, to one or a few people of a kind; but a *whole race of servants* are a degradation to that people.

Efforts made by men of qualifications for the toiling and degraded millions among the whites, neither gives offence to that class, nor is it taken unkindly by them; but received with manifestations of gratitude; to know that they are thought to be, equally worthy of, and entitled to stand on a level with the elevated classes; and they have only got to be informed of the way to raise themselves, to make the effort and do so as far as they can. But how different with us. Speak of our position in society, and it at once gives insult. Though we are servants; among ourselves we claim to be *ladies* and *gentlemen,* equal in standing, and as the popular expression goes, "Just as good as anybody"—and so believing, we make no efforts to raise above the common level of menials; because the *best* being in that capacity, all are content with the position. We cannot at the same time, be domestic and lady; servant and gentleman. We must be the one or the other. Sad, sad indeed, is the thought, that hangs drooping in our mind, when contemplating the picture drawn before us. Young men and women, "we write these things unto you, because ye are strong," because the writer, a few years ago, gave unpardonable offence to many of the young people of Philadelphia and other places, because he dared tell them, that he thought too much of them, to be content with seeing them the servants of other people. Surely, she that could be the mistress, would not be the maid; neither would he that could be the master, be content with being the servant; then why be offended, when we point out to you, the way that leads from the menial to the mistress or the master. All this we seem to reject with fixed determination, repelling with anger, every effort on the part of our intelligent men and women to elevate us, with true Israelitish degradation, in reply to any suggestion or proposition that may be offered, "Who made thee a ruler and judge?"

The writer is no "Public Man," in the sense in which this is understood among our people, but simply an humble individual, endeavoring to seek a livelihood by a profession obtained entirely by his own efforts, without relatives and friends able to assist him; except such friends as he gained by the merit of his course and conduct, which he here gratefully acknowledges; and whatever he has accomplished, other young men may, by making corresponding efforts, also accomplish.

We have advised an emigration to Central and South America, and even to Mexico and the West Indies, to those who prefer either of the last named places, all of which are free countries, Brazil being the only real slave-holding State in South America—there being nominal slavery in Dutch Guiana, Peru, Buenos Ayres, Paraguay, and Uraguay, in all of which places colored people have equality in social, civil, political, and religious privileges; Brazil making it punishable with death to import slaves into the empire....

Of the West India Islands, Santa Cruz, belonging to Denmark; Porto Rico, and Cuba with its little adjuncts, belonging to Spain, are the only slave-holding Islands among them—three-fifths of the whole population of Cuba being colored people, who cannot and will not much longer endure the burden and the yoke. They only want intelligent leaders of their own color, when they are ready at any moment to charge to the conflict—to liberty or death. The remembrance of the noble mulatto, PLACIDO, the gentleman, scholar, poet, and intended Chief Engineer of the Army of Liberty and Freedom in Cuba; and the equally noble black, CHARLES BLAIR, who was to have been Commander-in-Chief, who were shamefully put to death in 1844, by that living monster, Captain General O'Donnell, is still fresh and indelible to the mind of every bondman of Cuba.

In our own country, the United States, there are *three million five hundred thousand slaves;* and we, the nominally free colored people, are *six hundred thousand* in number; estimating one-sixth to be men, we have *one hundred thousand* able bodied freemen, which will make a powerful auxiliary in any country to which we may become adopted—an ally not to be despised by any power on earth. We love our country, dearly love her, but she don't love us—she despises us, and bids us begone, driving us from her embraces; but we shall not go where she desires us; but when we do go, whatever love we have for her, we shall love the country none the less that receives us as her adopted children....

One of our great temporal curses is our consummate poverty. We are the poorest people, as a class, in the world of civilized mankind—abjectly, miserably poor, no one scarcely being able to assist the other. To this, of course, there are noble exceptions; but that which is common to, and the very process by which white men exist, and succeed in life, is unknown to colored men in general. In any and every considerable community may be found, some one of our white fellow-citizens, who is worth more than all the colored people in that community put together. We consequently have little or no efficiency. We must have means to be practically efficient in all the under-takings of life; and to obtain them, it is necessary that we should be engaged in lucrative pursuits, trades, and general business transactions. In order to be thus engaged, it is necessary that we should occupy positions that afford the facilities for such pursuits. To compete now with the mighty odds of wealth, social and religious preferences, and political influences of this country, at this advanced stage of its national existence, we never may expect. A new country, and new beginning, is the only true, rational, politic remedy for our disadvantageous position; and that country we have already pointed out, with triple golden advantages, all things considered, to that of any country to which it has been the province of man to embark.

Every other than we, have at various periods of necessity, been a migratory people; and all when oppressed, shown a greater abhorrence of oppression, if not a greater love of liberty, than we. We cling to our oppressors as the objects of our love. It is true that our enslaved brethren are here, and we have been led to believe that it is necessary for us to remain, on that account. Is it true, that all should remain in degradation, because a part are degraded? We believe no such thing. We believe it to be the duty of the Free, to elevate themselves in the most speedy and effective manner possible; as the redemption of the bondman depends entirely upon the elevation of the freeman; therefore, to elevate the free colored people of America, anywhere upon this continent; forebodes the speedy redemption of the slaves. We shall hope to hear no more of so fallacious a doctrine—the necessity of the free remaining in degradation, for the sake of the oppressed. Let us apply, first, the lever to ourselves; and the force that elevates us to the position of manhood's considerations and honors, will cleft the manacle of every slave in the land....

The slave may become a lover of his master, and learn to forgive him for continual deeds of maltreatment and abuse; just as the Spaniel would couch and fondle at the feet that kick him; because he has been taught to reverence them, and consequently, becomes adapted in body and mind to his condition. Even the shrubbery-loving Canary, and lofty-soaring Eagle, may be tamed to the cage, and learn to love it from habit of confinement. It has been so with us in our position among our oppressors; we have been so prone to such positions, that we have learned to love them. When reflecting upon this all important, and to us, all absorbing subject; we feel in the agony and anxiety of the moment, as though we could cry out in the language of a Prophet of old: "Oh that my head were waters, and mine eyes a fountain of tears, that I might weep day and night for the" degradation "of my people! Oh that I had in the wilderness a lodging place of way-faring men; that I might leave my people, and go from them!"

The Irishman and German in the United States, are very different persons to what they were when in Ireland and Germany, the countries of their nativity. There their spirits were depressed and downcast; but the instant they set their foot upon unrestricted soil; free to act and untrammeled to move; their physical condition undergoes a change, which in time becomes physiological, which is transmitted to the offspring, who when born under such circumstances, is a decidedly different being to what it would have been, had it been born under different circumstances.

A child born under oppression, has all the elements of servility in its constitution; who when born under favorable circumstances, has to the contrary, all the elements of freedom and independence of feeling. Our children then, may not be expected, to maintain that position and manly bearing; born under the unfavorable circumstances with which we are surrounded in this country; that we so much desire. To use the language of the talented Mr. Whipper, "they cannot be raised in this country, without being stoop shouldered." Heaven's pathway stands unobstructed, which will lead us into a Paradise of bliss. Let us go on and possess the land, and the God of Israel will be our God.

The lessons of every school book, the pages of every history, and columns of every newspaper, are so replete with stimuli to nerve us on to manly aspirations, that those of our young people, who will now refuse to enter upon this great theatre of Polynesian adventure, and take their position on the stage of Central and South America, where a brilliant engagement, of certain and most triumphant success, in the drama of human equality awaits them; then, with the blood of *slaves,* write upon the lintel of every door in sterling Capitals, to be gazed and hissed at by every passer by—

> Doomed by the Creator
> To servility and degradation;
> The SERVANT of the *white man,*
> And despised of every nation!

Appendix.

A PROJECT FOR AN EXPEDITION OF ADVENTURE, TO THE EASTERN COAST OF AFRICA.

EVERY people should be the originators of their own designs, the projector of their own schemes, and creators of the events that lead to their destiny—the consummation of their desires.

Situated as we are, in the United States, many, and almost insurmountable obstacles present themselves. We are four-and-a-half millions in numbers, free and bond; six hundred thousand free, and three-and-a-half millions bond.

We have native hearts and virtues, just as other nations; which in their pristine purity are noble, potent, and worthy of example. We are a nation within a nation;—as the Poles in Russia, the Hungarians in Austria, the Welsh, Irish, and Scotch in the British dominions.

But we have been, by our oppressors, despoiled of our purity, and corrupted in our native characteristics, so that we have inherited their vices, and but few of their virtues, leaving us in character, really a *broken people.*

Being distinguished by complexion, we are still singled out—although having merged in the habits and customs of our oppressors—as a distinct nation of people; as the Poles, Hungarians, Irish, and others, who still retain their native peculiarities, of language, habits, and various other traits. The claims of no people, according to established policy and usage, are respected by any nation, until they are presented in a national capacity. . . .

The Eastern Coast of Africa has long been neglected, and never but little known, even to the ancients; but has ever been our choice part of the Continent. Bounded by the Red Sea, Arabian Sea, and Indian Ocean, it presents the greatest facilities for an immense trade, with China, Japan, Siam, Hindoostan, in short, all the East Indies—of any other country in the world. With a settlement of enlightened freemen, who with the immense facilities, must soon grow into a powerful nation. In the Province of Berbera, south of the Strait of Babel-mandel, or the great pass, from the Arabian to the Red Sea, the whole commerce of the East must touch this point.

Also, a great rail road could be constructed from here, running with the Mountains of the Moon, clearing them entirely, except making one mountain pass, at the western extremity of the Mountains of the Moon, and the southeastern terminus of the Kong Mountains; entering the Province of Dahomey, and terminating on the Atlantic Ocean West; which would make the GREAT THOROUGH FARE for all the trade with the East Indies and Eastern Coast of Africa, and the Continent of America. All the world would pass through Africa upon this rail road, which would yield a revenue infinitely greater than any other investment in the world.

The means for prosecuting such a project—as stupendous as it may appear—will be fully realised in the prosecution of the work. Every mile of the road, will thrice pay for itself, in the development of the rich treasures that now lie hidden in the bowels of the earth. There is no doubt, that in some one section of twenty-five miles, the developments of gold would more than pay the expenses of any one thousand miles of the work. This calculation may, to those who have never given this subject a thought, appear extravagant, and visionary; but to one who has had his attention in this direction for years, it is clear enough. But a few years will witness a development of gold, precious metals, and minerals in Eastern Africa, the Moon and Kong Mountains, ten-fold greater than all the rich productions of California.

There is one great physiological fact in regard to the colored race—which, while it may not apply to all colored persons, is true of those having black skins—that they can bear *more different* climates than the white race. They bear *all* the temperates and extremes, while the other can only bear the temperates and *one* of the extremes. The black race is endowed with natural properties, that adapt and fit them for temperate, cold, and hot climates; while the white race is only endowed with properties that adapt them to temperate and cold climates; being unable to stand the warmer climates; in them, the white race cannot work, but become perfectly indolent, requiring somebody to work for them—and these, are always people of the black race.

The black race may be found, inhabiting in healthful improvement, every part of the globe where the white race reside; while there are parts of the globe where the black race reside, that the white race cannot live in health.

What part of mankind is the "denizen of every soil, and the lord of terrestrial creation," if it be not the black race? The Creator has indisputably adapted us for the "denizens of *every soil,*" all that is left for us to do, is to *make* ourselves the "*lords* of terrestrial creation." The land is ours—there it lies with inexhaustible resources; let us go and possess it. In Eastern Africa must rise up a nation, to whom all the world must pay commercial tribute.

FREDERICK DOUGLASS

"What to the Slave Is the Fourth of July?"
(1852)

Frederick Douglass (1818–1895) was the foremost African-American leader of the early nineteenth century. He was also the author of three autobiographies that collectively, in their record of his relentless climb from slave to Republican party statesman, rivaled Franklin's as a great American exemplary saga. Hardly less important, though, was his role in defining a powerful philosophy of antislavery and American reform. Douglass's primary strength as a reform thinker was his ability to extract from the major traditions of post-Revolutionary American political thought both a sharply delineated argument for black emancipation and a culturally resonant vision of a just American society.

Nowhere was this dual exploitation better exemplified than in Douglass's oration on the Fourth of July. On one hand, Douglass used the egalitarian ideals of the Declaration of Independence and a humanistic Christianity to puncture the moral pretensions of a system that converted men and women into property and to excoriate Americans who in the overwhelming majority hypocritically celebrated the Fourth of July while tolerating a system that mocked it. On the other hand, in identifying antislavery with two of the most basic beliefs in American culture, along with the Constitution—which he interpreted, unlike Garrison, as a "Glorious liberty Document"—Douglass presented antislavery as almost the essence of American nationhood. Finally, linking antislavery's progress with the very forces most Americans associated with their nation's progress—knowledge, technology, and commerce—Douglass all but foretold the movements' ultimate triumph. All, then, that was needed was "a fiery stream of biting ridicule, blasting reproach, withering sarcasm, and stern rebuke" to awaken Americans to an urgent sense of their duty to do the right. And this the ex-slave Douglass gave them in heaping portions.

Discerning discussions of Douglass's social and political thought may be found in two collections: Eric J. Sundquist, ed., *Frederick Douglass: New Literary and Historical Essays* (Cambridge, 1990); and Bill E. Lawson and Frank M. Kirkland, eds., *Frederick Douglass: A Critical Reader* (Maiden, Mass., 1999). Peter C. Myers, *Frederick Douglass: Race and the Rebirth of American Liberalism* (Lawrence, Kans., 2008) focuses on Douglass's application of the doctrine of natural rights to antislavery. Nicholas Buccola, *The Political Thought of Frederick Douglass: In Pursuit of American Liberty* (New York, 2012) explores Douglass's multiple "liberalisms" and their connections to the manifold identities that he fashioned for himself.

An Address Delivered in Rochester, New York, on 5 July 1852

Mr. President, Friends and Fellow Citizens: He who could address this audience without a quailing sensation, has stronger nerves than I have....

The papers and placards say, that I am to deliver a 4th [of] July oration. This certainly sounds large, and out of the common way, for me. It is true that I have often had the privilege to speak in this beautiful Hall, and to address many who now honor me with their presence. But neither their familiar faces, nor the perfect gage I think I have of Corinthian Hall, seems to free me from embarrassment.

The fact is, ladies and gentlemen, the distance between this platform and the slave plantation, from which I escaped, is considerable—and the difficulties to be overcome in getting from the latter to the former, are by no means slight. That I am here to-day is, to me, a matter of astonishment as well as of gratitude. You will not, therefore, be surprised, if in what I have to say, I evince no elaborate preparation, nor grace my speech with any high sounding exordium. With little experience and with less learning, I have been able to throw my thoughts hastily and imperfectly together, and trusting to your patient and generous indulgence, I will proceed to lay them before you.

This, for the purpose of this celebration, is the 4th of July. It is the birthday of your National Independence, and of your political freedom. This, to you, is what the Passover was to the emancipated people of God. It carries your minds back to the day, and to the act of your great deliverance; and to the signs, and to the wonders, associated with that act, and that day. This celebration also marks the beginning of another year of your national life; and reminds you that the Republic of America is now 76 years old. I am glad, fellow-citizens, that your nation is so young. Seventy-six years, though a good old age for a man, is but a mere speck in the life of a nation. Three score years and ten is the allotted time for individual men, but nations number their years by thousands. According to this fact, you are, even now, only in the beginning of your national career, still lingering in the period of childhood. I repeat, I am glad this is so. There is hope in the thought, and hope is much needed, under the dark clouds which lower above the horizon. The eye of the reformer is met with angry flashes, portending disastrous times; but his heart may well beat lighter at the thought that America is young, and that she is still in the impressible stage of her existence....

Citizens, your fathers...succeeded; and to-day you reap the fruits of their success. The freedom gained is yours; and you, therefore, may properly celebrate this anniversary. The 4th of July is the first great fact in your nation's history—the very ring-bolt in the chain of your yet undeveloped destiny.

Pride and patriotism, not less than gratitude, prompt you to celebrate and to hold it in perpetual remembrance. I have said that the Declaration of Independence is the RING-BOLT to the chain of your nation's destiny; so, indeed, I regard it. The principles contained in that instrument are saving principles. Stand by those principles, be true to them on all occasions, in all places, against all foes, and at whatever cost.

From the round top of your ship of state, dark and threatening clouds may be seen. Heavy billows, like mountains in the distance, disclose to the leeward huge forms of flinty rocks! That bolt drawn, that chain broken, and all is lost. *Cling to this day—cling to it,* and to its principles, with the grasp of a storm-tossed mariner to a spar at midnight....

Source: The Frederick Douglass Papers, Series One: Speeches, Debates, and Interviews, vol. 2, ed. John W. Blassingame et al. (New Haven: Yale University Press, 1982), 359, 360, 363–88. Editors' notes omitted. Reprinted by permission of Yale University Press, Copyright © 1982.

Fellow Citizens, I am not wanting in respect for the fathers of this republic. The signers of the Declaration of Independence were brave men. They were great men too— great enough to give fame to a great age. It does not often happen to a nation to raise, at one time, such a number of truly great men. The point from which I am compelled to view them is not, certainly, the most favorable; and yet I cannot contemplate their great deeds with less than admiration. They were statesmen, patriots and heroes, and for the good they did, and the principles they contended for, I will unite with you to honor their memory.

They loved their country better than their own private interests; and, though this is not the highest form of human excellence, all will concede that it is a rare virtue, and that when it is exhibited, it ought to command respect. He who will, intelligently, lay down his life for his country, is a man whom it is not in human nature to despise. Your fathers staked their lives, their fortunes, and their sacred honor, on the cause of their country. In their admiration of liberty, they lost sight of all other interests.

They were peace men; but they preferred revolution to peaceful submission to bondage. They were quiet men; but they did not shrink from agitating against oppression. They showed forbearance; but that they knew its limits. They believed in order; but not in the order of tyranny. With them, nothing was *"settled"* that was not right. With them, justice, liberty and humanity were *"final;"* not slavery and oppression. You may well cherish the memory of such men. They were great in their day and generation. Their solid manhood stands out the more as we contrast it with these degenerate times.

How circumspect, exact and proportionate were all their movements! How unlike the politicians of an hour! Their statesmanship looked beyond the passing moment, and stretched away in strength into the distant future. They seized upon eternal principles, and set a glorious example in their defence. Mark them!

Fully appreciating the hardship to be encountered, firmly believing in the right of their cause, honorably inviting the scrutiny of an on-looking world, reverently appealing to heaven to attest their sincerity, soundly comprehending the solemn responsibility they were about to assume, wisely measuring the terrible odds against them, your fathers, the fathers of this republic, did, most deliberately, under the inspiration of a glorious patriotism, and with a sublime faith in the great principles of justice and freedom, lay deep the corner-stone of the national superstructure, which has risen and still rises in grandeur around you.

Of this fundamental work, this day is the anniversary. Our eyes are met with demonstrations of joyous enthusiasm. Banners and pennants wave exultingly on the breeze. The din of business, too, is hushed. Even Mammon seems to have quitted his grasp on this day. The ear-piercing fife and the stirring drum unite their accents with the ascending peal of a thousand church bells. Prayers are made, hymns are sung, and sermons are preached in honor of this day; while the quick martial tramp of a great and multitudinous nation, echoed back by all the hills, valleys and mountains of a vast continent, bespeak the occasion one of thrilling and universal interest—a nation's jubilee.

Friends and citizens, I need not enter further into the causes which led to this anniversary. Many of you understand them better than I do. You could instruct me in regard to them. That is a branch of knowledge in which you feel, perhaps, a much deeper interest than your speaker. The causes which led to the separation of the colonies from the British crown have never lacked for a tongue. They have all been taught in your common schools, narrated at your firesides, unfolded from your pulpits, and thundered from your legislative halls, and are as familiar to you as household words. They form the staple of your national poetry and eloquence.

I remember, also, that, as a people, Americans are remarkably familiar with all facts which make in their own favor. This is esteemed by some as a national trait—perhaps a national weakness. It is a fact, that whatever makes for the wealth or for the reputation of Americans, and can be had *cheap!* will be found by Americans. I shall not be charged with slandering Americans, if I say I think the American side of any question may be safely left in American hands.

I leave, therefore, the great deeds of your fathers to other gentlemen whose claim to have been regularly descended will be less likely to be disputed than mine!

The Present.

My business, if I have any here to-day, is with the present. The accepted time with God and his cause is the ever-living now.

> "Trust no future, however pleasant,
> Let the dead past bury its dead;
> Act, act in the living present,
> Heart within, and God overhead."

We have to do with the past only as we can make it useful to the present and to the future. To all inspiring motives, to noble deeds which can be gained from the past, we are welcome. But now is the time, the important time. Your fathers have lived, died, and have done their work, and have done much of it well. You live and must die, and you must do your work. You have no right to enjoy a child's share in the labor of your fathers, unless your children are to be blest by your labors. You have no right to wear out and waste the hard-earned fame of your fathers to cover your indolence. Sydney Smith tells us that men seldom eulogize the wisdom and virtues of their fathers, but to excuse some folly or wickedness of their own. This truth is not a doubtful one. There are illustrations of it near and remote, ancient and modern. It was fashionable, hundreds of years ago, for the children of Jacob to boast, we have "Abraham to our father," when they had long lost Abraham's faith and spirit. That people contented them under the shadow of Abraham's great name, while they repudiated the deeds which made his name great. Need I remind you that a similar thing is being done all over this country to-day? Need I tell you that the Jews are not the only people who built the tombs of the prophets, and garnished the sepulchres of the righteous? Washington could not die till he had broken the chains of his slaves. Yet his monument is built up by the price of human blood, and the traders in the bodies and souls of men, shout—"We have Washington to *our father*." Alas! that it should be so; yet so it is.

> "The evil that men do, lives after them,
> The good is oft' interred with their bones."

Fellow-citizens, pardon me, allow me to ask, why am I called upon to speak here today? What have I, or those I represent, to do with your national independence? Are the great principles of political freedom and of natural justice, embodied in that Declaration of Independence, extended to us? and am I, therefore, called upon to bring our humble offering to the national altar, and to confess the benefits and express devout gratitude for the blessings resulting from your independence to us?

Would to God, both for your sakes and ours, than an affirmative answer could be truthfully returned to these questions! Then would my task be light, and my burden easy and delightful. For *who* is there so cold, that a nation's sympathy could not warm him? Who so obdurate and dead to the claims of gratitude, that would not thankfully acknowledge such priceless benefits? Who so stolid and selfish, that would not give his voice to swell the hallelujahs of a nation's jubilee, when the chains of servitude had been torn from his limbs? I am not that man. In a case like that, the dumb might eloquently speak, and the "lame man leap as an hart."

But, such is not the state of the case. I say it with a sad sense of the disparity between us. I am not included within the pale of this glorious anniversary! Your high independence only reveals the immeasurable distance between us. The blessings in which you, this day, rejoice, are not enjoyed in common. The rich inheritance of justice, liberty, prosperity and independence, bequeathed by your fathers, is shared by you, not by me. The sunlight that brought life and healing to you, has brought stripes and death to me. This Fourth [of] July is *yours,* not *mine. You* may rejoice, *I* must mourn. To drag a man in fetters into the grand illuminated temple of liberty, and call upon him to join you in joyous anthems, were inhuman mockery and sacrilegious irony. Do you mean, citizens, to mock me, by asking me to speak to-day? If so, there is a parallel to your conduct. And let me warn you that it is dangerous to copy the example of a nation whose crimes, towering up to heaven, were thrown down by the breath of the Almighty, burying that nation in irrecoverable ruin! I can to-day take up the plaintive lament of a peeled and woesmitten people!

"By the rivers of Babylon, there we sat down. Yea! we wept when we remembered Zion. We hanged our harps upon the willows in the midst thereof. For there, they that carried us away captive, required of us a song; and they who wasted us required of us mirth, saying, Sing us one of the songs of Zion. How can we sing the Lord's song in a strange land? If I forget thee, O Jerusalem, let my right hand forget her cunning. If I do not remember thee, let my tongue cleave to the roof of my mouth."

Fellow-citizens; above your national, tumultous joy, I hear the mournful wail of millions! whose chains, heavy and grievous yesterday, are, to-day, rendered more intolerable by the jubilee shouts that reach them. If I do forget, if I do not faithfully remember those bleeding children of sorrow this day, "may my right hand forget her cunning, and may my tongue cleave to the roof of my mouth!" To forget them, to pass lightly over their wrongs, and to chime in with the popular theme, would be treason most scandalous and shocking, and would make me a reproach before God and the world. My subject, then fellow-citizens, is AMERICAN SLAVERY. I shall see, this day, and its popular characteristics, from the slave's point of view. Standing, there, identified with the American bondman, making his wrongs mine, I do not hesitate to declare, with all my soul, that the character and conduct of this nation never looked blacker to me than on this 4th of July! Whether we turn to the declarations of the past, or to the professions of the present, the conduct of the nation seems equally hideous and revolting. America is false to the past, false to the present, and solemnly binds herself to be false to the future. Standing with God and the crushed and bleeding slave on this occasion, I will, in the name of humanity which is outraged, in the name of liberty which is fettered, in the name of the constitution and the Bible, which are disregarded and trampled upon, dare to call in question and to denounce, with all the emphasis I can command, everything that serves to perpetuate slavery—the great sin and shame of America! "I will not equivocate; I will not excuse;" I will use the severest language I can command; and yet not one word shall escape me that any man, whose judgement is not blinded by prejudice, or who is not at heart a slaveholder, shall not confess to be right and just.

But I fancy I hear some one of my audience say, it is just in this circumstance that you and your brother abolitionists fail to make a favorable impression on the public mind. Would you argue more, and denounce less, would you persuade more, and rebuke less, your cause would be much more likely to succeed. But, I submit, where all is plain there is nothing to be argued. What point in the anti-slavery creed would you have me argue? On what branch of the subject do the people of this country need light? Must I undertake to prove that the slave is a man? That point is conceded already. Nobody doubts it. The slaveholders themselves acknowledge it in the enactment of laws for their government. They acknowledge it when they punish disobedience on the part of the slave. There are seventy-two crimes in the State of Virginia, which, if committed by a black man, (no matter how ignorant he be), subject him to the punishment of death; while only two of the same crimes will subject a white man to the like punishment. What is this but the acknowledgement that the slave is a moral, intellectual and responsible being? The manhood of the slave is conceded. It is admitted in the fact that Southern statute books are covered with enactments forbidding, under severe fines and penalties, the teaching of the slave to read or to write. When you can point to any such laws, in reference to the beasts of the field, then I may consent to argue the manhood of the slave. When the dogs in your streets, when the fowls of the air, when the cattle on your hills, when the fish of the sea, and the reptiles that crawl, shall be unable to distinguish the slave from a brute, *then* will I argue with you that the slave is a man!

For the present, it is enough to affirm the equal manhood of the negro race. Is it not astonishing that, while we are ploughing, planting and reaping, using all kinds of mechanical tools, erecting houses, constructing bridges, building ships, working in metals of brass, iron, copper, silver and gold; that, while we are reading, writing and cyphering, acting as clerks, merchants and secretaries, having among us lawyers, doctors, ministers, poets, authors, editors, orators, and teachers; that, while we are engaged in all manner of enterprises common to other men, digging gold in California, capturing the whale in the Pacific, feeding sheep and cattle on the hill-side, living, moving, acting, thinking, planning, living in families as husbands, wives and children, and, above all, confessing and worshipping the Christian's God, and looking hopefully for life and immortality beyond the grave, we are called upon to prove that we are men!

Would you have me argue that man is entitled to liberty? that he is the rightful owner of his own body? You have already declared it. Must I argue the wrongfulness of slavery? Is that a question for Republicans? Is it to be settled by the rules of logic and argumentation, as a matter beset with great difficulty, involving a doubtful application of the principle of justice, hard to be understood? How should I look to-day, in the presence of Americans, dividing, and subdividing a discourse, to show that men have a natural right to freedom? speaking of it relatively, and positively, negatively, and affirmatively. To do so, would be to make myself ridiculous, and to offer an insult to your understanding. There is not a man beneath the canopy of heaven, that does not know that slavery is wrong *for him*.

What, am I to argue that it is wrong to make men brutes, to rob them of their liberty, to work them without wages, to keep them ignorant of their relations to their fellow men, to beat them with sticks, to flay their flesh with the lash, to load their limbs with irons, to hunt them with dogs, to sell them at auction, to sunder their families, to knock out their teeth, to burn their flesh, to starve them into obedience and submission to their masters? Must I argue that a system thus marked with blood, and stained with pollution, is *wrong*? No! I will not. I have better employments for my time and strength, than such arguments would imply.

What, then, remains to be argued? Is it that slavery is not divine; that God did not establish it; that our doctors of divinity are mistaken? There is blasphemy in the thought. That which is inhuman, cannot be divine! *Who* can reason on such a proposition? They that can, may; I cannot. The time for such argument is past.

At a time like this, scorching irony, not convincing argument, is needed. O! had I the ability, and could I reach the nation's ear, I would, to-day, pour out a fiery stream of biting ridicule, blasting reproach, withering sarcasm, and stern rebuke. For it is not light that is needed, but fire; it is not the gentle shower, but thunder. We need the storm, the whirlwind, and the earthquake. The feeling of the nation must be quickened; the conscience of the nation must be roused; the propriety of the nation must be startled; the hypocrisy of the nation must be exposed; and its crimes against God and man must be proclaimed and denounced.

What, to the American slave, is your 4th of July? I answer; a day that reveals to him, more than all other days in the year, the gross injustice and cruelty to which he is the constant victim. To him, your celebration is a sham; your boasted liberty, an unholy license; your national greatness, swelling vanity; your sounds of rejoicing are empty and heartless; your denunciations of tyrants, brass fronted impudence; your shouts of liberty and equality, hollow mockery; your prayers and hymns, your sermons and thanksgivings, with all your religious parade, and solemnity, are, to him, mere bombast, fraud, deception, impiety, and hyprocrisy—a thin veil to cover up crimes which would disgrace a nation of savages. There is not a nation on the earth guilty of practices, more shocking and bloody, than are the people of these United States, at this very hour.

Go where you may, search where you will, roam through all the monarchies and despotisms of the old world, travel through South America, search out every abuse, and when you have found the last, lay your facts by the side of the everyday practices of this nation, and you will say with me, that, for revolting barbarity and shameless hypocrisy, America reigns without a rival.

The Internal Slave Trade.

Take the American slave-trade, which, we are told by the papers, is especially prosperous just now. Ex-Senator Benton tells us that the price of men was never higher than now. He mentions the fact to show that slavery is in no danger. This trade is one of the peculiarities of American institutions. It is carried on in all the large towns and cities in one-half of this confederacy, and millions are pocketed every year, by dealers in this horrid traffic. In several states, this trade is a chief source of wealth. It is called (in contradistinction to the foreign slave-trade) *"the internal slave-trade."* It is, probably, called so, too, in order to divert from it the horror with which the foreign slave-trade is contemplated. That trade has long since been denounced by this government, as piracy. It has been denounced with burning words, from the high places of the nation, as an execrable traffic. To arrest it, to put an end to it, this nation keeps a squadron, at immense cost, on the coast of Africa. Everywhere, in this country, it is safe to speak of this foreign slave-trade, as a most inhuman traffic, opposed alike to the laws of God and of man. The duty to extirpate and destroy it, is admitted even by our DOCTORS OF DIVINITY. In order to put an end to it, some of these last have consented that their colored brethren (nominally free) should leave this country, and establish themselves on the western coast of Africa! It is, however, a notable fact that, while so much execration is poured out by Americans upon those engaged in the foreign slave-trade, the men engaged in the slave-trade between the states pass without condemnation, and their business is deemed honorable.

Behold the practical operation of this internal slave-trade, the American slave-trade, sustained by American politics and American religion. Here you will see men and women reared like swine for the market. You know what is a swine-drover? I will show you a man-drover. They inhabit all our Southern States. They perambulate the country, and crowd the highways of the nation, with droves of human stock. You will see one of these human flesh-jobbers, armed with pistol, whip and bowie-knife, driving a company of a hundred men, women, and children, from the Potomac to the slave market at New Orleans. These wretched people are to be sold singly, or in lots, to suit purchasers. They are food for the cotton-field, and the deadly sugar-mill. Mark the sad procession, as it moves wearily along, and the inhuman wretch who drives them. Hear his savage yells and his blood-chilling oaths, as he hurries on his affrighted captives! There, see the old man, with locks thinned and gray. Cast one glance, if you please, upon that young mother, whose shoulders are bare to the scorching sun, her briny tears falling on the brow of the babe in her arms. See, too, that girl of thirteen, weeping, yes! weeping, as she thinks of the mother from whom she has been torn! The drove moves tardily. Heat and sorrow have nearly consumed their strength; suddenly you hear a quick snap, like the discharge of a rifle; the fetters clank, and the chain rattles simultaneously; your ears are saluted with a scream, that seems to have torn its way to the centre of your soul! The crack you heard, was the sound of the slave-whip; the scream you heard, was from the woman you saw with the babe. Her speed had faltered under the weight of her child and her chains! that gash on her shoulder tells her to move on. Follow this drove to New Orleans. Attend the auction, see men examined like horses; see the forms of women rudely and brutally exposed to the shocking gaze of American slave-buyers. See this drove sold and separated forever; and never forget the deep, sad sobs that arose from that scattered multitude. Tell me citizen, WHERE, under the sun, you can witness a spectacle more fiendish and shocking. Yet this is but a glance at the American slave-trade, as it exists, at this moment, in the ruling part of the United States.

I was born amid such sights and scenes. To me the American slave-trade is a terrible reality. When a child, my soul was often pierced with a sense of its horrors. I lived on Philpot Street, Fell's Point, Baltimore, and have watched from the wharves, the slave ships in the Basin, anchored from the shore, with their cargoes of human flesh, waiting for favorable winds to waft them down the Chesapeake. There was, at that time, a grand slave market kept at the head of Pratt Street, by Austin Woldfolk. His agents were sent into every town and county in Maryland, announcing their arrival, through the papers, and on flaming "*handbills*," headed CASH FOR NEGROES. These men were generally well dressed men, and very captivating in their manners. Ever ready to drink, to treat, and to gamble. The fate of many a slave has depended upon the turn of a single card; and many a child has been snatched from the arms of its mother by bargains arranged in a state of brutal drunkenness.

The flesh-mongers gather up their victims by dozens, and drive them, chained, to the general depot at Baltimore. When a sufficient number have been collected here, a ship is chartered, for the purpose of conveying the forlorn crew to Mobile, or to New Orleans. From the slave prison to the ship, they are usually driven in the darkness of night; for since the anti-slavery agitation, a certain caution is observed.

In the deep still darkness of midnight, I have been often aroused by the dead heavy footsteps, and the piteous cries of the chained gangs that passed our door. The anguish of my boyish heart was intense; and I was often consoled, when speaking to my mistress in the morning, to hear her say that the custom was very wicked; that she hated to hear the rattle of the chains, and the heart-rending cries. I was glad to find one who sympathised with me in my horror.

Fellow-citizens, this murderous traffic is, to-day, in active operation in this boasted republic. In the solitude of my spirit, I see clouds of dust raised on the highways of the South; I see the bleeding footsteps; I hear the doleful wail of fettered humanity, on the way to the slave-markets, where the victims are to be sold like horses, sheep, and swine, knocked off to the highest bidder. There I see the tenderest ties ruthlessly broken, to gratify the lust, caprice and rapacity of the buyers and sellers of men. My soul sickens at the sight.

> "Is this the land your Fathers loved,
> The freedom which they toiled to win?
> Is this the earth whereon they moved?
> Are these the graves they slumber in?"

But a still more inhuman, disgraceful, and scandalous state of things remains to be presented.

By an act of the American Congress, not yet two years old, slavery has been nationalized in its most horrible and revolting form. By that act, Mason & Dixon's line has been obliterated; New York has become as Virginia; and the power to hold, hunt, and sell men, women, and children as slaves remains no longer a mere state institution, but is now an institution of the whole United States. The power is co-extensive with the star-spangled banner and American Christianity. Where these go, may also go the merciless slave-hunter. Where these are, man is not sacred. He is a bird for the sportsman's gun. By that most foul and fiendish of all human decrees, the liberty and person of every man are put in peril. Your broad republican domain is hunting ground for men. Not for thieves and robbers, enemies of society, merely, but for men guilty of no crime. Your law-makers have commanded all good citizens to engage in this hellish sport. Your President, your Secretary of State, your *lords, nobles,* and ecclesiastics, enforce, as a duty you owe to your free and glorious country, and to your God, that you do this accursed thing. Not fewer than forty Americans have, within the past two years, been hunted down and, without a moment's warning, hurried away in chains, and consigned to slavery and excruciating torture. Some of these have had wives and children, dependent on them for bread; but of this, no account was made. The right of the hunter to his prey stands superior to the right of marriage, and to all rights in this republic, the rights of God included! For black men there are neither law, justice, humanity, nor religion. The Fugitive Slave *Law* makes MERCY TO THEM, A CRIME; and bribes the judge who tries them. An American JUDGE GETS TEN DOLLARS FOR EVERY VICTIM HE CONSIGNS to Slavery, and five, when he fails to do so. The oath of any two villains is sufficient, under this hell-black enactment, to send the most pious and exemplary black man into the remorseless jaws of slavery! His own testimony is nothing. He can bring no witnesses for himself. The minister of American justice is bound by the law to hear but *one* side; and *that* side, is the side of the oppressor. Let this damning fact be perpetually told. Let it be thundered around the world, that, in tyrant-killing, king-hating, people-loving, democratic, Christian America, the seats of justice are filled with judges, who hold their offices under an open and palpable *bribe,* and are bound, in deciding in the case of a man's liberty, *to hear only his accusers!*

In glaring violation of justice, in shameless disregard of the forms of administering law, in cunning arrangement to entrap the defenceless, and in diabolical intent, this Fugitive Slave Law stands alone in the annals of tyrannical legislation. I doubt if there be another nation on the globe, having the brass and the baseness to put such a law on the statute-book. If any man in this assembly thinks differently from me in this matter, and feels able to disprove my statements, I will gladly confront him at any suitable time and place he may select.

Religious Liberty.

I take this law to be one of the grossest infringements of Christian Liberty, and, if the churches and ministers of our country were not stupidly blind, or most wickedly indifferent, they, too, would so regard it.

At the very moment that they are thanking God for the enjoyment of civil and religious liberty, and for the right to worship God according to the dictates of their own consciences, they are utterly silent in respect to a law which robs religion of its chief significance, and makes it utterly worthless to a world lying in wickedness. Did this law concern the "*mint, anise* and *cummin*"—abridge the right to sing psalms, to partake of the sacrament, or to engage in any of the ceremonies of religion, it would be smitten by the thunder of a thousand pulpits. A general shout would go up from the church, demanding *repeal, repeal, instant repeal!* And it would go hard with that politician who presumed to solicit the votes of the people without inscribing this motto on his banner. Further, if this demand were not complied with, another Scotland would be added to the history of religious liberty, and the stern old Covenanters would be thrown into the shade. A John Knox would be seen at every church door, and heard from every pulpit, and Fillmore would have no more quarter than was shown by Knox, to the beautiful, but treacherous Queen Mary of Scotland. The fact that the church of our country, (with fractional exceptions), does not esteem "the Fugitive Slave Law" as a declaration of war against religious liberty, implies that that church regards religion simply as a form of worship, an empty ceremony, and *not* a vital principle, requiring active benevolence, justice, love and good will towards man. It esteems sacrifice above mercy; psalm-singing above right doing; solemn meetings above practical righteousness. A worship that can be conducted by persons who refuse to give shelter to the houseless, to give bread to the hungry, clothing to the naked, and who enjoin obedience to a law forbidding these acts of mercy, is a curse, not a blessing to mankind. The Bible addresses all such persons as "scribes, pharisees, hypocrites, who pay tithe of *mint, anise,* and *cummin,* and have omitted the weightier matters of the law, judgement, mercy and faith."

The Church Responsible.

But the church of this country is not only indifferent to the wrongs of the slave, it actually takes sides with the oppressors. It has made itself the bulwark of American slavery, and the shield of American slave-hunters. Many of its most eloquent Divines, who stand as the very lights of the church, have shamelessly given the sanction of religion and the Bible to the whole slave system. They have taught that man may, properly, be a slave; that the relation of master and slave is ordained of God; that to send back an escaped bondman to his master is clearly the duty of all the followers of the Lord Jesus Christ; and this horrible blasphemy is palmed off upon the world for Christianity.

For my part, I would say, welcome infidelity! welcome atheism! welcome anything! in preference to the gospel, *as preached by those Divines!* They convert the very name of religion into an engine of tyranny, and barbarous cruelty, and serve to confirm more infidels, in this age, than all the infidel writings of Thomas Paine, Voltaire, and Bolingbroke, put together, have done! These ministers make religion a cold and flinty-hearted thing, having neither principles of right action, nor bowels of compassion. They strip the love of God of its beauty, and leave the throne of religion a huge, horrible, repulsive form. It is a religion for oppressors, tyrants, man-stealers, and *thugs.* It is not that "*pure and undefiled religion*" which is from above, and which is *"first pure, then peaceable, easy to be entreated,* full of mercy and good fruits, *without partiality, and without hypocrisy."* But a religion which favors the rich against the poor; which exalts the proud above the humble; which divides mankind into two classes, tyrants and slaves; which says to the man in chains, *stay there;* and to the oppressor, *oppress on;* it is a religion which may be professed and enjoyed by all the robbers and enslavers of mankind; it makes God a respecter of persons, denies his fatherhood of the race, and tramples in the dust the great truth of the brotherhood of man. All this we affirm to be true of the popular church, and the popular worship of our land and nation—a religion, a church, and a worship which, on the authority of inspired wisdom, we pronounce to be an abomination in the sight of God. In the language of Isaiah, the American church might be well addressed. "Bring no more vain oblations; incense is an abomination unto me: the new moons and Sabbaths, the calling of assemblies, I cannot away with; it is iniquity, even the solemn meeting. Your new moons and your appointed feasts my soul hateth. They are a trouble to me; I am weary to bear them; and when ye spread forth your hands I will hide mine eyes from you. Yea! when ye make many prayers, I will not hear. YOUR HANDS ARE FULL OF BLOOD; cease to do evil, learn to do well; seek judgement; relieve the oppressed; judge for the fatherless; plead for the widow."

The American church is guilty, when viewed in connection with what it is doing to uphold slavery; but it is superlatively guilty when viewed in connection with its ability to abolish slavery.

The sin of which it is guilty is one of omission as well as of commission. Albert Barnes but uttered what the common sense of every man at all observant of the actual state of the case will receive as truth, when he declared that "There is no power out of the church that could sustain slavery an hour, if it were not sustained in it."

Let the religious press, the pulpit, the Sunday school, the conference meeting, the great ecclesiastical, missionary, Bible and tract associations of the land array their immense powers against slavery and slave-holding; and the whole system of crime and blood would be scattered to the winds; and that they do not do this involves them in the most awful responsibility of which the mind can conceive.

In prosecuting the anti-slavery enterprise, we have been asked to spare the church, to spare the ministry; but *how,* we ask, could such a thing be done? We are met on the threshold of our efforts for the redemption of the slave, by the church and ministry of the country, in battle arrayed against us; and we are compelled to fight or flee. From what *quarter,* I beg to know, has proceeded a fire so deadly upon our ranks, during the last two years, as from the Northern pulpit? As the champions of oppressors, the chosen men of American theology have appeared—men, honored for their so-called piety, and their real learning. The LORDS of Buffalo, the SPRINGS of New York, the LATHROPS of Auburn, the COXES and SPENCERS of Brooklyn, the GANNETS and SHARPS of Boston, the DEWEYS of Washington, and other great religious lights of the land, have, in utter denial of the authority of *Him,* by whom they professed to be called to the ministry, deliberately taught us, against the example of the Hebrews and against the remonstrance of the Apostles, they teach *"that we ought to obey man's law before the law of God."*

My spirit wearies of such blasphemy; and how such men can be supported, as the "standing types and representatives of Jesus Christ," is a mystery which I leave others to penetrate. In speaking of the American church, however, let it be distinctly understood that I mean the great mass of the religious organizations of our land. There are exceptions, and I thank God that there are. Noble men may be found scattered all over these Northern States, of whom Henry Ward Beecher of Brooklyn, Samuel J. May of Syracuse, and my esteemed friend[1] on the platform, are shining examples; and let me say further, that upon these men lies the duty to inspire our ranks with high religious faith and zeal, and to cheer us on in the great mission of the slave's redemption from his chains.

Religion in England and Religion in America.

One is struck with the difference between the attitude of the American church towards the anti-slavery movement, and that occupied by the churches in England towards a similar movement in that country. There, the church, true to its mission of ameliorating, elevating, and improving the condition of mankind, came forward promptly, bound up the wounds of the West Indian slave, and restored him to his liberty. There, the question of emancipation was a high[ly] religious question. It was demanded, in the name of humanity, and according to the law of the living God. The Sharps, the Clarksons, the Wilberforces, the Buxtons, and Burchells and the Knibbs, were alike famous for their piety, and for their philanthropy. The anti-slavery movement *there* was not an anti-church movement, for the reason that the church took its full share in prosecuting that movement: and the anti-slavery movement in this country will cease to be an anti-church movement, when the church of this country shall assume a favorable, instead of a hostile position towards that movement.

Americans! your republican politics, not less than your republican religion, are flagrantly inconsistent. You boast of your love of liberty, your superior civilization, and your pure Christianity, while the whole political power of the nation (as embodied in the two great political parties), is solemnly pledged to support and perpetuate the enslavement of three millions of your countrymen. You hurl your anathema at the crowned headed tyrants of Russia and Austria, and pride yourselves on your Democratic institutions, while you yourselves consent to be the mere *tools* and *body-guards* of the tyrants of Virginia and Carolina. You invite to your shores fugitives of oppression from abroad, honor them with banquets, greet them with ovations, cheer them, toast them, salute them, protect them, and pour out your money to them like water, but the fugitives from your own land you advertise, hunt, arrest, shoot and kill. You glory in your refinement and your universal education; yet you maintain a system as barbarous and dreadful as ever stained the character of a nation—a system begun in avarice, supported in pride, and perpetuated in cruelty. You shed tears over fallen Hungary, and make the sad story of her wrongs the theme of your poets, statesmen and orators, till your gallant sons are ready to fly to arms to vindicate her cause against her oppressors; but, in regard to the ten thousand wrongs of the American slave, you would enforce the strictest silence, and would hail him as an enemy of the nation who dares to make those wrongs the subject of public discourse! You are all on fire at the mention of liberty for France or for Ireland; but are as cold as an iceberg at the thought of liberty for the enslaved of America. You discourse eloquently on the dignity of labor; yet, you sustain a system which, in its very essence, casts a stigma upon labor. You can bare your bosom to the storm of British artillery to throw off a threepenny tax on tea; and yet wring the last hard-earned farthing from the grasp of the black laborers of your country. You profess to believe "that, of one blood, God made all nations of men to dwell on the face of all the earth," and hath commanded all men, everywhere to love one another; yet you notoriously hate, (and glory in your hatred), all men whose skins are not colored like your own. You declare, before the world, and are understood by the world to declare, that you *"hold these truths to be self evident, that all men are created equal; and*

---

1. Rev. R. R. Raymond. [F.D. note]

are endowed by their Creator with certain inalienable rights; and that, among these are,
life, liberty, and the pursuit of happiness;" and yet, you hold securely, in a bondage which,
according to your own Thomas Jefferson, *"is worse than ages of that which your fathers rose*
in rebellion to oppose," a *seventh part* of the inhabitants of your country.

Fellow-citizens! I will not enlarge further on your national inconsistencies. The existence of slavery in this country brands your republicanism as a sham, your humanity as
a base pretence, and your Christianity as a lie. It destroys your moral power abroad; it
corrupts your politicians at home. It saps the foundation of religion; it makes your name a
hissing, and a byword to a mocking earth. It is the antagonistic force in your government,
the only thing that seriously disturbs and endangers your *Union.* It fetters your progress;
it is the enemy of improvement, the deadly foe of education; it fosters pride; it breeds insolence; it promotes vice; it shelters crime; it is a curse to the earth that supports it; and yet,
you cling to it, as if it were the sheet anchor of all your hopes. Oh! be warned! be warned!
a horrible reptile is coiled up in your nation's bosom; the venomous creature is nursing at
the tender breast of your youthful republic; *for the love of God, tear away,* and fling from
you the hideous monster, and *let the weight of twenty millions crush and destroy it forever!*

The Constitution.

But it is answered in reply to all this, that precisely what I have now denounced is, in fact,
guaranteed and sanctioned by the Constitution of the United States; that the right to hold and
to hunt slaves is a part of that Constitution framed by the illustrious Fathers of this Republic.

Then, I dare to affirm, notwithstanding all I have said before, your fathers stooped,

> "To palter with us in a double sense:
> And keep the word of promise to the ear,
> But break it to the heart."

And instead of being the honest men I have before declared them to be, they were the
veriest imposters that ever practised on mankind. *This* is the inevitable conclusion, and
from it there is no escape. But I differ from those who charge this baseness on the framers
of the Constitution of the United States. *It is a slander upon their memory,* at least, so I
believe. There is not time now to argue the constitutional question at length; nor have I the
ability to discuss it as it ought to be discussed. The subject has been handled with masterly
power by Lysander Spooner, Esq., by William Goodell, by Samuel E. Sewall, Esq., and last,
though not least, by Gerritt Smith, Esq. These gentlemen have, as I think, fully and clearly
vindicated the Constitution from any design to support slavery for an hour.

Fellow-citizens! there is no matter in respect to which, the people of the North have
allowed themselves to be so ruinously imposed upon, as that of the pro-slavery character
of the Constitution. In *that* instrument I hold there is neither warrant, license, nor sanction of the hateful thing; but, interpreted as it *ought* to be interpreted, the Constitution is a
Glorious Liberty Document. Read its preamble, consider its purposes. Is slavery among
them? Is it at the gateway? or is it in the temple? It is neither. While I do not intend to argue
this question on the present occasion, let me ask, if it be not somewhat singular that, if the
Constitution were intended to be, by its framers and adopters, a slave-holding instrument,
why neither *slavery, slaveholding,* nor *slave* can anywhere be found in it. What would be
thought of an instrument, drawn up, *legally* drawn up, for the purpose of entitling the city of
Rochester to a track of land, in which no mention of land was made? Now, there are certain
rules of interpretation, for the proper understanding of all legal instruments. These rules are

well established. They are plain, common-sense rules, such as you and I, and all of us, can understand and apply, without having passed years in the study of law. I scout the idea that the question of the constitutionality or unconstitutionality of slavery is not a question for the people. I hold that every American citizen has a right to form an opinion of the constitution, and to propagate that opinion, and to use all honorable means to make his opinion the prevailing one. Without this right, the liberty of an American citizen would be as insecure as that of a Frenchman. Ex-Vice-President Dallas tells us that the constitution is an object to which no American mind can be too attentive, and no American heart too devoted. He further says, the constitution, in its words, is plain and intelligible, and is meant for the home-bred, unsophisticated understandings of our fellow-citizens. Senator Berrien tells us that the Constitution is the fundamental law, that which controls all others. The charter of our liberties, which every citizen has a personal interest in understanding thoroughly. The testimony of Senator Breese, Lewis Cass, and many others that might be named, who are everywhere esteemed as sound lawyers, so regard the constitution. I take it, therefore, that it is not presumption in a private citizen to form an opinion of that instrument.

Now, take the constitution according to its plain reading, and I defy the presentation of a single pro-slavery clause in it. On the other hand it will be found to contain principles and purposes, entirely hostile to the existence of slavery.

I have detained my audience entirely too long already. At some future period I will gladly avail myself of an opportunity to give this subject a full and fair discussion.

Allow me to say, in conclusion, notwithstanding the dark picture I have this day presented of the state of the nation, I do not despair of this country. There are forces in operation, which must inevitably work the downfall of slavery. "*The arm of the Lord is not shortened,*" and the doom of slavery is certain. I, therefore, leave off where I began, with *hope*. While drawing encouragement from the Declaration of Independence, the great principles it contains, and the genius of American Institutions, my spirit is also cheered by the obvious tendencies of the age. Nations do not now stand in the same relation to each other that they did ages ago. No nation can now shut itself up from the surrounding world, and trot round in the same old path of its fathers without interference. The *time* was when such could be done. Long established customs of hurtful character could formerly fence themselves in, and do their evil work with social impunity. Knowledge was then confined and enjoyed by the privileged few, and the multitude walked on in mental darkness. But a change has now come over the affairs of mankind. Walled cities and empires have become unfashionable. The arm of commerce has borne away the gates of the strong city. Intelligence is penetrating the darkest corners of the globe. It makes its pathway over and under the sea, as well as on the earth. Wind, steam, and lightning are its chartered agents. Oceans no longer divide, but link nations together. From Boston to London is now a holiday excursion. Space is comparatively annihilated. Thoughts expressed on one side of the Atlantic are distinctly heard on the other.

The far off and almost fabulous Pacific rolls in grandeur at our feet. The Celestial Empire, the mystery of ages, is being solved. The fiat of the Almightly, "*Let there be Light,*" has not yet spent its force. No abuse, no outrage whether in taste, sport or avarice, can now hide itself from the all-pervading light. The iron shoe, and crippled foot of China must be seen, in contrast with nature. *Africa must rise and put on her yet unwoven garment,* "*Ethiopia shall stretch out her hand unto God.*"

ABRAHAM LINCOLN

"Speech at Peoria, Illinois"
(1854)

"Address Before the Wisconsin State Agricultural Society"
(1859)

"Address Delivered at the Dedication of the Cemetery at Gettysburg"
(1863)

"Second Inaugural Address"
(1865)

Like Frederick Douglass, Abraham Lincoln (1809–1865) was a political moralist. But unlike that of Douglass, Lincoln's egalitarian philosophy was complicated by his commitment to a semi-historicist and sometimes mystical conception of democratic union.

In his Peoria speech against the Kansas-Nebraska Act, Lincoln demonstrated the ways in which such competing commitments both strengthened and weakened his antislavery outlook. Slavery, he argued, was intrinsically immoral and discontinuous with the founders' vision, and therefore Americans were both morally and historically obligated to take action to continue to keep the "cancer" isolated preparatory to some undefined later cutting. Meanwhile, social and historical circumstances justified not taking any further steps in the direction of either slave emancipation or black civil rights. A critical element in Lincoln's social thought was his concept of labor. Lincoln thought slavery particularly wrong because it allowed slaveholders to wring "their bread from the sweat of other men's faces." But it was not only a laborer's economic autonomy that defined Lincoln's idea of labor. In his Wisconsin address he presented an entire array of virtues democratic labor fostered—self-culture, small-scale capitalism, social mobility, even a hope of immortality.

Lincoln's most profound considerations of democracy's transcendent meaning were provoked, though, not by the labor question but by civil war. For Lincoln, in his two Civil War addresses, death was a tragic facilitator of democracy's consecration and rebirth. And not just death. In the Second Inaugural, Lincoln broke down this process further to a tension-filled synthesis of the war's multiple meanings—divine wrath, righteous human actions, atonement and redemption through human suffering, and finally, brooding over all, a hidden God's inscrutable purposes.

Several of the best recent studies of Lincoln emphasize his character as a moral and religious thinker. The most comprehensive, Allen C. Guelzo's *Abraham Lincoln: Redeemer President* (Grand Rapids, 1999), convincingly captures Lincoln's distinctive amalgam of political liberalism and "Calvinized deism." William Lee Miller, *Lincoln's Virtues: An Ethical Biography* (New York, 2002), charts Lincoln's hybrid "realist" and "idealist" political ethics. Garry Wills's *Lincoln at Gettysburg: The Words That Remade America* (New York, 1992) is a brilliant reading of Lincoln's Gettysburg Address in light of the intellectual traditions and rhetorical modes that he absorbed and reshaped in constructing it. Harry V. Jaffe, *Crisis of the House Divided: An Interpretation of the Issues in the Lincoln-Douglas Debates* (Garden City, N.Y, 1959) is a classic exegesis of the ideas expressed in the debates, but for a contrasting recent "pragmatist" reading, see John Burt, *Lincoln's Tragic Pragmatism: Lincoln, Douglas, and Moral Conflict* (Cambridge, Mass., 2013).

"Speech at Peoria, Illinois"
(1854)

[October 16, 1854]

This [Kansas-Nebraska Act] is the *repeal* of the Missouri Compromise. The foregoing history may not be precisely accurate in every particular; but I am sure it is sufficiently so, for all the uses I shall attempt to make of it, and in it, we have before us, the chief material enabling us to correctly judge whether the repeal of the Missouri Compromise is right or wrong.

I think, and shall try to show, that it is wrong; wrong in its direct effect, letting slavery into Kansas and Nebraska—and wrong in its prospective principle, allowing it to spread to every other part of the wide world, where men can be found inclined to take it.

This *declared* indifference, but as I must think, covert *real* zeal for the spread of slavery, I can not but hate. I hate it because of the monstrous injustice of slavery itself. I hate it because it deprives our republican example of its just influence in the world—enables the enemies of free institutions, with plausibility, to taunt us as hypocrites—causes the real friends of freedom to doubt our sincerity, and especially because it forces so many really good men amongst ourselves into an open war with the very fundamental principles of civil liberty—criticising the Declaration of Independence, and insisting that there is no right principle of action but *self-interest.*

Before proceeding, let me say I think I have no prejudice against the Southern people. They are just what we would be in their situation. If slavery did not now exist amongst them, they would not introduce it. If it did now exist amongst us, we should not instantly give it up. This I believe of the masses north and south. Doubtless there are individuals, on both sides, who would not hold slaves under any circumstances; and others who would gladly introduce slavery anew, if it were out of existence. We know that some southern men do free their slaves, go north, and become tip-top abolitionists; while some northern ones go south, and become most cruel slave-masters.

When southern people tell us they are no more responsible for the origin of slavery, than we; I acknowledge the fact. When it is said that the institution exists; and that it is very difficult to get rid of it, in any satisfactory way, I can understand and appreciate the saying. I surely will not blame them for not doing what I should not know how to do myself. If all earthly power were given me, I should not know what to do, as to the existing institution. My first impulse would be to free all the slaves, and send them to Liberia,—to their own native land. But a moment's reflection would convince me, that whatever of high hope, (as I think there is) there may be in this, in the long run, its sudden execution is impossible. If they were all landed there in a day, they would all perish in the next ten days; and there are not surplus shipping and surplus money enough in the world to carry

Source: The Collected Works of Abraham Lincoln, vol. 2, ed. Roy P. Basler, Marion Dolores Pratt, and Lloyd A. Dunlap (New Brunswick, N.J.: Rutgers University Press, 1953), 247, 254–56, 261–62, 264–66, 268, 270–71, 272–74, 275–76. Editors' notes omitted. Reprinted by permission of Rutgers University Press, Copyright © 1953 by the Abraham Lincoln Association.

them there in many times ten days. What then? Free them all, and keep them among us as underlings? Is it quite certain that this betters their condition? I think I would not hold one in slavery, at any rate; yet the point is not clear enough for me to denounce people upon. What next? Free them, and make them politically and socially, our equals? My own feelings will not admit of this; and if mine would, we well know that those of the great mass of white people will not. Whether this feeling accords with justice and sound judgment, is not the sole question, if indeed, it is any part of it. A universal feeling, whether well or ill-founded, can not be safely disregarded. We can not, then, make them equals. It does seem to me that systems of gradual emancipation might be adopted; but for their tardiness in this, I will not undertake to judge our brethren of the south.

When they remind us of their constitutional rights, I acknowledge them, not grudgingly, but fully, and fairly; and I would give them any legislation for the reclaiming of their fugitives, which should not, in its stringency, be more likely to carry a free man into slavery, than our ordinary criminal laws are to hang an innocent one.

But all this, to my judgment, furnishes no more excuse for permitting slavery to go into our own free territory, than it would for reviving the African slave trade by law. The law which forbids the bringing of slaves *from* Africa; and that which has so long forbid the taking them *to* Nebraska, can hardly be distinguished on any moral principle; and the repeal of the former could find quite as plausible excuses as that of the latter....

I now come to consider whether the repeal, with its avowed principle, is intrinsically right. I insist that it is not. Take the particular case. A controversy had arisen between the advocates and opponents of slavery, in relation to its establishment within the country we had purchased of France. The southern, and then best part of the purchase, was already in as a slave State. The controversy was settled by also letting Missouri in as a slave State; but with the agreement that within all the remaining part of the purchase, North of a certain line, there should never be slavery. As to what was to be done with the remaining part south of the line, nothing was said; but perhaps the fair implication was, that it should come in with slavery if it should so choose. The southern part, except a portion heretofore mentioned, afterwards did come in with slavery, as the State of Arkansas. All these many years since 1820, the Northern part had remained a wilderness. At length settlements began in it also. In due course, Iowa, came in as a free State, and Minnesota was given a territorial government, without removing the slavery restriction. Finally the sole remaining part, North of the line, Kansas and Nebraska, was to be organized; and it is proposed, and carried, to blot out the old dividing line of thirty-four years standing, and to open the whole of that country to the introduction of slavery. Now, this, to my mind, is manifestly unjust. After an angry and dangerous controversy, the parties made friends by dividing the bone of contention. The one party first appropriates her own share, beyond all power to be disturbed in the possession of it; and then seizes the share of the other party. It is as if two starving men had divided their only loaf; the one had hastily swallowed his half, and then grabbed the other half just as he was putting it to his mouth!...

Equal justice to the south, it is said, requires us to consent to the extending of slavery to new countries. That is to say, inasmuch as you do not object to my taking my hog to Nebraska, therefore I must not object to you taking your slave. Now, I admit this is perfectly logical, if there is no difference between hogs and negroes. But while you thus require me to deny the humanity of the negro, I wish to ask whether you of the south yourselves, have even been willing to do as much? It is kindly provided that of all those who come into the world, only a small percentage are natural tyrants. That percentage is no larger in the slave States than in the free. The great majority, south as well as north, have human sympathies, of which they can no more divest themselves than they can of their sensibility to physical pain. These sympathies in the bosoms of the southern people, manifest in many ways, their sense of the wrong of slavery, and their consciousness that, after all, there is humanity in the negro. If they deny this, let me address them a few plain questions. In 1820 you joined the north, almost unanimously, in declaring the African slave trade piracy, and in annexing to it the punishment of death. Why did you do this? If you did not feel that it was wrong, why did you join in providing that men should be hung for it? The practice was no more than bringing wild negroes from Africa, to sell to such as would buy them. But you never thought of hanging men for catching and selling wild horses, wild buffaloes or wild bears.

Again, you have amongst you, a sneaking individual, of the class of native tyrants, known as the "SLAVE-DEALER." he watches your necessities, and crawls up to buy your slave, at a speculating price. If you cannot help it, you sell to him; but if you can help it, you drive him from your door. You despise him utterly. You do not recognize him as a friend, or even as an honest man. Your children must not play with his; they may rollick freely with the little negroes, but not with "slave-dealers" children. If you are obliged to deal with him, you try to get through the job without so much as touching him. It is common with you to join hands with the men you meet; but with the slave dealer you avoid the ceremony—instinctively shrinking from the snaky contact. If he grows rich and retires from business, you still remember him, and still keep up the ban of non-intercourse upon him and his family. Now why is this? You do not so treat the man who deals in corn, cattle or tobacco.

And yet again; there are in the United States and territories, including the District of Columbia, 433,643 free blacks. At $500 per head they are worth over two hundred millions of dollars. How comes this vast amount of property to be running about without owners? We do not see free horses or free cattle running at large. How is this? All these free blacks are the descendants of slaves, or have been slaves themselves, and they would be slaves now, but for SOMETHING which has operated on their white owners, inducing them, at vast pecuniary sacrifices, to liberate them. What is that SOMETHING? Is there any mistaking it? In all these cases it is your sense of justice, and human sympathy, continually telling you, that the poor negro has some natural right to himself—that those who deny it, and make mere merchandise of him, deserve kickings, contempt and death.

And now, why will you ask us to deny the humanity of the slave? and estimate him only as the equal of the hog? Why ask us to do what you will not do yourselves? Why ask us to do for *nothing*, what two hundred million of dollars could not induce you to do?

But one great argument in the support of the repeal of the Missouri Compromise, is still to come. That argument is "the sacred right of the government." It seems our distinguished Senator has found great difficulty in getting his antagonists, even in the Senate to meet him fairly on this argument—some poet has said

"Fools rush in where angels fear to tread."

At the hazzard of being thought one of the fools of this quotation, I meet that argument—I rush in, I take that bull by the horns.

I trust I understand, and truly estimate the right of self-government. My faith in the proposition that each man should do precisely as he pleases with all which is exclusively his own, lies at the foundation of the sense of justice there is in me. I extend the principles to communities of men, as well as to individuals. I so extend it, because it is politically wise, as well as naturally just: politically wise, in saving us from broils about matters which do not concern us. Here, or at Washington, I would not trouble myself with the oyster laws of Virginia, or the cranberry laws of Indiana.

The doctrine of self government is right—absolutely and eternally right—but it has no just application, as here attempted. Or perhaps I should rather say that whether it has such just application depends upon whether a negro is not or is a man. If he is not a man, why in that case, he who is a man may, as a matter of self-government, do just as he pleases with him. But if the negro is a man, is it not to that extent, a total destruction of self-government, to say that he too shall not govern *himself?* When the white man governs himself that is self-government; but when he governs himself, and also governs *another* man, that is *more* than self-government—that is despotism. If the negro is a *man*, why then my ancient faith teaches me that "all men are created equal;" and that there can be no moral right in connection with one man's making a slave of another.

Judge Douglas frequently, with bitter irony and sarcasm, paraphrases our argument by saying "The white people of Nebraska are good enough to govern themselves, *but they are not good enough to govern a few miserable negroes!!*"

Well I doubt not that the people of Nebraska are, and will continue to be as good as the average of people elsewhere. I do not say the contrary. What I do say is, that no man is good enough to govern another man, *without that other's consent*. I say this is the leading principle—the sheet anchor of American republicanism. Our Declaration of Independence says:

"We hold these truths to be self evident: that all men are created equal; that they are endowed by their Creator with certain inalienable rights; that among these are life, liberty and the pursuit of happiness. That to secure these rights, governments are instituted among men, DERIVING THEIR JUST POWERS FROM THE CONSENT OF THE GOVERNED."

I have quoted so much at this time merely to show that according to our ancient faith, the just powers of governments are derived from the consent of the governed. Now the relation of masters and slaves is, PRO TANTO, a total violation of this principle. The master not only governs the slave without his consent; but he governs him by a set of rules altogether different from those which he prescribes for himself. Allow ALL the governed an equal voice in the government, and that, and that only is self government.

Let it not be said I am contending for the establishment of political and social equality between the whites and blacks. I have already said the contrary. I am not now combating the argument of NECESSITY, arising from the fact that the blacks are already amongst us; but I am combating what is set up as MORAL argument for allowing them to be taken where they have never yet been—arguing against the EXTENSION of a bad thing, which where it already exists, we must of necessity, manage as we best can....

Whether slavery shall go into Nebraska, or other new territories, is not a matter of exclusive concern to the people who may go there. The whole nation is interested that the best use shall be made of these territories. We want them for the homes of free white people. This they cannot be, to any considerable extent, if slavery shall be planted within them. Slave States are places for poor white people to remove FROM; not to remove TO. New free States are the places for poor people to go to and better their condition. For this use, the nation needs these territories....

Finally, I insist, that if there is ANY THING which it is the duty of the WHOLE PEOPLE to never entrust to any hands but their own, that thing is the preservation and perpetuity, of their own liberties, and institutions. And if they shall think, as I do, that the extension of slavery endangers them, more than any, or all other causes, how recreant to themselves, if they submit the question, and with it, the fate of their country, to a mere hand-full of men, bent only on temporary self-interest. If this question of slavery extension were an insignificant one—one having no power to do harm—it might be shuffled aside in this way. But being, as it is, the great Behemoth of danger, shall the strong grip of the nation be loosened upon him, to entrust him to the hands of such feeble keepers?

I have done with this mighty argument, of self-government. Go, sacred thing! Go in peace.

But Nebraska is urged as a great Union-saving measure. Well I too, go for saving the Union. Much as I hate slavery, I would consent to the extension of it rather than to see the Union dissolved, just as I would consent to any GREAT evil, to avoid a GREATER one. But when I go to Union saving, I must believe, at least, that the means I employ has some adaptation to the end. To my mind, Nebraska has no such adaptation.

"It hath no relish of salvation in it."

It is an aggravation, rather, of the only one thing which ever endangers the Union. When it came upon us, all was peace and quiet. The nation was looking to the forming of new bonds of Union; and a long course of peace and prosperity seemed to lie before us. In the whole range of possibility, there scarcely appears to me to have been any thing, out of which the slavery agitation could have been revived, except the very project of repealing the Missouri compromise. Every inch of territory we owned, already had a definite settlement of the slavery question, and by which, all parties were pledged to abide. Indeed, there was no uninhabited country on the continent, which we could acquire; if we except some extreme northern regions, which are wholly out of the question. In this state of case, the genius of Discord himself, could scarcely have invented a way of again getting [setting?] us by the ears, but by turning back and destroying the peace measures of the past. The councils of that genius seem to have prevailed, the Missouri compromise was repealed; and here we are, in the midst of a new slavery agitation, such, I think, as we have never seen before. Who is responsible for this? Is it those who resist the measure; or those who, causelessly, brought it forward, and pressed it through, having reason to know, and, in fact, knowing it must and would be so resisted? It could not but be expected by its author, that it would be looked upon as a measure for the extension of slavery, aggravated by a gross breach of faith. Argue as you will, and long as you will, this is the naked FRONT and ASPECT, of the measure. And in this aspect, it could not but produce agitation. Slavery is founded in the selfishness of man's nature—opposition to it, is [in?] his love of justice. These principles are an eternal antagonism; and when brought into collision so fiercely, as slavery extension brings them, shocks, and throes, and convulsions must ceaselessly follow. Repeal the Missouri compromise—repeal all compromises—repeal the declaration of independence—repeal all past history, you still can not repeal human nature. It still will be the abundance of man's heart, that slavery extension is wrong; and out of the abundance of his heart, his mouth will continue to speak....

The Missouri Compromise ought to be restored. For the sake of the union, it ought to be restored. We ought to elect a House of Representatives which will vote its restoration. If by any means, we omit to do this, what follows? Slavery may or may not be established in Nebraska. But whether it be or not, we shall have repudiated—discarded from the councils of the Nation—the SPIRIT of COMPROMISE; for who after this will ever trust in a national compromise? The spirit of mutual concession—that spirit which first gave us the constitution, and which has thrice saved the Union—we shall have strangled and cast from us forever. And what shall we have in lieu of it? The South flushed with triumph and tempted to excesses; the North, betrayed, as they believe, brooding on wrong and burning for revenge. One side will provoke; the other resent. The one will taunt, the other defy; one agrees [aggresses?], the other retaliates. Already a few in the North, defy all constitutional restraints, resist the execution of the fugitive slave law, and even menace the institution of slavery in the states where it exists.

Already a few in the South, claim the constitutional right to take to and hold slaves in the free states—demand the revival of the slave trade; and demand a treaty with Great Britain by which fugitive slaves may be reclaimed from Canada. As yet they are but few on either side. It is a grave question for the lovers of the Union, whether the final destruction of the Missouri Compromise, and with it the spirit of all compromise will or will not embolden and embitter each of these, and fatally increase the numbers of both.

But restore the compromise, and what then? We thereby restore the national faith, the national confidence, the national feeling of brotherhood. We thereby reinstate the spirit of concession and compromise—that spirit which has never failed us in past perils, and which may be safely trusted for all the future. The south ought to join in doing this. The peace of the nation is as dear to them as to us. In memories of the past and hopes of the future, they share as largely as we. It would be on their part, a great act—great in its spirit, and great in its effect. It would be worth to the nation a hundred years' purchase of peace and prosperity. And what of sacrifice would they make? They only surrender to us, what they gave us for a consideration long, long ago; what they have not now, asked for, struggled or cared for; what has been thrust upon them, not less to their own astonishment than to ours.

But it is said we cannot restore it; that though we elect every member of the lower house, the Senate is still against us. It is quite true, that of the Senators who passed the Nebraska bill, a majority of the whole Senate will retain their seats in spite of the elections of this and the next year. But if at these elections, their several constituencies shall clearly express their will against Nebraska, will these senators disregard their will? Will they neither obey, nor make room for those who will?

But even if we fail to technically restore the compromise, it is still a great point to carry a popular vote in favor of the restoration. The moral weight of such a vote can not be estimated too highly. The authors of Nebraska are not at all satisfied with the destruction of the compromise—an endorsement of this PRINCIPLE, they proclaim to be the great object. With them, Nebraska alone is a small matter—to establish a principle, for FUTURE USE, is what they particularly desire.

That future use is to be the planting of slavery wherever in the wide world, local and unorganized opposition can not prevent it. Now if you wish to give them this endorsement—if you wish to establish this principle—do so. I shall regret it; but it is your right. On the contrary if you are opposed to the principle—intend to give it no such endorsement—let no wheedling, no sophistry, divert you from throwing a direct vote against it.

Some men, mostly whigs, who condemn the repeal of the Missouri Compromise, nevertheless hesitate to go for its restoration, lest they be thrown in company with the abolitionist. Will they allow me as an old whig to tell them good humoredly, that I think this is very silly? Stand with anybody that stands RIGHT. Stand with him while he is right and PART with him when he goes wrong. Stand WITH the abolitionist in restoring the Missouri Compromise; and stand AGAINST him when he attempts to repeal the fugitive slave law. In the latter case you stand with the southern disunionist. What of that? you are still right. In both cases you are right. In both cases you oppose [expose?] the dangerous extremes. In both you stand on middle ground and hold the ship level and steady. In both you are national and nothing less than national. This is good old whig ground. To desert such ground, because of any company, is to be less than a whig—less than a man—less than an American.

I particularly object to the NEW position which the avowed principle of this Nebraska law gives to slavery in the body politic. I object to it because it assumes that there CAN be MORAL RIGHT in the enslaving of one man by another. I object to it as a dangerous dalliance for a few [free?] people—a sad evidence that, feeling prosperity we forget right—that liberty, as a principle, we have ceased to revere. I object to it because the fathers of the republic eschewed, and rejected it. The argument of "Necessity" was the only argument they ever admitted in favor of slavery; and so far, and so far only as it carried them, did they ever go. They found the institution existing among us, which they could not help; and they cast blame upon the British King for having permitted its introduction. BEFORE the constitution, they prohibited its introduction into the north-western Territory—the only country we owned, then free from it. At the framing and adoption of the constitution, they forbore to so much as mention the word "slave" or "slavery" in the whole instrument. In the provision for the recovery of fugitives, the slave is spoken of as a "PERSON HELD TO SERVICE OR LABOR." In that prohibiting the abolition of the African slave trade for twenty years, that trade is spoken of as "The migration or importation of such persons as any of the States NOW EXISTING, shall think proper to admit," &c. These are the only provisions alluding to slavery. Thus, the thing is hid away, in the constitution, just as an afflicted man hides away a wen or a cancer, which he dares not cut out once, lest he bleed to death; with the promise, nevertheless, that the cutting may begin at the end of a given time. Less than this our fathers COULD not do; and NOW [MORE?] they WOULD not do. Necessity drove them so far, and farther, they would not go. But this is not all. The earliest Congress, under the constitution, took the same view of slavery. They hedged and hemmed it in to the narrowest limits of necessity....

But NOW it is to be transformed into a "sacred right." Nebraska brings it forth, places it on the high road to extension and perpetuity; and, with a pat on its back, says to it, "Go, and God speed you." Henceforth it is to be the chief jewel of the nation—the very figurehead of the ship of State. Little by little, but steadily as man's march to the grave, we have been giving up the OLD for the NEW faith. Near eighty years ago we began by declaring that all men are created equal; but now from that beginning we have run down to the other declaration, that for SOME men to enslave (OTHERS is a "sacred right of self-government." These principles can not stand together. They are as opposite as God and mammon; and whoever holds to the one, must despise the other. When Pettit, in connection with his support of the Nebraska bill, called the Declaration of Independence "a self-evident lie" he only did what consistency and candor require all other Nebraska men to do. Of the forty odd Nebraska Senators who sat present and heard him, no one rebuked him. Nor am I apprized that any Nebraska newspaper, or any Nebraska orator, in the whole nation, has ever yet rebuked him. If this had been said among Marion's men, Southerners though they were, what would have become of the man who said it? If this had been said to the men who captured André, the man who said it, would probably have been hung sooner than André was. If it had been said in old independence Hall, seventy-eight years ago, the very door-keeper would have throttled the man, and thrust him into the street.

Let no one be deceived. The spirit of seventy-six and the spirit of Nebraska, are utter antagonisms; and the former is being rapidly displaced by the latter.

Fellow countrymen—Americans south, as well as north, shall we make no effort to arrest this? Already the liberal party throughout the world, express the apprehension "that the one retrograde institution in America, is undermining the principles of progress, and fatally violating the noblest political system the world ever saw." This is not the taunt of enemies, but the warning of friends. Is it quite safe to disregard it—to despise it? Is there no danger to liberty itself, in discarding the earliest practice, and first precept of our ancient faith? In our greedy chase to make profit of the negro, let us beware, lest we "cancel and tear to pieces" even the white man's charter of freedom.

Our republican robe is soiled, and trailed in the dust. Let us repurify it. Let us turn and wash it white, in the spirit, if not the blood, of the Revolution. Let us turn slavery from its claims of "moral right," back upon its existing legal rights, and its arguments of "necessity." Let us return it to the position our fathers gave it; and there let it rest in peace. Let us re-adopt the Declaration of Independence, and with it, the practices, and policy, which harmonize with it. Let north and south—let all Americans—let all lovers of liberty everywhere—join in the great and good work. If we do this, we shall not only have saved the Union; but we shall have so saved it, as to make, and to keep it, forever worthy of the saving. We shall have so saved it, that the succeeding millions of free happy people, the world over, shall rise up, and call us blessed, to the latest generations.

"Address Before the Wisconsin State Agricultural Society" (1859)

[Milwaukee, Wisconsin, September 30, 1859]

The world is agreed that *labor* is the source from which human wants are mainly supplied. There is no dispute upon this point. From this point, however, men immediately diverge. Much disputation is maintained as to the best way of applying and controlling the labor element. By some it is assumed that labor is available only in connection with capital— that nobody labors, unless somebody else, owning capital, somehow, by the use of that capital, induces him to do it. Having assumed this, they proceed to consider whether it is best that capital shall *hire* laborers, and thus induce them to work by their own consent; or *buy* them, and drive them to it without their consent. Having proceeded so far they naturally conclude that all laborers are necessarily either *hired* laborers, or *slaves.* They further assume that whoever is once a *hired* laborer, is fatally fixed in that condition for life; and thence again that his condition is as bad as, or worse than that of a slave. This is the *"mud-sill"* theory.

But another class of reasoners hold the opinion that there is no *such* relation between capital and labor, as assumed; and that there is no such thing as a freeman being fatally fixed for life, in the condition of a hired laborer, that both these assumptions are false, and all inferences from them groundless. They hold that labor is prior to, and independent of, capital; that, in fact, capital is the fruit of labor, and could never have existed if labor had not *first* existed—that labor can exist without capital, but that capital could never have existed without labor. Hence they hold that labor is the superior—greatly the superior—of capital.

They do not deny that there is, and probably always will be, a relation between labor and capital. The error, as they hold, is in assuming that the *whole* labor of the world exists within that relation. A few men own capital; and that few avoid labor themselves, and with their capital, hire, or buy, another few to labor for them. A large majority belong to neither class—neither work for others, nor have others working for them. Even in all our slave States, except South Carolina, a majority of the whole people of all colors, are neither slaves nor masters. In these Free States, a large majority are neither *hirers* nor *hired.* Men, with their families— wives, sons and daughters—work for themselves, on their farms, in their houses and in their shops, taking the whole product to themselves, and asking no favors of capital on the one hand, nor of hirelings or slaves on the other. It is not forgotten that a considerable number of persons mingle their own labor with capital; that is, labor with their own hands, and also buy slaves or hire freemen to labor for them; but this is only a *mixed,* and not a *distinct* class. No principle stated is disturbed by the existence of this mixed class. Again, as has already been said, the opponents of the *"mud-sill"* theory insist that there is not, of necessity, any such thing as the free hired laborer being fixed to

Source: *The Collected Works of Abraham Lincoln,* vol. 3, ed. Roy P. Basler, Marion Dolores Pratt, and Lloyd A. Dunlap (New Brunswick, N.J.: Rutgers University Press, 1953), 477–82. Editors' notes omitted. Reprinted by permission of Rutgers University Press, Copyright © 1953 by the Abraham Lincoln Association.

that condition for life. There is demonstration for saying this. Many independent men, in this assembly, doubtless a few years ago were hired laborers. And their case is almost if not quite the general rule.

The prudent, penniless beginner in the world, labors for wages awhile, saves a surplus with which to buy tools or land, for himself; then labors on his own account another while, and at length hires another new beginner to help him. This, say its advocates, is *free* labor— the just and generous, and prosperous system, which opens the way for all—gives hope to all, and energy, and progress, and improvement of condition to all. If any continue through life in the condition of the hired laborer, it is not the fault of the system, but because of either a dependent nature which prefers it, or improvidence, folly, or singular misfortune. I have said this much about the elements of labor generally, as introductory to the consideration of a new phase which that element is in process of assuming. The old general rule was that *educated* people did not perform manual labor. They managed to eat their bread, leaving the toil of producing it to the uneducated. This was not an insupportable evil to the working bees, so long as the class of drones remained very small. But *now,* especially in these free States, nearly all are educated—quite too nearly all, to leave the labor of the uneducated, in any wise adequate to the support of the whole. It follows from this that henceforth educated people must labor. Otherwise, education itself would become a positive and intolerable evil. No country can sustain, in idleness, more than a small percentage of its numbers. The great majority must labor at something productive. From these premises the problem springs, "How can *labor* and *education* be the most satisfactorily combined?"

By the *"mud-sill"* theory it is assumed that labor and education are incompatible; and any practical combination of them impossible. According to that theory, a blind horse upon a tread-mill, is a perfect illustration of what a laborer should be—all the better for being blind, that he could not tread out of place, or kick understandingly. According to that theory, the education of laborers, is not only useless, but pernicious, and danger- ous. In fact, it is, in some sort, deemed a misfortune that laborers should have heads at all. Those same heads are regarded as explosive materials, only to be safely kept in damp places, as far as possible from that peculiar sort of fire which ignites them. A Yankee who could invent a strong *handed* man without a head would receive the everlasting gratitude of the "mud-sill" advocates.

But Free Labor says "no!" Free Labor argues that, as the Author of man makes every individual with one head and one pair of hands, it was probably intended that heads and hands should cooperate as friends; and that that particular head, should direct and con- trol that particular pair of hands. As each man has one mouth to be fed, and one pair of hands to furnish food, it was probably intended that that particular pair of hands should feed that particular mouth—that each head is the natural guardian, director, and protec- tor of the hands and mouth inseparably connected with it; and that being so, every head should be cultivated, and improved, by whatever will add to its capacity for performing its charge. In one word Free labor insists on universal education.

I have so far stated the opposite theories of *"Mud-Sill"* and "Free Labor" without declaring any preference of my own between them. On an occasion like this I ought not to declare any. I suppose, however, I shall not be mistaken, in assuming as a fact, that the people of Wisconsin prefer free labor, with its natural companion, education.

This leads to the further reflection, that no other human occupation opens so wide a field for the profitable and agreeable combination of labor with cultivated thought, as agri- culture. I know of nothing so pleasant to the mind, as the discovery of anything which is at once *new* and *valuable*—nothing which so lightens and sweetens toil, as the hopeful pursuit of such discovery. And how vast, and how varied a field is agriculture, for such discovery. The mind, already trained to thought, in the country school, or higher school, cannot fail to find there an exhaustless source of profitable enjoyment. Every blade of grass is a study; and to produce two, where there was but one, is both a profit and a pleasure. And not grass alone; but soils, seeds, and seasons—hedges, ditches, and fences, draining, droughts, and irrigation—plowing, hoeing, and harrowing—reaping, mowing, and threshing—saving crops, pests of crops, diseases of crops, and what will prevent or cure them—implements, utensils, and machines, their relative merits, and [how] to improve them—hogs, horses, and cattle—sheep, goats, and poultry—trees, shrubs, fruits, plants, and flowers—the thousand things of which these are specimens—each a world of study within itself.

In all this, book-learning is available. A capacity, and taste, for reading, gives access to whatever has already been discovered by others. It is the key, or one of the keys, to the already solved problems. And not only so. It gives a relish, and facility, for successfully pursuing the [yet] unsolved ones. The rudiments of science, are available, and highly valuable. Some knowledge of Botany assists in dealing with the vegetable world—with all growing crops. Chemistry assists in the analysis of soils, selection, and application of manures, and in numerous other ways. The mechanical branches of Natural Philosophy, are ready help in almost everything; but especially in reference to implements and machinery.

The thought recurs that education—cultivated thought—can best be combined with agricultural labor, or any labor, on the principle of *thorough* work—that careless, half performed, slovenly work, makes no place for such combination. And thorough work, again, renders sufficient, the smallest quantity of ground to each man. And this again, conforms to what must occur in a world less inclined to wars, and more devoted to the arts of peace, than heretofore. Population must increase rapidly—more rapidly than in former times— and ere long the most valuable of all arts, will be the art of deriving a comfortable subsistence from the smallest area of soil. No community whose every member possesses this art, can ever be the victim of oppression in any of its forms. Such community will be alike independent of crowned-kings, money-kings, and land-kings.

But, according to your programme, the awarding of premiums awaits the closing of this address. Considering the deep interest necessarily pertaining to that performance, it would be no wonder if I am already heard with some impatience. I will detain you but a moment longer. Some of you will be successful, and such will need but little philosophy to take them home in cheerful spirits; others will be disappointed, and will be in a less happy mood. To such, let it be said, "Lay it not too much to heart." Let them adopt the maxim, "Better luck next time;" and then, by renewed exertion, make that better luck for themselves.

And by the successful, and the unsuccessful, let it be remembered, that while occasions like the present, bring their sober and durable benefits, the exultations and mortifications of them, are but temporary; that the victor shall soon be the vanquished, if he relax in his exertion; and that the vanquished this year, may be victor the next, in spite of all competition.

It is said an Eastern monarch once charged his wise men to invent him a sentence, to be ever in view, and which should be true and appropriate in all times and situations. They presented him the words: *"And this, too, shall pass away."* How much it expresses! How chastening in the hour of pride!—how consoling in the depths of affliction! "And this, too, shall pass away." And yet let us hope it is not *quite* true. Let us hope, rather, that by the best cultivation of the physical world, beneath and around us; and the intellectual and moral world within us, we shall secure an individual, social, and political prosperity and happiness, whose course shall be onward and upward, and which, while the earth endures, shall not pass away.

"Address Delivered at the Dedication
of the Cemetery at Gettysburg"
(1863)

[November 19,1863]

Four score and seven years ago our fathers brought forth on this continent, a new nation, conceived in Liberty, and dedicated to the proposition that all men are created equal.

Now we are engaged in a great civil war, testing whether that nation, or any nation so conceived and so dedicated, can long endure. We are met on a great battle-field of that war. We have come to dedicate a portion of that field, as a final resting place for those who here gave their lives that that nation might live. It is altogether fitting and proper that we should do this.

But, in a larger sense, we can not dedicate—we can not consecrate—we can not hallow—this ground. The brave men, living and dead, who struggled here, have consecrated it, far above our poor power to add or detract. The world will little note, nor long remember what we say here, but it can never forget what they did here. It is for us the living, rather, to be dedicated here to the unfinished work which they who fought here have thus far so nobly advanced. It is rather for us to be here dedicated to the great task remaining before us—that from these honored dead we take increased devotion to that cause for which they gave the last full measure of devotion—that we here highly resolve that these dead shall not have died in vain—that this nation, under God, shall have a new birth of freedom—and that government of the people, by the people, for the people, shall not perish from the earth.

Source: The Collected Works of Abraham Lincoln, vol. 7, ed. Roy P. Basler, Marion Dolores Pratt, and Lloyd A. Dunlap (New Brunswick, N.J.: Rutgers University Press, 1953), 23. Editors' notes omitted. Reprinted by permission of Rutgers University Press, Copyright © 1953 by the Abraham Lincoln Association.

"Second Inaugural Address"
(1865)

March 4, 1865

[Fellow Countrymen:]

At this second appearing to take the oath of the presidential office, there is less occasion for an extended address than there was at the first. Then a statement, somewhat in detail, of a course to be pursued, seemed fitting and proper. Now, at the expiration of four years, during which public declarations have been constantly called forth on every point and phase of the great contest which still absorbs the attention, and engrosses the energies of the nation, little that is new could be presented. The progress of our arms, upon which all else chiefly depends, is as well known to the public as to myself; and it is, I trust, reasonably satisfactory and encouraging to all. With high hope for the future, no prediction in regard to it is ventured.

On the occasion corresponding to this four years ago, all thoughts were anxiously directed to an impending civil-war. All dreaded it—all sought to avert it. While the inaugural address was being delivered from this place, devoted altogether to saving the Union without war, insurgent agents were in the city seeking to *destroy* it without war—seeking to dissol[v]e the Union, and divide effects, by negotiation. Both parties deprecated war, but one of them would *make* war rather than let the nation survive; and the other would *accept* war rather than let it perish. And the war came.

One eighth of the whole population were colored slaves, not distributed generally over the Union, but localized in the Southern part of it. These slaves constituted a peculiar and powerful interest. All knew that this interest was, somehow, the cause of the war. To strengthen, perpetuate, and extend this interest was the object for which the insurgents would rend the Union, even by war; while the government claimed no right to do more than to restrict the territorial enlargement of it. Neither party expected for the war, the magnitude, or the duration, which it has already attained. Neither anticipated that the *cause* of the conflict might cease with, or even before, the conflict itself should cease. Each looked for an easier triumph, and a result less fundamental and astounding. Both read the same Bible, and pray to the same God; and each invokes His aid against the other. It may seem strange that any men should dare to ask a just God's assistance in wringing their bread from the sweat of other men's faces; but let us judge not that we be not judged. The prayers of both could not be answered; that of neither has been answered fully. The Almighty has His own purposes. "Woe unto the world because of offences! for it must needs be that offences come; but woe to that man by whom the offence cometh!" If we shall suppose that American Slavery is one of those offences which, in the providence of God, must needs come, but which, having continued through His appointed time, He now wills to remove, and that He gives to both North and South, this terrible war, as the woe

Source: *The Collected Works of Abraham Lincoln*, vol. 8, ed. Roy P. Basler, Marion Dolores Pratt, and Lloyd A. Dunlap (New Brunswick, N.J.: Rutgers University Press, 1953), 332–33. Editors' notes omitted. Reprinted by permission of Rutgers University Press, Copyright © 1953 by the Abraham Lincoln Association.

due to those by whom the offence came, shall we discern therein any departure from those divine attributes which the believers in a Living God always ascribe to Him? Fondly do we hope—fervently do we pray—that this mighty scourge of war may speedily pass away. Yet, if God wills that it continue, until all the wealth piled by the bond-man's two hundred and fifty years of unrequited toil shall be sunk, and until every drop of blood drawn with the lash, shall be paid by another drawn with the sword, as was said three thousand years ago, so still it must be said "the judgments of the Lord, are true and righteous altogether."

With malice toward none; with charity for all; with firmness in the right, as God gives us to see the right, let us strive on to finish the work we are in; to bind up the nation's wounds; to care for him who shall have borne the battle, and for his widow, and his orphan—to do all which may achieve and cherish a just, and a lasting peace, among ourselves, and with all nations.

FRANCIS LIEBER

"Nationalism and Internationalism"
(1868)

Francis Lieber (1800–1872) was one of a group of young German liberal revolutionaries escaping political harassment in Prussia who in the 1820s immigrated to the United States. Well-schooled in his former country's pioneering human sciences, he now prided himself on being a citizen of a country that, though woefully lacking anything like the great universities of Germany, gave him the freedom to test, through public debate and political practice, what he had learned there. This dual focus of thought and action marked the rest of his career. Founder of the American discipline of political science, he was also, in the wake of the Union's victory, which his zealous pro-Union wartime propaganda helped secure, the country's most ardent and sophisticated theorist of nationalism. His ideas showed the clear markings of his studies in Kantian philosophy and German Romantic political theory. Only a society conscious of its organic identity and destiny, not a barren Lockean contract of self-protective individuals, could constitute an extensive autonomous nation productive of "institutional liberty" founded on its citizens' recognition of each other's reciprocal "rights" and "duties." Yet he also regarded himself, without contradiction, as an advanced internationalist. He most successfully demonstrated this other side of nationalism two months before the Battle of Gettysburg, when at the request of President Lincoln's Secretary of War, he drafted "General Orders, 100," the first official codification of the rules of war in Western history. Prohibiting acts of cruelty, revenge, torture, and other militarily unnecessary acts of violence directed at combatants and noncombatants on all sides, the Lieber Code would profoundly influence national manuals and international conventions on wartime conduct down to our own time. The most important are the Geneva Conventions and the subsequent international Convention Against Torture, which the United States ratified in 1994 and that twenty years later the U. S. Senate Intelligence Committee's report condemned the Bush administration for contravening during the Iraq War.

Nowhere did Lieber so succinctly tie together these two iconic concepts than in his fittingly titled "Nationalism and Internationalism." The address was the product of many years of thinking and writing on the subject, but he delivered it three years after the end of the war and dedicated it to General Ulysses S. Grant on the eve of Grant's first election to the presidency. Rejecting both the model of a deracinated trans-nationalism and that of a coercive supranationalism—whether of an empire, monarchy, or republic—he urged instead an "internationalism" that he claimed grew out of the same human impulse toward "interdependence" manifested in a nation's citizens' free exchanges of goods and ideas. However, his extensive list of voluntary agreements in culture and science evidencing expanding interdependence, he made an important exclusion: only "Cis-Caucasian" or white peoples would be in the vanguard of this advancing interdependent "civilization." But if Lieber was a racist—and he was—he was also a soft if not muddled one. His "Cis-Caucasian" "races" were by and large cultural rather than biological categories. Moreover they were peoples, he freely conceded, who had simply entered the march of civilization early and had regularly enslaved their inferiors "with a fiendish zeal." At the same time, this abolitionist Radical Republican did not seem very certain how long these lower orders would wallow in their primitive states. Africans and Asians did not provide their children with toys as the civilized nations did, he asserted, but sometime in the near future, he imagined, the civilized phalanx would connect Europe with Asia—fortuitously passing through America! Indeed, at the end he complacently reported that an American citizen had recently led a delegation of Chinese to New York and other Western cities for the purpose of attaching China to the community of nations dedicated to international law. It was only natural, Lieber evidently thought, that the freest nation would lead the non-West in the perhaps not-so-long climb toward worldwide interdependence.

Frank Friedel, *Francis Lieber: Nineteenth-Century Liberal* (Baton Rouge, 1947) is the still-standard biography. Excellent essays on Lieber's thought and intellectual character may be found in Charles R. Mack and Henry H. Lesesne, eds., *Francis Lieber and The Culture of The Mind* (Columbia, S.C., 2005). For a cogent discussion of the contribution of Lieber to a transatlantic liberal discourse that "Americanized" political science, see Robert Adcock, *Liberalism and the Emergence of American Political Science: A Transatlantic Tale* (New York, 2014), chap. 3. An elegant elucidation of Lieber's international thought may be found in David Clinton, *Tocqueville, Lieber, and Bagehot: Liberalism Confronts the World* (New York, 2003), chap. 3. John Fabian Witt, *Lincoln's Code: The Laws of War in American History* (New York, 2012) is a grippingly told story of the genesis and impact of "Lincoln's Code," so named by virtue of the president's approval and execution of the law.

ON THE EVE OF A MOMENTOUS NATIONAL ELECTION THE WRITER OF THESE
FEW PAGES MAKES BOLD TO DEDICATE THEM TO

GENERAL U. S. GRANT.

MAY THE AMERICAN PEOPLE

CONFER UPON HIM

THE CHIEF MAGISTRACY OF THIS NATION,

CONSCIOUS OF ITS FREEDOM AND ITS GRANDEUR

AND NOW ASSAILED AGAIN

IN ITS BEST AND NOBLEST INTERESTS

BY THOSE ENEMIES

AGAINST WHOM BUT A SHORT TIME AGO

HE LED THE NATIONAL HOSTS

TO VICTORY AND PATRIOTIC GLORY.

AND LET THE PEOPLE OF THIS CONTINENTAL REPUBLIC

ON THE COMING FOURTH OF MARCH

GREET HIM AS CHARLEMAGNE WAS HAILED AT ROME:

PACIFIC VICTOR.

I.

Normal Types of Government. Nationalization.

As the city-state was the normal type of free communities in antiquity, and as the feudal system must be considered as one of the normal types of government in the forbidding middle ages, so is the national polity the normal type of our own epoch—not indeed centralism.

The highest national polity yet developed is the representative national government, equally distant from the market-republic of old and the despotism of Asia or Europe, from absorbing centralism and dissolving communism, so-called. Centralism may be intensely national, even to bigotry; it may become a political fanaticism; it may be intelligent and formulated with great precision; but centralism remains an inferior species of government. It is no government of peaceful development, and decentralization becomes necessary as self-government or liberty are longed for and present themselves clearer to the mind of a people waxing in manliness and independence. Centralism may be national, but National Polity and Centralism are far from being equivalent terms. England, which has enjoyed a national polity long before other European countries, is to this day the least centralized state of Europe, and possesses a far higher degree of self-government than any people of the neighboring continent. Germany, although the Germans were called the German Nation in the early times of the emperors, never acquired a national polity, like the English, which dates from the days of Alfred, and is openly and liberally marked out by Magna Charta. There was an England with unbarred national intercommunication long before there was a national France, Spain, or Italy, or a political, national Germany.

The "Evil Tolls" of which the Great Charter of England speaks, and which included the arrogant extortion of tolls by feudal lords along the roads and rivers, and the custom-lines between the different provinces, were abolished on the continent at a much later period. The journal minutely kept by Albert Duerer, when called by Charles V. from Nuremberg to Ghent, gives an appalling picture of the former, and the latter were abolished in France only by the first revolution. Prussia has been at work ever since the Congress of Vienna to abolish the internal Evil Tolls in Germany, and at last succeeded in a measure. Happy, indeed, are we that our constitution forbids the "evil tolls" in this country.

Those large communities, which we call nations, were gradually formed on the continent of Europe out of the fragmentary peoples left by the disintegration of the Roman empire. The different processes of Nationalization form one of the most instructive subjects in the whole history of civilization. England dates the blessing of a national polity over a thousand years back, and in her alone liberty and nationality grew apace. Other nations are even now in the act of forming; others, already existing, are carrying out more distinctly or establishing more firmly the national elements of their polities. For this reason, and because the existence of many nations at the same time deeply influences our civilization, the present period will be called the National Period. It began plainly when so many other great things began—when great events happened and great ideas burst upon mankind, and when inventions and discoveries were made, which ushered in the modern era—in the middle of the fifteenth century; that age when the conquering Mussulman tore the fairest portion from Europe, and thereby forced the restoration of letters and revival of inquiry upon her; when Europe lost Greece in the East, and sent Columbus to the West

Source: Francis Lieber, *Fragments of Political Science on Nationalism and Inter-Nationalism* (New York: Charles Scribner & Co., 1868), 3–23. Notes altered.

to discover our continent, and when, close upon this event, the still greater Reformation began at home.

The process of nationalizing the many dialects and jargons had begun in some countries—geographically marked as countries, but wholly unnationalized otherwise—at an earlier time. Dante, singing in the Tuscan dialect, raised it thus to the dignity of the language for all Italy, as later Luther by his own translation of the Bible, made his dialect the German language; and Dante, the greatest poet of his country, which he calls *Italia mia di dolor ostello* (the very inn of grief), because torn to pieces and lacking her destined nationality, became thus the first nationalizer of Italy in the thirteenth and at the beginning of the fourteenth century—five hundred years before Cavour; and now only has Germany made a vigorous movement toward her political nationalization, in which may Heaven bless her leaders' boldest acts.

II.

What is a Nation in the Modern Sense of the Word?

The word Nation, in the fullest adaptation of the term, means, in modern times, a numerous and homogeneous population (having long emerged from the hunter's and nomadic state), permanently inhabiting and cultivating a coherent territory, with a well-defined geographic outline, and a name of its own—the inhabitants speaking their own language, having their own literature and common institutions, which distinguish them clearly from other and similar groups of people; being citizens or subjects of a unitary government, however subdivided it may be, and feeling an organic unity with one another, as well as being conscious of a common destiny. Organic intellectual and political internal unity, with proportionate strength, and a distinct and obvious demarcation from similar groups, are notable elements of the idea of a modern nation in its fullest sense. A nation is a nation only when there is but one nationality; and the attempt at establishing a nationality within a nationality is more inconsistent and mischievous even than the establishment of "an empire within an empire."

No groupings of human beings, short of nations, are adequate to the high demands of modern civilization. Without a national character, States cannot obtain that longevity and continuity of political society which is necessary for our progress. Even our patriotism has become preëminently national. Modern patriotism is not satisfied with the narrow bounds of a city, as of old, or the limits of a province, though it be the fairest. Nothing but a Country, that is the dwelling-place of a nation, suffices for the *patria* of modern men. But the noblest sentiments and deeds and victories of sword or mind, even of ancient Greece, were of a Pan-Hellenic character. Greece never got, in her political life, beyond frail confederacies with the unavoidable, undefined, but forcibly asserted hegemony of some one State, but her Hellenism—her nationalism in all other respects—in religion, in literature, in the arts, in language and poetry, in philosophy, in republicanism, in colonization and commercial spirit, and indeed in every branch of high culture, blossomed forth everywhere. She died of crushing State sovereignty, which proved so fatal to Germany; to which Napoleon III. strongly desired to reduce Italy, and which was near to be our grave.

In the organic unity lies the chief difference between the words Nation and People. People generally means the aggregate of the inhabitants of a territory, without any additional idea, at least favorable idea. In all European languages, except the English, the words corresponding to People had acquired the meaning of rabble, populace, the lowest and least respectable class. The French Dictionary of the Academy gave hardly another definition of the word *Peuple;* and in England alone, to her great honor, did it retain, or at any rate acquire at a very early period, an honorable meaning, as Populus had possessed a dignified meaning in the better times of Rome. While the French Academy thus ignominiously defined the word People, Chatham, when George III. had reluctantly appointed him premier, used to be called the People's Minister for "His Majesty's Secretary of State;" and, on the other hand, it was natural that Louis XV. was startled when first the word Nation came to be heard in the last century, in France. He is reported to have said: "Nation! What is Nation? Is there anything besides myself?" The remark seems to be too profound for a being such as he had sunk to be; but there can be no doubt that this supposed question indicated the sentiment of that portion of the French court which was led by the Jesuits, then as under the Spanish predominance, and as now, hostile to national organic unity and to nationalism in its varied manifestations.

Extensive and organized power over large populations does not suffice to make a nation. The Roman monarchy was no national empire; nor had the vast dominion of Charles the Fifth a national character. Prussia, ever since the Peace of Paris, in 1815, called one of the Five Great Powers, never formed a nation. She herself acknowledged, and still acknowledges, that the nation to which she belongs is the German nation, though not yet politically nationalized, as Martin Luther had called it in 1520, in his grand and inspiriting letter "To the Christian Nobility of the German Nation on the Bettering of the Ghostly Class" (Clergy). Nor does common extraction and demarcating institutions, not even a peculiar religion, necessarily constitute a nation in the modern sense. The modern Jews dispersed over the globe have never consolidated into a nation. The Armenians with their many characteristics, of religion, language, and culture, form no nation. Nor does a common language alone constitute a nation. If Panslavism were ever so successful, there would be no Panslavic nation; nor can we properly speak, at present, of a Russian nation, however distinct the Russian empire may be. The Russian system has rather the tendency to trample out nationalities and national characteristics for the benefit of a gigantic bureaucracy, called Russia.

In antiquity and the early middle ages there existed no nations in the modern sense, this side of China, with the only exception of the Israelites. There were Assyrian and Median and Persian empires, but no nations. The empires were called after the conquering and ruling tribe or race. Hence their sudden conquests and speedy annihilation.

The Mosaic constitution establishes the Israelites as different yet very closely related tribes wrought into a national sacerdotal government; but, either the untoward surroundings of that people in close propinquity to fully developed, conquering Asiatic despotism, or the inaptitude for political development and organic congregation which seems to be common to the whole Semitic family, led the Israelites to disruption and secession long before their national government had fully and comprehensively developed itself. The history of the Hebrews is a saddening account of national humiliation and suicide.

The appointed and historic work of the Hebrews was to guard, in spite of their pagan pruriency, the idea of one God, Creator and Sustainer of all things and beings, through centuries of alluring, sensuous, and sometimes æsthetic polytheism around them. Political nationality was subordinate with them; yet the fact ought to arrest our grave attention that the only monotheistic people, and the people for whom Moses legislated, formed, in the earliest times of history, a nation in the modern sense. The same cannot be said of ancient Egypt.

However striking a characteristic of a nation may be found in a separate language, and however important a separate name for a country or a nation may be, neither is absolutely necessary. We are an illustration. We have not our separate language; and more than two distinctly separate nations may speak the English tongue, before the Cis-Caucasian race passes into the twentieth century. But are we a nation?

III.

The Americans form a Nation. The Vein of Nationality crops out from our earliest periods, and the sacrifices of our Civil War have been made for two objects, one of which was to save our indispensable Nationality.

Some American publicists and statesmen consider the States, as now constituted, the preëxistent elements of our comprehensive polity; somewhat as though the present reluctance of Nova Scotia to join the Canadian Union indicated a Nova-Scotian sovereignty preordained from the beginning. This is a radical error. The first States arose, in a great measure, out of the colonial governments, while the genesis of the later and far greater number of States is absolutely national; and it is, indeed, a fact of moment in our history that thus comparatively small divisions of the country were formed and became normal, differing from the vice-royalties in Spanish America; but there was nothing in these demarcations of the colonies or in the charters or the crown gifts, that had any intrinsic connection with a future sovereignty. The motives of these charters were often reprehensible; the geographic demarcations frequently indicated by ignorance. What, however, really became important in the colonization of this portion of the globe, are the following things and circumstances which may be justly called factors of our growth and elements of our public life, in nearly all which our characteristics are the direct opposite to the elements of South American colonization.

The country in which our first colonists settled was an almost unbounded body of land, in the temperate zone, with an extensive coast and a dignified geography, a rewarding soil and rich in minerals; thinly peopled by rovers in the hunter's stage of civilization; extending from sea to sea, and situated between the Old and the Older World. The age at which our settlers came hither was the age marked by two characteristics—the formation of nations and the struggle of fierce Spanish Catholicism against Protestantism. In the Netherlands Freedom had been victorious against sinister absolutism; in Germany the direst of all wars, the Thirty Years War, was raging, and Hugo Grotius published at the same time the first portion of his immortal work. It was that period at which in Spain Absolutism in politics, and the Inquisition and unlimited persecution had been fully developed, while in England, whence our settlers came, the people accustomed to freedom were preparing for resistance to rising and tentative absolutism. Our colonists belonged to the virile branch of the Teutonic race in England; they were protestants, they rather fled for peaceful existence than that they conquered and slaughtered populous tribes; they came from a country in which a national government had existed for centuries; the feudal estates had long been shaped into a representative system with Two Houses, and in which a Common, that is a National Law, had evolved itself in a great measure independent of the executive, containing manly principles of individual independence and self-government, with a position of the judiciary and the advocate which soon expanded in the noblest dimensions and led to the independence of the judiciary and to the position of the lawyer in North America, which had and continues to have a marked influence on our public life.

The colonists brought no feudalism along with them; land was owned almost everywhere in fee simple; no lords, no peasants; and almost all the original settlers came from the independent middle class, from which nearly all freedom in the history of our race has come; and these settlers brought along with them that marked desire to establish common and higher schools with which the Reformation had everywhere leaped into life (the Bible and worship in the mother tongue, and grammar schools); they were experts in self-government; their country was in one of those periods which seem profusely gifted in literature—Shakspeare had but just died, and Milton began to lift his wings; and to all this must be added that dark feature in the history of our proud race, that while the people struggled bravely for liberty in many portions, and when Europe had abolished slavery within her bosom, she introduced negro slavery in her colonies in America.*

Our Cis-Caucasian race, which has been the keenest of all races in the pursuit of wealth, and the most systematically cruel in this pursuit and in religious persecution, developed this new slavery and slave-trade with a fiendish zeal and deplorable success. Slavery became thus also one of the factors of our public life, and we all know the bitter consequences to which it led—the bitterest of all anachronisms.

Long before the American Independence was actually declared, the consciousness of our forming a national entirety was ripening. The Continental Congress used the words Country and America in its official acts—in resolutions and appointments—before that day of mark, the Fourth of July. The very name Continental Congress, Continental Army and Money, shows that the idea of a national unity was present to the minds of all—at home as well as abroad. Unfortunately no name had formed itself for our portion of the globe. No one can say in what bed our history would have coursed, had there been a distinct name for our country, and had Philadelphia become the national capital. Nothing seemed to offer itself for the formation of a name so fit as Americus, of which the German schoolmaster Waldseemüller formed the beautiful but cruelly unjust name for our entire hemisphere. As it was, general names came to be used. North America was not unfrequently used to designate our country, as it is still in Germany and France. The bank which the Continental Congress established, May 25, 1781, in Philadelphia, after having received the all but desponding letter of General Washington, was called Bank of North America. It is called thus to this day. The seal of the Treasury of the United States, probably devised by Alexander Hamilton, as it may be seen on each of our legal tender notes, is: *Thesaur. Amer. Septem. Sigill.* (Seal of the Treasury of North America). If this seal is not of Hamilton's devising it must come from Robert Morris, but Robert Morris was Superintendent of the Finances; there was no Treasury before the year 1789, and it was in 1781 that the office of the "Superintendent of the Finances" was created. John Adams, and other writers of that period, frequently use North America. Chatham and his contemporaries always used the name America; Washington was appointed to the command in order to defend and protect "American liberty," before the Declaration of Independence. But whether there was a distinct name or not, all felt that we were a nation. United America, as the Italians now speak of United Italy, was another name used at the time, and later by Washington and others, for our country. John Adams ascribes to the speech of Otis against the Writs of Assistance, therefore before the outbreak of the Revolution, the power of having "breathed into this nation the breath of life;" and when Doctor Franklin, with Deane and Lee, were

---

* No more astounding fact exists in all history than this, that slavery was recognized as perfectly legal in the colonies, that is at a distance, but declared unable to stand before reason and justice at home. The case of Somerset was anticipated in France under Louis XIV.

received as Ministers of the United States of America by the king of France on March 19, 1778, after the conclusion of the treaty between the two governments, the king spoke to Franklin of "the two nations."

The pre-revolutionary speeches, specimens of which are given in a modest but very instructive school book ("Patriotic Eloquence," by the late Mrs. Kirkland), show that the leading men of America had at that early period no other idea than that of a country, of our land; and that of a nation, of our people. The puny provincialism which unfolded itself under the insufficient Articles of Confederation, came into vogue after the heroic period of the Revolution, and it led the country to the very brink of ruin and extinction. So at least Washington and his contemporaries, who knew the state of the country, with sympathetic patriotism and keen insight thought and wrote.

There were constant partial crystallizations of the colonies, united indeed under the British crown, but here demarcated by geographic lines the one from the other. Toward the end of the first half of the seventeenth century, the New England colonies confederated for common protection. Toward the end of the same century, in 1697, a proposition of union of the different colonies was made, as it is supposed with good reason, by William Penn, in "A brief and plain scheme, how the English colonies in the north parts of America, viz., Boston, Connecticut, New Hampshire, Rhode Island, New York, New Jersey, Pennsylvania, Maryland, Virginia, and Carolina, may be made more useful to the Crown and one another's peace and safety, with an universal concurrence." Equality of rights of property, and free ingress, egress, and abode, was proposed to be secured to all. In 1754, again fifty years later, Dr. Franklin drew up and proposed the (now called) Albany Plan of Union, unanimously adopted by the delegates at Albany, but not passed by the different assemblies—a plan which foreshadowed the later Union under the Continental Congress.

The time of resistance to England approached, and at every point it is to be observed that it is the "whole," as the Greeks called it, that moved and ultimately resisted; all exertions were instinctively national, or in the spirit of a nation to be born. Of the Declaration of Independence there shall be mentioned here three points only: It begins with calling the Americans *one people,* as contradistinguished to the people of the mother country, the other people; it calls Americans fellow-citizens, and it is Pan-American throughout. No separate independences, and, after this, no aggregate independence are spoken of; no separate complaint is even alluded to. The Americans had always the national comprehensive English Constitution before their eyes—no provincial polity—and repeatedly referred to it.

In 1777 The Articles of Confederation were adopted. They were called Articles, indeed, yet they are Articles of Confederation and Perpetual Union between the States; and in the official Letter of Congress, dated Yorktown, November 17, 1777, in which the States are advised to adopt the Articles, is this passage: "In short, the salutary measure can no longer be deferred. It seems essential to our very existence *as a free people.*" The Articles declare that "each State retains its sovereignty, freedom, and independence," but no State had or has ever since enjoyed what the law and all the world call sovereignty, and moreover, the Articles themselves contain numerous passages of a plainly national character, some of them directly antagonistic to separate sovereignty; for instance, that provision in Article IX., according to which nine out of the thirteen sovereigns can bind, in the most momentous measures, the four remaining sovereigns of the thirteen. The Articles themselves, having declared each State sovereign, take from the States those powers which are universally considered the main attributes of sovereignty. Nevertheless, the Articles provided for no national government, no broad and open political formulation of our nationality; yet Congress, "supported by the confidence of the people, but without any express powers, undertook to direct the storm, and were seconded by the people and by the colonial authorities;" and after the presentation of the Articles to the States (not adopted by all until the year 1781), Congress proceeded as if invested with the most explicit powers; it even went so far as to bind the nation by treaties with France; nor was it thought necessary that those treaties should be ratified by State legislatures. Under the Articles of Confederation, in 1782, the seal of the United States, with *E pluribus unum,* was adopted, and early in the year 1786 the oath of military officers and each one is made to swear that "he owes faith and true allegiance to the United States, and agrees to maintain its freedom, sovereignty, and independence."

The period between the adoption of the articles and the Constitution is the most humiliating in our history. All our leading men acknowledged it, and well-nigh lost hope and confidence. It is a period far too little studied. The Articles of Confederation are known by very few. Disorganizing provincialism became more and more active and destructive, until a stop was put to the nuisance by the Constitution of the United States, the genesis of which is at least as important as the instrument itself. It is a national work from beginning to end, conceived by the living national spirit of "one people," in spite of destructive provincialism, and establishing a National Government in the fullest sense of the word. The instrument is called a Constitution, not Articles; the word sovereign does not appear once; a national legislature, the members of which vote individually and personally, not by States, and an eminently national and individual Executive, in the person of one man, are established, and a portion of the people or of the States (though it must be a large majority) can oblige the smaller portion to adopt amendments to the Constitution. No minority of *sovereigns,* however small, can be made subject to a majority of sovereigns, however large. This single fact would annihilate *sovereignty.* We are a nation. The general government was always called in the earlier years of our present government, the National Government, and justly so. The Constitution makes our polity a National Representative Republic. Ever since the establishment of our government two political schools have existed, with varying distinctions, the National one and the Provincial one, which has often appeared to consider liberty to consist in a marring opposition to the National Government, which rejoiced in our not having a name for our country (which is a deficiency not quite unlike the deficiency of the English language itself in not possessing a word for *Patrie* or *Vaterland*), and openly declared the loosest possible confederacy the best of all governments, while the whole world was agreed to consider it in modern times the worst, and confederations good only in as far as they unite, and not as far as they sever.*

We have had State rebellions; we have had Nullification, and we had a territorial rebellion fomented by State-Rights doctrine, coupled with the dark declaration of the divinity of slavery. Our people have gone through a sanguinary and laborious war in order to save and establish more firmly our nationality. We are a nation, and we mean to remain one.

The magnificent words, We, the People, with which the Constitution begins, have often been denied a national character. This absence of national character it was said, was indicated by the words which follow, viz., of the United States. Mr. Calhoun denied even the national character in the President of the United States, and allowed only a joint

---

*   A prominent and bitter State-Rights man and, later, Secessionist, praised, within my hearing, in a public speech, returning from a foreign mission, the then existing Germanic Confederacy as the best polity! And the most prominent State-Rights man, when I once said to him what a pity it was that no American Nelson ever could signal so stirring an order as "England expects, etc.," because we have no name for our country, promptly replied: "We have no country, and need no name for one; we ought to have only a name for a mere political system, as you call it."

Preamble of the Constitution of the United States of America.	Preamble of the Constitution of the Confederate States of America.
We, the People of the United States,	We, the People of the Confederate States, each State acting in its sovereign and independent character,
in order to form a more perfect Union,	in order to form a permanent federal government,
establish justice, insure domestic tranquillity,	establish justice, insure domestic tranquillity,
provide for the common defence,	(*Left out.*)
promote the general welfare,	(*Left out.*)
and secure the blessings of liberty to ourselves and our posterity,	and secure the blessings of liberty to ourselves and our posterity,
	invoking the favor and guidance of Almighty God,
do ordain and establish this Constitution for the United States of America.	do ordain and establish this Constitution for the Confederate States of America.

representation of the many different State sovereignties within his individuality, by what mysterious process it is impossible to see. It seems, however, that the meaning of We the People of the United States, did not appear to the secessionists so absolutely clear as not to require an alteration in the preamble of their constitution, as the reader will perceive from the following comparison of the preamble of our Constitution and that of the constitution adopted by "the Congress of the Confederate States of America," March 11, 1861.

IV.

Political Characteristics of our Age.

The three main characteristics of the political development which mark the modern epoch are:

The national polity.

The general endeavor to define more clearly, and to extend more widely, human rights and civil liberty, (not unconnected as this movement is with the pervading critical spirit of the age, and the wedlock of Knowledge and Labor, which marks the nineteenth century.)

And the decree which has gone forth that many leading nations shall flourish at one and the same time, plainly distinguished from one another, yet striving together, with one public opinion, under the protection of one law of nations, and in the bonds of one common moving civilization.

The universal monarchy, whether purely political, as that of the Romans was, or that attempted again by Napoleon I.; or whether coupled with the papacy, as cruelly attempted by Charles V., and especially by Philip II., under whom the war-cry was: "One Pope and One King;" a single leading nation; an agglomeration of States without a fundamental law, with the mere leadership or hegemony of one State or other, which always leads to

Peloponnesian wars; regular confederacies of petty sovereigns; a civilization confined to one spot or portion of the globe—all these are obsolete ideas, wholly insufficient for the demands of advanced civilization, and attempts at their renewal have led and must lead to ruinous results, the end of all anachronisms recklessly pursued.

Even the course which civilization has steadily taken for thousands of years, from the southeast to the northwest, has ceased in our times. It now spreads for the first time in all directions, and bends its way back to the Orient. The old historic belt between 30° and 50° northern latitude, within which the great current of events has flown, shall confine history no more.

All great ideas which have set whole periods and entire races in motion, and which ultimately are established in great institutions, have their caricatures—often fierce and sanguinary. Communism is thus a caricature of one of these characteristics, and the recently proclaimed anti-nationalism another. All division into nations is to be done away with; all Europe is to be one ant-hill! But why only Europe? Let it be repeated, every idea in history, even the greatest and the holiest, has its hideous caricature.

V.

Inter-Dependence of Individuals and Nations.
The Commonwealth of Nations.

The multiplicity of civilized nations, their distinct independence (without which there would be enslaving Universal Monarchy), and their increasing resemblance and agreement, are some of the great safeguards of our civilization. Modern nations of our family have come to agree in much, and the agreement is growing. We have one alphabet; the same systems of notation, arithmetical and musical; one division of the circle and of time; the same sea-league; the same barometer; one mathematical language; one music and the same fine arts; one system of education, high and low; one science; one division of government; one domestic economy; one dress and fashion; the same manners, and the same toys for our children (Asia and Africa have no toys): we have a united mail system, and uniting telegraphs; we have an extending agreement in measures, weights, coinage, and signals at sea, and one financial conception, so that all merchants' exchanges have become meetings of international import, at least of equal effect with that of international diplomacy; we have a rapidly extending international copyright; perfectly acknowledged foreign individual property; we have a common international law, even during war. Add to this, that we really have what has been, not inaptly, called an international literature, in which a Shakespeare and a Kepler, a Franklin, Humboldt, Grotius, and Voltaire are belonging to the whole Cis-Caucasian race; we have a common history of Civilization; and Columbus and Frederic, Napoleon and Washington, for weel or woe, belong to all.

Formerly the process of nationalization was appearing as one of the novel things; now the process of inter-nationalization is going on; and yet there will be no obliteration of nationalities. If such were the case, civilization would be seriously injured. Civilization always dwelled preëminently in ancient times with one people, and one government always swayed and led. Hence the simplicity of chronologic tables presenting the events of that time; and all ancient States were short-lived. Once declining, they never recovered. Their course was that of the projectile: ascending, a maximum, a precipitate descent, and no more rising. Modern nations are long-lived, and possess recuperative energy wholly unknown to antiquity. They could neither be the one nor possess the other without national existence and comprehensive polities, and without the law of nations, in its modern and elevated sense, in which it is at once the manly idea of self-government applied to a number of independent nations in close relation with one another, and the application of the fundamental law of Good Neighborhood, and the comprehensive law of Nuisance, flowing from it, to vast national societies, wholly independent, sovereign, yet bound together by a thousand ties.

The all-pervading law of inter-dependence, without which men would never have felt compelled to form society, beyond the narrowest family ties—and it is even one of the elementary principles of the family—inter-dependence which like all original principles or characteristics of humanity, increases in intensity and spreads in action as men advance,—this divine law of inter-dependence applies to nations quite as much as to individuals.

The individual division of labor is no more impelled by it, than the production by territorial and climatic division of labor is quickened by the mutual dependence of the dwellers on the earth. This propitious and civilizing inter-dependence among nations is becoming daily more freely and willingly acknowledged, and the wise saying, *Ubi Societas ibi Jus,* finds constantly increasing application to entire nations. The civilized nations have come to constitute a community, and are daily forming more and more a commonwealth of nations, under the restraint and protection of the law of nations, which has begun to make its way even to countries not belonging to the Christian community, to which the Law of Nations had been confined. Our Wheaton's Law of Nations has been translated into Chinese, and is distributed by the government of that empire among its high officials. Soon it will form a subject of the Chinese higher state examination. The leading nations— the French, the English, the German, the American—they draw the chariot of civilization abreast, as the ancient steeds drew the car of victory: and these pages are writing at the time when the imperial chancellor of the German Union has been directed by the Union's parliament to propose to all nations the perfect security of private property on the high seas during war, even though belonging to an enemy; and when a citizen of the American Republic has entered our city, at the head of a Chinese embassy, sent to the great Western Powers in America and Europe, for the avowed purpose of attaching China to that Union of Nations among whom the Law of Nations has its sway in peace and in war.

Chronologies

The documents listed in the first column are texts often mentioned in studies of the intellectual history of the United States. The second column shows European works frequently discussed in America. The third column lists some of the significant social, cultural, and political events that took place simultaneously with the publication or production of the works listed in columns 1 and 2.

Year	American Documents	European Documents	Political, Social, and Cultural Events
1607			Jamestown settled
1609		Johannes Kepler, *De motibus stellae Martis*	
		William Shakespeare, *Sonnets*	
1611		King James Version of the Bible	
		William Shakespeare, *The Tempest*	
1615		Miguel de Cervantes *Don Quixote*, Part 2 (Part 1, 1605)	
1619		Synod of Dort (1618–19) Westminster Confession	First African slaves in North America brought to Virginia
			First American representative assembly meets in Virginia

Note: The date assigned to a document is generally the year of its first regular publication or, in the case of a single address, play, or opera, of its initial delivery or performance. Variations are noted in parentheses. Except for texts generally known by their original titles, foreign documents are in English.

Year	American Documents	European Documents	Political, Social, and Cultural Events
1620	Mayflower Compact	Francis Bacon, *Novum Organum*	Plymouth Colony established
1622		Jacob Boehme, *De signatura rerum*	
1623		William Ames, *Medulla sacrae theologiae*	
		John Webster, *The Duchess of Malfi* (published)	
1624		Lord Herbert of Cherbury, *De veritate*	
		John Smith, *The Generall Historie of Virginia, New England, and the Summer Isles*	
1625		Hugo Grotius, *The Rights of War and Peace*	Accession of King Charles I
1630	John Winthrop, "A Modell of Christian Charity"		Massachusetts Bay Colony established
1632		Galileo Galilei, *Dialogue on the Two Chief Systems of the World*	
1633		John Donne, *Poems* (posthumous)	
1634			Maryland settled
1635		Pedro Calderón, *Life's a Dream*	
1636			Harvard College founded
			Providence, Rhode Island, founded by Roger Williams

Year	American Documents	European Documents	Political, Social, and Cultural Events
1637		Pierre Corneille, *Le Cid* René Descartes, *Discourse on the Method*	Anne Hutchinson tried and banished
1639			First American printing press established in Cambridge, Massachusetts
1640	*The Whole Booke of Psalms (The Bay Psalm Book)*	Jansenius (Cornelius Jansen), *Augustinus* (posthumous)	
1641	John Cotton, *The Way of Life* (delivered c. 1624–32)		
1642			English Civil War begins
1644	Roger Williams, *The Bloudy Tenent of Persecution*		
1645	Roger Williams, *Christenings Make Not Christians* John Winthrop, "Speech to the General Court"		
1646	Peter Bulkeley, *The Gospel-Covenant* (enlarged edition, 1651) Thomas Shepard, *The Sincere Convert*		

Year	American Documents	European Documents	Political, Social, and Cultural Events
1647	Cotton Mather, *The Bloudy Tenent, Washed and Made White in the Bloud of the Lambe* Nathaniel Ward, *The Simple Cobbler of Aggawam in America*		
1648	Thomas Hooker, *A Survey of the Summe of Church-Discipline*		Cambridge Platform Society of Friends (Quakers) founded by George Fox
1649			Execution of King Charles I
1650	William Bradford, *History of Plimmoth Plantation* (written 1630–50) Anne Bradstreet, *The Tenth Muse Lately Sprung up in America*	Richard Baxter, *The Saint's Everlasting Rest*	
1651		Thomas Hobbes, *The Leviathan*	
1652		Gerrard Winstanley, *The Law of Freedom*	
1654	John Cotton, *The New Covenant* (delivered 1636; published 1659 as *A Treatise of the Covenant of Grace*)		

Year	American Documents	European Documents	Political, Social, and Cultural Events
	Edward Johnson, *The Wonder-Working Providence of Sions Saviour in New-England*		
	John Norton, *The Orthodox Evangelist*		
1656	Richard Hooker, *The Application of Redemption*	James Harrington, *The Commonwealth of Oceana*	
1660	Thomas Shepard, *The Parable of the Ten Virgins*		King Charles II restored to throne
1661	John Eliot, Algonquian translation of the Bible (1661–63)	Robert Boyle, *The Sceptical Chemist*	
1662	Michael Wigglesworth, *The Day of Doom* and "God's Controversy with New England"		Half-Way Covenant
1664		Molière, *Le Tartuffe*	English conquest of New Netherland
1665		François de La Rochefoucauld, *Maximes*	
1667		John Milton, *Paradise Lost*	
1668		Jean de La Fontaine, *Fables* (1668–94)	
1669	Increase Mather, *The Mystery of Israel's Salvation*	William Penn, *No Cross, No Crown*	

Year	American Documents	European Documents	Political, Social, and Cultural Events
1670		Blaise Pascal, *Pensées* (posthumous)	Charleston founded
1674		Boileau, *The Art of Poetry*	
		Nicolas Malebranche, *The Search for Truth* (1674–75)	
1675			King Philip's War (1675–76)
1676			Bacon's Rebellion in Virginia
1677		Jean Racine, *Phèdre*	
		Baruch Spinoza, *Ethics* (posthumous)	
1678		John Bunyan, *The Pilgrim's Progress* (1678, 1684)	
		Ralph Cudworth, *The True Intellectual System of the Universe*	
		Marie-Madeleine de La Fayette, *La Princesse de Clèves*	
		Richard Simon, *Historical Criticism of the New Testament*	
1680	Edward Taylor, Poems written c. 1680–1725 and first published in 1937		
1681		John Dryden, *Absalom and Achitophel*	
1682	Urian Oakes, *The Soveraign Efficacy of Divine Providence*		Pennsylvania settled

Year	American Documents	European Documents	Political, Social, and Cultural Events
	Mary Rowlandson, *A Narrative of the Captivity and Restauration of Mrs. Mary Rowlandson*		
1684	Increase Mather, *An Essay for the Recording of Illustrious Providences*		Massachusetts Bay charter rescinded
1685			Accession of King James II
1687		Isaac Newton, *Philosophiae naturalis principia mathematica*	
1688			Glorious Revolution (1688–89)
1689		Henry Purcell (libretto by Nahum Tate), *Dido and Aeneas*	King William's War (1689–97)
1690		John Locke, *An Essay Concerning Human Understanding* and *Two Treatises of Government*	
1691			Massachusetts given a new charter
1692			Salem witchcraft trials
1693	Cotton Mather, *The Wonders of the Invisible World*	John Locke, *Some Thoughts Concerning Education*	College of William and Mary founded
1694		George Fox, *Journal* (posthumous)	
1696		John Toland, *Christianity Not Mysterious*	

Year	American Documents	European Documents	Political, Social, and Cultural Events
1697	Samuel Sewall, *Phaenomena quaedam Apocalyptica*	Pierre Bayle, *Historical and Critical Dictionary*	
1699		François de Fenelon, *Télémaque*	
1700	Increase Mather, *The Order of the Gospel*	William Congreve, *The Way of the World*	
	Samuel Sewall, *The Selling of Joseph*		
	Solomon Stoddard, *The Doctrine of Instituted Churches*		
1701			Yale College founded
1702	Cotton Mather, *Magnalia Christi Americana*		Queen Anne's War (1702–13)
1705	Robert Beverley, *The History and Present State of Virginia*		
1706		Samuel Clarke, *A Discourse Concerning the Being and Attributes of God*	
1708	Ebenezer Cook, *The Sot-Weed Factor*		Saybrook Platform
1710	Cotton Mather, *Bonifacius*	George Berkeley, *A Treatise Concerning the Principles of Human Knowledge*	
		Gottfried Wilhelm von Leibniz, *Theodicy*	

Year	American Documents	European Documents	Political, Social, and Cultural Events
1711		Third Earl of Shaftesbury (Anthony Ashley Cooper), *Characteristics of Men, Manners, Opinions, Times*	
		The Spectator (1711–12, 1714)	
1713		Anthony Collins, *A Discourse of Free-Thinking*	
1714		Bernard Mandeville, *The Fable of the Bees*	
1715		Alain-René Lesage, *Gil Blas* (1715–35)	
1717	John Wise, *A Vindication of the Government of New-England Churches*		
1719		Daniel Defoe, *Robinson Crusoe*	
		Isaac Watts, *The Psalms of David Imitated*	
1721	Benjamin Franklin, *A Dissertation on Liberty and Necessity*		
	Cotton Mather, *The Christian Philosopher*		
1723		Johann Sebastian Bach, *St. John Passion*	
1725		Francis Hutcheson, *An Inquiry into the Original of Our Ideas of Beauty and Virtue*	

Year	American Documents	European Documents	Political, Social, and Cultural Events
		Giambattista Vico, *Principles of a New Science of Nations*	
1726	Samuel Willard, *A Compleat Body of Divinity*	Jonathan Swift, *Gulliver's Travels* James Thomson, *The Seasons* (1726–30)	
1728	William Byrd, *The History of the Dividing Line* (published 1841)	John Gay, *The Beggar's Opera*	
1732		Alexander Pope, *An Essay on Man* (1732–34)	
1733	Benjamin Franklin, *Poor Richard's Almanack* (1733–58)	Voltaire, *Letters Concerning the English Nation*	
1734			Revival in Northampton, Massachusetts: beginning of the First Great Awakening
1735	Jane Turell, *Reliquiae Turellae*	Carl Linnaeus, *Systema naturae*	John Peter Zenger tried and acquitted
1736		Joseph Butler, *Analogy of Religion*	
1738			John Wesley's conversion and founding of Methodism
1739		David Hume, *A Treatise of Human Nature* (1739–40)	George Whitefield's first preaching tour of America (1739–40)

Year	American Documents	European Documents	Political, Social, and Cultural Events
1740	Gilbert Tennent, *The Danger of an Unconverted Ministry*	Samuel Richardson, *Pamela* (1740–41)	
1741	Jonathan Edwards, *Sinners in the Hands of an Angry God*		
1742	Charles Chauncy, *Enthusiasm Described and Caution'd Against* Jonathan Edwards, *Some Thoughts Concerning the Present Revival of Religion in New England*	George Frideric Handel (libretto by Charles Jennens), *Messiah*	
1743	Charles Chauncy, *Seasonable Thoughts on the State of Religion in New-England*		American Philosophical Society founded
1744			King George's War (1744–48)
1745		Philip Doddridge, *The Rise and Progress of Religion in the Soul*	
1746	Jonathan Edwards, *A Treatise Concerning Religious Affections*		College of New Jersey founded (later Princeton University)
1748		Charles-Louis de Montesquieu, *The Spirit of Laws*	

Year	American Documents	European Documents	Political, Social, and Cultural Events
1749		Henry St. John Bolingbroke, *The Idea of a Patriot King* Henry Fielding, *Tom Jones* Georges-Louis Leclerc de Buffon, *Natural History* (1749–1804) David Hartley, *Observations on Man*	
1750	Joseph Bellamy, *True Religion Delineated* Jonathan Mayhew, *A Discourse Concerning Unlimited Submission*		
1751	Benjamin Franklin, *Experiments and Observations on Electricity* (1751–72)	Denis Diderot and Jean d'Alembert, eds., *Encyclopedia*	Philadelphia Academy founded (later University of Pennsylvania)
1752	Samuel Johnson, *Elementa philosophica,*		
1754	Jonathan Edwards, *Freedom of the Will*	David Hume, *History of Great Britain* (1754–62)	French and Indian War (1754–63) King's College founded (later Columbia University)
1755		Jean-Jacques Rousseau, *The Discourse on the Origin of Inequality* Samuel Johnson, *A Dictionary of the English Language*	

Year	American Documents	European Documents	Political, Social, and Cultural Events
1758	Joseph Bellamy, *The Millennium*	Claude-Adrien Helvétius, *Essays on the Mind*	
	Benjamin Franklin, Preface to *Poor Richard Improved*, 1758 ("The Way to Wealth")	Richard Price, *A Review of the Principal Questions in Morals*	
1759		Samuel Johnson, *Rasselas*	
		Adam Smith, *The Theory of Moral Sentiments*	
		Laurence Sterne, *Tristram Shandy* (1759–67)	
		Voltaire, *Candide*	
1760			Accession of King George III
1761		Denis Diderot, *Rameau's Nephew* (written c. 1761–74, published 1823)	
1762		Jean-Jacques Rousseau, *The Social Contract* and *Émile*	
1763	John Woolman, *A Plea for the Poor* (published 1793)	Emmanuel Swedenborg, *Divine Love and Wisdom*	
1764	James Otis, *The Rights of the British Colonies*	Thomas Reid, *An Inquiry into the Human Mind*	Rhode Island College founded (later Brown University)
		Voltaire, *Philosophical Dictionary*	
1765	John Adams, *A Dissertation on the Canon and the Feudal Law*	William Blackstone, *Commentaries on the Laws of England* (1765–69)	Stamp Act

Year	American Documents	European Documents	Political, Social, and Cultural Events
	Jonathan Edwards, *The Nature of True Virtue* and *Concerning the End for Which God Created the World* (both posthumous)		
1766		Oliver Goldsmith, *The Vicar of Wakefield* Gotthold Ephraim Lessing, *Laokoön*	
1767		Adam Ferguson, *An Essay on the History of Civil Society*	
1768	John Dickinson, *Letters from a Farmer in Pennsylvania*	Joseph Priestley, *An Essay on the First Principles of Government*	
1770			Boston Massacre
1771		Henry Mackenzie, *The Man of Feeling*	
1772	Hugh Henry Brackenridge and Philip Freneau, "The Rising Glory of America"		
1773	Phillis Wheatley, *Poems on Various Subjects*		Boston Tea Party
1774	Thomas Jefferson, *A Summary View of the Rights of British America* John Woolman, *Journal* (posthumous)	Johann Wolfgang von Goethe, *The Sorrows of Young Werther*	Arrival in America of Mother Ann Lee, founder of the Shakers

Year	American Documents	European Documents	Political, Social, and Cultural Events
1776	John Adams, *Thoughts on Government*	Edward Gibbon, *The Decline and Fall of the Roman Empire* (1776–88)	Declaration of Independence
	Thomas Jefferson, the Declaration of Independence	Adam Smith, *The Wealth of Nations*	
	Thomas Paine, *Common Sense*		
1777	Isaac Backus, *History of New England* (1777–96)	Richard Brinsley Sheridan, *The School for Scandal*	
1778		Richard Price and Joseph Priestley, *A Free Discussion of the Doctrines of Materialism and Philosophical Necessity Illustrated*	Friedrich Anton Mesmer's Paris lectures on "animal magnetism" (hypnotism)
1779		David Hume, *Dialogues Concerning Natural Religion* (posthumous)	
1780			American Academy of Arts and Sciences founded
1781		Immanuel Kant, *Critique of Pure Reason*	Articles of Confederation ratified
		Jean-Jacques Rousseau, *The Confessions* (posthumous, 1781–88)	
		Friedrich Schiller, *The Robbers*	
1782	J. Hector St. John de Crèvecoeur, *Letters from an American Farmer*		
1783			Treaty of Paris

Year	American Documents	European Documents	Political, Social, and Cultural Events
1784	Ethan Allen (and Thomas Young), *Reason the Only Oracle of Man* Charles Chauncy, *The Benevolence of the Deity*	Pierre-Augustin Beaumarchais, *The Marriage of Figaro* Hugh Blair, *Lectures on Rhetoric and Belles Lettres* Johann Gottfried Herder, *Ideas on the Philosophy of the History of Mankind* (1784–91)	
1785		William Paley, *The Principles of Moral and Political Philosophy*	
1786	"The Connecticut Wits," *The Anarchiad* (1786–87) Philip Freneau, *Poems*	Robert Burns, *Poems*	
1787	John Adams, *A Defense of the Constitutions of Government of the United States of America* Joel Barlow, *The Vision of Columbus* (revised as *The Columbiad,* 1807) "Essays of Brutus" *Letters from the Federal Farmer* Alexander Hamilton, James Madison, and John Jay, *The Federalist* (1787–88)		Federal Constitutional Convention

Year	American Documents	European Documents	Political, Social, and Cultural Events
	Thomas Jefferson, *Notes on the State of Virginia* Benjamin Rush, "Thoughts upon Female Education" Royall Tyler, *The Contrast*		
1788		Immanuel Kant, *Critique of Practical Reason* Hannah More, *Thoughts on the Importance of the Manners of the Great to General Society*	Constitution ratified
1789	David Ramsay, *History of the American Revolution* Noah Webster, *Dissertations on the English Language*	Jeremy Bentham, *Introduction to Principles of Morals and Legislation* The Declaration of the Rights of Man and Citizen Antoine-Laurent Lavoisier, *Elements of Chemistry*	George Washington inaugurated University of North Carolina founded French Revolution begins
1790	Benjamin Franklin, *Autobiography* (written 1771–90; first American edition, 1818)	William Blake, *The Marriage of Heaven and Hell* (engraved c. 1790–93)	

Year	American Documents	European Documents	Political, Social, and Cultural Events
	Judith Sargent Murray, "On the Equality of the Sexes" James Wilson, *Public Discourses upon Jurisprudence and the Political Science* (1790–92)	Edmund Burke, *Reflections on the Revolution in France* Immanuel Kant, *Critique of Judgement*	
1791	John Adams, *Discourses on Davila* Alexander Hamilton, *Report on Manufactures* Thomas Paine, *The Rights of Man* (1791–92) Susanna Rowson, *Charlotte Temple* (American edition, 1794)	James Boswell, *The Life of Samuel Johnson* Wolfgang Amadeus Mozart (libretto by Emanuel Schikaneder), *The Magic Flute*	Bill of Rights adopted
1792	Joel Barlow, *Advice to the Privileged Orders* Hugh Henry Brackenridge, *Modern Chivalry* (1792–1815)	Wilhelm von Humboldt, *The Limits of State Action* Dugald Stewart, *Elements of the Philosophy of the Human Mind* (1792–1827) Mary Wollstonecraft, *A Vindication of the Rights of Woman*	French Revolutionary and Napoleonic Wars (1792–1815)
1793	Samuel Hopkins, *The System of Doctrines*	William Godwin, *Enquiry Concerning Political Justice*	Eli Whitney invents the cotton gin

Year	American Documents	European Documents	Political, Social, and Cultural Events
1794	Thomas Paine, *The Age of Reason* (1794–95)	Johann Gottlieb Fichte, *The Science of Knowledge*	
		Ann Radcliffe, *The Mysteries of Udolpho*	
1795		William Blake, *Songs of Innocence and of Experience*	
		Antoine-Nicolas de Condorcet, *Sketch for a Historical Picture of the Progress of the Human Mind* (posthumous)	
		Johann Wolfgang von Goethe, *Wilhelm Meister's Apprenticeship* (1795–96)	
		Friedrich Schiller, *On the Aesthetic Education of Man* and *On Naive and Sentimental Poetry* (1795–96)	
		Friedrich August Wolf, *Prolegomena to Homer*	
1796	George Washington, "The Farewell Address"		
1797	Jonathan Boucher, *A View of the Causes and Consequences of the American Revolution* (delivered 1763–75)	Friedrich Hölderlin, *Hyperion* (1797–99) Ludwig Tieck, *Volkmärchen*	
1798	Charles Brockden Brown, *Wieland*	Maria and Richard Lovell Edgeworth, *Practical Education*	

Year	American Documents	European Documents	Political, Social, and Cultural Events
	Timothy Dwight, *The Duty of Americans, at the Present Crisis*	Franz Joseph Haydn (text from Genesis and *Paradise Lost*), *The Creation*	
		Thomas Robert Malthus, *An Essay on the Principle of Population*	
		August Wilhelm Schlegel and Friedrich Schlegel, eds., *Athenäum* (1798–1800)	
		William Wordsworth and Samuel Taylor Coleridge, *Lyrical Ballads* (second edition 1800)	
		William Wordsworth, *The Prelude* (1798–1805, final version published 1850)	
1799	Charles Brockden Brown, *Edgar Huntly*	Pierre-Simon Laplace, *Mécanique Céleste* (1799–1825)	
		Friedrich Schleiermacher, *Speeches on Religion to Its Cultured Despisers*	
1800		Jean Paul, *Titan*	Washington, D.C., becomes capital of United States
		Novalis, *Hymns to the Night*	
		Friedrich von Schelling, *System of Transcendental Idealism*	Library of Congress founded
1801	*New York Evening Post* (1801–)	Johann Heinrich Pestalozzi, *How Gertrude Teaches Her Children*	Jefferson's administration (1801–9)

Year	American Documents	European Documents	Political, Social, and Cultural Events
	Port Folio (1801–27)		Revival in Cane Ridge, Kentucky: beginning of the Second Great Awakening
1802	John Witherspoon, *Lectures on Moral Philosophy* (posthumous)	François-René de Chateaubriand, *The Genius of Christianity* William Paley, *Natural Theology*	
1803	Samuel Miller, *A Brief Retrospect of the Eighteenth Century* William Wirt, *Letters of the British Spy*	Jean-Baptiste Say, *A Treatise on Political Economy*	Louisiana Purchase *Marbury v. Madison*
1804		Antoine-Louis-Claude Destutt de Tracy, *Eléments d'idéologie*	
1805	Hosea Ballou, *A Treatise on Atonement* Mercy Otis Warren, *History of the Rise, Progress and Termination of the American Revolution*	Ludwig van Beethoven (libretto by Joseph Sonnleithner), *Fidelio*	Boston Athenaeum founded Pennsylvania Academy of the Fine Arts founded

Year	American Documents	European Documents	Political, Social, and Cultural Events
1807	Washington and William Irving and James Kirke Paulding, *Salmagundi* (1807–8)	Georg Wilhelm Friedrich Hegel, *The Phenomenology of Mind* Anne-Louise-Germaine de Staël, *Corinne*	
1808		John Dalton, *New System of Chemical Philosophy* (1808–27) Johann Wolfgang von Goethe, *Faust* (1808–32)	
1809	Washington Irving, *A History of New York*	Jean-Baptiste de Lamarck, *Zoological Philosophy*	
1810	Samuel Stanhope Smith, *An Essay on the Causes of the Variety of Complexion and Figure in the Human Species* (second edition, enlarged)	Heinrich von Kleist, *Prinz Friedrich von Homburg* (completed 1810; published posthumously 1821)	
1812	Benjamin Rush, *Medical Inquiries and Observations upon the Diseases of the Mind*	Lord Byron, *Childe Harold's Pilgrimage* (1812–18) Jacob and Wilhelm Grimm, *Fairy Tales* (1812–14)	American Antiquarian Society founded War of 1812 (1812–14)
1813		Jane Austen, *Pride and Prejudice* Robert Owen, *A New View of Society* Anne-Louise-Germaine de Staël, *On Germany*	

Year	American Documents	European Documents	Political, Social, and Cultural Events
1814	John Taylor, *An Inquiry into the Principles and Policy of the Government of the United States*	Sir Walter Scott, *Waverly*	
1815	*North American Review* (1815–1939)	E. T. A. Hoffman, *The Devil's Elixir* (1815–16)	Napoleon defeated at Waterloo
1816		Benjamin Constant, *Adolph*	
		Gioacchino Rossini, *The Barber of Seville*	
1817	William Cullen Bryant, "Thanatopsis" (revised 1821)	Samuel Taylor Coleridge, *Biographia Literaria*	American Colonization Society founded
		David Ricardo, *On the Principles of Political Economy and Taxation*	University of Michigan founded
1818	*American Journal of Science and Arts* (1818–)	John Keats, *Endymion*	
	Timothy Dwight, *Theology, Explained and Defended* (1818–19)	Mary Shelley, *Frankenstein*	
1819	William Ellery Channing, "Unitarian Christianity"	Lord Byron, *Don Juan* (1819–24)	Dartmouth College Case
	Washington Irving, *The Sketch Book* (1819–20)	Arthur Schopenhauer, *The World as Will and Idea*	*McCullough v. Maryland*
			University of Virginia founded
1820		Alphonse de Lamartine, *Méditations poétique*	Missouri Compromise

Year	American Documents	European Documents	Political, Social, and Cultural Events
		Percy Bysshe Shelley, *Prometheus Unbound*	
1821	William Cullen Bryant, *Poems* Timothy Dwight, *Travels in New England and New York* (1821–22)	Joseph de Maistre, *St. Petersburg Dialogues* Percy Bysshe Shelley, *The Defence of Poetry* (published 1840)	Troy Female Seminary founded by Emma Willard
1822		Charles Fourier, *Treatise on Agrarian-Domestic Fellowship*	
1823	James Fenimore Cooper, *The Pioneers* (First Leatherstocking Tale) Lyman Beecher, *The Faith Once Delivered to the Saints* Charles J. Ingersoll, *The Influence of America on the Mind* Daniel Raymond, *The Elements of Political Economy*	Alexander Pushkin, *Eugene Onegin* (1823–31)	Monroe Doctrine
1824	Lydia Maria Child, *Hobomok* *Christian Examiner* (1824–69)	Leopold von Ranke, *Critique of Modern Historical Writing*	Marquis de Lafayette's tour of the United States (1824–25)

Year	American Documents	European Documents	Political, Social, and Cultural Events
1825	*Biblical Repertory,* later *Biblical Repertory and Princeton Review* (1825–88)	Alessandro Manzoni, *The Betrothed* Claude-Henri de Saint-Simon, *The New Christianity*	
1826	Langdon Byllesby, *Observations on the Sources and Effects of Unequal Wealth* James Fenimore Cooper, *The Last of the Mohicans* (Second Leatherstocking Tale) *Graham's Magazine* (1826–58) James Kent, *Commentaries on American Law* (1826–30)	Benjamin Disraeli, *Vivian Grey* (1826–27) Friedrich Fröbel, *The Education of Man*	First American lyceum
1827	Catharine Maria Sedgwick, *Hope Leslie* Sarah Josepha Hale, *Northwood* (revised 1852) *Western Monthly Review* (1827–30)	Heinrich Heine, *Book of Songs* Victor Hugo, *Cromwell*	Disciples of Christ founded by Alexander Campbell
1828	William Ellery Channing, "Likeness to God" *Southern Review* (1828–32)	Edward Bulwer-Lytton, *Pelham*	

Year	American Documents	European Documents	Political, Social, and Cultural Events
	Nathaniel William Taylor, *Concio ad Clerum* Noah Webster, *An American Dictionary of the English Language*		
1829	Jacob Bigelow, *Elements of Technology* James Marsh, Edition of Coleridge's *Aids to Reflection* (1825) Thomas Skidmore, *The Rights of Man to Property!* David Walker, *An Appeal to the Colored Citizens of the World* Frances Wright, *A Course of Popular Lectures*	Thomas Carlyle, "Signs of the Times" Victor Cousin, *Cours de l'Histoire de la philosophie* James Mill, *Analysis of the Phenomena of the Human Mind*	
1830	Jeremiah Day and James L. Kingsley, *Reports on the Course of Instruction in Yale College* Edward Everett, "Fourth of July at Lowell" *Godey's Lady's Book* (1830–98)	Auguste Comte, *Course of Positive Philosophy* (1830–42) John Herschel, *Preliminary Discourse on the Study of Natural Philosophy* Charles Lyell, *Principles of Geology* (1830–33)	Senate debate between Robert Y. Hayne and Daniel Webster European revolutions

Year	American Documents	European Documents	Political, Social, and Cultural Events
	Joseph Smith, *Book of Mormon*	Stendhal, *The Red and the Black*	
1831	Lyman Beecher, *The Necessity of Revivals to the Perpetuity of Our Civil and Religious Institutions*	Victor Hugo, *Notre Dame de Paris*	Nat Turner's slave insurrection New York University founded
	Thomas R. Gray, *The Confessions of Nat Turner*		
	Liberator (1831–65)		
1832	Thomas R. Dew, *Review of the Debate in the Virginia Legislature of 1831 and 1832*	Karl von Clausewitz, *On War* Frances Trollope, *Domestic Manners of the Americans*	
	William Lloyd Garrison, *Thoughts on African Colonization*		
	John Pendleton Kennedy, *Swallow Barn*		
1833	Lydia Maria Child, *An Appeal in Favor of That Class of Americans Called Africans*		American Antislavery Society founded Oberlin College founded
	Knickerbocker Magazine (1833–65)		*Tracts for the Times* and Oxford Movement launched by John Henry Newman and others

Year	American Documents	European Documents	Political, Social, and Cultural Events
1834	George Bancroft, *History of the United States* (1834–76) *Southern Literary Messenger* (1834–64)	Honoré de Balzac, *Le Père Goriot* Félicité de Lamennais, *Words of a Believer* Adam Mickiewicz, *Pan Tadeusz*	
1835	George Bancroft, "The Office of the People in Art, Government, and Religion" William Ellery Channing, *Slavery* Charles Grandison Finney, *Lectures on Revivals of Religion* William Gilmore Simms, *The Yemassee* Francis Wayland, *The Elements of Moral Science* *Western Messenger* (1835–41)	David Friedrich Strauss, *The Life of Jesus* (1835–36) Alexis de Tocqueville, *Democracy in America* (1835–40)	
1836	Bronson Alcott, *Conversations with Children on the Gospels* (1836–37)	Thomas Carlyle, *Sartor Resartus* Heinrich Heine, *The Romantic School*	Mount Holyoke Seminary founded by Mary Lyon (later Mount Holyoke College)

Year	American Documents	European Documents	Political, Social, and Cultural Events
	Orestes A. Brownson, *New Views of Christianity, Society and the Church*		Transcendental Club (1836–40)
	Ralph Waldo Emerson, *Nature*		
	William Holmes McGuffey, *Eclectic Readers* (1836–57)		
1837	Robert Montgomery Bird, *Nick of the Woods*	Charles Dickens, *Pickwick Papers*	Chartist Movement (1837–48)
	Henry C. Carey, *Principles of Political Economy* (1837–40)	Georg Wilhelm Friedrich Hegel, *Lectures on the Philosophy of History* (posthumous)	Financial panic
	Ralph Waldo Emerson, "The American Scholar"	Harriet Martineau, *Society in America*	Accession of Queen Victoria
	Nathaniel Hawthorne, *Twice-Told Tales*	William Whewell, *History of the Inductive Sciences*	
	New York Review (1837–42)		
	United States Magazine and Democratic Review (1837–49)		
	Francis Wayland, *The Elements of Political Economy*		

Year	American Documents	European Documents	Political, Social, and Cultural Events
1838	*Boston Quarterly Review* (1838–42)		
	William Ellery Channing, *Self-Culture*		
	James Fenimore Cooper, *The American Democrat*		
	Ralph Waldo Emerson, "The Divinity School Address"		
	Sarah Grimké, *Letters on the Equality of the Sexes, and the Condition of Woman*		
	Abraham Lincoln, "Address Before the Young Men's Lyceum of Springfield, Illinois"		
1839	Henry Wadsworth Longfellow, *Voices of the Night*		Depression (1839–43)
	Andrews Norton, *A Discourse on the Latest Form of Infidelity*		
	Edgar Allan Poe, *Tales of the Grotesque and Arabesque*		

Year	American Documents	European Documents	Political, Social, and Cultural Events
	George Ripley, *The Latest Form of Infidelity Examined*		
	Jones Very, *Essays and Poems*		
	Theodore Dwight Weld, *American Slavery As It Is*		
1840	Albert Brisbane, *Social Destiny of Man*	Robert Browning, *Sordello*	
	Orestes Brownson, "The Laboring Classes"	Pierre- Joseph Proudhon, *What Is Property?*	
	Richard Henry Dana, Jr., *Two Years Before the Mast*		
	Dial (1840–44)		
	William Leggett, *Political Writings* (posthumous)		
1841	Catharine Beecher, *A Treatise on Domestic Economy*	Thomas Carlyle, *On Heroes, Hero-Worship and the Heroic in History*	Brook Farm (1841–47)
	Ralph Waldo Emerson, *Essays* (first series)	Ludwig Feuerbach, *The Essence of Christianity*	
	Charles Hodge, *The Way of Life*	Friedrich List, *The National System of Political Economy*	
	New-York Tribune (1841–1966)		

Year	American Documents	European Documents	Political, Social, and Cultural Events
	Theodore Parker, *A Discourse of the Transient and Permanent in Christianity*		
	Elizabeth Palmer Peabody, "A Glimpse of Christ's Idea of Society"		
1842	Elizabeth Palmer Peabody, "Plan of the West Roxbury Community"	Charles Dickens, *American Notes*	
	Southern Quarterly Review (1842–57)	Nikolai Gogol, *Dead Souls*	
		George Sand, *Consuelo* (1842–43)	
1843	John Hickling Prescott, *History of the Conquest of Mexico*	Søren Kierkegaard, *Either/Or*	
		John Stuart Mill, *A System of Logic*	
		John Ruskin, *Modern Painters* (1843–60)	
1844	*Brownson's Quarterly Review* (1844–75)	Robert Chambers, *Vestiges of the Natural History of Creation*	
	Ralph Waldo Emerson, *Essays* (second series)	Karl Marx, *Economic and Philosophical Manuscripts* (written 1844; published 1932)	
	Robert Baird, *Religion in America*		
	Parke Godwin, *Democracy, Constructive and Pacific*		

Year	American Documents	European Documents	Political, Social, and Cultural Events
	Samuel Tyler, *Discourse on the Baconian Philosophy*		
1845	*American Whig Review* (1845–52) Frederick Douglass, *Narrative of the Life of Frederick Douglass* Margaret Fuller, *Woman in the Nineteenth Century* Horace Mann, *Lectures on Education* Edgar Allan Poe, *The Raven and Other Poems* Philip Schaff, *The Principle of Protestantism*	Alexander von Humboldt, *Der Kosmos* (1845–62) Karl Marx and Friedrich Engels, *The German Ideology* (written 1845–46)	
1846	*De Bow's Review* (1846–80) Charles Grandison Finney, *Lectures on Systematic Theology* Margaret Fuller, *Papers on Literature and Art* Nathaniel Hawthorne, *Mosses from an Old Manse*		Mexican War (1846–48)

Year	American Documents	European Documents	Political, Social, and Cultural Events
	Herman Melville, *Typee* John Williamson Nevin, *The Mystical Presence*		
1847	Horace Bushnell, *Views of Christian Nurture* John Humphrey Noyes, *The Berean*	Charlotte Brontë, *Jane Eyre* Emily Brontë, *Wuthering Heights* Jules Michelet, *The French Revolution* (1847–53)	
1848	James Russell Lowell, *The Biglow Papers* (first series) and *A Fable for Critics* Edgar Allan Poe, *Eureka*	Karl Marx and Friedrich Engels, *Communist Manifesto* William Makepeace Thackeray, *Vanity Fair*	College of the City of New York founded European revolutions Oneida Community (1848–79) Seneca Falls women's rights convention University of Wisconsin founded
1849	Horace Bushnell, *God in Christ* William Goodell, *The Democracy of Christianity* (1849–52) Francis Parkman, *The Oregon Trail*	Thomas Babington Macaulay, *History of England* (1849–55)	

Year	American Documents	European Documents	Political, Social, and Cultural Events
	Henry David Thoreau, "Resistance to Civil Government"		
1850	Washington Allston, *Lectures on Art, and Poems* (posthumous) Ralph Waldo Emerson, *Representative Men* *Harper's Monthly Magazine* (1850–) Nathaniel Hawthorne, *The Scarlet Letter* Edwards Amasa Park and Charles Hodge exchange on "The Theology of the Intellect and That of the Feelings" Susan Warner, *The Wide, Wide World* John Greenleaf Whittier, "Ichabod" Herman Melville, "Hawthorne and His Mosses"	Charles Dickens, *David Copperfield* Alexander Herzen, *From the Other Shore* Herbert Spencer, *Social Statics* Alfred, Lord Tennyson, *In Memoriam*	Compromise of 1850 and Fugitive Slave Law
1851	Stephen Pearl Andrews, *The Science of Society*	Giuseppe Verdi, *Rigoletto*	Northwestern University founded

Year	American Documents	European Documents	Political, Social, and Cultural Events
	John C. Calhoun, *A Disquisition on Government* (posthumous)		
	Henry C. Carey, *The Harmony of Interests*		
	Nathaniel Hawthorne, *The House of the Seven Gables*		
	Herman Melville, *Moby-Dick*		
1852	Martin Delany, *The Condition, Elevation, Emigration, and Destiny of the Colored People of the United States*		
	Frederick Douglass, "What to the Slave Is the Fourth of July?"		
	Dwight's Journal of Music (1852–81)		
	Nathaniel Hawthorne, *The Blithedale Romance*		
	Louisa McCord, "Enfranchise-ment of Women" and "Woman and Her Needs"		
	The Pro-Slavery Argument		

Year	American Documents	European Documents	Political, Social, and Cultural Events
	Harriet Beecher Stowe, *Uncle Tom's Cabin* James Henley Thornwell, *Report on the Subject of Slavery*		
1853	Richard Hildreth, *Theory of Politics* Francis Lieber, *On Civil Liberty and Self-Government* Charles Eliot Norton, *Considerations on Some Recent Social Theories* *Putnam's Monthly Magazine* (1853–57)	Richard Wagner, *The Ring of the Nibelung* (composed 1853–74; produced 1869–76)	Antioch College founded
1854	George Fitzhugh, *Sociology for the South* Henry Hughes, *Treatise on Sociology* Abraham Lincoln, "Speech at Peoria, Illinois" Henry David Thoreau, *Walden*	Gérard de Nerval, *Les Filles du feu*	
1855	Walt Whitman, *Leaves of Grass* (enlarged editions, 1856–92)		

Year	American Documents	European Documents	Political, Social, and Cultural Events
1856	George William Curtis, " The Duty of the American Scholar to Politics and the Times" John Lothrop Motley, *The Rise of the Dutch Republic*	Hector Berlioz, *The Trojans* (composed 1856–58)	
1857	Louis Agassiz, *Contributions to the Natural History of the United States* (1857–62) *Atlantic Monthly* (1857–) Peter Cartwright, *Autobiography* George Fitzhugh, *Cannibals All!* Hinton R. Helper, *The Impending Crisis of the South* Henry James, Sr., *Christianity the Logic of Creation* Herman Melville, *The Confidence-Man*	Charles Baudelaire, *The Flowers of Evil* Elizabeth Barrett Browning, *Aurora Leigh* Gustave Flaubert, *Madame Bovary*	*Dred Scott* decision
1858	Horace Bushnell, *Nature and the Supernatural*	Henry Longueville Mansel, *Limits of Religious Thought Examined*	Lincoln-Douglas debates

Year	American Documents	European Documents	Political, Social, and Cultural Events
	Henry C. Carey, *Principles of Social Science* (1858–59)		
	James Henry Hammond, "mudsill" speech in U.S. Senate		
	Oliver Wendell Holmes, *The Autocrat of the Breakfast-Table*		
1859	Augusta Evans (later Wilson), *Beulah*	Charles Darwin, *On the Origin of Species*	John Brown's raid on Harpers Ferry
	Abraham Lincoln, "Address Before the Wisconsin State Agricultural Society"	John Stuart Mill, *On Liberty*	
	Harriet Beecher Stowe, *The Minister's Wooing*		
	Nathaniel William Taylor, *Lectures on the Moral Government of God* (posthumous)		
	Harriet E. Wilson, *Our Nig*		
1860	E. N. Elliott, ed., *Cotton Is King, and Pro-Slavery Arguments*	Jacob Burckhardt, *The Civilization of the Renaissance in Italy*	

Year	American Documents	European Documents	Political, Social, and Cultural Events
	James McCosh, *The Intuitions of the Mind*	George Eliot, *The Mill on the Floss*	
1861	Harriet Jacobs, *Incidents in the Life of a Slave Girl*		Civil War (1861–65)
			Lincoln's administration (1861–65)
			Vassar College founded
1862	Alexander Crummell, *The Future of Africa*	Herbert Spencer, *First Principles*	
	Julia Ward Howe, "The Battle Hymn of the Republic"	Ivan Turgenev, *Fathers and Sons*	
	Frederick Law Olmstead, *The Cotton Kingdom*		
	Elizabeth Stoddard, *The Morgesons*		
1863	Charles Hodge, "Aggressive Christianity"	Charles Lyell, *The Geological Evidences of the Antiquity of Man*	Emancipation Proclamation
	Abraham Lincoln, "Address Delivered at the Dedication of the Cemetery at Gettysburg"	John Stuart Mill, *Utilitarianism*	
		Ernest Renan, *Life of Jesus*	
	Henry David Thoreau, "Life Without Principle" (posthumous)	Leo Tolstoy, *War and Peace* (1863–69)	

Year	American Documents	European Documents	Political, Social, and Cultural Events
1864	Lyman Beecher, *Autobiography* (1864–65; published posthumously)	John Henry Newman, *Apologia pro Vita Sua* Fyodor Dostoevsky, *Notes from Underground*	
1865	*The Nation* (1865–) Abraham Lincoln, "Second Inaugural Address" Walt Whitman, *Drum-Taps*	Lews Carroll, *Alice's Adventures in Wonderland*	Cornell University founded Abraham Lincoln assassinated Thirteenth Amendment outlawing slavery ratified